D0842103

Vínland Revisited:
the Norse World at the Turn of the First Millennium

Vínland Revisited: the Norse World at the Turn of the First Millennium

SELECTED PAPERS FROM THE
VIKING MILLENNIUM INTERNATIONAL SYMPOSIUM,
15-24 SEPTEMBER 2000,
NEWFOUNDLAND AND LABRADOR

Edited by Shannon Lewis-Simpson

On the cover and this page: *Meeting of Two Worlds*. This bronze sculpture frames the reconstructed Norse settlement at L'Anse aux Meadows National Historic Site of Canada. The sculpture, created by Luben Boykov and Richard Brixel, was unveiled at the site in 2002 (photo: Erick Walsh).

VÍNLAND REVISITED: the Norse World at the Turn of the First Millennium
Selected Papers from the Viking Millennium International Symposium,
15-24 September 2000, Newfoundland and Labrador

Editor: Shannon Lewis-Simpson
Copyright: Historic Sites Association of Newfoundland and Labrador, Inc.

ISBN 0-919735-07-X

Published by: Historic Sites Association of Newfoundland and Labrador, Inc.
Box 5542
St John's, NL
A1C 5W4 Canada
www.historicsites.ca

Managing Editor: Catherine Dempsey
Cover Design: Ragged Harbour Design
Advisory Committee: James Hiller   Aileen MacDonald
Kevin McAleese   Paul O'Neill
Priscilla Renouf   William Schipper
Birgitta Wallace
Images: credited throughout the text

The Historic Sites Association of Newfoundland and Labrador (HSA) is a charitable organization which works to preserve, promote and interpret the history and heritage of our province. The HSA partnered with the Labrador Straits Historical Development Corporation and the Committee on Medieval Studies, Memorial University to organise the Symposium. The Committee is proud to publish this selection from the papers presented at the Viking Millennium International Symposium, and thanks its financial supporters: The Canada Millennium Partnership Program, The Government of Newfoundland and Labrador, Parks Canada, and St. Anthony Basin Resources Inc.

Contents

Preface

Paul O'Neill, C.M., LL.D., Chair, Symposium Committee

In February 1998 the Historic Sites Association of Newfoundland and Labrador (HSA) began discussing ideas for observing the millennium year 2000. Various proposals were made. The one adopted was a suggestion to hold an international symposium, in conjunction with the millennial anniversary of the voyage of Leifr Eiríksson to North America, which the Newfoundland and Labrador Government decided would be celebrated that same year. The HSA was already involved at L'Anse aux Meadows National Historic Site of Canada, so a congress seemed to suit the objectives of the Association.

A Viking Symposium Committee, of which I was Chair, was formed, and various organisations were invited to participate in planning an educational conference for the autumn of 2000, centred around the theme of the Viking explorations of the Newfoundland and Labrador coasts. Many ideas were proposed, adopted and abandoned before the agenda finally took shape. It was decided the conference should appeal to the general public, as well as the academic community. Banquets and entertainment were woven into the schedule of sessions, to take place in both Newfoundland and Labrador. Doug Robbins, of the Labrador Straits Historical Development Corporation, was invited to become co-chair of the Committee.

Funding was sought from and approved by the Millennium Bureau of Canada, with added assistance from all levels of government, federal, provincial and civic, as well as various organisations and individuals. A major ten day symposium was agreed upon, to open 15 September 2000 in St. John's and closing 25 September, in the city of Corner Brook, with other sessions in L'Anse aux Meadows, St. Anthony, Forteau, West St. Modeste and Red Bay. Taking part in lectures, panels and open discussions, on numerous topics, related to the Viking world and west Atlantic voyages, were scholars from Canada, the United States, Ireland, Britain, Iceland, Norway, Sweden, Denmark, Poland, and Japan. Participants came from 24 countries throughout North America and Europe. The sessions in St. John's were arranged in cooperation with the Department of Medieval Studies, Memorial University of Newfoundland. During the ten days of meetings, large numbers of contending views were expressed and discussed, regarding the location, interpretation and impact of the Norse in North America at the beginning of the last millennium.

As the Symposium was taking shape, the Government of Newfoundland and Labrador had its Provincial Museum staff organise a public exhibition, Full Circle-First Contact, supported by Parks Canada, which told the story of the coming east of the aboriginal peoples from Asia, and of the linking-up of the eastern and western worlds, when they made their first contact with the western-bound Norse in Vínland. Using sound and light, the exhibition displays featured artefacts, illustrations, and other materials, in an attempt to answer such questions as 'Who were the Vikings?' and 'How does L'Anse aux Meadows fit into their world?' The Museum organisers, and HSA, co-operated closely in timing the exhibition and the Symposium, so as to coincide with one another, in both the city of St. John's, and later in the city of Corner Brook.

Papers presented at sessions of the Symposium have been collected by a publication committee, and prepared for presentation in this volume, so as to reflect the character and wide range of opinions expressed by the participants. The HSA thanks all who helped make a success of the Viking Millennium International Symposium in AD 2000.

List of Figures

11

3. Chart, radiocarbon dates on the Norse occupation.
4. Photo, spruce board in situ.
5. Pie chart, types of slag at L'Anse aux Meadows.
6. Photo, water-smoothed piece with seaworm holes.
7. Photo, a small birchbark container sewn with spruce root
8. Photo, wood objects with undetermined function.
9. Overhead photo, the archaeological remains of the A-B-C building complex.

MARKEWITZ:
1. Photo, the 'Viking Encampment' programme at L'Anse aux Meadows NHSC uses costumed historic interpreters to bring the past to life.
2. Photo, the story of Vínland: a control station for exploration and timber gathering.
3. Photo, a female interpreter wearing the small cap discussed in the text at LAM

BELL, MACPHERSON AND RENOUF:
1. Oblique, three-dimensional digital elevation model with shaded relief showing the location of placenames used in the text.
2A. Photo, striated surface from the Strait of Belle Isle.
2B. Photo, view south to the White Hills with Route 340 in the foreground.
2C. Photo, former shorelines are marked by raised gravel beaches and terraces up to 140 m asl.
2D. Photo, at LAM, terraces occur at 16, 10.5, and 4 m asl, the lower one being the site of Norse occupation AD 1000.
3A-D. Approximate shoreline positions at selected time periods during postglacial emergence of the study region.
4A-D. Photographs, vegetation types in LAM National Historic Site
5. Graph, selected pollen taxa recorded from peat (0-2000 BP) and lake sediment (2000-8000 BP) are used to reconstruct the vegetation history of the L'Anse aux Meadows area.
6. Graph, variations of summer lake water temperature from present for approximately the last 7000 years based on chironomid remains in a sediment core from Bass Pond, Port au Choix.

GRAHAM-CAMPBELL:
1. The 'Great Beast' and snake motif from Harald Bluetooth's runestone at Jelling, Denmark.
2. The 'Great Beast', with a companion, from the Heggen vane, Norway.
3. Photo, fragment of a carved panel, with haloed figures, from Flatatunga, Iceland.
4. Photo, seated figure from Eyrarland, Iceland.
5. Ornament of beasts and snakes on the west gable of Urnes church, Norway.
6. Photo, silver openwork brooch, consisting of an Urnes-style beast and two snakes, from Tröllaskógur, Iceland.
7. Photo, carved wooden object, with animal-head terminal, from Sandnes, Greenland.

HAYEUR-SMITH:
1. Tongue-shaped brooch, Kornsá, Austur-Hunavatnsýsla, Iceland.
2. Strap-end from Kroppur, Eyjafjarðarsýsla, Iceland.
3. Oval brooch from Skogar í Flókadal, Iceland.
4. Oval brooch from Daðastaðir, Iceland.

STUMMANN-HANSEN:
1. Photo, Poul Nørlund and Aage Roussell in the Western Settlement of Norse Greenland, 1930.
2. Site-plan of the bishop's seat at Garðar in the Eastern Settlement.
3. Photo, black house in Shawbost, Lewis, 1936.
4. Site-plan, medieval farmstead at Samsstaðir in Þjórsárdalur, Iceland.
5. Site-plan, the First Phase of the Scandinavian settlement at Jarlshof, Shetland.
6. Site-plan, Viking-Age farmstead at Niðri á Toft, Kvívík, Faroe Islands.
7. Viking-Age longhouses of the ninth and tenth centuries.
8. Typology of houses from southern Scandinavia from the early Iron Age to the early medieval period.
9. Proposal for a reconstruction of a house of Trelleborg type excavated at Lejre, Seeland, Denmark.

GRÄSLUND:
1. Scandinavia. Map of places discussed in the text.
2. Photo, the Jellinge stone, Denmark, set up by king Harald Bluetooth.
3. Photo, the Frösö stone, Sweden.
4. Photo, the Kuli stone, Norway.
5. The woman's grave Bj 968.
6. The man's grave Bj 581.
7. The rune stone U 661 Håby, Håtuna parish, Uppland from the first half of the eleventh century.

PRICE:
1. Photo, three iron staffs from the Viking-Age cemeteries at Birka, Björkö, Sweden: graves Bj. 834 (1), 845 (2), 660 (3).
2. Photo, the silver 'weapon dancer' pendant from Birka grave Bj. 571.
3. A miniature silver chair, found in Birka grave Bj. 968.
4. Two Viking-Age picture stones from Gotland, with images of the eight-legged horse; from Alskog Tjängvide I, and Ardre VIII.
5. Weave 1a from Överhogdal, Härjedalen, Sweden, radio-carbondated to the Viking Age.
6. Photo, one of the two cloth masks found rolled up and used as caulking in a Viking-Age ship, wrecked in the harbour at Hedeby, Schleswig-Holstein.

MORRIS:
1. Aerial photograph of Birsay Bay, Orkney from SE with village in foreground and Brough of Birsay in background.
2. Aerial photograph of Brattahlíð / Qagssiarssuk, Greenland from SE.
3. Aerial photograph of the Brough of Deerness, Orkney, from the north.
4. Overall map of chapel sites, Unst, Shetland.
5. Overall map of chapel sites, Fetlar, Shetland.
6. Overall map of chapel sites, Yell, Shetland.
7. Map, medieval churches and chapels in Shetland.

STEFÁNSSON
1. Map, the world in accordance with Adam of Bremen's History.
2. Map, Eastern North America, demonstrating the southern limit of salmon and northern limit of wild grape vines.
3. The 1669 version of the 'Skálholt Map'.
4. The younger, 1706 engraving of the 'Skálholt Map'.
5. Map, the Eastern Arctic region.

POPE:
1. Map, places claimed as Cabot's landfall.
2. Map, the traditional Norse sailing itinerary with the winds prevailing in May.

MCALEESE:
1. Map, the North West Atlantic and northeast North America: the arena for skraelingar and Norsemen, c. eleventh to fourteenth centuries AD.
2. Photo, a driftwood carving, with distinctly non-Inuit features, c. mid-thirteenth century AD.
3. Photo, Dorset amulet made from a piece of smelted sheet copper possibly from Norse Greenland found in Richmond Gulf, Hudson's Bay.
4. Photo, Skraeling Island, in Alexandra Fjord, Ellesmere Island.
5. Photo, iron ship rivet, c. AD mid-thirteenth century, found in a Thule Inuit winter house ruin on Skraeling Island

WALLACE:
1. Photo, reconstructed sod houses at L'Anse aux Meadows National Historic Site of Canada
2. Photo, lagoons in Kouchibouguac National Park, New Brunswick.
3. Photo, North American dune grass, Elymus mollis.
4. Photo, grapevines growing on trees, the Saint John valley, New Brunswick.
5. Map, the route to Vínland.
6. Photo, Grand Lake, Hamilton Inlet, Labrador.

LARSSON:
1. 30-year median of ice concentration along Eastern Canada in the beginning of June.
2. 28-year median of ice concentration along Baffin Island and Northern Labrador in the beginning of August.
3. Sailing courses and distances in 'days' from Greenland to Helluland, Markland and Vínland.
4. Photo, the barrier beaches south of Cape Gabarus, Cape Breton Island.
5. Reports of wild grape vines in Nova Scotia.
6. Photo, the tidal flats at the estuary of Chegoggin River.
7. Reconstruction of the former tidal lake at Chegoggin River.

SHENDOCK:
1. The 1669 version of the 'Skálholt Map'.
2. Map, the Eastern Seaboard of North America.

List of Tables

List of Contributors

AHRONSON, KRISTJÁN

Currently Rhys Scholar at Jesus College, Oxford, and nearing completion of his doctorate in Celtic and Scottish Studies at the University of Edinburgh. A graduate of the University of Toronto, Kristján Ahronson has worked on a wide range of archaeological projects from in England, Scotland, Iceland, and the Ottawa Valley (Quebec and Ontario). As a 'Celtic Geoarchaeologist' and director of the Seljaland Project in southern Iceland, he explores cave use in Atlantic Scotland and Iceland. Using a multi-disciplinary approach, Kristján Ahronson applies tephrochronology to early human-environmental interactions and the archaeology of cultures in contact.

ALBRETHSEN, SVEND E.

Svend E. Albrethsen is with The National Cultural Heritage Agency, Department of Prehistoric Monuments in Denmark. He has extensive experience with excavations in the Arctic especially in Western Greenland and Svalbard.

ARNEBORG, JETTE

Jette Arneborg (PhD) is a senior researcher at the Centre for Greenland Research, National Museum of Denmark. She has conducted archaeological research and fieldwork in Greenland since 1980.

BAITSHOLTS, KENNETH

Born in Rochester, New York, Kenneth Baitsholts has lived and worked in Germany, Sweden and Iceland. In addition to translating Swedish and Icelandic poetry, he has delivered papers on topics ranging from the conversion of Iceland to Christianity, and Old Norse religious history, to Icelandic NATO membership. He currently works at Cornell University Library, USA, and is a user of the Fiske Icelandic Collection.

BATEY, COLLEEN

Lecturer in Archaeology, University of Glasgow and Finds Research Manager Archaeological Institute of Iceland, Reykjavik. She has excavated extensively in Northern Scotland, and worked with the International Fieldschool at Hofstadir since 2000. She has written extensively on the Vikings and Late Norse period in Scotland, publishing in 1998 *Vikings in Scotland: An Archaeological Survey*, with James Graham-Campbell.

BELL, TREVOR

Trevor Bell (PhD, University of Alberta, 1992) is an Associate Professor of Geography at Memorial University of Newfoundland, Canada. His research focuses on environmental change in northern and eastern Canada, with particular emphasis on landscape history. Since 1996 he has been collaborating with M.A.P. Renouf on prehistoric occupations and their environmental context in Newfoundland. In 2003, he received the Petro-Canada Young Innovator Award for his research on submerged landscapes of potential archaeological significance around the Newfoundland coast.

BLÖNDAL, SIGURÐUR

Born 1924, Sigurður Blöndal was the Director of the Iceland Forest Service 1977-1989, and has published many papers, educational pamphlets and books on forestry issues in Iceland.

CHRISTENSEN, ARNE EMIL

Arne Emil Christensen is a professor of Nordic Archaeology at the Viking Ship Museum, University Museum of Cultural Heritage, University of Oslo. His speciality is Viking-Age ships, and the history and technology of shipbuilding.

CROZIER, ALAN

Born in Northern Ireland 1953, now living in Sweden. MA in Anglo-Saxon, Norse and Celtic at Cambridge University. Ph.D. in Germanic Philology at Cambridge University. Teaching experience at Cambridge University and the University of Iceland. Now working as a full-time translator of Scandinavian academic texts.

ECKHOFF, NICOLAY

Nicolay Eckhoff is a professional engineer educated at the University of Toronto and Nova Scotia Technical College. He participated in five of Helge Ingstad's archaeological expeditions to Newfoundland, Labrador and Baffin Island. His varied work experience ranges from the Hospital for Sick Children to Mobil Oil. He is now employed by the Norwegian Civil Aviation Administration .He is also currently revisiting the sailing routes of the Greenlanders to North America, with specific reference to ice and meteorological conditions.

EYSTEINSSON, ÞRÖSTUR

Born 1955, Þröstur Eysteinsson is the Deputy Director of the Iceland Forest Service since 1994, and has published several papers on a variety of forestry related subjects.

GARDNER, DAVID

Toronto-born David Gardner is equally well known as a performer/director and an academic. In the 1960s and 70s he produced 75 TV dramas for the CBC; ran the Vancouver Playhouse; and then served as theatre officer for the Canada Council. He returned to the University of Toronto in the mid-70s to research a PhD in Canadian Theatre History. He subsequently taught at the University of Toronto and York University. He is currently working on a memoir entitled *The Adventures of a Shy Extrovert*.

GRAHAM-CAMPBELL, JAMES

Dr James Graham-Campbell is professor emeritus of Medieval Archaeology at University College London and author of numerous publications on the art and archaeology of the Viking Age.

GRÄSLUND, ANNE-SOFIE

Dr Gräslund is professor in archaeology at Uppsala University, Sweden, who has authored several articles on graves as ancient monuments, burial customs, Christianisation, rune stones, Viking Age art, Viking-Age women etc. Her doctoral thesis (1981) was entitled *Birka IV: the Burial Customs. A study of the graves on Björkö*.

HALL, RICHARD

Dr Hall is Deputy Director and Head of Academic Division at York Archaeological Trust, one of Britain's foremost archaeological units; he directed the internationally-known York 'Viking Dig'. He is currently Honourary Secretary of the Council for British Archaeology and President of the Society for Medieval Archaeology.

HAYEUR-SMITH, MICHÈLE

Michèle Hayeur Smith (PhD, University of Glasgow, 2003) researches the social use of jewellery in the North Atlantic in the Viking period, as well as theoretical questions of gender and identity. In 1998, she was hired as an archaeological illustrator for the Institute of Archaeology of Iceland, for the re-publication of Kristján Eldjárn's, *Kuml og Haugfe*. She has archaeological field experience in Native American prehistory, as well as the Viking period, and has excavated in Northern Quebec, Iceland and Sweden. She lives in Rhode Island, USA and is currently a Research Associate of Brown University's Haffenreffer Museum of Anthropology.

JASINSKI, MAREK

Dr Marek E. Jasinski is a professor in Maritime Archaeology at the Norwegian University of Science and Technology. His main focus is the comparative study of maritime cultures and arctic research. Dr Jasinski is also co-founder of Promare, a non-profit organisation dedicated to ocean exploration.

KELLER, CHRISTIAN

Dr Keller is a Professor of Nordic Archaeology at the Viking and Medieval Centre in Norway and is a co-founder of the research network NABO (North Atlantic Biocultural Organization). He is presently engaged in archaeological fieldwork in North West Iceland.

17

LARSSON, MATS G.

Born in Stockholm in 1946, Dr. Larsson is a senior lecturer at Lund University, Sweden. He is the author of several popular books on archaeology and Viking expeditions, and his research focuses on the Viking period social conditions and expeditions to the east and west.

LEWIS-SIMPSON, SHANNON

A Newfoundlander, Shannon Lewis-Simpson studied at Memorial University, and worked in publishing prior to commencing further academic research. She has completed a Masters degree in Early Medieval Studies at the Centre for Medieval Studies, University of York and is currently researching an interdisciplinary PhD concerning aspects of colonialism and cultural interaction in the western Viking-Age settlements.

LYNNERUP, NIELS

Dr Lynnerup (MD, PhD) is an Associate Professor, at the Laboratory of Biological Anthropology at the Panum Institute in Denmark. He has written articles on Norse biological anthropology, Inuit biological anthropological studies and studies of Danish archaeological skeletal finds.

MACPHERSON, JOYCE

Joyce Macpherson (PhD, McGill University, 1966) is Professor Emeritus in the Geography Department at Memorial University of Newfoundland, Canada. Her research interests are vegetation and climate change in Newfoundland from pollen analysis of lake sediments. Current projects include an investigation of environmental changes associated with prehistoric settlement at Port au Choix and post-glacial vegetation sequences on the Grey Islands, Northern Newfoundland.

MAGNUSSON, MAGNUS

Magnus Magnusson was born in Iceland in 1929 but has lived for most of his life in Scotland. He has written and broadcast several books and TV programmes on the Vikings, and translated the Vínland sagas and many other sagas into English. He has been Lord

Rector of Edinburgh University, and chairman of the Ancient Monuments Board for Scotland and of the government's environmental agency, Scottish Natural Heritage. He has been honoured in 'both of his countries': in Iceland, as Knight Commander of the Icelandic Falcon, and in Britain as Knight of the British Empire (KBE).

MARKEWITZ, DARRELL

Darrell Markewitz has over 20 years experience with Living History museums, and has worked as a demonstrator, interpretive trainer, and program designer. Recent work has included consulting on the Smithsonian's Vikings–North Atlantic Saga and the Newfoundland Museum's Full Circle–First Contact exhibits. He designed the 'Viking Encampment' program for L'Anse aux Meadows National Historic Site, along with creating the reproductions used and training the interpretative staff.

MCALEESE, KEVIN

Kevin McAleese has conducted archaeological research in both western and eastern Canada, particularly in 18th-century European and Aboriginal archaeology. He curated Kimatullivik, an exhibit on Thule Inuit in Labrador, part of which travelled (1998-1999) through coastal Labrador. He is the Senior Curator on the Full Circle—First Contact traveling exhibit (2000-2004), which celebrates Norse exploration and settlement in Vínland. As the Provincial Museum of Newfoundland and Labrador Archaeology & Ethnology Curator, Mr McAleese works with various groups throughout Newfoundland and Labrador on assorted research projects and exhibits.

MORRIS, CHRISTOPHER

Christopher Morris is Professor of Archaeology at the University of Glasgow and also currently Vice-Principal (Staffing and Arts-side Faculties). He has conducted extensive excavations and fieldwork in Northern Scotland, Orkney, Shetland, Isle of Man and Cornwall. He is the author/editor of numerous monographs and other publications concerning Viking, Late Norse and Late Celtic archaeology.

PÁSZTOR, EMÍLIA

Emília Pásztor graduated in astronomy and the archaeology of the prehistoric and Migration periods. She has taken part in several archaeoastronomical projects supported by Gothenburg University and the Soros Foundation. At present she is researching the significance of the sun, moon and celestial bodies to societies in the Carpathian Basin during the Bronze Age.

POPE, PETER

Peter Pope (BA., MLitt (Oxon.); MA, PhD), is an Associate Professor of Anthropology at Memorial University of Newfoundland, Canada, who teaches historical archaeology and has carried out excavations for several years on the St John's waterfront. He is interested in the early European fishery at Newfoundland and is currently finishing a book on 17th-century settlement for the Omohundro Institute of Early American History and Culture.

PRICE, NEIL

Neil Price began his archaeological career in 1983, developing his research interests in the Viking Age with studies at the universities of London and York. In 1992 he emigrated to Sweden and later took his doctorate at the University of Uppsala, where he is currently Reader in Viking and Early Medieval Studies. He has excavated extensively in Britain, Scandinavia and further afield, and has directed Viking research projects in France, Iceland and Russia. Neil has published widely on Viking subjects, mostly in his specialist fields of pagan religion, identity and ideology, landscape, Sámi (Lapp) archaeology, and the Vikings in Continental Europe.

RENOUF, PRISCILLA

M.A.P. Renouf (PhD, Cambridge, 1982) is a Professor and Canada Research Chair in North Atlantic Archaeology at the Archaeology Unit, Department of Anthropology, Memorial University of Newfoundland, Canada. Her research interests are northern coastal hunter-gatherers, and she has been conducting fieldwork at Port au Choix since 1984. Currently, she is co-directing, along with Trevor Bell, the Port au Choix Archaeology and Landscape History Project.

ROESDAHL, ELSE

Born 1942, Else Roesdahl is Danish and a Professor of Medieval Archaeology, at the University of Aarhus, Denmark. Litt. D., F.S.A. Special professor in Viking Studies, University of Nottingham 1989-97 and 2000-2003. Honorary Doctor of the University of Dublin, Trinity College, 1995.

ROSLUND, CURT

Curt Roslund is a senior lecturer in astronomy at the University of Gothenburg. While teaching there, he introduced a course in The History of Navigation in which field he is still doing research work after his retirement in 1995.

19

SAWYER, BIRGIT

Dr Sawyer is the author of numerous publications in her field and has been a research fellow, University of Gothenburg (Sweden) 1986-91; a senior lecturer, University of Gothenburg 1991-96; and is a Professor in the Department of History at NTNU (Norway's Technical and Natural-Scientific University) 1996-present.

SAWYER, PETER

His university appointments include Professor of Medieval History, Leeds University, 1970-82 (early retirement); Distinguished Visiting Professor of Medieval Studies, University of California, Berkeley, 1985; and Ford's Lecturer in English History, University of Oxford 1993. His scholarship includes being the editor of *The Oxford Illustrated History of the Vikings* (Oxford, 1997).

SEAVER, KIRSTEN

Kirsten Seaver was educated in Norway and in the U.S. and after working at the Harvard University Library and teaching Norwegian at Stanford University, she returned to her original academic interests: early North Atlantic exploration, the Greenland Norse, and early cartography. She is the author of *The Frozen Echo: Greenland and the Exploration of North America ca. A.D. 1000-1500*; *Maps, Myths, And Men: The Story Of The Vinland Map* (2004, Stanford University Press), and a number of scholarly articles.

SHENDOCK, GEORGE

George Shendock (BA, MS, MEd) is a classroom teacher of 29 years, currently on sabbatical as a full-time student of the graduate education department at the University of Scranton, USA. He has field experience to Newfoundland, Labrador, Quebec and Iceland.

SØREIDE, FREDRIK

Dr Fredrik Søreide works for the Norwegian University of Science and Technology as a consultant. His main research focus is deep-sea archaeology and applications of advanced technology in marine research. He is also President of Promare, a non-profit organisation dedicated to ocean exploration.

STEFÁNSSON, MAGNÚS

Born in Iceland, Magnús Stefánsson is a history professor emeritus from the University of Bergen, Norway. He has written several articles on Icelandic church and legal history, primarily dealing with the proprietary church system (*Eigenkirchenwesen*) of Iceland. His most important work in this field is *Staðir og staðamál. Studier i islandske egenkirkelige og beneficialrettslige forhold i middelalderen I* (Bergen 2000), written in Norwegian.

STUMMANN HANSEN, STEFFEN

Steffen Stummann Hansen has conducted surveys and excavations on Viking and early Medieval sites in Denmark, Norway, Shetland, Faroe Islands, Iceland and Greenland. He has worked with the University of Copenhagen and the Danish Polar Centre and is now the State Antiquary of the Faroe Islands. He has published a wide range of books and articles on the Viking Age and medieval period of the North Atlantic.

THIRSLUND, SØREN

Søren Thirslund is a retired master mariner. After retirement in 1982 he started researching into the history of navigation, and from 1985 especially on Viking navigation. Attached to the Danish Maritime Museum, he has published numerous books on historical navigation, and has demonstrated possible navigation aids.

URBAŃCZYK, PRZEMYSŁAW

Dr Urbańczyk is a Professor at the Institute of Archaeology and Ethnology at the Polish Academy of Sciences in Warsaw and the holder of a chair of prehistory at the Akademia Podlaska in Siedlce, Poland. He has been engaged in North Atlantic archaeology and history since 1981.

WALLACE, BIRGITTA

Born and raised in Sweden, Dr Wallace is a Staff Archaeologist (emeritus) for Parks Canada. She specialises in the subject of Vikings in North America with numerous publications on this topic. She worked on the L'Anse aux Meadows site in 1964 and 1968 and during the later Parks Canada excavations and has been affiliated with the site ever since.

WOXEN, TROND

Trond Woxen is an actor/writer/translator. Born in Norway, he lived in the United States and Norway until moving to Los Angeles, CA where he co-founded the Scandinavian Theatre Company, and serves as Hon. Cultural Representative at the Royal Norwegian Consulate General. An Ibsen scholar, he is a member of the Council of the Ibsen Society of Americ and has given many papers on the subject. With Astrid Oglivie he has produced many CDs of saga readings including *Vínland 1000* (2002).

Introduction: Approaches and Arguments

Shannon Lewis-Simpson

Since the Viking Millennium International Symposium was held in September 2000, some excellent volumes concerning the voyages of the Scandinavians throughout the North Atlantic have been published (Hagland and Supphellen 2001; Wawn and Sigurðardóttir 2001; Barrett 2003). While some topics in the present volume have also been discussed in these other works, this volume is presented as a compilation of diverse interpretations of the Viking Age which were presented at the Symposium, with a special focus being the Vínland episode as it pertains to wider Viking-Age studies. The contributions were selected for this volume to indicate the mixture of both established and upcoming scholars, and Viking-Age enthusiasts who attended and contributed to the Symposium.

This volume is decidedly interdisciplinary with literary, historical and archaeological evidence being examined to discuss what is in some respects a prehistoric period. The reader should recall that *Grœnlendinga saga* ('The Greenlanders' Saga) and *Eiríks saga rauða* ('The Saga of Eiríkr the Red'), colloquially termed the 'Vínland sagas', were transcribed approximately three centuries after the events which they relate. Some past scholars have treated these sagas as accurate historical accounts, sometimes leading to very problematic interpretations. For example, Halldór Hermannsson attempted to explain the *einfœtingr* or 'uniped' who killed Þorvaldr in *Eiríks saga* as a native dancing on one foot, a native woman in very long clothing, an amputee or a limping native (Hermannsson 1936, 23-4).

Perhaps a more accurate way to approach these specific texts and indeed all Icelandic sagas is to remember that they are products of the time in which they were written down. The twelfth- and thirteenth-century Icelandic scholars who transcribed these sagas were influenced by contemporary medieval learning as participants in a shared, European literary and cultural network (Frakes 2001, 163-4). With this in mind, the *einfœtingr* and other marvellous wonders should be expected to exist in Vínland. The Icelanders 'knew on the authority of such encyclopedists as the seventh-century Isidore of Seville that there were unipeds in Africa—so why not in Vinland too?' (Jones 1991, 10). Gísli Sigurðsson believes that the Vínland sagas reflect the social memory of the events which occurred in the past. They do not record the events as they actually occurred (Sigurðsson 2000, 218). As such, some information contained within them can be said to be based in past truths, while also reflecting the social reality of the day (see also Barnes 1995). This is common to all sagas, and not only those which describe the Vínland voyages. But, somehow, sagas such as *Örvar-Odds saga* ('The Saga of Arrow-Odd') have never been subject to the same sort of quest to discover where other strange lands, in this case Risaland ('Giantland') or Bjarmaland ('Permia'), might be nor what mysterious events occurred there (e.g. Ross 1941; Pálsson and Edwards 1971).

There are many reasons why Vínland has been the focus of so much study over the last century and a half. Perhaps the most important impetus of this interest came with the archaeological corroboration that the Norse explored and eventually settled in North America (Ingstad 1977). At the time of Anne Stine Ingstad's investigations, there were many 'crackpot archaeologists' attempting to locate Vínland and an overabundance of Norse hoaxes were brought to light, such as the Kensington rune stone (Wallace 1991). It became necessary for Ingstad to indubitably validate the site as Norse using scientific methods. L'Anse aux Meadows was proven to be a Norse settlement not so much because of the diagnostically Norse finds like the soapstone spindle whorl and ring-headed bronze pin (cf. Fanning 1994), but because so many of these finds which related to the Norse cultural milieu could be dated to the early eleventh century by radio-carbon dating (see Wallace, McAleese, this volume).

The more cautious view would be to treat the contemporary archaeological evidence as separate from the later saga accounts and not conflate the information from each evidence source. However, this is perhaps not the most fruitful approach. The site at L'Anse aux Meadows appears to support the saga narratives and this invites further research as to the details contained within the sagas. The site, read together with the saga narratives, creates more questions than answers. This volume seeks to address these questions and some possible answers.

The session order in which the contributions were presented at the Symposium is maintained here. Because of this, the reader will note connections amongst the various sections, and also various approaches by different authors to similar forms of evidence.

SECTION 1: VOYAGE TO VÍNLAND

The papers in Section One, 'Voyage to Vínland', can be divided into two discrete groups. The first group concerns the identity of those who settled in Iceland, Greenland and briefly in Vínland. The keynote address from Peter Sawyer summarises the history of Norwegian settlement in Scotland, Ireland and Iceland, and some reasons for this movement west. Sawyer is quick to note that the *landnámsmenn* who settled in uninhabited Iceland were not all Norwegians: there was a significant Irish contribution to the cultural milieu. This point of multicultural origins is addressed by Przemysław Urbańczyk. He challenges the assumption that the 'Scandinavian' settlers involved in the western expansion were a uniform ethnic group, noting that Viking-Age society was as ethnically diverse and dynamic as modern multicultural societies (see also Barth 1969; Jones 1997). This concept of being able to forge one's identity anew is also discussed by R.A. Hall in his paper on the Danelaw. The 'Danes' who raided and eventually settled in England adapted to their new homelands and forged a new Anglo-Scandinavian cultural identity in eastern England (see also Hadley and Richards 2000; Graham-Campbell *et al.* 2001).

But who were these people from the north, who came to raid, trade and settle? This is a question which Birgit Sawyer's first contribution seeks to answer. She discusses the political, economic and social structure of the Scandinavian homelands contemporaneous with the Viking-Age expansion.

Viking-Age settlement and expansion was the product of many immigrants in a multicultural environment. Colleen Batey discusses the importance of the Northern Isles and people to the Icelandic *lándnam* or 'land-taking', and asks whether we can ascertain the presence of British settlers in Iceland during the Viking Age. But before the *lándnam*, there may have been Irish monks, called *papar* in Old Norse, who preceded the Viking-Age settlers. Kristján Ahronson argues their presence may be seen through simple crosses incised in Icelandic caves. Complementing these papers on the diverse ethnic identities of the Vínland voyagers, Magnus Magnusson's first contribution introduces the voyagers themselves, as they are mentioned in the saga narratives of *Grænlendinga saga* and *Eiríks saga rauða*.

The contributions in the second half of Section 1 anticipate the voyages to Vínland and discuss the nature of settlement in Greenland. Svend Albrethsen surveys the earliest settlement sites and discusses the evidence for the Greenland *landnám*. Evidence and interpretations concerning the mysterious decline and demise of the Greenland colony are discussed in the following four contributions. Jette Arneborg discusses some common problems associated with reconciling the disparate literary and archaeological evidence concerning the Greenland colony. Marek Jasinski and Fredrik Søreide, having conducted seabed exploration near the Eastern Settlement, suggest that climatic deterioration, land erosion and

22

saline encroachment adversely affected the grass-growing potential of the area. They argue that the Norse population could not continue a traditional lifestyle of farming and animal husbandry under such conditions. Niels Lynnerup uses a demographic method to estimate how many people would actually have been living in the colony, and thus supporting themselves and also the voyages to Vínland. Else Roesdahl argues that changing world economics were partially responsible for Greenland's demise: as demand for narwhal and walrus ivory declined in Europe, so, too, did the colony decline.

Section 2: Society, Culture and Settlement

The Symposium moved to the Great Northern Peninsula where the contributions of Section Two, 'Society, Culture and Settlement' were heard. It is fitting that these discuss the settlement site at L'Anse aux Meadows, and also what sort of beliefs its inhabitants might have possessed, what games they enjoyed, and how they might have lived. The keynote address by Magnus Magnusson sets the tone by discussing the diverse nature of the Viking Age in the context of its recognised saints (saintly or otherwise), finally nominating Guðríðr Þorbjarnardóttir, a visitor to North America, for sainthood.

Archaeology is a discipline that attempts to recreate the past. This is a theme inherent in the following papers concerning L'Anse aux Meadows and surrounding area. The archaeological evidence of the site is summarised by Birgitta Wallace, who excavated at L'Anse aux Meadows as part of Anne Stine Ingstad's team, and directed further excavations for Parks Canada. Kevin McAleese discusses the history of the area, and the importance of World Heritage status to the local community of today. Nicolay Eckhoff shares his memories of what life was like for the residents of the Great Northern Peninsula and the archaeologists during the early excavations in the 1960s. Using the L'Anse aux Meadows National Historic Site as a case study, Darrell Markewitz discusses the challenges associated with representing the past as a living history interpreter. Trevor Bell, Joyce Macpherson and Priscilla Renouf use botanical, climatic and archaeological evidence to recreate what the landscape of L'Anse aux Meadows would have looked like to the Norse a thousand years ago, and who they might have encountered at that time.

23

Moving away from the specifics of L'Anse aux Meadows, the next eight contributions discuss Viking-Age society and culture more generally, adding to our picture of who these people were who travelled to North America. James Graham-Campbell summarises the diverse art styles that were present in the North Atlantic region at the turn of the millennium. Michèle Hayeur-Smith's contribution analyses the importance of the oval brooch to signify cultural identity within the dynamics of early Icelandic society. Steffen Stumman Hansen discusses house forms in the wider context of the North Atlantic region and situates the houses in a typology of Viking-Age buildings. This is of particular importance to L'Anse aux Meadows, as the site was partially identified by the distinctive forms of houses found there. Following from this, David Gardner speculates as to what games and entertainment may have been enjoyed in these Viking-Age houses.

The stories of the Æsir and Vanir, the pantheon of gods and goddesses, related in the prose and poetic Eddas should be familiar to most. What is not so easy to understand is how these gods were worshipped nor the processes whereby the Scandinavians were converted to Christianity. Upon examining runestones and burial evidence, Anne Sofie Gräslund believes this conversion was gradual: while the Scandinavians nominally adopted the rituals and doctrine of the Christian faith, they simultaneously maintained older pagan beliefs. Using literary, archaeological and comparative evidence, Neil Price introduces an aspect of these older pagan beliefs, *seiðr*, a complicated term which is of extreme importance to an understanding of Viking-Age beliefs.

The conversion to Christianity brought many changes to the Scandinavian world and the Church became very influential in later society. Birgit Sawyer's second contribution discusses the status of women in late Viking-Age Scandinavia and discusses the dichotomy of woman as pagan 'shieldmaiden' or Christian 'Madonna'. In a summary of his most recent work, Christopher Morris argues for an early Norse Christian community in Shetland and Orkney—not 'pre-Norse' or 'Celtic'—which was superseded by the growing power of an ecclesiastical church in the twelfth century.

The last two contributions of Section 2 from Magnús Stefánsson and Alan Crozier debate whether the Greenlanders intended the name of the place where they landed to be **Vinland** or **Vínland**. What appears to be a small, onomastic point is very important concerning the debate as to the location of the saga-place **Vínland** itself. (It should at this point be noted that unless otherwise specified for the purpose of individual argument, the name **Vínland** with a long í is used throughout the volume, as it is the form found in the saga manuscripts.)

Section 3: Exploration, Navigation and Cultural Interaction

This final part of the Symposium was held in Labrador and in Corner Brook. Peter Pope discusses the obsession with the 'discovery' of North America. Through the use of sailing itineraries from the sagas and later accounts, he speculates as to where the Norse may have sailed, while further questioning whether the Norse voyages should be called 'voyages of discovery' in the same sense as the later colonising European voyages. Kevin McAleese's second contribution investigates the nature of the *skrælingar* in saga sources and uses evidence from the high arctic and northern Scandinavia to determine what sort of cultural contact occurred between Norse and non-European peoples. Kenneth Baitsholts also explores these cultural interactions, agreeing with Pope that the nature of contact between Norse and native was markedly different that that between later European and native. It might be mentioned here that the preliminary findings from the ongoing 'Helluland Archaeology Project', currently led by Patricia Sutherland in the Canadian high arctic, appear to support more regular and intentional contact between native peoples and Norse than has been previously thought (P. Sutherland, pers. comm.).

Birgitta Wallace, Mats G. Larsson and George Shendock each read the two Vínland sagas in great detail to specifically locate places in the two sagas. Wallace argues that the site at L'Anse aux Meadows is probably Leifsbúðir / Straumfjörðr with Vínland being the whole of the eastern seaboard, including Newfoundland. Larsson argues Leifsbúðir/ Straumfjörðr is probably to be found in Nova Scotia and that Vínland corresponds generally with the St Lawrence waterway. Shendock also argues for Vínland in the St Lawrence region, more specifically that the original camp was in Ile D'Orleans, but as he states, the search for Vínland

is to a very large extent a personally subjective evaluation. But barring any other hard evidence of major importance since L'Anse aux Meadows, what other approach can be taken at this time?

Readers are invited to draw their own conclusions as to where Vínland might be, or if it is actually a physical place at all, or merely a state of mind, or a dream.

One of the reasons postulated for the Norse wishing to travel the dangerous sea road to North America was the search for timber, for ship-building and other needs. Þröstur Eysteinsson and Sigurður Blöndal discuss the importance of timber to the early Icelanders and the unfortunate environmental consequences of over-harvesting and sheep farming which resulted in the deforestation of the whole country.

Perhaps the need for timber and other goods was so great that it caused the Icelanders and Greenlanders to seek out their Vínland. The last three papers of the volume discuss the means by which the Norse might have sailed across the Atlantic. Curt Roslund, Søren Thirslund and Emília Pásztor discuss the possibility that a sun compass may have been used to indicate one's position at sea by means of the sun's shadow. A specific artefact found in Uunartoq, Greenland comprising of one-half of a notched wooden disc is described by them as a possible bearing dial for this purpose. Christian Keller and Arne Emil Christensen call into question this interpretation for the dial, suggesting it might actually be a medieval religious artefact and had nothing to do with navigation nor should it be dated to the Viking Age. The final paper in the volume also calls into dispute the validity of a well-known artefact. Kirsten A. Seaver summarises the history of the Vínland Map, and submits a candidate for the fabrication of that map.

EDITORIAL CONVENTIONS OF THE VOLUME

Modern Scandinavian place names are given as in modern Scandinavian usage except where a common anglicised version exists, e.g. Copenhagen. Icelandic personal names are listed by western conventions and not by patronymics in the bibliographies of each paper. Place names, such as Vínland, and personal names from the sagas are given in the normalised Old Norse nominative form as found in the *Íslenzk fornrit* editions of the saga texts. Readers unfamiliar with Old Norse should note the following equivalents:

25

Þ, þ   Modern English 'th' as in 'that'
Ð, ð   Modern English 'th' as in 'brother'

All texts are given in Modern English, but in some cases are also given in Old Norse. This is not meant to be a difficulty for the reader, but to allow the reader to experience more fully the culture of the Norse world at the turn of the last millennium.

The terms 'Viking Age' and 'Viking Period' are used interchangeably to refer to *c.* AD 800-1100. It should be noted, to the possible chagrin of Magnus Magnusson and Peter Sawyer (see this volume), that many authors have used the term 'Viking' as an easy way of describing those diverse ethnic groups who contributed in some way to the expansion westwards, and is used as such. The origin of the term 'viking' is ambiguous and may mean everything from a 'bayman' (although not strictly in the Newfoundland dialectal sense of the word), or a 'pirate'(see further Fell 1987). It is noted that the term, although not preferable, is the best one at the moment to describe the people and culture in question and as such is used here. Likewise, the plural Old Norse term *skrælingar* (sing. *skræling*) refers in the saga sources and in Ari Þorgilsson's twelfth-century *Íslendingabók* to the people who came into contact with the Norse in Vínland, and later in Greenland. The etymology of this word is far from certain, as is evidence of whom the *skrælingar* might have been (see Baitsholts, McAleese, this volume). Because of this scanty evidence, the word is left unanglicised in all instances in the volume when refering to saga events. Where specific parallels are made by the contributors to modern native peoples, the modern names for those peoples are used.

ACKNOWLEDGEMENTS

I thank Toby Simpson for producing some of the figures in the volume, and Judith Jesch and Neil Price for commenting upon this introduction. I also thank Julian D. Richards, William Schipper and Matthew Townend for introducing me to the Viking Age.

BIBLIOGRAPHY

Barnes, G. 1995. 'Vínland the Good: Paradise Lost?', *Parergon*, 12, 75-96.

Barth, F. ed., 1969. *Ethnic Groups and Boundaries: the Social Organization of Culture Difference*, Boston.

Barrett, J. ed., 2003. Contact, Continuity and Collapse: The Norse Colonization of the North Atlantic, Turnhout.

Fanning, T. 1994. *Viking-Age Ringed Pins in Dublin*, Dublin.

Fell, C. 1987. 'Modern English Viking', *Leeds Studies in English*, 18, 111-22.

Fitzhugh, W.W. and Ward, E.I., eds, 2000. *Vikings: The North Atlantic Saga*, Washington and London.

Frakes, J.C. 2001. 'Vikings, Vínland, and the Discourse of Eurocentrism', *Journal of English and Germanic Philology*, April, 157-99.

Graham-Campbell, J., Hall, R., Jesch, J. and Parsons, D.N., eds, 2001. *Vikings and the Danelaw: Select Papers from the Proceedings of the Thirteenth Viking Congress*, Oxford.

Hadley, D.M. and Richards, J.D., eds, 2000. *Cultures in Contact: Scandinavian Settlement in England in the Ninth and Tenth Centuries*, Turnhout.

Hagland, J.R. and Supphellen, S., eds, 2001. *Leiv Eriksson, Helge Ingstad og Vinland: kjelder og tradisjonar*, Trondheim, Norway.

Halldórsson, Ó. 2000. *Danish Kings and the Jomsvikings in the Greatest Saga of Óláfr Tryggvason*, London.

Hermannsson, H. 1936. *The Problem of Wineland*, Ithaca, NY.

Ingstad, A-S. 1977. *The Norse Discovery of America*, vol. 1, Oslo.

Jones, S. 1997. *The Archaeology of Ethnicity*, London.

Pálsson, H. and Edwards, P. 1971. *Legendary Fiction in Medieval Iceland*, Reykjavík.

Ross, A.S. 1941. *The Terfinnas and the Beormas of Ohtere*, Leeds.

Samson, R. ed. 1991. *Social Approaches to Viking Studies*, Glasgow.

Sigurðsson, G. 2000. 'An Introduction to the Vinland Sagas', in Fitzhugh and Ward 2000, 218-24.

Wallace, B.L. 1991. 'The Vikings in North America: myth and reality', in Samson 1991, 207-220.

Wawn, A. and Sigurðardóttir, Þ.,eds, 2001. *Approaches to Vínland: a conference on the written and archaeological sources for the Norse settlements in the North-Atlantic region and exploration of America*. Reykjavík: Sigurður Nordal Institute Studies 4.

Section One:
Voyage to Vínland

Scotland, Ireland and Iceland:

Norwegian settlers in the ninth century

Peter Sawyer

Keynote Address, St. John's, 15 September 2000

This paper is about the Norwegian emigration to the west in the ninth century, with particular attention to the role of the British Isles in the colonisation of Iceland. Much of what I have to say will be familiar to many readers, but I should like to take this opportunity to draw attention to some important recent studies that may not be so widely known (Helgason *et al.* 2000; 2001).

Some scholars have recently argued that there were direct contacts between Norway and Orkney long before the ninth century. This claim has had a sceptical reception, and even the most enthusiastic proponent of such early contacts must accept that the evidence for them is very slight, and that if there were any they were on a small scale (Myrhe 1993; Graham-Campbell and Batey 1998, 23, 54-67).

The situation changed dramatically in the last years of the eighth century when Scandinavians began raiding the coasts of the British Isles and western Europe (Whitelock 1979, 26-7; Coupland 1995; Sawyer 1997a; Ó Corráin 1998, 435-8). The first recorded raid was in 793 on Lindisfarne, an island monastery off the coast of Northumberland. In the next seven years at least three other monasteries on the coast of Northumbria were attacked. In 795 Vikings attacked island monasteries in the west: on Skye and Iona in the Hebrides, and Rathlin off the north-east coast of Ireland. In 798 the Annals of Ulster report that pagans plundered St Patrick's Island on the east coast of Ireland 'and made great incursions both in Ireland and Scotland', and by 807 Vikings had begun to raid the west coast of Ireland. The first recorded raid on the Continent, in 799, was also on an island monastery, St Philibert's on Noirmoutier, near the estuary of the Loire. One early incident that did not involve a church was in the reign of Brihtric, king of the West Saxons (786-802). The crews of three ships, later described as from Hordaland in Norway, landed in Portland on the south coast of England and killed a royal reeve who mistook them for merchants.

There must also have been raids on south-east England at this time, although none is reported until 835. As early as 792 the churches of Kent were obliged to contribute to defences against pagan seamen, an obligation that is also mentioned in early ninth-century Kentish charters, in one of which, dated 822, it is extended to include the duty to destroy forts built by the pagans. Another indication that the Vikings threatened that part of England before 835 is a charter dated 804 granting land within the walls of Canterbury as a refuge for the nunnery of Lyminge, an exposed coastal site near Romney Marsh (Brooks 1971, 79-80).

Across the Channel, in 800 Charlemagne organized defences along the coast north of the Seine estuary against pirates who 'infest the Gallic sea'. As no attack on that coast is reported before 810, it is not possible to say when the raids began. It is, however, clear that by the last decade of the century their raids had become so serious that rulers on both sides of the Channel took action against them.

The spate of reported raids suggests that they were a sudden, new phenomenon. That is confirmed by a letter that Alcuin, a Northumbrian who was then a leading adviser of Charlemagne, sent to the king of Northumbria about the Lindisfarne raid. Dorothy Whitelock's translation is usually cited: 'nor was it thought that such an inroad from the sea could be made'. The original reads *nec eiusmodi naufragium fieri posse putabatur*. In classical Latin *naufragium* normally meant 'shipwreck' but by the late eighth century it was being used to mean 'loss' or 'ruin' with no maritime association (Whitelock 1979, 842; Niermeyer 1954-76, 715). In other words, Alcuin was not referring to some unprecedented nautical exploit, but to an unprecedented depredation of the most famous shrine of Northumbria. Once Scandinavians discovered that there were wealthy communities on exposed sites from which wealth could be obtained as plunder, protection money, or by ransoming prisoners of high status, the news must have spread rapidly. It is not surprising that the first raids were followed by many others.

It has often been suggested that the main cause of this Viking activity was the pressure of increasing population in Scandinavia and the consequent shortage of land there. Some scholars have argued that the shortage was particularly acute in Rogaland in western Norway. Recent investigations, however, have shown that although a rapid expansion of settlement in Norway can be traced during the Roman and Migration periods and during the High Middle Ages, it was only on a small scale immediately before and during the early Viking Age. This suggests that the major expansion of settlement into marginal areas did not, as a rule, begin before the late Viking Age; there is, therefore, no evidence that population pressure was a serious problem in most parts of Norway or anywhere else in Scandinavia in the eighth and ninth centuries (Myhre 1998, 11-13; cf. Helle 1998, 244-50). Most of the first generations of Vikings were seeking wealth, not land.

The Norwegian archaeologist, Bjørn Myhre, has argued that 'conflicts between heathen Scandinavian kingdoms and the Christian powers on the Continent and in England may have been one of the main reasons for the plundering of churches and leading monasteries after 790' and that they were 'incidents in a conflict between powers around the North Sea' (1998, 27). This interpretation has won some support from scholars, but it is difficult to understand how raids on the Western Isles and Ireland can have been a response to conflicts between the Franks and the Danes.

A more plausible argument is that it was the remarkable expansion of commerce between western and northern Europe in the eighth century, and its consequences, that prepared the way for Viking activity (Sawyer 1997b, 3-8). In the first place, increased familiarity with western European sailing ships was an important factor in the adoption of sails in Scandinavia. Secondly, contacts with western merchants enabled Scandinavians to learn about the wealth of Christian Europe and about the conflicts between, and within, European kingdoms from which they were later able to profit. Thirdly, merchant ships in the Baltic provided opportunities for pirates who were in time tempted to extend their activities into the North Sea. However, none of these developments explain the sudden outburst of activity by both Danish and Norwegian Vikings in the 790s. The cause was probably the increasing power of the Danes at that time.

There are various indications that in the first half of the ninth century Danish kings were acknowledged as overlords by many of the local rulers and chieftains in the lands round Skagerrak and Kattegat (Sawyer and Sawyer 1993, 51-3). Any who were unable to resist Danish power and were unwilling to submit could choose exile, a prospect made more attractive by the newly discovered possibilities of winning fame and fortune by leading, or taking part in, raids on Christian Europe. The Danes were particularly eager to have hegemony over Viken, flanking Oslo Fjord, for it was there that they could obtain iron and whetstones produced in Norway. As overlords of south Norway, Danish kings also controlled the route along the Norwegian coast, the 'North Way', and could thus control the export of furs, walrus ivory, and other luxuries from the far north to markets in western Europe. If, as seems likely, the word *Viking* originally referred to the inhabitants of Viken, it could explain why the English, and only they, occasionally called Scandinavian raiders in the ninth century Vikings, for England was the natural objective for men from Viken who chose exile as raiders rather than accept Danish overlordship (Hødnebo 1987; Fell 1987).

Most of the raiders who attacked southern England and northern Frankia in the ninth century were Danes, or came from parts of southern Scandinavia that were under Danish overlordship. Most of those who operated in the north and west of the British Isles were from Norway, and by 820 Norwegians had not only gained control of most, if not all, of the Orkney Islands and the Hebrides, but had already begun to conquer, or at least make themselves overlords over, parts of the adjacent mainland, creating what can conveniently be described as Viking Scotland, from which raids were launched against Ireland and the western parts of Britain. By the middle of the ninth century there were extensive Norwegian settlements in the Hebrides as well as the Northern Isles (Graham-Campbell and Batey 1998). A recent study of the genetic evidence, mentioned below, suggests that a large proportion of the native population of these islands survived the conquest.

For several decades the Vikings, both Danes and Norwegians, mounted what were, in effect, hit and run raids on coastal targets by single ships or small groups. It was in the 830s that the scale and extent of Viking incursions increased dramatically, partly as a result of internal disputes in the Franish Empire. Dorestad was raided in 834 and in each of the next three years. In 835 the Isle of Sheppey in the Thames estuary was ravaged, and in 836 an English army was defeated by Vikings who landed on the north coast of Somerset. In the same year Vikings began to plunder monasteries in the interior of Ireland, and by then the monks of St Philibert had abandoned Noirmoutier to seek shelter in the Loire valley.

Although the main arena of Viking activity in the middle years of the century was Frankia, Ireland continued to suffer raids by Norwegians. They were led by several chieftains, acting independently (the Irish did not recognize them as kings), some of whom were probably based in Viking Scotland, but in the 840s they began to establish bases in Ireland. One group spent the winter of 840 on Lough Neagh in the north, and in the next year other groups overwintered in defended ship-enclosures they had constructed at Dublin and further north, at Anagassan. Before long there were Viking bases at Wexford, Waterford, Cork, Limerick and elsewhere, from which the surrounding areas were plundered. The booty they gathered included ornaments and elaborate caskets, but Irish monasteries were not so rich in gold, silver, and gems as those in Frankia and England. Captives, who could be sold to Muslims in Spain or North Africa were far more valuable. Viking activity in Ireland can be studied in some detail thanks to the contemporary Irish annals that have been preserved. They are also the only contemporary textual evidence for the Northern and Western Isles.

These annals report seven Viking raids in Ireland before 813, and sixteen between 821 and 836, but none in the years between those two periods. Donnchadh Ó Corráin has suggested that in that interval the Norwegians were consolidating their control of Viking Scotland. By the 840s, and possibly earlier, a Viking kingdom had been created in Scotland with its centre probably in Orkney (1999). In contemporary Irish sources it is variously called Lothlend or Laithlind. Its king apparently claimed to be overlord not only of the Scandinavians who had established themselves in the Hebrides, but also over the neighbouring parts of the Scottish mainland. In the eleventh century, when Norwegian kings claimed authority over that territory, this name, in the form Lochlainn, began to be used for Norway, a change that has been a cause of much confusion.

In 853 Olaf, son of the king of Laithlind, gained control of Dublin and for some twenty years he and his brother Ivar ruled in Dublin, exacting tribute from some Irish kings and claiming lordship over at least some of the Norwegian Vikings based in other parts of Ireland. The Dublin Vikings also extended their authority across the Irish Sea, and in 871, after a siege of four months, they took Dumbarton, the capital of the British kingdom of Strathclyde, and returned to Dublin with 'a great multitude of men, English, Britons, and Picts in captivity', a reminder of the importance of human booty.

Soon after that triumph, Olaf went to Laithlind to help his father, Gofraidh, deal with a revolt by the Lochlannaigh. This has been interpreted by many commentators as meaning that Olaf returned to Norway where his father was king. They have reinforced their argument by using the evidence of *Ynglingatal*, a poem supposed to have been composed *c.* 900 for the Norwegian king Haraldr *inn hárfagri* (Finehair). It has thirty stanzas, each devoted to a member of the Yngling dynasty to which Haraldr was believed to belong, beginning with mythological kings in Sweden whose descendants moved to Norway. One of the last of these kings is Óláfr, son of Guðrøðr. Several scholars have argued that they were the Olaf and Gofraidh in the Irish annals (Smyth 1977, 108-14).

Claus Krag has, however, questioned the antiquity of *Ynglingatal* and advanced good reasons for thinking that the Yngling tradition was a learned invention developed in Iceland in the eleventh century (1991). He has also shown how the tradition was altered during the twelfth century to transform kings who were originally said to have ruled Oppland in eastern Norway into kings of Vestfold. His interpretation of the relationship between the evolving versions of the tradition, ending with the poem, resolves many of the difficulties posed by accepting Snorri's claim that the poem was written in the early tenth century.

After Olaf went to help his father in Laithlind, that is in the Western or Northern Isles, Ivar remained in Dublin, and when he died in 873 the Annals of Ulster describe him as 'king of the Northmen of the whole of Ireland and Britain'. This suggests that Dublin was then regarded not only as the dominant power in Ireland, but also the capital of a kingdom extending from the Isle of Man to Orkney and Caithness (Duffy 1992).

The colonisation of Iceland by Norwegians began soon after a prolonged volcanic eruption that happened within a year or two of 871 when most of the country was covered with a layer of volcanic ash. With one exception the earliest traces of human activity in Iceland have been found above that layer and below another formed fifty years later. The exception, evidence showing that barley was cultivated in the south-west before the 871 eruption, suggests that some Scandinavians settled before that date, but they cannot have been numerous and no other trace of their presence has yet been found (Vésteinsson 2000).

Icelanders later claimed that their ancestors emigrated in order to escape the tyranny of Haraldr Finehair, who was traditionally remembered as the first king of a united Norway (Jones 1964, 19-20, 122). This explanation is unsatisfactory. Haraldr's reign cannot have begun so early. According to Ári, Haraldr died in 930 or 931 (*Íslendingabók* 1 in Jones 1964, 101-02). That is probably correct; there is independent evidence that he was alive after 927 (Page 1981). Ári is, however, not such a reliable source for the date of Haraldr's birth and the beginning of his reign. He claimed that Haraldr lived to be 80 years old and was king for 70. In this he was obviously influenced by the belief that the first settler in Iceland, Ingólfr, left Norway when king Haraldr was sixteen years old (*Íslendingabók* 1 in Jones 1964, 101-02). There is no independent evidence that Haraldr had such a long life or reign. It is more reasonable to assume that his success in Norway was when the Danes were temporarily weak at the end of the ninth century. Norwegians were still emigrating to Iceland during Haraldr's reign and some of them may well have chosen to leave Norway because they did not wish to submit to Haraldr's growing power.

It is far more likely that the first settlers came from the British Isles where they could have learned of Iceland's existence. A geographical treatise written in Frankia in 825 by an Irishman, Dicuil, shows that the existence of Iceland was known in Ireland and that some Irish priests had visited it, but did not settle (cited in Jones 1964, 8-9). Ári claimed that there was an Irish religious community in Iceland that withdrew when the Scandinavians arrived (*Íslendingabók* 1 in Jones 1964, 101-02). That appears to depend on the fact that an island off the south-east coast of Iceland was, and is, called *Papoy*, 'the Island of the Priests', but no evidence of Irish activity on that island or elsewhere in Iceland has been found (but see Ahronson, this volume). The most likely explanation for the name is that the profile of the island seen from the mainland is remarkably similar to that of Iona in the Hebrides where there was a major Irish religious community with which some of the settlers in Iceland were certainly familiar; it was raided by Viking several times in the early ninth century.

Irish annals suggest that Scandinavians based in Ireland had reason to look for new homes in the second half of the ninth century. By establishing permanent bases in Ireland the Vikings lost the advantage of mobility, and disputes between different groups meant that they were unable to present a united front of the kind that proved effective in England. They suffered many defeats. In 866 they were expelled from all their strongholds in the north (AU 320-1). It is not known where they went, but the evidence, discussed below, that there was a substantial proportion of Celts among the earliest Icelandic population makes it reasonable to assume that some of the Scandinavians driven from Ireland went to Iceland with their Celtic wives and their children, and with Celtic servants and slaves.

The factional conflict in Laithlind mentioned above, that led Olaf to leave Dublin to help his father, probably in 872, may also have encouraged some Norwegians who had set-tled in Scotland and its islands to move on to the new land. Genetic evidence noted below indicates that there were very close links between the female settlers in Iceland and the Western Isles. Towards the end of the century the Vikings of Limerick, Waterford and Wexford all suffered defeats and the Dublin Vikings, weakened by factional conflict, were overcome by the Irish in 902 and expelled. Some settled across the Irish Sea near Chester and possibly on the Isle of Man. Others probably emigrated to Iceland. Several leading fam-ilies in Iceland claimed to have ancestors who came from Ireland or the Hebrides. There are, moreover, several clear indications of early Irish influence in Iceland. Some Irish names were used in families of high status, for example, Njáll, Kormákr, and Kjartan. Irish nick-names were also given at an early stage and some other Irish names, such as Dufan and Melkólfr, were given to servants and slaves. There are also some place-names in Iceland that are either of Irish origin or reflect that Irishmen once lived in those places, for example, Brjánslökr, Patreksfjörðr and Iragerði. Even more revealing are the few Irish loan words in Icelandic. Two of them, *tarfr* 'a bull' from Irish *tarbh* and *súst* or *thúst* 'a flail' from Irish *súiste* imply that the Irish made a significant contribution to the development of farming in Iceland (Turville-Petre 1953).

33

These and other indications of early Celtic influence have led to attempts to estimate the proportion of Celts among the earliest settlers. Early discussions, based on such criteria as cranial indexes or hair colour were unhelpful. The hope that blood-groups would provide a sound quantitative basis have proved unfounded; the wildly divergent results that have been reached—98 per cent Celtic, 86 per cent Scandinavian—are evidence enough that blood groups are an unsatisfactory guide. More reliable results are being reached by analysis of DNA in the populations of Scandinavia, the British Isles, and Iceland. The proportion of Scandinavians among the ancestors can be estimated by studying the Y chromosome, that is only transmitted by fathers to sons, and the mitochondrial chromosome (mtDNA), that is only transmitted by females. Recent studies have indicated that while at least 75 per cent of the male ancestors of the Icelanders were from Scandinavia, the proportion of female ances-tors from Scandinavia was only 37.5 per cent. Most of the women who settled in Iceland in the ninth and tenth centuries were from the Celtic parts of the British Isles. The proportion of Scandinavian female ancestors in Orkney was even smaller, 35.5 per cent, which means that many native women survived the Scandinavian colonisation. The proportion of Scandinavian female ancestors in the Western Isles was only 11 per cent, but two mtDNA sequence types were only found in Iceland and the Western Isles. The leader of the investi-gation, Agnar Helgason, comments that such exclusive sharing of lineages between popula-tions is very rare, which suggests that there was a strong matrilineal link between the Western Isles and Iceland. This is consistent with the fact that the Western Isles are men-tioned many more times than any other North Atlantic islands in *Landnámabók* (Helgason *et al.* 2000; 2001).

This evidence raises questions about the role of the Celts in the development of Iceland. Several scholars have commented on indications that Irish influence left its mark on the themes and even on the form of some Icelandic literature (Ól. Sveinsson 1957; 1975; Turville-Petre 1971; Lukman 1977; McTurk 1977-79). I would like to suggest that this topic is worth closer study. The intellectual and cultural achievements of the Icelanders before they submitted to the Norwegian king in the mid-thirteenth century were truly remarkable. Most of the skaldic verse of the tenth and eleventh centuries was composed by Icelanders, in the twelfth century they studied chronology and produced histories, laws, itineraries, and, perhaps most remarkable of all the linguistically precocious *First Grammatical Treatise* (Holtsmark 1936). The sagas they wrote in the thirteenth century rank highly in medieval European literature. Iceland was, indeed, the leading cultural centre in the Scandinavian world. This intellectual productivity seems often to have been taken for granted. It is, however, worth remembering that it was accomplished by a very small population, at most 30,000 people, living on a remote Atlantic island; the cathedral schools of Scandinavia, including the archiepiscopal sees of Lund and Nidaros, produced nothing comparable.

I should like to conclude by suggesting that it was Irish influence that explains the intellectual predominance in Iceland. I hope that this symposium will encourage experts in different disciplines to re-examine the ways that the Celtic peoples of the British Isles contributed to the society and advanced culture of early medieval Iceland.

34

ABBREVIATION

AU   Mac Airt, S. and Mac Niocaill, G., eds, 1983. *Annals of Ulster*, Dublin.

BIBLIOGRAPHY

Brooks, N. 1971. 'The Development of Military Obligations in Eighth- and Ninth-Century England', in Clemoes and Hughes 1971, 69-84.

Chase, C. ed., 1981. *The Dating of Beowulf*, Toronto.

Clarke, H.B. *et al.*, eds, 1998. *Ireland and Scandinavia in the Early Viking Age*, Dublin.

Clemoes, P. and Hughes, K., eds, 1971. *England before the Conquest: Studies in Primary Sources presented to Dorothy Whitelock*, Cambridge.

Coupland, S. 1995. 'The Vikings in Francia and Anglo-Saxon England to 911', in McKitterick 1995, 190-201.

Duffy, S. 1992. 'Irishmen and Islesmen in the Kingdoms of Dublin and Man, 1052-1171', *Ériu*, 43, 93-133.

Faulkes, A. and Perkins, R., eds, 1993. *Viking Revaluations*, London.

Fell, C.E. 1987. 'Old English *Wicing*; A question of Semantics', *Leeds Studies in English*, 18, 111-23.

Fitzhugh, W.W. and Ward, E., eds, 2000. *Vikings: The North Atlantic Saga*, Washington and London.

Graham-Campbell, J. and Batey, C. 1998. *Vikings in Scotland: an Archaeological Survey*, Edinburgh.

Helgason, A. *et al.* 2000. 'Estimating Scandinavian and Gaelic Ancestry in the Male Settlers of Iceland', *American Journal of Human Genetics*, 67, 697-717.

Helgason, A., Hickey, E., Goodacre, S., Bosnes, V., Stefánsson, K., Ward, R., and Sykes, B. 2001. 'mtDNA and the Islands of the North Atlantic: Estimating the Proportions of Norse and Gaelic Ancestry', *American Journal of Human Genetics*, 68, 723-37.

Helle, K. 1998. 'The History of the Early Viking Age in Norway', in Clarke *et al.* 1998, 239-58.

Hødnebo, F. 1987. 'Who were the First Vikings?', in Knirk 1987, 43- 54.

Holtsmark, A. 1936. *En islandsk scholasticus fra det 12. århundre*, Oslo.

Jones, G. trans., 1964. *The Norse Atlantic Saga*, London.

Knirk, J.E. ed., 1987. *Proceedings of the Tenth Viking Congress: Larkollen, Norway, 1985*, Oslo.

Krag, C. 1991. *Ynglingatal og Yngingasaga*, Oslo.

Lukman, N. 1977. 'An Irish Source and some Icelandic fornaldarsögur', *Mediaeval Scandinavia*, 10, 41-57.

McKitterick, R. ed., 1995. *The New Cambridge Medieval History*, II, Cambridge.

McTurk, R. 1977-79. 'An Irish Analogue to the Kráka-Episode of *Ragnars saga Loðbrokar*', *Éigse*, 17, 277-96.

Myhre, B. 1993. 'The beginning of the Viking Age—some current archaeological problems', in Faulkes and Perkins 1993, 182-204.

Myhre, B. 1998. 'The Archaeology of the Early Viking Age in Norway' in Clarke *et al.* 1998, 3-36.

Niermeyer, J.F. 1954-76. *Mediae Latinitatis Lexicon Minus*, Leiden.

Ó Corráin, D. 1998. 'Viking Ireland—Afterthoughts' in Clarke *et al.* 1998, 421-52.

——1999. 'The Vikings in Scotland and Ireland', *Peritia*, 12, 296-339.

Page, R.I. 1981. 'The Audience of Beowulf and the Vikings' in Chase 1981, 113-22.

Sawyer, B. and Sawyer, P. 1993. *Medieval Scandinavia: from Conversion to Reformation circa 800-1500*, Minneapolis and London.

Sawyer, P. ed., 1997a. *The Oxford Illustrated History of the Vikings*, Oxford.

——1997b. 'The Age of the Vikings, and Before',in Sawyer 1997a, 1-18.

Smyth, A.B. 1977. *Scandinavian Kings in the British Isles, 850-880,* Oxford.

Sveinsson, E. Ól. 1957. 'Celtic Elements in Icelandic Tradition', *Béaloideas: The Journal of the Folklore of Ireland Society*, 25, 2-24.

——1975. *Löng ser För,* Reykjavík.

Turville-Petre, G. 1953. *Origins of Icelandic Literature*, Oxford.

——1971. 'Dróttkvæt and Irish Syllabic Measures, *Ériu,* 22, 1-22.

Vésteinsson, O. 2000. 'The Archaeology of Landnám: Early Settlement in Iceland' in Fitzhugh and Ward 2000, 164-74.

Whitelock, D. ed., 1979. *English Historical Documents c. 500-1042*, 2nd edn, London and New York.

35

Drengs, Vikings, Countrymen:

raiding, conquering and settling in ninth-

and tenth-century England

R.A. Hall

Introduction

In 793, 'bloody rain [was seen] in Lent in the City of York in the church of St Peter… falling in a clear sky menacingly'; afterwards, 'on 8 June, the ravages of heathen men miserably destroyed God's church on [the island monastery of] Lindisfarne with plunder and slaughter' in the first Viking raid of which we know any detail (ASC, *s.a.* 793; Allott 1974, 18). In 1066, at Stamford Bridge in Yorkshire, the invading army of the Norwegian king Haraldr *harðráði* (Hard-ruler) was surprised by the Anglo-Saxons under their king, Harold Godwinson. In an epic battle Haraldr *harðráði* was killed and his army routed. These two events in the north of England, in the Anglo-Saxon kingdom of Northumbria, may be said to mark the beginning and the end of the Viking Age in England. In the two and a half centuries in between, however, there were several distinct phases of Scandinavian activity.

First came a period given over exclusively to sea-borne raiding by *drengir*, the crew of fighting ships (Foote and Wilson 1970, 105-08), in which the looting of coastal monasteries was often the objective. Then came land-based campaigns by what the annalist in the Anglo-Saxon Chronicle described as a 'great heathen army'. This invaded England in 865 and maintained a continuous presence for fifteen years, overwintering each year in a defensive encampment. In generally successful warfare the army captured three of the four great kingdoms—Northumbria, Mercia and East Anglia—which made up Anglo-Saxon England. This success was followed in 876-80 by the settlement of those areas by sections of the 'great army'. Estates in the three captured kingdoms were, apparently, allocated to individuals from the conquering armies and, in the words of the contemporary *Anglo-Saxon Chronicle* (ASC), 'they began to plough and to support themselves'. These events created a swathe of territory beyond the control of the Anglo-Saxon king of Wessex, King Alfred, where Scandinavian laws and customs predominated.

Alfred's heirs gradually recaptured and unified the country politically, but this was a process that took several generations. It was not finally accomplished until 952-954; its result was the creation of the kingdom of England. Political subjugation did not, however, prevent the Scandinavian settlers in England and their descendants from continuing to exert a cultural influence. Later still, from the 980s, another wave of invaders from Denmark, led by King Sveinn and his son Knútr / Cnut, extorted large sums of *danegeld*, and eventually placed Cnut and then his two sons on the throne of England during the period 1016-1042.

Contemporary English writers—mainly monks—recorded the headline events of these years in annals which survive to the present, and the impact of Scandinavians on England has never been forgotten. Some English antiquaries, historians and archaeologists have had a tendency to blame the direct action of Viking raids for every change they see (or think they see) in the historical or archaeological record; for example, the decline of individual monasteries, even where there is no evidence that the monastery in question was ever raided. English archaeologists of past generations have also interpreted some discoveries in a sensational manner; for example, an axe dug up beside the Anglo-Saxon church at Repton

(Derbyshire) was interpreted as having been damaged and discarded in disgust by a Viking frustrated in trying to break down the church (Brown 1925, 318-9).

Historical and archaeological enquiry over the last thirty years, however, has considerably refined our understanding of the Viking Age in England. Significant and recent discoveries are now shedding light on the critical events of the later ninth and early tenth century, and the contribution made by the Vikings as catalysts for change in Anglo-Saxon society. Much current academic work is focussed on identifying archaeological traces of Scandinavians, and on recognizing how Vikings, and second/third/fourth generation settlers of Scandinavian descent, chose to define and portray their identity (Hadley 2000).

RAIDING AND CONQUERING

The early raids were part of a wave of Viking attacks throughout north-west Europe but, contrary to popular opinion, Viking raiders sometimes worked much more subtly than by mere smash and grab tactics. For example, the Codex Aureus (now, with historical irony, in the Royal Library Stockholm), was a valuable church treasure which Vikings seized from a Kent monastery in the mid ninth century. Fortunately, an annotation written in the margins of folio 11 records how ealdorman Æelfred and his wife Werburg 'ransomed' it for gold (Alexander 1978, 56-7; Roesdahl *et al.* 1981, 63). Vikings could see its value to the English, and were prepared to negotiate its return to them.

Just as Viking raiders were subtle in their financial stratagems for raising capital through extortion, so the 'great army' of 865 and later seems to have been efficient and well-organized in provisioning its forces during the next phase of Viking activity. This can be inferred thanks to the discovery of a hoard of silver, including Anglo-Saxon and Arab coins and hacksilver (fragments of Scandinavian silver ornaments/jewellery), which was found near London at Croydon in the mid nineteenth century (Brooks and Graham-Campbell 1986). The coins date the hoard to 871/2, and allow its deposition to be related to the 'great army': who else is likely to have had Arab coins and Scandinavian hacksilver? There is other evidence that Croydon was a manor house and estate owned by the Archbishop of Canterbury at this time, and it looks as if the Vikings were taking advantage of the existing Anglo-Saxon system of collecting surplus food and other renders at aristocratic manors (the tax system of the time), and extorting these resources to feed themselves. Why exactly some Viking buried the hoard is not known, but it is one of several hoards found on the route taken by the 'great army', which archaeologically confirm its progress around England.

An even more remarkable insight into the activities of the 'great army' in a hostile foreign country has come from discoveries made by Martin Biddle and Birthe Kjølbye-Biddle in central England at Repton (the site of the axe find and its lurid if fanciful interpretation mentioned above). Repton is well known to historians and archaeologists. There are documentary records that in the ninth century this was a burial place for kings of the Anglo-Saxon kingdom of Mercia, and there are standing remains of an Anglo-Saxon stone church, and of an even more remarkable crypt (Taylor and Taylor 1965, 510-16; Taylor 1987). It is also recorded in the ASC that Repton was where the 'great army' spent the winter of 873/4.

Immediately off the south-east corner of church the Biddles discovered a massive ditch which presumably once had an earthen rampart thrown up on its inner side. Through a combination of geophysical prospecting and limited excavation they were able to trace its course (Biddle and Kjølbye-Biddle 1992). It enclosed a D-shape, with its straight edge along the shallow cliff of the River Trent, and with the Anglo-Saxon church at the centre of the landward arc, presumably a gatehouse or strongpoint. This earthwork, which enclosed 1·46 ha/3.65 acres, is interpreted as the Vikings' winter camp—the first in England to be identified with certainty.

Excavations around the east end of church also uncovered a cluster of graves which can be dated to the ninth century, among them one in which the famous 'door-breaking axe' was probably originally buried. They also include one where the body was interred with a series of weapons and other objects—a classic Viking warrior burial. There is no doubt about the cause of the warrior's death—the top of his left thigh bone had been cleft by a sharp-edged weapon, resulting in a severed artery. The objects buried in his grave include weapons, belt fittings and, between the legs, a container, totally decayed, in which were items best interpreted as lucky charms/ amulets/ talismans—a rare insight into personal or family beliefs.

These graves confirm that there were Vikings at Repton in the ninth century, but there are also other indications of a Scandinavian presence. In 1726, an antiquarian talked to an 88 year old local man who, about forty years earlier, had been 'cutting Hillocks' in a close just west of the church, in what is now the vicarage garden (Biddle *et al.* 1986, 111-2). The old man recalled how he had come across a large number of human bones, and a giant in a stone coffin. The soil was backfilled, he said, and a tree planted; subsequent re-investigations of the spot added nothing that has been recorded. A low mound was, however, still visible in the vicarage garden, and the Biddles' excavation revealed a series of later burials around it, which seem to have the mound as their focus. These include the graves of people buried in fine costumes, and they suggest that the mound retained an importance into the tenth century. The mound's original significance and, perhaps, the foundation of this later reverence, was emphasised when clearance of the turf on top of the mound revealed a bizarre burial. Four youths had been laid out in a communal grave in such unusual juxtaposition as to suggest that their grave represented the culmination of a ritual which might even have involved their sacrificial death.

Within the mound itself was the outline of a two-roomed stone building. Lead from windows and plaster from the walls indicate that this was a high status structure, possibly an Anglo-Saxon royal mausoleum. In the east room was a mass of bones, representing 249 skeletons. Subsequent analysis has shown that 82 per cent were males aged 15-45, and 18 per cent were female. The bones had been stacked as charnel around the walls—this was not their primary burial. Neither, apparently, were they the dead of battle, for none of them bore any sign of injury on their bones. Nonetheless, coins of 873/4 found with them clearly indicate that their re-burial took place at the time when the Viking army was in control of Repton. It has been suggested that some of them may be part of the Viking 'great army' re-interred around the stone coffin of a very important Viking leader (Biddle and Kjølbye-Biddle 2001); another interpretation is that they are predominantly the remains of individuals originally interred in the monastic graveyard, disturbed when the Vikings dug their defensive ditch'(Richards 2003, 390).

Several suggestions may be made about the motivation for these actions and rituals. In taking over the Anglo-Saxon royal church at Repton, the Vikings signalled their takeover of the surrounding country. Cutting down the royal mausoleum for their own burials was perhaps symbolic of how they had defeated the Mercian royal dynasty. Using the church as a strongpoint in their defences demonstrated to themselves and their Anglo-Saxon enemies just how ineffective was the alliance of Christian church and state. And what now seem bizarre burials, perhaps sacrifices, at the top of the mound, hint at other rites and rituals which were presumably designed and undertaken to cement the Viking army's cohesion, traditions and esprit de corps.

One suggestion about the origin of the bones in the mass grave was that they could perhaps be linked to a site four miles away, at Ingleby. There, until recently in deep woodland, is a series of inconspicuous mounds. A handful were opened in the 1940s and 1950s; some were apparently empty, while others contained layers of charcoal and burnt bone. In these latter were objects including, most conspicuously, a Viking sword. This appears, therefore, to be the only Viking cremation cemetery in England.

A recent survey has shown that there is a total of 59 barrows (Richards *et al.* 1995). Excavation of one has revealed traces of a cremation pyre, fragments of burnt human bone, parts of many small metal objects apparently burnt in a fire, and animal bones, perhaps graveside sacrifices representing pagan Scandinavian rituals. Another excavated mound was initially thought to be empty and, like the previously excavated mounds which had no obvious remains of any burials, to represent a cenotaph for someone buried elsewhere. However, the discovery of a small patch of burnt human bone and a ring-headed pin at the very edge of this mound, and its interpretation as a burial, casts doubt on the long-held theory that these are empty mounds which were cenotaphs. Only careful and total excavation has revealed this new evidence which, if this interpretation is correct, would sever any obvious connection between the bones in the Repton mass grave and the cemetery at Ingleby. Nonetheless, it remains possible that Ingleby was the cemetery of a part of the great Viking army who wanted nothing at all to do with burials in the nearby Repton (Christian) graveyard. This would suggest factionalism in the 'great army', another possible insight into that army's composition, tensions and modus operandi. These are new and fascinating perspectives which current studies of both the Repton and the Ingleby data may be able to sharpen.

SETTLEMENT

40

The settlement of part of the 'great army' in 876, 877 and 879 created politically distinct areas which eventually became known as the Danelaw. The effect of that settlement and its aftermath is recognised today in village names of characteristically Scandinavian forms e.g. Danby, Normanby, Copmanthorpe, Scagglethorpe, Upsall, Lund—the geographical limits of these name-forms correspond well with the documented limits of Danelaw. However, when looking for evidence of settlements by Scandinavians within (let alone beyond) the Danelaw, there are very few burials of classic Scandinavian form, where objects were put into the grave, to attest the presence of immigrants. Either this was not a popular means of signalling identity, or there were relatively few Scandinavian settlers, or such graves have not come to light.

There is rather more evidence, in the form of pieces of stone sculpture which functioned as gravemarkers in cemeteries, for a change in rural settlement and ideology at about this time. Compared to the pre-Viking period, stone sculpture is now found at a multiplicity of church sites. Some stones have figures of warriors, some display animal interlace patterns, and others even incorporate Scandinavian mythology (Bailey 1980). Another form of evidence for settlement in the countryside, growing with the activities of people using metal detectors, is the quantity of small objects, particularly second-rate/base metal jewellery, which can be dated to this period. The increasing quantities show that there was much more of this stuff in circulation than previously thought, and also that there was mass production of popular types, which were widely distributed (e.g. Bailey 1993; Leahy and Paterson 2001).

Only recently, however, have the sites of houses, hamlets, villages and manor houses where people lived during these centuries been located and investigated; and the picture that is emerging is that the ninth and tenth centuries, the time around and after the Viking settlement reported in the ASC, was an era of change, re-arrangement and even upheaval in the pattern of rural occupation. This can be demonstrated through a summary of discoveries made at several Danelaw sites.

In Lincolnshire, excavations undertaken at the deserted site of a medieval village referred to as Goltho (Beresford 1987) have shown that a totally new manor house complex was founded in the mid ninth century, and was eventually transformed into a Norman castle. As a new element in the countryside, the manor house may indicate the presence of new landlords, perhaps the Viking settlers mentioned in the ASC or, alternatively, native English opportunistically grasping a new social status under a new regime.

In North Yorkshire, at an open field site known by the parish name of West Heslerton, there is no visible trace that anyone ever lived there. Large-scale archaeological excavation has, however, brought to light a village that existed from the Roman period for many hundreds of years until it disappeared by about 900—just after the Vikings settled. At that time the landscape was re-arranged and all the people moved away from the traditional site, perhaps to found the medieval and modern village of West Heslerton (Powlesland 2000).

Not far away, at a site known as Cottam, in East Yorkshire, there is evidence for Anglo-Saxon occupation before the Vikings (Richards 1999). Then, *c.* 900, a new settlement was established nearby, distinguished by what is interpreted as an impressive, 'ranch-style' gateway, which was not a viable defence but a statement of social status, wealth and superiority. The suggestion is that this new settlement was initiated by landlords only recently enabled to display their position in society, and responding to new political, social and economic circumstances. In the case of Cottam this aggrandised 'ranch-house' appears to represent a transitional phase in the location of the settlement, which lasted only a generation before its site was deserted, perhaps in a move which created the nearby medieval villages of Cottam or Cowlam.

Wharram Percy, also in East Yorkshire, is one of the most famous archaeological sites in England thanks to excavations every summer over several decades which have investigated the long-term history of the now deserted medieval village. There is evidence for occupation on the village plateau from the eighth century onwards, and field walking in the Wharram area suggests a network of dispersed middle Saxon settlements (Richards 1999, 88). Although there is not yet certainty about when the medieval village was laid out, the most likely date for this landmark event is the late ninth or tenth century; the tenth-century foundation of what was later the parish church is certainly an indicator of change at that time (cf. Stamper and Croft 2000). A high quality belt-set decorated in Scandinavian Borre style, thought to have been made in Scandinavia may, it is suggested, point to the presence of a high-status Scandinavian immigrant at this time, perhaps a new landowner who initiated the change in settlement.

At each of these sites—Goltho, West Heslerton, Cottam and Wharram Percy—there is evidence which suggests changes in the settlement pattern in the decades around 900. The earliest forms, layout and economies of the hypothetical 'new' settlements of *c.* 900—that is, the proposed new villages at Wharram Percy, Cottam/Cowlam, West Heslerton, and their like—now need investigation. Here lies the key to defining and comprehending the fundamental movement to the nucleated villages and open field agriculture well known as the enduring medieval settlement pattern in this part of England. It may be that this familiar patterning of the landscape was instigated by the competitive need to maximise the output of new, relatively small estates, deploying a critical mass of manpower to better advantage. These relatively small estates had their origins in the prizes of successful war, given by Viking kings and warlords to their followers, when these rulers sub-divided the apparently much larger pre-Viking estates.

It is not only the discovery of villages and houses, or the objects used/worn by their inhabitants, which is broadening our understanding of the Viking impact on Anglo-Saxon society: it is also a fresh look at aspects of religious belief that can be detected archaeologically. In particular, it is becoming clear that the origins of many of England's parish churches can be dated to the tenth century. Although some complete churches or parts of churches over 1000 years old still stand today, only a handful can be dated using documentary sources or inscriptions such as that on a sundial at Kirkdale, North Yorkshire (Taylor and Taylor 1965, 357-61; Rahtz and Watts 2003), and few have been excavated as comprehensively as St Peters, Barton-upon-Humber, Lincolnshire (Rodwell and Rodwell 1982), or St Martins,

Wharram Percy (Bell *et al.* 1987). Even at Wharram Percy later alterations to the church, and the continual use of the graveyard for burials into the modern era, have limited the survival of the earliest remains. However, at Raunds, Northamptonshire, excavations before redevelopment uncovered traces of a totally unknown parish church and its burial ground which were in use from *c.* 900 until *c.* 1300 (Boddington 1996). This unencumbered site allowed a total excavation which was undisturbed by later medieval and modern intrusions, and which yielded a complete picture of the church's evolution. As well as remains of the earliest church, a graveyard with several hundred burials was investigated, but among all these burials there were just two interred beneath decorated tomb slabs. It is suggested that one of these should be interpreted as marking the grave of the church's founder.

The recognition that in such a large cemetery there were only two marked graves, and the suggestion that they go back to church's origin, has prompted re-evaluation of the distribution of the hundreds of such grave markers in the Danelaw. It has just been recognized that there is a remarkably consistent pattern of only one or two such markers per church, and it has recently been suggested that this is not just a product of the chance of survival, but the norm—and that, as at Raunds, these monuments probably marked the graves of the church's founder and his family (Stocker 2001). In Yorkshire and Lincolnshire such grave markers are dated 900-950, and it seems that, once again, in the second or third generation after the political and social upheaval brought about by the Viking conquest and settlement, new landlords there were signalling their status through ostentatious foundation of their own, proprietorial, churches.

This building of churches and erection of stone monuments is seen also in the towns of the Danelaw. At York, for example, investigations at the site of the long-lost church of St Helen-on-the-Walls suggest a tenth-century origin (Magilton 1980), and the presence of tenth-century sculpture at other churches attests their existence at that time (Lang 1991). These are the churches and monuments of new urban landowners and property developers, perhaps originally the same people who owned rural estates, perhaps new, nouveau riche entrepreneurs. They catered for a newly expanded urban population who lived, as excavations at Coppergate in York have shown, in newly defined property blocks on newly laid out streets created in the early tenth century, and who were the progenitors of a new era of industrial-scale mass production of goods for a newly created market economy (Walton 1989; Bayley 1992; Ottaway 1992; Hall 1994: Walton Rogers 1997; Mainman and Rogers 2000; Morris 2000; Mould *et al.* forthcoming). The cycle of production was based on the supply of raw materials from rural estates to the city, where a new expanded cadre of specialist craftsmen provided essentials and luxuries for use both by their fellow townsfolk and by the majority of the population who were now living on the smaller, rural estates which, because of their diminished size when compared to the pre-Viking period, were less able to maintain a range of craft specialists.

In all, the period of the late ninth and tenth century does seem to have been a watershed, changing the face of the Danelaw countryside, fermenting town life, and creating the basic underlying framework of much that survives to this day. The coincidence of this period of change with the documented Viking takeover and settlement of the 870s seems too great to ignore. It looks as if the Scandinavians were crucial catalysts for change—dismantling the previous social and economic order, and creating their own.

Their strategy was, by and large, not to proclaim their distinctive Scandinavian identity by employing old, traditional symbols such as overtly pagan burial. Rather, they blended into and adapted Anglo-Saxon traditions, this masking the fact that they were a highly significant, politically dominant and economically successful element in the population of northern and eastern England. This policy helped to forge a new, Anglo-Scandinavian, identity.

ACKNOWLEDGEMENTS

I wish to thank the organizers of the Viking Millennium International Symposium, the Newfoundland Historic Sites Association and Memorial University, St John's, Newfoundland for affording me the opportunity to present a version of this paper at the Conference. I am particularly grateful to Dr Julian Richards, Department of Archaeology, University of York, for updating me on his recent discoveries at Ingleby, to others who have contributed to my understanding, and to Heather Dawson for assistance in preparing this text.

ABBREVIATION

ASC   Whitelock, D. ed., 1965. *The Anglo-Saxon Chronicle*, 2nd edn, London.

BIBLIOGRAPHY

Alexander, J.J.G. 1978. *Insular Manuscripts 6th to the 9th century*, London.

Allott, S. 1974. *Alcuin of York*, York.

Bailey, R.N. 1980. *Viking Age Sculpture*, London.

——1993. 'An Anglo-Saxon strap-end from Wooperton', *Archaeologia Aeliana*, 5th series, 21, 87-93.

Bayley, J. 1992. *Non-ferrous Metalworking from 16-22 Coppergate*. York: The Archaeology of York, 17/7.

Bell, R.D., Beresford, M.W. *et al.* 1987. *Wharram Percy: The Church of St Martin*. London: Society for Medieval Archaeology Mongraph Series 10.

Beresford, G. 1987. *Goltho: The development of an early medieval manor, 850-1150*. London: English Heritage Archaeological Report 4.

Biddle, M. and B. Kjølbye-Biddle. 1992. 'Repton and the Vikings', *Antiquity*, 66, 36-51.

——2001. 'Repton and the "great heathen army", 873-4', in Graham-Campbell et al. 2001, 45-96.

Biddle, M., Kjølbye-Biddle, B., Northover, J.P. and Pagan, H. 1986. 'A parcel of pennies from a mass-burial associated with the Viking cemetery at Repton in 873-4', in Blackburn 1986, 111-24.

Blackburn, M.A.S. ed., 1986. *Anglo-Saxon Monetary History*, Leicester.

Boddington, A. 1996. *Raunds Furnells. The Anglo-Saxon Church and Churchyard*. London: English Heritage Archaeological Report 7.

Brooks, N.P. and Graham-Campbell, J. 1986. 'Reflections on the Viking-Age Silver Hoard from Croydon, Surrey', in Blackburn 1986, 91-110.

Brown, G.B. 1925. *The Arts in Anglo-Saxon England II. Anglo-Saxon Architecture*, 2nd edn, London.

Carver, M.O. ed., 2003. *The Cross Goes North*, Woodbridge.

Foote, P.G. and Wilson, D.M. 1970. *The Viking Achievement*, London.

Frazer, W.O and Tyrrell, A., eds, 2000. *Social Identity in Early Medieval Britain*, London.

Geake, H. and Kenny, J., eds, 2000. *Early Deira. Archaeological Studies of the East Riding in the fourth to ninth centuries AD*, Oxford.

Graham-Campbell, J., Hall, R.A., Jesch, J. and Parsons, D., eds, 2001. *Vikings and the Danelaw: Select Papers from the Proceedings of the Thirteenth Viking Congress*, Oxford.

Hadley, D. 2000. '"Cockles amongst the Wheat": The Scandinavian Settlement of England', in Frazer and Tyrrell 2000, 111-136.

Hadley, D. and Richards, J.D., eds, 2000. *Cultures in Contact: Scandinavian Settlement in England in the Ninth and Tenth Centuries*, Turnhout.

Hall, R.A. 1994. *Viking Age York*, London.

Lang, J.T. 1991. *York and Eastern Yorkshire. British Academy Corpus of Anglo-Saxon Stone Sculpture*, III, Oxford.

Leahy, K. and Paterson, C. 2001. 'New light on the Viking presence in Lincolnshire: the artefactual evidence', in Graham-Campbell *et al.* 2001, 181-202.

43

Magilton, J.R. 1980. *The Church of St Helen-on-the-Wall, Aldwark*. York: The Archaeology of York, 10/1.

Mainman, A.J. and Rogers, N.S.H. 2000. *Anglo-Scandinavian Finds* York: The Archaeology of York, 17/14.

Morris, C.D. 2000. *Wood and Woodworking in Anglo-Scandinavian and Medieval York*. York: The Archaeology of York, 17/13.

Mould, Q., Cameron, E. and Carlisle, I. forthcoming. *Leather and Leatherworking from Anglo-Scandinavian and Medieval York*. York: The Archaeology of York, 17/16.

Ottaway, P.J. 1992. *Anglo-Scandinavian Ironwork from 16-22 Coppergate*. York: The Archaeology of York, 17/6.

Powlesland, D. 2000. 'West Heslerton Settlement Mobility: a case of static development', in Geake and Kenny 2000, 19-26.

Rahtz, P. and Watts, L. 2003. 'Three ages of conversion at Kirkdale, North Yorkshire', in Carver 2003, 289-309.

Richards, J.D. 1999. 'Cottam: An Anglian and Anglo-Scandinavian settlement on the Yorkshire Wolds', *Archaeological Journal*, 156, 1-110.

——2003. 'Pagans and Christians at a frontier: Viking burial in the Danelaw', in Carver 2003, 383-96.

Richards, J.D., Jecock, M., Richmond, L. and Tuck, C. 1995. 'The Viking barrow cemetery at Heath Wood, Ingleby, Derbyshire', *Medieval Archaeology*, 39, 51-70.

Rodwell, W. and Rodwell, K. 1982. 'St Peter's Church, Barton-upon-Humber: excavation and structural study 1978-81', *Antiquaries Journal*, 62, 283-315.

Roesdahl, E. *et al.* 1981. *The Vikings in England*, London.

Stamper, P. and Croft, R., eds, 2000. *The South Manor Area*. York: York University Archaeological Publications 10.

Stocker, D. 2001. 'Monuments and Merchants: Irregularities in the distribution of stone sculpture in Lincolnshire and Yorkshire in the tenth century', in Hadley and Richards 2000, 179-212.

Taylor, H.M. 1987. 'St Wystan's Church, Derbyshire: a reconstruction essay', *Archaeological Journal*, 144, 205-45.

Taylor, H.M. and Taylor, J. 1965. *Anglo-Saxon Architecture*, Cambridge.

Walton, P. 1989. *Textiles, Cordage and Raw Fibre from 16-22 Coppergate*. York: The Archaeology of York, 17/5.

Walton Rogers, P. 1997. *Textile Production at 16-22 Coppergate*. York: The Archaeology of York, 17/11.

Breaking the monolith:

multi-cultural roots of the North Atlantic settlers

Przemysław Urbańczyk

T here is a deeply rooted premise underlying most of the North Atlantic settlement studies, which causes scholars to assume a uniform Scandinavian ethnicity of people who
colonised the new-found-lands during the Viking Age, and among Scandinavians it is
Norwegians who especially claim the inheritance of that heroic trans-oceanic venture's tradition.

Such an attitude derives from the romantic times of building national identity by referring to own specific glorious and heroic past. This was a strategy typical of all nations
emerging in the nineteenth and early twentieth century in various parts of Europe that was
dominated by several multinational 'empires', e.g. Turkey, Austro-Hungary, tsarist Russia,
Prussian Germany, and Sweden. Historical sources and archaeological discoveries were
commonly used in order to justify territorial rights and to distinctively discern nations by
giving them clear identity. Today, also, we can observe similar manipulations with the past
in the areas where contemporary multinational states of the Soviet Union and Yugoslavia
broke down in the early 1990s.

In the case of the Viking-Age colonisation of the North Atlantic islands, Norwegian
claims for 'primary rights' were built upon Sturla Þordarson's explicit declaration that
'Iceland was discovered and settled by Norwegians' (*Landnámabók*, chap. 2). According to
the same tradition it was also Norwegians who discovered Greenland. Hence, a clear
transoceanic leap-frog progress was constructed with Norway as the 'homeland' and subsequent stages at the Faeroes, Iceland, Greenland and finally Vinland. Medieval westward
expansion of the Norwegian political domination reinforced this mono-ethnic model, which
was yet supported by archaeological discoveries that showed 'obvious' cultural affiliations
of the vernacular architecture and the mixed economy system characteristic of Viking-Age
insular societies.

All this well illustrates a rather typical process of a politically promoted process of the
mythicisation of the past that is used to legitimate actual needs for national identity by referring to the possibly distant and linearly organized past. This is a tendency typical of the most
contemporary historical and archaeological research, which results in interpretations producing homogenous, uniform, and unproblematic visions of the more or less distant past.
Within this paradigm a strategic position is occupied by the premise of ethnic continuity and
purity of cultural development that may be connected directly with contemporary nations.
Such an attitude results from the lack of theoretical consideration of the problem of ethnicity that is crucial for any anthropological but also for historical and archaeological studies
(Urbańczyk 2000).

Contemporary anthropology suggests that

> ethnicity is fundamentally political, and ethnic boundaries are, to some extent at least, permeable and
> osmotic, existing despite the flow of personnel or interaction across them. Thus criteria for ethnic
> ascription and subscription are variable (Jenkins 1997, 52).

Ethnicity appears to be differentiated, multidimensional, gradual, and contextual (Babiński
1998, 8).

Thus, the traditional concept of an ethnic group as a relatively isolated and stable population that is objectively discerned by its common culture is revealed as irrelevant. It was
first undermined in 1922 by Max Weber who stressed the decisive function of the 'belief' in

common origin, which is shared by members of an ethnic group (1978). Such belief is not a cause but a result of group cooperation, which promotes construction of a common identity. This 'subjectivist' approach was further developed in 1969 by Fredrik Barth who viewed culture not as some reality that shapes daily life of people but as a dynamic 'product' of interpersonal contacts. Group identity results from both the feeling of internal similarity and also external dissimilarity. Thus, ethnic identity may be situational and negotiable since it results from continuous relating of a 'self' to 'another' person(s) and it is not a passive reflection of some 'objective' norms of cultural tradition (Jones 1997, 115).

Anthropological expertise suggests that closed homogenous societies are very rare and most areas are characterized by multi-ethnicity (Jenkins 1997, 50), because 'group ideologies rarely or almost never are shared by all or even by the majority of the group members'(Babiński 1998, 25). The criteria of ethnic identity have never been absolute because they are based on similarities and differences that were meaningful for 'somebody' who used them to define his/her intra- and inter-group relations. Thus, 'boundaries' dividing ethnic groups might change in space and over time in result of the 'strategic manipulation of identity' connected to the execution of economic and political goals (Jones 1997, 110).

Armed with such a theory let us reconsider the 'ethnicity' of the Viking Age settlers of the North Atlantic new-found-lands. In this case an important argument may be raised against the anthropologists' claims of multi-ethnicity of almost all human societies. It is the insular character of the areas in question, which must have somewhat determined organization and development of local societies there (cf. Urbańczyk 1998 for yet another aspect of the life in the islands). Extremely small (as in the Faeroes) or small (as in Greenland) habitation zones available for sedentary societies with their rather uniform ecological conditions usually do stimulate development of cultural diversity, which is promoted as self-identification of groups competing over rare and/or unevenly distributed resources. For, if ethnicity is a reflection of the collective strategy of execution of various interests—including economic ones (Barth 1969a, 19)—then lack of clearly differentiated niches prevents the social need to express inter-group differences. Ecological diversity should not be equaled with differentiated productivity of various localities, which usually results in social stratification, but not in ethnic diversification of sedentary populations.

However, the primary target of my concern in this paper are not socially and economically stabilized societies of the Medieval and later periods but the phase of the colonisation, before the power relations were established and before social order was institutionalized. It was the time of the 'land rush' when not the social structure but geographical space was the main range for competition. Let us then analyze socioeconomic and political aspects of the settlement process by referring to available historical and archaeological sources of information relevant for discussion of 'ethnicity'. Due to the quality and quantity of data most references must be made to Iceland but I think that the following observations have some more general value and may be applied also to other islands of the region.

Settlement of the North Atlantic lands that were discovered in the late first millennium AD was a complex process, which took place in a specific political situation. During the tenth century, Northern Europe (i.e. the lands around the North Sea and the Baltic Sea) was undergoing quick and often radical political, ideological, economic, and territorial changes. Traditional decentralized and dynamic power structure was being replaced by organization based on supremacy of the 'royal' dynasties who claimed their sovereignty over larger and larger areas. Flexible polytheistic religions rooted in local traditions were giving way to expanding Christianity with its missionary zeal and promotion of strictly hierarchical structure of society organized by and around paramount power center supported by ecclesiastical institutions. Subsistence economy involved mostly in local exchange of unspecialized products was being stimulated towards greater effectiveness in order to achieve politically consumable surplus and to offer 'export' commodities. Geographic space that was subject to

collective control expressed by economic claims of local power centers was being extensively reorganized into politically and militarily maintained territories divided by more and
more stable borders.

Such processes involved also voluntary and coerced migrations of both, whole populations and families but also individuals. In contrast to the Migration Period they occurred
mostly in the border zones and involved relatively short distances. However, numerous
long-distance voyages were also undertaken along the sea routes. They were stimulated by
the above-mentioned socio-political changes and made possible by the development of the
open-sea means of transport and spread of navigation knowledge.

There were no authorities capable of controlling those movements. Probably, there were
also no authorities willing to control overseas migrations. The only real limits were personal determination, access to sea-going vessels and some knowledge of the destination of the
expedition to be undertaken. There were no mechanisms of any selection due to cultural
background, religious commitment, language or political preferences. Almost anyone could
engage in such venture although the final success was difficult to foresee.

Those preconditions, of a technical rather than social or ethnic nature, favoured
Scandinavians who entered the Viking Age with all necessary knowledge, technical skills
and entrepreneurial attitude. No wonder than, that it was them who dominated the heroic
period of the westward colonisation of the North Atlantic. Discovery of the uninhabited and
fertile Iceland opened quite new opportunities because it could 'host' many thousands of
newcomers.

47

The news quickly spread through the coastal ports of trade and the focus for those ready
to take necessary risks was clearly established. 'Every' capable man or woman could join
the land claiming rush with no respect to his/her ethnic background. For, what really mat-
tered was not persons' origin but their adaptability to the pioneer conditions of life.
However, the ability to cooperate and accept rules necessary to maintain social order was
decisive. For, in an agricultural subsistence economy there was no place for free competition over resources that are exploited within a delayed-return strategy. Access to land must
be carefully regulated according to socially accepted rules.

Establishment and execution of such rules is the more successful when the society is the
better developed and organized. Development of social institutions depends, among other
factors, on the number of people involved. 'Sufficient' quantity of participants was especially important for hierarchical societies of the Early Middle Europe. For, there was no
leadership without the necessary support which depended on the number of followers.
Therefore, those striving for dominant positions in uninhabited areas had to organize such
support by attracting, persuading or coercing people to settle within their more or less real
domains.

Landnamabók offers some accounts of such strategies on the part of ambitious individuals who came to Iceland in already well organized 'convoys' (*Sturlubók* (S) 113; 211; 214),
who made land pre-claims for the newcomers scheduled to come later (S. 184; 274), who
'granted lands' to their relatives and friends (S. 280) but also of some who apparently
attracted settlers to inhabit their domains (S. 30). These are all reflections of the competition
for power that was present already at the early stage of the colonisation. This competition
involved ambitious and/or charismatic individuals who must have felt challenged by the situation that offered unusual perspective but also faced them with constraints that were related to demography. One can, therefore, easily imagine even some recruitment along the
North European sea shores as well as a tendency to bribe and coerce people to resettle.

Thus, both the political circumstances and social dynamism of that society in formation must have resulted in the peopling of the North Atlantic islands with settlers of various
cultural/ethnic backgrounds. This should not be seen as an obstacle for organizing a well-
functioning society because early medieval people were culturally much more open than we

are today. They did not live in monopolistic states, which would impose uniform behaviors. They were used to quite frequent changes of the geopolitical situation, which often resulted in cultural, religious, economic, and even linguistic dynamism—especially in the border zones.

There is no reason to believe that settlers of the North Atlantic islands showed less cultural flexibility during the colonisation period, even if it was mostly western Scandinavians who played the organisational role and who subsequently managed to impose their socioeconomic preferences. Of the 435 named immigrants only *c.* 130 are clearly derived from the western and northern shores of the Scandinavian Peninsula, i.e. Norway and Hålogaland (Rafnsson 1974, 222). Almost 50 are said to have come from the British Isles (Ireland, Hebrides and Northern Isles). Some came also from Denmark, Sweden and Gotland.

Historical sources are explicit to show that many of the newcomers were of non-Scandinavian origin. Thus, there was substantial wave of Celtic people present especially among the slaves and freedmen but also among wives (cf. Pálsson 1996). The question still persists of the pre-Viking presence of Irish *papar* which is suggested in the literary evidence but is not yet confirmed archaeologically. Less distinct but detectable is the contribution of the Sámi whose participation in the settlement process and cultural legacy may also be traced in written sources (Pálsson 1997).

There were also some 'Germans' (= West Franks or Saxons) who can be identified indirectly by their names, e.g. Svavarr (= Swabian warrior?; S. 4), Viligisl (*Hauksbók* 16), Saxi (S. 76), Thjodrek (= Theoderic; S. 302) and Vilbald (S. 324). One, however, is directly mentioned by the author of the *Grœnlendinga saga* (chapter 4) who wrote that Leifr Eiríksson's 'foster father' came to Vínland as a member of the first exploring expedition. He even spoke German there when depressed by some unexpected events. Given this clear 'ethnic' definition it is strange to hear that his name was Tyrkir (=Turk or Southerner). Such an obvious contradiction should make us very careful with hasty interpretations of names that are devoid any explanatory context.

Somewhere else we may spot an opposite situation when there is a strange name mentioned in a context that allows some 'ethnic' inferences to make. A good example is the mysterious Nattfari who was brought to Iceland by Gardar Svavarson (S. 4). Struck by bad luck, Nattfari involuntarily became the first permanent inhabitant of Iceland accompanied by one slave and a woman whose names were not recorded. His subsequent behavior suggests a non-Scandinavian origin, which may be inferred from his ignorance of the knowledge necessary to properly secure the land claim. This ignorance resulted in his later removal from his land that was taken over by some later pretender for the land ownership (S. 247).

Of course, reliability of both of these saga stories may easily be questioned when their accuracy is discussed. What remains important for this discussion, however, is that the sagas indicate that early settlers of the North Atlantic islands were 'ethnically' open and could incorporate both newcomers and individuals who were coerced to join the transoceanic expeditions. To support such conclusion one may quote yet another story written into the early Icelandic version of the discovery of Vínland. For, it is written in *Eiríks saga rauða* (chpt. 12) that the Greenlanders kidnapped two *skrœling* boys who were later baptized and included in their society.

Also, archaeology may furnish some insights into the 'ethnic' backgrounds of the early settlers. This direction of studying the problem in question needs further development of comparative studies but there are some finds available that are so specific that they allow 'ethnic' interpretations. A striking example is offered by *c.* 18 sunken huts that were discovered at various Icelandic settlements dated to the Viking Age. They are all near- or subrectangular with vertical walls dug into the ground, with flat floors and stone ovens placed in one of the corners, post-holes dug in the corners and along the walls and no visible entrances. The most recent structures of this type were excavated in 2000 in Hofstaðir by

Orri Vesteinsson (Edvardsson, Lucas and Vesteinsson 1999, 36-40), in Háls by Kevin Smith (pers.comm.), and in Sveigakot (2001-02) by the present author.

They are usually dated to the tenth century. Characteristic is their relative chronological position in the local settlement sequence. Whenever relative stratigraphy is available they are always proved to be the earliest buildings at given sites. Later they were replaced by standard long houses built according to the classical Scandinavian tradition.

Although I formulated the hypothesis already five years ago I did not hear yet any explanation of this phenomenon that would be more convincing than connecting these unusual constructions with Slavic traditions (cf. detailed description in Urbańczyk 2002). Such houses are extremely typical for all lands inhabited by the early medieval Slavs. And they are distinctively different from the *gruben-hauser* known from many areas settled by the Germanic populations. Thus, I cannot imagine that they could have been built in Iceland by people who did not live in such houses and who were not well acquainted with their construction. Alternative hypotheses that explain these houses that were excavated also in Scandinavia, as temporary sheds, specialized workshops or steam baths, are not convincing at all.

What I suggest here is not, of course, any massive Slavic 'invasion' in Iceland but the presence of some Slavs who took part in the settlement of the island together with Celts, Germans and Sámi who were all, from the beginning, dominated or quickly fell under political and economic domination of Western Scandinavians. It was the need for social cooperation that later imposed a rather uniform cultural pattern over all insular populations who developed a specific tradition made up of various Scandinavian elements.

49

Conclusion

The conclusion of this paper must be that we should not transfer the Medieval and later North Atlantic homogeneity back to the Viking Age when insular cultures took their form in result of the choices made by people who decided to stay in those outposts of the European civilization. We should refrain from responding to modern political demands to prove ethnic continuity and for legitimating geopolitical claims. It is important to discern ethnicity, which is historically changeable from the demographic continuity of concrete populations (Shennan 1989a, 19). Understanding historical circumstances is always crucial to understand how, why and when ethnicity could have been manifested or constrained. It makes sense to talk of ethnicity in an individual sense only when the identity is collectively recognizable and expressed in culturally specified practices (Jenkins 1997, 53) that are subject to changes.

We cannot project our contemporary concept of nation-states into a distant past when such an idea was absent. This is the way of thinking that is completely irrelevant for the studies of the Viking Age. For, in the tenth century there were no nations in Europe—no Norwegians, Danes or Swedes, just like no Germans, Poles, Italians or Spaniards, and obviously no Icelanders although the latter quickly achieved a nation-like stage due to the specific geographic conditions. There were only locally bound societies characterized by the dynamism of both the internal organization and also inter-group relations. It was with the development of the monopolistic political centers capable of effective control over stable territories that more and more uniform cultural patterns could have been imposed, maintained and produced within populations 'trapped' in stately borders.

BIBLIOGRAPHY

Babiński G. 1998. *Metodologiczne problemy badań etnicznych* [*Methodological problems of ethnic studies*], Kraków.

Barth F. 1969a. 'Introduction', in Barth 1969b, 9-38.

——ed., 1969b. *Ethnic groups and boundaries: the social organization of culture difference*, Boston.

Buko, A. and Urbańczyk, P., eds, 2000. *Archeologia w teorii i w praktyce* [*Archaeology in theory and practice*], Warsaw.

Crawford, B.E.C. ed., 2002. *Papa Stour and 1299. Commemorating the 700th anniversary of Shetland's first document*, Lerwick.

Edvardsson, R., Lucas, G., Vesteinsson, O. 1999. 'The Viking settlement', in Lucas 1999, 20-41.

Jenkins, R. 1997. *Rethinking ethnicity. Arguments and explorations*, London.

Jones, S. 1997. *The archaeology of ethnicity. Constructing identities in the past and present*, London.

Lucas, G. ed., 1999. *Hofstaðir 1999. Interim report,* Reykjavík.

Pálsson, H. 1996. *Keltar á Íslandi*, Reykjavík.

——1997. *Úr landnorði. Samar og ýstu rætur íslenskar menningar*, Reykjavík.

Rafnsson S. 1974. *Studier i Landnámabók. Kritiske bidrag til de isländska fristatidens historia*, Lund.

Shennan, S. J. 1989a. 'Introduction', in Shennan 1989b, 1-32.

——ed., 1989b. *Archaeological approaches to cultural identity*, London.

Urbańczyk P. 1998. 'Human response to environmental change in North Atlantic insular situations', *Fróðskaparrit*, 46, 149-153.

——2000. 'Archeologia etniczności— fikcja czy nadzieja?' ['Archaeology of ethnicity—fiction or hope?'], in Buko and Urbańczyk 2000, 137-146.

——2002. 'Ethnic aspects of the settlement of Iceland', in Crawford 2002, 155-65.

Weber M. 1978 [1922]. *Economy and society*, Berkeley.

50

Scandinavia in the Viking Age

Birgit Sawyer

W hat do we know about the society, from which the Vikings—raiders, traders, explorers, and colonisers—came? Scandinavia is poorly provided with written evidence for its early medieval history. Before the late eleventh century the only vernacular texts preserved are runic inscriptions and some coin legends; historians are therefore dependent on information gleaned from sources written outside Scandinavia, e.g. in Frankia, England, and Germany such as Rimbert's *The Life of Anskar* (*c.* 870); Widukind's *Saxon Chronicle* (968); and Adam of Bremen's *History of the Archbishops of Hamburg-Bremen* (*c.* 1075). The problem with most of these foreign sources is, however, that they let us meet Scandinavians outside their home-lands, and—apart from Rimbert and Adam—do not give much information about the political and social situation within Scandinavia itself.

It was not until the mid-twelfth century that literary texts and collections of laws began to be produced within Scandinavia. The Icelandic sagas, as well as the historical works by the twelfth-century Icelandic scholar Ári Þorgilsson and works written during the late twelfth to early thirteenth centuries, e.g. by the Dane Saxo Grammaticus, give a lot of information, but since they were written several hundred years after the beginning of the Viking Age, we can never be sure to what extent the picture they give reflects their own time, rather than that of the Viking Age. We have the same problem with the medieval law codes from the same period; no doubt they contain many older rules, but again the difficulty is to know which they are (Sawyer and Sawyer 1993, chapters 1 and 10).

Considering the problems posed by the foreign—and late—vernacular texts, the following study is as far as possible based on contemporary Scandinavian sources, provided by archaeology, place names and runic inscriptions. Numismatic evidence based on the study of coinage is very important but is excluded in this study (Sawyer and Sawyer 1993, 6-8). Archaeological excavations provide information about life and death in Viking-Age Scandinavia, e.g. about settlements, buildings, tools, and burial habits. Improved dating techniques help us to place the finds in a historical context, and osteology contributes with knowledge about life expectancy and illnesses (Sawyer and Sawyer 1993, 5, 41-2). Place-names can provide much information, although their interpretation poses problems. Most were first recorded in the fifteenth and sixteenth centuries, long after they were coined and when their original meaning had been forgotten. Despite some uncertainties they can cast light on a wide range of topics, including the development of language, pre-Christian religion, changes in the landscape, boundaries, communications, and, above all, the development of settlement. So, for example, thousands of names describing clearings dramatically reflect the extensive colonization of forest in many parts of Scandinavia between the tenth and fourteenth centuries. The rune-stones have hitherto not been much used as a historical source, and therefore it may be helpful briefly to describe them (Sawyer 2000).

In late Viking-Age Scandinavia the custom of commemorating the dead with runic inscriptions carved on raised stones or natural rock faces was widespread. From this period more than 3000 such inscriptions are known, but their distribution is very uneven; about 50 are known in Norway, about 200 in (medieval) Denmark (including Bornholm), and as many as 1750 in (medieval) Sweden. There are no Viking-Age runic inscriptions found from Iceland. The inscriptions vary, but they all say who commissioned or sponsored them and who was honoured. In most cases the relationship between sponsor and deceased is indicated, and sometimes a parent or other relative of the latter is also named. This commemoration formula, which often also contains some description of the dead person, is sometimes followed by a Christian prayer or, rarely, a curse. Information is also occasionally given about how and where the death happened. These inscriptions are an invaluable source of knowledge about the Viking Age; they throw light on such varied matters as the development of the language and poetry, kinship and habits of name-giving, settlement and communications, Viking as well as trading expeditions, and, not least, the spread of Christianity. They are also a source for political, social, economic, and legal history, although this large corpus of contemporary evidence has hitherto been largely untapped by historians.

POLITICAL SITUATION

During the Viking Age, the only well-established kingdom in Scandinavia was that of the Danes; already by the early eighth century there are both literary and archaeological indications that powerful Danish rulers were based in South Jutland, and towards the end of the tenth century Harald Bluetooth and his son Sven Forkbeard extended their power to include the eastern border areas—the 'march' of the Danes. Thus by *c.* 1000 the territorial kingdom of the Danes encompassed what is today Denmark plus the western and southern regions of modern Sweden. Danish kings ruled a relatively numerous population, and by ship had easy access to all parts of their territory. These were important factors in their power. What is more, by controlling the entrance to the Baltic they were able to regulate and benefit from the trade between western Europe and the lands round that sea, and by extending their authority in southern Norway they also profited from the trade along the Norwegian coast (the 'North way'). Their domination of southern Scandinavia can be traced back to the eighth century.

The formation of both the Norwegian and the Swedish kingdoms, which started later and were more long drawn-out processes, should be seen against this background of Danish hegemony and the fact that the Viking raids, having for more than two hundred years enabled chieftains and their retainers to enrich themselves, were now coming to an end. The first known attempt to create a Norwegian kingdom (mainly in western Norway) was by Haraldr *inn hárfagri* (Finehair) *c.* 900, but it soon fell apart. From the middle of the tenth century Norway remained under Danish overlordship for almost a century, with short periods of independence (during the reigns of Óláfr Tryggvason, *c.* 995-999, and Óláfr Haraldsson, 1015-1028). In Sweden the first king known to have been acknowledged by the two main groups, the *Götar* and the *Svear*, was Olof Eriksson (*c.* 995-1020), who was probably under Danish overlordship for most of his reign. The territorial consolidation of the Swedish kingdom was delayed by the tensions and differences between the *Götar*, who occupied the plains of central southern Sweden, and the *Svear*, whose territory was around Lake Mälaren and along the east coast (Sawyer and Sawyer 1993, chapter 3).

In Viking-Age Norway and Sweden, and even in Denmark royal power was limited and did not affect the society in the way it was to do later. How, then, was society structured?

SOCIAL STRUCTURE

The conventional interpretation is that early Scandinavian society was fundamentally egalitarian with free landowners and chieftains, who were believed to have common interests, and who were supported by unfree men and women who did the menial work.

This picture of early Scandinavian society was given a mythological basis in *Rígsþula*, a poem that describes the god Rígr visiting three households, representing three generations-great-grandparents, grandparents and parents (KHL XIV, 234-6; Karras 1988, 60-3, 208-10). He shares the bed of each couple in turn and fathers a son in all three. The first son, Þræll (slave) lives with a woman called Þír (servant) and their children, both boys and girls, have names describing their ugliness or the heavy and dirty work they do. The second son, Karl (free man) marries Snör (daughter-in-law); he ploughs and she weaves. They are good-look-ing and prosperous, as are their many children, who have names meaning e.g. warrior, farmer, and wife. Rígr's third son Jarl and his wife Erna only have sons with names mean-ing noble, heir, king); none of them works, they live in luxury, eating and drinking, hunting and fighting.

The poem only survives in an incomplete fourteenth-century copy and has been vari-ously dated between the late ninth and the thirteenth centuries. The place of composition is equally uncertain; Norway, Denmark, the British Isles and Iceland have all been suggested. Those who accept that it is an early poem have taken it as a description of early Germanic social structure, in which the *bönder* (=landowners) had pride of place. The presence of a distinct aristocratic class would, however, have been more appropriate in the thirteenth cen-tury. The indications of an early date, such as the prominence given to the slaves, the absence of overt Christian influence, the vocabulary and the apparent description of old-fashioned dress, could all be deliberate archaisms. Moreover, it is unlikely that slaves would be described as masterless at a time when slavery was a flourishing institution.

Instead of the picture given by *Rigsþula* we should envisage a much more complicated and hierarchical society; we have no evidence supporting the idea of a free and equal farmer society in Scandinavia. On the contrary: in all parts of Scandinavia, except perhaps among the Saami, society was highly hierarchical. In the early Middle Ages some men and women were unfree, and at all times there were various grades of freemen, ranging from those who had been freed to men of superior status who had lordship not only over their own house-holds, as all freemen had, but also over other freemen.

53

THE UNFREE: 'THRALLS'

Medieval Scandinavian laws and sagas have many references to unfree men and women. The word for such men was *þræll*, and for a woman *ambátt*. For simplicity I shall use the modern English word thrall for both (Danish *træl*, Norwegian *trell*, Swedish *träl*). In modern works they are often called slaves. It is true that some can properly be called slaves, that is people who were the property of others who had absolute power over them. Some were apparently killed and buried with their owners. The Arab Ibn Fadlan described such a custom among the Rus in the tenth century and that may be the explanation of a few double burials that have been found in Scandinavia. It is, however, misleading to describe all the unfree as slaves for that encourages the belief that they all had the same status as slaves in the ancient, Mediterranean world. It is significant that the Scandinavian words used for a thrall and thraldom basically meant servant or service in a household. The laws compiled in the twelfth century and later that contain most information about thralls were deeply influ-enced by Church and Roman Law. One American scholar has indeed suggested that 'per-haps those who framed the law codes saw in the Roman laws on slavery a convenient way of defining the status of thralls, and in so doing altered that status to that of slaves' (Karras 1988, 120).

The rules concerning thralls, which are most elaborate in Norwegian and Icelandic laws, must have been at best no more than oral tradition when they were compiled, for thral-dom had then ended. In Norway it was virtually ignored in the National Law issued in 1274. It is remarkable that in Sweden, where thraldom was not formally abolished until 1335, the earlier provincial laws are very much less elaborate in their treatment of thralls than are the Norwegian laws.

Most thralls seem to have been the children of unfree parents, but some were captives taken in conflicts or who had surrendered their freedom because of debts. It is, however, important to emphasize that thralls could buy or be given freedom. Freedmen of the Danes are mentioned in ninth-century England. According to Norwegian laws, a freedman and his children remained in some degree of subordination for several generations and a distinction was made between freedmen and their children who were still under obligation to their former masters (or their heirs), and those who had been completely freed. The latter were, nevertheless, treated differently from people whose ancestors had always been free. It is, therefore, possible that one purpose of those who compiled these laws was to explain and justify the existence in their own days of a large group of people who were legally free, but economically very dependent, even depressed. Many Scandinavians cherished the notion that their ancestors had enjoyed a great degree of freedom and full control over their own land. One explanation for the supposed change, current in medieval Norway and Iceland, was that kings, in particular Haraldr inn hárfagri (Finehair), had tyrannically deprived many people of their ancestral rights. By suggesting that many people were descendants of slaves, and consequently had no right to inherit free land, the compilers of the laws offered an explanation for, and justification of, the control some exercised over others.

There is no reliable information about the number or proportion of thralls in individual households or in the whole population of any part of Viking-Age Scandinavia. Some early households are described in thirteenth-century sagas as having had twelve, eighteen or even thirty thralls, but there were no thralls in Iceland after the twelfth century (KHL XIX, col. 17), and it is improbable that these figures were accurately remembered for a century or more; they are perhaps based on the number of landless labourers and servants employed by great men in the thirteenth century. Just as the status of such labourers and servants varied, so too did that of thralls earlier, some of whom had arduous or dirty tasks, while others had great responsibilities as stewards of the estates of kings or other major landowners.

FREE—BUT DEPENDENT

A much debated question is when thralls and impoverished landowners became tenants. Some scholars think this development did not normally happen before the twelfth century, while others think it had started during or even before the Viking Age (Sawyer and Sawyer 2002, chapter 4.2). The question of tenancy is closely connected with the question of thraldom; those who are convinced that thralls were very common in early Scandinavian society have found it difficult to believe that there were many tenants at the same time, while those who do not think thraldom was so important argue that there must always have been many more or less dependent farmers who were forced to rent all or part of the land they cultivated.

No doubt all over Scandinavia tenants were recruited from both former thralls and poor landowners, but there are different opinions concerning the proportion of each group; the fact that in medieval Scandinavia tenants were considered legally free has led many scholars to suppose that a large proportion of the tenants had originally been free and independent landowners (Iversen 1994, 33-4). If most of the tenants had originally been recruited from the thralls, it has seemed difficult to explain why the status of tenants in Scandinavia, especially in Norway and Sweden, was so much higher than in other parts of Europe.

We cannot, however, assume that most Scandinavian farmers were originally free and independent landowners. The legal freedom they enjoyed in the Middle Ages could have been the result of political developments in the twelfth and thirteenth centuries, when it was in the interest of kings to have as many free subjects as possible so that they could be taxed. It was also in the interest of the landlords to free their thralls, so that, as freedmen, they could pay fines and taxes themselves. What is more, the increasing population made tenants more practical and lucrative for landlords than thralls (Iversen 1994, 464-81; Helle 1995, 116).

The original meaning of the term *bonde* is a 'settled man', in contrast to people who did not own land. The runic inscriptions of the tenth and eleventh centuries show clearly that a bonde was a landowner with responsibility for a household. Only ten per cent of the men named in the inscriptions are called *bönder*, and as almost all of the people named in inscriptions belonged to the social *élite*, it is arguable that bönder only comprised three to four per cent of the population. In Denmark and Sweden the term *bonde* was only used for this top level of society well into the fourteenth century, but in Norway it went out of use much earlier, probably because its meaning changed. The reason Norwegian laws use *þegnr* or *hauldr* instead of *bonde*, is most likely because, by the twelfth century, a man could be both a landowner and a tenant at the same time; other terms thus had to be used about those who only cultivated their own land.

It seems reasonable to conclude that we should not draw too sharp a line between 'unfree' and 'free' in Viking Scandinavia, but rather think in terms of a scale of dependence, from free and wealthy landowners who were dependent on their chieftains, the less wealthy, but free, landowners who rented land, and the impoverished farmers who owned no land, down to the bottom level: the thralls. Not only were the border lines between these forms of dependence blurred, it was possible for one and the same person to belong to more than one category.

55

LORDS AND OVERLORDSHIPS

There were also lords/rulers, and these too were ranged in hierarchies in which some were acknowledged as overlords by others. Such overlordships were inherently unstable and could be ended by defeat or the death of an overlord; few lasted more than a couple of generations.

Although the earliest reliable, direct evidence for such an overlordship in Scandinavia is from the early ninth century (that of the Danes over southern Norway), there can be no doubt that they were a normal phenomenon long before that, as they were in most other parts of Europe (*Annales Regni Francorum s.a.* 813). Conflicts between communities and their leaders must have created a succession of overlordships among the Scandinavians. Some exceptionally powerful, or lucky, rulers probably claimed exceptionally extensive overlordships and these may have been responsible for at least some of the cultural contacts revealed by archaeological and linguistic evidence.

SETTLEMENTS

The economic basis was land, and the majority of the population lived from cultivating it, even though fishing and hunting also played a big role. There was a high degree of subsistence economy, supplemented by exchange of goods and other kinds of trade, controlled by local chieftains. Long distance trade especially in luxury goods (e.g. precious metals, glass, wine, fine fabrics) is documented long before the Viking Age, but it was not until the eighth century that permanent trading places such as Ribe, Kaupang, and Birka were established.

The core of society was the farm, situated either on its own or in villages. The single farms were most common in Norway and northern Sweden, while villages were established early in Denmark and southern Sweden. The village of Vorbasse in Jutland, for example, can be traced as far back as the fourth century, when it consisted of twenty farms, one of them much bigger than the others (Hedeager and Kristiansen 1988, 132-34). A characteristic for these early villages is that they often moved short distances: Vorbasse moved eight times before it settled where it still is. Such moves offered an opportunity to cultivate the fertilized ground where the cattle had been housed. Most Danish settlements were, however, permanently established in the eleventh or twelfth centuries on sites that had not previously been occupied and that seem to have been chosen to be close to land suitable for arable farming.

HOUSEHOLDS AND FAMILIES

In all households there was a master, normally the husband, but in households of siblings with their families, normally the eldest brother. Sagas and rune-stones show that there was only one master (*bonde*) at a time: his wife, children, other relatives in the household as well as any thralls were under his authority, and he was responsible for them and their actions in the outside world. The wife, however, was not without influence; there is abundant evidence that, while the husband ruled 'beyond the threshold', the wife, being in charge of the locks and keys, ruled inside it.

In Viking-Age Scandinavia this responsibility of the wife meant much more than it would today; in fact, many women held a key position:

> While women may not have had power over people like men, we must be allowed to assume that in the domestic sphere women had power to make decisions of far-reaching consequences to the entire household. As managers of all kinds of farm products, such as food, textiles, and hides, it was in the hands of the wife to see to it that the often quite big household of many generations, servants, and animals came safely through the winter. In this capacity she must have had decisive influence in the disposition of these goods and thereby over family economy (Dommasnes 1991, 71).

What is more, in pagan Scandinavia, the mistress of the house seems to have had an important religious role, especially in rituals connected with the fertility cult (Steinsland 1985).

Even when husbands were alive, many wives exercised also power 'beyond the threshold' when their husbands were away from home raiding, hunting, fishing, or trading. Women then had to take responsibility for everything at home, including a certain amount of trading. In many Scandinavian graves women were buried with scales (or weights). These have often been interpreted the graves of professional 'tradeswomen'. The Norwegian archaeologist Anne Stalsberg, however, suggests that they were matrons who stayed in the home farm or the town property, while the men were away. In such circumstances, women had to buy what was needed, or sell produce, transactions in which it must often have been necessary to weigh payments of silver (Stalsberg 1991, 81).

Widows had even greater responsibilities and remained in charge of their households as long as their children were under age. This is well illustrated by the many rune-stones that were sponsored by widows. These show that it was quite common for women to survive not only their husbands but also their children, so that they were left as independent property owners. This evidence is consistent with indications that after about AD 1000 the number of women who lived longer than men tended to increase, partly thanks to the increased cultivation of beans and other leguminous crops that were rich in iron. As the rate of infant mortality was high they also often survived their children. This, together with the fact that Church condemned infanticide—which affected girls more than boys—led to demographic changes, with a higher proportion of women in the population than earlier (Sawyer and Sawyer 1993, 40-42). On the other hand, many women often died when they were young, but this cannot be blamed on complications in pregnancy and childbirth, because high mortality connected with childbearing has been shown to be a modern phenomenon, largely due to infections and complications that were rare or unknown in Europe before the nineteenth century (Sellevold 1989, n.6). Instead, it seems more likely that girls were not as well cared for as boys in childhood and were ill prepared for the strain of childbirth. Those who survived their fertile period, however, now had better chances of outliving their male contemporaries (Sawyer and Sawyer 1993, 42).

MARRIAGE AND OTHER FORMS OF COHABITATION

Sagas and runic inscriptions show that families were formed by monogamous marriages. A man may have had relationships, and children, with several women, but when he died, only one wife was acknowledged. We do not know how couples were married but there is no doubt that then, as later, marriage was based on a contract between families. Reciprocally binding agreements were needed, especially between wealthy families, for reverse inheritance could result in the transfer of large estates from one family to another.

Contracted marriages, however, were not the only form of cohabitation. Concubinage, or informal relationships without legal consequences, were very common later, and although the inscriptions do not provide evidence for this custom, many rulers in the eleventh and twelfth centuries had concubines and there is no doubt that it was a common practice, especially among wealthy landowners. Concubinage should not be confused with brief relationships; a concubine was a permanent, or at least long-term, partner of a man, and their children could inherit from him if he acknowledged them. In the higher levels of society a man could hope to ensure that he would have one or more sons to survive him by having a concubine as well as a legal wife; in lower levels such informal relationships may have been the normal form of partnership between men and women. There is nothing to suggest that these relationships were considered improper at any social level before the Church condemned them and only approved relationships that met its requirements for a Christian marriage.

57

THE FAMILY

A woman did not sever the links with her own family when she married. In the new family that she and her husband created, they both, together with their children, had property rights or expectations. There is no proof that wives owned a share of the household property at that time as they did later, but it does seem likely that they did. The fact that many rune-stones were sponsored by widows, either on their own or together with other members of the family, suggests that, as wives, they had a leading role in their families, most probably as co-owners. With some regional exceptions it seems to have been the widow's task to sponsor her husband's memorial if his sons, brothers or father did not survive him, or if his sons were too young. In such a situation the widow apparently took over the leadership of the household, the guardianship of minors and control of the property, suggesting that she had well-defined rights as co-owner when her husband was alive. The many memorials sponsored jointly by a widow and sons confirm the nuclear character of families and possibly imply that in those families the inheritance had not yet been divided among the heirs.

THE SIZE OF FAMILIES

Runic inscriptions also provide some information about the size and composition of families in eastern Sweden where men and women jointly acted as sponsors. Inscriptions with more than three or four children are rare, but as a high rate of infant mortality can be assumed, many more children must have been born. Daughters are significantly fewer than sons. In Uppland inscriptions with both, the ratio of sons to daughters is 3:2. This cannot be explained by the exclusion of married daughters, for they are sometimes named. It was probably the result of a deliberate attempt to control the size of the population by limiting the number of girls who were allowed to survive.

Christian missionaries condemned this practice, and in Iceland it was prohibited soon after conversion. Christianity was certainly responsible for many other changes that affected families. Too little is known about the pre-Christian situation to say much about the immediate impact of the new religion. The runic inscriptions, most of which are Christian, may give some clues to the early stages of transition at least in the upper levels of society. They may, however, give a misleading impression of circumstances in general; only a small number of Scandinavians were rich or Christian. Later evidence does show how many Scandinavians reacted to and resisted the policy of the church on families, inheritance and property in the twelfth and thirteenth centuries. The struggle between secular and ecclesiastical interests has left many traces, and the thirteenth-century laws show that the church was then still meeting determined resistance.

KINSHIP AND INHERITANCE

A widely held interpretation of early Scandinavian society has been that it was based on clans (Sw. *ätter*) in the sense of descent groups that were responsible for many of the functions that were later taken over by kings and the church, an encroachment that the clans are supposed to have vigorously resisted. This view of Scandinavian and other Germanic societies is frequently repeated in modern text-books. There is, however, no evidence for such well-defined descent groups in Scandinavia (nor in any other Germanic societies: Murray 1983). Belief in their existence largely depends on interpreting the provincial laws as reflecting such a clan-society in the last stages of dissolution (Sawyer and Sawyer 1993, 166). Some provisions in these laws have been taken to be relics of a time when rights and obligations were matters not for individuals but for the clan, which is supposed at some time to have owned land collectively and been collectively responsible for protecting its members. In the absence of any superior authority, conflicts between members of different clans are assumed to have been resolved (or not) by blood feud; if an individual was dishonored, injured or killed, the clan took revenge on the clan of the wrong-doer.

For such a society to function each clan would have to be a well-defined, distinct group, which in turn requires that descent was traced from either fathers or mothers. The Scandinavian clans are supposed to have been patrilineal. If they were, a woman must have left her own clan to join her husband's. As a consequence, women are supposed to have had no right to inherit land; otherwise clans could not have had permanent rights over their own land. The existence of such a society in Scandinavia, however, cannot be proved at any time; the assumption of a clan society is based on an interpretation of the medieval laws that cannot be supported (Sawyer and Sawyer 1993, 167f). As far back as we have evidence, the character of kinship in Scandinavia was fundamentally bilateral. The runic inscriptions of the tenth and eleventh centuries confirm this, for they show that kinship was then bilateral and that families were nuclear. Most rune-stones were erected in memory of people by their closest relatives-by children after their parents, by siblings or spouses after each other. Men sponsor memorials to their brothers-in-law and other relatives by marriage, and there are even memorials after mothers-in-law (SRI Uppland 897 and 914b). Many inscriptions name the wife, mother or daughter of the dead man and in some, a husband, when commemorating his wife, named her father and occasionally even her grandfather. The fundamentally bilateral character of kinship is further underlined by the words used in inscriptions for some relatives; an uncle, for example, is called either a 'mother-brother' or a 'father-brother', and a grandfather is called either a 'mother-father' or a 'father-father'.

INHERITANCE

The rune-stones were sponsored by the heirs (or the guardians) of the persons commemorated and they therefore yield information about customs of inheritance current in the tenth and the eleventh centuries (Sawyer 2000, chapter 3). A systematic study of the inscriptions has shown that, in general, men had much stronger inheritance rights than women; daughters were postponed by sons in cases of paternal inheritances, the right of a brother was generally stronger than that of the mother. Customs were, however, not the same in all regions; in Denmark, Norway, and parts of southern Sweden women seem to come even further down in the order of inheritance, while in Uppland they could apparently inherit together with men, e.g. daughters together with sons, and sisters together with brothers.

Even where inheritance by women was postponed, individual inscriptions show that in practice daughters and sisters inherited from their fathers and brothers much more often than is suggested by their frequency as sponsors. Many heiresses are hidden behind their husbands, fathers, uncles, or other male relatives, who sponsored the stones on their behalf. It can also be seen that many women left property, which they are likely to have inherited (e.g. from fathers, brothers or other relatives).

With some regional exceptions reverse inheritance was very frequent; fathers and mothers commemorating their sons constitute almost eighteen per cent of the relationships in the inscriptions. Thus there seems to be many parents in Viking-Age Scandinavia who survived their offspring, and in reality reverse inheritance might well have been even more common; in *c.* 190 inscriptions widows commemorated their husbands, and if they survived their sons they would have be entitled to inherit from them.

59

COMMUNITIES AND THINGS

The transfer of property or rights to an heir had to be publicly recognized. In medieval Scandinavia this was customarily done in one or more of the assemblies or things in which local communities regulated their affairs (Sawyer and Sawyer 2002). Little is known about these assemblies before the thirteenth century when contemporary texts begin to provide detailed information about them. By then churchmen and royal officials had wrought many changes, but some common and apparently ancient features can be discerned. Something can also be learnt from the arrangements made in the ninth and tenth centuries by the Scandinavians who settled in the British Isles and the Atlantic islands, especially Iceland.

It appears that in the ninth century the main assemblies were known as allthings because all the freemen of the community had the right to attend. The recognition of heirs was only one of their many functions. They also dealt with accusations of theft and disputes about the ownership of land, or boundaries. They were occasions for political decisions, for social contacts, for buying and selling, for sporting contests, and, most important of all, for religious ceremonies. It is significant that many of the places in which major assemblies met were, to judge by their names, cult centres. There is, however, no doubt that all assemblies were associated with cults. Inherited rituals were an essential element in the sense of community, and were performed in special places, some of which can be identified by names that incorporate words that meant 'a place of worship', for example *-vi* in Odensvi, or that are named after a god, for example Óðínn in Onsjö in Skåne, Þor in Torsø in Sjælland or Þi (r) in Tislund in Jutland. There are also places named after gods collectively, such as the major cult centre at Gudme in Fyn. Religion in pagan Scandinavia is discussed in the final section of this study (see also Price, Gräslund, this volume).

By the thirteenth century, churches and markets had taken over many of the diverse activities of earlier things; assemblies were then largely concerned with legal matters.

Proceedings were highly ritualistic. Accusations and responses had to be made in traditional formulas. Decisions were sometimes made by appeals to the supernatural, for example by casting lots, a procedure that gave power to those responsible for interpreting the signs. Decisions could also be made by a duel between the parties in dispute or their representatives. Another method was by compurgation, a procedure in which an individual was supported by oaths sworn by other people. As the value of oaths depended on status, it was an advantage to have the support of men of high rank.

In the early Middle Ages, assemblies had no executive power; their effectiveness depended on social pressures, reinforced by religious sanctions. The ultimate sanction was outlawry, exclusion from the society represented by the assembly. The imposition of lesser penalties and the implementation of decisions about, for example, landownership, lay in the hands of the individuals concerned. For the protection of their rights individuals therefore depended on their own resources or what help they could obtain from others. One source of support must often have been the family, but many disputes were within families, and then the support of friends was needed, if possible by the more powerful men in the community. The support of a lord who could call on his sworn followers was particularly valuable. By acknowledging such a lord, a man could gain protection for himself and his family without losing his free status, and lords gained in prestige and influence. The most prestigious and normally most powerful lords were kings whose function as the best guarantors of individual rights was an important factor in the extension of royal authority and the formation of the medieval kingdoms.

60

It was in local communities, presumably in assemblies, that some men were recognized as especially trustworthy and were described as good. The only evidence for them in early Scandinavia is provided by runic inscriptions in which over 250 men who are decribed as good (*kuþr*). In these contexts the word has been translated variously as 'well-born' or simply 'good'. There are, however, reasons for thinking that it did not refer to the excellence of husbands or the skill of farmers, but was, rather, a mark of status. These 'good men' were the equivalent of the *boni homines*, familiar in other parts of early medieval Europe. They were men who were acknowledged as trustworthy members of local communities, who had a leading role in local affairs, in assemblies, in making legal decisions, and as witnesses. They were not chosen or designated by rulers, but their willingness to cooperate with kings, even to act as royal agents, was an important factor in the enlargement of royal authority and its extension in remote regions of the developing Scandinavian kingdoms. Their status was normally hereditary, but it naturally affected the standing of the whole family, and it is therefore not surprising that the *epithet* 'good' was also sometimes given to sons, brothers, even sisters and daughters of 'good men' (Sawyer 2000, 107-11).

MOBILITY

Many people must have spent most of their lives in their home districts, but there were times when some of them had to visit markets elsewhere or go on fishing or hunting expeditions. Some travelled far for peaceful purposes; the winter festival at Uppsala, for example, was attended by people from the Arctic. Others who joined bands of Vikings returned home with their winnings, although some found new homes abroad.

The mobility of some Scandinavians in the tenth and eleventh centuries is confirmed by runic inscriptions, although only a tenth of the inscriptions commemorate people who travelled, or died, abroad. Some did so in the service of Danish kings or other leaders of expeditions to both East and West, a few were traders, and two inscriptions refer to pilgrims to Jerusalem. These monuments were, however, not erected to display pride in foreign adventures (Sawyer 2000, 116-22). Most commemorated men who died abroad and reflect the concern of their families or companions about the inheritance of their property. Medieval laws include rules for dealing with the problems that could arise in such situations. It was, for example, sometimes necessary to decide when an absent landowner could be presumed dead. A very serious problem was posed if a father and son both died on an expedition abroad; the fate of the father's inheritance depended on who died first. If it was the son, the inheritance would go to the father's kin, both paternal and maternal, but if the son survived his father, he inherited, and after him, his mother. The careful formulation of inscriptions commemorating men who died abroad shows that they were concerned with the resolution of such problems. The main issue in these monuments, as in virtually all the others, was inheritance. In effect, they proclaimed the decisions that must have been made in communal assemblies.

Even if the rune-stones do not give a representative picture of Viking activities, we can, however, learn something about some of the Vikings. A special group of these travellers' stones consists of those who had served a (Danish) king, in one case Svein Forkbeard, in five cases Knútr *inn mikli* (the Great: Sawyer 2000, 118). There were, however, other leaders than kings, the most famous of whom was Ingvarr (mentioned in 25 inscriptions!) who led an expedition to the east that ended in total disaster. This expedition has been interpreted as a summoning of a fleet that took part in prince Jaroslav's conflicts with the Petchenegs in 1036, and later went on to Georgia and the Caspian Sea, where the majority of the participants died *c.* 1041, most likely from diseases (Larsson 1990, 106).

61

Towards the end of the Viking Age there seems to have been more room for private enterprises in eastern Sweden, where royal power was still weak, than in western Scandinavia, where, from the time of Svein Forkbeard, the expeditions were led by the Danish kings. It goes without saying, however, that all these leaders—kings and others— must have had much larger bands of warriors than is indicated by the rune-stone material, but since they were not commemorated we will never know who these people were.

RELIGION

It was religion that bound society together before the medieval kingdoms were established. Scandinavian society then consisted of many local communities, each kept together by a common religious cult which was led by local chieftains. The cult was ethnic and integrated into the whole culture (Steinsland 1995). The gathering around the inherited rituals constituted the religious community, which was identical not only with the social but also the political and juridical community. A characteristic of Scandinavian paganism is that it was tolerant as far as different ideas and beliefs were concerned but intolerant about its cult, which had to be respected and performed in the proper way. There was no distinction between profane and sacred; the cult rituals took place in people's homes, in the halls of chieftains, and out of doors. There was no special 'clergy'; the husband and wife of a family, the chieftain and king were the natural cult leaders.

It is clear that in many parts of Scandinavia there was a long period, in some places as much as 200 years, in which the old and new religions overlapped. Pagan beliefs and rituals must have been affected by contact with Christianity. It is, for example, likely that the concept of Valhalla, which is first evidenced in the mid-tenth century, was shaped under Christian influence. Poetry and pictures provide good evidence for some Scandinavian myths and the attributes of a few of their gods, but most of that evidence is not early enough to have escaped the risk of some Christian contamination. The main source of information about pre-Christian religion in Scandinavia (other than what can be deduced about burial customs) is provided by Christian authors some of whom, including Adam of Bremen and Saxo Grammaticus, were very hostile and prepared to believe that pagans indulged in obscene, inhuman rituals. The most authoritative source of information is the Prose Edda of

Snorri Sturluson, who had a more positive attitude to the old religion. Although he was obviously influenced by Classical as well as Christian authors, his account of pagan myths and interpretation of the poetry is the starting point for most discussions of the subject.

Norse mythology

In Norse mythology both male and female deities were abundant. Goddesses were considered as holy and powerful as the gods; there were *Disir* (sing. *dis* 'woman') whose cult was particularly important in Uppsala; sibyls, such as Þor's wife Sif and the prophetess of *Völuspá*; valkyries, who conducted selected dead warriors to Valhalla; *fylgjur* 'accompaniers', spirits who were attached to particular families or individuals; demonic giantesses; and, especially significant, the Norns, supernatural women who determined the success or failure of both gods and men.

There were two groups or families of gods and goddesses, the *Æsir* and the *Vanir*. Conflict between them had been resolved, and later commentators could treat all these deities as Æsir, but they seem originally to have been associated with different cults. One was an essentially masculine, warrior-cult centered on Óðinn and his descendants, the Æsir; the other, in which women had a key role, worshipped the Vanir. The main Vanir deities were Njörðr, his wife Freyja, the guarantor of health, wealth and fertility, and her brother Freyr, a pair whose names originally meant 'lady' and 'lord'. The natural emphasis of the Vanir cult on kinship took different forms in the privacy of the home, where housewives seem to have had the main responsibility, from the large annual assemblies when sacrifices were offered to the Disir, the most important of whom was Freyja, known as Vanadis, 'Lady of the Vanir', accompanied by her maidens. It has been suggested that the Disir cult was connected with the worship of ancestral mothers of powerful families or clans. Women seem to have had a leading role in it, but not as priestesses, for there is no reliable evidence of priests in pagan Scandinavia. It is uncertain whether women could act publicly in cult celebrations or were represented by men, as happened later with the legal and political responsibilities of a woman who inherited a *godord* in Iceland.

The Óðinn cult emphasized comradeship and loyalty, not kinship. Its dissociation from things female was demonstrated by the belief that Óðinn himself learned the magic known as *seiðr* (a ritual in which the sorcerer fell into a trance) that was supposed until then to have been the preserve of women (see Price, this volume). It was this that led Óðinn to become *argr*, 'unmanly, effeminate'. Selected dead warriors were conducted by valkyries to Valhall, 'Hall of the slain' and home of the gods. That was a totally male world of feasting and fighting. Most of the dead, women and men who were chosen, were assigned to Helheim, ruled by the goddess Hel. They were not destined to spend eternity with the gods. For most people life after death was a family matter, for it was in the family that the dead, buried in the family cemetery, were best remembered by their descendants and kin.

Transition period

Mutual influence of the old and new religions on each other makes it difficult to assess what contribution the old made to the new, but there are some fairly clear signs of continuity. Many places where pagan cults had been celebrated continued to be religious centres after conversion, and some pre-Christian rituals survived conversion in a Christian guise, including the custom of taking holy objects in procession to ensure good harvests, but much was suppressed or treated with contempt as mere superstition.

The acceptance of Christian ideas and values meant the abandonment of most pagan beliefs. The church prized chastity more than fertility; concern for the family was less significant than concern for the salvation of the individual soul; Christians were taught to be tolerant and merciful, not vengeful; humility was a greater virtue than honour, and the new cult was in the hands of professionals, i.e. a completely male priesthood; women could only participate passively.

THE END OF THE VIKING AGE

Scandinavians who visited Christian Europe in the ninth century as raiders, settlers, merchants or envoys, must have been impressed by the enormous wealth and elaborate rituals of the great churches in the Frankish empire and the British Isles, and when Viking leaders came to terms with Christian rulers they normally accepted baptism. In the ninth century missionaries were encouraged by kings of the Danes and the *Svear* to work in the trading places of Hedeby, Ribe and Birka, apparently in order to reassure Christian merchants that it was safe to visit them. Although these ninth-century missionaries were unable to convert rulers, they claimed to have baptized many people, including some of high status. They were, however, unable to establish the infrastructure of bishoprics, churches and priests needed to instruct converts, and sustain their faith. As a result, some Scandinavians regarded Christ as a God, but not the only one.

In the early eleventh century the situation was very different; Christian evangelism had now begun to influence a growing number of people. The hundreds of Christian runic inscriptions in eastern Sweden clearly show that many were converted long before pagan cults were abolished. This suggests that the initiative was often taken by chieftains who supported the missionaries. The missionaries said little about such theological subtleties as the Virgin birth or the Trinity but concentrated on the power of a militant Christ to ensure success in this world and salvation from eternal damnation in the next. Their main purpose was to demonstrate that their God was not just more powerful than other gods, but was indeed the only true God and that all others were demons.

This period of religious toleration prepared the way for the next stage of Christianization, the formal acceptance of the exclusive claims of the Christian God. Such a dramatic break with the past required the support of powerful forces, especially of kings who were before their conversion closely linked with the traditional cults. Gradually Scandinavian rulers came to recognize that Christianity had much to offer them; it not only exalted their status, but also provided practical help. Missionary bishops were literate and those who had experience of royal government in Germany and England could be valuable advisers. Thus in most parts of Scandinavia the public acceptance of Christianity occurred in the late tenth and the early eleventh centuries.

Viking activity caused many changes within Scandinavia, the most fundamental being the conversion to Christianity. The basis was laid for the development of the three medieval kingdoms of Denmark, Norway and Sweden. The expanding commerce resulted in the development of towns, functioning not only as centres of secular authority but also as places in which royal churches symbolized the new, Christian kingship, early examples being Lund in Denmark, Trondheim in Norway, and Sigtuna in Sweden.

Birgit Sawyer

ABBREVIATIONS

Annales Regni Francorum Pertz, G.H. and Kurze, F., eds, 1891. *Annales Regni Francorum. Monumenta Germaniae historica; Scriptores rerum Germanicarum in usum scholarum*, Hanover.

KHL 1956-78. *Kulturhistorisk leksikon for nordisk middelalder*, 22 vols, Copenhagen.

SRI 1911. *Sveriges Runinskrifter. Kungl. Vitterhets Historie och Antikvitetsakademien*, Stockholm.

BIBLIOGRAPHY

Andersen, R. *et al.*, eds, 1985. *Kvinnearbeid i Norden fra vikingtiden til reformasjonen; foredrag fra et nordisk kvinnehistorisk seminar i Bergen, augusti 1983*, Bergen.

Bjørn, C. *et al.*, eds, 1988. *Det danske landbrugs historie 4000 f.Kr - 1536*, Odense.

Dommasnes, L.H. 1991. 'Women, kinship, and the basis of power in the Norwegian Viking Age', in Samson 1991, 65-73.

Gunneng, H. *et al.*, eds, 1989. *Kvinnors Rosengård: föredrag från nordiska tvärveten-skapliga symposier i Århus aug. 1985 och Visby sept. 1987*, Stockholm.

Hedeager, L. and Kristiansen, K. 1988. 'Oldtid, omkr. 4000 f.Kr -1000 e.Kr.', in Bjørn *et al.* 1988, 11-108.

Helle, K. 1995. *Under kirke og kongemakt 1130-1350*. Oslo: Aschehougs Norges historie 3.

Iversen, T. 1994. *Trelldommen; norsk slaveri i middelalderen*, Bergen.

Karras, R.M. 1988. *Slavery and Society in Medieval Scandinavia*, New Haven and London.

Larsson, M.G. 1990. *Runstenar och utlandsfärder: Aspekter på det senvikingatida samhället med utgångspunkt i de fasta fornlämningarna*. Lund: Acta Archaeologica Lundensia 18.

Lidén, H.E. ed., 1995. *Møtet mellom hedendom og kristendom i Norge*, Oslo.

Murray, A. 1983. *Germanic Kinship Structure: Studies in Law and Society in Antiquity and the Early Middle Ages*, Toronto.

Samson, R. ed., 1991. *Social Approaches to Viking Studies*, Glasgow.

Sawyer, B. 2000. *The Viking-Age Rune-Stones: Custom and Commemoration in Early Medieval Scandinavia*, Oxford.

Sawyer, B. and Sawyer, P. 1993. *Medieval Scandinavia: from Conversion to Reformation circa 800-1500*, Minneapolis and London.

——2002. *Die Welt der Wikinger*, Berlin.

Sellevold, B.J. 1989. 'Fødsel og død: kvinners dødelighet i forbindelse med svangerskap og fødsel i forhistorisk tid og middelalder, belyst ut fra studier av skjelettmaterialer', in Gunneng *et al.* 1989, 79-86.

Stalsberg, A. 1991. 'Women as Actors in North European Viking Age Trade', in Samson 1991, 75-83.

Steinsland, G. 1985. 'Kvinner og kult i vikingetid', in Andersen *et al.* 1985, 31-42.

——1995. 'Hvordan ble hedendommen utfordret og påvirket av kristendommen?', in Lidén 1995, 9-27.

64

The Islands of Scotland:

their role in the Western Voyages

Colleen E. Batey

Introduction: The arrival of the Vikings

In common with many other areas of Western Europe at the end of the eighth century, Scotland suffered seasonal raiding activities along its extensive coastline. As in England, with the raid on Lindisfarne in 793, the raiding Vikings were in search of not only adventure but also loot; their attention was focused on the rich monastic houses or trading centres (Morris 1998, 80-82). In Scotland attacks are noted on a number of monastic centres, most particularly Iona on the west coast off Mull, the foundation of St Columba, which was raided three times in 795, 802 and 806. The *Annals of Ulster* (AU) records in 795:

> Devastation of Iona of Columcille, and of Inishmurray and of Inisboffin […]. The burning of Rechru [Rathlin Island, Co. Antrim] by the gentiles; and Skye was pillaged and devastated (AU I, 255).

65

Under 798, the comment was added that the Hebrides and Ulster were plundered by Scandinavians. These actions presumably represented the predations of Viking bands sailing down the west coast of Scotland *en route* to the seemingly greater prizes to be had from the Irish monastic houses.

Figure 1. Iona Abbey as it is today. Its predecessor was the scene of repeated Viking raids (photo: Colleen Batey).

Rich pickings and good farmland

The advent of the Vikings on the Scottish scene therefore would seem to fit the stereo-typical view of the 'vicious Vikings'—all rape and pillage and little else. There can be no doubt that fine metalwork, originally from the monastic centres, found its way back to the homelands as a result of these activities. Take for example the gilt bronze fragment from Sunndal in Norway with its distinctive serpent design and amber inset, probably originally part of a book mount from a Western Scottish or Irish monastery (Martins and Wilson 1992, 259). More spectacular are the pair of Irish gable end finials which were originally part of a large house shrine from St Germain en Laye, and other pieces from the same original object from the grave at Gausel in Norway (Bakka 1965; Youngs 1989, 145)—items torn asunder in some great division of booty and ending up in both Norway and France as warring bands broke and re-formed elsewhere.

In order to overturn or modify such a black and white view of the Viking arrival in Scottish waters, we need to turn to a consideration of the other archaeological evidence, in the form of settlement remains. If the Vikings met and fought with the indigenous peoples, the Picts in both monastery or settlement, we ought to be able to see it in the archaeological record. Destruction by burning or defacement would leave its mark and if we are to believe the assertions of the twelfth century source the *Historia Norwegiae* that the native inhabitants of Orkney (*Peti/Papae*) were utterly destroyed by members of Rognvald's family (*Historia Norwegiae* I, 331), this most certainly should be clear in the archaeological record. The fact that it is not so should be some cause for concern amongst those historians who look only at the written record, as well as those archaeologists who generally tend to avoid the complexities of the written word!

However, only a small handful of sites have so far produced evidence of the actual inter-face between the Picts and the Vikings. Ongoing excavations by Martin Carver at Portmahomack (Tarbat Ness) in Easter Ross perhaps provide a rare glimpse of massive dis-ruption of a Pictish monastic house due to interaction with the Vikings (Carver 2000; 2001). The results in general, however, apparently present a varied picture. Discoveries at Birsay and nearby Buckquoy in Orkney indicate that at least to some extent relations were harmo-nious, with Vikings continuing to occupy the sites of the Picts, possibly adopting and adapt-ing local styles, intermarrying with the native women (Curle 1982; Ritchie 1977). Elsewhere in Orkney, at Skaill to the east, a more violent meeting has been postulated, although since somewhat retracted (discussed in Graham-Campbell and Batey 1998, 170). And at the site of Pool on Sanday, Hunter (1990) had noted the levelling of the site at the arrival of the Vikings and a subsequent re-building programme. In the west, at the Udal in North Uist, a violent arrival has been mooted since excavations began at the site some decades ago. The problem of interpretation is a major issue and hampered somewhat by the lack of sites which have both Pictish and early Viking settlement remains. New excavations at Bornais on South Uist, where a succession of structures lie, tell like, on top of one another in the dunes, may well have much to offer in the ongoing debate. These excavations, to be completed in 2003, focused on the unexpectedly rich remains of Norse material culture remaining in the floor deposits. The recovery of combs and fragments of imported types as well as nearby comb-making debris is a significant development and the evidence of both ceramics and metal-work including a coin of Olav Kyrre and a bone cylinder decorated with Ringerike animal style reinforce the links which must have existed between the Western Isles and Scandinavia itself (N. Sharples pers. comm.).

That there was a take-over, violent or otherwise is clear in the place-name record for the region. In the north, elements such as *bólstaðr* can be seen in Caithness at Scrabster, Kirbister in Orkney and Embo in Sutherland. In the west, the place names of Lewis, for example, have been studied in depth (Oftedal 1954; Fellows Jensen 1984) and show that roughly eighty per cent of the names are of Norse origin, e.g. Uig (ON *vik* 'bay'); Ness (ON *nes* 'headland'); Bostahd (ON *bólstaðr*); and Mealasbhall (ON *Nialls fjall* 'mountain or fell') with a Gaelic overlay. In Orkney, Norn (essentially a Norwegian dialect), survived into the eighteenth century as an understood language.

The extent of the settlement and cultural supremacy is largely defined by the place name record—essentially the Western Island groups, the Northern Isles of Shetland and Orkney and parts of the Scottish Mainland (Caithness and Sutherland in particular). Within these areas, the place name concentration varies from almost one hundred per cent Old Norse-derived names in Shetland to slightly less in Lewis in the west, and the distribution of the archaeological evidence largely reflects areas of concentrated fieldwork. So, for example, there is a preponderance of settlement and grave evidence from Orkney because it has long been a honey-pot for archaeologists, in addition to being a rich farming area where the plough frequently disturbs invisible burials or heaps of ancient kitchen debris (garbage). Whereas, Shetland to the far north has only in recent years attracted increased archaeological interest, with for example field survey by a team from Copenhagen revealing on Unst, the most northerly island, potentially tens of new settlement sites of the period and renewed interest in the Norse Christian heritage through a team from Glasgow (Morris 2001; see this volume). Likewise, detailed work in South Uist and elsewhere in the west is revealing traces of Norse presence on a scale larger than previously suspected.

I will here provide a brief outline of the evidence for just a handful of the major settlements in the area under scrutiny: Birsay in Orkney; Jarlshof in Shetland; Freswick in Caithness; and Bornais and Drimore in South Uist. For these people and their neighbours at least may well have been part of the brain drain to Iceland between 870 and 930! Although, as Crawford has pointed out, there is a lack of any mention of Orcadian slaves or otherwise in the Icelandic sources for the settlement period (1987, 210), the focus is always on the Hebrides and Ireland, a point to which we shall return.

67

BIRSAY

The unparalleled settlement focus of Birsay, at the north west tip of Mainland Orkney, has the Brough of Birsay, a tidal island which was to become the home of the mighty Earl Þorfinnr, and the lands nearby peopled by his retinue and extended household. Viking period settlement has been identified at Buckquoy on top of the Pictish settlement and nearby along the Brough Road and subsequently Late Norse occupation into the more modern village at Beachview. This extensive Norse presence at this political centre has been investigated in considerable detail over the recent decades, first by Anna Ritchie (1977) at the Pictish site of Buckquoy, and then more extensively by John Hunter (1986) and Christopher Morris (1996), revealing the homes and yards of the settlers as well as something of their external contacts. No doubt in line with the other settlements excavated in both Orkney and Shetland—although the preponderance of evidence so far recovered is from the Late Norse phases of occupation—these settlements contained a mix of peoples of both local and Scandinavian stock. It is hard to believe that the glossy black tresses of a Pictish girl would not have been attractive to the blonde incomers—if only for the novelty factor!

JARLSHOF

The farming settlement of Jarlshof in southern Shetland is probably visually one of the most impressive sites for the period in Scotland. Located on a narrow isthmus, adjacent to a portage route where the dangerous waters of the Roost could be avoided, this site was occupied from early Prehistory to the Medieval period, with several generations of Viking and

Figure 2. The Brough of Birsay from Mareick Head, Orkney, the island base of the Orkney Earls (photo: Christopher Morris).

Figure 3. Eroding fish middens at Freswick Kinks, Caithness (photo: Colleen Batey).

Late Norse houses superimposed on each other (Hamilton 1956). Excavated many decades ago, the detailed stratigraphy of the site is confused due to the constant rebuilding and re-use of stone there, but ninth- to tenth-century occupation must be indicated amongst these remains. Beginning with a single farmstead, the number of dwellings grew as the family expanded, exploiting as best they could the surrounding farmland and resources of both the sea and the rock—in the form of steatite (the soft soapstone which would have been famil-iar from their homelands). The location is spectacular and may well have seemed familiar to the incoming settlers from Norway.

FRESWICK

The wide sweep of Freswick Bay is the location of another multi-period site, settled from early Prehistory to the modern day. Extensive excavations both in the past and in more recent years—by Christopher Morris and myself—have revealed the site to have been occu-pied by Picts and Late Norse, harvesting both the land and the seas alike (Morris *et al.* 1995); with detailed examination of eroding middens revealing cultivation and extensive fishing debris. Unlike the other sites previously mentioned, there is little evidence here for early Viking activity and, as seems to be the case for Caithness, it is likely that the area was settled by Scandinavian speakers from Orkney, just a few miles to the north. As is the case with both Birsay and Jarlshof, this area is dominated by Scandinavian place names, testa-ment to large-scale presence but which is harder to locate on the Scottish mainland. The importance of Freswick and nearby Robert's Haven in our story of Norse expansion to Iceland is that this area is an obvious candidate for the adopted home region of exiled Auðr *inn djúpúðga* (the Deep Minded), of whom we shall hear more.

DRIMORE AND BORNAIS

Despite ongoing work in the Hebrides, in archaeological terms there is still an apparent dearth of identified settlement for this period. It is possible that since these islands played a significant role in providing folk for the movements to Iceland, the settlements themselves may not have been long-lived (if abandonment is the scenario), a generation or so at most, and consequently are somewhat more elusive. However, total abandonment throughout the island chain is not an option to consider, since the islands continued in Scandinavian power until 1266!

Excavations in 1956 at the site of Drimore on South Uist were amongst the first to iden-tify Norse building in the Western Isles. Briefly excavated and succinctly published in 1974 (MacLaren 1974), this was identified as a single unit dwelling. Little examination of either the floor deposits or the surrounding middens suggest that this was a lost opportunity. It has been suggested more recently that the structure incorporates a pre-Viking building, and as such therefore this may be part of a larger settlement of the Viking Age (Graham-Campbell and Batey 1998, 175-77). In North Uist, the important excavations at the Udal by Ian Crawford remain largely unpublished but it is clear that the site was multi-period and did include the crucial Pictish-Viking interface period. Full publication is awaited (Graham-Campbell and Batey 1998, 173-75).

Since 1993, the western coastal machair margins of South Uist have been a focus of fieldwork by Cardiff and Sheffield Universities. Excavation is being undertaken on two of the many new sites, Cille Pheadair and Bornais (Sharples and Parker Pearson 1999) and indications are that good preservation of rich deposits suggests occupation in the tenth cen-tury and, pending further examination of the earliest phases of activity, may stretch back into the elusive ninth century. So finally, here at last we may have a settlement which is broadly

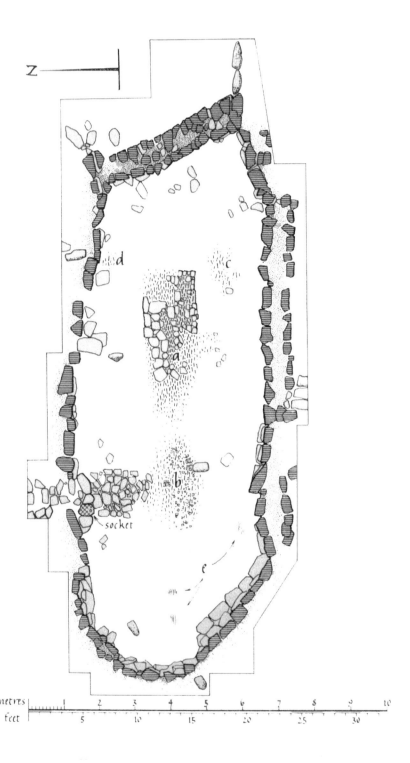

70

Figure 4. Plan of the Norse house at Drimore, South Uist (after MacLaren 1974).

contemporary with the *landnám* phase in Iceland and in an area, geographically at least, which may have provided settlers for the new colony.

In Lewis to the north, a single settlement has been excavated to date, at Barvas Machair (Trevor Cowie pers. comm.; Armit 1996, 192-3) possibly dating to the tenth or eleventh centuries, and ongoing excavations at Bostadh seem to have identified an early Viking-Age site on top of a Pictish horizon (T. Neighbour pers. comm.).

The evidence for Viking-Age settlement in the west is gradually increasing, and provides a glimpse of conditions at the time when some of the population was being wooed to Iceland. The economic evidence for the settlements suggest a mixture of farming and fishing, with the cultivation of barley and also oats as well as exploitation of large gadids such as cod. These early generations of Scandinavian settlers had already made the transition from farming in Norway, perhaps learning to be more flexible with the climatic vagaries and different crop yields, so it would not have been unthinkable that they could make a further move from Scotland. They had already made the mental leap of transferring their economy and lifestyle to a different context, albeit topographically familiar, they would be in a stronger position to chance their future in a virgin land. Indeed, their experiences may have been sought out for the new colony and certainly could have contributed to the selection of some of the better sites in Iceland.

THE MOVES TO ICELAND

The frequent references to the Hebridean origins of the settlers who moved away from the Scottish Islands is of considerable interest. Could it be that the writers of the twelfth-century *Landnámabók* ('The Book of the Settlements') considered all Scottish people to be Hebrideans? This would bring a smile today, but how likely is it that a culture for whom genealogy was of such importance could make this mistake? In my view it is not likely, since one's point of origin is an integral part of personal identity. To interject a modern slant on the situation: on the first day at University, modern students faced with a new peer group in a new environment hasten to create a formula for gathering information, asking each new encounter: where do you come from? what school did you go to? what do your parents do? what football team do you support?, etc., etc. In this they are establishing a framework for communication and expressing their own need to identify with this new cultural grouping and their own position within it. This must surely have been the case in Iceland at the time of the land taking.

Crawford has made the point that *Landnámabók* makes scant reference to settlers coming to Iceland from Orkney, citing the rare example from *Laxdæla saga* of Erp, son of Earl Meldun, whose mother, Muirgeal, had been taken into captivity to serve Earl Sigurd of Orkney's wife. Muirgeal was bought 'for a high price' by Auðr *inn djúpúðga* (the Deep-Minded) who took both Erp and Muirgeal to Iceland (*Laxdæla saga* chapter 6; Crawford 1987, 210). Crawford views the lack of Orcadian settlers as a reflection of the success of farming prime lands which the Vikings had taken in Orkney and which, she implies, presumably they did not have in the Hebrides to the same extent. In this case, both the Western Isles and Shetland ought to have contributed to the supply of new settlers.

The story of Auðr *inn djúpúðga* is in the true historical novel tradition. The daughter of Ketil *flatnefr* (Flat-Nose), who conquered the Hebrides and then lived there, she married Óláfr *hvíti* (the White, likely to be the King of Dublin of this name), and her son, Þorsteinn *rauða* (the Red) took lands in Northern Scotland. Newly widowed, she fled to Caithness to stay with her son, being forced to move on again, this time to Iceland when her son was killed (*Landnámabók* 136; Crawford 1987, 216-7). She epitomises the Viking heroic ideal and political interweaving of the dynasties at this period. Some of Ketil's family from the Hebrides had already settled in Iceland (*Laxdæla saga* chapter 5; Crawford 1987, 48), and so it is not surprising she turned there, to the strength of her extended family, a focus in her next exile, despite being renowned in the saga sources for being a woman of exceptional fortitude. She was accompanied by her grand-daughters, some of whom she married off as she travelled north (including leaving one in Orkney), and by her slaves who she freed once in Iceland. The remaining unmarried grand-daughters were married in Iceland, and the freed slaves also presumably owed some informal allegiance to her. In combination these would have made Auðr a force to be reckoned with in the emergent Icelandic state. Indeed, *Íslendingabók*, 'The Book of the Icelanders', states that Auðr was one of the four most important settlers of Iceland, and settled in Breiðafjörðr in the west of Iceland (chapter 2, 6 and *Ættartala*, 26).

CAN WE RECOGNISE SETTLERS FROM BRITAIN IN ICELANDIC EVIDENCE?

In order to identify the settlers who went to Iceland from the British Isles, excluding for the moment Irish monks or *papar* (see Ahronson this volume), it is necessary to accept that probably both artefactual and genetic work will identify the Celtic peoples, most particularly the women who went either as wives or as slaves to the new colony. The potential artefactual elements are considered elsewhere by Michèle Hayeur-Smith in this volume, but recent advances have focussed on the examination of the distinctive mitochondrial DNA sequence transmitted through the female line. Earlier genetic studies have been attempted (Thompson 1973), but current work being undertaken by Agnar Helgason and colleagues (Helgason *et al.* 2000) suggests a major input in the female gene group from the British Isles, although the precise percentage is open to varied interpretation, depending on whether you are a scientist or a journalist! *Landnámabók* supplies an extensive name list of over 400 of the primary settlers, and it is clear that the vast majority were males and most of course came direct from Norway. Amongst the settlers were several with Celtic names—Bekan, Brjann, Domnall, Kalman, Kormakr for example (cited in Gudmundsson 1997)—many are of recognisably Irish origin. However, although there are a handful of examples where the first settlers cited are women, they possess Norse names and are presumably Scandinavians despite having come from the British Isles.

> Hildir and Hallgeirr and their sister Ljót came from the British Isles; they went to Iceland and claimed land between Fljótr and Ránga (cited in Jesch 1991, 82).

This would perhaps therefore confirm the interpretation that the Celtic mtDNA is derived from the slave population brought to Iceland or Celtic wives, rather than the main settlers themselves.

Ongoing scientific analysis of trace elements from teeth in the pagan cemetery at Cnip on Lewis is of relevance to this point (Dunwell *et al.* 1995). Work by Janet Montgomery at Bradford University focussing on the element Strontian has shown in preliminary results that two of the graves without grave goods in the cemetery have different chemical signatures suggesting that they had been brought up away from Lewis, perhaps in Skye, Mull or North Antrim (Janet Montgomery conference presentation March 2000). Could these have been local slaves, buried in the Norse cemetery and without distinctive grave goods? Members of their surviving peer group may have been taken to Iceland.

In conclusion therefore, the presence of settlers from the Scottish Isles (and also Ireland) cannot be doubted, saga information and genetic studies go hand in hand towards this conclusion. It is however, just worth remembering that the western parts of Iceland, particularly Breiðafjörðr were relatively popular destinations in Iceland for these Celtic settlers (Sigurdsson n.d., 13). In years to come, these areas provided some of the settlers who travelled further to Greenland and perhaps beyond. They may have had dark hair, and, through their mothers, they may have had Celtic genes. It would be exciting to prove that these great explorers of the North Atlantic just may have had more than a touch of Scottish blood in their veins.

ABBREVIATIONS

AU   *Annals of Ulster*, in Anderson, A.O. ed., 1922. *Early Sources of Scottish History*, vol. I: AD 500-1286, Edinburgh.

Historia Norwegiae   Anderson, A.O. ed., 1922. *Early Sources of Scottish History*, vol. I: AD 500-1286, Edinburgh.

Íslendingabók   Benediktsson, J. ed., 1968. *Íslendingabók, Landnámbók*. Reykjavík: Íslenzk fornrit 1.

Landnámabók   Benediktsson, J. ed., 1968. *Íslendingabók, Landnámbók*. Reykjavík: Íslenzk fornrit 1.

Laxdæla saga   Sveinsson, E.Ó. ed., 1934. *Laxdæla saga*. Reykjavík: Íslenzk fornrit 5.

BIBLIOGRAPHY

Armit, I. ed., 1990. *Beyond the Brochs,* Edinburgh.

——1996. *The Archaeology of Skye and the Western Isles*, Edinburgh.

Bakka, E. 1965. 'Some Decorated Anglo-Saxon metalwork found in Norwegian Viking Graves', in Small 1965, 32-40.

Carver, M. O. H. ed., 2000. 'Bulletin of the Tarbat Discovery Programme 5', <http://www.york.ac.uk/depts/arch/staff/sites/tarbat> (Site visited 24 April 2002).

Carver, M. O. H. ed., 2001. 'Bulletin of the Tarbat Discovery Programme 6', <http://www.york.ac.uk/depts/arch/staff/sites/tarbat> (Site visited 24 April 2002).

Clarke, H.B., Ní Mhaonaigh, M. and Ó Floinn, R., eds, 1998. *Ireland and Scandinavia in the Early Viking Age,* Dublin.

Crawford, B.E. 1987. *Scandinavian Scotland*. Leicester: Scotland in the Early Middle Ages 2.

Curle, C.L. 1982. *Pictish and Norse Finds from the Brough of Birsay 1934-74*. Edinburgh: Society of Antiquaries of Scotland Monograph Series 1.

Dunwell, A.J., Cowie, T.G., Bruce, M.F., Neighbour, T. and Rees, A.R. 1995. 'A Viking Age cemetery at Cnip, Uig, Isle of Lewis', *Proceedings of the Society of Antiquaries of Scotland*, 125, 719-52.

Fellows Jensen, G. 1984. 'Viking settlement in the Northern and Western Isles: the place-names evidence as seen from Denmark and the Danelaw', in Fenton and Pálsson 1984, 148-68.

Fellows-Jensen G. ed., 2001. *Denmark and Scotland: the cultural and environmental resources of small nations.* Copenhagen: Historisk-filosofiske Meddelelser 82, The Royal Danish Academy of Sciences and Letters.

Fenton, A. and Pálsson, H., eds, 1984. *The Northern and Western Isles in the Viking World. Survival, Continuity and Change*, Edinburgh.

Graham-Campbell, J. and Batey, C.E. 1998. *Vikings in Scotland. An Archaeological Survey*, Edinburgh.

Gudmundsson, H. 1997. *Um Haf Innan. Vestraenir Menn og Íslenzk Menning á Miðöldum*, Reykjavík.

Hamilton, J.R.C. 1956. *Excavations at Jarlshof, Shetland*. Edinburgh: Ministry of Works Archaeological Report 1.

Helgason, A, Sigurðardóttir, S., Gulcher, J.R., Ward, R. and Stefánsson, K. 2000. 'MtDNA and the Origin of the Icelanders: Deciphering Signals of Recent Population History', *American Journal of Human Genetics*, 66, 999-1016.

Hunter, J.R. 1986. *Rescue Excavations on the Brough of Birsay 1974-82*. Edinburgh: Society of Antiquaries of Scotland Monograph Series 4.

Hunter. J.R. 1990. 'Pool, Sanday, a case study for the Late Iron Age and Viking periods', in Armit 1990, 175-93.

Jesch, J. 1991. *Women in the Viking Age*, Woodbridge.

MacLaren, A. 1974. 'A Norse house on Drimore Machair, South Uist', *Glasgow Archaeological Journal*, 3, 9-18.

Martins, I. and Wilson, D.M. 1992. '129. Mount (Sunndal)', in Roesdahl and Wilson 1992, 259.

Morris, C.D. 1996. *The Birsay Bay Project, Volume 2. Sites in the Birsay Village and on the Brough of Birsay, Orkney*. Durham: University of Durham, Department of Archaeology, Monograph Series 2.

73

——1998. 'Raiders, Traders and Settlers: the Early Viking Age in Scotland', in Clarke *et al.* 1998, 73-103.

——2001. 'Norse Settlement in Shetland: the Shetland chapel-sites project', in Fellows-Jensen 2001, 58-78.

Morris, C.D., Batey, C.E. and Rackham, D.J. 1995. *Freswick Links, Caithness. Excavations and Survey of a Norse Settlement.* Inverness and New York: Highland Libraries in association with the North Atlantic Biocultural Organisation.

Oftedal, M. 1954. 'The village names of Lewis in the Outer Hebrides', *Norsk Tidsskrift for Sprogvidenskap*, 17, 363-409.

Ritchie, A. 1977. 'Excavations of Pictish and Viking-age farmsteads at Buckquoy, Orkney', *Proceedings of the Society of Antiquaries of Scotland*, 108, 174-227.

Roesdahl, E. and Wilson, D.M., eds, 1992. *From Viking to Crusader. Scandinavia and Europe 800-1200,* Uddevalla.

Sharples, N. and Parker Pearson, M. 1999. 'Norse Settlement in the Outer Hebrides', *Norwegian Archaeological Review*, 32, 1, 41-62.

Sigurdsson, G. n.d. *Vikings and the New World.* (Exhibition catalogue to accompany an exhibition in The Culture House, opened April 20, 2000), Reykjavík.

Small, A. ed., 1965. *The Fourth Viking Congress, York, August 1961*, Edinburgh.

Thompson, E.A. 1973. 'The Icelandic admixture problem', *Annual of Human Genetics*, 37, 69-80.

Youngs, S. ed., 1989. *'The Work of Angels': Masterpieces of Celtic Metalwork, 6th - 9th centuries AD*, London.

The Crosses of Columban Iceland:

A Survey of Preliminary Research

Kristján Ahronson

S
candinavian groups are believed to have settled the northern North Atlantic islands of Iceland and the Faroe Islands in the late ninth century of their own pioneering initiative. Recent archaeological and environmental research in southern Iceland calls for a reassessment of this scenario. Several artificial caves and rock shelters in southern Iceland have features paralleled in early Christian western Scotland. Little is known about the 170 artificial caves of southern Iceland. These caves may be related to the earliest settlement of the island and thus have important implications for study of the Viking North. The Norse longhouse, a Viking Age house-type built of turf and found as far west as L'Anse-aux-Meadows in Newfoundland, is understood as one of the earliest medieval house-structures of Iceland. In contrast, while cave sites are thought to be old (Holt and Guðmundsson 1980, 16-17), the origins and history of these caves are enigmatic.

In 1991, Hjartarson *et al.* published a survey of the numerous artificial caves of Iceland, carved out of the soft sandstone and volcanic rocks of eastern Arnarssýsla, Rangárvallasýsla and in Mýrdalur. This book, along with a series of articles (Hjartarson and Gísladóttir 1983, 1985, 1993) and *Um Manngerða Hella á Suðurlandi* (Holt and Guðmundsson 1980), is a significant step forward for the subject since Matthías Þórðarson's 1931 study. Nonetheless, the origins of the caves and their role in Iceland's settlement archaeology remain poorly understood. This rare situation in Atlantic archaeology, of investigating a well-represented site-type that is without a place in the settlement sequence, provided the impetus for the investigations discussed here. Figure 1 illustrates the distribution of artificial caves across Iceland.

Hjartarson and Gísladóttir (1983, 133) describe the southern Iceland caves as including a number of 'the oldest housebuildings in Iceland'. Many caves are listed in 1709 land registers (Hjartarson and Gísladóttir 1983, 133), while the description of Bishop Þórlakur's miracles in the late twelfth-century *Biskupa sögur* mentions the collapse of a cattle cave (cited in Friðriksson 1994, 25). It is noteworthy that cave use is described at such an early date, for the twelfth century is the period of the oldest Icelandic writing. From a north-central European perspective, Adam of Bremen provides the earliest known depiction of Icelandic cave use. In an eleventh-century account, Adam describes the people of Iceland (Thule) thus,

> *in subterraneis habitant speluncis, communi tecto et strato gaudentes cum pecoribus suis.*
> [they live in underground caves, glad to have roof and food and bed in common with their cattle]
> (Schmeidler 1917, 272; Tschan 1959, 217).

A feature of numerous southern Iceland caves as well as some Westmen Island rock shelters are stylistically distinctive cross carvings that, taken together, form a coherent body of data. Figure 2 illustrates a small selection of this cross sculpture, sculpture discussed more fully elsewhere (Ahronson 2000; 2002).

In figure 2, the three crosses on the left were found in sheltered alcoves of the exposed cliff Heimaklettir, Vestmannaeyjar (Westmen Islands). The largest cross, carved into its own alcove, is found alongside hand- and foot-holds cut into the soft rock. The Westmen Islands lie off the southern Iceland coast, opposite the region in which the artificial caves are found. The two crosses on the right of figure 2 are cut into a soft sandstone wall of Skollhólahellir

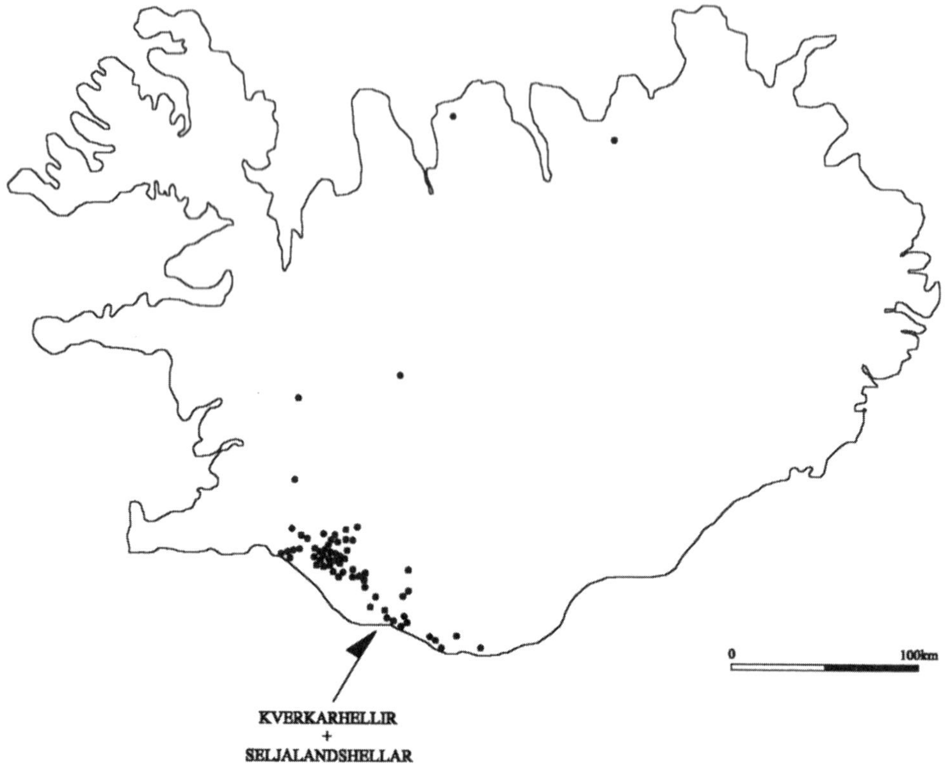

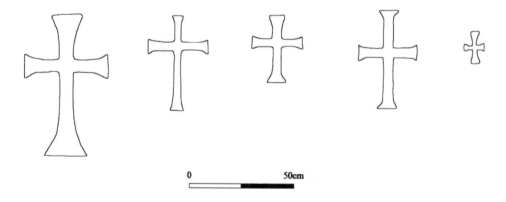

0
100km
KVERKARHELLIR
+
SELJALANDSHELLAR

Figure 1. Distribution of artificial caves across Iceland (T. Simpson based on Hjartarson *et al.* 1991, 12).

Figure 2. Selection of expanded terminal crosses from southern Iceland (T. Simpson).

0
50cm

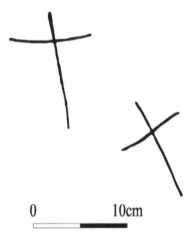

0   10cm

Figure 3. Simple incised crosses from Skollhólahellir, Rangárvallasýsla (T. Simpson).

Figure 4. Argyll expanded terminal crosses from Iona (T. Simpson after Campbell 1987, 110).

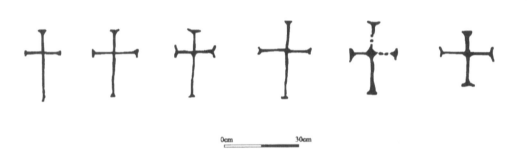

0cm   30cm

in mainland southern Iceland. The cave is discussed by Hjartarson and Gísladóttir (1983, 130). Simple incised crosses also decorate the walls of Skollhólahellir and are illustrated in figure 3. On a comparable note, Holt and Guðmundsson (1980, 16-17) studied the cross carvings in the cave Efri-Gegnishólar and cautiously dated the cross forms to the sixth to tenth centuries.

On typological and contextual grounds, specific comparisons have been drawn between the Icelandic expanded terminal crosses and the Argyll expanded terminal type, a style linked to the Columban familia of monastic houses of the seventh and eighth centuries (Campbell 1987, Ahronson 2000, 119). Rock-cut early Christian crosses (Fisher 2001, 8-13), including a number of the Argyll expanded terminal crosses, are found in caves, sites which Campbell (1987, 108-9) suggests as 'retreats or deserta for anchorites or penitents'. Figure 4 illustrates a selection of the comparable expanded terminal crosses from Iona.

The stone carvings of Scotland's West Highlands and Islands have been subjected to academic attention for many years, the most recent contribution providing a sophisticated presentation of comparative data and analysis (Fisher 2001). Fisher (pers. comm.) consulted published drawings of a number of southern Iceland crosses (Hjartarson *et al.* 1991, 248) and noted the possibility of several styles finding close parallels in early Christian West Scotland, though specialised illustrations are needed before further comment can be made.

It has long been recognised that expanded terminal crosses, incised into stone, were characteristic of the early Church in western Scotland and Ireland (Fisher 2001, 12-13). But in 1987, Ewan Campbell made significant advance upon this observation. What Campbell did was set about a detailed and comprehensive examination of Argyll crosses. This investigation enabled him to identify the expanded terminal cross-form as a coherent group, a group he linked with areas in which the monks of St Columba, based in Iona, were active (Campbell 1987, 111). This is consistent with Charles Thomas' view that simple crosses incised into stone are

> essentially a western and north-western facet of post-Roman Britain, the source being apparently Ireland, and the spread a reflection of the work of Irish monastic missions. The crosses themselves are of a limited range of linear forms, and are usually incised with a knife or point (1973, 28).

The expanded terminal cross-form central to discussion here belongs to what Campbell describes as a 'larger group of simple incised crosses which are commonly found on recumbent slabs, upright pillars, boulders and rock faces throughout the Celtic west' (1987, 106). Though likely the earliest form of stone crosses, scholars agree this group has often been ignored because of its simplicity (Thomas 1971, 112-4; Henderson 1987, 46). It nonetheless appears such simple crosses form a distinctive stage in the development of Early Christian decoration in northern Britain and Ireland.

Thomas (1971, 112-6; Campbell 1987, 107) sees primitive cross-marked stones as emerging in late sixth- and seventh-century Britain from ultimately Mediterranean models of the fifth and sixth centuries. Looking to Pictland, Henderson (1987, 48) is in agreement by seeing simple cross-markings as a seventh-century phenomena logically preceding the eighth-century relief cross-slabs.

The basic premise of Campbell's study is that,

> While it is possible that the very simplest of these crosses, consisting of plain vertical and horizontal lines, are not amenable to any analysis, the slightly more complex forms may reflect changing fashions in particular regions (1987, 107).

Originally suggested by Hamlin (1982, 290), this premise has proven a valid one for a pattern does emerge in Argyll.

Argyll, because of its excellent and comprehensive inventory of Early Christian monuments, provides a good geographic distribution from which significant archaeological information can be recovered (Campbell 1987, 107). Campbell (1987, 108) maps the roughly 50 sites from which 150 cross-marked stones have been identified and a discrete clustering of expanded terminal crosses is revealed. This clustering of crosses is significant and reinforced by a strong similarity of form and dimension among the expanded terminal group members. The clustering is important because these crosses can now be associated in time and space with areas in which we know the Columban familia to have been active (Campbell 1987, 107-8).

The Columban association with the expanded terminal cross-form is reinforced by an analysis of Adomnán's *Life of St Columba*. Study reveals that, aside from locations along the sea route to Ireland and those associated with Columba's travels in Pictland or Skye, all identified places lie in Tiree, Mull, Morven, Ardnamurchan and Lorne. This is the same portion of northern Argyll in which the expanded terminal crosses were found (Campbell 1987, 110). The idea of a monastic age for the northernmost North Atlantic is not new and has been advanced in the adventurous writings of Lethbridge (1948, 85-8; 1950, 79-85). An Ionan identification for these North Atlantic monastic communities has also previously been forwarded in the arguments of Smyth (1984, 166-74).

The dating evidence for each carving elaborates the discussion. Individually, the 17 expanded terminal crosses of Argyll offer dates between the late sixth and early ninth centuries. Noting the restricted range of the cross-form, mentioned above, Campbell suggests the expanded terminal cross finds its home at the earlier end of the period (1987, 112). This dating is consistent with Thomas' general simple cross-form dates for northern Britain and Henderson's Class IV Monument dates for Pictland, both mentioned earlier. It is then reasonable, on geographic and temporal grounds, to link this cross form with the Columban *familia* of monastic houses specifically of the seventh and eighth centuries.

As for the general distribution of the form, it appears largely exclusive to Ireland (likely the coastal west), western Scotland and both the Western and Northern Isles (Hamlin 1982, 289-93; Campbell 1987, 111). This dating is consistent with a barred terminal cross found on St Ninian's Isle, Shetland, and dating to *c.* AD 700 (Thomas 1973, 28) as well as an expanded terminal cross from Papil, Shetland, dated to the mid-eighth century (Thomas 1973, 29).

Folklore and onomastics associate some of southern Iceland's artificial caves with Papar. Icelandic folk tradition and medieval texts hold that early North Atlantic Christian Gaels, called *papar* by the Norse, inhabited Iceland previous to Scandinavian-led settlement in the late ninth century. The cave Seljalandshellar (West Eyjafjalla-district), for example, was known under the alternate 'child's name' of Papahellir, 'cave of the Papar' (Hálfdan Ómar Hálfdanarson pers. comm.). Papar are described in the earliest documentary sources of the island as being present: *Í þann tíð vas Ísland viði vaxit á miðli fjalls ok fjøru* [At that time when Iceland was covered with woods between mountains and shore] (ÍF 1968, 5), or *áðr Ísland byggðisk af Nóregi* [before Iceland was built from Norway] (ÍF 1968, 31). These Papar, or *Vestmenn* ('Westpeople'), find context within the northwards-looking monastic communities of western Scotland, related to the Columban *familia*, and appearing in Gaelic documentary traditions (Tierney 1967, 72-7; Anderson and Anderson 1991; Morris 1991, 65) as well as to a limited degree in the North Atlantic archaeological record (Bourke 1983, 464-468; 1997a, 163-165; Ahronson 2000; Fisher 2001; 2002). The cross sculpture of the Northern and Western Isles of Scotland preserve a record of early Christianity before the Norse presence in the Scottish Islands. Comparable early Christian Faroese carved stones have recently been reassessed by Fisher (2002; forthcoming) and previously discussed by Radford (1962, 163), Kermode (1931, 373-378), and Arge (1991, 104-105). The southern Iceland cross carvings and caves may be related to the *papa-*, *vestmanna-*, and *íra-* place-names found across the North Atlantic islands from the Hebrides to Iceland. The distribution of *papa-*names argues for a group known among the Norse as 'papar' having some role in the early Norse North Atlantic—at a time when the landscape was being appropriated and 'named' by the Norse. Modern folklore and place-names, however, cannot establish a connection between southern Iceland's artificial caves and Vestmenn communities without further archaeological investigations.

Research at Seljaland (Ahronson 2002, forthcoming a; Smith and Ahronson forthcoming), in the West Eyjafjalla-district, may test this hypothesis by providing a chronology of cave construction and occupation combined with a rich environmental record of land use. By looking at the cross-marked caves of Seljaland (Kverkarhellir and Seljalandshellar), investigations hope to construct a model for artificial cave use in southern Iceland—thus addressing this long ignored and very substantial body of housebuildings. Initial results are surprising and may date a construction phase of the cave Kverkahellir to *c.* AD 800—many decades before the Norse colonisation of Iceland. Preliminary archaeological and environmental fieldwork in 2001 (Ahronson forthcoming a) concentrated along three lines of investigation: initial attempts at dating a construction phase of the cave Kverkarhellir, archaeological survey and development of a new technique for environmental research—the *tephra contour*. Fieldwork from 2002 (in prep) also followed three lines: further investigation of cave construction at Kverkarhellir, recording 19 of the larger cross sculptures in the cave group Seljalandshellar, and refinement of the tephra contour technique. Investigations attempt to answer three questions: *When was the cave Kverkarhellir constructed?; How did*

79

early human populations interact with the environment?; and *Where is the cross sculpture in the cave group Seljalandshellar best paralleled?*

Working in the Eyjafjalla-district of southern Iceland, we are fortunate to be able to use tephrochronology so extensively. Tephrochronology, the study of volcanic airfall deposits, is a powerful dating technique that is particularly applicable to the excellent tephra sequence at Seljaland. Tephrochronology has been used to support a model of late ninth-century Icelandic settlement: when present, a volcanic ash deposit dated to AD 871±2 lies beneath virtually all early Norse sites in Iceland. 50 cm below the AD 871±2 tephra, excavations in 2002 identified a *c.* AD 800 deposit of gravels and fractured palagonite 50-75 cm in thickness. This *c.* AD 800 deposit is concentrated immediately outside of and slightly downslope from the Kverkarhellir cave mouth. This gravel and fractured palagonite deposit was column sampled and processed in the field as well as in the laboratory and is currently under analysis in Edinburgh and Oxford.

Seljaland investigations seek to identify a human interaction with the environment. When a deposit of volcanic ash (tephra) falls upon a landscape, it 'photographs' that land surface. The tephra contour exposes volcanic airfall deposits of known age to reveal forest and vegetation cover. In 2002, the tephra contour technique was applied to three soil horizons from AD 1500 to AD 871 and revealed surfaces consistent with heavily frost-hummocked open grazing land (*c.* AD 1500), young birch woodland with slender 5-9 cm trunks and heavy under storey (*c.* AD 920), as well as an AD 871±2 surface consistent with open level grassland. A parallel study by Ashburn *et al.*, of magnetic susceptibility at Seljaland, confirmed a localized environmental change *c.* AD 800 first noted by Dugmore and Erskine (1994, 69-73). The magnetic susceptibility readings of this deposit are suggested as a record of the introduction of grazing animals in the post-AD 871 period. Highlighting its potential for study, Ashburn *et al.* call for further investigation of the AD 800-871 deposit. Ashburn *et al.* also identified a susceptibility 'spike' which they propose records burning of woodland after AD 920—this is a burning of the young woodland the tephra contour technique 'photographs'.

For this article, a relevant aim of Seljaland investigations in 2002 was to document with precision the 19 larger crosses of the Seljalandshellar cave group. High quality photographs, scale drawings and wax rubbings recorded this sculpture in the field. Publication illustrations are generously being prepared by Ian Scott (formerly of the RCAHMS) and have begun to be studied by Ian Fisher. This work is in progress: the Seljaland crosses appear to have parallel features with early Christian crosses in Scotland—though conservatism of style in later Scandinavian cross traditions is also a possibility. A further complicating factor is the Gaelic origin of many Scandinavian-led settlers in Iceland, well documented by place-names and documentary accounts.

Bearing in mind all our evidence, then, it may be sensible as a provisional measure to follow the stylistic similarity between Campbell's 'Columban' cross-form and the Icelandic examples. Realising this, then, perhaps we should begin to rethink the mechanics of the Norse settlement of Iceland, Faroe, Shetland and Orkney in terms of real contact with early Gaelic Christianity. Consider the example of Bishop Patrick of the Viking-Age Hebridean Church. According to *Landnámabók*, this bishop, in whose honour Patreksfjörður in the Icelandic westfjords is named, gave the late ninth-century Norse settler Örlygur directions to Esja, near Reykjavík. Upon arrival, Örlygur kept a promise to Bishop Patrick and erected a church to St Columba (ÍF 1968,53-5; Smyth 1984, 163, 171-2; Anderson 1922, 340 n.1, 343-4 n.1). Perhaps the ideas discussed here, coupled with future work, will put this Patrick into a context which we can comfortably understand.

ACKNOWLEDGEMENTS

The advice and assistance of Tõnno Jonuks (Rakvere Museum, Estonia), Alex Woolf (University of St Andrews), Professor William Gillies (University of Edinburgh), Andy Dugmore (University of Edinburgh), Fraser Hunter (National Museums of Scotland), Professor Gísli Pálsson (Háskóli Íslands/University of Iceland), and Páll Marvin Jónsson (Háskóli Íslands í Vestmannaeyjum/University Field Station in the Westmen Islands) is gratefully acknowledged. This work was fostered by the interest and support of Professor Ann Dooley (University of Toronto).

ABBREVIATIONS

ÍF	Benediktsson, J. ed., 1968. *Íslendingabók og Landnámabók*. Reykjavík: Íslenzk fornrit 1.
Life of Columba	Anderson, A.O. and Anderson, M.O., eds and trans, 1991. *Adomnán's Life of Columba*, Oxford.
RCAHMS	Royal Commission on the Ancient and Historic Monuments of Scotland.

BIBLIOGRAPHY

Ahronson, K. 2000. 'Further Evidence for a Columban Iceland: Preliminary Results of Recent Work', *Norwegian Archaeological Review*, 33, 2, 117-124.

——2002. 'Testing the Evidence for Northernmost North Atlantic Papar: A Cave Site in Southern Iceland', in Crawford 2002, 107-20.

——forthcoming a. 'One North Atlantic Cave Settlement: Preliminary Archaeological and Environmental Investigations at Seljaland, South Iceland', in Ahronson forthcoming b.

——forthcoming b. *Atlantic Peoples between Fire, Ice, River and Sea. Past Environments in Southern Iceland.* Edinburgh: Northern Studies 37.

Anderson, A.O., ed. and trans. 1991. *Early Sources of Scottish History A.D. 500 to 1286: Volume 1*, Edinburgh.

Arge, S.V. 1991. 'The Landnam in the Faroes', *Arctic Anthropology*, 28, 2, 101-120.

Ashburn, D.I., Kirkbride, M.P. and Dugmore, A.J. forthcoming. 'Post-settlement land disturbance indicated by magnetic susceptibility of aeolian soils at Seljaland, southern Iceland', in Ahronson forthcoming b.

Bourke, C. 1983. 'The handbells of the early Scottish church', *Proceedings of the Society of Antiquaries of Scotland*, 113, 464-468.

——1997a. 'Insignia Columbae II', in Bourke 1997b, 162-183.

——ed., 1997b. *Studies in the Cult of Saint Columba*, Bodmin, Cornwall.

Campbell, E. 1987. 'A cross-marked quern from Dunadd and other evidence for relations between Dunadd and Iona', *Proceedings of the Society of Antiquaries of Scotland*, 117, 105-117.

Crawford, B. ed., 2002. *The Papar in the North Atlantic: Environment and History. Proceedings of the St. Andrews Dark Age Conference*, St Andrews.

Dugmore, A.J. and Erskine, C.C. 1994. 'Local and regional patterns of soil erosion in southern Iceland', in Stötter and Wilhelm 1994, 63-78.

Fisher, I. 2001. *Early Medieval Sculpture in the West Highlands and Islands*. Edinburgh: RCAHMS & SOC ANT SCOT Monograph 1.

——2002. 'Crosses in the Ocean', in Crawford 2002, 39-58.

——forthcoming. 'Cross-currents in North Atlantic sculpture', in Thorsteinsson forthcoming.

Friðriksson, A. 1994. *Sagas and Popular Antiquarianism in Icelandic Archaeology*, Avebury.

Hamlin, A. 1982. 'Early Irish stone carving: content and context', in Pearce 1982, 283-296.

Henderson, I. 1987. 'Early Christian monuments of Scotland displaying crosses but no other ornament', in Small 1987, 45-58.

Hjartarson, Á. and Gísladóttir, H. 1983. 'Skollhólahellir', *Árbók hins Íslenzka fornleifafélags*, 1982, 123-133.

——1985. 'Hellamyndir Johannesar S. Kjarval', *Árbók hins Íslenzka fornleifafélags*, 1984, 167-182.

——1993. 'Hellarannsókna leiðangur Einars Benediktssonar 1915', *Árbók hins Íslenzka fornleifafélags*, 1992, 135-144.

Hjartarson, Á., Guðmundsson, G.J. and Gísladóttir, H. 1991. *Manngerða Hellar á Íslandi*, Reykjavík.

Holt, A. and Guðmundsson, G.J. 1980. *Um Manngerða Hella á Suðurlandi*, Reykjavík.

Karkov, C. and Farrell, R., eds, 1991. *Studies in Insular Art and Archaeology*, Oxford, Ohio.

Kermode, P.M.C. 1931. 'Note on Early Cross-slabs from the Faroe Islands', *Proceedings of the Society of Antiquaries of Scotland*, 65, 373-378.

Morris, C.D. 1991. 'Native and Norse in Orkney and Shetland', in Karkov and Farrell 1991, 61-80.

Radford, C.A.R. 1962. 'Art and Architecture: Celtic and Norse', in Wainwright, 163-187.

Pearce, S.M. ed., 1982. *The Early Church in Western Britain and Ireland*, Great Britain.

Schmeidler, B. 1917. *Adam von Bremen, Hamburgische Kirchengeschichte,* Hannover.

Small, A. ed., 1987. *The Pict: A New Look at Old Problems*, Dundee.

Small, A., Thomas, C. and Wilson, D.M. *et al.* 1973. *St. Ninian's Isle and its Treasure*, vol. 1, Oxford.

Smith, K.T. and Ahronson, K. forthcoming. 'Dating the Cave? The Preliminary Tephra Stratigraphy at Kverkin, Seljaland', in Ahronson forthcoming b.

Smyth, A.P. 1984. *Warlords and Holy Men: Scotland AD 80-1000*, Edinburgh.

Stötter, J. and Wilhelm, J.F., eds, 1994. *Environmental Change in Iceland*, Munich.

Thomas, C. 1971. *The Early Christian Archaeology of North Britain*, London.

——1973. 'Sculptured stones and crosses from St. Ninian's Isle and Papil', in Small *et al.* 1973, 8-44.

Thorsteinsson, A. ed., forthcoming. *Proceedings of the Fourteenth Viking Congress*, Tórshavn.

Þórðarson, M. 1931. 'Manngerðir hellar í Rangárvallasýslu og Árnessýslu', *Árbók hins íslenzka fornleifafélags,* 1930-1931, 1-76.

Tierney, J. J. ed., 1967. *Dicuili: Liber de mensura orbis terrae*, Dublin.

Tschan, F.J. trans., 1959. *Adam of Bremen: History of the Archbishops of Hamburg-Bremen*, New York.

Wainwright, F.T. ed., 1962. *The Northern Isles*, Edinburgh.

82

Vínland: the Ultimate Outpost

Magnus Magnusson KBE

Henrietta Harvey Lecture, Memorial University of Newfoundland, 15 September 2000

I stand before you with a sinking feeling in the pit of my stomach. Here I am, an honoured guest at this thousand-year party, realising that I may well turn out to be the spoilsport of the millennium, the ultimate wet blanket, the party-pooper of the age. I use the term 'party-pooper' as a somewhat racy translation of the classical term *advocatus diaboli*, 'devil's advocate'—not, I hope, in the contemporary sense of a mean-minded and carping critic, but as the person appointed by the Catholic church to oppose with scrupulous rigour the claims of a candidate for canonisation.

The candidate for canonisation in this instance is the alleged 'viking' discovery of Vínland one thousand years ago. I trust you will find it a consolation that, if I am the *advocatus diaboli*, all of you (or at least most of you) are by definition the *advocati dei*, 'God's advocates'.

So why am I so foolhardy as to embark on this highly prestigious annual lecture on such a cantankerous, not to say carnaptious, note? The derivation of the word 'carnaptious', meaning 'ill-tempered', is unknown; but in a spirit of craven self-defence, I would like to associate the word with the name of Rudolf Carnap, the American apostle of logical positivism, who attempted to construct a formal language for the empirical sciences which would eliminate all ambiguity. A hopeless cause, you might think. But that is what I want to try to do—to discuss some of the ambiguities and ambivalences which shroud the whole issue of the Norse discovery of a place named, in the Icelandic saga sources, *Vínland hit góða*—'Vínland the Good'. What I want to argue, as advocatus diaboli, is that the Vínland whose discovery we are celebrating so rapturously this year may not have existed at all in the strictly physical, geographical sense—that it was essentially an intellectual concept, not a place on the map; and furthermore that, if it did exist, we are celebrating it in the wrong year, and under the wrong title: the Viking Millennium International Symposium. 'Millennium International Symposium' it certainly is, but—and I say this with all due diffidence—'Viking Millennium International Symposium' it is not.

Would you just like me to go away now, before I get into any worse trouble?! No? All right—but having dug a hole for myself, I shall ignore all the conventional advice, and carry on digging!

So why do I dare to suggest that 'Viking Millennium' is a misnomer? Perhaps I just have a bee in my bonnet about it but, when you think about it, the word 'viking' is all too often misused as a generic term for all Scandinavians—Danes, Faroese, Finns, Greenlanders, Icelanders, Norwegians, Swedes. It may be all right as a means of selling lager or cruise holidays, but it is not all right as a serious descriptive term for the northlands of the period from the end of the eighth century to the end of the eleventh. It gives a very misleading impression indeed.

It's little wonder that the term 'viking' is misused—after all, we do not even know for certain what it means! The Old Norse word *víkingr* may be related to the word *vík*, meaning a 'bay' or a 'creek', so that a viking may have meant someone who kept his ship in a bay, either for trading or for raiding. I have always found this rather far-fetched, I have to admit. Or it may be related to the Old English word *wic*, borrowed from the Latin *vicus*, meaning a camp or a fortified trading place, so that a viking might mean an armed trader. Certainly, in the Norse language the term *víkingr* came to denote a pirate—that is how it is always used in the Icelandic sagas. To the peoples of the rest of Europe of that period, a 'viking' was synonymous with barbarian paganism, associated only with horrendous atrocities perpetrated by armed Scandinavian bands—even armies—in the British Isles and continental Europe during the so-called Viking Age. The Victorians, who loved nothing better than a Gothic frisson or two, the tourist trade and Hollywood have all exploited and reinforced this use of the term 'viking'.

But I think you will find that all the scholars taking part in this symposium are careful not to use the term 'viking' as a generic term for 'Scandinavian', although many of them have published innumerable books and articles about the 'Viking Age'.

Does it matter, you may well be asking, whether we talk about the 'viking' discovery of Vínland, or (to a lesser extent) the 'Norse' discovery of Vínland? Yes, I believe it does. To call it a 'viking' discovery is to suggest that North America was discovered during some piratical expedition across the Atlantic by a disciplined band, or even army, of Scandinavian warriors, like the conquistadors of five centuries later. And to call it a 'Norse' discovery implies an element of conscious Scandinavian expansionism which is equally misleading. The quest for some 'Ultimate Outpost' in the west was not a national or ethnic venture; it was the outcome of individual entrepreneurialism by merchants from the smallest, newest and remotest of all the Scandinavian settlements—exclusively Iceland and Greenland.

So, having got that gripe off my chest, what are we looking at here in the Millennium International Symposium? We are looking at stories about the discovery and attempted settlement of an area in North America by Icelanders and second-generation Greenlanders sometime after the year 1000, five centuries (as we are always told, with a certain triumphalism) before Christopher Columbus stumbled across South America. These stories were given the patina of ancient authenticity by saga sources written in Iceland a couple of centuries or so after the alleged event. But is that patina simply an applied veneer?

There can be no doubt whatsoever that seafaring Scandinavian traders, sailing from Greenland, made land in several places on the eastern littoral of north America about ten centuries ago, give or take a couple of decades. That is not at issue here. What is at issue is the location, the purpose and the nature of their fleeting presence.

The two major sources for the events we are celebrating this month are two Icelandic sagas, *Grænlendinga saga* (Greenlanders' Saga: GLS) and *Eiríks saga rauða* (Saga of Eiríkr the Red: ESR). They are not two versions of the same saga, but two separate sagas incorporating different and often conflicting traditions about the same or similar events. It is important to be clear in our minds about that.

Let us take GLS first, because it seems to have been the earlier of the two—not necessarily 'better', not necessarily 'more authentic', but earlier—written in the first years of the thirteenth century. It can be broken down into seven sections:

Section 1 tells how Eiríkr *rauði* and his father, outlawed from Norway, came to Iceland, and how Eiríkr founded an Icelandic colony on the western coast of Greenland. This was in AD 985 or 986.

Section 2 tells the story of a young Icelandic merchant named Bjarni Herjólfsson, the son of one of the settlers who had gone with Eiríkr *rauði* to Greenland. Bjarni returned to Iceland from a trading voyage to Norway to find his father gone to Greenland, and hastened across the Denmark Strait in his father's wake. He was blown blindly off-course, far beyond his planned destination. He sighted three unknown lands, but made no attempt to go ashore until he found Greenland, where he settled with his father.

Section 3 is about a very renowned name in these sagas: Leifr *heppni* (the Lucky), the eldest son of Eiríkr *rauði*. Leifr bought Bjarni's ship, hired a crew of thirty-five and put to sea in search of the lands Bjarni had sighted. By retracing Bjarni's homeward route (but now in a south-westerly arc), he touched lands he named Helluland (probably Baffin Island) and Markland (doubtless Labrador). The most southerly point he reached was a large island on which he built some houses (later to be known as Leifsbúðir, or 'Leifr's Houses'), which would become a focal point for later explorers in GLS.

This is a key section in the Vínland story. When the explorers landed, the saga says

> The weather was fine. There was dew on the grass, and the first thing they did was to take some of it in their hands and put it to their lips, and it seemed to them the sweetest thing they had ever tasted (GLS 250).

What a wonderful evocation of sea-weary mariners coming ashore! The river and the lake teemed with enormous salmon, there was no frost all winter. And as a rough geographical indication, the saga says that

> On the shortest day of the year the sun was already up by about 9 a.m., and did not set until after 3 p.m. (GLS 251).

This means that the explorers reckoned that they were somewhere south of latitude 50 and north of latitude 40—anywhere between the Gulf of St Lawrence and New Jersey. It's not all that helpful.

Leifr Eiríksson happened to have a foster-father named Tyrkir, who is said to have been a German (*suðrmaðr*, 'southern man'). Not far away from 'Leifr's Houses' he got lost one day, and came back jabbering excitedly, 'rolling his eyes in all directions and pulling faces'. What had so intoxicated him was that he had found *vínvið ok vínber* ('vines and grapes')— and he should know, he claimed, because where he came from there were plenty of vines and grapes (GLS 252).

85

Next spring Leifr loaded his ship with timber and grapes (no doubt raisins by then) and sailed away: 'Leifr named the country after its natural qualities—Vínland' (the Land of Wine, or the Land of Vines).

On his way back to Greenland, Leifr rescued fifteen people from a Norwegian boat which had been wrecked on a reef; the captain's name was Þórir, and his wife was named, simply, Guðríðr. For that happy exploit Leifur earned the nickname *heppni*, 'the Lucky'. That winter in Greenland disease killed Þórir and many of his crew died; but Guðríðr survived.

Section 4 concerns the voyage of one of Leifr's brothers, Þorvaldr Eiríksson. Þorvaldr reckoned that this Vínland place had not been properly explored. Leifr lent him his boat, and Þorvaldr hired a crew of thirty and sailed to Leifsbúðir where they settled for the winter and, says the saga, 'caught fish for their food' (GLS 254). They did some exploring, but found no traces of human habitation apart from a wooden stack-cover. A couple of years later Þorvaldr and his men came across three upturned skin-boats, with three men under each; they killed eight of them, but the ninth got away. These men the explorers called *skrælingar*, the Norse term for the indigenous inhabitants both of Greenland and of North America. Soon the explorers were attacked by a host of *skrælingar* in a huge swarm of skin-boats; Þorvaldr was fatally wounded by an arrow in his armpit. He was buried at a place they had earlier admired for its beauty and which they had named Krossanes. His surviving companions filled their boat with vines and grapes and sailed back to Greenland.

Section 5 tells the story of another of Leifr's brothers, Þorsteinn Eiríksson. While Þorvaldr Eiríksson was living out his last days in Vínland, his brother Þorsteinn married Guðríðr (now given the patronymic of Þorbjarnardóttir), the widow of the Norwegian skipper Þórir whom Leifr *heppni* had rescued from the skerry. When Þorsteinn Eiríksson heard of his brother's death he decided to go to Vínland to fetch the body. They had a hazardous journey—'throughout the summer they were at the mercy of the weather and never knew where they were going'(GLS 258). Eventually, late that autumn, they limped back to Greenland, to Lýsufjörður in the Western Settlement, where Þorsteinn died. Guðríðr, now widowed for a second time, went to stay with her brother-in-law, Leifr *heppni,* at Brattahlíð in the Eastern Settlement.

Section 6 is the second major section in GLS; it carries an account of the major expedition led by Þorfinnr Karlsefni (his by-name means 'Makings of a Man'), a wealthy Icelandic merchant who had come to Greenland to trade. He spent the winter with Leifr Eiríksson at Brattahlíð, fell in love with the widowed Guðríðr and married her.

There was still much talk of voyaging to Vínland, and Þorfinnr set sail with Guðríðr and a crew of 60 men and 5 women. It was a strictly mercantile venture. The saga says

> He made an agreement with his crew that everyone should share equally in whatever profits the expedition might yield. They took with them livestock of all kinds, for they intended to settle in the country if possible (GLS 261).

Þorfinnr had also made an agreement with Leifr Eiríksson over 'Leifr's Houses'—Leifr said that he would lend them, but would not give them, making Leifr the first realtor we know of from those parts. When they arrived at 'Leifr's Houses' they put the livestock out to grass. A whale—a rorqual (*reyðarhvalr*)—had been driven shore, providing a plentiful supply of fresh meat. Þorfinnr ordered timber to be felled and cut into lengths for a cargo, and, according to the saga, 'they made use of everything nature provided there, grapes and fish and game of all kinds and other good things' (GLS 261).

The following summer they had their first encounter with the *skrælingar*, who were alarmed by the bellowing of a fractious bull the would-be colonists had brought with them. Nevertheless they came back to do some bartering, exchanging furs and pelts for dairy produce; but they were refused the weapons they wanted to buy.

About this time Guðríðr gave birth to a son, and he was named Snorri Þorfinnsson (the son of Þorfinnr Karlsefni).

Early next winter the *skrælingar* returned to do some more bartering. One of them tried to steal weapons, and was killed. Soon they were back, this time with hostile intent. A pitched battle ensued, in which the *skrælingar* lost many of their men before retreating.

That was the end of the encounter—and, eventually, the end of the colonising venture. The saga says

> Karlsefni and his men spent the whole winter there, but in the spring he announced that he did not wish to stay there any longer and wanted to return to Greenland. They made ready for the voyage and took with them much valuable produce, vines and berries and pelts (GLS 264).

From Greenland Þorfinnr Karlsefni and his wife Guðríðr sailed first to Norway. Here he sold an artefact off his ship, which had been made from what is called in Icelandic *mösurr*; this is usually translated as 'maple', but is also a word for a kind of warty growth or burl which occurs on some trees. After that they went back to Iceland, where they made their home.

Section 7 tells the story of Freydís Eiríksdóttir, an illegitimate daughter of Eiríkr *rauði.* She, too, wanted to get in on the Vínland bonanza, if bonanza it was. Two Icelandic traders had arrived in Greenland, and Freydís persuaded them to join her and her husband on another expedition to Vínland, the profits to be shared. But Freydís broke faith with them, accused them of treachery and had all of them slaughtered, including five women, whom she herself butchered with an axe.

That curiously macabre episode was the last of the Vínland adventures in GLS. But there is also a postlude, or epilogue, which details some of Þorfinnr Karlsefni's famous twelfth-century descendants, and gives additional details about the later life of Guðríðr, who made a pilgrimage to Rome and became a nun at Glaumbær, in the north of Iceland. This postscript ends with a specific claim to authenticity:

It was Karlsefni who told more fully than anyone else the story of all these voyages, some of which has been written here (GLS 269).

I have given the GLS account in some detail, so that we can compare it with the account given in ESR which, as I said earlier, seems to be the later of the two sagas and shows marked dissimilarities as well as some tantalising similarities with the earlier saga.

ESR is a carefully crafted saga—much more coherent and tidy than GLS—and it, too, can be broken down into seven separate sections.

Section 1 tells the story of the principal settler in the Breiðafjörður (Broadfjord) region of western Iceland, which was the place of origin of most of the colonists who followed Eiríkr *rauði* to Greenland. The first settler there was the matriarchal Auðr *inn djúpúðga* (the Deep-Minded—what a wonderful nickname!), a resourceful Norwegian woman of high birth who married a Norwegian war-chief named Ólafr *hvíti* (the White) who conquered Dublin (see Batey, this volume). After her husband's death in battle in Ireland, Auðr went to Scotland with her son Þorsteinn *rauði*, where Þorsteinn conquered much of the mainland before he, too, was killed in battle. Auðr the Deep-Minded thereupon sailed with her grand-children and a large retinue from Caithness, in the north of Scotland, to Iceland, which was then in the early stages of Norse settlement. Here she took possession of the Dalir (Dales), district in the Breiðafjörður region and granted lands to her loyal supporters. She made her home at Hvammur, where her descendants lived for many years.

Now, this section is more than a nostalgic wallow in genealogy. Its significance lies in the fact that one of Auðr's descendants was Ari *fróði* (the Learned, 1068-1148), the found-ing father of Iceland's historical tradition. In the 1120s he wrote the first brief history of Iceland in the vernacular—a priceless little book known as *Íslendingabók* ('Book of Icelanders'). In *Íslendingabók* we find the first written reference to the name Vínland in the Icelandic sources—a glancing reference to the *skrælingar* who inhabited Vínland being the same as those who had been the aboriginal inhabitants of Greenland. Remember, this was written down only a century after the Vínland adventure.

Section 2 recounts the story of Eiríkr *rauði* and his discovery and colonisation of Greenland from his base in Breiðafjörður. It is only slightly more detailed than the account in GLS, and both accounts seem to have been lifted directly from another major historical work with which Ari *fróði* was closely connected—*Landnámabók* ('Book of Settlements'). There seems little doubt that Ari *fróði*, descendant of Auðr *inn djúpúðga*, was responsible both for the story of Auðr's settlement in Breiðafjörður and of Eiríkr *rauði*'s colonisation of Greenland in *Landnámabók*.

Section 3 gives a much fuller account of Guðríðr Þorbjarnardóttir, the ultimate heroine of the saga, whom we have already met in GLS. Her grandfather, Vífill, had gone to Iceland with Auðr the Deep-Minded; he was a man of noble lineage (of course!), who had been taken prisoner in the British Isles and was a slave until Auðr gave him his freedom. His son, a proud but impecunious farmer named Þorbjörn Vífilsson, emigrated to Greenland in order to forestall what he considered an unsuitable marriage proposal for his daughter Guðríðr.

There was a severe famine in Greenland at the time. The man who owned the farm where Þorbjörn and his family spent their first winter hired a sibyl, a sorceress, to perform a pagan ritual to find out how long the current hardships would last. The scene is described by the saga-writer with all the passion and detail of a true antiquarian. Guðríðr, although she was a Christian, was persuaded (for the good of the community) to assist in the ritual by singing an old pagan song which she had been taught by her foster-mother in Iceland. The old witch rewarded her by foretelling her destiny—she would marry a fine husband in Greenland but eventually return to her native Iceland where she would have glorious prog-eny; oddly enough, she made no mention of Guðríðr's forthcoming adventures in Vínland.

87

Section 4 is devoted to the founding family in Greenland—Eiríkr *rauði* and his son Leifr Eiríksson—Leifr *heppni*. This section also introduces the formidable personage of King Óláfr Tryggvason, the Christian evangelist who was king of Norway for five lurid years from AD 995 to 1000. Here the two sagas diverge very significantly indeed; there is no mention whatsoever of an earlier voyage to the west by Bjarni Herjólfsson, or anyone else for that matter. And this is where we start warming to the millennial theme.

Leifr Eiríksson, we are told, was a member of King Óláfr's court in Norway. Mindful of his duties as a courtier, Leifr had sailed from Greenland for Norway. He was blown off course and landed in the Hebrides, where he had an *affaire* with a woman named Þórgunna. She was of noble Hebridean lineage, and skilled in magic. She gave birth to a son, named Þorgils, and wanted to go with Leifr to Norway, but Leifur refused and went off to Norway without her. In Norway Leifr is received with all due honour (like all promising young Icelanders in the sagas, I might say).

The king had a mission in mind for Leifr. He had already converted Norway to Christianity at sword-point, and he had eyes on other countries as well. He asked Leifr to return to Greenland and bring the Christian gospel to the settlers there.

> Leifr said it was for the king to command, but said he thought this mission would be difficult in Greenland. The king replied that he could think of no one more suitable for it than him— 'and your good luck will see you through' (ESR 211).

We are now at the nub of the story—one of the stories—about the discovery of North America. Here it comes, from ESR, chapter 5.

> Leifr put out to sea; he had a long and difficult voyage, and finally came upon lands where he had not expected any to be found. There were fields of wild corn there, and vines growing; there were also trees known as maples. They took some samples of all these things. Some of the trees were so large that they could be used for house-building (ESR 211).

(We should notice in passing that there is no mention here of Leifr giving the land he had found the name of Vínland).

> Leifr also came across some shipwrecked seamen and brought them home to Greenland with them; he looked after them with all hospitality during the winter. In this as in other things he showed his great magnanimity and goodness; he brought Christianity to the country and he rescued these men. From then on he was known as Leifr *heppni* [...]. He quickly began preaching Christianity and the true Catholic faith throughout the country; he revealed to the people King Óláfr Tryggvason's message, and told them what excellence and what glory there was in this faith (ESR 211-12).

Leifr's mother, Þjóðhildr, and many others in Greenland are said to have embraced Christianity, but his father, Eiríkr *rauði*, refused to abandon the old religion. Þjóðhildr defiantly built a church 'not too close' to the farmstead at Brattahlíð (Kagssiarssuk), which came to be known as 'Þjóðhildr's Church', and refused to sleep with the old pagan any more.

From then on, Leifr *heppni* is virtually out of the Vínland story—in ESR, anyway.

Section 5 describes the next stage—an abortive expedition in search of the unnamed land Leifr had found. It was mounted by Leifr's brother, Þorsteinn Eiríksson. He made ready the ship which Guðríðr's father Þorbjörn Vífilsson had brought from Iceland. This was not to be a colonising expedition: the crew of 20 took only weapons and provisions with them. They sailed off in high spirits, but had a long and difficult voyage and never reached their destination. 'Their ship was driven back and forth across the ocean,' says the saga. They got back to Greenland late in the autumn, worn out and exhausted. That winter Þorsteinn married Guðríðr, but they were not destined to enjoy married life for long: Þorsteinn soon succumbed to a disease. In another eerie scene heavy with folklore, Þorsteinn's corpse sits up and foretells Guðríðr's future, saying that she would have a great destiny, but warning her against marrying a Greenlander. The widowed Guðríðr now moved into Brattahlíð to stay with her in-laws.

Section 6 forms the major part of the saga account of Vinland. The spotlight now falls on Þorfinnr Karlsefni, the Icelandic merchant who sailed on a trading expedition to Greenland, where he met and married Guðríðr. And now, says the saga, there were great discussions at Brattahlíð about going in search of Vínland (the country had apparently been named by then).

The expedition consisted of three ships, carrying 160 people, led by Þorfinnr Karlsefni and his bride. It included several named Icelanders, as well as another of Eiríkr's sons, Þorvaldur, Eiríkr's illegitimate daughter Freydís, and a member of the Brattahlíð household named Þórhallr *veiðimaðr* (Hunter), a curmudgeonly old pagan—an echo, perhaps, of the German Tyrkir in GLS.

Þorfinnr's sailing route in search of Vínland is described in some detail. From Brattahlíð in the Eastern Settlement of Greenland they sailed north-east up the coast to the Western Settlement, and then to the Bjarneyjar (Bear Isles)—possibly Disco Island. From there they sailed for two days before a northerly wind to a land they named Helluland (Slab-Land)—presumably Baffin Island. From there they sailed for another two days before a northerly wind and came to a heavily-forested country they named Markland (Forest-land)—presumably Labrador. After another two days' sail they came to a stretch of coast-line of such remarkably extensive reaches of sand that they named it Furðustrandir ('Marvel Strands'), which has a distinct whiff of fable about it. At the end of this marvellous stretch of coast they put ashore a Scottish couple, named Haki and Hekja, who could run faster than deer, according to the saga; the two Scots were told to run south for three days in order to explore the country's resources. They came back with grapes and wild wheat, and Þorfinnr said that they claimed to have found good land.

89

From there, according to the saga, they sailed on until they reached a fjord. At its mouth lay an island around which there flowed very strong currents, and so they named it Straumey (Stream Island). It teemed with nesting birds. This is where they settled for the summer, which was so beguiling that they made no provision for the winter. The winter, however, was very severe, and they ran out of food. They prayed to God to send them something to eat, but to no avail.

At this point Þórhallr *veiðimaðr* disappeared. He was found three days later in a bit of a state (just as Tyrkir had been): he was twitching and mumbling to himself, staring at the sky with eyes and mouth and nostrils agape. He seems to have gone into some kind of shamanistic trance in order to attract a whale to beach itself. Sure enough, they came across a stranded whale of some previously unknown genus—an echo, perhaps, of the rorqual which Karlsefni's expedition in GLS had found; but when they fell upon it and cut it up, the meat proved to be poisonous.

This was clearly not the Promised Land of Vinland. They decided to look elsewhere. Þórhallr *veiðimaðr* and nine other men insisted on heading north, but they ran into fierce headwinds and were driven right across to Ireland, where they were brutally beaten and enslaved, according to the saga. And there Þórhallr died.

Þorfinnr, on the other hand, sailed south along the coast, 'for he believed that the country would improve the farther south they went' (ESR 226). And he was right. They came to a place they named Hóp (Tidal Lake).

Here they found fields of wild wheat growing on all the low ground and grape vines on all the higher ground. Every stream was teeming with fish. They dug trenches at the high-tide mark, and when the tide went out there were flounders trapped in the trenches. In the woods there were animals of all kinds (ESR 226-27).

Was this the elusive Vínland at last? The saga does not say so. But it was certainly the last point of their search. Soon they started trading with the indigenous people who arrived on the scene in their skinboats. At first the bartering went well. The natives traded their grey pelts for red cloth, but as the supplies of red cloth dwindled, the explorers began to give smaller and smaller strips of cloth in exchange for larger and larger numbers of pelts. At that point a bull belonging to Þorfinnr came running out of the woods, bellowing furiously; the natives took fright and fled.

Three weeks later the natives returned, in overwhelming numbers. The explorers were forced to retreat, but now Freydís (a very different Freydís, this) showed her true mettle. Snatching up a sword from a fallen Greenlander, she bared one of her breasts and slapped it with the sword. It must have been some breast, because the natives took fright and fled.

Þorfinnr realised that his ambitious mercantile venture was doomed. The saga says

> Karlsefni and his men now recognised that although the land was excellent they could never live there in safety or freedom from fear, because of the native inhabitants; so they made ready to leave the place and return home (ESR 230).

Section 7 presents an account of the return home and some of the unlikely adventures which befell them. On the way back north to Straumfjörðr, Þorfinnr came upon a group of five natives sleeping under their skin-boats, and killed them on the bland assumption that they must be outlaws. He then sailed off with one ship in search of Þórhallr *veiðimaðr*; the only outcome of this unavailing effort was an extraordinary encounter with a uniped (*einfætingr*), a one-legged man who came bounding down to where the ship lay and mortally wounded Leifr's brother Þorvaldr with an arrow through the groin.

They all over-wintered at Straumfjörðr— their third winter in the New World. But now tensions broke out in the settlement—over women. The saga notes that it was all right for Þorfinnr Karlsefni: his wife Guðríðr had given birth to a son, Snorri, during the first autumn of the expedition. Not so the others.

> But now quarrels kept breaking out, as those with no wives sought to take those of the married men (ESR 233).

Next spring they set off for home. On Markland they captured two *skræling* children: 'they took the boys with them and taught them their language and had them baptised.' This episode is particularly notable for a reference to Irish and Icelandic folklore which has intrigued every scholar. The boys told them that across from their own land there was a country whose people wore white clothing and uttered loud cries and carried poles with patches of cloth attached. This, says the saga, is thought to have been a place called Hvítramannaland (Land of the White People)—which, according to *Landnámabók*, lay six days' sail west of Ireland.

Meanwhile one of the ships came to grief in a maggot-infested ocean identified in the saga as the Greenland Sea.

And so the Vínland venture came to a somewhat inglorious close. A brief postlude to the saga notes that Þorfinnr Karlsefni and his wife Guðríðr went back to Þorfinnr's home in the north of Iceland (not Glaumbær, as in GLS, but Reynistaðr in Skagafjörður). It also notes that three of their descendants in the twelfth century were bishops.

So much for the saga narratives. You will have noted how tantalisingly similar and yet dissimilar they are, in terms of the people, the expeditions, the outcomes. They are clearly recalling events whose details have become blurred and confused with the passage of time and the telling and retelling of the yarns. The key differences we should focus on concern the role of Leifr Eiríksson—Leifr the Lucky— in these events, and consequently the story of Guðríðr and, above all, the role of 'Leifr's Houses' (Leifsbúðir): the settlement which

90

Eiríkr is said to have built but which figures in only one of the sagas, GLS, and not at all in the other.

I am tempted here to call in support from that old friend of old hack newspaper reporters like me, Rudyard Kipling. In a little ditty called 'The Elephant's Child', published in the *Just-So Stories*, he penned the journalists' creed

> I keep six honest serving men
> (they taught me all I knew):
> their names are What & Why & When
> and How & Where & Who.

Well, we know the first honest serving man—the What: a series of accounts, based on traditions in the west and north of Iceland, of a number of voyages of exploration and mercantile expeditions to the eastern seaboard of North America.

And we know the last of them—the Who: Eiríkr *rauði* of Iceland and Greenland with his son Leifr Eiríksson, and the merchant Þorfinnr Karlsefni of Iceland with his wife Guðríðr Þorbjarnardóttir.

The How is pretty clear, too—by boat: not the lean and predatory longship of inshore warfare, but the buxom-breasted *knörr*, the tireless maid-of-all-work of the Scandinavian trade-routes.

The Why is also made clear in the saga sources. These individuals, the Who, were motivated by a restless curiosity—and an eye on the main chance. They had moved from Iceland at a time of famine and founded two Icelandic colonies on the west coast of Greenland (the Eastern Settlement and the Western Settlement). They lived reasonably well—certainly as well as they had lived in Iceland. But always there was the natural human aspiration for something better, a better place in a better sun. Whether by chance or by calculation, these individuals went in search of that better place in a better sun. Whether by chance or calculation they found their Promised Land—or almost found it: paradise was glimpsed, at least, if not actually found, somewhere in that golden west. And with it came the promise of untold wealth by exploiting the abundant natural resources of the lands they had found.

And that leaves us with the last two questions, the two questions I dared to raise at the outset of my address: the When and the Where.

Let's take the When first. It goes without saying that there are no dates given in the saga accounts, and that the sagas themselves are based on oral traditions (perhaps stiffened with some early written notes, or *schedae*), and that these sagas were written some two centuries after the events they purport to describe. So dating is going to be a matter of conjecture based on speculation about any internal evidence which can be inferred from the texts.

And as we consider the texts, we should remind ourselves that no text is ever strictly neutral. Everything is written for a particular audience and for a particular purpose—the knack is to identify and understand that audience and that purpose in order to be able to assess the degree of editorialising which inspires it.

The key factor in any attempt to date the events precisely is the role played by Leifr *heppni* Eiríksson. Here the two sagas are at the greatest variance with one another. In the earlier saga, GLS, Leifr makes a purposeful voyage of exploration to follow up the chance discovery of unknown lands by Bjarni Herjólfsson; in ESR, on the other hand, it is Leifr, not Bjarni Herjólfsson, who makes the first chance discovery. This version offers the opportunity of attaching a specific date to Leifr's fortuitous discovery; for in ESR, Leifr is portrayed as a Christian evangelist commissioned by King Óláfr Tryggvason of Norway to convert the new inhabitants of Greenland to Christianity. Since Óláfr Tryggvason's death in battle is conventionally dated to the autumn of 1000, a month or two after he had engineered the conversion of Iceland to Christianity, then Leifr's evangelising mission to Greenland must have

91

been undertaken in the spring of the year 1000. Ergo, Vínland was discovered in that momentous millennial year.

But—and it is a very large but indeed—the literary evidence suggests very strongly that Leifr's missionary journey from Norway never took place at all—that it was, in fact, a pious fiction invented by early Icelandic historians and picked up by others.

I had better explain that.

Back in the 1950s, an Icelandic scholar named Jón Jóhanneson published a brilliant piece of literary detective work on the two sagas. It was contained in an essay entitled 'Aldur *Grænlendinga sögu*' in 1956. The nub of his argument was that the key to this seemingly intractable puzzle lay with that enigmatic character, King Óláfr Tryggvason. He was the darling of the Icelandic court poets and saga-historians, and was hailed as the great champion of Christianity, having played a major role in the conversion of Iceland in the year 1000. He was credited with having been instrumental in the conversion of four other lands besides Iceland—Norway, Shetland, the Orkneys and the Faroes.

(This fulsome attitude towards King Óláfr in the Icelandic sources stands in stark contrast, I may say, with the view of him expressed by medieval continental historians such the eleventh-century German cleric Adam of Bremen, or the twelfth-century Danish historian and poet Saxo Grammaticus. To them, he was anathema: no evangelist, not even a proper Christian, more like Anti-Christ—a foreign usurper who had seized the throne of Norway by force and wrought untold harm in that country before his unlamented death in AD 1000. One could perhaps trace this ungenerous attitude to the fact that the Bishopric of Hamburg was keen to apportion to itself the prestige and perquisites of having Christianised the northlands through its own missionaries, rather than allowing the credit to be given to an upstart usurper king. But that is by-the-by.)

The Icelandic church historians, however, wanted a patron saint of their own, and who better than Óláfr Tryggvason, whose ruthless power-politics had helped to bring Iceland out of paganism to the true faith? And so, to give further polish to King Óláfr's lustre as the evangelist of the Northlands, and to embellish his claim for canonisation, round about the year 1200 an Icelandic monk named Gunnlaugr Leifsson wrote a Latin biography (the original is now lost, alas) of the king which, for the first time, added Greenland to the list of Óláfr's Christianising achievements. Earlier Icelandic historians of greater repute, like Ari *fróði* in his *Íslendingabók* (*c.* 1120), had made no mention of this; nor did the *Historia Norvegiae*, the Latin history of Norway written in Norway early in the thirteenth century.

Once this late fiction was given currency in Iceland, however, it meant that history and saga alike had to be re-written. The story, however implausible, was picked up by the great Icelandic saga-historian Snorri Sturluson (1179-1241) in his monumental work on the history of the kings of Norway, *Heimskringla*.

Accordingly, the story of Vínland as given in GLS had to be re-cast in ESR. Out went Bjarni Herjólfsson as the accidental discoverer of North America. Out went Leifr Eiríksson in his much more robust and admirable role as the deliberate explorer of North America. And out, I regret to say, went the nicely pat dating of the event to the year 1000.

So where does that leave the question, When? The precise chronology can only be a matter for speculation: you pay your money and you take your choice. If you rely on GLS, much depends on how many years elapsed after the first colonisation of Greenland in 985 or 986 before the first accidental discovery of the New World by Bjarni Herjólfsson or whoever, and how many years it took for Leifr Eiríksson to grow to manhood and undertake the planned exploration of Bjarni's sighting (after all, we do not know in which year Leifr was born).

But there is another way of looking at it—through those genealogies of which Icelanders are so passionately (and perhaps genetically) addicted. We know that one of the most eminent of the descendants of Guðríðr, mother of the first European child born in the

New World, was the historian Ari *fróði*. The Icelandic scholar Ólafur Halldórsson, who has produced what is to my mind the most authoritative interpretation of the sagas to date in his book *Grænland í miðaldaritum* ('Greenland in medieval sources'), calculated from the genealogical information that both Þorfinnr Karlsefni and his wife Guðríðr were born around the year 995. By this reckoning, their Vínland voyage, the most significant of the expeditions in both the sagas, therefore probably took place around 1020.

And so to the final question—the Where. This is the one which I confess I have been secretly dreading, because of the circumstances of this International Symposium in Newfoundland and Labrador. It's not that I am more of a coward than other men, but I have a lively interest in survival.

Let me iterate that I have no doubt whatsoever that North America was discovered and explored by Scandinavians from Greenland and Iceland about a thousand years ago. Whatever one might think about the Icelandic sagas as historical sources (and opinions vary greatly), no serious scholar would gainsay the incontrovertible archaeological evidence uncovered by Helge Ingstad and his wife Anne Stine at L'Anse aux Meadows here in Newfoundland in the 1960s. The site has been exhaustively re-excavated and re-studied and has stood up to the most rigorous examination: L'Anse aux Meadows is incontrovertibly an Iron Age Norse site dating to about 1000 years ago.

But archaeology is not quite, even yet, the strict historical '-ology' discipline it would like to be. There is always an almost irresistible temptation to try to relate any archaeological discovery to whatever written sources might exist, however meagre or misleading. Think of the great German archaeologist, Heinrich Schliemann, who unearthed a golden face mask in one of the celebrated shaft-graves at Bronze-Age Mycenae in Greece and sent an impulsively romantic telegram to the King of Greece, announcing unequivocally, 'Today I have gazed upon the face of Agamemnon.' Great telegram—pity about the fact that his find was later dated to a period six centuries before Homer's Agamemnon led his confederation of bronze-clad warriors against Troy. Archaeology always likes to place a visiting card on site to 'prove' its provenance.

93

And forgers and wishful thinkers have never been slow to exploit the perceived need for 'proof' of the Vínland venture. The bizarre Kensington Stone with its alleged Swedish runic inscription is as irrelevant to our discussion as the so-called 'Vinland Map' which has left nothing but egg on the faces of the solemn scholars of Yale University, despite their unceasing attempts to prove its authenticity (see Seaver, this volume). The so-called Maine Penny, minted in the reign of King Óláfr *kyrri* ('The Peaceful') of Norway in 1067-1093 and found during the excavation of an Amerindian site in 1957, is certainly authentic, but cannot be cited as proof of Scandinavian presence there. Coins have a habit of travelling on their own—another Óláfr *kyrri* silver penny turned up in England in a flower-bed outside the Art Gallery in Lincoln!

It is a very real problem. And I believe it has positively bedevilled the quest for Vínland. *One* saga—GLS—refers to some houses which Leifr Eiríksson is said to have built as a temporary encampment. And when, after decades of fakes and false archaeological hopes, an authentic site of some Norse-type buildings *was* discovered, it was instantly and uncritically identified as the site of Leifsbúðir (Leifr's Houses), and therefore of Vínland itself.

It could well be the site of the Leifsbúðir of GLS—at least until another incontrovertible Norse site is found; I look forward to that with unholy glee! But I do not for a moment believe that it was the Vínland envisaged in the traditions enshrined by the saga-writers. Enthusiasts have twiddled the texts, selected from the texts, conflated the texts and compromised the texts in endless attempts to create a coherent story which will 'prove' their particular hypothesis. But frankly, the sailing directions which dozens of eager researchers have tried to follow are not much more explicit than the old Icelandic adage for getting to North America: sail south until the butter melts, and then turn right.

The saga traditions of Vínland, I personally believe, are irretrievable in terms of fact. One can only admire the colossal energies which have been expended on the search for Vínland by enthusiasts of all kinds, excavators, forgers, mariners, numismatists, palaeographers, patriots and meteorologists like Páll Bergþórsson of Iceland who has perfected the opposite of weather forecasting—weather back-casting—to deduce sailing conditions a thousand years ago. His book on the subject has now been translated into English as *The Wineland Millennium, Saga and Evidence*—and I warmly commend it. Between them all they have 'identified' Vínland in places as far apart as Hudson Bay and Florida—with New York (for good commercial reasons) one of the front runners nowadays.

Support for a New York location has also come from a more unlikely academic source—animal genetics. It concerns the populations of *cats* in New York and Boston, which have been studied by one of Iceland's most eminent livestock experts, Dr Stefán Aðalsteinsson. The results of his researches appeared in 1983 in a learned journal with the catchy title of *Zeitschrift für Tierzüchtung und Züchtungsbiologi*.

What Dr Stefán Aðalsteinsson found was that the colour combinations among cats in the cities of New York and Boston are very similar to those found among cats in Iceland and other Nordic areas in north-western Europe; furthermore, the genetic properties of the New York and Boston cat populations are very similar to those of cat populations in former 'viking' areas, like Iceland and Shetland.

94

It is not unlikely that the Karslefni expedition had taken cats with them, to defend their storehouses against the native rodent population; but cats were also valuable for their pelts in those days, as well as being nice pets to have around. Domestic cats feature in several of the Iceland sagas. In *Vatnsdæla saga*, for instance, a villainous thief named Þórólfr *sleggja* ('Sledgehammer') is feared by his enemies because of the twenty fierce black cats he owned. And in GLS we read of a pagan sorceress in Greenland whose ceremonial outfit included gloves fashioned from catskin with the hair turned to the outside and white on the inside, along with a black lambskin hat which was lined on the inside with white catskin. Around AD 1200 such pelts were lawful currency, and one skin from an adult tomcat was equal in value to three fox-skins or three skins from autumn lambs.

The thesis is that in North America, the cats which jumped ship or were left behind when the Vínland voyagers left went feral; when Europeans arrived there in a second wave of immigration in the seventeenth century, the feral males would have dominated in matings to domestic cats, and these would have carried Icelandic and Greenlandic colour genes into the households of the settlers. The cat population would then have gradually attained an Icelandic profile of colour combinations, without anyone really noticing it, until Dr Stefán Aðalsteinsson smelled a rat, or at least a mouse.

It's all very intriguing. Frankly, I do not know the answer to the Vínland puzzle. I don't think *anyone* does. But I must confess that I have a lurking suspicion that Vínland, as such, as opposed to the North American littoral, never existed *as an actual place*. The name itself, 'Vínland the Good', carries too many overtones of romance and fable: fables of the Hesperides, of the Fortunate Isles (*Insulae Fortunatae*), of Hvítramannaland (Land of the White People), of the Irish *Immrama* (Voyages) in their Lives of Saints—indeed, I suspect we are going to see a lot more emphasis on the Irish literary and genetic influence on Iceland's history and literature in the future. Indeed, iconoclasm is much in the air, as in this volume, for instance, my compatriot and namesake Professor Magnús Stefánsson of Bergen University revives an old argument about the very name 'Vínland', arguing that the place was originally called *Vinland* ('Meadowland'), not Vínland ('Wineland') (see Stefánsson, Crozier, this volume).

For my own part, for what it's worth, 'Vínland the Good' smacks much more of a wistful and wishful concept than of a geographical reality.

Chairman, learned masters and doctors, ladies and gentlemen—the search for the Ultimate Outpost has become a major industry. In the summer of 2000, Greenland celebrated its part in the discoveries to the west with a royal visit by the queen of Denmark to handsel the construction of replicas of Eiríkr *rauði*'s farmstead and Þjóðhildr's Church at Brattahlíð. At L'Anse aux Meadows, Parks Canada has constructed a rather grandiose version of Leifr's Houses which draws visitors in droves. From Iceland, a replica of the Gokstad ship, named of course the *Íslendingur* (Icelander), is making its way towards its ultimate destination in New York. And why not? The building and sailing of replicas of the Gokstad ship has been an industry ever since Captain Magnus Anderson of Norway sailed one to Chicago in 1893 for the World Fair to publicise the continuing virility of Norwegian ship-building.

Good on them, say I! Good on all of them! But let us not confuse honest commercialism with the more scrupulous disciplines of scholarship.

The Vínland event, however we read it, was both insignificant and highly important: as a footnote to history it may have been no big deal, but as a chapter in the story of man's aspirations it has a fascination which will never die.

What we are doing at this Viking Millennium International Symposium is celebrating the spirit of adventurous endeavour and exploration which imbued those early pioneers of the sea-routes across the Atlantic around the time of the last millennium. What we are also doing is celebrating man's unending quest to discover the truth about the past. It doesn't matter a jot whether or not we celebrate it in the millennial year of 2000; we should be celebrating it every year, every month, every day of every year, millennium or not.

These are essentially saga-stories, not historical reports or geographical treatises. They are more concerned with people than with places; they are explorations of people's responses to ordeal—hence, I suspect, the very different versions of the behaviour of Freydís in the two sagas.

So when people ask, 'Are the Sagas true? Are they history? Is this what really happened?', these questions ultimately do not matter. Ultimately, the past is not a stable entity which can ever be properly recovered. The 'past' as we perceive it is an ever-changing combination of contemporary evidences and testimonies, whether of the word or the spade, constantly under review in the light of new theories, new preoccupations, new interpretations, new methodologies, new systems, new translations even. But let us never forget the voice of the past in all this: the voice of the story-tellers, the saga-writers. The sagas they wrote, the stories they told, are 'true' in the one way which really matters: true to something deep within us all as human beings, true to the profoundest imperatives of human action and feeling.

So let me leave you with a final quotation, not from the sagas but from a modern Scandinavian who knew a thing or two about story-telling. It comes from Isak Dinesen (Karen Blixen), from *The Blank Page* in her book of *Lost Tales*:

> If the story-teller is faithful to the story, in the end the silence will speak; if the story-teller is not faithful to the story, in the end there will be nothing but silence.

And now, chairman, ladies and gentlemen, if you want to run me out of town, I promise I shall go quietly.

Magnus Magnusson

ABBREVIATIONS

ESR 'Eirik's Saga', in Magnusson, M. and Pálsson, H., trans, 1965. *The Vinland Sagas: The Norse Discovery of North America*, Harmondsworth, 73-105.

GLS 'Grœnlendinga Saga', in Magnusson, M. and Pálsson, H., trans, 1965. *The Vinland Sagas: The Norse Discovery of North America*, Harmondsworth, 47-72.

BIBLIOGRAPHY

Bergþórsson. P. 2000. *The Wineland Millennium, Saga and Evidence,* Reykjavík.

Halldórsson, Ó. 1978. *Grœnland í miðaldaritum*, Reykjavík.

96

The Early Norse Farm Buildings in Western Greenland:

Archaeological evidence

Svend E. Albrethsen

Since the first scientific excavations were conducted in Norse ruins in Greenland by Gustav Holm in 1880 (Holm 1883) and Daniel Bruun in 1895 (Bruun 1896), there have been deliberations among researchers over how the Norse farm developed from the *landnám* or first settlement shortly before the year 1000 until the end of the colony in the first half of the fifteenth century.

It was Daniel Bruun's view that there must be a close connection between the development of the dwelling and thus of the farm itself in Iceland and Greenland, and that this development presumably must have proceeded from a relatively simple form, i.e. a longhouse, to a more complex one like the Icelandic passage-house. He thought, on the basis of his reconnaissances and excavations in the Norse Eastern Settlement, that he could demonstrate certain types in the Greenlandic material. This view of the development of the Norse dwelling has in principle not changed much since.

97

The material on which Daniel Bruun could base his theories was in the nature of things very deficient, and it was only with the big systematic excavations, in Iceland as well as Greenland in the first half of this century, that it became possible to make any progress with the problem.

In his doctoral dissertation, Aage Roussell (1941) dealt in detail with the problem of the development of the dwelling and the farm, and believed he could distinguish three main types that could be ascribed chronological value:

Type I: The *longhouse* with one room or several extending lengthwise, dating throughout most of the eleventh century; and a subtype, the *expanded longhouse*, where one or two smaller rooms have been added on one of the long sides. The entrance was placed in the middle of one of the long sides of the house and led into an antechamber or corridor from which there was access to the other rooms of the house. The expanded longhouse was said to date from the late eleventh century until about 1300. The other buildings of the farm such as barns, animal sheds, storage rooms and forge were in independent buildings separated from the dwelling.

Type II: The *passage house* with rooms in rows behind one another around one or more passages. This dwelling type was said to have gradually replaced the longhouse from the late thirteenth century onwards. In this case the functions of the farm, with the exception of the sheds, barns and similar buildings, were gathered in one block, which meant substantially fewer independent buildings.

Type III: The *centralized farm*, where dwelling and utility buildings were built together in one large block. The actual dwelling was in this case arranged more or less like the passage-house with the utility buildings placed around it. The centralized farm in its fully developed form was dated from the early fourteenth century.

This development of the Norse farm corresponded on the whole, in Roussell's view, to the development of the farm in Iceland—apart from the fact that the centralized farm does not seem to occur in the Icelandic material and therefore had to be regarded as a peculiarly Greenlandic phenomenon. However, there were great problems with the synchronization of the datings from the two areas, since substantially different dating methods had been used.

In Iceland the chronology had mainly been drawn up on the basis of the written sources and tephrochronology (dating of a site from volcanic ash deposit), while the Greenlandic datings were almost exclusively based on estimates since, in 1941, it had not been possible to draw up a local Greenlandic chronology.

It is unlikely that there will be important changes in the main features of the course of development outlined above for the Greenlandic dwelling/farm in the future, but further research has shown that Roussell's chronology for the development of the dwelling, including the farm, cannot be used in practice for dating purposes. It appears evident from the Greenlandic material that all three farm types were in use and were perhaps even built all the way up until the end of the Norse colony.

Instead of regarding the farm types as clearly demarcated types as Roussell did, perhaps one should see them as different stages of a steady development, since one can very well imagine a dwelling which through expansion and rebuilding gradually changes from a long-house to a passage-house to a centralized farm. The most recent form of a given farm should therefore be regarded as interplay of needs, function, terrain and dating, rather than solely as an expression of dating, as has been done earlier.

There is much to suggest that the view of Norse society has earlier been much too simplistic, since with a few exceptions the Norse settlements have mainly been seen as consisting of a number of fairly uniform individual units (farms), each of which 'lived its own life'. The question is, however, whether one should not rather regard the individual farms as elements in a strongly differentiated social structure where each farm complex had a quite precisely defined function. In that case this function must have been determined by the location in relation to hunting, pasturage, navigation, trade and the like—factors which would have played a crucial role in the specific forming and development of the individual farm.

THE OLDEST NORSE FARMS

In the following I will give an overview of the material from Greenland in terms of building remains, which with greater or lesser likelihood can be ascribed to the earliest period of the Norse colony. From the pre-1960 large excavations made by Bruun (1896), Nørlund (1934), Roussell (1936; 1941) and Vebæk (1943), there is minimal evidence of early Norse buildings and the few remains found by them are normally difficult to date and interpret.

RUIN GROUP Ø[1] 17 A NARSSAQ

The farm comprises at least ten buildings, of which only the dwelling has been subjected to systematic investigation (Vebæk 1993).

The house ruin consists of a north-south oriented longhouse whose facade lies parallel with the coastline. The ruin has inside measurements of 33-34 x 4-6 m, and in its last phase was divided into four rooms extending lengthwise. The excavation revealed that the four rooms had different construction periods.

The oldest construction phase consists of a building with only one room, with inside dimensions of *c.* 11 x 5.5 m. Because of later rebuilding and additions it is difficult to say anything with certainty about the arrangement of this first building. It appears that the oldest construction phase had a stone-built long hearth in the middle of a wholly or partially flagged floor, and that the floor level in the eastern part of the room was somewhat higher than in the western part. A system of partially flagged drainage gutters, probably meant to channel rain and meltwater away from the house, also belongs to the oldest construction

1. Ø = Eastern Settlement. V = Western Settlement.

phase. In one of these gutters, running down through the middle of the house, a small oval wooden barrel was found; it probably functioned as a kind of well.

The dating of the oldest construction phase is based first and foremost on the runological dating of an inscription on a four-sided pine stick 40 cm long, which cannot have been made much later than the year AD 1000 (Moltke 1961, 411ff). This early dating is supported by other finds from the investigation, including some arrowheads of a Late Viking-Age/Medieval type made of reindeer antler (Rygh 1885: type R 538-539). Two C^{14} dates made from local wood gives a date about AD 1000 for the oldest building phase (Vebæk 1993).

RUIN GROUP Ø 20

The farm comprises ten buildings in the most recent construction phase; only the dwelling has been subjected to a detailed archaeological investigation (Bruun 1896, 264ff). The dwelling ruin is an approximately E-W-oriented longhouse consisting of three rooms running lengthwise, with a smaller annex towards the north. The entrance was in the middle of the southern long wall. The ruin has outside dimensions of 23.5 x 6.5-8 m. The westernmost room has a stone-built cooking pit in the northeastern corner. Along the outer walls excavation revealed a number of stones which probably represent the foundations of the walls of an older construction phase when the building was rather narrower than in the last phase of use.

99

The dwelling in its most recent form is a typical example of an expanded longhouse, but the traces of older foundations show that this form was not the original one.

Unfortunately the excavation and the finds made do not permit us to date the two construction phases more accurately.

RUIN GROUP Ø 29 A QASSIARSUK (BRATTAHLÍÐ)

On the northernmost of the three farms on the Brattahlíð plain we know of the remains of at least three buildings which must be dated to the *landnám* period or a very early phase of Norse colonisation.

Ruin 2. In connection with the excavation in 1932 (Nørlund and Stenberger 1934) of the dwelling ruin of the Brattahlíð farm the remains of a longhouse (A) were identified below the medieval ruins (fig. 1). Oddly enough the remains were not investigated further, and despite this find the excavators stated that the large hall (Room I)—often called 'Eric the Red's Hall'—must originally have been a longhouse and was probably the oldest building in Greenland. In 1964 a small follow-up investigation was conducted at the edge of the excavation field from 1932. This investigation revealed that there were very well preserved remains of a longhouse in the form of a building with metre-thick turf walls on a foundation of stone. The house had an outside length of some 13 m and a width of no less then 8 m. It had slightly curving long walls and straight-cut gables. There are no finds from Ruin A, but it seems likely that this house may go all the way back to the first period of the colonization.

In general the plan drawing of the large medieval dwelling is typified by showing the remains of many phases, but the excavation in 1932 by no means clarified the interrelationships of the different construction phases.

Ruin 59. This ruin is in all probability the remains of Greenland's oldest Christian church, and was excavated in 1962-65 (Krogh 1967). The church building, with inside dimensions of *c.* 3.5 x 2 m, consists of a slender wooden building with an entrance in the west gable. The roof was partly borne by the walls, partly by six pairs of posts; the floor was

Figure 1. Plan of ruin group Ø 29a (Brattahlíð), ruin 2. Ruin A which represents a building clearly older than the rest of the complex, has been drawn on the basis of the original plan from 1932, together with information obtained during the investigation in 1964 (after Albrethsen 1982).

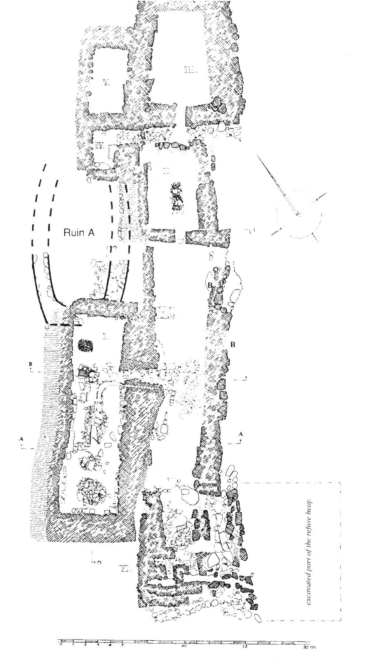

100

once covered with red sandstone tiles, and along the walls towards the north and south there appear to have been wooden benches.

The U-shaped turf wall that protected the thin wooden building to the north, south and east had slightly curving long walls and a straight-cut gable. The wall measures 1.3 m in thickness at the bottom and had a height of *c.* 1.5 m.

The ground plan of the church makes it reasonable to assume that it was built shortly after the year AD 1000, when Christianity was introduced in Greenland. C[14] dating of skeletons from the churchyard indicates that there was activity at the churchyard from about AD 1000 (Arneborg 2001).

It is probably reasonable to suppose that this was the church that the saga literature ascribes to the wife of Eiríkr *rauði*, Þjóðhildr.

Ruin 60. About 45 m NW of the church lie the remains of an approximately north-south oriented longhouse with curving long walls and straight-cut gables. The house was some 20 m long and 8 m wide at the widest point. The entrance was in the northern part of the eastern long wall. The building seems to have had an internal wooden structure, the walls of which rested on foundation stones; this was surrounded on all sides by a 1.2 m thick turf wall built directly on the surface without the use of a stone foundation. The excavation, which was begun in 1974, but was never finished, seems to show that these are the remains of a dwelling from the very first period of the colony. This building along with the other two buildings mentioned may very well represent the remains of Eiríkr *rauði*'s *landnám* farm.

RUIN GROUP Ø 64A

The farm consists in its last phase of a centralised farm complex and seven smaller buildings and pens. At several points the excavation revealed the presence of older building remains. These were the remains of slightly curving walls consisting of turf walls on double rows of foundation stones. A smallish area with flagstones and a hearth seems to belong to one of these buildings, which must presumably be regarded as the remains of a dwelling (Vebæk 1943).

101

The investigation does not permit a dating of the various construction phases, but the slightly curving turf walls seem to suggest that these may be buildings that go all the way back to the earliest period of the colony.

RUIN GROUP Ø 83 QAQORTOQ (HVALSEY)

The farm, which includes the famous church ruin, was partly investigated in 1935 (Roussell 1941). The investigation concentrated mainly on the dwelling, but the work and the interpretation of the results were made considerably more difficult by the collapsed state of the ruin. The excavation showed that the dwelling complex in its last phase must be described as a passage-house, but that several construction phase could be observed.

In the view of the excavator Room IX was the oldest part of the dwelling complex. This room has been interpreted as the remains of an east-west-oriented longhouse with inside dimensions of *c.* 14 x 3.5-4 m. Along the north wall a *c.* 1 m wide earth bench had been recessed, and in the middle of the room the remains of a partly flagged long hearth were found. In the southeastern corner a cooking pit had been built. On both sides of the long hearth a number of post-holes were found, ten of which were so large that they could be described as traces of roof-bearing posts with a diameter of *c.* 30-40 cm. In the western part of the room there were remains of two drainage channels in the floor.

No dated finds were made in connection with the investigation of this presumed longhouse, but the excavator takes the view that this was the oldest dwelling of the farm, and that its construction may go back to the first period of colonisation.

RUIN GROUP Ø 149 NARSARSUAQ

This group is probably the Benedictine convent mentioned by Ívarr Bárðarson. The ruin group include a church, two large building complexes and many small buildings all surrounded by a fence. The ruins was partly excavated by C. L. Vebæk in 1945-46 and 1948 (Vebæk 1991). Below the last phase of the large house complex (ruin 2) a cultural stratum and the remains of a storehouse with seven large wooden barrels were identified, both were

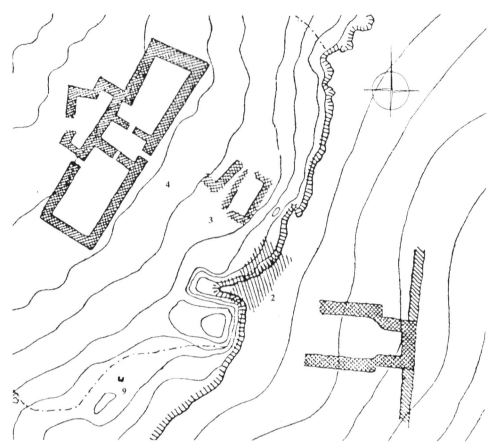

Figure 2. Ruin group V 51 (Sandnes). Detail of Roussell's original plan from 1934, the only existing drawing of ruin 3 (after Roussell 1936).

older than the house complex. C^{14} dating made on local wood indicate that there have been Norse activity at the site from about AD 1000.

RUIN GROUP Ø 167

Remains of an older building complex with a fireplace partly below the last dwelling (Vebæk 1992). There are no artefacts related to these old ruins.

RUIN GROUP V 51 KILAURSSAFIK (SANDNES)

The farm complex excavated in 1930-34 by P. Nørlund and Aa. Roussell (Roussell 1936) consists in its last phase of a dwelling ruin; two large shed units built together, a couple of smaller buildings, and a church. The dwelling ruin in its most recent form is a typical example of an expanded longhouse with a small central room and two larger living rooms as well as an annex at 'the back'. This building was in all probability in use to the beginning of the fourteenth century. The excavation shows that below the expanded longhouse there were remains of an older building, probably a smaller longhouse oriented southwest-northeast. Of the house, which is probably the remains of a dwelling, most of the northeastern gable was preserved as well as *c.* 5 m of the southeastern long wall (fig. 2). In the northeastern corner of this older longhouse the remains of a circular hearth were found. The entrance to the house was in the southeastern corner, where the remains of a flagged door arrangement were found, with a doorstep in the form of a flagstone placed edgeways. On each side of this stone a post-hole was found. The inside width of the house was at least 4.5 m. A row of stones along the southeastern wall of the room may also belong to an older building. There are no artifacts related to this oldest phase of the dwelling.

Just under 10 m south east of the dwelling ruin—overlaid by a midden—the remains of two almost obliterated buildings were found (Roussell 1936).

Of the southernmost, best preserved building, only an inside row of very fine foundation stones was found; the rest of the walls were probably made of turf. The building has inside dimensions of *c*. 4.9 x 2.3 m. Of the northernmost building only an angled section of a 1.3 m thick wall has been preserved. It is the view of the excavator that these two buildings and the oldest phase of the dwelling ruin go back to the time around the beginning of colonization. An early dating of these ruins is based partly on the position of the buildings below the midden of the more recent dwelling ruin, partly on the objects that were found in and around the last two ruins mentioned. In this connection the so-called 'chair arm'—more likely to be a tiller—is of the greatest importance, since it must be placed stylistically in the Late Viking Age/Early Post-Viking Middle Ages (Roussell 1936). Today we must greatly lament the lack of interest the excavator showed in these early building traces. In a follow-up excavation at Sandnes in 1984 it was not possible to find further evidence for the dating of the early building remains, but the radiocarbon dates of skeletons from the graveyard and animal bones from the midden indicate that there was Norse activity at the site during the first decades of the eleventh century.

103

RUIN GROUP V 48 NIAQUSSAT

Partly excavated 1976-77. Radiocarbon dates show that there have been Norse activity at the site during the first part of the eleventh century (Arneborg 1991), but the excavation showed no building remains from this early activity (Andreasen 1982).

RUIN GROUP V52 A UMIVIARSSUK

Below the large centralized farm complex, which represents the most recent construction phase at the site, the excavation of 1934 (Roussell 1936) found the remains of at least four buildings from two different construction phases older than the centralized farm.

Building A. The remains of a presumed cattle shed with inside dimensions of 4 x 1.7 m. The preserved gable wall was 0.8 m thick. Of the other walls only the inside foundation stone row was preserved. The floor consisted of an irregular layer of flagstones covered by a thick layer of sheep manure. In the central axis of the room two stumps of posts were found; the posts had probably borne the roof ridge.

Building B. Building remains that seem to come from a smallish longhouse with rounded corners, whose greatest inside width was 5.8 m; the length was slightly more than 7.5 m. Close up against the west gable and placed more or less in the longitudinal axis of the house there was probably a hearth.

Building C. The remains of a smallish longhouse. All that was preserved was a rounded corner and a short section of wall. The width of the building must have been a good 6 m, but nothing can be said about the length.

Building D. Only preserved in the form of a *c.* 1.5 m thick wall section, which along with a somewhat thinner wall section and a cooking pit, may constitute the remains of a building. The various parts cannot be related to one another with certainty.

Looking at the published overall plan of the farm, one can see in many parts of the walls structure the remains of older construction phases, although it has not been possible to separate these clearly. The results of the excavation do not permit a relative or absolute dating of the buildings described above. It is likely that several of these older building remains belong to the oldest construction phase of the farm.

RUIN GROUP V 54 NIPAITSOQ

Partly excavated 1976-77. Radiocarbon dates show that there have been Norse activity at the site during the first part of the eleventh century, but the excavation made in the old traditional way gave only weak indications of building remains from this early activity (Andreasen 1982).

THE FARM BENEATH THE SAND/GÅRDEN UNDER SANDET (GUS)

104

In 1990, at the edge of a river bed in the southeasternmost part of the Western Settlement, the remains of a hitherto unknown Norse farm called 'Gården under Sandet' ('the Farm Beneath the Sand'), or in everyday speech GUS, were found by chance. In the subsequent excavation, which took place in the years 1991-96, it was established that this was a very large and particularly well preserved farm complex which, a relatively short time after the farm was abandoned, probably in the first half of the 1300s, was covered by a sand layer up to 1-1.5 m thick (Arneborg and Gulløv 1998).

Thanks to the perma-frost the preservation conditions at GUS were extraordinarily good, and this has been especially important for the interpretation of the construction details and the find material.

On the basis of the investigations it has been possible to demonstrate—not surprisingly—that GUS underwent a long series of changes and rebuilding over the 2-300 years the farm complex was in use. As a whole, the preserved part of the building complex has an impressive area of *c.* 70 x 18 m and a permafrozen culture layer of as much as *c.* 1.5 m, but the river has eroded away a not inconsiderable portion of the western part of the farm. Thanks to analyses of the excavation results, it has been possible to demonstrate that there were at least eight construction phases in the investigated part of the farm, and to identify a total of more than 38 rooms, and to show that at least twelve rooms were in use during the last phase of the farm.

Because of the extremely difficult excavation conditions, it has so far only been possible to a limited extent to link the constructional analysis with the find material and the C^{14} datings. In the following only the oldest construction phase of the farm will be discussed.

The first building at the locality—a longhouse or hall—was sited on a grassy plateau on a south-west-facing slope. The subsoil of the plateau consists of yellow, clayey meltwater sand which would have made for a well-drained building site. This oldest building was, despite much damage associated with later rebuilding of the farm, relatively well preserved, but the south gable, the north-west corner and much of the north part of the house were disturbed to varying extents during later construction.

The hall was built with turf walls up to 1.9 m thick, with inside dimensions of about 12 x 5 m (oriented NW-SE). The house was three-aisled with the floor level of the middle aisle sunk some 15-20 cm below the original surface. The entrance was in the eastern long wall. The long hearth was placed in the center of the house. The side aisles have a width of *c.* 1.5

m. The roof was borne by two rows of posts, partly sunken, partly standing on stone flags. The roof covering had consisted of large rafters with horizontal joists covered by wattles and long thin turfs.

The walls of the hall were constructed with cofferwork technique from yellow turf blocks, with inside filling of soil and turf fragments. The turf blocks are placed on edge in a herringbone pattern, with longitudinal horizontal turfs between them. The western long wall is about 1.2-1.6 m wide, while the eastern long wall has a width of about 1.8-1.9 m. In a few places this wall has been preserved up to 0.6 m in height. The walls were built on a grassy surface, which shows no traces of previous building. It is notable that no stones what-soever were used in the walls of the hall, a feature that often is considered to belong to the earliest settlement phase in Iceland.

The hall seems to have been built according to the following plan: (1) the contour of the walls was marked off with small sticks; (2) the lowest course of the turf wall was laid direct-ly on the field surface; and (3) the grass surface inside the walls was peeled off and proba-bly used in the construction of the walls. The rest of the turf was probably peeled off in the immediate surroundings of the house from a grassy surface, which shows no trace of human activity ('virgin' field). Finally the level of the central section of the house was dug down a further 10 to 15 cm.

During the excavation of the hall two phases of use could be established. The original function of the house was as a dwelling, a function that changed, after a relatively short time, to animal shed/storeroom.

105

Oldest phase of use (fig. 3). In the dwelling phase the floor layer was about 1-2 cm thick and contains fragments of burnt and unburnt animal bones, but few actual objects. At the bottom of the floor layer large quantities of wood chips, which must come from the build-ing work, were found.

In the northern part of the eastern long wall there had been a 1 m wide entrance partly covered with thin flagstones placed on a *c.* 2 cm thick layer of wattles and finely chopped twigs. Flush with the outside edge of the long wall a wooden threshold had been placed, con-sisting of a board placed edgeways and kept in place by two hammered-in pegs. Flush with the inside of the wall there was a door arrangement consisting of a vertically placed sill board and a threshold made of two thin flagstones placed on edge.

As a continuation of the entrance there was probably a kind of entrance hall with the dwelling room to the south and a utility room to the north. The entrance hall had partly been dug away for later construction.

The dwelling room consists of a central section and long benches. The central section was 2 m wide and delimited to the east and west by the front edges of the benches and to the north by the entrance hall. The dwelling room was probably separated from the entrance hall by a partition wall that can only be seen as a row of buried stakes and sticks. The door opening between the entrance hall and the dwelling room is marked by a narrow oblong depression, which are probably the remains of a threshold. The floor level in the central sec-tion of the dwelling room is 5-10 cm lower than the long benches. The central section seems to have continued all the way to the south gable.

The majority of the objects found in the hall were on the floor of the central section. The most important objects are textile fragments and parts of a wooden vessel.

In the middle of the floor in the central section there was a long hearth. The fireplace was *c.* 1.7 m long and 0.5 m wide, and partly edged with vertical flagstones. South of the long hearth was an ashpan. The fireplace and ashpan were partly covered by flat, greatly burnt slabs, the biggest perhaps a baking plate.

On both sides of the central section there are benches *c.* 1.5 m wide, the front edges of which are marked by a large number of small hammered-in pegs. Presumably the benches

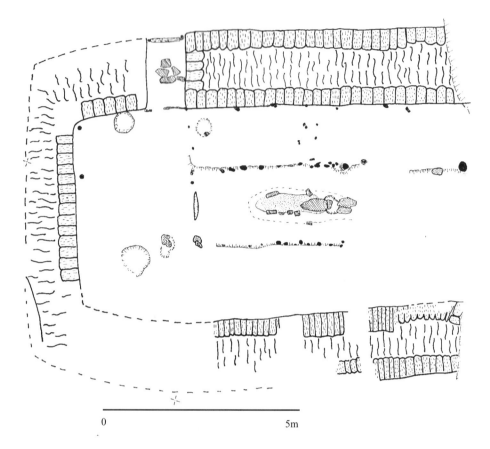

0   5m

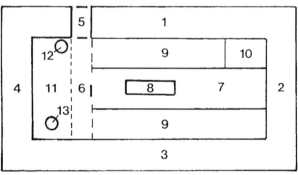

Figure 3. 'The Farm beneath the Sand'. Ground plan of the first phase of the longhouse (room XVII) (T. Simpson after Albrethsen and Ólafson 1998).

1-4. Turf walls; 5. Entrance; 6. Entrance hall; 7. Central section; 8. Long hearth; 9. Long benches; 10. Sleeping alcove?; 11. Storage room; 12. Barrel; 13. Cooking pit?

were covered by wood during the phase when the room functioned as a dwelling. This is supported by the fact that the floor layer is considerably thinner on the benches than in the central section. Very few objects were found on the benches—the most important is a whetstone.

On the southern part of the eastern bench some charred boards were found. Some of these boards are the remains of a door. The door forms part of an arrangement that could possibly be interpreted as a sleeping alcove at the southern end of the long bench.

North of the entrance hall is a room 2 m wide that presumably functioned as a storage room and kitchen. It has not been possible to show that there was a partition wall between the entrance hall and the utility section, although it seems likely. Along the gable wall there may have been some kind of wooden paneling, since some charred pieces of board up to *c.* 0.26 m wide lay there.

In the south-east corner of this room, just north of the entrance, a small circular pit dug in the floor was found. It may have contained a small barrel—the position and shape strongly resemble those of similar pits known from Icelandic farms. From this pit come a bone hook and a fragment of a bone pin.

In the western part of the room a flat pit (cooking pit?) filled with peat ash was found. It was *c.* 1 m in diameter and *c.* 15 cm deep. From this came a few finds: a loom weight, a fragment of a possible spindle whorl and a strike-a-light (?) of chalcedony.

The quantity of turf needed to build the hall, and the area of grass that had to be peeled off to get enough turf, have been tentatively calculated. If we assume that the inside dimensions of the hall were 12 x 5 m, which gives us an inside floor area of *c.* 60 m², and that the walls were *c.* 1.5 m wide and at least 1 m high, it would have been necessary to peel off *c.* 1000 m² of turf to obtain enough building material. The high consumption of turf is remarkable.

According to AMS datings the hall was used in the period *c.* 1020-1200. The archaeological dating of the hall suggests a date in the first half of the eleventh century, that is in the earliest part of the period indicated by the AMS datings.

If one were to suggest an absolute date on purely typological criteria—with reference to houses in Scandinavia and the North Atlantic islands—the hall must have been built in the first half of the eleventh century (Òlafsson 1998).

107

Most recent phase of use. After the hall had been used as a dwelling for a relatively short period its function changed to an animal shed, as can be seen from a *c.* 5 cm thick brown floor layer mixed with sheep dung, plant remains, bone fragments, chopped twigs and a single-sided comb. The fireplace was no longer used and was covered by the animal shed floor layer. It appears that the wooden benches and perhaps part of the partition walls were removed in this phase. In front of the entrance outside the house several large flagstones were placed, partly covering the doorstep of the older phase.

The most recent phase of the use of the hall ended with a serious fire, which seems to have started in the southern part of the house. All wooden structures in the house were burnt down to floor level. On the floor a compact layer of charcoal and charred pieces of plank from the roof construction, up to 8 cm thick, was formed, and above this was a layer, some 5-10 cm thick, of red-burnt turf ash from the roof turf. After the fire the ruin was partly leveled, but parts of the turf wall were still used in later constructions.

The hall from GUS represents a house type which was very common in the North Atlantic area in the Viking Age and the post-Viking Middle Ages, but the hall described here is the first house of this type from Norse Greenland to be excavated. It must be regarded as pure chance that such large parts of the house have been preserved, considering the intense building activity on the site during the *c.* 300 years of the farm's history.

It is important to emphasize that it was only possible to offer a correct interpretation of the relationships among the various elements of the hall at the end of the excavation, when the whole central part of the excavation field had been cleared down to the subsoil. Given these results it can come as no surprise that in the major farm investigations of the 1920s-1950s, there were very few cases, and these mostly accidental, where it was possible to identify construction traces from the oldest phases of Norse settlement. These older investigations are all characterized by an excavation method, which only emptied the rooms that could be identified at the beginning of the excavation. The result was a quite incorrect picture of the developmental history of the farm, since the topmost rooms can belong to quite different construction phases. Furthermore, such a method makes it impossible to identify the changes and rebuilding in the individual rooms.

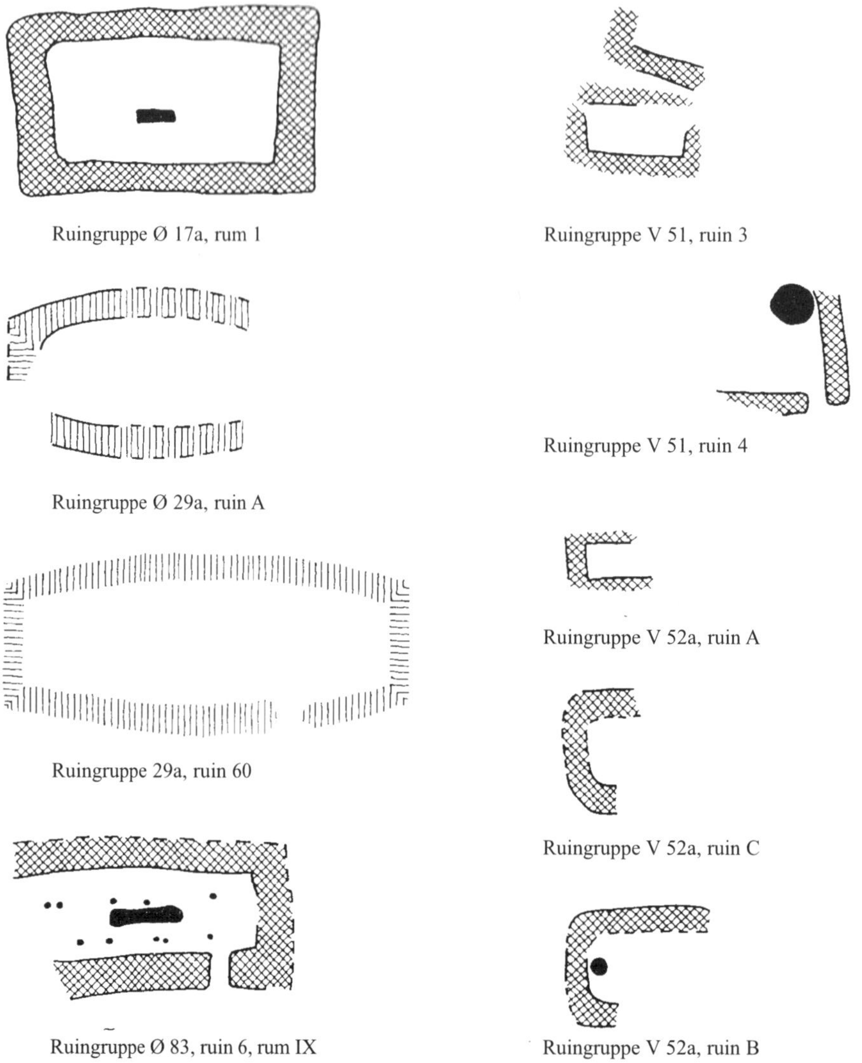

Ruingruppe Ø 17a, rum 1

Ruingruppe Ø 29a, ruin A

Ruingruppe 29a, ruin 60

Ruingruppe Ø 83, ruin 6, rum IX

Ruingruppe V 51, ruin 3

Ruingruppe V 51, ruin 4

Ruingruppe V 52a, ruin A

Ruingruppe V 52a, ruin C

Ruingruppe V 52a, ruin B

Figure 4. Ground plan sketches of the buildings assumed with some probability to have been erected in the first period of the Norse colonisation about 1:300 (after Albrethsen 1982).

This has only touched on a small part of the whole body of material from GUS. But the overall results of the excavation at GUS are unique among the Norse farm investigations in Greenland, since most of the complex has been excavated stratigraphically from top to bottom. In its entirety the GUS excavation is the only investigation in Greenland, which affords us an opportunity for anything like realistic insight into the construction history of the Norse farms from establishment to desertion. This makes it one of the most important investigations ever in North Atlantic archaeology.

CONCLUSION

As will be evident from this review, there is very little archaeological material available when one is to attempt to assess the form of the oldest Norse dwellings and farms in Greenland, but despite this tenuous basis it does seem possible to infer certain conclusions from the material.

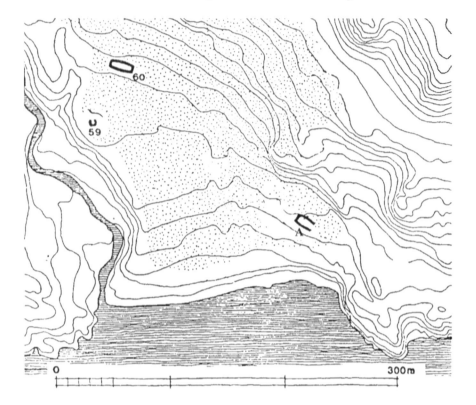

Figure 5. Site Plan of ruin group Ø 29a (Brattahlíð). Only the buildings assumed to date from the earliest period of Norse colonisation, have been included (after Albrethsen 1982).

DWELLING

It is likely that the oldest dwellings consisted of relatively simple longhouses. In a few cases the ground plan shows a typical 'Trelleborg shape' with curved long walls and straight-cut gables, but in most cases the dwelling is just a simple rectangular building with more or less rounded corners (fig. 4), best illustrated by the oldest building at GUS.

No partitioning of the inside space with transverse walls has been noted in any of the older excavations, but this is clearly documented in the oldest phase at GUS.

The size of the oldest dwelling ruins varies somewhat: the width is in most cases around 5-8 m, while the length varies from 10 m to *c*. 20 m. The walls usually seem to be pure turf walls, in some cases placed on an inside and/or outside row of foundation stones. In the few places where a door opening has been identified, it is placed in one of the long walls of the house near one of the gables. The material from the older excavations affords very little opportunity to assess the furnishings of these early dwellings. In a few cases the presence of earth benches along one or both long walls has been noted, and a couple of dwelling ruins seem to show that the walls were wholly or partly clad with wooden paneling.

In some cases the walls appear to have been clad with flagstones and a flagged long hearth was placed in the middle of the floor and/or there was a circular hearth or cooking pit placed by one of the walls of the house.

In a couple of cases flagged drainage gutters were noted in the floor of the dwelling, gutters that seem to have had a combined drainage and water supply function.

Only in the excavation of GUS has it been possible to gain any insight into the roof construction. There is no evidence of the presence of annexes in the form of storehouses or animals sheds in direct association with the oldest dwelling ruins.

Svend E. Albrethsen

Our almost total ignorance of the utility buildings on the oldest Norse farms leaves us little scope for assessing the plan of the *landnám* farms. Only at Brattahlíð can one get a certain impression of the form of the farm, since this site has the remains of at least three buildings from the oldest period of colonisation (fig. 5).

An important reason for our inadequate knowledge of the *landnám* buildings is that precisely at the places where the *landnám* men settled, we must as a rule expect continuous settlement all the way down to the end of the Norse colony. The buildings of the earlier farms must be presumed to have been placed at the most suitable localities and one must suppose—as also seems to be evident from the sparse archaeological material available—that where the *landnám* men placed the various buildings of the farm, there they usually remained throughout the whole succession of construction periods.

Given the excavation methods that were used in the large investigations at the beginning of the twentieth century, when only the rooms of the most recent construction phase were excavated, it is not surprising that the material available to shed light on the nature of the oldest Norse farm is still as tenuous as it is.

BIBLIOGRAPHY

Albrethsen, S.E. 1982. 'Træk af den norrøne gårds udvikling på Grønland', in Myhre *et al.* 1982, 269-287.

Albrethsen, S.E. and Òlafsson, G. 1998. 'A Viking age hall', in Arneborg and Gulløv 1998, 19-26.

Andreasen, C. 1982. 'Nipaitsoq og Vesterbygden', *Grønland*, nr. 5-6-7 (Copenhagen), 177-188.

Arneborg, J. 1991. 'The Niaqusat excavations reconsidered', *Acta Borialia*, 1, 82-92.

——2001. 'The Initial Period of the Norse Settlement in Greenland—in Written Sources and in Archaeology', in Wawn and Sigurðardóttir 2001, 122-134.

Arneborg, J. and Gulløv, H.C., eds, 1998. *Man, Culture and Environment in Ancient Greenland*, Copenhagen.

Bruun, D. 1896. 'Arkæologiske Undersøgelser i Julianehaab Distrikt: 1895', *Meddr Grønland*, 16, 3, 173-461.

Holm, G. F. 1883. 'Beskrivelse af Ruinerne i Julianehaab Distrikt, der ere undersøgte i Aaret 1880', *Meddr Grønland*, 6, 3, 57-221.

Krogh, K.J. 1967. *Viking Greenland*, Copehagen.

Moltke, E. 1961. 'En grønlandsk runeindskrift fra Erik den Rødes tid', *Grønland*, 401-410.

Myhre, B., Stoklund, B., and Gjærder, P., eds, 1982. *Vestnordisk byggeskikk gjennom to tusen år.* Stavanger: Museums Skrifter 7.

Nørlund, P. and Stenberger, M. 1934. *Brattahlid.* Copenhagen: Meddr Grønland, 88, 1.

Òlafsson, G. 1998. *Eriksstaðir í Haukadal. Fornleifannsókn á skálarúst*, Reykjavík.

Roussell, Aa. 1936. *Sandnes and Neighbouring Farms.* Copenhagen: Meddr Grønland, 88, 2.

——1941. *Farms and Churches in the Mediaeval Norse Settlement of Greenland.* Copenhagen: Meddr Grønland, 89, 1.

Rygh, O. 1885. *Norske Oldsager*, Kristiania.

Vebæk, C. L. 1943. *Inland Farms in the Norse East Settlement.* Copenhagen: Meddr Grønland, 90, 1.

——1991. *The Church Topography of the Eastern Settlement and the Excavation of the Benedictine Convent at Narsarsuaq in the Unatoq Fjord.* Copenhagen: Meddr Grønland. Man & Society, 14.

——1992. *Vatnahverfi. An inland district of the Eastern Settlement in Greenland.* Copenhagen: Meddr Grønland. Man & Society, 17.

——1993. *Narsaq—a Norse* landnáma *farm.* Copenhagen: Meddr Grønland. Man & Society, 18.

Wawn, A. and Sigurðardóttir, Þ., eds, 2001. *Approaches to Vínland.* Reykjavík: Sigurður Nordal Institute Studies 4.

Norse Greenland Archaeology: The Dialogue
Between the Written and the Archaeological Records

Jette Arneborg

INTRODUCTION

In the year 2000, several places in Scandinavia, Iceland and North America celebrated the Millennium of the acceptance of Christianity by the Icelandic *Alþing* and the Millennium of Leifr Eiríksson's visit to North America. The Greenlanders have been celebrating with great festivities the Millennium of the building of the first Christian church in Greenland as well as the journeys of the Norse Greenland settlers to the North American continent.

At the little sheep-farming settlement of Qassiarsuk in South Greenland (fig. 1b), with financial support from the West Nordic Foundation, copies have been built of the small Viking Age church attributed to the wife of Eiríkr *rauði* (the Red), Þjóðhildr and a Viking longhouse marketed as 'Eric the Red's Farm'(fig. 2).

Qassiarsuk has further been blessed with a 4.5 metre tall bronze statue, allegedly showing Eiríkr's and Þjóðhildr's son Leifr—the one later given the by-name *inn heppni* (the Lucky). From his rock a little behind the settlement Leifr looks out over the wide new world that he has either already discovered or is about to discover.

The two copy buildings were built by Icelandic experts, and they are very well executed and beautiful. The church was built on the basis of available survey plans from the archaeological investigations of the remains of the small church building that was found in front of the settlement's present-day church in 1961. Wherever the plans were not sufficient, the Icelandic experts drew on their experience from Icelandic investigations.

The longhouse was built on the basis of plans of the oldest building on the Norse farm complex known as the Farm Beneath the Sand, which was excavated in the Norse Western Settlement near Nuuk in the period 1991-1996 (see Albrethsen, this volume). In this case the builders also drew on experience from Iceland, and Gudmunður Ólafsson of the Icelandic National Museum was the expert consultant on the project. Gudmunður himself took part in the investigation at the Farm Beneath the Sand.

At Qassiarsuk there was a great deal about the personalities of Eiríkr *rauði*, Þjóðhildr his wife and their son Leifr, and the world to which the visitor is introduced is quite unreservedly that of the Icelandic sagas. Eiríkr *rauði* built his farm at Brattahlíð when he arrived in Greenland at the end of the 900s. After discovering America Leifr, at the behest of the Norwegian king Óláfr Tryggvason, brought Christianity to Greenland. Eiríkr was loth to accept the new faith, but Leifr's mother Þjóðhildr was converted, and she built a little church some distance from the dwelling so that Eiríkr would not be too annoyed by her decision.

The fixation on personalities and the exciting stories from the Icelandic sagas are not peculiar to the tourism promoters at Qassiarsuk—you only have to look at the impressive catalogue (Fitzhugh and Ward 2000) from the exhibition 'Vikings: the North Atlantic Saga' at the Smithsonian, National Museum of Natural History in Washington D.C. Several of the articles in the catalogue refer to the exciting stories in the Icelandic sagas. However, the strong influence of the sagas on the perception of the historical process of Norse settlement in Greenland prompts certain reflections on both the very assured way they are used in Greenland Norse archaeology and—not least—on the role of archaeology in the writing of history.

Figure 1a. Greenland.

Figure 1b. The central part of
the Eastern Settlement.

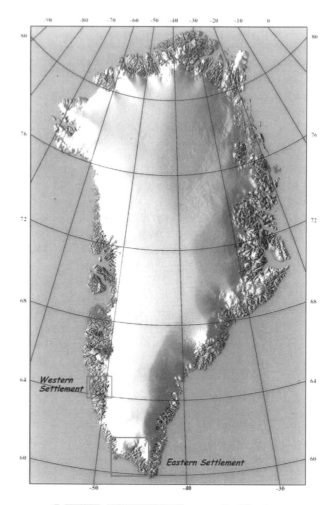

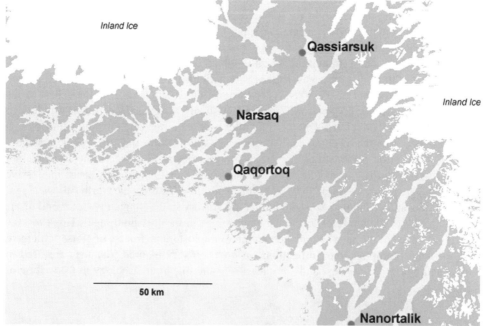

Figure 2. Replica buildings of Þjóðhildr's Church and a Norse Viking long house in Qassiarsuk, Brattahlíð (photo: J. Arneborg 2000).

THE RELATIONSHIP BETWEEN WRITTEN AND ARCHAEOLOGICAL SOURCES

The relationship between texts and things, or between written and archaeological sources, has in recent years been discussed by medieval archaeologists in Scandinavia (e.g. Andrén 1998). Some regard the existence of written sources as a great advantage, since after all archaeology depends on analogies to put the archaeological finds in perspective. Others see the written sources as a disadvantage, because they are seen as limiting the archaeological interpretation. Between the two extremes lies the discussion of the interplay between the two source groups. If one does not choose—as some medieval archaeologists have done— to wholly disregard the written sources, or if one does not work with subjects where there is no relevant written information, two kinds of interaction between the source groups emerge. One is the unquestioning belief in the evidence of the written sources. The archaeological finds are interpreted within the framework of what the sources say. The other is that the two source groups are interpreted in an ongoing dialogue.

This order of relationships reflects the history of Norse Greenland archaeology. Unquestioning belief in the evidence of the written sources —in the Greenlandic context first and foremost the Icelandic sagas—primarily belongs to the historiography of the nineteenth century. In the case of Greenland the three-volume work *Grønlands Historiske Mindesmærker* ('The Historical Monuments of Greenland': GHM) represents this attitude. But the historical-topographical investigations whose leading figures were the philologist Finnur Jónsson (1858-1934) and the archaeologists Poul Nørlund (1888-1951) and C.L. Vebæk (1913-1993) also took their point of departure from the written sources. The Norse settlements were thus systematically identified by comparing the finds in the field with the topographical information, first and foremost in Ívarr Bárðarson's *Description of Greenland* (cf. Vebæk 1991, 6), but also in other written sources where Greenlandic place-names are mentioned (cf. Langer Andersen 1982).

The dialogue between the two source groups became necessary, as archaeology was gradually able to show more and more results. However, it was never a dialogue of equals, since it was to a great extent the written information that had the last word when the synthesis was to be written. I cannot think of a single example where the information in a written source has been rejected on an archaeological basis.

The new tendencies in archaeology—the 'New Archaeology'—made their debut in earnest in Norse Greenland archaeology in the 1970s. In 1975-76 Knud Krogh (1982) headed a major Nordic project in the Qorlortoq valley in the Norse Eastern Settlement, the object of which was to map the resource area and the vegetation potential for the farms of the valley, and in 1976-77 Jørgen Meldgaard organized the 'Inuit-Norse Project' in the Western Settlement, where the main aim was to elucidate the cultural encounter between the Norsemen and the Inuit on the basis of resource utilization and possible competition, especially over the marine resources. The project assumed a safe demonstration of the contemporaneity of the two population groups in the Norse Western Settlement, and although this particular part of the project did not hold water, the Inuit-Norse Project was of great importance to Norse Greenland archaeology in the subsequent years. Methods, issues and researchers who had been introduced to Norse archaeology through the Inuit-Norse Project have later made a strong impact—especially with research themes like social structure and economics. However, despite the new methods and approaches, and ground-breaking achievements in archaeology, there is still a clear tendency to fall back on the evidence of the written sources when the conclusions are to be drawn and the synthesis formulated.

In my view the issue is not whether one should use the written sources or not as an archaeologist; but the time must be ripe to discuss the two source groups in a dialogue where they are in principle regarded as equal. The confrontation could lead to several results (cf. Andrén 1998, 162): (1) the source groups could agree; (2) the interpretations of one source group could lead to new interpretative options for the other; or (3) the sources do not agree, in which case the task must be to explain the discrepancies.

I would like to illustrate with a couple of examples why there is a basis for asking new questions and confronting the source basis for Norse Greenland archaeology. First I will very briefly return to the events around the introduction of Christianity in Greenland, and then I will give a few selected examples from the discussion of the reasons for the depopulation of the Norse settlements in the Late Middle Ages.

THE INTRODUCTION OF CHRISTIANITY TO GREENLAND—
ACCORDING TO THE WRITTEN SOURCES

It is well known that there is no agreement on the course of the introduction of Christianity in Greenland in the two Greenland sagas *Grœnlandinga saga* (GLS) and *Eiriks saga rauða* (ESR) (Arneborg 2001). The story of Leifr's mission on behalf of Óláfr Tryggvasson, and the circumstances surrounding the building of Þjóðhildr's Church, are described in ESR, while GLS only sporadically mentions the introduction of Christianity in Greenland and adds that this only happened after Eiríkr rauði was dead. Other sources, like the little history of Norway *Historia Norvegiae* from the end of the 1100s, say that Greenland received Christianity from Iceland.

The Icelandic sagas have special problems, and the discussion of their value as sources has gone on for decades. I won't go into that discussion here: I will only say that today the sagas are granted some degree of historical source value, and that there are—as I understand it—two attitudes to the authorship question. For some people the sagas contain historical accounts, which before they were written down in the thirteenth and fourteenth centuries, were kept alive by the oral tradition. Uncertainties and obscurities are attributed to the centuries that passed between the time the events took place and the time they were written down (e.g. Sigurðsson 2000, 218).

Others see the sagas as manipulated history-writing which must first and foremost be understood in the context of the age in which they were written (cf. Meulengracht Sørensen 1993, 18-19). The late Icelandic historian Jón Jóhannesson (1962) thus argued that the story of Leifr the Lucky's mission to Greenland—and as a result also his Vinland voyage—are most probable unhistorical and never took place. According to Jón the stories were invented by the Icelandic monk Gunnlaugr Leifsson around 1200, when he wrote the Latin Saga of Óláfr Tryggvason, and needed background descriptions for his story of how King Óláfr christianized not only Norway, Iceland, the Faroes, the Shetlands and the Orkneys, but also Greenland. As support for his claim Jón points to among other things the information in *Historia Norvegiae*.

THE INTRODUCTION OF CHRISTIANITY IN GREENLAND—
THE ARCHAEOLOGY

But what does archaeology say? The identification of Qassiarsuk as the Norsemen's Brattahlíð was established by Finnur Jónsson (1899) as early as 1898 with his point of departure in the information in the topographical sources about fjords and churches in the Eastern Settlement. The sources are certainly not unambiguous in their descriptions, and several new churches have been localized in the area since Jónsson put forward his theory, no one has argued convincingly against it, and at present I do not think either that there is any reason not to keep Jónsson's identification.

Several ruins have been localized on the plain in Qassiarsuk (fig. 3), but most must be assigned to the latest settlement phase. In a few places, for example beneath the late dwelling at the so-called North Farm, traces of older houses have been registered which may have belonged to a very early phase in the history of the place (Albrethsen 1982, 273f; see this volume). Similarly, older remains of buildings have been found near Þjóðhildr's Church, which can perhaps be assigned to the very earliest phase of construction at the place. Like the building under the dwelling in the North Farm, the small Þjóðhildr's Church had slightly curved long walls—a feature that is assigned to the building custom of the Viking Age, and C^{14} datings of the skeletons from the churchyard support an early dating of the church (Arneborg *et al.* 1999).

THE DIALOGUE

Do the written sources and the archaeological finds agree? Is there a discrepancy or does the interpretation of the one group of sources give rise to renewed consideration of our understanding of the other group of sources?

Direct comparison is difficult, since even the evaluation of the written information creates problems, which I do not think archaeology can solve—but perhaps it can throw them into relief. Common to the information in GLS and ESR is the fact that they both say that the first colonists in Greenland were heathens. The C^{14} datings from Þjóðhildr's Church on the other hand suggest that among the colonists at least some people were given a Christian burial, and were thus presumably Christian before Leifr's mission is said to have taken place. That there were Christians among the colonists is of course not to say that Leifr's and Óláfr Tryggvason's mission cannot have taken place. The datings cannot be taken directly as support for Jón Johannesen's theory that the stories about Leifr are fictional; but the early datings shed new light on the stories in the saga, and this should form a basis for reconsid-

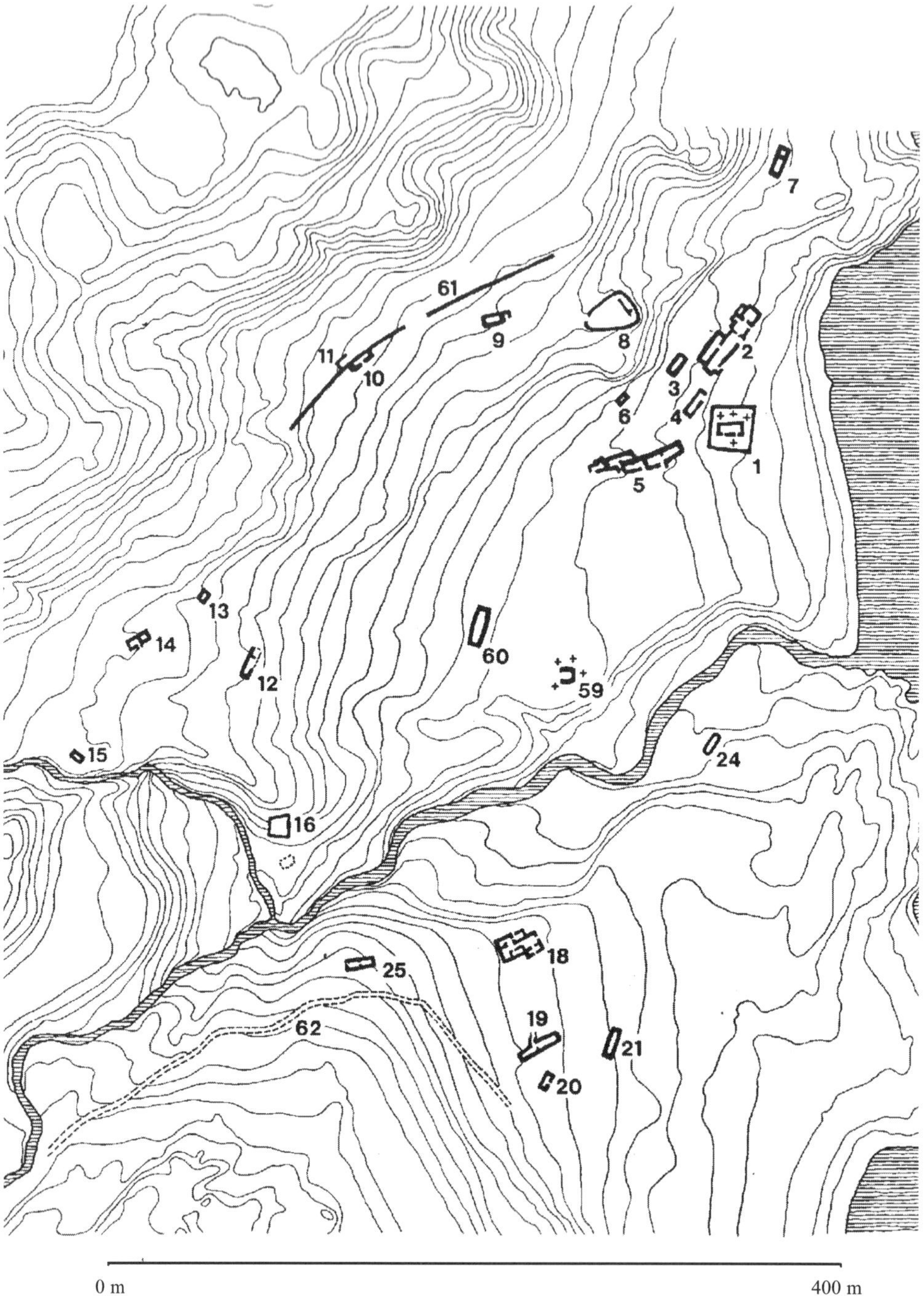

0 m   400 m

Figure 3. Norse ruins on the Qassiarsuk plain (after Krogh 1982).

eration, not only of the course of events around the year 1000, but also of the possible manipulation of history in the 1200s of which the texts also seem to be a result.

THE DEPOPULATION OF NORSE SETTLEMENTS: THE CONFRONTATION THEORY

Moving on from the landnám period I will now turn the focus on the last period of the Norsemen in Greenland. In the course of time several theories have been proposed for why and how the Norse settlements in Greenland were depopulated in the latter half of the 1400s, but here I will only deal with the theory that it was the Inuit population of Greenland that waged war on and actually wiped out the Norsemen (fig. 4).

The theories have roots all the way back in the first half of the 1700s, when it was put forward as the only explanation of the fate of the Norse settlers. In time the discussion has become subtler, and today there is no one who believes Inuit attacks were crucial, but the theory is still proposed as one factor among many when the depopulation is to be explained, among other reasons because it has been preserved by a rich Inuit legendary tradition (see for example Petersen 2000).

Norse and Inuit sources both mention the relations between the two population groups. An Icelandic chronicle says under the year 1379 that the *skrælingar*—the Norsemen's name for Inuit in Greenland—attacked the Norsemen, killed 18 and took two men as slaves (GHM III, 464). The event is not localized. The information can be traced back to two copies of the chronicle from the end of the 1500s. The two copies are independent of each other, but it must be assumed that they had a common original. When this original was written is unknown, but there seems to be no reason to reject the source.

The source that has undoubtedly been of the greatest importance for the theory that it was Inuit who killed the Norsemen is the above-mentioned Ívarr Bárðarson's *Description of Greenland* (cf. Jónsson 1930). There are two passages in it that refer directly to *skrælingar*. In one passage, which is at the end of the topographical description of the Eastern Settlement, it is said that the *skrælingar*, at the time when Ívarr Bárðarson was in Greenland, 'now have the whole Western Settlement'. In the same sentence it also says—rather contradicting the first item of information—that there are neither 'heathen nor Christian people' left in the settlement. The second passage clearly begins a postscript to Ívarr Bárðarson's original story, since it says that all the above was told by Ívarr Bárðarson, who was the steward of the bishop's seat at Garðar for many years, and who was sent to the Western Settlement 'to drive the *skrælingar* out' from the settlement. The Description of Greenland is preserved in several variants, all translated from the presumably originally Norwegian text, and all from the period after the latter half of the 1500s. The interrelationships among the different copies have not been clarified, nor is it clear which parts of the text can be attributed to Ívarr Bárðarson and which are later additions (Jónsson 1899).

Although the *Description of Greenland* in fact says nothing directly about Inuit attacks on the Norsemen in the Western Settlement, the source has later been regarded as if it did. The Norwegian-Danish missionary Hans Egede, who went to Greenland in 1721, already committed this error. In a description of Greenland from 1724 Egede concluded, after quoting the *Description of Greenland*, that the ancient Norsemen in the Western Settlement 'are said to have been destroyed by the savage heathens'. He adds that the Greenlanders in the area, whom he regards as the descendants of these savage heathens, incidentally have no information on what happened to the Norsemen (Egede 1729, 5).

Hans Egede reissued his book about Greenland 17 years later in 1741. The new edition is more or less identical to the 1724 edition, but a few changes have been made, and one of these is precisely in the passage about the end of the Norsemen, where Egede has now added

117

that the Greenlanders confirm what is said in the Old Norse writings, that their ancestors had waged war on the Norsemen and killed them (Egede 1741, 6-7).

What had happened in the intervening period? One could of course always claim that Hans Egede had gained a better knowledge of the Greenlandic language, and that communication thus improved, but it is worth noting that what the Greenlanders confirm is Egede's own preconceived opinion of the course of events.

INUIT LEGENDS ABOUT THE NORSEMEN

In the years after Egede several Greenlandic stories about the end of the Norsemen were written down. The culmination came in the mid-1800s when H.J. Rink took the initiative for a grand collection of Inuit legends and tales, and got Aron from Kangeq to illustrate the legends (cf. Thisted 1999). The basic theme was the same in all the legends of the Norsemen: they were all about the end of the Norsemen, and in all of them—except one—it was the Inuit who killed the Norsemen (Thisted 2001, 288). But in time the content of the tales changed character: from short legends where for example place-names were explained, they became longer epic stories. The explanation of this development must be sought in the audience to whom the tales were addressed. The Danish interest in the fate of the Norse Greenlanders was great in the same period, as was the activity related to the relics of the Norsemen in South Greenland. The Greenlanders were asked high and low about what they knew, and in some cases they were even promised large rewards for new information about the Norsemen. In an environment like this the tales would have had good conditions to thrive in (for more arguments see Arneborg 1991). Let me give a single example.

In 1824 the Greenlander Pelimut found this Norse runic stone on the small island of Kingittorsuaq, slightly north of Upernavik in northern West Greenland (fig. 5), and the very next year, in 1825, the minister in Aasiat, Peder Kragh (1794-1883) was pointed to a group of rocks between Upernavik and Kangersusiaq which according to an allegedly very ancient Greenlandic tradition was two petrified Norse Greenlanders, a man and his wife, who had escaped to the mountains when the *skrælingar* attacked and murdered the Norse settlers in the area (Kragh 1875, 73). The tale was later included in a longer tale that was published in 1915, now with the addition, among others, that the Norsemen lived on the island of Inussuk near Kingittorsuaq (Rossen 1916, 98-99). In fact the story was one of the reasons Therkel Mathiassen chose to excavate houses precisely at Inussuk when he began his Inuit-archaeological excavations in Greenland in 1929 (Mathiassen 1930, 146ff).

The text on the runic stone mentioned three men, probably hunters, who visited the island of Kingittorsuaq at one time in the 1200s. The find, along with other archaeological finds, reflects Norse activity from Disko Bay on the west coast of Greenland in the south to Thule and Ellesmere Island in the High Arctic area in the north (see for example Arneborg 1997; Schledermann 2000), but there was no question of permanent settlement, and there can presumably be little doubt that it was the finding of the runic stone in 1824 that sparked off people's imagination.

If nothing else, the lateness of the period when the stories were written down compared with the time when the events are supposed to have taken place weakens the tradition and thus the value of the Inuit legends as historical sources. Given that in addition one cannot ignore the very probable Danish influence on both the origin of the tradition and the content and later development of the tale, the source value of the Greenlandic legends of the Norsemen must be considered so low that they must be disregarded as historical sources— at all events for medieval history.

119

Figure 4. The Norsemen in Ameralik fjord (in the Western Settlement) are burnt by the Inuit (woodcut: Aron of Kangeq).

Figure 5. Runic stone from Kingottorsuaq in northern Greenland. The stone is *c.* 10 cm long (photo: The National Museum of Denmark).

ARCHAEOLOGY AND THE CONFRONTATION THEORY

If we now turn to archaeology, it can briefly be said that the archaeological finds show no evidence that the Norse settlers were attacked by the Inuit. We have not yet been able to document with full certainty a contemporary Inuit and Norse presence in the Eastern Settlement, although there may have been such a presence in the Western Settlement (Arneborg 2003), and not one of the farms or churches investigated can be said to have been attacked and burnt down as narrated in several of the Inuit legends.

THE DIALOGUE

Comparing the two source groups one must conclude that it is the written sources alone that tell us of hostilities between the Norsemen and the Inuit, and in fact only one source, the chronicle entry from 1379, is invoked in favour of the theory of Inuit attacks on the Norsemen. The absence of archaeological finds is of course not sufficient to disprove a theory that takes its point of departure in other sources, but on the available basis the conclusion must be that in 1379, allegedly, there was an Inuit attack on a group of Norsemen— somewhere or other. Perhaps in the settlements in South Greenland, perhaps in connection with the Norsemen's hunting trips north along the west coast of Greenland.

SUMMARY

In the first of the two examples I have presented here, one notes a certain disagreement in the sources when it comes to the introduction of Christianity in Greenland. The archaeology suggests that the colonists or at least some of the colonists may have been Christian already when they arrived in Greenland, while the Icelandic sagas would have us believe that the christianisation of Greenland was organized centrally from Norway. Archaeology gives us no reason to reject the possibility that such an initiative may have been taken; but the focus in the sagas on the initiative of the King could prompt us to reconsider the relations between the Norse colonies in Greenland and the Norwegian monarchy in the 1200s, when the sagas were written down.

The theory of bloody clashes between the Inuit and the Norsemen finds little confirmation in the source material. A single written source mentions an Inuit attack on Norsemen in 1379, while the Inuit legendary tradition about the Norsemen must be assumed to be so late that it can be attributed no source value in the discussion of the Norsemen and their fate in Greenland.

Here I have only dealt with two kinds of written sources: the Inuit legendary tradition and the Icelandic sagas. What is common for all involved sources, both the written and the archaeological sources, is that the even-handed dialogue requires us to deal with each source group on its own terms, and only then to confront them with each other.

Several disciplines are involved in the discussions, which require open-mindedness within the disciplines in question, and interdisciplinary collaboration is essential. The many events in the year 2000 helped to strengthen the existing interdisciplinary research in North Atlantic archaeology, and several new configurations have arisen, so personally I am looking forward to the exciting challenges of the coming years in Greenlandic archaeology and in North Atlantic archaeology as a whole.

ABBREVIATION

GHM   Anon. 1838-45. *Grønlands Historiske Mindesmærker* I - III. Copenhagen: Det
                                      Kongelige Nordiske Oldskrift-Selskab.

BIBLIOGRAPHY

Albrethsen, S.E. 1982. 'Træk af den norrøne gårds udvikling på Grønland', in Myhre *et al.* 1982, 269-287.

Andrén, A. 1998. *Between Artifacts and Texts: Historical Archaeology in Global Perspective*, Lund.

Arneborg, J. 1991. Kulturmødet mellem nordboer og eskimoer, Unpublished PhD dissertation, University of
     Copenhagen.

——1997. 'Cultural Borders: Reflections on Norse-Eskimo Interaction', in Gilberg and Gulløv 1997, 41-46.

——2001. 'The Initial Period of the Norse Settlement in Greenland—in Written Sources and in Archaeology', in
     Wawn and Sigurðardóttir 2001, 122-134.

——2003. 'Norse Greenland: Reflections on the Discussion of Depopulation', in Barrett 2003,

Arneborg, J., Heinemeier, J., Lynnerup, N., Nielsen, H.L., and Sveinbjörnsdóttir, Á.E. 1999. 'Changes of Diet of
     the Greenland Vikings Determined from Stable Carbon Isotope Analysis and 14C Dating of their Bones',
     Radiocarbon, 41, 2, 157-168.

Barrett, J.H., ed., 2003. *Contact, Continuity and Collapse: The Norse Colonization of the North Atlantic*, Turnhout.

Egede, H. 1729. *Udg. Gelmeyden. Det gamle Grønlands Nye Perlustration; Eller: En kort Beskrivelse om de gamle
     Nordske Coloniers Begyndelse og Undergang i Grønland, Grønlands Situation, Luft og Temperament, og dets
     itzige Indbyggeres klædedragt, handtæring, Spise, Sprog, Ægteskab, og andre deres isaavel i Samquem som
     i egne Huuse nu brugelige sæder, først Anno 1724 forfattet af Hr. Hans Egede, Missionarius ved den dersidst
     oprettede Colonie, og nu Anno 1729 efterseet og efter forfarenhed noget forandret af én der paa nogen Tiid
     har været i Grønland*, Copenhagen.

——1741. *Det gamle Grønlands NyePerlustration, eller Naturel=Historie, og Beskrivelse over det gamle
     Grønlands Situation, Luft, Temperament og Beskaffenhed; De gamle Norske Coloniers Bebyggelse og
     Undergang der Samme=Steds, de i.ige Indbyggeres Oprindelse, Væsen, og Leve=Maade og Handtæringer,
     samt hvad ellers Landet yder og giver af sig, saasom Dyer, Fiske og Fugle &c. med hosføyet nyt Land=Caart
     og andre kaaber=Stykker over Landets Naturalier og Indbyggernis handtæringer, forfattet af Hans Egede.
     Forhen Missionair udi Grønland*, Copenhagen.

Fitzhugh, W.W. and Ward, E.I., eds, 2000. *Vikings:The North Atlantic Saga*, Washington and London.

Gilberg, R. and Gulløv, H.C., eds, 1997. *Fifty Years of Arctic Research*. Copenhagen: Publications of The National
     Museum Ethnographical Series 18.

Jóhannesson, J. 1962. 'The Date of the Composition of the Saga of the Greenlanders', *Saga-Book*, 16, 1, 54-66.

Jónsson, F. 1899. 'Grønlands gamle Topografi efter Kilderne', *Meddelelser om Grønland*, 20, 265-331.

——1930. *Det Gamle Grønlands Beskrivelse af Ívar Bárðarson*, Copenhagen.

Kragh, P. 1875. *Udtog af Missionair P. Kraghs Dagbog* (2den Deel), Haderslev.

Krogh, K.J. 1982. *Erik den Rødes Grønland*, Copenhagen.

Langer Andersen, E. 1982. 'De norrøne stednavne i Østerbygden', *Grønland*, 5-6-7, 163-176.

Mathiassen, T. 1930. 'Inugsuk, a medieval Inuit settlement in Upernivik district, W. Greenland', *Meddelelser om
     Grønland*, 77, 4, 147-340.

Meulengracht Sørensen, P. 1993. *Fortælling og ære*, Århus.

Myhre, B., Stoklund, B., and Gjærder, P., eds, 1982. *Vestnordisk byggeskikk gjennom to tusen år*. Stavanger:
     Museums Skrifter 7.

Petersen, H.C. 2000. 'The Norse Legacy in Greenland' in Fitzhugh and Ward 2000, 340-349.

Rossen, H.C. 1916. 'Nordboerne ved Upernivik', *Det Grønlandske Selskabs Aarsskrift 1915* (Copenhagen), 98-
     101.

Schledermann, P. 2000. 'Ellesmere: Vikings in the Far North', in Fitzhugh and Ward 2000, 248-257.

Sigurðsson, G. 2000. 'An introduction to the Vinland Sagas', in Fitzhugh and Ward 2000, 218-224.

Thisted, K. 1999. *Således skriver jeg, Aron*, vols I-II, Atuakkiorfik, Nuuk.

121

——2001. 'On narrative Expectations: Greenlandic Oral Traditions about the Cultural Encounter between Inuit and Norsemen', *Scandinavian Studies*, 73, 3, 253-297.

Vebæk, C.L. 1991. 'The Church Topography of the Eastern Settlement and the Excavation of the Benedictine Convent at Narsarsuaq in the Uunartoq Fjord', *Meddelelser om Grønland - Man and Society* 14, Copenhagen.

Wawn, A. and Sigurðardóttir, Þ., eds, 2001. *Approaches to Vínland*. Reykjavík: Sigurður Nordal Institute Studies 4.

The Norse Settlements in Greenland from a Maritime Perspective

Marek E. Jasinski and Fredrik Søreide

Introduction

The aim of this article is to discuss the Norse settlements in Greenland from a maritime perspective. Our study is based on already published archaeological and historical sources and new marine geological and marine archaeological data obtained by an international team during fieldwork in Greenland in 1998. This project utilised advanced technology such as sidescan sonars, seabed corers, sub-bottom profilers, a remotely operated vehicle etc., to collect geological and archaeological data from the seabed in close vicinity to the Eastern Settlement in Greenland.

Íslendingabók indicates that the first colonisation of south-west Greenland took place '15 years before Christianity was introduced in Iceland', i.e. about AD 985 when Eiríkr *rauði* sailed from Iceland and settled at Brattahlíð, while Garðar was established in the next fjord (fig. 1). Garðar later became the first and only episcopal residence in Greenland, under Lund from 1125, and Nidaros from 1152-53. Garðar and Brattahlíð were the centres of the so-called Eastern Settlement, while a so-called Western Settlement was established near the present capital Nuuk. It has been estimated that as many as 5000 people can have lived in these two settlements in Greenland (cf. Lynnerup, this volume).

In the fourteenth century the Western Settlement ceased to exist, followed by the Eastern Settlement in the fifteenth century, and the Norse disappeared from Greenland. The last piece of written evidence concerning the Norse in the Eastern Settlement describes a wedding in Hvalsey church in AD 1408. The exact date of the final extinction is, however, unknown and so far no satisfactory explanation has been given as to the cause. Several possible causes have been suggested including climate deterioration, emigration to Newfoundland, Iceland or Europe, raids by European pirates or abduction by European slave-traders, battles with Inuit and diseases (e.g. Bruun 1915; 1918; Nørlund 1923; 1928; 1935; Krogh 1982; McGhee 1984; Arneborg 1988; Seaver 1996; Keller 1989).

Favourable ice conditions for transatlantic shipping between Iceland and Greenland prevailed at the time of Norse colonisation of Greenland. However, numerous indications have been found in the Northern Hemisphere pointing to severe climate deterioration (or the Little Ice Age, AD 1350-1850) by which conditions with vineyards in England and fields of wheat and barley in south Iceland came to an end. Both Icelandic sagas and annals mention that after the first period of colonisation, sea ice off south-east Greenland significantly expanded, causing growing problems to Norse shipping between Iceland and Greenland (e.g. Storm 1888).

As described by Dansgaard *et al.* (1989), the cold climate conditions in central Greenland, as revealed by ice core records, are characterised by dry and very stormy weather conditions, thus providing further evidence for adverse sailing conditions. Stuiver *et al.* (1995) found in their study of ice cores that cold conditions prevailed between *c.* AD 1350 and 1800, with the extremes of temperature lowering dated at AD 1720. They dated the warm peak at AD 975, i.e. close to the time of the Norse *landnám*.

Several indicators therefore point to climatic deterioration as the main cause for deterioration of the Norse settlements in Greenland, but firm evidence for a direct link between the climate deterioration and the deterioration of the Norse coastal settlements has not existed. Onshore palynological investigations on the sites of the Greenland settlements have

Figure 1. Site location and places mentioned in the text.

Figure 2. The research vessel *Poseidon* in a fjord of the Eastern Settlement, south-west Greenland

mainly failed to demonstrate an abrupt and dramatic climate change in this area (Kuijpers *et al.* 1997; 1999). However, new evidence obtained from the seabed by the 1998 project team definitively shows that the climatic conditions deteriorated in the period, with serious consequences for the fjord's environment.

FIELD WORK 1998

The main goal of the fieldwork was to conduct the first marine investigations in the central waters of the Eastern Settlement. The project was carried out between 24 August and 10 September 1998, using the 61 m long German research vessel *Poseidon* (fig. 2). The project entitled 'Climate change and the Viking-Age fjord environment of the Eastern Settlement, south-west Greenland' was an investigation in two fjords off the Eastern settlement, near Brattahlíð and Garðar (Kuijpers *et al.* 1997). The primary goal was to reconstruct the Late Holocene marine environmental changes focusing on the transition from the medieval warm period to the Little Ice Age in the immediate vicinity of the Eastern Settlement.

The main task was to collect sediment cores from south-west Greenland inshore and coastal waters to study the impact of a large-scale climate change on the hydrographic conditions of the Eastern Settlement waters. It is evident that impacts like a more persistent ice cover could have had large effects on the availability of living resources, and on navigation, both crucial factors for the survival of the local population. Using primarily acoustic techniques a further objective was to locate possible underwater cultural heritage as for example shipwrecks, lost cargo, submerged constructions etc. from the Norse period and document targets further with a remotely operated vehicle (ROV).

125

The target area was the waters immediately adjacent to the largest and most important Norse living centres in the Eastern Settlement, Qassiarsuk and Igaliku, i.e. Brattahlíð and Garðar. These settlements were inhabited by the most distinguished members of the community and church. It is therefore a possibility that these areas contain underwater remains from the Norse period that can improve the knowledge of the cultural and maritime history of the period, and add to what is already known from previous studies carried out on land. As shipping has been a prerequisite for transport, the main target was shipwrecks, particularly sites in deep water, that have been better preserved and protected from destruction of ice. The route from Iceland to Greenland was considered extremely rough and the sagas mention special ships that were used for this route. The sagas also mention several shipwrecks but their positions are usually given as only 'on the way to Greenland' or 'in Greenland'.

Because of the relative sea level rise due to subsidence of southern Greenland since the Norse period, it should also be possible to find submerged constructions from the Norse period. This is most clearly observed in the vicinity of Ikigaat or Herjolfsnes, where most ships bound for Greenland would have arrived (fig. 1). Here, most of the southern parts of the graveyard have been inundated. Also at V-51 in Sandnes in the Western settlement, the church and churchyard are presently located in shallow water.

SHIPBOARD TECHNIQUES

Since the target areas were mainly uncharted, bathymetric information had to be collected by the Royal Danish Administration of Navigation and Hydrography in 1998 prior to the project. The water depth in the Tunnuliarfik fjord (fig. 1) is on average 300 m, but in some areas the depths can reach almost 400 m. The southern part of the Igaliku fjord is around 415 m, but it gradually becomes shallower towards the north. The water temperature at around 285 m was found to vary between 1-3 degrees Celsius (Hoffmann *et al.* 1999).

Information was first collected on the upper subsurface structure of the seafloor in the survey areas to locate suitable coring sites with high sediment accumulation rates. A high resolution sediment echo-sounding (sub-bottom profiling) system consisting of an 18 kHz pinger as well as a CHIRP system were used for this purpose. Concurrently a deep-tow 59 kHz EG&G sidescan sonar with a 600 m range was used in the deep parts of the fjords, to about 300 m depth. To avoid reworked sediments not suitable for high resolution paleoenvironmental reconstruction, the cores had to be collected from depths larger than the ice grounding depth, and the sidescan sonar was used to determine the late Holocene maximum ice grounding depths, or possible areas with trawling marks.

When suitable coring sites had been discovered, the coring was done using a 6 m long gravity corer (fig. 3) and a Reinecke box-corer. The collected sediment samples have been partially analysed by Risø National Laboratory in Denmark and Aarhus University (Kuijpers *et al.* 1999).

ARCHAEOLOGICAL SITE INVESTIGATIONS

The sidescan data was analysed continuously on board to locate possible cultural remains on the seabed. However, only one possible archaeological site was located in 80 m depth, in the Igaliku Fjord. This site was investigated with the ROV (fig. 4), based on methods that have been developed at the Norwegian University of Science and Technology in the past few years (Søreide and Jasinski 1998; Jasinski 1999; Søreide 1999; 2000).

A scanning sonar mounted on the ROV was used to relocate the site on the seafloor and the video cameras were used to document the site features. The target turned out to be a 30 m long and 2 m high pile of sediment on the seabed, very similar in shape to a wreck-site but with no visible traces of man-made objects on the surface of the mound (Jasinski and Søreide 1999; 2000).

However, from information obtained by Pb-210 and Cs-137 measurements of the box-cores from the northern part of the Igaliku Fjord, it has now been established that the recent (last 150 years) sedimentation rate is on average 1-2 mm/year, which implies 1-2 m in the past 1000 years. This means that any wreck remains from the Norse period are covered by 1-2 m of sediment, which makes the 'ridge structure' more than interesting.

Also the results from the AMS (Accelerator Mass Spectrometry) C^{14} dating of 2 levels in a selected reference core (PO-243-443) confirm the Pb-210 measurements of the recent (150 years) sedimentation rates, i.e. an age of AD 1450 at 1.63 m below the top of the core (sediment surface), and an age of AD 535 at 4.69 m core depth. This implies that a mass (turbidity) flow process occurred at the transition from warmer to colder climate (middle part of the core), and any cultural remains from before AD 1450 will be covered by at least 1.60 m of sediment, as was suggested by the Pb-210 data.

It cannot be definitely said at the present stage that the mound covers a Norse shipwreck, but the sidescan sonar records of the wide surroundings of the 'structure' do indicate a smooth and flat seabed, without any evidence of larger (natural) ripplemarks or comparable structures around the site. It is therefore very likely that the mound covers a man-made object.

RECONSTRUCTING DETAILS OF THE HYDROGRAPHIC CHANGES

Figure 5 shows a bathymetric map of the Igaliku Fjord with the location of core 443, which was selected for detailed studies. Figure 6 shows a diagram of the latter core showing evidence of a marked (undersea) land slide activity around the time of the beginning of the Little Ice Age (marked by arrows), at around AD 1300 to AD 1400. That age is inferred from the Pb-210 information referred to above.

126

Figure 3. Coring with a 6 m long gravity corer.

Figure 4. Seabed anomalies was investigated using a remotely operated vehicle (ROV).

The possible causes for widespread (submarine) sliding at the transition from warmer to colder climate, i.e. around AD 1300 to AD 1400 include overstepping of sediments accumulated at shallow water depth induced by the trapping of windblown silt and sand. A distinct increase of windblown 'eolian' sedimentation has been found to have occurred onshore at that time, presumably resulting from the reduction of vegetation and enhanced 'freeze-drying' of (barren) soils. Other factors to explain sliding could have been increased storminess, i.e. wave action and storm surges. As for the temperature, we can indirectly deduct higher temperatures in the time interval before sliding from the fact that the magnetic susceptibility values are lower than in the upper part of the core, but that is based on rather complex reasoning.

Probably the reason for the significantly lower magnetic susceptibility values near the bottom of the core must be sought in sedimentary and physico-chemical conditions that were different from those having prevailed in the period when the silty and clayey sediments of the top unit were deposited. Tentatively, we may conclude that climate conditions, being a primary factor governing the fjord hydrography and the more regional (onshore) sedimentary processes, must have been different, i.e. most likely characterised by higher temperatures than those from the last centuries. Similar evidence comes from microfossils preserved in the sediments and from stable (oxygen) isotope data.

128

COASTAL DROWNING AND CLIMATIC EFFECTS ON FARMING

During a shallow water sidescan sonar survey in Tunnuliarfik off Qassiarsuk or Brattahlíð, the presence of a drowned beach was recorded at 3-4 m below present mean sea level. Although at this occasion no material was sampled for dating, it is likely that the age is not in excess of 1000 years BP. This implies that during the 500 years of the Norse settlement era large areas of the fertile lowlands along the fjords were lost to the sea. For example, in the case of the drowned beach zone off Brattahlíð, the relative sea level rise probably resulted in a coastal regression over a distance of about 100 m. A gradual loss of useful land areas due to the fast relative sea level rise must have had an adverse effect on the farming and (grass) cultivation potential for the successive Norse generations living there. Seen in combination with reduced temperatures and increased winds the effects on the grass-production, and consequently the husbandry potential of the Norse must have been dramatic.

Major regional hydrographic changes, like for instance a more permanent ice cover, can also be assumed to have had major consequences for the fjord flora and fauna, and, therefore, for the standing stocks available for hunting and fishing. The distinct increase of windblown sedimentation may have degraded the soils and further reduced

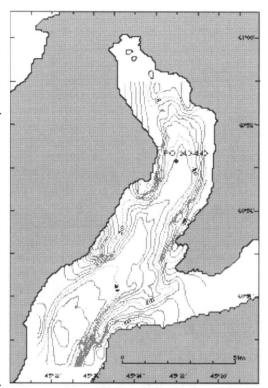

Figure 5. Bathymetric map of the Igaliku Fjord with the location of core 443, which was selected for detailed studies (courtesy of the *Poseidon* expedition, 1998).

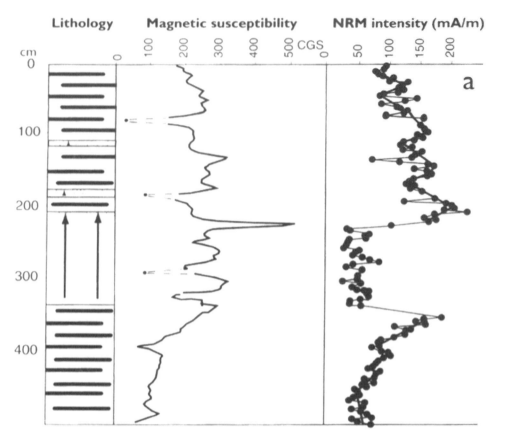

Figure 6. A diagram of core 443 showing evidence of a marked (undersea) land slide activity around the time of the beginning of the Little Ice Age, marked by arrows (courtesy of the *Poseidon* expedition, 1998).

crops and farmland. Enhanced freeze-drying of soils will have made farming further difficult as plants suffered from cold-stress. It can also be postulated that increased wind probably also increased salinity levels in the soil.

THE EFFECTS OF THE CLIMATIC DETERIORATION FROM A MARITIME PERSPECTIVE

The results from the core samples taken from the sea floor in the immediate vicinity to the Norse settlements confirm a considerable climatic deterioration in the coastal areas of south-west Greenland in the period when the Norse settlements were abandoned. The Norse were 'attacked' by forces of nature and had to adapt.

The development of modern European society has been, almost without exceptions, based on the principle of land ownership or terrestrial resource ownership. Ownership of land and its resources establishes terrestrial-oriented social structures, including economical and political control. The land ownership principle can, however, only exist as long as the land can deliver the resources needed to keep the society alive and accumulate a resource surplus. For most populations that have surpassed the purely hunting-gathering level of cultural development this has been the case in areas where farming or animal husbandry has been possible.

For coastal areas the situation is somewhat more complicated. Populations living along the coasts also utilise marine resources, which in fact are richer and easier accessible than land resources for populations with the adequate technology at their disposal. But still the sea is a dynamic element, which it is difficult to include into the ownership principle. Therefore most coastal populations have also based their social structure on land-ownership as long as the land at least has delivered parts of the necessary supplies and resources. Even in less fertile areas such as the Arctic (Jasinski 1993; Jasinski and Ovsyannikov 1998), this has clearly been the case.

But what happens if the land no longer delivers any valuable resources and the population is forced to turn totally to the marine way of living? The established land based social structure, the whole ontological world order, social co-existence, organisation and perception will disintegrate and collapse. What such destruction would mean for a particular population is not difficult to imagine.

A survey of the archaeological literature regarding the Norse period and Greenland's history clearly illustrates that these effects have not been fully explored. Research efforts related to the Norse society in Greenland have primarily focused on farming and animal husbandry, although some attempts within zoo-archaeology have focused on the maritime aspect of the settlements (McGovern 1980; 1981; 1985; 1992). Most archaeologists and historians have used a purely terrestrial perspective, forgetting that the reality in an Arctic region is in fact determined by the maritime sphere. Greenland, by virtue of its natural environment, belongs to those regions of the world whose connections and interaction with the sea have been the strongest (Jasinski 1992). Even if aspects such as fishing and sea-mammal hunting are mentioned as an important part of the Norse survival strategy in Greenland, the maritime perspective is very limited in the studies of the historical processes (e.g. Bruun 1915; 1918; Nørlund 1923; 1928; 1935; Krogh 1982; Arneborg 1988; Keller 1989; Seaver 1996).

130

However, some early publications by Nansen (1911) and Ingstad (1959) argue that the Norse settlements in Greenland were probably more dependent on maritime hunting than on animal husbandry. Midden investigations have failed to recover more than a handful of fish-bones, but seal-bones are abundant, indicating that seal-meat provided as much as 70% of the diet. Nansen and Ingstad included this point in their divagations concerning the decline of the Norse settlement, concluding that a growing interaction between the Norse and the Inuit had to have had, in one way or another, an impact on the Norse settlements.

The findings described here show that the Norse population had to adapt to deteriorating climatic conditions. Decreasing temperatures reduced the production potential, while the increasing sea levels slowly reduced the available area. Overall, this had a destructive effect on the farming and (grass) cultivation potential of the successive Norse generations living there. It seems likely that the terrestrial sphere of the environment eventually could no longer supply the population with important resources needed.

In this situation the established system based on land ownership lost its role as the prestige and social power provider. This in turn accelerated the devastation of social structure and ontological order.

In this position the Norse population in Greenland had in fact only two possible solutions: to leave Greenland and resettle in other areas, or to adopt a purely maritime lifestyle where the social structure and hierarchy would be based on personal hunting and fishing skills—i.e. adapt to the social structure of their neighbours, the Inuit.

With the Norse operating on the same hunting and fishing grounds as the Inuit, it would have been impossible to avoid competition. This competition could (but not necessarily) have had a character of aggressive confrontation, as suggested by Inuit tales (Rink 1866-71; Arneborg 1988; Seaver 1996). The Inuit could on the other hand just as easily have assimilated the remaining Norsemen into their population as suggested by Nansen (1911).

There were undoubtedly chances to leave. Parts of the Norse population could easily have migrated to Vínland (as suggested by Ingstad 1959), Norway or Iceland where the population could find available farmland due to the major plagues which decreased populations living there in that period. We know for instance from the sagas that the couple that was married in Hvalsey church left for Iceland in 1410.

CONCLUSION

The bearing idea of this article has been to study the Norse settlements in Greenland from a maritime perspective based on already published archaeological and historical sources and new marine geological and marine archaeological data obtained by an international team of scientists during fieldwork in Greenland in 1998. Seabed samples taken in the close vicinity of the Eastern Settlement show that the climatic conditions deteriorated in the period, with serious consequences for the fjord's maritime environment. Declining temperatures affected the fauna, farming and grass cultivation potential of the Norse. Increased winds further eroded the farmland and cultivation potential. Sea level changes drowned fertile lowlands along the fjords and further decreased the cultivation potential and a more permanent ice cover had serious consequences for marine hunting and shipping.

Building on these results, the authors propose a scenario where the Norse population either had to leave or to assimilate to a more maritime lifestyle. We hope that this approach and the results can contribute to the general understanding of the destiny of the Norse population, and become a foundation for future studies of the maritime aspects of the Norse settlements in Greenland.

131

ACKNOWLEDGEMENTS

The Poseidon expedition was a co-operation between the Geological Survey of Denmark and Greenland, GEOMAR Institute for Marine Geosciences, the National Museum of Denmark, the National Museum and Archive of Greenland, the Alfred-Wegener-Institute for Polar and Marine Research, Southampton Oceanography Center, University of Iceland and the Norwegian University of Science and Technology.

BIBLIOGRAPHY

Arneborg, J. 1988. *Nordboerne i Grønland—et bidrag til diskusjonen om eskimoernes rolle i Vesterbygdens affolkning.* Hikuin 14.

Bruun, D. 1915. *Erik den Røde og Nordbokolonierne i Grønland*, Copenhagen.

——1918. *The Icelandic Colonization of Greenland and the finding of Vineland.* Copenhagen: Meddelelser om Grønland 57.

Dansgaard, W., White, J.W.C. and Johnsen, S.J. 1989. 'The abrupt termination of the Younger Dryas climate event', *Nature*, 339, 532-534.

Hoffmann, G., Kuijpers, A., Thiede, J. and the Shipboard Scientific Party. 1999. 'Poseidon Cruise No. 243 (Reykjavík-Greenland-Reykjavík, 24 August - 11 September 1998), Climate change and the Viking-Age fjord environment of the Eastern Settlement, south-west Greenland', *Berichte zur Polarforschung*, 331/1999, Alfred-Wegener-Institute for Polar and Marine Research.

Ingstad H. 1959. *Landet under Leidarstjernen*, Oslo.

Jasinski, M.E. 1992. 'European Arctic: Maritime aspects of cultural development', *Specimina Sibirica*, 1992, 127-136.

——1993. Pomors in Grumant. Archaeological studies of Russian hunting stations in Svalbard. Unpublished PhD thesis, University of Tromsø.

——1999. 'Which way now? Maritime archaeology and underwater heritage into the 21st century', unpublished paper, Maritime Archaeology Symposium, World Archaeological Congress 4, Cape Town.

Jasinski, M.E. and Ovsyannikov, O.V. 1998. *Vzgljad na evropeiskuju arktiku, Arkhangelskij sever: problemy i istotsniki*, vols 1-2, St. Petersburg.

Jasinski, M.E. and Søreide, F. 1999. 'Noen benkestokker, inuiter og den lille istid—et norrønt mysterium på Grønland', *Spor*, 1, 24-27.

——2000. 'Poseidon-ekspedisjonen 1998—marin forskning på Grønland', *Spor*, 1, 50-51.

Keller, C. 1989. The Eastern Settlement Reconsidered. Unpublished DPhil thesis, University of Oslo.

Krogh, K.J. 1982. *Erik den Rødes Grønland*, Copenhagen.

Kuijpers, A. and Project Group Members. 1997. Climate change and the Viking-age fjord environment of the Eastern Settlement, south-west Greenland. Marine geological and archaeological investigations in south-west Greenland fjords and coastal waters off the Eastern Settlement of the Norse, Unpublished Project description, September 1997.

Kuijpers, A. *et al.* 1999. 'Climate change and the Viking-age fjord environment of the Eastern Settlement, South Greenland', *Geology of Greenland Survey Bulletin*, 183, 61-67.

Lamb, H.H. 1984. 'Some studies of the Little Ice Age of recent centuries and its great storms', in Mörner and Karlen 1984, 309-329.

Nansen, F. 1911. *Nord i tåkeheimen*, Kristiania.

McGhee, R. 1984. 'Contacts between Native North Americans and the Medieval Norse: A review of evidence', *American Antiquity*, 49, 1, 4-26.

McGovern, T.H. 1980. 'Cows, harp seals and churchbells: Adaptation and Extinction in Norse Greenland', *Human Ecology*, 8, 3, 245-77.

——1981. 'The economics of extinction in Norse Greenland', in Wigley *et al.* 1981, 404-33.

——1985. 'Contributions to the Paleoeconomy of Norse Greenland', *Acta Archaeologica*, 54, 73-122.

——1992. 'Bones, buildings and boundaries: palaeoeconomic approaches to Norse Greenland', in Morris and Rackham 1992, 157-86.

Morris, C.D. and Rackham, J. 1992. *Norse and Later Settlement and Subsistence in the North Atlantic*, Glasgow.

Mörner, N. and Karlen, W., eds, 1984. *Climatic changes on a yearly to millenial basis: Geological, historical and instrumental records*, Dordrecht.

Nørlund, P. 1923. *The first Scandinavian Settlers in Greenland*. New York: The American-Scandinavian Review, 11.

——1928. *Nordboproblemer i Grønland*. Copenhagen: Geografisk Tidskrift, 31.

——1935. *De gamle Nordboers Saga paa Grønland.* Helsinki: Nya Argus.

Rink, H.J. 1866-71. *Eskimoiske eventyr og sagn*, Copenhagen.

Seaver, K. 1996. *The Frozen Echo*, Stanford, California

Storm, G. 1888. *Islandske Annaler indtil 1578*, Christiania.

Stuiver, M., Grootes, P.M. and Braziunas, T.F. 1995. 'The GISP d18O climate record of the past 16,500 years and the role of the sun, ocean and volcanoes', *Quaternary Research*, 44, 341-354.

Søreide, F. and Jasinski, M.E. 1998. 'The Unicorn wreck, central Norway—Underwater archaeological investigations of an 18th-century pink, using remotely controlled equipment', *The International Journal of Nautical Archaeology*, 27, 2, 95-112.

Søreide, F. 1999. Applications of underwater technology in deep water archaeology. Principles and practice. Unpublished DEng thesis, Department of Marine Systems Design, Norwegian University of Science and Technology.

Søreide, F. 2000. 'Cost-effective deep water archaeology: preliminary investigations in Trondheim Harbour', *The International Journal of Nautical Archaeology*, 29, 2, 284-293.

Wigley, T.M.L. *et al.*, eds, 1981. *Climate and History*, Cambridge.

132

Paleodemography of the Greenland Norse

Niels Lynnerup

INTRODUCTION

According to the Icelandic sagas, Eiríkr *rauði* founded the Greenlandic Norse settlement in the year AD 986 (Bekker-Nielsen 1982; Jones 1986). This first settlement (the Eastern settlement) was augmented with another settlement (the Western settlement), situated about 400 km to the north of the first settlement. However, after nearly 500 years of settlement decline set in, and the settlements were depopulated in the fifteenth century (e.g. Meldgaard 1965).

The aim of this study was to establish a paleodemographic profile of the Norse Greenlandic settlements and to estimate total population size. This was achieved by the construction and analysis of various mathematical population models, and this constitutes the first part of this paper. In order to evaluate the estimates of total and average population size, calculations of the projected total number of burials were performed, and this constitutes the second part of this paper. Finally, a general discussion is given concerning the results.

133

POPULATION MODELS

The settlement period was arbitrarily divided into two parts: a first part with population increase and a second part with population decrease. This was based on the following assumptions: (1) the initial settlement population had a size of about 400-500 individuals; (2) the peak population level had to reach at least 2000 individuals; and (3) the population size had to decrease below 500 after the peak level.

The starting population was set arbitrarily at 400-500 individuals. A starting population of a minimum of about 500 people would be in accordance with the accepted minimum levels for sustainable populations of about 400-500 (Geist 1978). As an interesting point, it may be noted that according to the *Grænlendinga saga* ('The Saga of the Greenlanders') and *Eiríks saga rauða* ('Eiríkr the Red's Saga') account that '35 ships sailed to Greenland…, but only fourteen made it there'(GHM I, 179; GHM I, 207). Allowing for a capacity of about thirty individuals (it is estimated that some of the larger Viking cargo ships in AD 1000 had a capacity of 40 tonnes (Crumlin-Pedersen *et al.* 1992), this means that about 300-400 people could have settled in Greenland in the first wave (Meldgaard 1965). Keller has mentioned that the capacity of the ships may have been smaller, but that there was more ongoing immigration, leading to a 'start' population of about 300-800 people (Keller 1986).

The simplest form of population growth modeling is to express population size as a function (usually exponential) of time (Renshaw 1991; Keen and Spain 1992; Hiorns 1972). This is the approach often used when population size forecasts are made. If it is assumed that a starting population of 500 had to increase to 2250 in the course of 200 years, this would mean that the growth rate (r) would be 0.0075 (0.75%). This curve is shown in figure 1. Given an average female life span of 29 years, an average length of female reproductive period of 13 years, and 4.5 live births per female, Hassan (1981) calculated a gross reproduction rate of 2.22 based on model life tables. With a corresponding net reproduction rate of 1.11, this leads to a rate of potential natural increase of 0.52%, which is in general accordance with other studies and with ethnographic data (Hassan 1981). Applying this value means that the Norse population would not reach a level of 2250 until after 289 years (fig. 1).

The above model assumes no immigration or emigration. However, it would seem natural to assume some continuing immigration throughout the beginning of the settlement period. Even if the majority of the population came over in one major wave, minor waves consisting of small groups may have followed. Indeed, such a 'drip-wise' immigration would be very well facilitated by the probably very de-centralized trading structure at the times, with merchants trading directly with the farms (Arneborg 2000). Assuming a low immigration rate (a) of 1 person per year on average over 200 years, results in the curve shown in figure 2. A population level of 1700 individuals is reached after 200 years, assuming r = 0.0052. Assuming a slightly higher (r) of 0.0065, a population level of 2250 is reached after 200 years.

While population increases often seem to fit well with exponential functions, one must not infer some biological 'law'. Furthermore, these exponential models only fit for limited time spans; e.g., while exponential growth can be postulated for the beginning of the settlement period, simple extrapolation beyond this initial phase would result in a Norse population in excess of 14,000 individuals by the year AD 1450. Another widely used function is the logistic growth curve or the Verhulst-Pearl Logistic (Renshaw 1991; Keen and Spain 1992; Hiorns 1972; Kingsland 1982). This function incorporates the 'carrying capacity' parameter (i.e., the population size reaches a maximum at some point). The logistic growth curve models population increase so that the rate of increase falls as the population reaches the maximum carrying capacity. The function may be modeled so that it follows the previously noted exponential growth in the beginning, but as the carrying capacity limit is reached, the rate of increase drops and the population size comes asymptotically near the carrying capacity (fig. 3).

If it is assumed that the population decreased from 2000 individuals to 0 inside about 200 years, the formula of exponential increase and immigration may be changed to assume negative (a), i.e., emigration. Since a positive growth rate must still be assumed (i.e., due to child births), the values for growth and emigration rate have to be balanced so as to produce a net. Assuming a constant growth rate in the order of the population increase period, the emigration rate would be at least 13 people per year in order to drive population numbers below sustainable levels within 200 years (fig. 4). If it is assumed that the growth rate was not constant as in the above model, but rather decreased over 200 years, extinction could be accomplished by an emigration rate of 8 individuals/year (fig. 5). Such a decrease in growth would be due to the fact that in an emigration scenario, it is mostly young people who leave. Thus, not only do the emigrants lessen the population numbers directly, but being in the fertile age they also lower the number of childbirths and thereby lower population numbers further.

Stochastic models incorporate an element of chance, which is why they are also known as Monte Carlo models. While deterministic functions such as the above are basically linear functions, stochastic models are event-based (Howell and Lehotay 1978). By setting the chances of birth and death so that they roughly reflect overall birth and mortality rates, the computer 'chooses' an event (i.e., either birth or death) at some given point in time. This is usually implemented by generating random numbers, and based on these random numbers the event is chosen (Renshaw 1991; Keen and Spain 1992). This gives random variation to the overall population curve. By making many runs or simulations, it may be seen that while most runs probably lie close to deterministic models, there is now much fluctuation. For small populations, a chance series of death 'events' may lead to extinction. If the outcomes of many stochastic simulations generally lie close to deterministic curves, then one can be satisfied that the determinstic approach will provide an adequate description of population development (Renshaw 1991). Figure 6 shows two runs. While generally most simulations more or less lay close to the deterministic models, several runs gave other results. The lower of the two curves in fig. 6 practically shows a pronounced population decrease, while the

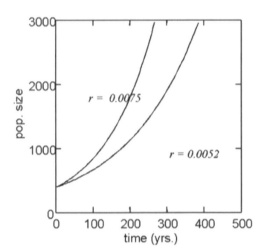

Figure 1. Simple exponential growth (r = 0.0075 (line) and 0.0052 (broken line)). N(t) = population at time t; N(0) = starting population (t = 0); r = growth rate; and t = time.

$$N(t) = N(0)\exp(rt)$$

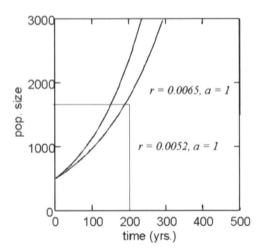

Figure 2. Exponential growth with immigration (r = 0.0065 (line) and 0.0052 (broken line). Same variables as in fig. 1, except a = immigration rate.

$$N(t) = N(0)\exp(rt) + a/r\,(\exp(rt)-1)$$

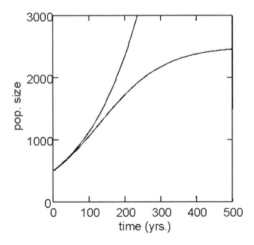

Figure 3. Logistic growth model. Growth rate decreases as carrying capacity limit is approached. An exponential growth curve (cf. fig. 1) has been overlaid for comparison (broken line). Same variables as in fig. 1, except K = carrying capacity.

$$N(t) = K/(1 + \exp(-rt))$$

Figure 4. Depopulation assuming constant growth rates (as in figs 1-2). Extinction is accomplished within 200 years assuming an emigration rate of 15 persons per year.

N(t) = N(0)exp(rt) - a/r (exp(rt) -1)

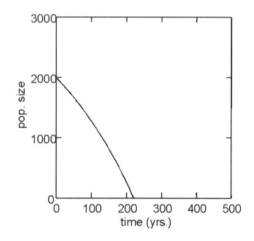

$$N(t) = N(0)\exp(rt) - a/r(\exp(rt)-1)$$

136

Figure 5. Depopulation assuming decreasing growth rates. Extinction is accomplished assuming an emigration rate of 8 persons per year.

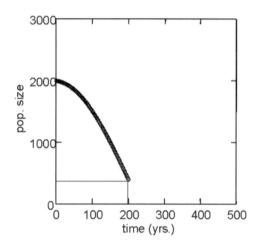

Figure 6. Stochastic modeling of population events (see text).

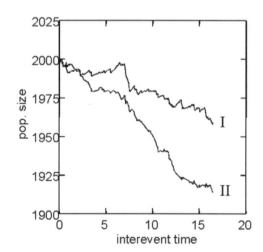

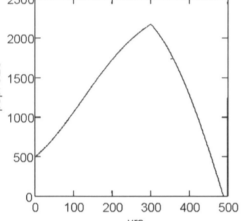

Figure 7. Population profile throughout 500 years of settlement.

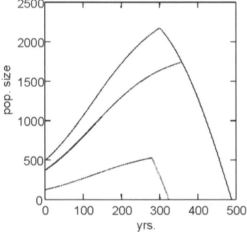

Figure 8. Same as figure 7, but an attempt has been made to divide the population into Western and Eastern settlement. The uppermost curve is the cumulative curve for both settlements, the middle curve is the population profile for the Eastern settlement, while the lowermost curve refers to the Western settlement.

upper curve shows a much smaller decrease, even though the same probabilities are used. If a smaller starting population had been assumed, such a course may conceivably have led to extinction (Ward and Weiss 1976).

Based on the above models of population change a total population profile was made (fig. 7). This makes it possible to calculate the total population that lived throughout the settlement period and the average population per year. The average population was simply calculated by generating the population number per year, and summing these numbers and dividing them by 500 years. This yields an average yearly population of 1377 individuals. The total population was then calculated based on this model, yielding a total of approximately 26,500 individuals. This figure is thus based *inter alia* on growth rates which seem in accordance with a calculated population increase in Iceland in the period AD 970-1095 (calculated using population figures from Thorarinsson 1961). A small rate of continuing immigration (1 individual per year) was also assumed. Probably this rate dropped to zero (or rather the net rate of immigration and emigration was zero), during the years AD 1100-1200. This, along with a slowing of population increase (due to the population nearing the carrying capacity and hence straining resources), could be consistent with some kind of level being reached by AD 1200. While in the logistic model (fig. 3), the population level approaches the carrying capacity asymptotically, population studies seem to show that 'real' populations often experience much fluctuation around the carrying capacity (Renshaw 1991). This would also be the case for the Norse, so the model in fig. 7 must be taken as representative of some sort of 'average'. Such fluctuations are best seen when performing stochastic modelling, as was shown in fig. 7, where the initial population increase is much more fluctuating than if simply assuming linear functions.

Having shown that a population of some 2000 individuals can be reached within 250 years, assuming realistic figures for growth and immigration, the question then remained if the reverse can be modeled. Is it possible, still assuming realistic parameters, to model an 'extinction' curve? Given a positive growth rate, emigration remains as an explanation for a decreasing population. Emigration may occur when a population exceeds its optimum level of living (Hassan 1981). This could be because the Norse population reached the carrying capacity of their land. Several analyses point to a shift in climate, which may have restricted the Norse ecological niche and lowered the carrying capacity (Berglund 1986; McGovern 1979). Even allowing for a decreasing rate of growth over 200 years, as shown in fig. 3, this still means that the emigration rate would have to be about eight individuals per year. For a small population such as the Norse, such a level of emigration would certainly seem massive. The question is, of course, whether such rates are realistic. It must first be remembered that these rates represent averages. Probably emigration proceeded in waves, comprising 100 people every 10 years. Furthermore, there may be stochastic variation; once the population is sufficiently small, it becomes vulnerable to fluctuations in fertility and mortality (Weiss and Smouse 1976). A beginning decline may thus have been precipitated, and the population may have fallen sharply, perhaps with short periods of relative stability. Most important is the size difference between the Western and Eastern settlements. Judging by numbers of farmhouses (West: 80, East: 250 (Kleivan 1984)), and by churches, and leaving out the minor 'prayerhouses' (West: 3, East: 11), there seems to be a 1:3 ratio between population size of the settlements. Viewed by itself, the Western settlement would rapidly approach the 500 level minimum population size. Indeed, the population, assuming the above emigration rates and lowered fertility rates, would pass below this level after only 20 years. Thus, it is possible that decline set in at around AD 1300, and some 50 years later most had emigrated from the Western settlement, leaving perhaps only a few, mainly old, settlers. The Western settlement could thus be completely depopulated during the fourteenth century. Perhaps the Eastern settlement experienced some immigration due to resettlement, which for some years offset the rate of decline, whereby decline proceeded at the same rate as it had in the Western settlement. This would leave the Eastern settlement depopulated in the mid-fifteenth century.

Decline may also have been brought about by exceptionally high mortality rates. High mortality rates are usually linked with war and with epidemics. However, even killing rates of up to 10% of young adults in warfare would not substantially decrease birth rates, unless strict monogamy had prevailed and widow remarriage were prohibited (Polgar 1972). It has also been mentioned that perhaps the introduction of monasticism with a Benedictine convent in Narsarsuaq and an Augustinian monastery in Ketilsfjord may have played a role in declining population numbers. The real limiting factor here would be the number of nuns, or rather how large a part of the female population did not marry and bear children. There are no historical sources to indicate the monastic population number, but judged on the basis of the ruins of the probable monastic buildings it has not been big and thus only had a marginal effect if any.

This virtually leaves highly lethal epidemics as a causative factor for drastically reducing a population within a short time span. Plague hit both Iceland and Norway in the fourteenth and fifteenth century, and total mortality rates of between 30% to 50% have been suggested. Clearly, a halving of the Norse population inside just one or two years would be disastrous for such a small population. Based on the numbers alone, epidemic diseases could quite plausibly explain the population reduction.

NUMBER OF INTERRED NORSE

Corroboration of the presented numbers was sought by a rather simple calculation: in theory, the cumulative number of individuals over the settlement period should be approximately equal to the total number of interred in the graveyards. In order to give an estimate of the total number of interred, two key parameters must first be established: the total burial area and the burial density. Although it cannot be expected that the total number of interred should be exactly equal to the total cumulated population, the numbers should none the less be roughly on the same scale.

Most Norse churchyards have been excavated to a degree allowing reasonably exact estimation of size (Lynnerup 1996; 1998). Burial density was calculated from the single excavation areas divided by the amount of specimens. As an example, Vebæk excavated an area of 3.25 m² at E23 Sillisit (Vebæk 1969). In this area five specimens were found, resulting in a density of 1.54 burials/m². Excavation areas and number of encountered interments are listed in Table 1. The calculated site burial densities were further divided by the estimated function period of the church yard. The function period denotes the approximate timespan during which the churchyard was in use. Since there are no exact datings pertaining to the function periods for the various churchyards, the values of 400 years for Eastern settlement churchyards and 300 years for Western settlement churchyards were set arbitrarily. Based on these assumptions, the average burial density was calculated to be 0.709 bodies/square meter/100 years.

139

We see some variation in burial densities among the single sites. However, the individual values for burial density are comparable to other medieval churchyards; e.g., at the cemeteries at Torup, Tryglsjö, Risby, and Rathhausmarkt (Kieffer-Olsen 1993). The average density at these churchyards was approximately 0.73 burials/m²/100 yrs (values calculated by this author). The burial densities of W51 Sandnes, W7 Anavik and E149 Undir Høfda are thus higher when compared to other medieval churchyards, and this seems amply reflected in the remarks by the archaeologists who excavated the Norse churchyards (Lynnerup 1996; 1998).

Site	Part	Excavated Area m²	Interments N	Burial density N/m²	Func. period years	Burial density N/m²/100yrs
E23	NE	3.25	5	1.54	400	0.385
E29a	All	300.50	155	0.52	100	0.520
E66	S	4.80	6	1.25	400	0.313
E111	N	290.00	200	0.69	400	0.172
E149	N	12.00	45	3.75	400	0.938
W7	N	2.20	7	3.18	300	1.060
W51	NW	26.00	123	4.73	300	1.577

Table 1. Excavated areas and calculation of average burial density.

Based on the calculated burial density, the total amount of burials per churchyard was calculated (Table 2). A major source of potential error is the function period of the churchyard. Again, the function period for churches in the East settlement has been set arbitrarily at 400 years, while the corresponding period for West settlement churches was set at 300 years (E29a Þjóðhildr's Church was set at 100 years). While these figures are probably not too far off for the bigger parish churches (e.g. E111 Herjolfsnes, E47 Garðar, etc.), the function periods for the smaller circular churches may well have been shorter. Even though burials have been found inside a church structure, these are few. By far the highest number was found at E111 Narsarsuaq where 20 bodies were observed.

The total number of burials in Norse Greenland is calculated to represent approximately 22,000 individuals. However, this figure basically stems from calculations using the number of retrieved specimens. This number has to be corrected for underrepresentation of subadults, where after the total buried number of individuals can thus be estimated at about 26,000 to 30,000.

Reasons for over- or underenumeration may be undiscovered churchyards or burial outside the churchyards. While there possibly may be unrecognized church sites (perhaps at the sites of the so-called Middle Settlement), this can hardly amount to more than a few. Even assuming that these might be large churches with big churchyards, this would not represent an underenumeration of more than 2000-5000 individuals. Likewise, while it must be assumed that some Norse died due to drowning or on expeditions, even high estimates (10%) would not markedly influence the grand total. Furthermore, only the remains of three individuals have been found outside the churchyards. It seems that the Norse were insistent in having their dead buried in consecrated earth, as evidenced by some secondary burials (Lynnerup 1998).

DISCUSSION

Earlier estimates of the Norse population have ranged from a peak level of about 3000 (Gad 1984), 4000 (Berglund 1986), 4000-5000 (Meldgaard 1965) and 5000-6000 (McGovern 1979). In his article on paleodemography, Keller (1986) operates with a larger starting population, and calculates a 'maximum' population level of about 6,000 reached by AD 1300. Keller relates this figure to the number of farmsteads, and estimates of number of people per farmstead (15 individuals per farmstead). Keller (1986) mentions that there is some uncertainty in such a direct calculation, since, not all farmsteads were in use simultaneously and were of different sizes. Indeed, only very few farms have been dated in order to establish function periods (see Albrethsen, this volume). Furthermore, the Norse have probably used *saetters* (livestock moved to out-lying grasslands during part of the grazing season). This may explain why the numbers given by archaeologists and others seem much higher than the numbers arrived at in the previous sections. The calculated cumulated number of individuals, assuming a peak population of 5000 to 6000, is in excess of 70,000 individuals and this seems to indicate that these estimates are too high. It would be almost impossible to expect more than three times as many graves existed, even if all churches have not been located or a high percentage of non-churchyard burials are assumed. While the results of this paper indicate a cumulated number of 28,000 individuals with remarkable consistency by two independent methods, this should not be taken as an exact estimate per se. Rather, the consistency indicates the probable population size: that cumulated population numbers lie in the 25,000 to 35,000 range, with a corresponding peak level of 2000-3000 individuals at a given point in time.

The population models used in this study show that depopulation was possible assuming a steady emigration rate. Theories of migration have mostly centered on the Norse population in Greenland 'returning' to Iceland, after a first relocation of the people of the

Site	Burial Area m²	Func. period years	Burials N	Church N	Total N
E1	416	400	1180	-	1180
E23	195	400	553	-	553
E29a	300	100	213	-	213
E47	753	400	2136	16	2152
E66	578	400	1639	7	1646
E111	530	400	1503	2	1505
E149	365	400	1032	20	1052
W7	469	300	998	-	998
W51	552	300	1174	-	1174
E18	962	400	2728	-	2728
E29	297	400	842	-	842
E33	68	400	193	-	193
E35	101	400	286	-	286
E48	210	400	596	-	596
E64	198	400	562	-	562
E78	180	400	511	-	511
E83	647	400	1835	-	1835
E105	723	400	2050	-	2050
E162	274	400	777	-	777
W23a	597	300	1270	-	1270
Total	8417.00	-	22,078	45	22123

141

Table 2. Number of individuals are shown as whole numbers. Site numbers refer to the Greenland National Museum denomination for Norse sites.

Western settlement to the Eastern Settlement (Berglund 1986). A few also have entertained the thought that the Norse moved on to the North American continent or northern Britain and Ireland (Fyllingsnes 1990). While it has been proved, based on the finds at L'Anse aux Meadows in Newfoundland by Ingstad (1970), that the Norse did indeed reach the North American continent (Vínland), there are absolutely no indications of any major settlements to this continent. This also goes for resettlements to the British Isles and Ireland.

Resettlement to Iceland would be more plausible. While there is no direct archaeological or cultural historical evidence of resettlement to Iceland, the complete absence of finds such as valuable sacramental objects in the Norse settlements in Greenland is puzzling. Only common and everyday items have been found (Berglund 1986). This could well indicate an 'ordered' resettlement, rather than some dramatic change and extinction. Berglund (1986) concludes that such an 'ordered' resettlement must have been to Iceland. Arneborg (1993, 193) also makes this point, based on her cultural historical research, proposing a scenario of 'slow and quite un-dramatic emigration from the Norse settlements in Greenland.' Such an 'ordered' resettlement would also explain the lack of find of precious items in the Norse settlements.

Resettlement movements did take place in Late Medieval Europe on a large scale. This was probably caused by the plague epidemics, which literally eradicated whole villages and settlements. In Iceland and Norway this lead in the aftermath to large scale resettling and abandonement of the least profitable farmsteads (Krogh 1982; Benedictow 1990; McEvedy 1988). Plague in Norway and Iceland laid waste many farmsteads (37 of 99 holdings in the hands of nine churches in Northern Iceland were still deserted 20 years after the plague epidemic hit the island; Benedictow 1990). This massive depopulation had enormous demographic, economic and societal repercussions. In the wake of the plague, largescale population resettlement took place, inhabitants of the more meager places leaving for the 'vacant' better places. Whether Norse Greenland was directly affected by plague or not, it most certainly has been affected by the derived effects of plague. For instance, export prices for several Icelandic comodities fell dramatically (Keller 1986), something which may well also have had economic consequences for Greenland. Such vacancies may have prompted the Greenlandic Norse to resettle there, if better economic prospects were perceived.

Also worsening climate, straining of resources and fear of cultural isolation may have been the prime 'movers' for the Norse. Indeed, evidence of a cooling climate may be found even in the dental tissue of the Norse themselves (Fricke *et al.* 1996). The climatic changes must be seen in connection with studies on resource use. It has been indicated that the Norse probably already were straining the carrying capacity of the land, and more and more becoming reliant on marine resources (McGovern 1979). It has also been mentioned that large herds of sheep may have overgrazed the lands to such a degree that the top soil was eroded (Krogh 1982). There is both archaeological and anthropological evidence in support of these theories. Studies of kitchen middens have confirmed changes in resource use, and the discovery of irrigation canals at E47 Garðar could very well point to an attempt at 'technical' adaptations in order to increase land output (Krogh 1982). Recent radiocarbon analysis of Norse skeletal remains (Lynnerup 1998) show a clear dietary shift over the settlement period, thus confirming the above points.

But if the Greenland Norse resettled in Iceland (or Norway) over perhaps a two hundred year time span, what then of the seemingly indifference to the fate of the Norse settlements in Greenland? There is a lack of written accounts relating the demise of the populations in Greenland, and surely such an influx to Iceland would have been noticed. However, the peak population size of the Greenland settlements, probably at most 2500 people, must be compared to the Icelandic population, which has been estimated at 70,000 people (pre-plague). Even allowing for a 30-50% decrease due to plague, an influx of perhaps 10 people a year would hardly be noticeable, especially if some turmoil in the midst of plague and internal resettlement was concurrent. And the rest of the world, also in the throes of plague and its repercussions, probably had other concerns. In AD 1453 Constantinople fell and the Turks advanced up to Vienna. Such events probably also served to divert the Church's attention from the small settlements, which were smaller than many European country villages.

I also think we here may be at the core of the whole 'Norse Enigma'. Today we devote much attention to the fate of the Norse settlements in Greenland, and see them as something unique. Maybe thousands of small and outlying villages and farmsteads throughout Europe were being abandoned (the so-called medieval agrarian crisis), but by giving up the Norse settlements, Greenland was in effect 'given up', which somehow today is seen as rather incomprehensible. Indeed, today, and for much earlier Norse research, there is a presumption of Greenland as a distinct entity. The Norse may not have held such a view themselves. To them, Greenland was probably simply an extension of inhabitable lands and fjords stretching from Norway over the Shetlands, Orkneys, Faroes and Iceland, all the way to Labrador and Newfoundland. For example, the Norse were not aware of having 'discovered' a new continent when they arrived in Vínland; they had simply set out to look for exploitable land. This they found, but, probably as a result of a decrease in population pressure and the uneconomically long distances, they never formed a proper settlement there. It is perhaps distinctly 'modern' (or at least post-medieval) to see Greenland as a distinct entity, and hence the abandonment of the settlements as not just internal population movements in Northern Europe, but as the abandonment of nearly a whole continent.

In other words, the Norse did not give up Greenland, they gave up some land and fjords which had become less and less profitable for their way of life, and moved back to more auspicious shores where new opportunities had arisen.

ABBREVIATION

GHM   Anon. 1838-45. *Grønlands Historiske Mindesmærker* I-III, Copenhagen [reprinted 1976 by Rosenkilde & Bagger].

BIBLIOGRAPHY

143

Arneborg, J. 1993. 'Vikingerne i Nordatlanten: De nordiske samfund i Island og Grønland og Europa', in Lund 1993, 179-94.

———2000. 'Greenland and Europe', in Fitzhugh and Ward 2000, 304-317.

Bekker-Nielsen, H. 1982. 'Islandske sagaer om Grønland', in Krogh 1982, 197-245.

Benedictow, O. J. 1992. *Plague in the Late medieval Nordic Countries*, Oslo.

Berglund, J. 1986. 'The decline of the Norse Settlements in Greenland', *Arctic Anthropology*, 23, 109-35.

Crumlin-Pedersen, O., Schou Jørgensen, M. and Edgren, T. 1992. 'Skibe og Samfærdsel' in Roesdahl 1992, 42-51.

Damas, ed. 1984. *Handbook of American Indians 5: The Arctic*, vol. 3, Washington, D.C.

Fitzhugh, W. W. and Ward, E.I., eds, 2000. *Vikings: The North Atlantic Saga*, Washington and London.

Fricke, H.C, O'Neil, J. P and Lynnerup, N. 1995. 'Oxygen Isotope Composition of Medieval Human Tooth Enamel from the Medieval Greenland: Linking Climate and Society', *Geology*, 23, 869-72.

Fyllingsnes, F. 1990. *Undergongen til dei norrøne bygdene på Grønland i seinmellomalderen*. Oslo: Forum Mediaevale, Skrifter 2.

Gad, F. 1984. 'History of colonial Greenland', in Damas 1984, 556-76.

Geist, V. 1978. *Life strategies, human evolution, Environmental design*, New York.

Harrison, G. A. and Boyce, A. J., eds, 1972. *The Structure of Human Populations*, Oxford.

Hassan, F.A. 1981. *Demographic Archaeology*, New York.

Hiorns, R.W. 1972. 'Mathematical models in demography', in Harrison and Boyce 1972, 110-27.

Howell, N. and Lehotay, V.A. 1978. 'AMBUSH: A computer program for stochastic microsimulation of small human populations', *American Anthropologist*, 80, 905-922.

Ingstad, A.S. 1970. 'The Norse settlement at L'Anse aux Meadows, Newfoundland', *Acta Archaeologica*, 41, 109-154.

Jones, Gwyn. 1986. *The Norse Atlantic Saga*, Oxford and New York.

Keen, R.E. and Spain, J.D. 1992. *Computer simulation in biology*, New York.

Keller, C. 1986. 'Nordboerne på Grønland 985-1350: Bidrag til en demografisk økologisk diskusjon', *Universitetets Oldsaksamling Årbok*, 1984/1985, 145-57.

Kieffer-Olsen, J. 1993. Grav og gravskik i det middelalderlige Danmark. 8 kirkegårdsudgravninger. Unpublished PhD thesis Afd. for Middelalder-arkæologi og Middelalder-arkæologisk Nyhedsbrev, Moesgård, Aarhus, Denmark.

Kingsland, S. 1982. 'The refractory model: The logistic growth curve and the history of population ecology', *The Quarterly Review of Biology*, 57, 29-52.

Krogh, K. ed., 1982. *Erik den Rødes Grønland*, Copenhagen.

Lynnerup N, 1996. 'Paleodemography of the Greenland Norse', *Arctic Anthropology*, 33, 122-137.

——1998. 'The Greenland Norse: A Biological-anthropological Study', *Meddelelser om Grønland, Man & Society,* Series 24, 1-148.

Lund, N. ed., 1993. *Norden og Europa i vikingetid og tidlig middelalder,* Copenhagen.

McEvedy, C. 1988. 'The bubonic plague', *Scientific American*, 258, 74-83.

McGovern, T.H. 1979. The Paleoeconomy of Norse Greenland: Adaptation and extinction in a tightly bounded ecosystem. Unpublished PhD thesis, University of Michigan.

Meldgaard, J. 1965. *Nordboerne i Grønland*, Copenhagen.

Polgar, S. 1972. 'Population history and population policies from an anthropological perspective', *Current Anthropology*, 13, 203-11.

Renshaw, E. 1991. *Modelling biological populations in space and time*, Cambridge.

Roesdahl, E. ed., 1992. *Viking og Hvidekrist,* Copenhagen.

Thorarinsson, S. 1961. 'Population changes in Iceland', *Geographical Review*, 51, 519-33.

Vebæk, C.L. 1969. 'Excavation report of the Site E23 Sillisit', unpublished site report, The Norse Archives, The Danish National Museum, Copenhagen.

Ward, R.H. and Weiss, K.M. 1976. 'The demographic evolution of human populations', *Journal of Human Evolution*, 5, 1-25.

Weiss, K.M. and Smouse, P.E. 1976. 'The demographic stability of small human populations', *Journal of Human Evolution*, 5, 59-74.

Walrus ivory and other northern luxuries: their importance for Norse voyages and settlements in Greenland and America

Else Roesdahl

Expanding from my previous work in this area (1995; 1998), I wish to discuss the importance of northern luxury products, particularly walrus ivory and narwhal tusks, to the Norse in Greenland. I wish also to suggest that the voyages to America were undertaken partly in order to investigate possibilities of discovering further luxury products. The basis of my argument is that the Norse in Greenland needed frequent and continuous contact with Scandinavia and western Europe in order to maintain their Scandinavian lifestyle and identity. This was only possible so long as the outside world retained a major interest in the products provided by the Greenland Norse, an interest strong enough to send ships to Greenland with the products (and ideas and news) needed there—timber, iron, fashions and much more—which would be exchanged for the products of that distant land (Arneborg 2000).

A number of written sources provide examples and lists of 'exports' from Greenland—some of which were extremely valuable and exotic. The thirteenth-century *King's Mirror* mentions skins of buck, cattle and seal, rope of walrus hide and walrus tusks (1926, 49f). Other sources add the skins of polar bear and indeed live polar bears, according to *Hungrvaka* one of which was presented to the German emperor Henry III by the Icelander Isleif in 1055 (*Hungrvaka* 1989, 34). The prestigious white hunting falcons sent from Iceland and then exported from Norway, possibly also came from Greenland, where, we are told, they were abundant. It seems obvious that quality furs were exported, and, according to the sagas, furs were among the goods bartered by the natives in Vínland (Magnusson and Pálsson 1965, 65, 99). Recent investigations by Else Østergaard of the Danish National Museum have shown that specialised textiles should be added to the list of northern goods (pers. comm.).

The very special importance of walrus tusks, ivory, is clear from many sources. It was a rare material, because walrus—a circumpolar species—lives only in Greenland and Canadian waters and in the waters along the distant northern coasts of Norway, Russia and Alaska (Muus *et al.* 1981, 405). It was in great demand in continental western Europe and in England, especially from the mid ninth to the early thirteenth century. It was used there, as in Scandinavia, for all sorts of ecclesiastical and vernacular high-status carvings (figs 1-4)—for example, mounts for book-bindings and boxes, crucifixes, crozier-heads, seals, gaming-pieces, belt-buckles and much else (Goldschmidt 1914-26; Gaborit-Chopin 1978; 1992; Liebgott 1985; Magerøy 1993). The famous Cloisters Cross, or Bury St Edmunds Cross, now in New York, is one of these carvings (Parker and Little 1994; cf. Baxter 1995).

Tusks of narwhal, which live almost exclusively in the waters between Greenland and Canada, though they also occur to the north of Iceland, along the eastern coast of Greenland and in the Western Arctic Sea (Muus *et al.* 1981, 438), seem not to be mentioned in written sources as exports, although they were immensely valuable in medieval Europe and were to be found in a number of royal and ecclesiastical treasuries. But, as they were believed to be horns of the mythical and highly symbolic unicorn (and illustrated as such on tapestries, murals and other pictures), and because the horn itself was believed to be a medium with which to detect poison in food and drink, there was very good reason why their true origin should not be revealed and committed to writing (figs 5-6). Only in the early seventeenth century was the true nature of the beast divulged (see, for example Bernström 1975, 448-50; Rosing 1986; Bencard 1989a; 1989b; Cherry 1995a).

Most of the recorded traded commodities are of organic materials which would rarely be preserved today—and, even if they were preserved, it would seldom be possible to identify their Greenland origin. I have chosen here to concentrate on the tusks of walrus and narwhal, because these were two of the most valuable commodities, because a considerable amount survives, and because new archaeological finds of walrus turn up all the time. Until now, these materials have mainly been dealt with by art historians, who have concentrated on their aesthetic quality and stylistic interest, and have naturally not examined implications more normally dealt with by archaeologists. I have been working in my spare time on the subject of walrus and narwhal tusk for some years (Roesdahl 1995; 1998), but this paper is still a preliminary study. My interest was initially born of the realisation that there is a huge number of ornamented objects of walrus ivory in European museums. I then became intrigued by their date in relation to the occurrence of objects made of elephant ivory, and in relation to the history of Norse settlement in Greenland.

There is a remarkable increase in the number of (preserved) objects made of walrus ivory from around AD 1000. Earlier objects are rare. This increase suggests that new sources were being exploited, and, interestingly, it coincides in terms of date with the settlement of Greenland. Walrus ivory was clearly most popular during the eleventh to early thirteenth centuries (figs 1-3) during a time when access to elephant ivory was still difficult (Goldschmidt 1914-26; Gaborit-Chopin 1978; 1992). The two materials could be substituted for each other, although elephant ivory has great advantages in that the tusk is much larger (a huge walrus tusk is only about 60-70cm long) and elephant tusks, unlike those of the walrus, are also solid to the core providing a uniform raw material (MacGregor 1985, 14ff.).

In the thirteenth century, elephant ivory became a more popular medium for the artist, while in the fourteenth century elephant ivory was so readily available that it totally dominated the market. Ornamented objects of ivory were now mass produced and became accessible to wealthy burghers and others—thus the prestige of ornamented ivory declined. From around AD 1400, ivory objects fell entirely out of fashion; hardly any fifteenth-century ivory objects, from either elephant or walrus, save for gaming pieces and a few finely-carved whole horns, were produced in northern and western Europe (Gaborit-Chopin 1978; Magerøy 1993; Roesdahl 1998, 41f.). There is thus a striking coincidence between the time of serious decline in the use of walrus ivory and the decline of Norse settlement in Greenland. There is an equally striking coincidence between the disappearance of all sorts of ivory in European art and the extinction of the Norse in Greenland.

But was walrus ivory really so crucial to the Greenland economy as this might suggest? Greenland was not the only source for this material. It could sometimes be obtained in the far north of Norway, and research by Lyoba Smirnova has now shown that walrus ivory—undoubtedly from the arctic waters to the north—was being worked in Novgorod and other places in northern Russia in the early Middle Ages (Smirnova 1997; 2001). This chimes with the Anglo-Saxon account of the Norwegian chieftain Ohthere (*c.* AD 890), and with Arab accounts of walrus tusk ('fish teeth') from the north which were traded south to Persian and Arab lands (*Two Voyagers* 1984, 18-21, 56; Tegengren 1962).

Greenland was, however, almost certainly the dominant source of the walrus ivory used in Scandinavia and western Europe. There is much written evidence of trade in the material to western Europe, mainly by way of Norway or Iceland (Roesdahl 1995, 33; 1998, 40; for Iceland also see Kristjánsson 1986, 93-107), and there is good archaeological evidence of walrus tusk on the farms of Greenland, evidence which includes fragments produced when the tusks were removed from the skull of the animal (Roesdahl 1998, 19-21, n.18). The main hunting grounds for walrus were probably those in Disko Bay, about 800 km to the north of the Western Settlement. Walrus are most easily killed on land or on ice, a method of hunting familiar to the Norse. The expeditions would have been dangerous, but profitable. The evidence mentioned suggests that tusks were often brought back while still in place on the frontal, which had been cut from the rest of the skull. The Norse of Greenland used little ivory. A few finished objects have been found. Although they include a bishop's crozier and a chess queen, generally only small and rather plain objects of this material have been found—gaming pieces and the like (Roesdahl 1998, 21). Recent excavations have also shown that belt buckles were carved there (G. Nyegaard, pers. comm.). The vast majority of tusks must have been exported and carved outside Greenland by highly sophisticated artists.

As has been mentioned, there is plenty of evidence of objects carved from this material in Europe: in Scandinavia (especially in Norway and Denmark); in England; western Germany (including Cologne); the Netherlands and northern France; and in the Paris region. Various art workshops have long ago been identified by art historians on the basis of the style and distribution of the objects (Gaborit-Chopin 1978). These include one in western

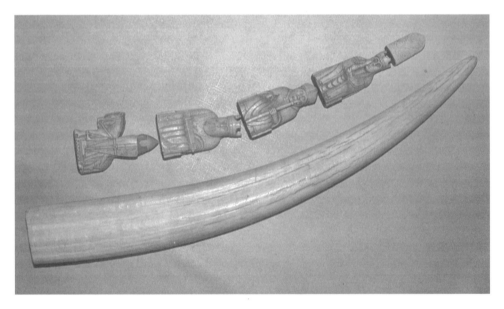

147

Figure 1. Modern walrus tusk (length 59cm; weight 1.5kg) with replicas of five of the 78 chessmen found at the Isle of Lewis, Outer Hebrides, Scotland. They were carved in western Norway in the second part of the 12th century. The replicas are placed in relation to the tusk in order to show how such a tusk might be used for chessmen of different sizes (photo: Lene Stevns Jensen 1992).

Figure 2. Anglo-Saxon pen case of walrus ivory found in the City of London. Carved in high relief on the lid and four sides with figural scenes. Length 23.2cm. Mid-11th century (photo: The British Museum).

Figure 3. The Sibylle
Cross. Composite cross of
walrus ivory made for a
book cover *c.* 1130-50.
Height 18.5cm. The name
of Sibylle, who was
countess of Flanders and
died as abbess of St.
Lazarus in Jerusalem, is
inscribed on the lower
mount. (photo: Musée du
Louvre).

148

Figure 4. Walrus skull
(frontal) from excavations
at Christchurch Place,
Dublin, 12th-13th centu-
ry. The tusks and all other
teeth were removed. The
photo also shows a the
sawn-off and discarded
hollow root end of a tusk,
which has here been
placed in the skull. This is
from the excavations at
Fishamble Street, Dublin,
c. AD 1000 (photo:
National Museum of
Ireland).

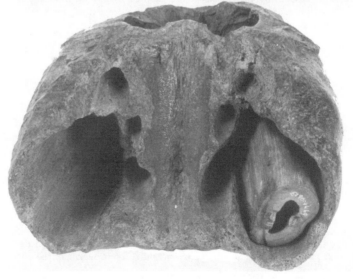

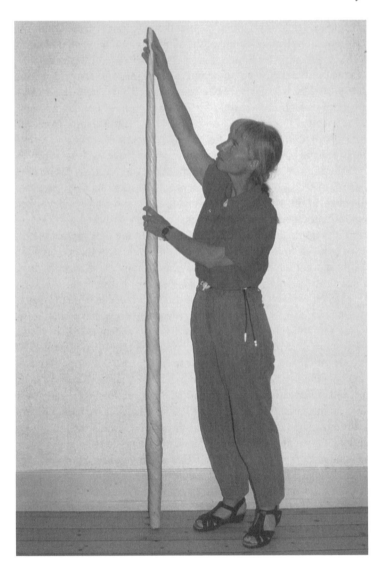

Figure 5. Modern narwhal tusk. Length *c.* 220cm (photo: Kjeld Stevns Jensen 1992).

149

Norway, probably in Trondheim (Stratford 1997, 41); one in Roskilde or somewhere else in Sjælland, in Denmark (Liebgott 1985); one in Canterbury (Beckwith 1972); and one in Cologne (Kölner Schatzbaukasten 1997).

Archaeological finds of workshop debris demonstrate that the material was also carved in other places, although products may have been merely plain pieces. Such waste occurs, as well as in Greenland (G. Nyegaard, pers. comm.), at Hedeby and Ribe in Jutland; Lund in Skåne; Sigtuna in central Sweden, and Trondheim in western Norway. In western Europe waste has been identified in Canterbury, Dublin and Cologne (Roesdahl 1998, 26-39) providing nice confirmation of the workshops identified by art historians. When dated, the waste is from the eleventh to thirteenth centuries—the heyday of the interest in walrus ivory.

There is also interesting evidence of the fascination for complete tusks and for the animal itself: frontals of walrus skulls, which have been found in many places where walrus ivory was appreciated. Few other skeletal parts of walrus have been found, save some penis bones. I have information on such skulls (or large fragments of skulls) from the bishop's seat at Gardar in Greenland, from Trondheim, Bergen and Oslo in Norway, from Uppsala and

Sigtuna in Sweden, from Lund and Schleswig, in what was then Denmark, from Dublin in Ireland (fig. 4) and from Novgorod in Russia. Some of the skulls are ornamented, and a few carry a runic inscription. They were almost certainly hunting trophies or exotica for display; written sources tell that skulls with tusks were sometime used as prestigious gifts (Grieg 1933, 380-85; Roesdahl 1998, 19-22). It has recently been noticed that there is an ornamented skull which retains both tusks in the museum in Le Mans, central France; one tusk has a runic inscription which reads, 'Orm Goat(?) owns this skull' (information from and preliminary reading by Marie Stoklund, National Museum of Denmark).

There was, as I hope I have shown, an enormous demand for walrus ivory in Scandinavia and Western Europe during part of the Middle Ages, and a great fascination concerning this strange animal. Archaeological finds increasingly illuminate the story of walrus ivory; from the slaughter of the walrus in Greenland to the much admired decorated objects in Trondheim, Lund, Canterbury, Cologne or Paris.

Narwhal tusk (figs 5-6) was in many ways a different matter. Today the narwhal is normally killed by Inuit in the open sea from a kayak, or at breathing holes in the ice, and the Norse in Greenland probably did not have the technical ability to hunt this mammal. It is, therefore, reasonable to suppose that the Norse acquired tusks by barter from the Inuit (Rosing 1986, 17, 51ff., 66ff.), possibly in the manner described in the Vinland sagas (Magnusson and Pálsson 1965, 65, 99). Narwhal tusks may, consequently, have been difficult for the Greenland Norse to obtain; indeed there is hardly any evidence of it in Norse contexts there, save for some narwhal skulls buried with the walrus skulls already mentioned at Gardar. It has, however, recently been proposed by Jørgen Meldgaard that a long-known unusual stone building, the so-called 'Bear-trap' on the north side of Disko Bay, was used for storing narwhal tusks and other valuables: its location, construction, size and inner arrangements would fit such an interpretation (Meldgaard 1995). Whatever the case, unicorn horns in European treasuries must have come mainly from Greenland, as this mammal lives chiefly in the waters west of Greenland, and it is abundantly clear that the tusks were extremely valuable. To sell one in Europe must have been like striking gold—a horn belonging to Elizabeth I of England was in 1598 valued at £10.000.

A systematic study of the information on these tusks is not yet available. They were, however, among the most coveted exotica in European treasuries and are occasionally mentioned in written sources (see, for example, Bernström 1975; Quak 1984; Rosing 1986; Bencard 1989a; Bauer *et al.* 1991, no. 138; Cherry 1995a). Most tusks seem to have been left unworked, though sometimes mounted for display, but two of uncertain provenance (perhaps from Lincoln Cathedral; one of them is now in the Victoria and Albert Museum), are finely carved in Romanesque style. Smaller pieces would be used for testing food and drink for poison. The preserved tusks include one in the Imperial Treasury at Vienna (a splendid two and a half meters long horn). Others are in St Marco in Venice, in Utrecht (one of which has a runic inscription, the reading of which is uncertain) and in the Cluny Museum in Paris. A bishop's staff of *c.* 1200 of narwhal tusk with crozier-head of ivory comes from Roskilde Cathedral in Denmark. One of the earliest references is to a horn owned by Edward I of England *c.* 1300, which was stolen, but then recovered. The earliest reference in France is to a horn owned by Charles VI in 1388. The Duc de Berry also owned one, as did Lorenzo il Magnifico in Florence and other men of fame.

To conclude, the reason why the Greenland settlements flourished during the eleventh to thirteenth centuries is probably best understood through the many walrus ivory carvings now found throughout European and American museums, and through the waste material and the skulls found in increasing numbers in northern and western Europe—a very small part of what once existed. One of the important reasons for the abandonment of Norse settlement in Greenland must be that the demand for its most valuable commodity, walrus tusk, vanished during the fourteenth century. To flood the market with unicorn horns would not

Figure 6. Lady with unicorn. Detail of tapestry from the series 'La Dame et la licorne'. Flanders, late 15th century (photo: Le Musée de Cluny, Paris).

151

have solved the problem, even if lots of horns could have been acquired; such an expansion would have broken the unicorn myth and the market would have collapsed.

From the very beginning of the Norse settlement of Greenland it became obvious that the export of northern exotica was of crucial importance. The travels to Vinland—voyages for 'fame and fortune', as told in *Grœnlendinga saga*—were almost certainly also undertaken in order to investigate what unknown exotica suitable for the European market might be found in these vast unknown lands. Here they found nothing important of that; the land of 'wines and grapes' could provide timber, iron, furs, good land and hostile *skraelingar*. The Norse decided not to settle.

ABBREVIATIONS

Hungrvaka   Loth, A., trans., 1989. *To islandske bispekrøniker, oversat med indledning, noter og efterord*, Odense.

King's Mirror   Jónsson, F., trans., 1926. *Kongespejlet. Konungs Skuggsjá*, Copenhagen.

Two voyagers   Lund, N. and Fell, C., ed. and trans. 1984. *Two voyagers at the Court of King Alfred: the ventures of Ohthere and Wulfstan*, York.

Else Roesdahl

BIBLIOGRAPHY

Arneborg, J. 2000. 'Greenland and Europe', in Fitzhugh and Ward 2000, 304-17.

Bauer, R. *et al.* 1991. *Kunsthistorisches Museum Vienna. The Secular and Ecclesiastical Treasuries*, Vienna.

Baxter, R. 1995. 'Review of *The Cloisters Cross. Its Art and Meaning,* by E.C. Parker and C.T. Little, 1994', *The Antiquaries Journal*, 75 (Book Review Supplement), 71-72.

Beckwith, J. 1972. *Ivory Carvings in Early Medieval England*, London.

Bencard, M. 1989a. 'Enhjørninger, narhvaler og gamle grønlændere', *MIV. Museerne i Viborg amt*, 13, 114-25.

——1989b. 'Two 17th-century Eskimos at Rosenborg Palace', *Meddelelser om Grønland, Man and Society*, 12, 47-55.

Bernström, J. 1975. 'Valar', *Kulturhistorisk Leksikon for Nordisk Middelalder* XIX, Copenhagen, col. 439-54.

Cherry, J. 1995a. 'Unicorns', in Cherry 1995b, 44-71.

——ed., 1995b. *Mythical Beasts,* London.

Choyke, A.M. and Bartosiewicz, L., eds, 2001. *Crafting Bone: Skeletal Technologies through Time and Space.* London: BAR International Series 937.

De Boe, G. and Verhaeghe, F., eds, 1997. *Material culture in Medieval Europe. Papers of the 'Medieval Europe Brugge 1997 Conference'*, vol. 7, Zellik.

Fitzhugh, W. and Ward, E., eds, 2000. *Vikings. The North Atlantic Saga*, Washington, D.C.

Gaborit-Chopin, D. 1978. *Ivoires du Moyen Age*, Fribourg. (German edition, 1978, *Elfenbeinkunst im Mittelalter*, Berlin.)

——1992. 'Walrus ivory in Western Europe', in Roesdahl and Wilson 1992, 204-5.

Goldschmidt, A. 1914-26. *Die Elfenbeinskulpturen,* vols I-IV, Berlin (new edn Berlin 1969-75).

Grieg, S. 1933. *Middelalderske byfund fra Bergen og Oslo*, Oslo.

Kristjánsson, L. 1986. *Íslenzkir Sjávarhættir* V, Reykjavík.

Kölner Schatzbaukasten. Die Grosse Kölner Beinschnitzwerkstatt des 12. Jahrhunderts, 1997, Mainz.

Liebgott, N.K. 1985. *Elfenben fra Danmarks Middelalder*, Copenhagen.

MacGregor, A. 1985. *Bone, Antler, Ivory and Horn. The Technology of Skeletal Materials Since the Roman Period*, London.

Magerøy, E.M. 1993. 'Carving: Bone, horn, and walrus tusk', in Pulsiano 1993, 66-71.

Magnusson, M. and Pálsson, H., trans, 1965. *The Vinland Sagas. The Norse Discovery of America*, London.

Meldgaard, J. 1995. 'Eskimoer og Nordboer i Det yderste Nord', *Nationalmuseets Arbejdsmark*, 1995, 199-214.

Muus, B. *et al.* 1981. *Grønlands fauna*, Copenhagen.

Parker, E.C. and Little, C.T. 1994. *The Cloisters Cross. Its Art and Meaning*, New York.

Pulsiano, P. ed., 1993. *Medieval Scandinavia: An Encyclopedia*, New York and London.

Quak, A. 1984. 'Eine nordische Runeninschrift in Utrecht', *Amsterdamer Beiträge zur älteren Germanistik*, 21, 73-83.

Roesdahl, E. 1995. *Hvalrostand, elfenben og nordboerne i Grønland,* Odense.

——1998. 'L'ivoire de morse et les colonies norroises du Groenland', *Proxima Thulé*, 3, 9-48.

Roesdahl, E. and Wilson, D.M., eds, 1992. *From Viking to Crusader: Scandinavia and Europe 800-1200*, Copenhagen.

Rosing, J. 1986. *Havets enhjørning*, Højbjerg.

Smirnova, L. 1997. 'Antler- and bone-working in Nerevsky and Lyudin ends of Medieval Novgorod. Evidence from Waste Analysis', in De Boe and Verhaeghe 1997, 137-46.

——2001. 'Utilization of rare bone materials in medieval Novgorod', in Choyke and Bartosiewicz 2001, 9-15.

Stratford, N. 1997. *The Lewis Chessmen and the Enigma of the hoard*, London.

Tegengren, H. 1962. 'Valrosstanden i världshandeln', Helsingfors: *Nordenskiöld-samfundets Tidsskrift* XXII, 3-37.

Section Two:
Society, Culture and Settlement

The Vikings—Saints or Sinners?

Magnus Magnusson KBE

Keynote Address, St Anthony, 18 September 2000

Saints or Sinners, eh? The vikings? Well, ask a silly question and you might well get a few silly answers. A few years ago, this would have been thought a silly question to pose, a positively unrealistic question to pose—unless you were one of those charitable folk who felt instinctively that the vikings were innocent, peace-loving gentlemen of leisure who were quite extraordinarily lucky in what they found fallen off the back of a long-ship.

It's all changed now. The vikings are in vogue. Indeed, the vikings are a vogue in themselves, especially here in North America. In 2000, we have had this prestigious Viking Millennium International Symposium. We have had the magnificent exhibition entitled 'Vikings: the North Atlantic Saga' at the Smithsonian Institute in Washington, in New York, and at the Museum of Civilisation in Hull, Québec. Indeed, *Time-Canada* devoted much space to an article about 'The Amazing Vikings' designed to rehabilitate (or even white-wash) those 'violent brutes' of history whose reputation, according to *Time-Canada*, has been 'wildly skewed': 155

> The Vikings were indeed raiders, but they were also traders whose economic network stretched from today's Iraq all the way to the Canadian Arctic. They were democrats who founded the world's oldest surviving parliament [in Iceland, let me smugly add] while Britain was still mired in feudalism. They were master metalworkers, fashioning exquisite jewellery from silver, gold and bronze. Above all, they were intrepid explorers whose restless hearts brought them to North America some 500 years before Columbus.

So that's all right, then. Vikings Rule OK.

This encomium contrasts quite vividly with the outraged rhetoric written eight centuries ago in the *Irish* equivalent of *Time-Canada*. The twelfth-century Irishman who wrote it, who had clearly been kissing the Blarney Stone with unbridled passion, called his dispatch, *Cogadh Gáedhel re Gallaibh* ('War of the Irish with the Foreigners'):

> In a word, although there were an hundred hard-steeled iron heads on every neck, and an hundred sharp, ever-ready, never-rusting brazen tongues in every head, and an hundred garrulous, loud unceasing voic-es from every tongue, they could not recount, nor narrate, nor enumerate, nor tell, what all the people of Ireland suffered in common, both men and women, laymen and priests, old and young, noble and ignoble, of hardship and injury and oppression from these ruthless, wrathful, foreign, purely pagan peo-ple (Todd 1867).

In a word! Some word! Even for an Irishman.

It was this sort of spluttering and gibbering which helped to inspire the perception of the vikings as a race of cruel and bloodthirsty assassins, intent only on plundering the wealth of a serenely Christian Europe, delighting only in rape and pillage and murder. To the liter-ate monks of the medieval church, the vikings were pagan devils, anti-Christ personified: men without mercy or morality who died as brutally and carelessly as they had lived, imbued with a ferocious faith in manic war-gods and a blind fatalism which inured them to the prospect of death.

The trouble is that the vikings became the victims of their own success. In a turbulent age when violence and piracy and casual raiding and cattle-rustling were endemic all over Europe (including Ireland), the vikings happened to be better at it than the rest, mainly because of their marvellous ships; and they paid the price by being given an extremely bad press. History is written by the victors, as we know, and ultimately the vikings were not the victors. And anyway the vikings were more or less illiterate at the time.

When the 'vikings' (and I am vainly trying to have that word stricken from the English language)—when the Scandinavians, I prefer to say, became fully literate, the Viking Age as a historical period (AD 800-1100) was over. And I fear we can blame my ancestors, the Icelanders, in their medieval sagas for giving a boost to the lurid reputation of the vikings. Iceland had never been a viking nation as such; it had never launched armed expeditions against other countries; as a republic it had never been ruled by kings with covetous designs on the lands and resources of their wealthy neighbours. Individual Icelanders had joined foreign courts and occasionally taken part in viking raids as mercenaries, but that was all.

The Icelandic sagas were not written until the thirteenth century. By that time the early pioneering days of Settlement had become a golden memory. The young Icelanders who had gone abroad to prove their mettle and seek fame and fortune were regarded as models of heroism and valour. The viking life was regarded with nostalgic hindsight as an open-air university of the manly arts, something to which every youngster worth his salt aspired.

In what one would call the 'classical' Icelandic sagas of the thirteenth century, the *Íslendingasögur* or so-called 'Family Sagas' like *Njáls saga*, *Laxdœla saga* and *Egils saga Skalla-Grímssonar*, the problems of law and order in a pioneering society were explored in an outpouring of intellectual creativity which is one of the great marvels of medieval literature. Later on, however, in the fourteenth and fifteenth centuries, the sagas degenerated into a genre known as 'Legendary Sagas' (*Fornaldarsögur* or *lýgisögur*—'Lying Sagas'—as they were called); these were mostly set in pre Viking-Age days. Their writers revelled in fantasy and folklore and buckets of gore. These were the horror comics of their day and you will not be surprised to hear that they were immensely popular, although the sterner literary critics tut-tut over them.

The literature of the north was re-discovered in Britain in the nineteenth century and found immediate favour with the general public. They lapped up the blood-and-thunder aspects of the viking world. How they loved their Gothic horrors—think of the Dracula vogue, and of Mary Shelley writing *Frankenstein*. The Victorians shuddered with delight at all the stories of carving blood-eagles on their victims' backs, and drinking blood from the skulls of defeated enemies, and wearing silly helmets adorned with bull's horns. Like Wagner, they loved the idea of Amazonian warrior-maidens, the Valkyries, 'Choosers of the Slain', who waltzed around on Óðinn's eight-legged steed Sleipnir deciding warriors' destinies in battle and carting them off to Valhalla to spend the rest of eternity roistering and brawling until the Last Trump.

On a rather higher level, the 'discovery' of Iceland and its medieval literature had a considerable impact on the 'thinking' Victorian. Let me illustrate this from the cultural contributions of two eminent Victorians. One was the historian and social philosopher Thomas Carlyle, the author of *Sartor Resartus* and the monumental *History of Frederick the Great*; the other was the socialist artist-craftsman and pre-Raphaelite poet, William Morris, the first major translator of the Icelandic sagas. Carlyle and Morris found in the saga and Edda literature of Iceland totally differing social messages for their own crusades to the Victorian people. Each discovered in the sagas something spiritual which they felt their 'modern age' needed.

Thomas Carlyle, in a celebrated essay in 1840 entitled 'On Heroes, Hero-Worship and the Heroic in History', enunciated his cure for the sceptical age which had explained away everything which had once been an object of reverent and innocent wonder. He found his ideal Great Man in Óðinn, the All-Father of the Norse pantheon, patron god of poetry and the Lord of the Slain—the poet-prophet sensitive to the mysteries of the universe, the firm-willed man of action, the saviour of his people. In Carlyle's eyes, Óðinn was the emblem of the strong, inspired leader his country required; while Óðinn's worshippers, those 'strong sons of nature', were the epitome of admiring, trusting, unquestioning obedience.

For William Morris, on the other hand, this kind of benevolent despotism to provide the smack of firm government was absolute anathema. To Morris, the Norseman was the emblem of the hard-working socialist who respected individuality but had no time for individualism; the Norsemen of the sagas personified resilient acceptance of life's hazards, stoic defiance of personal suffering and an unflinching defence of liberty and independence

And thus, lo and behold, the viking sinners had suddenly been imbued with virtues which I wager had never occurred to them as being theirs.

So now, having sorted out the vikings as sinners, I want to turn your attention to the viking saints (yes, there *were* some, I assure you). And I intend to close my talk by bringing to your attention a woman who I think *should* be regarded as a saint—an Icelandic housewife who became the farthest-travelled woman in the world a thousand years ago—Guðríður Þorbjarnardóttir, mother of the first European child born in North America.

Practically every Scandinavian country can boast a 'viking' saint or two. Sweden has a royal saint from the twelfth century, of whom little is known for certain: King Erik Jedvardsson (his father's name suggests English decent somewhere along the line: Jedvard > Edward). He is one of the two patron saints of Sweden, but has been almost totally eclipsed by the eminent St Birgitta (Bridget) of the fourteenth century, a formidable power-broker in royal circles who founded the Bridgettine Order and was canonised in 1391. Poor St Erik Jedvardsson doesn't even merit a mention in the *Oxford Dictionary of Saints*; but he is said to have led an armed 'crusade' into Finland to convert the population there to Christianity. He is also said to have got his come-uppance by being been murdered by a Danish prince during divine service at Uppsala on Ascension Day, 1160. His death was regarded as martyrdom, and from the spot on which his blood was spilled a spring gushed forth. He was never formally canonised, but he was much venerated as a national saint of the Swedes, especially by the people of Stockholm, who 'appropriated' him from Uppsala.

157

Iceland has a couple of canonised bishops lurking in the undergrowth of medieval church history. If the Swedes are feeling miffed at the *Oxford Dictionary of Saints*, what about us Icelanders? Oxford doesn't mention either of them. They were both early bishops of the Icelandic church—Bishop Þorlákur Þórhallsson and Bishop Jón Ögmundsson—and much as I like them I cannot by any stretch of semantics call them 'viking' bishops and so, regretfully, I feel I ought to give them a miss on this occasion.

Denmark, too, has a viking saint of sorts, from right at the end of the Viking Age—Knud II, who reigned, rather briefly, from 1080-86 and was murdered by his fractious subjects at the altar of the cathedral in Odense which he had just founded. Knud had his eye on the throne of England and had raised taxes steeply to finance an invasion. No one ever becomes popular through raising taxes, and Knud got the chop. But miracles were soon reported at his tomb in Odense, and in 1101 the Pope was persuaded to canonise him.

I must confess that I believe that the Pope canonised the wrong Knud. My candidate would have been his much more illustrious uncle and predecessor, Knútr *mikli*, better known in English as Canute/Cnut the Great, king of Denmark, England and Norway in the first half of the eleventh century, when he welded these countries under one crown into a viking empire of the North Sea. His reign (1016-35) gave England nearly twenty years of sorely-needed peace, and new laws which emphasised justice and the rights of individuals.

His mortal remains are said to be interred in one of the six mortuary chests which rest in Winchester Cathedral, on whose altar he had once hung up his gold crown in humility to the only true king of mankind, Jesus Christ.

And while we are on that subject, do you know *why* he hung up his crown there? It's a fascinating little story which I cannot resist telling you. It is to do with the only thing which people think they know about Canute—his apparent attempt to turn back the tide; and that gives me the chance of doing some late proselytising for him.

The story of 'Canute and the Waves' was first recorded a century after his death by the English chronicler Henry of Huntingdon. He wrote that when Canute was at the height of his political power he gave orders for his throne to be placed on the seashore as the tide came in. He seated himself upon the throne at the water's edge, surrounded by a group of puzzled courtiers. And he said to the rising tide, according to Henry of Huntingdon:

> 'You are within my jurisdiction, and the land on which I sit is mine; no one has ever resisted my command with impunity. I therefore command you not to rise over my land, and not to presume to wet the king's feet and legs without respect.' But the sea rose as usual, and wetted the king's feet and legs without respect.

That is about as much of the story as most people know, getting the impression that Canute had grown much too big for his boots, which got a good soaking in consequence. But in Henry of Huntingdon's version the story didn't end there; that is only the first half. The second half of the story makes it quite clear that the king intended the tide to give him a wetting, as an object lesson in humility for the benefit of the assembled courtiers. It goes on:

> And so the king jumped back on to dry land, and said, 'Be it known to all inhabitants of the world that the power of kings is empty and superficial, and that no one is worthy of the name of king except for Him whose will is obeyed by Heaven, earth and sea in accordance with eternal laws.'

And with that he took off his golden crown and never put it on his head again. Poor old Canute! Throughout his reign he had courted the Church zealously as the only institution which could reconcile the long-standing and virulent ethnic tensions between 'vikings' and Anglo-Saxons. The ecclesiastical sources speak glowingly of his generosity, his humility, his devotion to Christianity. To a nation exhausted with horrors he brought balm; to a land saturated with blood he brought security from external attack; to a realm which had lost all confidence in kingship he restored respect for the crown. Those whom he trusted, prospered; those whom he did not, died. Yet he is popularly remembered only for a vainglorious attempt to turn back the tide! I reckon the English have never forgiven him for being a Dane.

Norway has perhaps the most celebrated viking saint of them all: Óláfr *inn helgi* Haraldsson (Óláfr the Stout as he was known during his lifetime), whose cult spread remarkably quickly throughout the northlands and across the North Sea to England.

I rather like old St Óláfr. He had been a professional viking (a real one) since the age of 12, fighting all over the viking world from the Baltic to the Thames in England. He fought in Normandy as well, and it was in Rouen that he was converted to Christianity.

His claim to the throne of Norway was as tenuous as those of most other viking pretenders to thrones. However, he managed to seize it in 1015, and for the whole of his reign he was intent on converting his fellow-Norwegians to Christianity with ruthless single-mindedness. Those who opposed him were either killed, or maimed, or blinded. And it worked. Norway became a country governed by church authorities no less than by the crown.

Eventually, Óláfr was driven from the throne by his disaffected nobles in league with foreign powers—in this case, our old friend Canute. He took refuge in Sweden, and in 1030 he came back, leading a rag-tag peasant army to try to win back his crown. The fateful battle took place on a day of high summer at Stiklestad in the Trøndelag in northern Norway, its sunshine dimmed by a solar eclipse. The result was a foregone conclusion. Óláfr's motley muster numbered fewer than 4,000 men; facing him was the largest host ever assembled in Norway.

We are told that battle was joined just before half past one; by three o'clock it was all over. Óláfr's men surged forward, desperately shouting their war-cry of *Fram, fram, Kristsmenn, krossmenn, kongungsmenn* ('Forward, forward, Christ's-men, cross-men, king's-men'); but they broke almost at once and were routed. The king fought on with ferocious courage, but as the sky darkened ominously he was brought to bay with his back against a rock, and was cut down by three fearsome blows to leg, belly and neck. Around him the men of his shield-wall, scorning flight or surrender, fought to the last.

After the carnage of Stiklestad was over, the king's body was spirited away from the scene; and at once the miracles began. A wounded courtier who wiped the blood from the king's face and covered his body had his injuries instantly healed. A blind man who, that night, accidentally rubbed his eyes with the water in which the king's body had been washed, had his sight restored.

Within two years an Óláfr cult had sprung up. The patriotic warrior-hero had been transformed through death into a martyr and national saint. His body was exhumed and found to be uncorrupted. Very soon the centuries of pilgrimage to his shrine in Trondheim had begun.

But during his lifetime, the posthumously sainted Óláfr had manifestly been doing some sinning on the side—especially with a young lady named Álfhildr. The fruit of that liaison was a baby son who was the first Scandinavian to bear the hallowed name of 'Magnús'. And this is how it came about, according to Snorri Sturluson's 'History of the Kings of Norway' known familiarly as *Heimskringla*:

159

There was a woman named Álfhildr, who was called the king's concubine; but she was of good birth, and very beautiful, and she was at King Óláfr's court. That spring [the spring of 1024] it became apparent that Álfhildr was with child, and the king's confidantes knew that he was the father. One night, Álfhildr went into labour. There were very few people at hand, just some women and a priest and an Icelander named Sighvatr, who was one of the king's court poets, and one or two others. It was a very difficult birth, and Álfhildr nearly died. Eventually she gave birth to a boy-child, and for a while no one knew whether there was any life in the infant.

When the child at last started to draw breath, but very feebly, the priest asked Sighvatr the Poet to go and tell the king.

Sighvatr replied, 'I don't care to wake the king on any account, for he has forbidden anyone to disturb his sleep until he wakes up of his own accord.'

The priest said, 'But it is essential that the child should be baptised at once. I do not think it has any chance of surviving.'

Sighvatr replied, 'Rather than wake the king, I would rather take the risk of baptising the child: I shall take the responsibility for giving him a name.'

So the child was baptised, and christened Magnús. Next morning, when the king arose, he was told what had taken place during the night, and thereupon had Sighvatr summoned to his presence.

'How dare you have my child baptised without my knowledge?' he thundered.

'Because,' replied Sighvatr, 'I preferred to give two souls to God rather than one to the Devil.'

'What do you mean?' asked the king.

Sighvatr replied, 'The child was at death's door, sire, and if he had died unbaptised he would have belonged to the Devil; but now his soul belongs to God. And secondly, I knew that if you were so angry with me that you had me put to death, I reckoned that if I lost my life on this account I, too, would belong to God.'

The king said, 'But why did you name the boy Magnús? That is not a family name.'

Sighvatr replied, 'I named him after the Emperor Charlemagne, Carolus Magnus; for to my mind he is the greatest man the world has ever seen.'

Whereupon the king said, 'You are a man of remarkably good luck, Sighvatr. It is hardly surprising that luck should go with good brains; but it is odd that good luck can also attend men with no brains at all, so that witless schemes can turn out well.'

And with that the king was now well pleased.

I'm glad to report that the baby not only survived but did very well, despite his fraught beginnings. As a six-year-old boy he was smuggled to Russia after his father was killed at Stiklestad in 1030, and brought back to Norway by popular acclaim to assume the throne in 1035, at 11 years of age. He had a brief but busy reign, and by the time he fell ill and died during a military campaign in Denmark in 1047 at the age of 23 he had acquired the sobriquet of Magnús *góði*—Magnús the Good. And with that, 'Magnús' became a common and fortunate name in the northlands.

Indeed, another viking Magnús also became a saint—Magnús Erlendsson, Norse Earl of Orkney in the early twelfth century, when the earldom of Orkney was still a great power in the politics of the north. The story of how he became a saint is marvellously told in one of the Icelandic sagas, *Orkneyinga saga* (Saga of the Men of Orkney). The saga does not stint the superlatives about my namesake:

> St Magnús, Earl of Orkney, was a man of extraordinary distinction, tall, and with a fine, intelligent look about him. He was a man of strict virtue, successful in war, wise, eloquent, generous and magnanimous, open-handed with money, sound with advice, and altogether the most popular of men. He was gentle and agreeable when talking to men of wisdom and goodwill, but severe and uncompromising towards thieves and vikings, putting to death most of the men who plundered the farms and other parts of the earldom. He had murderers and robbers arrested, and punished the rich no less than the poor for their robberies, raids and other transgressions (OS, 89-90).

No doubt about it—this was a saint in the making:

> He lived according to God's commandments, mortifying the flesh through an exemplary way of life in many ways which, though revealed to God, remained hidden from the sight of men (OS, 90).

160

In only one aspect of his blameless life would I find a little fault: he married a Scottish girl named Ingigerður with whom he lived, according to *Orkneyinga saga*, 'for ten years without allowing either to suffer by way of their lusts, and so remaining chaste, without stain of lechery. Whenever the urge of temptation came upon him, he would plunge into cold water and pray to God for aid' (OS, 90). It is not recorded what his wife thought about this ultra-ascetic behaviour; but sometimes I am tempted to think that being a saint's wife must have been a darned sight harder than being a saint.

It is because of Earl Magnús Erlendsson that we now have in Kirkwall, the capital town of the Orkneys, the most impressive and enduring viking monument in the British Isles: St Magnus Cathedral, founded in 1137—a handsome, solid building of red sandstone glowing warmly in the northern sun.

It came about because early in the twelfth century the earldom of Orkney was shared between two cousins, two joint earls, Magnús Erlendsson and Hákon Pálsson. Tension soon developed between the two earls. After two years of feuding and squabbling they agreed to hold a peace-meeting to try to resolve their differences and come to an agreement over the future of the earldom.

The site chosen for the summit meeting was the tiny island of Egilsay, just off the east coast of the Mainland of Orkney, shortly before Easter; the year, as far as we can tell, was 1117. Each earl agreed to bring only two ships and an equal number of men, and they both swore binding oaths to keep whatever terms might be agreed between them.

Earl Magnús and his men set off in their two longships, rowing across a calm and sunlit sea. Suddenly, from nowhere, a huge breaker reared up over the ship the earl was steering and crashed down over him. No one had ever seen anything like it before.

'I think,' said Magnús, 'that this forebodes my death.' Deeply disturbed by this ominous occurrence his men urged him not to trust Earl Hákon, and to turn back, 'No,' said Magnús. 'On with the journey. Let it turn out as God wills'(OS, 92).

Earl Magnús was the first to reach Egilsay with two ship-loads of tried and trusted followers. But when they caught sight of Earl Hákon approaching across the sound late that evening, they saw that he had with him not *two* ships, but *eight*. Earl Magnús now realised that there was treachery afoot. He went up with his men to the church on Egilsay to pray, and there he spent the night.

There is a hauntingly beautiful ruined church on Egilsay today, situated high in the centre of the island, and conspicuous for its tall round tower at the west end of the nave. It is not the church in which Earl Magnús spent his last night on earth, although it may well stand on the same site; this one was built in the middle of the twelfth century in honour of his memory after his sanctity was formally recognised. It has a barrel-vaulted chancel at the east end, and above it there used to be an apartment known as the 'Grief House'; this is not a poignant reminder of Magnús and his vigil on Egilsay (although one feels it ought to be), but a corruption of the Old Norse word *grið*, meaning 'sanctuary'.

On that fateful night, Earl Magnús's men offered to defend him with their lives. 'No,' said Magnús, 'I do not want to put your lives at risk for my sake; and if there is not to be peace between us kinsmen, then be it as God wills'(OS, 93). He already seemed to have foreknowledge of the allotted hours of his life-span, and would neither flee nor shrink from a meeting with his enemies.

Early next morning Earl Hákon and his men hurried ashore and ran to the church and searched it, but found no trace of Earl Magnús, who had already gone to ground elsewhere on the island with two companions. He saw his enemies searching for him and called out to them, telling them where he was. When Earl Hákon and his men caught sight of him they rushed towards him with a great clamour and clangour of weapons.

The leaders parleyed. Earl Magnús offered his treacherous cousin three choices which would enable him to avoid violating his oaths by killing an innocent man. First, he offered to go on pilgrimage to Rome and never return to Orkney. This was refused. Then he offered to accept imprisonment for life in some dungeon in Scotland. This, too, was refused. Finally, Earl Magnús offered to accept mutilation and blinding, and then life-long incarceration.

161

Earl Hákon liked that idea, and accepted. But his lieutenants did not. 'We're going to kill one or other of you,' they said. 'From this day forward we're having no more joint rule'(OS, 94).

'Better kill [Magnús] then,' said Earl Hákon. 'I don't want an early death; I much prefer ruling over people and places'(OS, 94).

And so the die was cast. It is said that Earl Magnús was as blithe as if he had been invited to a feast, and uttered not a word of bitterness or anger.

Once it had been decided that Magnús was to die, Earl Hákon told his standard-bearer, a man named Ófeigr, to perform the execution, but Ófeigr angrily refused. So Hákon ordered his cook, Lífólfr, to kill Magnús. At that, Lífólfr began to sob loudly. But Earl Magnús said to him:

> 'This is nothing to weep over. A deed like this can only bring fame to the man who carries it out. Show yourself a man of spirit and you can have my clothes according to the old laws and customs…. Stand in front of me and strike me hard on the head', said Magnús, 'it's not fitting for a chieftain to be beheaded like a thief. Take heart, poor fellow, I've prayed that God grant you his mercy.' With that he crossed himself and stooped to receive the blow. So his soul passed away to Heaven (OS 94-5).

According to the saga, the place where Magnús was killed was rocky and overgrown with moss, but overnight it turned into a green and verdant field (OS, 95). The traditional site of the execution, about half a kilometre from the church, is now marked by an inscribed stone pillar.

And now politics came into play. Magnús had a nephew, Rögnvaldr Kali, who harboured ambitions for the earldom himself. In a shrewd move he vowed that if he ever became earl with the support of the people, he would build in his martyred uncle's memory the most magnificent minster in the Northern Isles. It was one of the few election promises in history which have been honoured to the letter.

But what of Magnús himself? When the cathedral in Kirkwall was ready for use, his relics were translated thither and enshrined 'above the high altar'. After that—silence. No more was heard of his remains.

Early in the nineteenth century a cache of bones was discovered in a crude cavity high up in the large pier of the *north* arcade of the choir, close to the original position of the high altar. It was popularly assumed that these must be the missing relics of St Magnús; others argued that they were more likely to be those of the cathedral's founder, Rögnvaldr Kali.

It was not until a hundred years later that the mystery was finally resolved. In March 1919 the cathedral's Clerk of Works was checking the stonework of the corresponding pier of the *south* arcade of the choir. He noticed that some of the facing-stones, high above floor-level, appeared to be loose. So he went up a ladder with his foot-rule, which he pushed into a crack between the stones. A long way in, it struck something which sounded like wood. And that was what it turned out to be. The loose stone was prised out, revealing a carefully excavated cavity behind the facade; and inside this cavity there lay a wooden casket made of oak, about 75 cm long.

When the casket was opened it was found to contain the skull and most of the bones of a man of medium height (about 170 cm), rather poorly developed physically, and aged between 25 and 35. What excited attention was the condition of the skull, because it brought irresistibly to mind the account of St Magnús's death in *Orkneyinga saga*—'Strike me hard on the head'. The skull had a clean-cut perpendicular gash through the parietal bones towards the back of the head, 'evidently produced by a swift blow from a heavy, sharp, cutting instrument such as an axe', according to the official report.

There was only one conclusion possible: the relics of St Magnús had been found at last. Presumably his bones had been hidden away in the pillar for safety during the time of the Protestant Reformation.

Every time I visit Kirkwall, I marvel at this brooding, wise old cathedral preserving its own saint in such security against all vicissitudes; and it delights me to know that in this most enduring of the monuments of the Viking Age in the British Isles, my namesake, Earl Magnús the Holy, still superintends those Northern Isles of Scotland which he had once ruled. Indeed, when a quiz programme called *Mastermind* which I presented for 25 years came to an end in 1997, I was allowed to choose the location for the final Final—and it had to be St Magnus Cathedral in Kirkwall.

Finally, ladies and gentlemen, as I promised, I want to talk about one of my very favourite women from the period which is of over-riding interest to all of us at this international symposium—the period of the expeditions to North America in search of Vínland. So I want you to accompany me, in your minds' eyes, to an eighteenth century farmstead, in Skagafjörður in the north of Iceland. Its name is *Glaumbær*, which means, literally, 'Merry-making Farm', and it was built on the site of the very first Glaumbær, back in the tenth century. It is one of Iceland's few surviving stone-and-turf-built farmhouses, and it now houses the Skagafjörður Folk Museum.

Inside, we can see what rural life in Iceland was like more than two centuries ago. A farmhouse was, in effect, a series of houses set side by side, with a linking passage inside; from a distance they looked like grassy mounds. The more substantial houses sported a row of carved wooden gables.

The only fireplace was in the kitchen; other rooms were not heated, apart from the *baðstofa* (literally, 'bathroom' or 'sauna'), but this one came to be used as a living-room and dormitory combined. It was an upper story room, so that the heat from the kitchen rose towards it; sometimes the cows were housed under the *baðstofa*; this added to the warmth. The better houses were often panelled with wood.

These houses provided the ideal atmosphere for the evening gatherings (*kvöldvökur*), when the paterfamilias would read sagas or homilies aloud, and the women would busy

162

themselves with carding, spinning and knitting while the menfolk carved utensils or repaired tools and farm equipment. Several generations lived together in the same house.

Outside the Glaumbær farmstead there is a fine monument carved by Iceland's outstanding twentieth-century sculptor, Ásmundur Sveinsson. It depicts a woman standing amidships in a stylised viking longship, gazing at far horizons. On her shoulder stands a small boy. The woman is Guðríðr Þorbjarnardóttir—Guðríðr, the daughter of Þorbjörn—and the boy is her son, Snorri: the child she bore in Vínland to her husband, Þorfinnr Karlsefni.

She was born in the west of Iceland around the year 950, as far as we can deduce; *Eiríks saga rauða* (ESR) describes her as 'very beautiful and a most exceptional woman in every respect'—a verdict with which posterity has no difficulty in agreeing. As a nubile girl in her early teens she emigrated with her father from Iceland to Greenland, a new country which had recently been colonised by Eiríkr *rauði*. In Greenland she married into the family of the first settler, but she was soon widowed and was married a second time, to a gallant and wealthy Icelandic merchant who had come to Greenland on a trading voyage. He had a sonorous name and by-name: Þorfinnr Karlsefni—the 'Makings of a Man'. With him she made an expedition to the fabled land of Vínland, somewhere in North America, which had been discovered, or glimpsed, or guessed at, some years before. The purpose of this large expedition—three ships, 160 people, and all the necessary livestock to provide for a self-sufficient, permanent settlement—was to colonise the New World, no less.

163

Where they went, and where they tried to settle, is a matter of feverish conjecture still. But wherever it was, Guðríðr arrived here in North America sometime soon after the beginning of the millennium we are celebrating this year—probably sometime between 1010 and 1020.

They reached the New World by taking the course followed by earlier explorers—across to Baffin Island, down past Labrador and then—where? Frankly, I don't think anyone knows. But wherever they went, in the first autumn Guðríðr gave birth somewhere over here to a boy named Snorri—the first European child born on this great continent, as far as can be ascertained. But their plans for permanent settlement were abandoned after three years, due mainly to the hostility of the aboriginal inhabitants. Guðríðr and her husband returned with their three-year-old son, first to Greenland and then, after a trading trip to Norway, back to Iceland, where they founded a dynasty whose fecund members still inhabit Iceland to this day.

To the medieval Icelandic writers Guðríðr's importance lay mainly in the fact that from her were descended no fewer than three Icelandic bishops who played a large part in Iceland's affairs in the thirteenth century. The accomplishments of a person's grandchildren or even more distant descendants may not impress us all that much nowadays (although I find myself changing my mind about this as time goes by!), but Guðríðr had some supernatural experiences which were unrelated to biological imperatives and which caught the imagination of the story-tellers as eminently worthy of recording.

When she was in Greenland as a young unmarried woman there came a period of severe famine. The local farmers hired a sibyl, a sorceress, to perform a pagan ritual to find out how the current hardships would last. Guðríðr was a Christian, but for the good of the community she was willing to use her knowledge of pagan lore which she had acquired in childhood from her old foster-mother; she was persuaded to sing some ancient songs ('Warlock songs', they were called) the sorceress required for her incantations. The forecast turned out well, and the old witch rewarded Guðríðr by prophesying a glorious destiny for her.

Later, in Vínland, just after the birth of her son, Guðríðr had another uncanny experience when the native Americans had started bartering with the would-be colonists. *Grænlendinga saga* (GLS) says:

> Guðríðr was sitting in the doorway beside the cradle of her son Snorri. A shadow fell across the door and a woman entered, wearing a black, close-fitting tunic; she was rather short, and had a head-band round her chestnut-coloured hair. She was pale, and had the largest eyes ever seen in a human head. She went to where Guðríðr was sitting and spoke.
> 'What is your name?' she asked.
> 'My name is Guðríðr. What is yours?'
> 'My name, too, is Guðríðr,' the woman replied (GLS 66).

At that moment there was a tremendous crash, and the woman disappeared: at the same instant one of the natives was killed for trying to steal the colonists' weapons. The apparition had presumably been Guðríðr's *fylgja*, her guardian angel, who had come to warn her of the dangers which lay ahead for her son and herself.

When Guðríðr returned to Iceland with her husband and child and settled at Glaumbær, her mother-in-law did not think her good enough for her son and refused to stay in the same house for the first year; but Guðríðr's manifest qualities soon won her over.

After Þorfinnr Karlsefni's death, Guðríðr went on a pilgrimage to Rome, which was quite a journey for those days. When she returned to Glaumbær she became a nun—one of the first women in Iceland known to have taken the veil. By that time she must have been the most widely-travelled woman in the world, having journeyed to the farthest corners of the known physical and spiritual world.

164 Yes, she was quite a woman, was Guðríðr. Iceland's most eminent scholarly expert on the Vínland saga texts, Ólafur Halldórsson, thinks that ESR should have been called *Guðríðar saga*! Indeed, Iceland's Nobel Prize-winning novelist, Halldór Laxness, refers to her in his novel *Íslands klukkan* ('Iceland's Bell'); it was set in the seventeenth century and concerned Iceland's great manuscript-collector, Árni Magnússon, and Laxness has Árni dreaming of making what would have been the find of a lifetime—some ancient manuscript which Guðríðr herself had written.

Don't we all! In my giddy youth I once embarked on a film script abut Guðríðr, which was set in a seminary in Rome and had Guðríðr telling the story of her adventures to one of her great-grandsons. It came to nothing, like so many of my more grandiose schemes. But in the summer of 2000, a book was published in Scotland called *The Sea Road*, by a Glasgow novelist named Margaret Elphinstone. And guess what? It is a retelling of the Vínland adventure from the viewpoint of Guðríðr, as transcribed by an Icelandic monk who had been commissioned to write up her life-story by his superiors in Rome!

So three cheers for Guðríðr Þorbjarnardóttir, that fascinating role-model for women from an earlier millennium. No viking sinner, she. She may never have been canonised—but she is surely as worthy of veneration as many another candidate who passed muster with one or other medieval Pope.

Ladies and gentlemen, I commend her to your earnest and affectionate attention as the saintly flavour of this momentous week of discussions and deliberations about Vínland.

ABBREVIATIONS

OS   Pálsson, H. and Edwards, P., trans, 1978. *Orkneyinga saga: the history of the Earls of Orkney*, London.

ESR   *Erik the Red's Saga,* in Magnusson, M. and Pálsson, H., trans, 1965. *The Vinland Sagas: The Norse Discovery of America*, London.

GLS   *Greenlanders' Saga,* in Magnusson, M. and Pálsson, H., trans, 1965. *The Vinland Sagas: The Norse Discovery of America*, London.

BIBLIOGRAPHY

Todd, J.H. ed. and trans., 1867. *Cogadh Gaedhel re Gaillaibh: The War of the Gaedhill with the Gaill, or, the Invasions of Ireland by the Danes and Other Norsemen*, London.

The later excavations at L'Anse aux Meadows

Birgitta Linderoth Wallace

W hen Helge and Anne Stine Ingstad announced, in the fall of 1961, that they had found a Norse settlement, few Norse scholars believed them. During the 120 years or so the Vínland sagas had been known in North America, numerous claims had been made of the finding of Vínland *hit goði*, and none had been able to withstand scrutiny. However, as subsequent excavations revealed more and more of the site, it became clear that the Ingstads had indeed uncovered a Norse settlement dating to the eleventh century, and still the only authenticated Norse settlement in the New World. As its historic significance came to be recognized, the Historic Sites and Monuments Board of Canada formally declared it a National Historic Site (fig. 1). It was also the first site to be proclaimed a UNESCO World Heritage Site.

As a National Historic Site, L'Anse aux Meadows (LAM) was acquired by the Government of Canada, under the management of Parks Canada. Because Parks Canada had no expertise in Norse archaeology, an International Advisory Committee was established consisting of the Ingstads, archaeologists from all the Nordic countries, a representative from Memorial University of Newfoundland, the Director of the Canadian National Museum of Man (now the Canadian Museum of Civilization), and Parks Canada staff. It was the purpose of the Committee to decide how the site should be protected and presented to the public, both essential aspects of Parks Canada's mandate. The International Advisory Committee found that there were still many unanswered questions about the site and recommended further excavations. How long had the site been occupied? What was its function? Was there a cemetery? Where had the iron been smelted? How had the topography been affected by factors such as land rise? Had the sedge bog beside the buildings been a lagoon when the Norse arrived? What was the relationship between the Norse settlement and the many Aboriginal cultures on the site? Anne Stine Ingstad declined leadership of the proposed excavations. Instead a Swedish archaeologist, Dr. Bengt Schonback, then Head of the Iron Age Department of the Swedish Museum of National Antiquities (Statens Historiska Museum, Stockholm), was chosen as their director. These excavations took place from 1973 to 1976. I served as his assistant during the first three excavation seasons. When Dr. Schonback returned to Sweden in 1975, I became the director of the final season of excavation. Most of the crew were from the local area, wonderful people who were among the best archaeological workers I have ever worked with. Their sharp eyesight and fine digging technique allowed them to recover items as small as strawberry seeds, *in situ*!

All of the areas between the buildings were excavated as well as significant sections of the sedge peat bog immediately west of the Norse houses (fig. 2). Extensive areas north of the Norse buildings, on the terrace closest to the shore and on the southern shore of Epaves Bay were also covered. In addition, the sphagnum bog east of the building terrace was tested, as well as areas along the brook, and north and south of the immediate site area. There were surveys via foot, helicopter, and aerial photography of the entire park area and nearby coves and islands. Bengt Schonback and Helge Ingstad also surveyed selected areas of both shores of the Northern Peninsula for Norse sites (Schonback field notes).

When the Ingstad expedition finished the excavation the Norse building ruins in 1962, the floors had been left open and covered with wooden sheds on the model of the Norse site Stöng in Iceland. The purpose was to preserve the building remains in their excavated condition and make them available to public viewing. Unlike Stöng, however, which is in a high, well-drained area, the LAM site is occasionally flooded by Black Duck Brook in the spring. The sheds became a trap for snow build-up in the winter, which, when melting, made

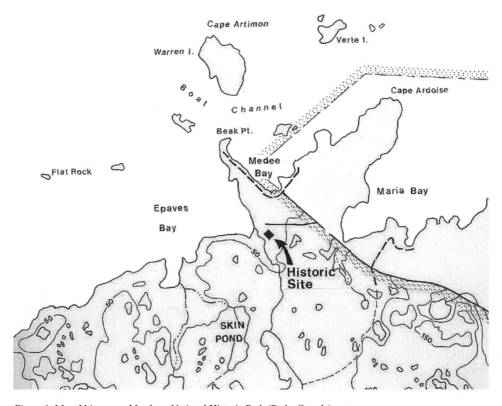

Figure 1. Map, L'Anse aux Meadows National Historic Park (Parks Canada).

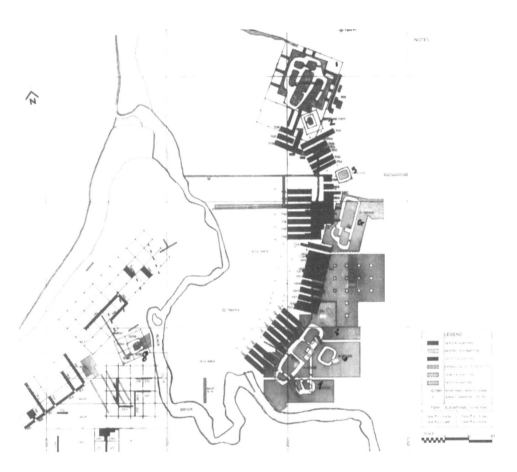

Figure 2. Map, the Parks Canada excavations (B. Gallant and B. Wallace).

Figure 3. Chart, radiocarbon dates of the Norse occupation.

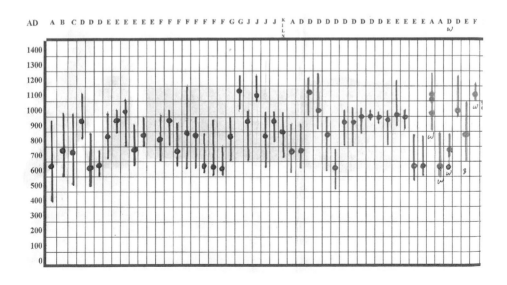

such flooding a yearly event. As a result, moss quickly formed over the excavated areas, disturbing the archaeological remains. On the advice of the International Advisory Committee, the sheds and moss were removed in 1975. The building ruins were subsequently sodded over and left more or less as found by the Ingstads.

The creation of LAM National Historic Park and the continued study came when financial resources were far more available than is the case today. To protect the site from modern encroachments a surrounding eighty-two square-kilometer area had been included in the new National Park, including Great Sacred Island to the north, South Road to the west, Foirou Island (a small island 4 km west of Cape Bauld) to the east, and Northwest Bay to the south. A wide range of natural science studies performed for Parks Canada on the entire area gave the archaeologists an exciting opportunity to incorporate ecological data: a geological study (Cummings 1974-1975); landrise study (Grant 1975); vegetation study (Pollett *et al.* 1975a; 1975b); fish inventory (Rombough *et al.* n.d.); bird inventory (Lamberton and Maunder 1976); sea mammal inventory (Northcott 1976); and a historical study (Matthews 1974). Summaries of these studies were published in 1977 by Paul Gimbarzevsky (1977) of the Department of Lands and Forests, Ottawa.

The past ecological setting was of vital interest, and, as excavation proceeded, an incredible amount of ancillary analyses followed: new faunal analyses (Rick 1977; Spiess 1990); additional pollen analyses (Mott 1974; Kuc 1975; McAndrews and Davis 1978; Davis 1985; Davis *et al.* 1988); seed analyses (Dawson 1976); shell analyses (Smith 1978); petrographic analyses (Pride 1978); soil analyses (Nowland 1977); and wood identifications of both worked and unworked wood (Douglas 1977; 1978a; 1978b; 1978c; 1979; Kuc 1973; Laflèche 1981; Laflèche and Douglas 1977; Moore 1978; Moore and Daley 1976; Perem 1974; 1978a; 1978b). An extensive phosphate analysis was also undertaken (McCawley 1973; 1975a; 1975b).

168

RESULTS
DATE OF OCCUPATION

Thanks to the high profile of LAM, we were also allowed to gather one of the highest number of radiocarbon dates determined for any site in the world at that time. An additional 118 dates were added to the 22 dates obtained by the Ingstad expedition, for a total of 140 dates, at the time when five or six dates per site was often considered sufficient. This sequence led to significant new insight into the nature of radiocarbon dates. About 50 of these pertain to the Norse occupation (fig. 3). They range in age from the seventh to eleventh century AD. This did not fit the archaeological data. The stratigraphy of the site was unequivocal that the Norse occupation had been one single, short-lived episode. How then could we explain the long range of dates?

From study of the individual dated pieces, it became clear that the nature of the samples influenced the dating. The age of a tree when cut is a primary factor. Depending on their origin within the tree, samples can indicate the earliest to the last years of a tree's life. Peat samples included grasses both older and younger than the event to be dated, as peat development had been slow and, at the time of the research, samples for dating had to be much larger than today. Finally, dates on sea mammal bone are unreliable because of the marine reservoir effect.

The wood age effect is amply illustrated. The oldest date comes from a spruce board worked with a metal broadaxe (fig. 4). It has an intercept date of AD 640±90 (S-1093). The board was found next to a small stake of Balsam fir with an intercept date of AD 980±65 (S-1093). Spruce can become very old, up to a thousand years in northern Sweden (Zachrisson 1979), and over six hundred years in Labrador (Jacoby and Ulan 1981). This particular board was cut from the very centre of the tree, hence the oldest section, and the sample submitted for dating was taken from the centre of that oldest part. Obviously it reflects the earliest date for the tree, not the time the board was produced. We looked at six dated samples (S-1111, 1113, 1118, 1340, 1355, 1357) from pieces which could not have been older than ten years, and, indeed, not only were the plus/minus factors generally short for these pieces, but the intercept dates lay close to AD 1000. The high profile of the LAM site also made it possible for us to take advantage of some of the earliest AMS dating in Canada, when the Icotrace laboratory in Toronto offered to run several dates for free. Here we had a new opportunity to test the effect of the wood age on small samples from young growth. Three samples in the Norse deposits were selected for AMS dating from young branches with about ten to twenty tree rings. The dates obtained were 1030±50, 990±30, and 1040±30 BP respectively (TO-117, 118, 119), confirming the general dating around AD 1000.

The radiocarbon dates are consistent with the architectural features of the buildings. Traits such as interior walls of sod, the placement of doors and fireplaces and number of rooms show that the structures could not have been built before the eleventh century.

LENGTH OF OCCUPATION

The small size of the middens indicates short occupation, the largest midden having been only about 3 by 4 m and 25 cm deep. Their insignificance becomes evident when compared to Niaqussat, a small farm in the West Settlement in Greenland (W48) occupied for about 350 years where the garbage deposits were 150 m long and about 1.5 to 1.7 m deep close to the house (McGovern and Bigelow 1977). To test if there had been large amounts of bone and ashes dumped from the houses on the bog side and dissolved from the acidity of the soils, Alexander Robertson (1978) performed chemical analyses of the peat. The results indicate that there was no chemical alteration of the peat in this area indicative of materials such as bone and ashes. Phosphate testing also indicates little alteration of the chemical composition of the soils beyond the actual garbage heaps on the terrace itself. The sparsity of artifacts

169

Figure 4. Photo, spruce board *in situ* (courtesy of Parks Canada; photo: C. Lindsay).

and shallow cultural deposits inside and outside the houses are also consistent with a short occupation.

Another indication of a short occupation is the lack of burial grounds, pagan or Christian. Pagan burials would likely have been in cairns or low mounds. Christian graves might have been visible as slight dips in the grounds, or more or less rectangular low mounds. One would also expect that burials from either religion would be in close proximity to the site, Christian ones perhaps within a walled cemetery. A rectangular feature north of the site, outlined by a low sod wall looked intriguingly as if it could have been such a cemetery. Excavation was begun with great anticipation, until Lloyd Decker, the caretaker for the site, informed us with some amusement that this was his old turnip garden! No cemeteries were found anywhere, in spite of extensive testing of areas from the southern shore of Epaves Bay to the present village. We therefore concluded that no burials existed and that settlement had been short.

Although the exact time of the Christianisation of Greenland cannot be determined, it is likely that the Norse had become Christian before their arrival in Greenland (Arneborg 2000, 311). Had any Christian died in such a far-away location as LAM, the body would probably have been brought back to Greenland for burial in consecrated ground. This is in line with the saga evidence in which a whole Vínland expedition is mounted by Þorsteinn simply to recover the body of his brother Þorvaldr (*Grænlendinga saga*).

170

RELATIONSHIP OF THE NORSE TO THE ABORIGINAL GROUPS ON THE SITE

Many Aboriginal groups were found to have occupied the site, both before and after the Norse. Most of the Aboriginal sites were simple tent floors, cooking pits, and linear fireplaces on the southern shore of the bay, but there were also Aboriginal fireplaces inside and outside the Norse houses. Several small hearths were found below the Norse hall D and immediately east of the building. Some of these were 5000 years old. Surveys in other coves show that there are Aboriginal sites all along the shore.

The earliest group was the Maritime Archaic, distinguished by diagnostic polished stone artifacts and a series of fireplaces east of and below the Norse hall D which was radiocarbon-dated to 5080±110 BP (Qu-365). Later Groswater Dorset people are marked by characteristic endblades and other chert artifacts encountered in and around hall D, and on the south shore of Epaves Bay. A harpoon shank of wood, radiocarbon-dated to 2795±100 (S-1094) from the bottom of the sedge peat bog, as well as a small fireplace, 'Feature 6', just north of hall F with a radiocarbon date of 2320±80 (S-1349) obtained after its excavation by the Ingstad expedition (Ingstad 1977, 102, 223), must also belong to this phase. Over all, the radiocarbon dates indicate parameters for Groswater Dorset of about 1000 to 400 BC (S-1094, 1116, 1117, 1130, 1341, 1344, 1349. 1356, 1359, 1360, 1362, 1363, 1748, 1749, 1754; GSC-1987; WAT-409). Middle Dorset were prevalent on the site *c.* AD 400-700 (Qu-360, 361; S-1096, 1097, 1100, 1122, 1124, 1126, 1168). Diagnostic artifacts of this date were primarily associated with a dense cluster of fireplaces and tent rings on the south shore of Epaves Bay at what would have been the water's edge at the time. These clusters were overlaid by a string of linear fireplaces associated with 'recent' Indian artifacts. Similar artifacts had been found by the Ingstad expedition in large firepits ('cooking pits' 1 and 2; Ingstad 1977, 56-58). Radiocarbon dates on charcoal from small twigs and branches indicated that the occupation had taken place in the ninth century (S-1098, 1099, 1121, 1123; T-365, 368; TO-116). From then, until the late twelfth or early thirteenth century there appear to have been no Aboriginal people on the site (Qu-348, 352, S-1129, 1166, 1167, 1354, 1361, 1364; GSC-2051; T-410). From this later period we find a habitation feature on the building terrace east of hall D, fireplaces on the shore terrace southwest of the Norse furnace hut, and a hut bottom west of hall F. They appear related to Point Revenge and proto- Beothuk.

Historical sources record that the French were present on the site from the seventeenth century until 1904, but the only evidence found on the Norse site from this period was a piece of a glass bottle and an iron nail. The French shore station was located on Beak (Colbourne) Point, separating Epaves Bay from Medee Bay, where brick ovens, tools and clay pipes have been found.

The fact that there were no Aboriginal people occupying the site in the eleventh century may have contributed to the choice of settlement here by the Norse. Later excavations at Bird Cove *c.* 125 km south of LAM have shown that there were Aboriginal people there close to the time of the Vinland voyages, but the radiocarbon dates are still too few and ambiguous to ascertain their presence in the eleventh century.

CLIMATE

The pollen analyses on monoliths from the bog, combined with radiocarbon dates, indicate that, at the time of the Norse presence, the climate was slightly warmer than now (McAndrews and Davis 1978; Davis 1985; Davis *et al.* 1988). They also show a severe climate deterioration beginning rather suddenly about 400 BC, a warming beginning around the eighth century AD, followed by another, less drastic, cooling period in the thirteenth century (see Bell, MacPherson and Renouf this volume).

171

TOPOGRAPHIC FEATURES

The pollen analyses and the radiocarbon dates show that the bog adjacent to the Norse buildings had *not* been a lagoon at the time of the Norse, but that the bog had begun to form already about two thousand years earlier. Alexander Robertson's study (1978) revealed that the trees at the bottom of the peat had died as a result of paludification, or increased moisture, as the bog began to form. The bog had, however, been considerably wetter in the Norse period than now (see Bell, MacPherson and Renouf this volume). Evidence from the walls of the Norse buildings shows that some of their sods had come from this bog. Sod stripping would have made conditions even wetter. The fact that Norse wood waste has been perfectly preserved (see below) indicates that, at the time, there would have been standing water in the bog.

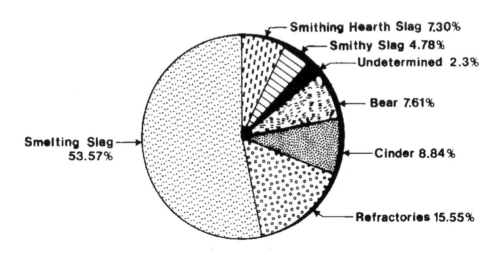

Figure 5. Pie chart, types of slag at L'Anse aux Meadows.

Land rise studies by Douglas Grant (Grant 1975) indicate that the land here has risen since the eleventh century, possibly as much as 1.5 m. This agrees with the earlier conclusions formed by the Norwegian palynologist Kari Henningsmoen (1977, 327).

IRON MANUFACTURE

The discovery of iron slag by the Ingstads was evidence of iron manufacture and smithing on the site. A metallurgical analysis of the slag by Anne M. Rosenquist in Oslo had determined that the mode of iron manufacture was consistent with Viking-Age methods (Rosenqvist 1977). One task of the continued excavations was to locate the furnace where the smelting had taken place and to examine if the iron smelting had been a major enterprise and reason for settlement. The extensive surveys located no additional slag piles. Meanwhile, evidence from Norwegian and Swedish smelting sites showed that Viking-Age and medieval iron smelting furnaces are usually found inside the slag piles or in their immediate vicinity (Johansen 1973, 96; Martens 1982, 30), since it would not have been worth

Figure 6. Photo, coiled spruce roots (courtesy of Parks Canada; photo: D. Brown).

the effort to move them. A re-examination of the LAM evidence showed that this had been the case here as well (fig. 5). A new, more extensive metallurgical analysis by Parks Canada's Conservation Division was aimed at separating the smelting slag from the smithing slag. The results showed that 86% of the slag were from smelting or associated products such as cinders, refractories, and bear. The smelting temperature had been between 1000 and 1100 degrees C, and the raw material had been local bog ore from the brook area (Salmon 1975; Stewart and Unglik 1976; Unglik and Stewart 1978; 1979a; 1979b; 1999a; 1999b). The distribution of the slag showed that about 87% of the smelting slag came from the small building on the seaside terrace above and around a low-shaft furnace of the kind found at Erlandsgård at Møsstrond in Telemark, Norway (Martens 1972, figs 7 and 9), Dokkfløy in Norway (Larsen 1989) and Grelutóttir in Iceland (Ólafsson 1980). The production had been small, only a one-time firing, resulting in about 15 kg of slag. The skills of the iron workers had not been great as 4/5 of the iron remained in the slag. This means that the total amount of iron produced could only have been about 3 kg. The yield could have been slightly higher if discarded nails and any other available iron stock had been added as smelting of finished iron products would have produced little or no slag. Smithing, as discussed below, actually took place in the hall A complex.

SITE FUNCTION

173

Attempts were made to locate additional buildings, especially barns, byres and enclosures for livestock, so prevalent on Iceland and Greenland sites. None were found. Nor were there any bones of domestic animals. The absence of such structures made it clear that LAM had not been a colonising settlement. If domestic animals were brought by the Norse, the animals had been few in number and either consumed or kept outside in the winter.

The overall faunal analyses of identifiable bones indicated that a great proportion of the food bones had been sea mammals, whale, seal, and, possibly, walrus (Rick 1977; Spiess 1990). Meaningful quantifications cannot be done because of the poor condition of the unburnt bone and the fact that the calcined bone had not been fully or systematically collected. Of the identified mammal bone, whale dominated but this is likely the effect of animal size rather than numbers consumed. Species could not be determined, except for a couple of seal bones, which were tentatively identified as harp seal (*Phoca groenlandica*), or harbour seal (*Phoca vitulina*) (Spiess 1990). Re-analysis of a posterior scapula border bone identified as a pig bone by the Norwegian zoologist Rolf W. Lie (Ingstad 1977, 266; although considered unidentifiable by another Norwegian zoologist Haakon Olsen (Ingstad 1977, 267)), showed that it is more likely that of a small seal (Rick 1977; Spiess 1990). A single cod vertebra indicated that some off-shore fishing had taken place.

The function of the settlement was limited to accommodations for people (65%), storage of goods (12%), and workshop space (23%). The site had not been a regular Norse settlement based on farming. Yet the sturdiness, size, and layout indicate that the buildings were not temporary búðir but year-round houses, meant to withstand winter. The sod-laying technique in each is the same, with skin walls of sod over an earth core. The end walls were straight, with slightly rounded outer corners. The corners had all been built from sods from the sedge peat bog, which yielded the sturdiest sods.

The narrow range of building function, together with the artifacts and their distribution, indicate that the site had served as a base for further exploration, a gateway to Vinland (Wallace 1991), and a place where crews could store their acquired supplies from Vinland and rest over the winter months. The most evident activity in the archaeological record is boat repair. Maintenance of boats would have been critical for expeditions so far from home.

Much of the evidence for site activity was the result of the excavations in the sedge peat bog. A secret wish to find the skeletons of the Icelandic crew killed by the vicious Freydís may have been part of our drive for digging here, but, although we found no such grisly evidence, the bog excavations were essential for understanding the site. An additional 644 Norse artifacts plus a couple of hundred Aboriginal wood pieces were found here. In the bog were massive layers of wood. At first we thought that it might all be driftwood, but, except for the wood closest to the brook, this was not the case. The wood was rather neatly separated into three layers, which we termed the Upper, Middle, and Lower, each layer separated from the other by peat development. The Upper Layer, which in part covered the Norse walls, contained roots from modern vegetation but also worked wood radio-carbon-dated to the thirteenth to fifteenth century. Worked wood dominated the Middle Layer. It began at the outer edges of the Norse house walls and extended about 30 m into the bog, thinning in depth with the distance from the houses. The radiocarbon-dates ranged from the seventh to the eleventh centuries (35 dates, see above for discussion of the range). The position of this layer indicated that it was associated with the Norse buildings. The Lower Layer contained only a few worked pieces but large quantities of wood from trees that had died *in situ*. The dates on the trees ranged from BC 1000 to 400 (15 dates; fig. 3).

174

Figure 7. A small birchbark container sewn with spruce root rope (courtesy of Parks Canada; photo: S. Vandervloogt).

Most of the wood consisted of cut-off ends of wood, stakes, posts, and various kinds of wood shavings. Since much of it was not diagnostic, the entire wood material was turned over to Paul Gleeson who was then working on a doctoral dissertation dealing with tool marks on wood from the water-logged Ozette site in Washington state. Questions posed were whether the tool marks had been metal tools or stone tools, and what particular tools had been used. With no knowledge of the provenance for individual pieces, Gleeson found three categories of tool marks. Of 184 pieces with identifiable tool marks, the largest category (122 pieces) consisted of pieces worked with sharp metal tools, mostly broadaxes but also some knives. Another much smaller category (40 pieces) consisted of pieces worked with stone chopping tools. A third category (22 pieces) consisted of pieces with ambiguous marks which could have resulted either from very sharp stone tools or dull metal tools. As the pieces then were sorted into their layers of provenance, it became evident that all the metal-worked wood stemmed from the Middle Layer. The stone-worked material came from either the Lower or Upper layers (Gleeson 1979). The identification of the Middle Layer

0 _____ 5 cm

with metal tools, together with the dating to *c*. AD 1000, confirmed its association with the Norse occupation.

Some of the Norse wood pieces were broken and discarded objects which probably had been replaced with new ones. Some were boat parts such as the floor board from a small boat. One, a water-smoothed piece, was full of seaworm holes. There were also treenails made of fir (*Abies*, species not determined; figs 6-7), pieces of ropes made from fine spruce roots, and a large spruce root coil. A small bow for an auger, which has an exact parallel from Coppergate, York (Jorvik), is an indication of carpentry work, presumably for replacing the discarded wood pieces. The function of other pieces, such as those in figure 8 is unclear. The cone-shaped piece appears to be Scots pine, a species not introduced into North America until the arrival of Europeans in the sixteenth century.

Many wooden skewers were found. Skewers are common on late Viking-Age and early medieval Scandinavian town sites. They have been interpreted as tying devices for cargo to be shipped (Christensen 1968), or stakes for holding sods onto sloping roofs (Thor Magnusson pers. comm.). Another suggestion is that they were used for tying sausages (Weber 1981).

175

Figure 8. Photo, wood objects with undetermined function (courtesy of Parks Canada; photos: S. Vandervloogt).

Figure 9. Overhead photo, the archaeological remains of the A-B-C building
complex (courtesy of Parks Canada;
photo: B. Schonback).

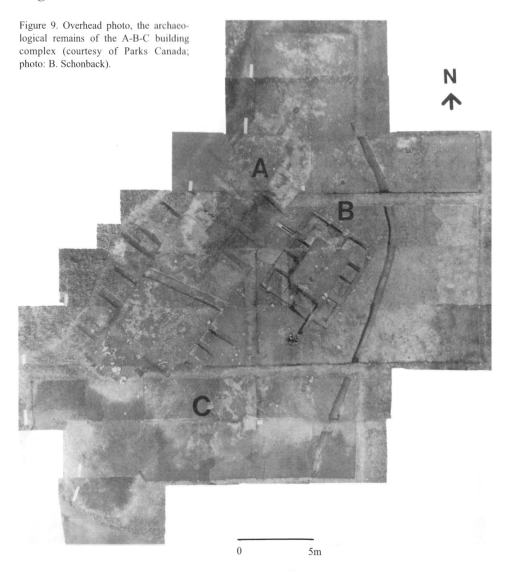

N

0   5m

The distribution of artifacts forms a striking pattern, supporting the evidence that this
was an organized base camp rather than a colonizing effort. The artifacts form four categories: smelting slag from iron manufacture, smithing slag from the forging of finished iron
objects, iron nails, and worked wood. The smelting slag is chiefly associated with the small
furnace hut on the west side of the brook, where iron was manufactured from local bog ore.
The smithing slag is chiefly in the southernmost hall (hall A), especially inside and outside
one particular room. It was here that the actual forging took place.

All iron artifacts found on the site are discarded nail fragments. The nails are concentrated chiefly in the northernmost complex (hall F and hut G). Of eighty-two nail fragments,
over 66% came from here, especially in and outside a shed attached to the eastern side of
the hall. Since nails are primarily associated with ship construction, the shed must have been
used for boat repair. The West Norse did not use iron nails in their house construction.
Whenever quantities of nails are found, they indicate boat repair as outlined by the
Norwegian archaeologist Per Rolfsen (1974), later corroborated with finds such as those at
Fribrødre Å in Denmark (Skamby-Madsen 1984) and Paviken on Gotland, Sweden

(Lundström 1981, 74-89). X-rays of the LAM nail fragments showed that their roves had been split with a chisel blow, so the nails could be removed, the same way as was the case at Paviken. Thus boat repair must have taken place here. Its size suggests that it was a small boat of *faering* size that needed repairs.

Finally, practically all the Norse worked wood came from the middle complex (hall D and hut E). This must have been where the carpentry took place. Among the waste from woodworking are the discarded pieces from boats, perhaps copied by the carpenters for repairs. The small floorboard is further evidence that the repairs were for a *faering*-sized boat.

Iron production was probably not planned but arose when one of the boats had been damaged. The various duties were then divided among the three households, perhaps on the basis of expertise. The need for new boat nails to replace the discarded ones is probably the explanation for the small one-shot and unskilled iron production. Aside from the ninety-eight discarded nail fragments, only one whole nail was found. This nail differed in composition from the fragments found elsewhere on the site, and was the only iron object found amongst the wood working waste outside hall D. It was probably manufactured on site and lost at the time new wood parts were made to replace old cracked ones, like the discarded floorboard.

The even spacing of the three clusters of buildings, and the integration of specific functions in each, indicates that the buildings were all part of a single, organized occupation. Our original theory that hall A predated the other two halls proved to be wrong. Our assumption had been that the northernmost room, room IV, which is narrower than the others, had been a later addition on an earlier structure. The excavation along the outer edges of the walls proved that this was not the case. The building stood on the very edge of the terrace along the sedge peat bog, and the narrowing of the room occurred only on the bog side. The construction must have begun on the landward side and had evidently not been well planned. As the seaward wall was laid, the builders must have discovered a sudden bend in the terrace at the northern end. The wall was therefore made thinner and stepped in. On the landward side, the wall forms one continuous line, and this side of the room is not constricted (fig. 9).

177

A limited number of personal objects, including the ringed pin and spindle whorl had been found by the Ingstads. The only additional personal artifact found by Parks Canada was a white glass bead, which lay directly outside the middle hall. Unfortunately this bead was lost during conservation. Typically all artifacts not associated with boat repair and carpentry are small, personal items, accidentally lost on the site. There are no typical domestic objects. The buildings must have been abandoned in an orderly manner, the owners taking their belongings with them as they left.

CONCLUSION

The questions posed by the International Advisory Committee have been addressed and answered. The story of LAM has unfolded through detailed studies to show that LAM was a short-lived settlement, probably only a decade or so, from *c*. AD 1000. It served as a gateway to the riches of Vínland, a base camp for storing goods to take home and for overwintering on the long journey to and from Greenland. There was no cemetery, perhaps because of the Christian faith but also because of the short occupation span. Iron had been made on site in the small furnace and worked into nails in the southern building complex. The rising land mass did not mean that a lagoon had existed in the bog, but that conditions were somewhat wetter than today. The climate had also been a little warmer and more favourable.

There were no Aboriginal people on the site when the Norse were there, perhaps one factor which made it a desirable location.

Archaeologists made a startling find during the later excavations, which held the key to the Vínland mystery. Three butternuts and a burl of butternut wood, a piece of *mösurr*, were found in the Middle Layer in the bog, in every case in context with the dated Norse wood. The butternut burl also has a cutmark made with a metal knife. These unassuming nuts and wood shed light on the purpose of the LAM settlement and its role in the Vínland sagas, and show that the people at LAM had indeed been to regions where grapes grew wild. But that is the story of another paper.

BIBLIOGRAPHY

Arneborg, J. 2000. 'Greenland and Europe', in Fitzhugh and Ward 2000, 304-317.

Christensen, A.E. 1968. 'The Sjøvollen Ship: Preliminary Report on the Excavation and Reconstruction of a Medieval Merchantman', *Viking*, 32, 131-154.

Cummings. L.M. 1974-1975. Geology of the L'Anse aux Meadows National Historic Park, Newfoundland, 3 vols, unpublished report, Parks Canada Atlantic Service Centre, Halifax.

Davis, A.M. 1985. Historical Biogeography and Archaeology: Reconstructing Past Environments at the L'Anse aux Meadows Site, Northern Newfoundland, unpublished report, Department of Geography, University of Toronto.

Davis, A.M., McAndrews, J.H. and Wallace, B. 1988. 'Paleoenvironment and the Archaeological Record at the L'Anse aux Meadows site, Newfoundland', *Geoarchaeology: An International Journal*, 3, 1, 53-64.

Dawson, J.E. 1976. Identification of Samples of Archaeological Seeds from L'Anse aux Meadows, Newfoundland, unpublished file, National Historic Parks and Sites Branch, Parks Canada, Ottawa.

Douglas, A. 1977. Wood from L'Anse aux Meadows, unpublished report, Conservation Division, Parks Canada, Ottawa.

——1978a. Wood Analysis, 4A Driftwood, unpublished report, Conservation Division, Parks Canada, Ottawa.

——1978b. L'Anse aux Meadows Wood Species Identification, unpublished report, Conservation Division, Parks Canada, Ottawa.

——1978c. Identification of Wood by Species of some L'Anse aux Meadows Artifacts, unpublished report, Conservation Division, Parks Canada, Ottawa.

——1979. Identification of Wood Species of a Wooden Stick from L'Anse aux Meadows, unpublished report, Conservation Division, Parks Canada, Ottawa.

Fitzhugh, W.W. and Ward, E.I., eds, 2000. *Vikings: The North Atlantic Saga*, Washington and London.

Gimbarzevsky, P. 1977. L'Anse aux Meadows National Historic Park Integrated Survey of Biophysical Resources, unpublished Information Report, FMR-X-99, Forest Management Institute, Environment Canada, Ottawa.

Gleeson, P. 1979. Study of Wood Material from L'Anse aux Meadows, unpublished report Parks Canada, Ottawa.

Grant, D.R. 1975. 'Surficial Geology and Sea-Level Changes, L'Anse aux Meadows National Historic Park, Newfoundland'. Ottawa: Paper 75-1, Part A, Geological Survey of Canada.

Harrington, C.R. ed., 1981. *Climatic Change in Canada*. Ottawa: Syllogeus 33.

Henningsmoen, K.E. 1977. 'Pollen-analytical Investigations in the L'Anse aux Meadows Area, Newfoundland', in Ingstad 1977, 289-340.

Ingstad, A-S. 1977. *The Discovery of a Norse Settlement in America: Excavations at L'Anse aux Meadows, Newfoundland, 1961-1968*, Oslo.

Jacobi, G.C. and Ulan, L. 1981. 'Review of dendrochronology in the forest-tundra ecotone of Alaska and Canada', in Harrington 1981, 97-128.

Johansen, A. 1973. 'Iron Production as a Factor in the Settlement History of the Mountain Valleys Surrounding Hardangervidda', *Norwegian Archaeological Review*, 6, 2, 84-101.

Kuc, M. 1973. Description with appendix of a fossilium collected by Marian Kuc 1973 in the archaeological trench at the Viking Site, L'Anse aux Meadows, Newfoundland, Canada, unpublished report, Parks Canada, Ottawa.

——1975. 'Paleoecological Inventory of the Norse Settlement at L'Anse aux Meadows, Newfoundland,' Project 690044. Ottawa: Geological Survey of Canada, *Terrain Science Division, Paper 75-1, Paper A*, 445-450.

178

Laflèche, L. 1981. Wood Identifications from L'Anse aux Meadows, unpublished report, Parks Canada, Ottawa.

Laflèche, L. and Douglas, A. 1977. Wood from L'Anse aux Meadows, unpublished report, Conservation Division, Parks Canada, Ottawa.

Lamberton, R.D. and Maunder, J.E. 1976. An Avifaunal Survey of L'Anse aux Meadows National Historic Park, unpublished report, Parks Canada, Ottawa.

Larsen, J. H. 1989. 'To jernvinneplasser fra middelalderen ved Dokkfløvatn', *Viking*, 52, 91-113.

Lundström, P. 1981. *De kommo vida...Vikingars hamn vid Paviken, Gotland*, Stockholm.

Martens, I. 1982. 'Recent Investigations of Iron Production in Viking Age Norway', *Norwegian Archaeological Review*, 15, 1-2, 29-44.

Matthews, K. 1974. Notes on the History of L'Anse aux Meadows, unpublished report, Parks Canada, Ottawa

McAndrews J. and Davis, A.M. 1978. Pollen Analysis at the L'Anse aux Meadows Norse Site, unpublished report, Archaeological Research Section, Canadian Parks Service, Environment Canada, Halifax.

McCawley, J.C. 1973. Results of Phosphate Analysis of Soils from L'Anse aux Meadows, unpublished report Conservation Division, Parks Canada, Ottawa

——1975a. Soil Phosphorous Levels at L'Anse aux Meadows, unpublished report, Conservation Division, Parks Canada, Ottawa.

——1975b. Examination of Charcoal and Other Burnt Material from L'Anse aux Meadows, unpublished report, Conservation Division, Parks Canada, Ottawa.

McGovern, T.H. and Bigelow, G.F. 1977. Report on midden excavations at V48 Niaqussat, Godthaab District, West Greenland 1977, unpublished research report.

Moore, J. 1978. L'Anse aux Meadows Wood Samples, unpublished report, Conservation Division, Parks Canada, Ottawa.

Moore, J. and Daley, T. 1976. Wood Species Identifications, L'Anse aux Meadows, unpublished report, Conservation Division, Parks Canada, Ottawa.

Mott, R. 1975. 'Palynological Studies of Peat Monoliths from L'Anse aux Meadows Norse Site', Ottawa: Geological Survey of Canada, *Paper 75-1, Part A*, 451-454.

Northcott, T.H. 1976. *The Land and Sea Mammals of L'Anse aux Meadows National Historic Park, Newfoundland*, Ottawa.

Nowland, J.K. 1977. Soil Analysis Report., unpublished report, Parks Canada, Ottawa.

Ólafsson, Guðmundur. 1980. 'Grelutóttir. Landnámsbær á Eyri við Arnarfjörð', *Árbók hins íslenzka fornleifafélags, 1979*, 25-73.

Perem, E. 1974. Observations on Wood Material from the Norse Habitation Site at L'Anse aux Meadows, Newfoundland, unpublished report, Parks Canada, Ottawa.

——1978a. Wood identification, unpublished report, Parks Canada, Ottawa.

——1978b. L'Anse aux Meadows Wood Samples, unpublished report, Parks Canada, Ottawa.

Pollett, F.C, Meades, W.J. and Robertson, A.W. 1975a. The classification and interpretation of the vegetation resource within L'Anse aux Meadows National Historic Park, unpublished report, Parks Canada, Ottawa.

——1975b. The vegetation of L'Anse aux Meadows National Historic Park with photography by Kevin Veigh, unpublished colour photographs selected for Parks Canada, Ottawa.

Pride, C. 1978. Petrological-Geochemical Report on Archaeological Samples from L'Anse aux Meadows, Newfoundland, unpublished report, Parks Canada, Ottawa.

Rick, A.M. 1977. Analysis of Bone Remains from L'Anse aux Meadows, Newfoundland, unpublished report, Parks Canada, Ottawa.

Robertson, A. 1978. Chemical-Analytical Investigations of the Archaeological Site at L'Anse aux Meadows National Historic Park, unpublished report, Parks Canada Atlantic Service Center, Halifax.

Rolfsen, P. 1974. 'Båtnaust på Jærkysten', *AmS-Skrifter* 8 (Stavanger), 1-155.

Rombough, P.J, Barbour, S.E. and Kerekes, J.J. n.d. Untitled and Unpublished report for Parks Canada by Peter J. Rombough and Stephen E. Barbour, Biology Department, Dalhousie University and Joseph J. Kerekes, Department of Fisheries and Environment Canada Wildlife Service, Halifax, Parks Canada, Ottawa.

Rosenqvist, A. M. 1977. 'Material Investigations. Report concluded 1971', in Ingstad 1977, 373-402.

179

Salmon, M.E. 1975. Interim Report on Slag and Bog Ore from L'Anse aux Meadows, unpublished report, Conservation Division, Parks Canada, Ottawa.

Skamby-Madsen, J. 1984. 'Et skibsværft fran sen vikingetid/tidlig middelalder ved Fribrødre Å på Falster', *Hikuin,* 10, 261-274.

Smith, M. 1978. Identifications of Shell from Newfoundland Peat Bog, unpublished report, Parks Canada, Ottawa.

Spiess, A.E. 1990. Identifications of Calcined Bone from L'Anse aux Meadows, unpublished report, Parks Canada Atlantic Service Center, Halifax.

Stewart, J. and Unglik, H. 1976. Examination of Slags and Bog Ores from L'Anse aux Meadows, unpublished report, Conservation Division, Parks Canada, Ottawa.

Unglik, H. and Stewart, J. 1978. L'Anse aux Meadows Iron Working Study, unpublished report, Conservation Division, Parks Canada, Ottawa.

——1979a. Metallurgical Examination of Archaeological Material from L'Anse aux Meadows, unpublished report, Conservation Division, Parks Canada, Ottawa.

——1979b. Metallurgical Investigation of Archaeological Material of Norse Origin from L'Anse aux Meadows, Newfoundland, unpublished report, Conservation Division, Parks Canada, Ottawa.

——1999a. *The Metallurgy of Norse Material from L'Anse aux Meadows, Newfoundland*, Ottawa.

——1999b. *Atlas of Microstructures of Norse Material from L'Anse aux Meadows, Newfoundland*, Ottawa.

Wallace, B.L. 1991. 'L'Anse aux Meadows: Gateway to Vinland', *Acta Archaeologica,* 61 (1990), 166-197.

Weber, B. 1981. 'Heita, feita pylsa!', *Viking*, 44, 91-111.

Zachrisson, O. 1979. 'Dendroekologiska metoder att spåra tidigare kulturinflyttande i den norrländska barrskogen', *Fornvännen*, 74, 4, 259-268.

L'Anse aux Meadows: Rediscovered and Remade

Kevin McAleese

Introduction

A millennial year, as a juncture of time, provides a good opportunity to review how ancient histories are presented to the public in this modern world. At the tip of the Northern Peninsula lies an ancient Norse and Aboriginal site, L'Anse aux Meadows (LAM). A thousand years ago Norse Greenlanders landed there, established an outpost and, according to their sagas, met some of the region's Aboriginal residents. There is no direct archaeological evidence for this meeting, but it is clear that the Norse left after about a decade.

A thousand years later the Norwegian Helge Ingstad rediscovered the place, led there by local resident George Decker. Since that significant event in 1960, our understanding of Viking-Age life at LAM has grown substantially. Both Canada and UNESCO recognize the site's important historical and cultural position, granting it National Historic and World Heritage Site status, respectively. This paper examines the process which led to that status by profiling certain milestones of research and public recognition.

This public recognition highlights a curious twist of fate: a growing number of local people now work seasonally as Viking-Age 'living history' interpreters. This new and potentially lucrative type of employment will be discussed in terms of 'sustainable development.'

Current Interpretation

The UNESCO commemorative Plaque at LAM lists the reasons for World Heritage status (1978). The Plaque states that it is the Norse landfall and settlement that makes LAM 'the only authenticated Norse site in North America'. There is no doubt that this episode is of great historic and cultural significance. Not surprisingly, the short, but significant Norse episode in Newfoundland and Labrador history is featured at LAM. But the UNESCO Plaque also describes the site as one of the world's major archaeological places because it is 'the base from where they [the Norse] launched expeditions resulting in the first contact between Aboriginal North Americans and Europeans'.

World Heritage status has had a profound influence on contemporary northern Newfoundland society and culture. Similarly, LAM research has had a positive effect on northern Newfoundland society over the last few decades. This is due in part to a relatively new phenomena, described here as 'bringing back the Vikings'. In other words, many Northern Peninsula residents have recently become quite attached to Viking-Age culture. This attachment is primarily economic, as much of their own cultural heritage is British, French or Irish, none of which is highlighted in the formal presentations at the LAM interpretation centre.

Great Northern Peninsula Prehistory

LAM and the surrounding area has significant Aboriginal and post-Viking Age European cultural resources, yet this history has generally been downplayed by Parks Canada, the federal agency that manages LAM.

For example, various groups of Aboriginal people have visited and lived at LAM and its surrounding area for thousands of years (Renouf 1999, 20). Stone tools manufactured by

Maritime Archaic Indians and recovered in the National Historic Site date as early as 5000-6000 years ago (Wallace 2000, 214).

Well-made artifacts knives, projectile points and scrapers from the site, and also from other locations around the Island of Newfoundland, attest to a vibrant hunting and fishing way of life. Maritime Archaic Indians also had a sophisticated spiritual life. At Port au Choix, approximately 175 km southwest of LAM, amulets, pendants and other grave goods including two stone effigies of killer whales (*Orca*) were excavated (Tuck 1976, 61, 62). These cult objects date to *c.* 3900 years old.

These maritime hunters were followed at LAM by various Palaeoeskimo peoples. Known to archaeologists as the Groswater and Dorset cultures, these arctic people lived in Newfoundland and Labrador from 3800 to 1200 years ago (Renouf 1999, 28). During that time they moved south along the coast of Labrador, onto the Island of Newfoundland and even settling on the Island of St. Pierre off the south coast of Newfoundland (LeBlanc 1999). Small, finely made Dorset tools have been found at LAM (Wallace 2000, 214), and in abundance throughout the Northern Peninsula (Renouf 1999, 28).

Towards the end of the Dorset occupation of the Island about 1900 years ago, people known to archaeologists as 'Recent Indians' began living in the Strait of Belle Isle and along the Northern Peninsula. 'Recent Indian' artifacts found at Bird Cove, on the Northern Peninsula about 125 km southwest of LAM, date to *c.* 1020 years ago (Hull 1999). Thus, Bird Cove was probably occupied when the Norse occupied LAM. However, Recent Indian artifacts at LAM itself do not date to the Viking Age, indicating that only the Norse occupied the site at that time (Wallace 2000, 214). This occupation at LAM was brief, with sod houses built, occupied and abandoned within a few decades of the early eleventh century.

This brevity was due to a number of reasons. The relatively small numbers of Norse settlers were inadequate to provide a solid, and secure, economic base. Second, there was only a limited number of valuable trade goods they could send back to their Nordic world, a fairly long, challenging and seasonally restricted journey (Wallace 1991; 1993). Third, their relations with the relatively large, resident Aboriginal population (*skraelingar* to the Norse) were, according to sags records, unstable and prone to conflict (McGhee 1993, 44, 50).

The short term Norse occupation at LAM may have characterised that of all Vínland. Vínland's boundaries are vague, and its occupation controversial (see Wallace, Larsson, Shendock, this volume). But many scholars assume the territory to at least include the Strait of Belle Isle and the Gulf of St. Lawrence. The exact details on why the Norse Greenlanders abandoned the area are unknown, but in combination the above factors resulted in only a brief sojourn for the Norse in Vínland, an area which faded from recorded history once abandoned by them (Wallace 1993, 42; Seaver 1996, 9).

Post Viking-Age History

Following its abandonment by Greenlanders and Icelanders, the LAM area did not cease being a place where people lived. Aboriginal people continued to use it for most of this millennium. By at least the fifteenth century Europeans such as the Spanish and Portuguese began their exploration of the North Atlantic's western edge. Did these later Europeans know of the Icelandic/Norse sagas?

The sagas contain stories written about Vínland approximately 300 years after it had been abandoned. This Vínland information, though not common knowledge, may have been known by a small number of European mariners. Information about marine resources such as codfish and whales, and how to sail to where they could be caught or where routes might be found to take explorers further west (i.e. to India), may have been exchanged amongst these mariners at European ports involved in the North Atlantic trade (Williams 1996, 11;

see Pope, this volume). However at present there is no clear evidence for that interpretation (Seaver 1996, 5; see this volume). In any case, later European explorations eventually led to European settlement of LAM, culminating with the British in the mid-nineteenth century.

In the late fifteenth century European trade was characterised by people sailing westward along the North Atlantic seaways to fish for cod and to hunt sea mammals. Some made landfall in the Strait of Belle Isle, for which there is clear evidence in the cartographic record (Morison 1971, 227). For example there are various Basque, Breton and French toponyms for Newfoundland and Labrador places: *Puerto Nuevo* = Pleasure Harbour (Basques); *Hable des Buttes* = Red Bay (Basques); *Terra de Lavrador* = Labrador (Basques); and *le Karpont* = Quirpon Harbour (Breton) (Tuck and Grenier 1989, 16,17).

The four-hundred-year French use of the area is also evident through cartography. Near Quirpon Island just northeast of LAM there are French places such as: *Le Degrat* = Degrat; *Ille de Ficho* = Fichot; *Ille St. Jullient* = St. Julien; and *Conche* (Morison 1971, 347-359).

Between *c.* AD 1500 and AD 1800, Basque and French fishermen, particularly the latter, used LAM as a fishing station. The French caught and processed codfish in the bays and coves around the site up to 1835. This migratory fishery on the 'French Shore' continued under British sanction throughout their two-hundred-year direct control of the Island of Newfoundland.

But when William Decker, an English speaking settler, arrived in 1835, the demise of French use of the LAM area began. Decker initially worked for the French, managing some of their shore stations until 1904. His arrival heralded further English settlement and, coincidentally, his descendants played a significant role in the 1960 discovery of the Norse occupation by the Norwegian, Helge Ingstad.

183

THE SAGAS: A FINDING AID FOR REDISCOVERY

Grœnlendinga saga and *Eiríks saga rauða*, first translated and published in English in 1838 (Rafn 1837), are very significant literary and historic bodies of knowledge. They were used by various adventurers and scholars to try to locate Vínland, or to investigate probable Viking-Age sailing routes. For example, sailing accounts from the sagas and other sources were used in 1893 by a group of Norwegians to sail a replica ship from Norway to North America. They built the 23 m *Viking* based on data collected during the 1880 excavation of the Gokstad Viking ship burial mound in Oslo Fjord (Vinner 1993, 95, 96). In it they traveled to New London, Connecticut in 44 days, sailing along seaways pioneered by the Viking-Age Norse.

Early in the next century Norse history was used just this way in northern Newfoundland. W.H. Munn, a Newfoundlander and amateur historian, studied the sagas in 1914 to better understand Viking-Age geography and travel means. He noted that Vínland had wild grapes, an environmental indicator of a temperate, not sub-arctic climate.

Munn studied saga sailing times and distances, as well as historic and contemporary maps. Based on his studies he suspected that sub-arctic Labrador, and the Island of Newfoundland's Northern Peninsula must have been part of Vínland . He suggested Pistolet Bay, approximately 25 km west of LAM, as a possible location. In true prescient form he also suggested 'Lancey Meadows,' as it was then known, as a likely landfall for Leifr Eiríkson.

The Danish archaeologist Hovgaard also used the sagas in 1915 (Hovgaard 1915) in an attempt to locate Vínland. He suggested the stretch of sandy beach coastline near Cape Porcupine was the *furðustrandir* or 'wonderstrands' of the sagas.

A few decades later the Finnish geographer Vaino Tanner, during his substantive 1940s study of Labrador geography, also speculated that a number of Vínland and Markland places referred to in the sagas were Labrador and Island of Newfoundland sites (Meldgaard 1993, 9).

That same decade Arlington Mallery, an American engineer, did more than speculate. He conducted brief archaeological survey work in Pistolet Bay near LAM, but without finding any Viking artifacts (Wallace 2000, 208).

A decade later the Danish archaeologist Jorgen Meldgaard, began a systematic search for ancient Viking settlements along the coasts of Labrador and the Island of Newfoundland. Using saga information and, apparently, W.A. Munn's book, Meldgaard surveyed and test excavated in and around Pistolet Bay in 1956 (Meldgaard 1993, 9; Wallace 2000, 208). He also planned to dig at Milan Arm, a few kilometres southwest of LAM, but instead started an excavation of a Greenland Viking site, never returning to LAM.

Coincidentally the lawyer turned explorer, Helge Ingstad, was also looking for remains of Viking sites in Labrador and on the Island of Newfoundland. Not surprisingly he used the sagas as a finding aid as well.

Norse Site 'Discovered' at L'Anse aux Meadows

Ingstad had been looking for Viking ruins in Atlantic Canada in the late 1950s. Using his own boat, the *Halten*, Ingstad cruised the Atlantic/Gulf of St. Lawrence coast searching for a Norse site. He also undertook aerial surveys of the Labrador coast.

By the summer of 1960 he was near LAM in the community of Raleigh, when he paid a visit to LAM. Apparently the *Halten* came to the wharf of Mr. George Decker, a community leader. Mr. Decker was the grandson of William Decker, the first English settler in LAM. He and Ingstad met on the wharf, and then Decker directed the inquisitive Ingstad to the site area.

Like other LAM residents, George Decker knew of some mounds and depressions which he referred to as 'the Indian mounds'. This was a sound interpretation based on local knowledge of Newfoundland and Labrador Aboriginal history. George Decker showed Ingstad the peculiar ground features, and Ingstad recognized the possibility of these being the remains of Norse turf-walled buildings.

L'Anse aux Meadows' Archaeological Research /
Public Interpretaton

In 1961 Ingstad and his archaeologist wife, Anne Stine, began excavations. Under her supervision, and with other archaeologists from Scandinavia, artifacts of wood, iron, soapstone and bronze, along with architectural remains were recovered, confirming LAM as a Viking-Age site.

However there was controversy surrounding the site's authenticity. Despite the Norse architectural remains it took some time for the few clearly diagnostic Norse artifacts to surface. Anne Stine also took considerable time to publish the definitive report detailing the site research and finds. As the controversy continued the government of Newfoundland and Labrador invited archaeologists from the Nordic countries to visit the site, review the ongoing research and, hopefully, help settle the debate.

Nordic Viking-Age specialists Dr Bjorn Hougen and Dr Marken Stenbergen responded to the invitation. They were quickly persuaded that it was indeed an authentic Norse site. Yet because of this controversy, other visiting Nordic archaeologists, like Dr Sigrid Kaland from Norway, knew they were getting involved in a controversial project. Kaland, a Norse archaeologist working in the Orkney Islands, was warned by some colleagues not to work at LAM for fear it would hurt her reputation. Despite the warnings, Kaland came to LAM to excavate in 1968, and recovered a number of the important Norse finds (Kaland, pers. comm.).

In these early years of site research, many scientists visited LAM. Junius Bird was a respected American archaeologist known for his excavations of ancient Inuit sites near Hopedale, Labrador. Another occasional site visitor was the amateur archaeologist J. Hartness Beardsley, a member of the 'Early Sites Foundation', an American heritage group. Beardsley took samples of tree stumps from outside the LAM site boundaries, which were later used in tree dating research. During another visit Beardsley's son Anthony excavated the one and only Norse spindle whorl found at LAM.

Dr Birgitta Wallace, originally from Sweden, came to work with the Ingstads in the 1960s. Her research continued there over two decades. As a Parks Canada Archaeologist Emeritus, she has become the leading scholar for LAM. It was largely because of her work that the site is now accepted as the 'gateway' to Vínland (Wallace 1993; 1991; 2000; see this volume).

Various Newfoundlanders worked at the site as principal research assistants, especially the Deckers and Andersons from the LAM community. The government of Newfoundland and Labrador managed the site during these early years of research. In 1966 Premier Joseph R. Smallwood, a long supporter of the Ingstads, assigned David Webber, Chief Curator at the Provincial Museum, to visit the Ingstads and assess the site.

185

One of Webber's projects was to redirect the flow of Black Duck Brook at the site's western end. In the spring the Brook flooded the adjacent Viking house ruins, and Mr. Webber developed plans to counter this damaging activity. He also helped maintain and improve temporary structures built to protect the sod house features. Finally, in 1966 he developed plans for the site's first formal interpretation centre, though it was never built (Webber pers. comm.).

Site interpretation was becoming a problem by the mid-1960s, given the increasing number of visitors. The resident caretaker, Lloyd Decker, was hard pressed to keep up with the growing public interest. In response to this expansion in visitation, an interpretation 'team' began the first site interpretive program in 1967.

Under the direction of Mr Ross Elliott, this team of university students, funded by an Opportunities For Youth grant, guided tourists/visitors around the site. Helge Ingstad gave these students ideas for displays on the walls of a building they called the Information Centre, and they also developed a 'library' of resource materials for local use.

The new interpreters came to realize, as many others have, that in addition to Viking - Age ruins, the area had many attractions to offer visitors. They became aware that 'the history of LAM, in the different cultural remains it has, shows a profile of the history of the province' (Elliott 1973, 10).

As a result of the Ingstads' work, and the acceptance of the research by the academic community, LAM's importance and outstanding significance as a heritage site for all of humanity was recognized. An International Advisory Committee was formed in 1972 to assist with research planning, with representatives from Scandinavia, the United States and Canada (see Wallace, this volume).

Concurrently, administration of LAM was passed over to the federal government, especially Parks Canada. The first formal interpretation centre was opened by Prime Minister Pierre Trudeau in 1975. The site was designated a National Historic Site by the Historic Sites and Monuments Board of Canada in 1977, while UNESCO designated it their first World Heritage cultural site in 1978.

Kevin McAleese

The New Millennium

Adjacent to the Viking cultural site is the modern community of LAM. Like other small Northern Peninsula communities, the economy of this settlement is growing very slowly. The residents continue to struggle with declining populations and economic hardships. For example, as a result of outmigration the adult population of LAM has dropped from 75 to 36 over the last eighteen years. The phrase 'there's nothing for me here' is heard often, a phrase hated and feared by the shrinking number of permanent residents.

But the growing cultural heritage business is good news for the Northern Peninsula. Although there is no Norse-descended population in the LAM area, local people have taken 'ownership' of the site and its Viking history. Some work as 'living history' interpreters dressed in period clothing at the National Historic site, a relatively new approach to presenting Viking-Age life (see Markewitz, this volume). More residents were recently trained to do similar work at the adjacent new tourist attraction, Norstead.

Norstead is a recreated port and trading place reflecting Norse life in the Viking Age. According to its Vision Statement, developed by the Viking Trail Tourism Association, Norstead's purpose is 'to foster knowledge and appreciation of Viking/Norse history through an interactive educational environment'. Four Norse-style buildings have been constructed at Garden Point near LAM, including a boat shed, a chieftain's hall, a church and a blacksmith shop.

Interpreters there demonstrate a Norse way of life practiced throughout the North Atlantic in the eighth to eleventh centuries. As part of Newfoundland and Labrador's year 2000 celebrations, these living history interpreters were visited by thousands of tourists and by numerous Scandinavian re-enactors from around the world.

Conclusion

It has been argued that an important reason for Newfoundland's pivotal position in world history is that 'geographically, Newfoundland lies just past the end of the Old World, at the beginning of the new' (Dyer 2000). Depending on perspective, this place is both a cultural juncture, as well as a cultural bridgehead.

As a juncture/bridgehead, LAM is not unique in the world as a place of human occupation with great time depth. But it is special in terms of multi-cultural use by people moving into the area from all points of the compass. Beside the Norse this special 'crossroads' has witnessed visitors from many cultures, some occupying the area for hundreds, if not thousands of years. The Maritime Archaic people arrived about five millennia ago, and were eventually followed by a variety of Europeans about five centuries ago. They all came to partake of the natural bounty of a northern marine environment. We do not know what they or the later Aboriginal groups called it, but we do know it was their homeland, and a giant influence on their life.

The promotion of the Norse site's rediscovery, and the subsequent Viking-Age research by international scholars, has overshadowed the histories of other former resident populations. Yet the area's Aboriginal history, and the later European settlement, provide the context in which the Norse episode can be fully understood. Public understanding of the Northern Peninsula past would benefit from a more comprehensive presentation of this context, with greater emphasis on LAM's non-Viking Age history.

This resource-rich land and sea was a magnet for the Norse in the Viking Age, who named it *Vínland hit góði*. People from other cultures were drawn to it as well, and today this 'magnet' draws the visitor from away. For the people who live here today, that is a good news story.

Local presentation of the Norse past bodes well for the long term future of the community and area. Norse heritage tourist related businesses, such as boat tours and hotels/cafes, are slowly expanding. As they expand they strive for a high level of Norse culture presentation, an interplay of culture history and culture tourism that needs to be well managed. This repackaging and presentation of the past has become part of 'sustainable development' for the LAM community's future.

ACKNOWLEDGEMENTS

For sharing their experiences of L'Anse aux Meadows I wish to thank the following people: Dr Birgitta Wallace, Loretta Decker, Debbie Anderson, Dr Benedicte Ingstad, Dr Sigrid Kaland and David Webber. Thanks also to the many local residents who offered valuable insight about the past, present and future of L'Anse aux Meadows.

BIBLIOGRAPHY

Clausen, B.L. ed., 1993. *Viking Voyages to North America*, Roskilde.

Dyer, G. 2000. *Full Circle—First Contact. Vikings and Skraelings in Newfoundland and Labrador,* St. John's.

Elliott, R. 1973. Project Vinland: A Final Report, unpublished manuscript, on file with author.

Hull, S.H. 1999. The Recent Indians at North Cove: The 1998 Field Season. Preliminary Site Report, unpublished manuscript, Provincial Archaeology Office, St. John's.

Hovgaard, W. 1915. *The Voyages of the Norsemen to America*, New York.

McGhee, R. 1993. 'The Skraellings of Vinland', in Clausen 1993, 43-53.

Meldgaard, J. 1993. 'Preface; Vinland Research 1832-1992', in Clausen 1993, 95-108.

Morison, S.E. 1971. *The European Discovery of America: The Northern Voyages*, New York.

Munn, W.H. 1914. *The Wineland Voyages: Location of Helluland, Markland and Vinland*, St. John's.

Rafn, C.C. 1837. *Antiquitates Americaenae*, Copenhagen [abstracted in English 1838].

Renouf, M.A.P. 1999. *Ancient Cultures-Bountiful Seas. The Story of Port au Choix*, St. John's.

Seaver, K. 1996. *The Frozen Echo: Greenland and the Exploration of North America, ca. AD 1000-1500*, Standford, CA.

Tuck, J.A. and Grenier, R. 1989. *Red Bay, Labrador. World Whaling Capital A.D. 1550-1600*, St. John's.

Tuck, J.A. 1976. *Ancient People of Port au Choix. The Excavation of an Archaic Indian Cemetery in Newfoundland*, St. John's.

Vinner, M. 1993. 'Unnasigling: The Seaworthiness of the Merchant Vessel', in Clausen 1993, 95-108.

Wallace, B.L. 1991. 'L'Anse aux Meadows: gateway to Vinland', *Acta Archaeologica*, 61, 166-197.

——1993. 'L'Anse aux Meadows, the Western Outpost', in Clausen 1993, 30-42.

——2000. 'The Viking Settlement at L'Anse aux Meadows', in Fitzhugh and Ward 2000, 208-16.

Williams, A. 1996. *John Cabot and Newfoundland*, St. John's.

Modern fishing stage with 'Viking' longship in the background on the Great Northern Peninsula (photo: N. Webster).

A Norseman's encounter in Vínland, a millennium later

Nicolay Eckhoff

Introduction

It was a great adventure to participate in five expeditions, travelling with Helge Ingstad along the coast of Newfoundland, Labrador and Baffin Island, and to meet the fine people living at L'Anse aux Meadows (LAM) in a vast green landscape without trees and birds. What follows are my own recollections of my time there during excavations at the Norse site. Today that Norse site looks like a well-kept lawn. Gone are the sheep and the cows that stood for the maintenance for many years. The sod does not only conceal the turf walls and fireplaces, but the years of blood, sweat and tears. The blood was extracted by blackflies and horse flies, the sweat from backbreaking work seven days a week, the tears, well, the site did not come on a silver platter—both the climate and the scientific environment were hostile. The hard work for Anne Stine and Helge Ingstad was not only to spend the summer months looking for the needle in the haystack, but also to spend the rest of the year securing financial backing for the next expedition. We were fortunate to have generous assistance from the Grenfell Mission. They often provided us with transport and in a region without roads this was great help.

St Anthony

LAM was a remote spot and was unmarked on most maps. After crossing the Atlantic, we flew over the top of Newfoundland at 30,000 feet on our way to Montreal. Then we spent up to two weeks backtracking to LAM. In Gander we could spend a few days waiting for good flying weather, passengers and a favourable distribution of the icebergs in St Anthony harbour so the seaplane could land.

My first encounter with the Inuit was in St Anthony. Tuberculosis was a common disease in the villages and Inuit from Labrador were sent to the Hospital in St Anthony for treatment. The Grenfell Mission did much to combat the disease. I remember being woken up by loud music from the hospital ship in LAM harbour, informing the people it was time for health checks. St Anthony was built around the Grenfell Mission and was dominated by the white and green Grenfell Mission buildings, some of them with huge billboards with quotations from the Bible. The hospital steam plant supplied the town with electricity. Every evening at ten o'clock the steam whistle would sound and one minute later the power was gone until the next morning. In St Anthony we picked up the 6 to 8 wooden crates of supplies we had shipped in the spring and it was our last chance to stock up on fresh food and supplies. As soon as the ice conditions around LAM were favourable, we took the coastal steamer to Quirpon. Here two fishing boats took our supplies and us the final stretch to LAM. For us the crates contained the bare necessities of life: archaeological / surveying equipment; tents; sleeping bags; and food. To the people of LAM they contained magic, messages of things to come such as nylon fish net and nylon fish line, new tools and bright kerosene lanterns, chocolate and bug repellent.

The settlers and the village

LAM is a good place to settle. It has a sheltered harbour, fresh water, good fishing and good hunting The first English settler was William Decker. He came from the Channel Islands around 1850 and was hired by the French to look after their fishing equipment, when they sailed back to Europe in the fall, with a valuable cargo of dried cod. It was his grandson, George Decker, who showed Ingstad the strange formations by Black Duck Brook. Later the Andersons arrived. They are descendants of Torsten Andersen (1834 -1904) who emigrated from Norway around 1870 to work for the Hudson's Bay Company in Labrador.

The village was not completely cut off from the outside world; it had a telegraph and radio connection to the hospital in St Anthony. In the early sixties LAM had less than seventy inhabitants. They lived off what the land and the sea provided such as berries, fish, birds, seals and small whales that got caught in the fishnets. Large families often with six to ten children were normal.

I recall asking a girl walking together with a small boy how old her little brother was. 'It is my uncle, Sir', was the answer.

In Northern Newfoundland it is the youngest son who inherits from his father. This is common sense since his elder brothers would be already established. The youngest son would first fish together with his father, and later take over the father's house and boat while caring for his ageing parents.

With a great amount of work to be done in the fishing season, interaction during the summer months between the families was limited to putting out the boats in the spring and pulling them ashore in the fall. The villagers also did not like to travel after it got dark during the winter months, and this placed great limitation on their movement. Some villagers told of stories about ghosts and mermaids. Except for the Sunday Church service there was little interaction between the different villages. People were religious and each summer the Pentecostals would gather at the local pond to baptise the new members.

FISHING — IN COD WE TRUST

The fishing season lasts from June to October, but the good fishing only lasts for two months. The rest of the year they received unemployment insurance. Fresh cod was sold for $0.04 a pound and $0.35 a pound if it was dried. The families had an annual income of $3000-5000 before squaring up with the merchant for expenses. They would fish 40,000 lbs. a year and up to 800 lbs. on a good day. There were four wharves—one for each surname—where the fish was landed and gutted. The liver was tossed into large barrels and fermented into cod liver oil. Every morning the old-timers would stop by the barrel, drink a mouthful and at the same time dip their southwester into it for waterproofing.

Each cod trap was tailor-made for a particular fishing spot and the spot had to be reclaimed every year. To secure a spot you had to toss out a marker and have your trap in the water within four days. The mysterious disappearance of markers combined with the unpredictable break up of the ice often resulted in arguments over fishing spots which were the roots of some discontent between the villages.

The fine for catching lobster out of season was one week in jail or a $10 fine. The enterprising offenders took the week in jail. They were sent to St. John's by steamer and served their days in jail. While awaiting transport home, they were put up in a hotel and used the opportunity to buy spare parts and look around.

LANGUAGE

The local dialect was fascinating specially the negative use of the word 'wonderful'. On a day with little wind: 'The flies are wonderful bad today'. It was no compliment to be described as 'a wonderful size of a woman, just like a sleeping bag'.

Like cockney, they dropped and added the 'H'. For breakfast it was 'am and heggs. In the church it was '…hand the 'oly Spirit, Hamen'. One summer we found a large piece of whalebone, that looked like an oar. The following Sunday a large number of men took sudden interest in archaeology. They all wanted see the 'Viking hoar'.

THE SITE / ARCHAEOLOGY

I guess the locals wondered how people could make a living by digging trenches. First remove the turf, then carefully scrape away some inches of soil, that was taken away and sifted. Finally put everything back and move five yards to the side and start all over again. We found few, but important artefacts, one summer we only found a single nail.

In 1962, houses were erected to protect the old sod houses. But the rain and snow combined with the high water table made it difficult to provide proper drainage and the houses were removed some years later. The snow comes late and in large quantities, every spring the snow and ice snow would block Black Duck Brook and flood a large area.

CLIMATE

Regular maps give a false impression of a permanent summer. They often hide the fact that the coast is covered in ice for parts of the year and that the navigational season can be very short. The top of Newfoundland is enclosed in ice from January until May and as late as midsummer the ice limits your movement. Labrador is covered in ice from December until July and Baffin Island from November until August.

Anne Stine Ingstad used to say that in her next life she would study classical archaeology and do field work in a warmer climate. In 1963, I recorded the temperature for 55 days, from the end of June until the beginning of September. The average daytime temperature was 13 degrees C (55 degrees F). In six days the temperature exceeded 20 degrees and this was compensated by the six days were the temperature stayed below 10 degrees. I never repeated this exercise and the subsequent summers felt much warmer. The weather was quite stable. It was sunny 1/3 of the time, overcast 1/3 of the time and rain the other third. Most of the time there was a constant strong wind from the north buzzing in our ears. Fortunately there were few windless days and this limited the effect of the blackflies and the horseflies.

ROYAL MAIL

The mail came to Henderson's shop in Straits View twice a week and it was over an hour and a half walk to pick it up. The opening hours were strictly enforced, if you came a little late, you returned empty handed. But not everybody was allowed to pick up all the mail for LAM, because the postmaster had problems getting the empty mailbags returned.

A friend had two undershirts, one grey winter shirt, made from the regular Royal Mail bags and one thin blue summer shirt made from the AirMail bags.

Most adults did not enjoy writing; when Ingstad wanted a receipt for transport in a fishing boat, it was noticeable how many fishermen had just hurt their right hand and were unable to sign.

The Eaton Mail Order Catalogue had an important impact on the isolated villages. Or, as the old timers would put it: 'I have to write to Canada for it'. The catalogue was indeed very useful. After a wedding or a movie it was interesting to go through the latest catalogue and notice how quick and how many had ordered new outfits. When the men got together over a few pails (the only bottles they had were medicine bottles) of home-made beer, the catalogue was often passed around and we enjoyed looking at the latest in ladies' bras and underwear. Finally it was nailed to the inside of the outhouse.

Entertainment

Each summer a man would travel from village to village with a generator and a projector and show movies. He had problems fine tuning the old boat engine that was powering the generator. Either it was running so fast that we had time to see the movie twice or so slow that the celluloid started to burn. All this was great entertainment, when the light came on to change the reels, we observed who was sitting with whom and finally we saw the movie backwards.

One benefit of having large families was the frequent weddings and this was the easiest way of meeting people. Everybody was invited to a good meal inside and there were always some very nice drinks outside. At the reception there were far more guests than seats and there was a line up behind your chair. If you sat too long and did not know the technique of extending your range by putting butter on your knife before dunking it into the plate of crackers, a hand would appear from behind and help you to finish the meal.

Ship wreck

During a snowstorm in 1947 the ship Lagley Crag was tossed so far up on Great Sacred Island, that the crew were able to rig a bos'n's chair to reach land. Years afterwards, the ship was gradually pushed up on shore. The ship is a constant reminder of the dangerous waters and the reason for the following prayer: 'Oh God, if there is a shipwreck, let it take place outside our coast.'

On a visit to Quirpon I noticed a woodpile of large, perfectly round pieces of firewood that looked like rigging from a ship. And this is the story. On a foggy day in 1968 a schooner ran aground in the harbour. It was not dramatic; the skipper tossed out the anchor and was gone for some days looking for a boat that could pull him off. The fog was thick and lasted for days and it was impossible for the Royal Wreck Commissioner to travel to the site and do his duty.

The locals did not want this opportunity to pass and appointed a retired skipper as temporary wreck commissioner. He did only one thing. 'It is a wreck', he declared.

Suddenly all the small boats headed for the schooner. With saws and axes they relieved it of the rigging and much of the cargo.

The road comes

The road made its way slowly from the south. Finally they got access to hospital and the shops. It was no longer eight-hours' walk. Now they were free to sell their fish when and where they wanted. The girls got jobs and took off. The RCMP came in and some of the old handicrafts like making beer and moonshine disappeared.

The road was unpaved and we seldom made it to St Anthony without having a flat tire. Suddenly 'Canadian Tire', the name of the automotive chain store, made sense.

A few villagers got a job in St Anthony and moved into rented accomodation. In the beginning people would pile into the cars and drive down for a visit. Here many villagers got their first hands-on experience with the future. First the light switch was turned on and off several times, later the water tap got the same treatment.

For a short time I was afraid that all the villagers would use the road and leave LAM. But they adapted fast. Some new signs that can be seen were 'Milk 10 cents', 'Iceberg Ice for sale', 'Handmade socks and quilts'. I think that the people of LAM are the living proof of Darwin's words: it is not the strongest, but the one who can adapt who will survive.

The 'Viking Encampment' at L'Anse aux Meadows National Historic Site of Canada: Presenting the Past

Darrell Markewitz

A Brief History of the 'Norse / Viking Encampment' Series

The current 'Viking Encampment' living history program is the result of ongoing modifications of the original program as it was designed and installed in 1997 at L'Anse aux Meadows (LAM) NHSC. Every aspect of the physical presentation is the result of a conscious design, with the academic facts of the Viking Age being filtered through an understanding of effective public programming. Costumed staff members portray aspects of daily life utilizing a collection of reproduction objects. Physical demonstrations consist primarily of small textiles (spinning) and cooking, along with limited use of woodworking tools. The interpreters use a 'floating' system of interpretive delivery, where the presentation of information can range from 'role playing' as a voice from the past, through to 'third person' commentary from a modern perspective, as suited the needs of individual visitors (Markewitz, 1996).

The development sequence of the program is important, since many aspects of the physical presentation are a result of direct experience with the demands of the visiting public. The current program is itself based on an earlier series of presentations originally (and more correctly) called 'The Norse Encampment' which were originally presented as a special educational presentation as part of the Orangeville Medieval Festival in Ontario. Commencing in 1992, they were quite limited in scope, utilizing two costumed historic interpreters. The staff were surrounded by approximately 200 artefact reproductions, centered on two major assemblages: an 'A' frame tent containing a bed and various sea chests, and a fire pit set with a tripod and equipped with various cooking tools, with a focus on objects illustrative of 'daily life'.

From its first inception, information concerning the Norse Encampment in Ontario had been sent to Parks Canada at LAM NHSC. In 1996, the Viking Trail Tourism Association (VTTA), in concert with Parks Canada, sponsored a two week demonstration of this type of living history program, with the name changed to 'The Viking Encampment'. This first program at LAM utilized a core group of four 'professional' interpreters, surrounded by a collection of approximately 200 individual artifact reproductions. Six local volunteers assisted after receiving a crash course on the relevant history and crafts skills. On the part of Parks Canada, it was an opportunity to evaluate the potential suitability and usefulness of a living history presentation at a very low cost.

In early 1997, I was contracted directly by the VTTA, who were working in partnership with Human Resources & Development Canada and again Parks Canada, to develop a regular seasonal presentation for the site. Six local staff underwent a two and a half week training program, the overall interpretive program was designed and implemented, and artifact reproductions were researched and created (or commissioned as required). The physical presentation as originally designed was equipped with a selection of about 150 replica artefacts and opened in mid June, 1997. A second week-long training session was held in 1998. The Viking Encampment program has remained a regular feature of the LAM NHSC over its normal operating season (approximately mid June to end September), at first under the control of the VTTA and Parks Canada since 2001.

A GENERAL OR SPECIFIC IMAGE OF THE VIKING AGE?

Any living history program is only one possible vision of the past, never an exact representation (Markewitz, 1999, 268). The Viking Encampment program had both its content and presentation shaped by a number of defining points of view: (1) the Norse 'outpost station' of LAM was to serve as point source for presenting the rough outlines of the entire Viking Age; (2) interpreters' characters would be bold and overly cosmopolitan to allow for an easy introduction to a wide range of social and historical topics; and (3) a wider selection of artifacts in type and quality than was likely to have been physically present at LAM would be included to present as full a picture of Norse material culture as possible.

From its conception and original design, the Norse Encampment was never intended to be a precise duplication of what may have been seen in 'Leifsbuðir' at the Vínland outpost in summer of AD 1000. Instead, the Encampment was both broader in scope and also less detailed, reflecting the general structure of Norse material culture near the close of the Viking Age.

To allow the staff to work effectively over several levels of interpretive delivery, especially with full role playing, a set of inter-related character descriptions and an overall scenario were written. These descriptions were deliberately written as sketches, allowing individual staff to refine the details based on their own personalities. Past experience has shown that providing for some personal input increases interest and enthusiasm, thus effectiveness of delivery. Also, some of the characters' details were contradictory, so as to create realistic, multiple 'points of view' over shared events. These characters were intentionally designed to reflect the Viking Age in general, rather than the situation at LAM. Thus, reflecting the importance of the defining artifact of the Viking Age, the longship, the characters consisted of the crew of a merchant ship-traders rather than farmers or explorers. The crew also dis-

194

Figure 1. The 'Viking Encampment' programme at L'Anse aux Meadows NHSC uses costumed historic interpreters to bring the past to life (photo: D. Markewitz).

played a range of origins and viewpoints, coming from Norway, Ireland, England and Iceland. This permitted discussion of topics that could not be easily introduced by focusing solely on Vínland. The characters themselves were admittedly 'larger than life', but again this has been deliberately done to make it easier for the public to relate to the personalities, and thus the historic era.

The prototype objects were also based on artifacts from widely diverse contexts. These were selected to create a complete set of equipment to make up the physical body of the presentation. It is quite obvious that the direct archaeology of LAM was not going to be great guidance in this selection, with so few artifacts available (Ingstad 1977). Of course the bronze ring pin and soapstone spindle whorl were represented and used, with iron process-ing portrayed with the basic tools necessary to form rivets. The total selection also includes a much wider range of both object types and quality that are likely to have been present in Vínland. Primary sources for the other replica objects used were: the Oseberg ship burial, Norway (Roesdahl and Wilson 1992); the Mastermyr tool box, Gotland (Ardwidsson and Berg 1983); and various everyday objects found during excavation at Coppergate, York, England (Hall 1994), and Wood Quay, Dublin, Ireland, plus an assortment of objects from other locations (Graham-Campbell 1980).

The problems of production costs, suitable raw materials and availability of trained arti-sans became important factors as to what artifacts could be recreated. Rather than attempt to detail every distortion that was the result of these interlocked factors, only a few of the more glaring examples will be briefly mentioned here, along with the rational for their inclu-sion.

195

Several items of glazed ceramic were part of the cookware. These included a medium jug, loosely based on those found at Birka, Sweden, plus a bowl with similar patterning but totally without provenance. It is unlikely that ceramics of any kind were ever present at

Figure 2. The story of Vínland: a control station for exploration and timber gathering (photo: D. Markewitz).

196

Figure 3. A female interpreter wearing the small cap discussed in the text at LAM. Any living history programme can only illustrate a generalised view of the past. Fine details are blurred by modern considerations (photo: D. Markewitz).

LAM, and certainly the glaze used is very modern. Despite this, these items were included to provide for the very real modern day problem of cleanliness related to food safety. (Part of the daily physical demonstrations carried out by the interpreters involved cooking 'flat cakes' using period type ingredients, which were distributed to the public.)

The anvil included as part of the blacksmith's equipment is in fact a modern steel casting rather than the historically correct forged wrought iron. This production method was chosen for pure ease of fabrication. Further, it is my opinion that the large physical size and pattern of this anvil based on a sample from Novgorod, Russia, makes it unlikely that the type would have been present at LAM. Despite this, physical depictions of iron working already on display at the site featured this specific object and it was decided to 'agree' with the earlier depictions.

The bed is based on one of the plainer ones found in the Oseberg ship burial. Although such a high status item may not have existed at LAM, the inclusion of the bed was to indicate status, so important to Norse society. The bed also allows for an easy introduction to the subjects of raw material production, timberwork and household furnishings.

Similarly, the cauldron hanger and the associated 'bronze' pot (actually formed of brass) are also high status items. Although the pot itself is based on the much worn sample found inside the Mastermyr tool box, it has been suggested since the installation of the presentation that such pots were most commonly used to serve wine to important guests, not used to cook daily soups (B. Wallace, pers. comm.). Again, problems related to fabrication and raw materials are the reasons for the use of this object rather than the far more typical and likely cauldron of iron segments.

197

Generally with all the physical objects that make up the presentation, there has been substitutions made for the original raw materials. Mild steel replaces wrought iron; commercially sawn North American woods replace quarter-split European varieties, commercially-blended fabrics replace hand spun and woven textiles. In each case, the related problems of availability and raw cost were the main reason for the substitutions. In some cases these exchanges are only apparent to the true expert, and they do not intrude upon the public's perception of authenticity. The individual craftsmanship as indicated in the quality of each object often varies considerably. This is not considered significant, but in fact lends an aura of authenticity to the entire collection. The Norse who came to Vínland were not high kings, and their personal gear would range both in quality and condition.

ROLE OF LIVING HISTORY

The intent of the program from its inception was to provide the museum visitor with a general insight into the overall culture of the Norse, to create an impression of what a people and their world was like. Artifacts would be contextualised; characters would be larger than life to better portray specific attitudes. In this way, what was included in the presentation, and how each element was employed, was part of an overall design.

Past experience has shown that many academics do not fully understand the basic principles of living history, or what such programs are designed to achieve (Markewitz 1998). This unfortunately often leads to an overall negative impression of any physical presentation that utilizes these techniques. It is true that it is simply impossible for any modern attempt to perfectly duplicate the past. There are a wide number of reasons why this is so, with changes to physical environment, available raw materials, human condition, social attitudes, and basic skills all forming barriers. There are a number of factors concerning the artifacts and the interpreter presentations which in the strictest sense may be seen as distortions of the Viking Age. By specifically detailing the origin of such distortions, one may illustrate some of the larger problems involved with converting pure research into physical programming.

Caps, Necklines and Fabrics—Reality over the Ideal

The physical objects that make up the body of any living history program are what sets the atmosphere perceived by the visiting public. Front and center are the costumes and accessories worn by the interpreters themselves which create the impression that an interpreter represents a voice from the past. At the same time, it is here that so many modern practicalities of mounting effective programming can be the most intrusive. In an ideal situation, each piece of costume would be created with painstaking detail. Ideally Viking-Age costumes would be created from raw fibres with natural dyes, hand spun, woven on warp weighted looms and sewn by hand. Finishing details would be supplied through similarly crafted tablet weaving and embroidery. As might be supposed, the production cost for complete staff costuming at this level would be extreme. In almost any living history presentation, restrictive budgets always control what degree of detailing is possible.

For the Viking Encampment, the staff were each issued with two sets of under clothes and two sets of over clothes, one heavy and one lightweight to provide for the variation in weather over the operating season (which is considerable in Northern Newfoundland!). The women each had a single apron, and each person had a single wool cloak. The choice of fabrics had to also reflect not only historic prototypes, but the practical necessities of modern life as well. Although it was desirable to use pure wool fabrics, it was well understood that these require special washing and drying methods, care that could not be expected to be undertaken. For this reason, the actual fabrics selected were mainly of wool / cotton or linen / cotton blends. Time and cost also determined production. The original issue of costumes was all machine sewn, with strong 'French seams' used to reinforce cut edges, modern methods that were intended to remain hidden. Considerable care was taken to use hand sewing finish work on things like necklines on the assumption these would be in clear view.

Another detail of the costume construction that relates to practical concerns rather than strict historic accuracy is the use of single buttons as neck closures. The majority of the tunics and dresses were constructed with oval or circular necklines with a short slit at the middle front. Historically, these slits would have been most commonly held closed with a small wire or cast metal pin, often a 'pennanular' type (Graham-Campbell 1980). Instead, costumes were designed with a single button, often a bead or antler disk, using a braided loop. Small brooches were not considered since past experience proved they are easily and quickly lost. Although not as historically accurate, at least the use of a single button proved a practical solution to these problems—especially since the costumes were produced before staff were hired and sizes known.

One last item of costume that has unintentionally resulted in some debate over its use is the small 'Jorvik' style cap, based on the original from Coppergate of imported silk and found in a cess pit (Hall 1994; fig. 3). The original costume issue for each female staff member included one of these, made of white linen. Since the start of the Viking Encampment, exactly what the wearing of this cap indicates has undergone several revisions. Is it a symbol of a married woman instead of a single? Is it a sign of a Christian practitioner over a pagan? Is it even a woman's accessory at all? The simple truth is that this cap was included into the costume of the female interpreters for entirely different and much more practical reasons. The female staff all had short hair, yet during the Viking Age long hair seems to have been the norm for women. Anticipating this, the decision was made very early in the program's design to hide this modern style with one of the small caps. A second function of the cap was to limit smoke damage and scent to their hair from open fires. Yet often staff members now were seen to tie the cap strings around their necks, but then fold it back to let it hang down their backs. This use satisfies no useful purpose, as physical protection, a historical element or as effective camouflage.

CHRISTIAN OR PAGAN?

One of the best examples of a distortion of historic fact that was introduced into the presentation for specific cause was with how the issue of religion was dealt. The 'date' of the Viking Encampment has always been fixed at AD 1000, a 'nice round number' that easily can be communicated to the public and which agrees with the archaeological interpretation of the site. This also marks the date of the well-documented 'official' conversion to Christianity in Iceland. Saga evidence indicates that both Leifr and his mother were Christians, physical evidence from Greenland suggests Christian churches were structures built early in the life of the colony. All these things would suggest that it is most probable that most, if not all, the members of any expedition to Vínland would have been Christians (Wallace 1991).

One of the basic elements that shaped the design of the program was that the Viking-Age cultural milieu was partially defined by a general belief in a basically similar and much older religious system than Christianity. This worldview of the Norse, shaped by their environment, was considered fundamental to any attempt at understanding or portraying the culture. The changes in attitude and daily conduct as determined by Christianity were considered to have been a shell over the older belief in a pantheon of gods, goddesses, giants and monsters. To have portrayed a purely Roman Catholic population would have made it extremely difficult to introduce the topic of these original Norse pagan systems and practices to the public.

199

For that reason alone, the original character sketches for the interpreters included a range of religious attitudes, from purely pagan to purely Christian, with the majority being portrayed as some blend of the two (see Gräslund, this volume). Although the initial staff training covered both the 'ancient pagan' and the 'new Christian' points of view, the intention was not to make religion a major or central topic of the presentation. Instead, the issue was raised by the subtle wearing of an amulet. In some cases this would be a small cross, in others a Thor's hammer, with others both. This allowed for an easy entry into discussion on the subject should a member of the public notice and inquire. Interpreters were not intended to launch into a description of 'their' religious beliefs any more than people do in the modern day.

BEADS, BUDGETS AND PERSONAL MODIFICATIONS

The amulets were attached to leather thongs for wear at the neck, each of which were further embellished by the addition of various glass beads. Originally, the men's costume included no more than a couple of beads, with women issued with both a larger number and wider selection of types. The exception to this was the 'chieftain', who wore a silver hammer pendant with about a dozen beads based on that from Skåne, Sweden. Along with the silver coins, glass beads could serve as a means to introduce the extent and nature of trade, rise of local production centers, even how colour relates to natural dye types on textiles. These factors also suggested the content of individual necklaces could be measured against social / economic status of the various characters portrayed. Taken altogether inside a living history framework, these necklaces can thus serve as an opening point to at least a half dozen individual topic areas for further discussion. The beaded necklaces here amply illustrate a number of problems that can arise within living history programs.

The first problem posed by attempting to introduce the correct type and collection of glass beads accurate to the Viking Age is with actual supply. Ideally, the solution to acquiring the correct types would be to employ suitably trained artisans to duplicate the originals, but once again the dual problem of availability and raw cost intruded. For the 'Viking

Encampment', it was necessary to carefully select commercially purchased glass beads. The end result was not perfect, but at least close to original Norse artifact samples.

When viewing the Viking Encampment presentation as existed in autumn, 2000, the beaded necklaces being worn were a clear indication of another of the most basic problems with the proper maintenance of any living history program. What I refer to is the requirement for experienced, knowledgeable, and close supervision of interpretive staff.

Effective living history interpreters are by their very nature a very difficult group to supervise. The qualities of personal creativity, breadth of knowledge, self direction and flair for the dramatic that are the mark of the best interpreter also make them prone to modify even the best established program. Ideal staff members continue to research and develop skills. They are most often the ones who breathe true life into a living history museum. The problem lies with finding the correct balance between maintaining control, and at the same time not destroying this personal initiative. This ideal balance is so difficult to achieve that its presence is more a rarity than the standard among living history museums, obviously a situation well understood by those who design interpretive programs. Too much control, and the best interpretive staff become frustrated and often leave, leaving a site dull and uninteresting. Too little control, and the carefully designed historic presentation will quickly become distorted.

200   It has been my personal experience that the very best on-site interpretive supervisors are those who have 'come up from the ranks'—former working interpreters with long experience, and considerable skills acquired over time. This has certainly been my observation within North America, where living history sites originated and are most common. I would suggest much of the dissatisfaction that academics find with living history as a method of museum presentation can be traced back to distortions resultant from this situation.

Having said this, what does our examination of the state of the Viking Encampment program suggest about this issue? The beaded necklaces being worn by male staff certainly indicated some problems. In autumn 2000, one could observe an absolute explosion in the size, complexity and number of beads on the necklaces from what had originally been issued. Most of these modified necklaces now included a large number of metal pendants, including those based on period objects, but also those that were clearly modern designs.

This situation clearly demonstrates a lack of the precise type of close supervision required to maintain historical accuracy and overall content. Direct daily supervision was provided by one of the interpretive staff themselves, acting as a 'team leader', with only infrequent assessments from outside consultants. Overall control of the program rested at that point with what was in fact 'an arms length government agency dedicated to the promotion of tourism and development of local business'—not an educational organization of any kind. Even on the most generous analysis, a situation existed where continued distortion of historic fact was likely to continue without the required close supervision of the program's content.

TOURISM VERSES HISTORY

From the very earliest work with the 'Encampment' series of educational programs, there has been a very careful distinction made between 'Norse' and 'Viking'. The term 'Norse' has been used to refer to a specific culture, the term 'Viking' to a specialized activity carried out by only a few members of that group. Although this may appear to be a fine point of distinction, there is in fact considerable argument (as demonstrated at the Viking Millennium International Symposium itself) over the appropriate use of these terms (see Magnusson, this volume).

It is suggested here that the change of name to 'Viking' Encampment was done for reasons that do not relate to historical education, but instead primarily as a direct reference to the tourism requirements of the modern 'Viking Trail' region in Newfoundland (see McAleese, this volume). The use of the term 'Viking' only serves to reinforce the North American cultural stereotype of the Norse as bloodthirsty raiders in horned helmets. As part of a larger presentation within a museum context, there is absolutely no need to pander to this misconception. A case can be made that it is the responsibility of any educational program to specifically address and attempt to destroy such incorrect stereotypes.

CONCLUSION

The Viking Encampment program as seen at LAM NHSC today is a modified version of the physical presentation as was originally designed and installed in June, 1997. Since this paper was originally presented in fall of 2000, Parks Canada as assumed overall control of the Viking Encampment programme. The improved supervision of the staff and increased ability to direct resources has resulted in the correction of a number of the problems detailed in this paper. In 2001, Parks also added a reconstruction of an iron-smelting hut to the physical presentation.

The Viking Encampment was the end result of a longer series of programs, stretching back to 1993, that allowed for trials, corrections, and the evolution of effective methods to portray the Viking Age to the general public. In its original form, the Norse Encampment was never intended to be an exact duplication of the specific events that took place at the Norse outpost at LAM about AD 1000. Instead, the presentation was intended to portray a much wider and generalized view of Norse material and social culture in the late Viking Age. As with all living history programs, the Norse Encampment was specifically designed to create an impression of 'what it was like' in the minds of the general public. 201

Inaccuracies in specific documented facts, most commonly as related to the specific details of individual objects, were sometimes allowed to enter into the physical presentation. This was almost always done with cause, as the primary objective of any living history program must remain to be historic accuracy. As has been examined through specific examples, the reasons for these inaccuracies are varied. The restrictions of limited budgets, modern considerations such as safety, practical factors such as material availability and durability; all effect what level of detail can be achieved. An important consideration remains the suitability of available staff, what training is provided to them, and what level of enthusiasm they are able to maintain as they work in a very demanding environment.

It is of fundamental importance that any living history program, even one that is the result of such a long development process as the Norse Encampment series, be professionally monitored, constantly upgraded, and properly supported. The very best historic interpreters are self-motivated, creative and enthusiastic. Too much control will kill the spirit and thus the 'life' of the program—too little and wide distortions of historic fact are sure to intrude. Living History remains one of the most effective tools for presenting the often complex cultural framework of a past time period. Academic researchers are reminded that even the best interpretive program can never be a perfect duplication of a lost age. Many factors from the philosophical to the practical make this impossible. Instead, a Living History program can only create a general impression of 'what it was like'. Hopefully the three elements of detailed and accurate program design, well-trained and motivated staff, and effective supervision and support, all combine to provide a historically accurate and memorable experience for the visiting public.

Darrell Markewitz

BIBLIOGRAPHY

Ardwidsson, G. and Berg, G. 1983. *The Mastermyr Find: A Viking-Age Tool Chest from Gotland*, Stockholm.

Graham-Campbell, J. 1980. *Viking Artefacts*, London.

Hall, R.A. 1994. *Viking Age York*, London.

Ingstad, A-S. 1977. *The Discovery of a Norse Settlement in North America*, Oslo.

Jones, C. 1999. *Proceedings of the 27th Meeting and Conference of the Association for Living Historical Farms & Agricultural Museums*, vol. 21, North Bloomfield, Ohio.

Markewitz, D. 1996. Working in the Middle Ages, Historic Interpretation and Experimental Archaeology in the Society for Creative Anachronism, unpublished paper, McMaster University.

——1998. Recreating the Viking Age: the Viking Encampment at L'Anse aux Meadows, unpublished paper, 33rd International Medieval Congress, Kalamazoo, Michigan.

——1999. 'Lessons from the Viking Age—Development of an Interpretive Program for L'Anse aux Meadows NHSC', in Jones 1999, 268-76.

Roesdahl, E. and Wilson, D. 1992. *From Viking to Crusader: The Scandinavians and Europe, 800-1200*, New York.

Wallace, B. 1991. 'L'Anse aux Meadows—Gateway to Vinland', *Acta Archaeologica*, 61, 166-97.

202

'Wish you were here...':

A Thumbnail Portrait of the Great Northern Peninsula AD 1000

Trevor Bell, Joyce B. Macpherson and M.A.P. Renouf

INTRODUCTION

Souvenir postcards from L'Anse aux Meadows (LAM) National Historic Park typically show a view from near the Visitors' Centre looking over a treeless landscape with icebergs grounded in the shallow water of Sacred Bay. If the native Indians or the Norse visitors 1000 years ago had been able to send a postcard, would the scene have been different? In this paper we attempt to address this question by examining records of past environmental change on the tip of the Great Northern Peninsula, focusing primarily on landscape and vegetation history and, to a lesser degree, climate. As much of the landscape we see today is a product of events and processes that go back much earlier than AD 1000, our story begins as the glaciers receded at the end of the last Ice Age, about 12,000 years BP (uncalibrated radiocarbon years before present).

203

The tip of the Northern Peninsula is bounded by the Strait of Belle Isle to the northwest, the Labrador Sea (Atlantic Ocean) to the north and east, and Hare Bay to the south (fig. 1). Local uplands include the White Hills on the north shore of Hare Bay which reach an elevation of 320 m and isolated hills along the east coast up to 100 m high. Elsewhere the land is low-lying and many areas are boggy. St. Anthony (pop. ~3000) is the largest of eighteen communities that are broadly distributed along the east and north coasts.

LANDSCAPE EVOLUTION

The region is a typical glacial landscape dominated by erosion. Bare bedrock which makes up the largest surficial unit, with up to 90% exposure in some areas (Grant 1986), is commonly moulded and etched to form abundant rock basins and knobs. In detail these rock surfaces preserve abundant evidence of ice movement and sculpting, including grooves and striations (fig. 2a). Erratic boulders of all sizes litter the surface. Ice flow features record the activity of both Laurentide (mainland) and Newfoundland ice masses during different glacial phases of the last (Late Wisconsinan) glaciation (Grant 1992). Briefly, for the study region these include: (i) a glacial maximal phase when Laurentide ice from Labrador extended southeastward across the Strait of Belle Isle and the northern tip of the Northern Peninsula, terminating some distance offshore in the Labrador Sea (*White Hills* phase); (ii) retreat of Laurentide ice back across the Strait of Belle Isle prior to 13,000 BP while a remnant ice mass persisted over Hare Bay, White Hills (fig. 2b) and coastal uplands farther north (*Hare Bay* phase); and (iii) stabilization and later readvance of Laurentide and Newfoundland ice margins between 13,000 and 11,000 BP (*Bradore/Piedmont* and *Ten Mile Lake* phases).

Following glacial retreat much of the landscape below the present 150 m contour was submerged by the sea because the earth's crust was depressed by the former ice load (glacioisostasy). As relative sea level returned to its present position, due primarily to crustal rebound, former shorelines were marked by raised marine landforms and sediments (fig. 2c). Gravel beach ridges and terraces are fairly common for several kilometres inland of the present coast (fig. 2d) and extensive deposits of deepwater mud occur between Sacred Bay and

Figure 1. Oblique, three-dimensional digital elevation model with shaded relief showing the location of placenames used in the text. Vertical exaggeration is 7 times and elevation is shown in increments of 35 m. East-west scale is *c.* 1:200 000. The distance from St. Anthony to Saddle Hill Pond is ~25 km. The elevation of the east summit of the White Hills is roughly 320 m.

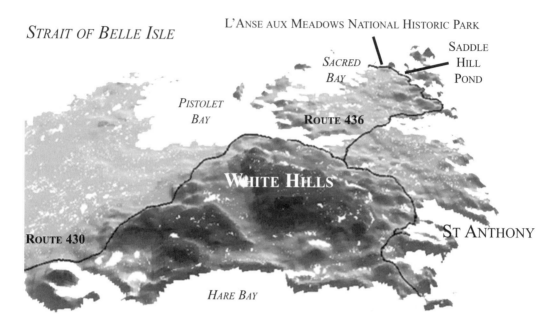

LABRADOR SEA

STRAIT OF BELLE ISLE

L'ANSE AUX MEADOWS NATIONAL HISTORIC PARK

SACRED BAY

SADDLE HILL POND

PISTOLET BAY

ROUTE 436

WHITE HILLS

ROUTE 430

ST ANTHONY

HARE BAY

204

Pistolet Bay. Occurrences of mud are likely more widespread but tend to be blanketed by bog due to poor drainage.

A preliminary shoreline displacement curve was constructed by Grant (1992) to demonstrate how relative sea level changed through postglacial time. He plotted the elevation of radiocarbon-dated marine fossils from beach and deepwater sediments (Grant 1992) and freshwater organic material from bogs and lake basins (Henningsmoen 1977; Davis *et al.* 1988). Unfortunately, many of these samples originated from either far above or below their contemporary sea level and therefore provide weak control on the elevation of sea level at the time of deposition. Nevertheless, the general sea level trend has an exponential form typical of a glacioisostatically rebounding coast, with rapid emergence until about 8000 BP (average of 2.9 m/century), followed by a much slower rate since about 6000 BP (average 0.16 m/century). The magnitude and direction of recent sea level change is unclear. Erosion of 1000-2000 year old raised beaches by modern shore processes suggests that emergence may have given way to submergence in recent time.

What was the effect of these higher relative sea levels on the paleogeography of the region? Using the generalized shoreline displacement curve for the Strait of Belle Isle from Grant (1989) and a digital elevation model (DEM) created from 1:50,000 scale topographic maps (50 ft contour interval; vertical error margin is ±20 m), we reconstructed the approximate palaeoshoreline positions at 2000 year intervals between 12,000 and 6000 BP (fig. 3). This age range was selected because by 12,000 BP most of the region was ice-free, except for some local ice masses on the White Hills (Grant 1992), while after 6000 BP the palaeoshorelines cannot be reliably distinguished from the present coastline given the vertical error margins inherent in the topographic data.

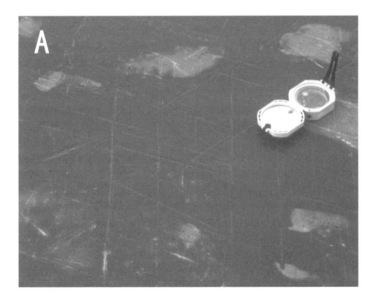

Figure 2.
A. Striated surfaces like this one from the Strait of Belle Isle indicate the direction and sequence of ice flows across the study region.

B. View south to the White Hills with Route 340 in the foreground. These hills were one of the few areas of land that remained above sea level at ~12,000 BP.

205

The 12,000 BP palaeoshoreline roughly shows the limit of marine inundation in the region (fig. 3a). At this time only the flanks and summits of the White Hills and neighbouring uplands were above sea level and they existed as islands offshore from the Northern Peninsula mainland. The sea reached a height of 140 m asl and extended inland up to ten kilometres from the present coast. By 10,000 BP up to 80 m of land emergence had occurred, creating a large single island of the White Hills and surrounding slopes, and raising above sea level the summits of coastal uplands along the Atlantic coast (fig. 3b). By 8000 BP relative sea level had fallen to 25 m asl and the region was reconnected to the Northern Peninsula (fig. 3c). In Hare Bay the configuration of the steep coastline was roughly as it is at present, whereas the gently shelving shore of Pistolet Bay was displaced inland by up to 5 km. By 6000 BP relative sea level had fallen to 10 m asl and the shoreline was within a

Figure 2.

C. Former shorelines are marked by raised gravel beaches and terraces up to 140 m asl (photo: I.A. McKnight).

D. At LAM, terraces occur at 16, 10.5, and 4 m asl, the lower one being the site of Norse occupation AD 1000 (reconstructed house left background).

206

C

D

kilometre or so of the present coast (fig. 3d). Only the heads of Sacred and Pistolet bays showed significant departures from the current coastline configuration.

VEGETATION HISTORY

LAM at 51°N is at the southeastern limit of the sub-arctic Forest-Tundra vegetation zone, which extends from north of the Arctic Circle at the mouth of the Mackenzie River, east and south across Labrador-Ungava to the Strait of Belle Isle. As the Canadian climatologist Dr. Kenneth Hare has stated, 'nowhere else on earth does the arctic verge drive so far south into middle latitudes'(Hare 1952). Why do we find sub-arctic vegetation at LAM, which is at the same latitude as London, England? The answer is provided by the icebergs shown in the souvenir postcard, or rather by the Labrador Current that carried them south from Baffin Bay.

Vegetation Type	Cover	Composition
Boreal forest (marginal)	4.6%	fir (*Abies balsamea*), larch (*Larix laricina*), black spruce (*Picea mariana*), white birch (*Betula papyrifera*), alder (shrub; *Alnus crispa* [now *Alnus viridis* (Hay and Brouillet 2000)]), heaths (*Ericaceae*).
Tall tuck	22%	fir (*Abies balsamifera, A. phanerolepis* [now included in *Abies balsamea*]), birch (*Betula papyrifera*), spruce (*Picea mariana*), larch (*Larix laricina*), alder (*Alnus crispa*), heaths (*Ericaceae*).
Low tuck	9%	spruce (*Picea mariana, P. glauca*), heaths (*Ericaceae*), *Sphagnum*.
Rock barrens	27%	heaths (*Empetrum nigrum, Arctostaphylos alpina* [now *Arctorus rubra*]), mosses, lichens.
Soil barrens		heaths (*Empetrum nigrum*), bakeapple (*Rubus chamaemorus*), mosses, lichens.
Beach berms		grass (*Elymus arenaria*), beach pea (*Lathyrus japonicus*), other herbs.
Snow beds		alder (*Alnus crispa*), birch (*Betula papyrifera, B. pumila*), other shrubs, herbs, mosses.
Bogs	>30%	*Sphagnum*, mosses, lichens, heaths (*Ericaceae*), sedges (*Cyperaceae*), bakeapple (*Rubus chamaemorus*).
Fen		sedges (*Cyperaceae*), *Sphagnum*, birch (*Betula michauxii*), heaths (*Ericaceae*), sweet gale (*Myrica* gale).
Marsh		sedges (*Carex*), birch (*Betula pumila, B. michauxii*), sweet gale (*Myrica* gale), herbs.
Tidal marsh		sedges (*Carex*), grasses (*Gramineae*), other herbs, *Sphagnum*.

207

Table 1. Vegetation types, percent cover and composition in the L'Anse aux Meadows area (Gimbarzevsky 1977; Davis 1980).

The water of the Labrador Current is cold, and the coastal sea ice which forms in December persists until June. Winds off the ocean are cool, and freezing temperatures have been recorded in every month except August. Snow-cover normally persists from November until May. Summers are short, cool, windy and damp, and where there is any depth of soil it tends to remain moist.

It is not surprising that more than one-third of the area of the National Historic Park is classified as Wetland: bog, fen and marsh (Table 1; fig. 4a background; Gimbarzevsky 1977); peat may remain frozen at depth throughout the summer (Gimbarzevsky 1977; Henningsmoen 1977). A similar area is classified as Heath (Barrens; fig. 4b foreground, fig. 4c) and the remaining one-third supports Marginal Forest (fig. 4a), and Tall and Low Tuckamore (Tuck or *Krummholz*; fig. 4b). Cut stumps are found on some of the barrens,

A   **~12 000 BP**

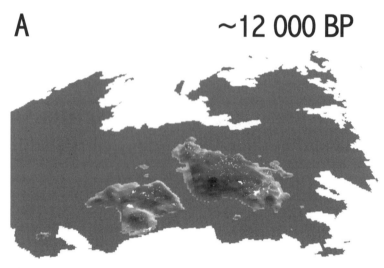

Figure 3A-D. Approximate shoreline positions at selected time periods during postglacial emergence of the study region. The dark grey fill outlines the present coastline for comparison and indicates the extent of formerly submerged land at each time period.

B   **~10 000 BP**

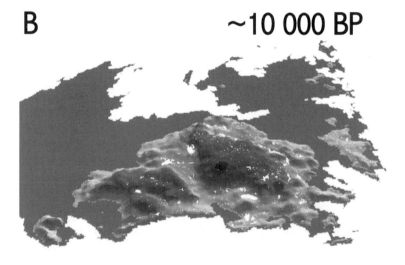

indicating that they supported forest or tuck not too long ago. The forest, with trees more than 5 m tall, covers only 5% of the area of the Park, and is found in more sheltered inland areas. Trees in exposed situations are shorter: less than 3 m in Tall Tuck and less than 2 m (to as little as a few centimetres) in Low Tuck. Here the branches are deformed by the wind or abraded by blowing snow if they rise above the snow-pack.

POLLEN DIAGRAMS

How can we learn what the vegetation was like in the past? Individual plants have life-spans of a few hundred years at most, and when they die their tissues decay and the nutrients they contain are recycled to build new plants. None of the plants we see today in the Park, even the largest tree, was living much more than 200 years ago. Fortunately there is one part of a plant, the wall of the microscopic pollen grain or spore, which is resistant to

C

~8000 BP

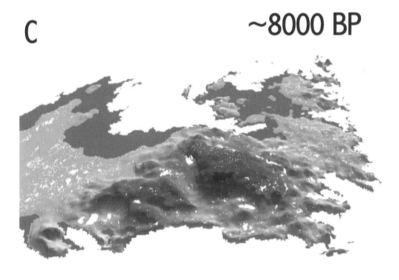

D

~6000 BP

decay under certain conditions; for instance, in the peat accumulating in a bog or fen or in the sediment (mud) at the bottom of a pond. As the peat or sediment accumulates year by year it incorporates pollen grains and spores from plants living nearby with a few blown in from greater distances. Using a microscope the pollen grains and spores can be identified by their size, shape and surface texture. By identifying the pollen grains and spores at different levels in the sediment we can make a pollen diagram which shows how the vegetation has changed over time.

Two sets of pollen graphs give us a partial record of the vegetation at LAM since 8000 BP (fig. 5). The graphs were selected to represent the major vegetation types; the data were extracted from work by A.M. Davis and J.H. McAndrews of the University of Toronto (Davis *et al.* 1988; J.H. McAndrews, pers. comm.). The upper set records some of the pollen preserved in the peat from the fen sloping down to Black Duck Brook from the terrace with the Norse house sites (Davis *et al.* 1988). This record extends back in time to about 2000

Figure 4. Photographs of vegetation types in LAM National Historic Site (photos: K. McVeigh; courtesy of Dr. A.W. Robertson).

A. Scrub Forest consisting of larch and balsam fir, 5-10 m tall, forms a fairly continuous cover in the foreground, whereas Sphagnum dominated Bog occupies poorly drained depressions in the background.

B. Tall Tuck grows in the shelter of a rock cliff near the coast. The tops of trees that project above the protective snow cover in winter are wind abraded. Spongy mats of Soil Barren occur in more open areas.

210

BP; the peat was more than 50 cm thick, and accumulated at a mean rate of about 1 cm in 33 years. Beneath this is a set of graphs from Saddle Hill Pond, at 32 m above sea level (J.H. McAndrews, pers. comm.); because this site is higher it emerged earlier from the postglacial sea; we show the pollen record back from 2000 to about 8000 BP; the sediment accumulated at a mean rate of about 1 cm in 23 years. An earlier pollen diagram from the bog adjacent to Saddle Hill Pond was published by K.E. Henningsmoen (1977); McAndrews' work on the pond sediments carries the record back closer to the time of emergence from the postglacial sea.

To make the pollen diagram from the peat, a block of peat was extracted from the wall of a trench cut across the terrace when the archaeological excavations were under way, and small samples (about 1 cm³) were extracted at intervals of 1 cm, with no gaps. For the pond, where the sediment is more than 4 m deep in the centre, a core of sediment 5 cm in diame-

C. Rock Barren vegetation grows in protected hollows of weathered bedrock where moisture and a favourable microclimate persist.

D. Beach Pea and Silverweed make up the dominant vegetation on beach berms.

211

ter was obtained from a boat in one-metre increments using a piston corer. The core was split and small samples (0.9 cm³) were extracted at intervals of 10 cm. Each sample in the bog represents a mean of 33 years of accumulation, whereas each sample for the pond represents a mean of about 23 years of accumulation once in about 230 years. In both cases the samples were treated chemically to remove organic materials, as well as inwashed mineral soil particles in the case of the pond, leaving the resistant pollen grains and spores. A sample of about 300 pollen grains is normally counted at each level, from the up to 500,000 that may be present.

Pollen Representation

The plant groups selected for display in the pollen diagram represent the major vegetation types in the Park. There are many species of grass and sedge. Grass represents plant communities on damp mineral soil, particularly beach berms and stream-side marshes (fig. 5d). Sedges occur on a variety of wetter sites, again normally with mineral soil: fens and marshes. The Heaths (*Ericaceae*), of which the black crowberry (*Empetrum nigrum*) is the most common, are typical of the treeless barrens (fig. 4c foreground), and also occur to some extent on *Sphagnum* bogs and in low tuck. Birch occurs as a tree (white birch) in the forest and tall tuck, and as several shrub species on barrens and wetlands. Mountain alder occurs as a shrub in the forest and in tall tuck; on the barrens it occurs in gullies in rocky areas where it is protected by snow in winter (snow beds; Table 1). Black spruce is dominant in low tuck, but also occurs in tall tuck and forest (figs 4a and 4b).

Although birch and spruce are strongly represented in the pollen record, neither is the most common tree in the region—in fact balsam fir is more common. But birch is a prolific producer of pollen, as are alder and spruce; all are wind-pollinated, and require the production of very large numbers of pollen grains for the method to be successful. There can be as many as 6 million pollen grains in one birch catkin. The great majority of the pollen grains fail to land on a female flower, landing instead on the soil (from where they can be washed into a pond) or on the surface of a pond or wetland. Eventually some are preserved in the sediment.

Grasses and sedges are also wind-pollinated, but because their pollen grains are released closer to the ground they do not travel as far as pollen released from a taller shrub or tree, so that a high pollen value indicates a high proportion of those plants in the vicinity of the site. For these diagrams the proportions of the pollens of these herbs have been calculated separately from proportions of the pollens of trees and shrubs (the regional pollen rain). The proportions of the spores of the moss, *Sphagnum*, have also been calculated separately.

Pollen grains of the heaths such as crowberry (*Empetrum*) and blueberry (*Vaccinium*) are much less common than those of the wind-pollinated trees, although the crowberry is very widespread in the park; these plants are pollinated by insects and produce less pollen than plants that are wind-pollinated. In order to understand what the pollen diagram can reveal the analyst has to consider these differences in pollen representation.

If we examine the pollen diagrams from the base up we can see how these components of the vegetation have changed over time. About 8000 BP, soon after Saddle Hill emerged from the sea as an island or group of islands and the history of Saddle Hill Pond began, grass, sedge and heaths grew nearby. The grass probably grew at the back of a beach, and the sedge on wetland surrounding the pond. There were barrens, indicated by the heath pollen, on the higher parts of the island. By about 7000 BP birch, probably shrubs, grew in the area, crowding out the heaths, and grass declined as the shoreline retreated. The proportions of alder and spruce pollen increased slowly; at first the pollen was probably blown from plants at a distance. Alder and spruce probably arrived in the area around 6000 BP, when they in turn crowded out some of the shrub birch. We cannot tell whether the spruce pollen was produced by trees in a forest or by low-growing tuckamore plants, but the number and/or size of spruce trees increased between about 6000 and 2000 BP. Alder decreased between 4000 and 2000 BP; spruce may have crowded out some of the alders. The amount of birch pollen was fairly constant between 5000 and 2000 BP. The slight increase in sedge and *Sphagnum* from *c.* 5000 BP indicates the development of wetland around the pond; the heaths may have grown on the bog.

After 2000 years BP the peat from near the Norse site provides a much more detailed record. The rate of sea-level change had decreased by the time this site had emerged, and it has always been near the shore, so grass pollen from shoreline plants is common. The much higher amounts of sedge pollen compared with Saddle Hill Pond were produced by plants growing on the wetland. The irregular record for *Sphagnum* is attributed to disturbance, both physical (by the ocean and by the nearby Black Duck Brook) and by native people (Davis *et al.* 1988). After *c.* 700 BP there was a general decline in spruce, with an increase first of birch (which decreased again after about 500 BP) and then of alder. These changes suggest a decrease in the area of forest and tuckamore, and a corresponding increase in the area of barrens, borne out by increased amounts of heath pollen. Cutting of trees by local people has had some effect, but the trend began before European settlement, and must have been related to deteriorating climate and the expansion of wetland (paludification) (Davis 1984; 1985; Davis *et al.* 1988). It is not possible to identify from the pollen record any effects of the brief Norse occupation on the local vegetation, whether in terms of timber extraction, peat excavation or the introduction of alien plant species.

TEMPERATURE RECONSTRUCTION

In addition to pollen, lake sediment contains the remains of organisms living in the lake. Some of these, like midges (Chironomids), are able to fly and can move quickly to suitable habitats if the climate changes, unlike plants.

213

Midges live part of their life cycle as larvae in lakes, moulting four times before emerging as adults at the surface and flying away. The microscopic moulted mouth parts of the larvae are preserved in the lake mud, and can be identified as to species, much as pollen grains are. By sampling lakes in many parts of Canada, it has been found that particular groups of midges are typical of particular summer water temperatures. The chironomid remains in the sediment from a small lake near Port au Choix, 160 km southwest of LAM on the west coast of the Northern Peninsula, were examined by Rosenberg (1998) and show that for much of the past 6000-7000 years summer temperatures were warmer than at present (fig. 6). The earlier part of this period was consistently warmer, and represents the 'climatic optimum' of the middle part of our current interglacial period. Only two relatively short periods between 3500 and 1500 BP were cooler than at present. The last warm period coincides with the time of the Norse expansion across the North Atlantic Ocean.

If the temperature reconstruction is compared with the pollen record, the only clear correlation is between declining temperatures and decreasing forest cover (spruce) in the last 1000 years. During the earlier 'climatic optimum' the boreal forest was becoming established on the Northern Peninsula, and the pollen record (including trees that are not shown in the diagrams) indicates a forest cover which included contemporary species, and no species which are not present today. The forest has always been of a boreal nature, and trees such as pine, which grow today in more favoured parts of the island of Newfoundland, have never been present.

It is not to be expected that pollen evidence would be found in northern Newfoundland of the presence of plants such as the butternut (*Juglans cinerea*) associated with the Norse occupation level at the LAM site or the 'grapes' (*Vitis sp.*) referred to in the saga accounts, and indeed none is found. The range of these plants does not extend today beyond the limits of the mixed Acadian Forest Region of New Brunswick (Hosie 1969; Rowe 1972), where the growing season is longer and warmer than any in Newfoundland.

The butternuts were most probably carried to Newfoundland by humans, for although driftwood from across the Gulf of St. Lawrence finds its way to Newfoundland there is no record of nuts being washed ashore. A radiocarbon date from a butternut might eliminate the possibility that they were carried to the site by native people after the Norse occupation. A date falling within the Norse period would not, however, confirm that it was the Norse, rather than native people, who had carried the nuts to the site.

There is no physical evidence for the 'grapes', and no means of determining whether the fruit referred to was truly *Vitis* (i.e. could not have been local), or was the edible berry of a plant growing locally, or indeed was fictional. A summary of the extensive literature on this topic is beyond the scope of this paper.

CHANGING TEMPERATURES, SHIFTING CULTURES

The proxy water temperature record from Bass Pond shows a broad correspondence with prehistoric occupation of the Northern Peninsula (fig. 6). Maritime Archaic Indians were the earliest inhabitants of the Province, arriving from Labrador around 5000 BP (Carigan 1975, Reader 1996) and possibly as early as 5500 BP (Renouf and Bell 2000). The richly accoutred Port au Choix cemetery site (Tuck 1976) suggests that these Archaic Indians flourished on the Northern Peninsula, although we have little direct evidence of their settlement or subsistence (cf. Reader 1998; 1999; Renouf and Bell 1999; 2000). Their disappearance from the Newfoundland archaeological record by 3200 BP is unexplained. Maritime Archaic Indians were present in the Northern Peninsula during the latter half of the climatic optimum and their disappearance coincides with the onset of cooler temperatures around 3300 BP.

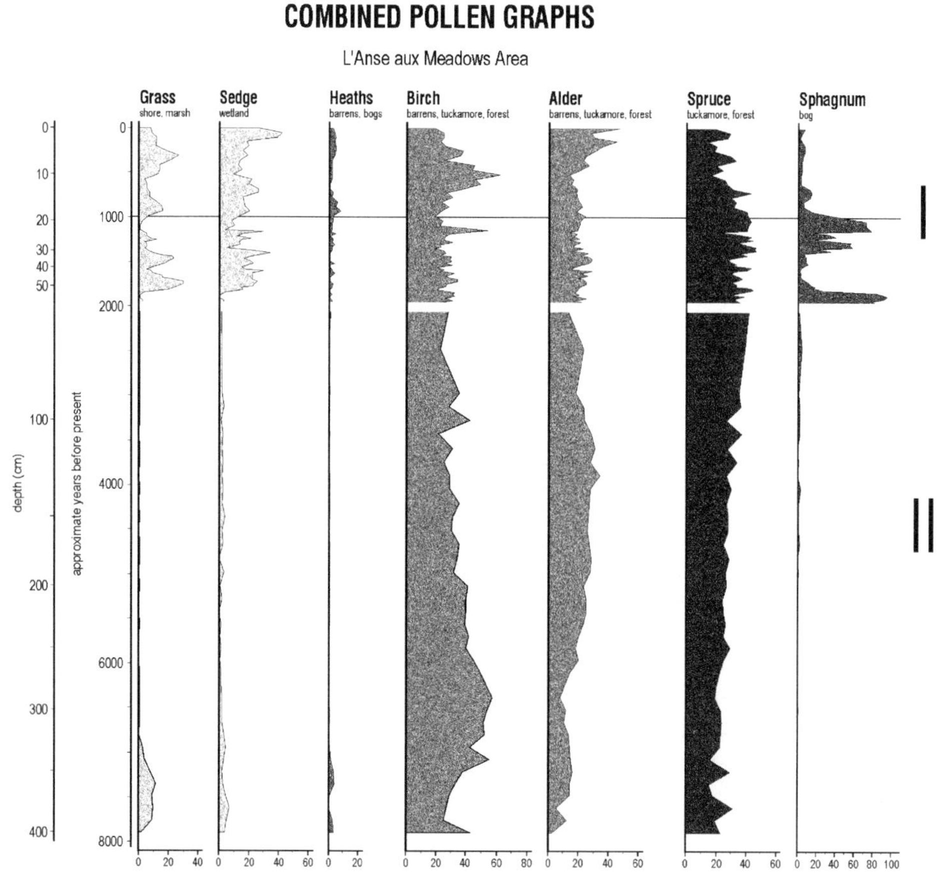

214

Figure 5. Selected pollen taxa recorded from peat (0-2000 BP) and lake sediment (2000-8000 BP) are used to reconstruct the vegetation history of the L'Anse aux Meadows area. See text for discussion. I. L'Anse aux Meadows Monolith 17 (Davis *et al.* 1988). II. Saddle Hill Pond (J.H. McAndrews, pers. comm.).

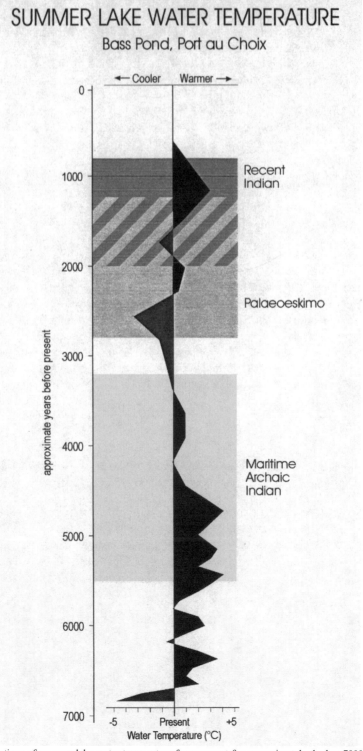

Figure 6. Variations of summer lake water temperature from present for approximately the last 7000 years based on chironomid remains in a sediment core from Bass Pond, Port au Choix. Chironomid data and temperature reconstructions are from Rosenberg (1998). The prehistoric cultural record from Port au Choix is superimposed on the temperature record for comparison. See text for discussion.

Arctic-adapted Palaeoeskimo populations were the next inhabitants of Newfoundland, coming south from the Canadian Arctic via Labrador. Palaeoeskimos lived in Newfoundland from 2800 to 1250 BP and their sites are well represented on the Northern Peninsula, including LAM (Tuck 1978; Auger 1984; Renouf 1993; 1994; Reader 1998; 1999; Wallace 1990). Like the Maritime Archaic people before them, Palaeoeskimos flourished on the Northern Peninsula, relying heavily on harp seal populations. These occupations coincided with marked climate cooling and variability, probably associated with more winter sea-ice and lower summer water and air temperatures. By 1500 BP the climate began to warm, with summer temperatures reaching a peak by 1250 BP, when Palaeoeskimos left the Northern Peninsula and soon after the Island of Newfoundland. It is possible that increasingly warm temperatures affected sea ice and seal hunting conditions.

Recent Indians are the prehistoric Amerindian people who lived in Newfoundland from 2000 BP to the historic period. Current data suggest that they came from interior Quebec and coastal Labrador. The Recent Indian period is sub-divided into three sequential complexes, the Cow Head complex (*c.* 2000-1500 BP), the Beaches complex (*c.* 1500-1000 BP) and the Little Passage Complex (1000 BP-historic period) (Penney 1981, Pastore 1992). Like the Palaeoeskimo, Recent Indian sites are also well represented on the Northern Peninsula, including LAM (Tuck 1978; Renouf 1992; Renouf and Bell 1999; Hull 1999; Reader 1998; 1999; Wallace 1990). Cow Head groups lived on the Northern Peninsula during a period of cold and Beaches and Little Passage people were present during warmer temperatures.

216

We cannot say how these temperature changes at the large temporal scale translated into the smaller time scale of individual experience and decision-making. Nevertheless, the broad congruence in temperature and prehistoric cultural records for the Northern Peninsula suggests that a changing climate, with attendant changes in vegetation, ice conditions and food resources, might well have been a significant factor in the ebb and flow of cultures in the archaeological record.

WISH YOU WERE HERE...

So, what would the landscape at LAM have been like 1000 years ago? Recent Indian occupations are dated at LAM from about 1200-900 BP and again from 700 to 400 BP (Ingstad 1977; Wallace 1990). The coastline would have been much the same as it is today, with sea level perhaps only slightly higher than present (1 m; Henningsmoen 1977; Grant 1992). The vegetation 1000 BP would have looked very similar to today's, perhaps with slightly more extensive forest cover. Sea ice extent during late winter and spring may have been reduced and summer water (and air?) temperature may have been several degrees higher. Such a landscape and the native people in it would certainly have been something for the Norse to write home about.

ACKNOWLEDGEMENTS

We would like to thank Dr J.H. McAndrews, University of Toronto for providing the raw pollen data from Saddle Hill Pond. Kelley Power used the resources of the Geographic Digital and Image Analysis Laboratory, Memorial University of Newfoundland, to generate the landscape images in figures 1 and 3. The vegetation photographs in figure 4 were taken by Kevin McVeigh, Department of the Environment, Ottawa, during the resource inventory of L'Anse aux Meadows National Historic Site in 1974. They are reproduced here courtesy of Dr A.W. Robertson, St. John's. Figures 5 and 6 were modified by Memorial University of Newfoundland Cartographic Laboratory. Our research on the Great Northern Peninsula was funded by Natural Sciences and Engineering Research Council of Canada (TB), Social

Sciences and Humanities Research Council of Canada (MAPR), Parks Canada and Memorial University of Newfoundland.

BIBLIOGRAPHY

Auger, R. 1984. Factory Cove: Recognition and Definition of the Early Palaeoeskimo Period in Newfoundland, unpublished MA thesis, Department of Anthropology, Memorial University of Newfoundland, St. John's

Carignan, P. 1975. *The Beaches: a Multi-component Habitation Site in Bonavista Bay*. Ottawa: National Museums of Canada, Archaeological Survey of Canada. Mercury Series, 39

Davis, A.M. 1980. 'Modern pollen spectra from the tundra-boreal forest transition in northern Newfoundland', *Boreas*, 9, 89-100.

——1984. 'Ombrotrophic peatlands in Newfoundland, Canada: their origins, development and trans-Atlantic affinities', *Chemical Geology*, 44, 287-309.

——1985. 'Causes and character of paludification in Newfoundland', *The Canadian Geographer*, 29, 361-364.

Davis, A.M. McAndrews, J.H. and Wallace, B. 1988. 'Paleoenvironment and the Archaeological Record at the L'Anse aux Meadows Site, Newfoundland', *Geoarchaeology*, 3, 53-64.

Fulton, R.J. ed., 1988. *Quaternary Geology of Canada and Greenland*, Geological Survey of Canada, Geology of Canada No. 1.

Gimbarzevsky, P. 1977. *L'Anse aux Meadows National Historic Park integrated survey of biophysical resources.* Information Report FMR-X-99, Forest Management Institute, Environment Canada.

Grant, D.R. 1986. *Surficial Geology, St. Anthony—Blanc-Sablon, Newfoundland and Québec*. Geological Survey of Canada, Map 1610A, scale 1:125 000.

——1988. 'Quaternary Geology of the Atlantic Appalachian region of Canada', in Fulton 1988, 391-440.

——1992. *Quaternery Geology of St. Anthony—Blanc-Sablon Area, Newfoundland and Québec*. Geological Survey of Canada, Memoir 427.

Hare, F.K., 1952. 'The climate of the island of Newfoundland: a geographical analysis', *Geographical Bulletin*, 2, 36-87.

Henningsmoen, K.E., 1977. 'Pollen-analytical investigations in the L'Anse aux Meadows area, Newfoundland', in Ingstad 1977, 289-340

Hosie, R.C., 1969. *Native Trees of Canada*, 7th edn. Ottawa: Canadian Forestry Service, Department of the Environment.

Hull, S. 1999. The Recent Indians at North Cove: 1998 Field Season, unpublished report, Culture and Heritage Division, Department of Tourism, Culture and Recreation, Government of Newfoundland and Labrador, St. John's,

Ingstad, A-S. 1977. *The Discovery of a Norse Settlement in America: Excavations at L'Anse aux Meadows, Newfoundland*, Oslo.

Meades, S.J., Hay, S.G., and Brouillet, L. 2000. 'Annotated Checklist of the Vascular Plants of Newfoundland and Labrador; digital publication of the Provincial Museum of Newfoundland and Labrador' <http://www.nfmuseum.com/meades.htm> (Site visited 5 Febraury 2003).

Morrison, D. and Pilon, J-L., eds, 1994. *Threads of Arctic Prehistory: Papers in Honour of William E. Taylor, Jr.* Hull: Archaeological Survey of Canada, Mercury Series, 149.

Pastore, R. T. 1992. *Shanawdithit's People*, St. John's, Newfoundland.

Penney, G. 1981. 'A Preliminary Report on the Excavation of the L'Anse à Flamme Site (CjAx-1)', in J. Sproull and Ransom 1981, 95-110.

Reader, D. 1998. Report of the 1997 Bird Cove Archaeological Site Survey, unpublished report, Culture and Heritage Division, Department of Tourism, Culture and Recreation, Government of Newfoundland and Labrador, St. John's.

——1999. Report of the 1998 Bird Cove Archaeological Project, unpublished report, Culture and Heritage Division, Department of Tourism, Culture and Recreation, Government of Newfoundland and Labrador, St. John's.

——1996. '"Interior" Occupation: A Maritime Archaic Site at South Brook Park Western Newfoundland', *Canadian Journal of Archaeology*, 20, 123-28.

217

Renouf, M. A. P. 1992. The 1991 Field Season at the Port au Choix National Historic Park, unpublished report, Parks Canada, Atlantic Region, Halifax.

——1993. 'Palaeoeskimo Seal Hunters at Port au Choix, Northwestern Newfoundland', *Newfoundland Studies*, 9, 2, 185-212.

——1994. 'Two Transitional Sites at Port au Choix, Northwestern Newfoundland', in Morrison and Pilon 1994, 165-196.

Renouf, M.A.P. and T. Bell. 1999. Report of Port au Choix Archaeology and Sea Level History Project, Preliminary Report of the 1998 Field Season, unpublished report, Culture and Heritage, Department of Tourism, Culture and Recreation, Government of Newfoundland and Labrador, St. John's.

——2000. Gould Site, Port au Choix, 1999 Report of Field Activities, unpublished report, Culture and Heritage Division, Department of Tourism, Culture and Recreation, St. John's.

Rosenberg, S., 1998. Chironomids and their relationship to the archaeological record and sea level change at Bass Pond, Newfoundland, Canada, unpublished B.Sc. dissertation, Okanagan University College.

Rowe, J.S., 1972. *Forest Regions of Canada*. Ottawa: Canadian Forestry Service Publication 1300, Department of the Environment.

Sproull Thomson, J. and Ransom, B., eds, 1981. *Archaeology in Newfoundland and Labrador 1980*. St. John's: Annual Report, 1. Historic Resources Division, Department of Culture, Recreation and Youth, Government of Newfoundland and Labrador.

Tuck J. A. 1976. *Ancient Peoples of Port au Choix Newfoundland*. St John's: Institute of Social and Economic Research, Memorial University of Nfld, Social and Economic Studies 17.

——1978. 'Excavations at Cow Head, Newfoundland. An Interim Report', *Etudes/Inuit/Studies*, 2, 1, 138-141.

Wallace, B. 1990. 'L'Anse au Meadows, Gateway to Vinland.', *Acta Archaeologica*, 61, 166-197.

Viking Art at the Millennium in the North Atlantic

James Graham-Campbell

During the second half of the tenth century, the Viking-age art of Scandinavia underwent a transformation arising out of the, by then, long-established contacts with Western Europe. In particular, the conversion of Denmark to Christianity opened up Southern Scandinavia to direct influences from the church art of both Anglo-Saxon England and the Continent, including the introduction of carved stone monuments, stone carving, as such, having previously been confined to the cutting of runic inscriptions (with the obvious exception of the unique 'picture-stones' from Gotland (see, for example, Wilson and Klindt-Jensen 1966, 46-7 and 79-82, fig. 42, pls v,c and xxvi). Hence the erection by the Danish king, Harald Bluetooth, of a great memorial stone at Jelling, in central Jutland, to commemorate not only his dead parents (who had died pagans and been buried there), but also his own conversion of his kingdom to Christianity, in about AD 965 (Roesdahl 1998, 161-5).

The massive Jelling monument, thought to be the first of its kind in Denmark, is a pyramidal granite boulder with three sides (Fuglesang 1991, no. 1). The first is filled with the greater part of the runic inscription, although this continues around the bottom of the other two sides. It reads:

219

> King Harald commanded these monuments to be made in memory of Gorm, his father, and in memory of Thorvi [Thyre], his mother—that Harald who won the whole of Denmark for himself, and Norway, and made the Danes Christian.

On the third and final side of the Jelling stone is depicted a stylised representation of the Crucifixion, but that in-between is occupied by a single 'Great Beast', entwined with a snake (fig. 1). This is executed in the so-called *Mammen style* of late Viking art (Wilson and Klindt-Jensen 1966, 119-21, pls xlviii-xlix; Fuglesang 1991, no. 1), named after the decoration on both sides of a parade axe from a Danish chamber-grave at Mammen, in Jutland, which has been dated by dendrochronology to 970/71 (Wilson and Klindt-Jensen 1966, 119, pls lii-liii; Fuglesang 1991, no. 23; Fitzhugh and Ward 2000, fig. 4.9).

The Mammen style represents an important phase in the development of Viking-age art in Scandinavia, not just because of its use of the lion-like 'Great Beast' motif, which represents a departure from the ribbon-like animals employed in the preceding Jellinge style (Wilson and Klindt-Jensen 1966, 95-118), but also because it incorporates Western European foliate motifs into its designs, as can be seen in the lobe and tendril treatment of the mane and tail of the 'Great Beast' at Jelling. Indeed, one side of the Mammen axe itself is fully occupied by a straggling plant motif.

The Mammen style was disseminated abroad to a limited extent. In fact, the two other most notable instances of artifacts in this style are both finely carved and mounted caskets, which were most probably made in southern Scandinavia at the end of the tenth century, but which seem to have been exported as royal gifts intended for use as Christian reliquaries: the well-known caskets from Cammin, Poland, and from Bamberg, Germany (Wilson and Klindt-Jensen 1966, 124-6, pls liv-lvi; Fuglesang 1991, nos 14-15; Roesdahl and Wilson 1992, nos 266-7).

By the turn of the millennium, the Mammen style was undergoing a transition into the *Ringerike style*, so-called after the geological name for a region in south-eastern Norway from which came the sandstone used for most of the Norwegian stones ornamented in this style, such as those from Alstad and Vang (Wilson and Klindt-Jensen 1966, 130-2, fig. 59, 136, 138, pl. lvii; Fuglesang 1980, nos 58 and 60). The Ringerike style is characterised by

Figure 1. The 'Great Beast' and snake motif from Harald Bluetooth's rune-stone at Jelling, Denmark (after Roesdahl, 1982, drawing: Sue Bird).

the continued use of the 'Great Beast' motif, but also by a far more confident and abundant use of the fleshy foliate motifs which had been experimented with in the preceding Mammen style (Wilson and Klindt-Jensen 1966, 134-46; Fuglesang 1980).

A fine example of Fuglesang's 'classic phase' of the Ringerike style is presented by a vane from the church at Heggen, Buskerud, Norway, on one side of which is engraved a 'Great Beast' (fig. 2) and its companion (Wilson and Klindt-Jensen 1966, 136, fig. 61, pl. lix,a-b; Fuglesang 1980, no. 42; Roesdahl and Wilson 1992, no. 417). The Ringerike style was influential in the south of England when the Danish king, Cnut (1016-35), was on the throne—its most notable expression being a gravestone from St Paul's churchyard in London, with a 'classic phase' composition of a greater and lesser beast, akin to that on the Heggen vane (Wilson and Klindt-Jensen 1966, 135-6, pl. lviii,a; Fuglesang 1980, no. 88; Roesdahl and Wilson 1992, no. 416).

The Ringerike style was also influential on the development of Irish art during the eleventh century. In addition to the well-known pieces of ecclesiastical metalwork, such as the book-shrine for the Cathac of St Columba, with its donor inscription dateable to 1062-98 (Wilson and Klindt-Jensen 1966, 143-4, pl. lxvi,b; Fuglesang 1980, no. 56), there is an interesting group of wood-carvings and 'motif-pieces' from the Dublin excavations (Fuglesang 1980, no. 102; Lang 1988, 46-7 and catalogue; Roesdahl and Wilson 1992, nos 397a and 398).

Some of the earliest wood carvings to have survived from Iceland, consisting of a series of planks from Möðrufell and one from Hólar (Fuglesang 1980, nos 104-5; 1991, no. 13), seem to belong to what may be considered as the Mammen/Ringerike transitional period, having scroll and tendril decoration, but these are sadly incomplete so that the overall designs cannot be reconstructed. More important, however, are the four fragmentary panels, discovered in 1952, at Flatatunga (Fuglesang 1980, no. 106; Roesdahl and Wilson 1992, no. 454; Fitzhugh and Ward 2000, fig. 12.13). The Möðrufell, Hólar and Flatatunga planks of fir were all discovered during the course of the last century, re-used as rafters in the ceilings of farm buildings. The latter represent what are presumably the earliest surviving remains of church decoration in Iceland, so identified because of the row of haloed figures (fig. 3) above which are incised the foliate patterns that are particularly characteristic of the 'classic phase' of this Scandinavian art style. Wilson and Klindt-Jensen (1966, 138) have commented that 'it would be difficult to imagine a more competent piece of wood-carving than the simply engraved Ringerike tendrils which appear on panels from the ancient Viking farm at Flatatunga in Iceland'. The most recent discovery in Iceland of a plank decorated with foliate ornament, in the Ringerike style, is a stray find (1974) from a demolished outhouse at Gaulverjabær; this is part of a composite object, most probably a piece of furniture (Roesdahl and Wilson 1992, no. 563).

221

The conversion of Iceland was declared official at the annual meeting of the Alþing (General Assembly) held in the year 999 or 1000, when the Lawspeaker declared, in the words of Dag Strömbäck (1975, 16-17) that

> Everyone should be Christian and all who had not been baptised should receive baptism. But the old law should stand as far as the exposure of children and the eating of horse-flesh were concerned...[and] that under the new law people could sacrifice in secret if they wanted to.

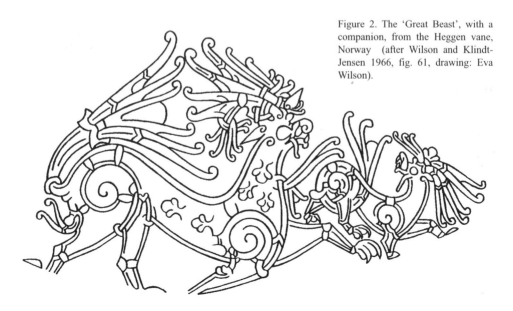

Figure 2. The 'Great Beast', with a companion, from the Heggen vane, Norway (after Wilson and Klindt-Jensen 1966, fig. 61, drawing: Eva Wilson).

Figure 3, below. Fragment of a carved panel, with haloed figures, from Flatatunga, Iceland (The National Museum of Iceland).

Figure 4, right. Seated figure from Eyrarland, Iceland. Height: 6.7 cm, scale 1:1 (The National Museum of Iceland).

222

The pagan gods chiefly worshipped in Iceland appear to have been Þor and Freyr, but the veneration of Þor was predominant (Strömbäck 1975, 49-50). These two factors, in combination, may account for the manufacture of the three-dimensional human figure from Eyrarland (fig. 4) which Kristján Eldjárn (1981, 74) has described as 'probably the best known and widely printed object now existing from early medieval times in Iceland'.

This cast bronze image (6.7 cm high) is of a seated man wearing a helmet or cap, but apparently otherwise naked because there are no obvious indications of clothing and his toes are clearly depicted (Graham-Campbell 1980, no. 101; Eldjárn 1981). He has a fine moustache and a forked beard, grasped in his hands, which terminates in a curious tripartite form, likened by some to a stylized Þor's hammer. The moustache is treated as a lobe and tendril, with a tightly curled terminal, exactly according to the principles of the Ringerike style (cf. fig. 2). This detail is sufficient to suggest a date for the Eyrarland image in the eleventh century, thus post-dating the official conversion of Iceland, as described above. Eldjárn proposed therefore that the conventional identification of this figure as a representation of Þor should be queried, suggesting instead that it might perhaps be a version of the main piece used in the board-game of *hneftafl*, citing the whalebone image of a squatting, beard-clutching figure from a tenth-century grave at Baldursheimur, Iceland, which was buried together with a set of twenty-four gaming pieces and a die (Graham-Campbell 1980, no. 100; Eldjárn 1981, 82-4, fig. 8; Roesdahl and Wilson 1992, no. 71; Fitzhugh and Ward 2000, fig. 12.11).   223

It remains the case, however, that the only closely comparable, three-dimensional, bronze figure of similar size (6.9 cm high) and date is that from Rällinge, in Sweden (Eldjárn 1981, 81, fig. 7; Roesdahl and Wilson 1992, no. 182; Fitzhugh and Ward 2000, fig. 3.4). This is of a squatting, beard-clutching man, also naked apart from a helmet or cap, as is evident

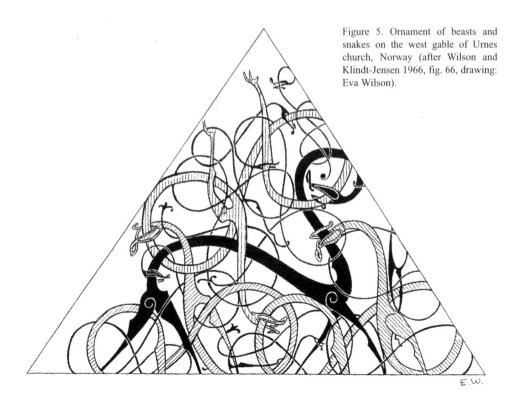

Figure 5. Ornament of beasts and snakes on the west gable of Urnes church, Norway (after Wilson and Klindt-Jensen 1966, fig. 66, drawing: Eva Wilson).

E.W.

Figure 6, left. Silver openwork brooch, consisting of an Urnes-style beast and two snakes, from Tröllaskógur, Iceland. Scale 1:1 (The National Museum of Iceland, photo: James Graham-Campbell).

Figure 7, below. Carved wooden object, with animal-head terminal, from Sandnes, Greenland (The National Museum of Denmark, photo: Arnold Mikkelsen).

224

from his large erect phallus. This latter attribute clearly associates him with a fertility cult, thus suggesting identification with the god Freyr.

On balance, it has become my opinion (contra Graham-Campbell 1980, no. 101), that the Eyrarland figure should be identified with the image of a pagan god, presumably Þor. As such, it would have been commissioned by an individual of some standing, given the quality of the workmanship, for the purpose of 'secret' devotion in the immediately post-conversion period (see now Perkins 2001).

The Ringerike style flourished during the first half of the eleventh century, before developing into the so-called *Urnes style*. The Urnes style is named for the fine wood-carvings which decorated the first stave-church to have been built at Urnes in western Norway (fig. 5); some of these have survived because they were incorporated into its twelfth-century successor where they can still be seen today (Wilson and Klindt-Jensen 1966, 147-9, fig. 66, pl. lxix). This is the last of the Viking-age art-styles and it flourished during the second half of the eleventh century, although elements were carried over into the Romanesque art of Scandinavia during the twelfth century (see, for example, the Lisbjerg altar-frontal from Denmark which has recently been dated by dendrochronology to *c.* 1135: Roesdahl and Wilson 1992, no. 467).

The Urnes style largely turned its back on plant motifs and depended for its decorative effect on intertwining stylised animals (Wilson and Klindt-Jensen 1966, 147-60), much as had the artists and craftsmen of the earlier Viking Age. Animals and snakes are combined to create looping compositions of great elegance, with constantly flowing lines which often form figures-of-eight (cf. figs 5 and 6).

The popularity of the Urnes style was such that it too spread across both the North Sea and the North Atlantic, being influential in both England and Ireland. It is represented in Iceland in the form of a couple of characteristically Scandinavian animal-shaped brooches. One of these openwork brooches, a stray find from the deserted farm of Tröllaskógur (fig. 6), is made of silver and the main animal, with its open jaws, is intertwined with two snakes (Roesdahl and Wilson 1992, no. 588; Fitzhugh and Ward 2000, fig. 12.10).

Also from Iceland, and of fine quality, is the cast bronze, T-shaped, head of a 'tau' crozier, found by chance at Thingvellir in 1957, which has a pair of Urnes-style animal-head terminals. One must, however, be cautious as to supposing that this crozier head is necessarily of Icelandic workmanship given that the wood preserved in its socket shows that the actual staff was fashioned from dogwood, a species foreign to Iceland (Graham-Campbell 1980, no. 540; Roesdahl and Wilson 1992, no. 335). Dogwood would have been available from only as far north as England (and south-eastern Scotland), Denmark and southern Sweden (Dr Jon Hather, pers. comm.).

225

From the Norse settlements in Greenland there is so far but one artifact which can be seen to be decorated in the tradition of Viking art, if not in the mainstream of its development. This is a piece of carved wood (38 cm long) which was found during excavations in 1930-32 of a turf and stone house, thought to be of eleventh-century date, at Sandnæs (Kilaursarfik) in the Western Settlement (Roesdahl and Wilson 1992, no. 565; Fitzhugh and Ward 2000, fig. 25.10). It terminates in a three-dimensional animal head (fig. 7), with an open mouth displaying large teeth and pear-shaped eyes which have their tapered ends extended into a small, tendril-like, scroll; incised behind its left jaw is a runic inscription, *halki*, which probably represents the man's name Helgi. In addition, there are three animal heads (or cat-like masks) carved in low relief towards the opposite end of its upper surface. It has been suggested that this well-executed example of the wood-carver's art may be either the arm of a chair or the tiller from the side-rudder of a boat, but the former identification is undoubtedly the more probable of the two, given that the animal heads along part of its 'shaft' would seem somewhat incompatible with its two-handed use as a tiller.

Turning, finally, to Newfoundland we can but note the absence of 'art' amongst the excavated finds from L'Anse aux Meadows, although there is evidence of wood carving in the form of a decorative (but plain) finial made of pine (Fitzhugh and Ward 2000, fig. 14.8). While visiting the Reception Centre at L'Anse aux Meadows with its display of artefacts from the site, I was asked by a member of the Symposium why I do not include the bronze ringed pin in my discussion. Although such might be considered a piece of ornamental metalwork, it is in fact lacking in any decoration (Roesdahl and Wilson 1992, no. 346; Fitzhugh and Ward 2000, fig. 14.5).

In conclusion, Viking art dating from either side of the millennium can be seen as a reflection of not only the current political and religious developments within Scandinavia, but also of external contacts and overseas expansion. During the period when the Scandinavian countries achieved nationhood—and the individual North Atlantic settlements took hold—Viking art can also be seen to have remained a reflection of their common cultural heritage.

ACKNOWLEDGEMENTS

I am most grateful to the Organizing Committee for the invitation to deliver a paper at the Viking Millennium International Symposium, in September 2000, which made possible for me to have such a memorable first visit to Newfoundland (and special thanks to Else Roesdahl for having driven me safely around the Northern Peninsula!).

INTRODUCTORY NOTE TO REFERENCES

In order to reduce the number of references, I have largely confined them to the two most recent Viking exhibition catalogues (Roesdahl and Wilson 1992; Fitzhugh and Ward 2000), both of which illustrate most of the artifacts under discussion, with the former providing associated bibliographies for further reading, including references to fuller descriptions of many of the pieces in Graham-Campbell 1980. For the general background, see Roesdahl 1998, whereas the standard survey of Viking art, in English, remains Wilson and Klindt-Jensen 1966, although it is worth noting that a slightly revised edition (with an updated bibliography) was published by the University of Minnesota Press in 1980. However, those with access to the multi-volume publication, *The Dictionary of Art*, edited by Jane Turner (London: 1996), may well find it useful to consult the section on 'Viking art' by Signe Horn Fuglesang and others.

BIBLIOGRAPHY

Dronke, U. *et al.*, eds, 1981. *Specvlvm Norroenvm. Norse Studies in Memory of Gabriel Turville-Petre*, Odense.

Eldjárn, K. 1981. 'The bronze image from Eyrarland', in Dronke *et al.* 1981, 73-84.

Fitzhugh, W.W. and Ward, E. I., eds, 2000. *Vikings. The North Atlantic Saga*, Washington and London.

Fuglesang, S. H. 1980. *Some Aspects of the Ringerike Style*, Odense.

——1991. 'The axehead from Mammen and the Mammen style', in Iversen *et al.* 1991, 83-107.

Graham-Campbell, J. 1980. *Viking Artefacts. A Select Catalogue*, London.

Iversen, M. *et al.,* eds, 1991. *Mammen. Grav, kunst og samfund i vikingetid*, Højbjerg.

Lang, J. T. 1988. *Viking-Age Decorated Wood. A Study of its Ornament and Style*, Dublin.

Perkins, R. 2001. *Thor the Windraiser and the Eyrarland Image*, London.

Roesdahl, E. 1982. *Viking-Age Denmark*, London.

——1998. *The Vikings*, 2nd edn, London.

Roesdahl, E. and Wilson, D. M., eds, 1992. *From Viking to Crusader. Scandinavia and Europe 800-1200*, Copenhagen.

Strömbäck, D. 1975. *The Conversion of Iceland. A Survey*, London.

Wilson, D. M. and Klindt-Jensen, O. 1966. *Viking Art*, London.

Dressing the Dead: Gender, Identity, and Adornment in Viking-Age Iceland

Michèle Hayeur-Smith

The most widespread use of jewellery is as body adornment. This paper will address the social dimension of jewellery and will look at the Icelandic mortuary material from the Viking period and its place in the North Atlantic context. In this paper, I am putting forth a hypothesis on the function of the oval brooch and similar Scandinavian 'type' objects in the settlement and early Commonwealth periods of Iceland. The focus will therefore be placed on female adornment rather than male, though data regarding both genders will be reviewed. This hypothesis may be applicable to other areas colonised by the Norse. I am suggesting that oval brooches (along with pagan burial practice in general) in the early part of the settlement may have changed social significance from that which they represented at home, to become symbols associated with personal and cultural identity, as well as being symbolic items connecting the settlers to their cultural past.

THE HISTORICAL CONTEXT OF EARLY ICELAND

The settlement of Iceland extended from AD 870-930. By 930 the country is presumed to have been fully inhabited (Hastrup 1985, 8). Early medieval literary sources (e.g. *Íslendingabók* and *Landnámabók*) suggest that most settlers came from south-west Norway, particularly from Sogn, Hordaland, and Rogaland and that Norwegian settlers fled Norway due the growing power of the king Haraldr *inn hárfagri* (Finehair) (Jones 1986, 44). Haraldr was attempting to subjugate local leaders, free farmers, and petty kings to his authority, in order to claim rulership over all of Norway (Byock 1993, 53).

When they arrived in Iceland the Norwegian settlers were foreigners in a new country, and far from their familiar homeland. At the same time they encountered no native populations with whom to compete for resources (Byock 1993, 2). As pointed out by Byock (1993), despite its seemingly large size the interior of Iceland is largely uninhabitable, due to its distance from the Gulf Stream which warms the coastal regions (Byock 1993, 10). The task of the newcomers was therefore to create a society on this empty island with a limited area of habitable space (Byock 1993, 10). According to Byock, the lack of indigenous populations enabled the first settlers to claim huge portions of land, thus creating disputes with later settlers (Byock 1993, 55).

Although there were many Norwegian settlers, it has long been acknowledged that not all settlers of Iceland came from Norway, though the dominant culture was distinctly 'Scandinavian' (see P. Sawyer, this volume). Language, religion, social organisation, and a chieftain-based society were similar to the homeland. Many settlers are said to have come from the British Isles, either from Norway via the British Isles, or directly (Jones 1986, 49). Crawford (1987), argued that the Icelandic sources make continuous reference to men and women from the Hebrides and Ireland (Crawford 1987, 210). Kristjánsson estimated the number of settlers from the British Isles at 20% (Kristjánsson 1998, 265). Whatever the exact numbers of Celtic immigrants, Iceland was not settled by a homogeneous population of people from Norway. These different cultural groups were, in effect, sharing the resources of a limited area.

In the first 300 years of settlement, Iceland was a chieftain-based society. It has been described as having a decentralised government and an absence of 'institutionalised hierarchical structures' (Byock 1993, 5). In broad terms there were two social groups: free-men and slaves. Slavery is said to have disappeared with the Christianisation of Iceland thus increasing the number of freeborn men in the population (McGovern *et al.* 1988, 251) There were no kings, or lords, but, despite this apparent classlessness, social divisions did exist among the settlers.

One cannot sufficiently stress the unique nature of this colony. The settlers of Iceland arrived on an empty island, derived from a mixed background of Norwegian, Hebridean, Irish and possibly even some Swedish and Danish settlers (Jones 1986, 44). It was in this social setting that these populations together created a society which came to be known as Icelandic.

FEMALE JEWELLERY, ADORNMENT, AND VIKING BURIAL CUSTOMS.

Through the visual clues of adornment humans are able to convey subtle messages about their social and cultural identity. This information may be of a particularly personal nature, decipherable only by members of a closed group, or it may operate a cultural level conveying information about group identity to other groups at large. According to some anthropologists, jewellery and adornment, by stressing unique physical features, are expressions of individuality and a means by which human societies can display information regarding group affiliation, values and standards of the group (Cannon 1998, 24; Polhemus and Procter 1978, 11). They constitute part of the vast tool kit used in marking issues of personal and cultural identity.

Despite the seeming similarities amongst all forms of adornment, they differ in their degrees of importance. A look at past scholarship reveals that jewellery has been given more weight than clothing in most cultures. I believe this to be the result of its permanence. Jewellery survives time, clothing does not. Furthermore, jewellery is often made of materials which themselves are loaded with symbolic meanings of 'preciousness'. Regardless of time and of cultural context, it is jewellery that we offer to mark society's rites of passage and the important moments of life. Jewellery is given at marriage, at birth, at death; jewellery is inherited.

Jewellery is a constant reminder of events not only to those who experienced them, but also to their kin. Most of us can relate to having inherited a piece of one's great-grandmother's jewellery and felt pride and a connection with one's past. Jewellery as heirloom, therefore, becomes a connecting agent with one's ancestral group. It establishes an emotional rapport with the past in providing the individual with a sense of belonging, a sense of group identity. Barley described the heirloom in the following manner:

> Their link with the dead may turn them into inalienable heirlooms or relics, kept by the living as witness to a bond between themselves and the departed (Barley 1995, 85).

FEMALE DRESS AND ADORNMENT OF THE VIKING AGE

From the archaeological data we know that Viking-Age women wore long garments, the basic outfit consisting of a long chemise with long sleeves fastened at the neck with a brooch (Hägg 1974, 108). A pair of oval brooches were worn at shoulder level attached to the straps of a sleeveless apron or dress, which was worn on top of the long dress underneath (Hägg 1974, 108). A string of beads or a pendant was frequently hung between the brooches along with other useful implements: knives, scissors and sometimes keys (Jesch 1991, 17). A wrap or a shawl could be been worn over this outfit; and from evidence recovered at Hedeby, well-to-do women often wore an ankle length coat over their dress (Jesch 1991, 18).

Oval brooches, are widespread in the burials of Scandinavia. They are considered as being among the most typical items of female Viking dress found throughout Scandinavia and the Viking world (Dommasnes 1982, 73; Owen and Dalland 1999, 147). They are so standardised that they have been used as gender identifiers in Viking burials (Dommasnes 1982, 73). Their designs are equally standardised. It is common to find specific brooch types (such as a Petersen 51), in such remote areas as Iceland or Gnezdovo in Russia, wherever the Viking presence was felt. Oval brooches are thought to have been produced in the Scandinavian trade centres, such as Hedeby, Birka, Ribe, where metalworking of gold, silver, bronze, and iron were said to be among the most important urban activities (Clarke and Ambrosiani 1991, 162-163). The archaeological record offers evidence of this local production through discarded moulds, tools, unfinished objects, raw materials, crucibles, and overall workshop debris (Clarke and Ambrosiani 1991, 163). There is no such archaeological evidence from Iceland for the local production of oval brooches indicating, in all probability, that the Icelandic examples were imported. Oval brooches went out of fashion in the Scandinavian homelands and the western settlements during the mid-tenth and early eleventh centuries (Jansson 1985, 228; Owen and Dalland 1999, 147), yet James Graham-Campbell has noted that these brooches became more fashionable in Finland, Lagoda and Latvia (1980, 28).

FEMALE ADORNMENT, BURIAL, AND STATUS

In the burial material from Scandinavia, oval brooches appear to be associated with women from a particular stratum of society. According to Gräslund (1980), oval brooches are found predominantly in female inhumation burials at Birka, less frequently in cremation burials (Gräslund 1980, 81). Furthermore, as was pointed out by Gräslund, Arbman estimated that 50% of Birka burials contained this type of brooch while the graves from Adelsö had none (Gräslund 1980, 81). Gräslund attributed this situation to different burial customs in Adelsö and offered the hypothesis that the grave goods in the inhumation burials of Birka reflect more the customs of central Uppland from which the more affluent members of Birka's population may have originated (Gräslund 1980, 82).

Bergliot Solberg (1985) conducted an analysis of gender and status on Merovingian and Viking-Age burials from northern, western, and eastern Norway. She attempted to rank social status on the basis of grave goods. From 833 female-gendered graves, Solberg's division of status was as follows:

Group 1:   5 beads or more, and/or the presence of textile implements

Group 2:   at least one conical brooch, or one oval brooch, beads, textile or agricultural implements, miscellaneous items like keys.

Group 3:   a conical and/or oval brooch, and the presence of a third brooch as well as beads, keys, agricultural and textile implements (Solberg 1985, 247-248).

For female graves, Group 3 represented the richest graves and encompassed only 16% of all female graves in western Norway and 13% in eastern Norway (Solberg 1985, 247-248). Group 2 represented the most common category with 40% in western Norway, 60% in central Norway and 54% in eastern Norway (Solberg 1985, 247). Solberg's analysis also included a study of male graves following a similar methodology. Her results proved similar to that of females with Group 3 graves representing the highest status burials but the least representative of the categories.

A similar study was carried out by Dommasnes (1982), for the region of Sogn in western Norway. Dommasnes attempted to rank female roles and status in her sample of 264 graves, of which only 213 were suitable for analysis. Although there was no mention of the frequency of oval brooches in her description, as they were incorporated under the heading of 'jewellery', she did notice that jewellery ranked as a constant artefact category with higher values in women's burials while weapons were preferred to jewellery in male burials (Dommasnes 1982, 77-78).

What is indicated by these various studies is that the oval brooch is an item of jewellery reserved for women of a certain status. The distribution of oval brooches in Scandinavia indicates that they were given to women who had reached a particular stage in life without necessarily belonging to the princely class. They were definitely not slaves but should perhaps be seen as the quintessential Viking housewife, married, with children, running her own household and farm in the absence of her husband, wife of a *bondi* or yeoman farmer, undoubtedly with slaves under her care. One might even suggest that her married status itself may have been displayed by her oval brooches, similar to the wedding ring today.

THE ARCHAEOLOGICAL DATA FOR ICELAND:
MALE AND FEMALE GRAVES AND THEIR JEWELLERY

This section will present the archaeological data for Iceland, looking first at the osteological basis for determining male and female graves in the Icelandic context. This discussion is followed by my own data relating to the frequency of jewellery in male and female graves.

In the most recent edition of *Kuml og Haugfé*, Eldjárn and Friðriksson (2000) established that for all the pagan burials known from Iceland, of which there are 316, only 181 skeletons exist, and of those, only 108 could be sexed. Forty-five are definitely male and another twenty-eight may be male (the sexing here is uncertain based on biological sexing). Another twenty are definite females, with an additional 15 that are potentially female (Table 1; Eldjárn and Friðriksson 2000, 595).

The total number of items of jewellery recorded from graves amounts to 162 separate objects (Hayeur-Smith 2002b). Five male graves contained at least one item of jewellery, while 40 osteologically sexed male graves did not. In contrast, 12 of the 20 graves with osteologically sexed females contained jewellery, while only 8 did not. While some jewellery was found in both male and female graves, the predominant association of jewellery with women's graves is significant at any reasonable of statistical significance, when this distribution is analysed using a simple chi-square test (Table 2: $X^2 = 17.35$, df = 1, p < 0.001).

Additionally, within this data set 38 individual items of jewellery could be attributed to female graves and 24 to men's graves (Table 3). An additional 100 pieces of jewellery came from 'indeterminate graves' for which no definite sexing was available.

The apparent association of more jewellery in women's graves is statistically significant ($X^2 =11.91$, df =1, p < 0.001), suggesting not only that women were more likely to receive jewellery as funerary accompaniments, but also that they were likely to receive more items of jewellery per grave than were men.

Total	Male	Male?	Female	Female?
316 Graves	-	-	-	-
181 Skeletons	-	-	-	-
108 sexed skeletons	45 (41.7%)	28 (25.9%)	20 (18.5%)	15 (13.9%)

Table 1. Distribution of male/female graves from Iceland (based on research by Eldjárn and Friðriksson 2000).

	Male	Female	Row totals
Graves with jewellery	5	12	17
	[11.8]	[5.2]	
Graves without jewellery	40	8	48
	[33.2]	[14.8]	
Column totals	45	20	65

Table 2. Contingency table of male and female Icelandic Viking-Age graves with and without items of jewellery. Bracketed figures indicate expected values for each cell, based on the row and column totals. The Chi-square value for this distribution ($X^2 = 17.135$), at one degree of freedom, indicates that jewellery is more frequently recovered as a funerary offering in women's graves than in men's, at any reasonable level of statistical confidence ($p < 0.001$).

	Males	Females	Row totals
Number of graves	45	20	65
	[35.3]	[29.7]	
Number of items of jewellery	24	38	62
	[33.7]	[28.3]	
Column totals	69	58	127

Table 3. Contingency table comparing the number of male and female Icelandic Viking-Age graves with the number of items of jewellery associated with each sex in those graves. Bracketed figures indicate expected values for each cell, based on the row and column totals. The Chi-square value for this distribution ($X^2 = 11.91$), at one degree of freedom, indicates that women's graves contain more jewellery, on average, than men's graves, at any reasonable level of statistical confidence ($p < 0.001$).

What these results indicate is that females were given significantly more jewellery in death than males. Some scholars may find this normal behaviour, yet completely neglect the fact that wearing jewellery along with other forms of adornment is sensitive to cultural variation, and in some societies it is the men who make greater use of jewellery than women. In the Norse context, Petré recognised that a common feature for Norway's early Iron Age and late Iron Age graves was that weapons were associated with male graves and jewellery with females (Petré 1993, 149). A similar pattern is noted for Iceland.

STATUS IDENTIFICATION IN ICELANDIC GRAVES

In order to establish a system of status identification for Iceland I have taken Solberg's criteria of status distinction and adapted it to the Icelandic context. I adapted her tripartite division of Group 1,2,3, with Group 3 reflective of the highest status and Group 1 the lowest. Table 4 indicates the defining characteristics of these groups for both men and women.

Using these criteria, the Icelandic burials with jewellery can be divided as shown in Table 5. Note that the graves presented therein are only the graves containing jewellery and which were recorded as part of this particular research project. I was not able to conduct a similar division for all of Icelandic burials as I did not possess information on the entire burial record.

	Male		Female	

Group 3
—3 weapons: sword, spear, axe
—2 weapons: sword, spear
—1 weapon: sword
—shield boss
—tools agricultural, carpentry etc 1 or more
—jewellery: 1> items of jewellery (round brooch, ringed pin, belt buckle, strap end, pendant)
—beads 1>
—animals (1 or more), and harness equipment
—miscellaneous (gaming pieces, ice spurs, weights, fish weights, knife etc.)

Group 3
—2 oval /or tongue shaped brooches
—1 central brooch, trefoil or round brooch
—additional items of jewellery
—beads 1>
—agricultural, cooking or weaving implements, all or any combination
—miscellaneous items (keys, weight scales, shears, combs etc)
—animals (1 or more) and harness equipment

Group 2
—2 weapons: spear/axe
—shield boss
—tools
—miscellaneous item
—1 item of jewellery
—beads 1>
—1 animal

Group 2
—1 oval brooch, or other brooch
—other item of jewellery
—beads 1>
—textile implements or other (1 only)
—miscellaneous items (same as above)
—1 animal and harness

Group 1
—1 weapon: axe or shield boss
—beads, or 1> or 1 item of jewellery
—1 animal or none

Group 1
—1> beads or simple item of jewellery
—additional implement such as a knife, comb etc
—1 animal or none

Table 4. Status identification for Icelandic graves.

	Group 1	Group 2	Group 3	Uncertain	Total
Male	2	2	1	0	5
Male?	2	2	1	0	5
Female	6	5	1	0	12
Female?	3	0	1	0	4
*Double grave**	1	0	3	0	4
Unknown	10	7	9	18	44
Totals	24	16	16	18	74

Table 5. Recorded number of graves with jewellery. (In my sample of graves with jewellery certain graves were double graves, 2 of which were male/female graves and two of which were male/male graves with the inclusion of a young male child in the latter category.)

As with Norway, Group 1 burials are more frequent for both sexes, (whether sexed or uncertain); Group 2 burials are slightly less common; and Group 3 burials are the least common. Furthermore, double graves appear to be associated with higher status. This could be explained in two ways: 1) double graves such as graves from Kaldarhöfði, and Vatnsdalur (both boat burials) have more artefacts than other graves; or 2) one of the individuals in the double grave may have been of high status such as the grave of Hafurbjarnarstaðir where a boy is interred with an adult male, and Surtstaðir where a woman is interred with a man.

OVAL BROOCHES AND STATUS IN ICELAND

We have seen that in the Icelandic burials males outnumber females although female graves contain more jewellery than males. This is similar to what was found in western Norway where only one fourth of burials were thought to be female (Dommasnes 1982, 73). One might argue from the ratio of male/female burials that possibly only the top echelons of females in society received burials while the remaining may have been disposed of in another manner. In this light even the 'poorest' of female graves with grave goods should be considered higher status burials in comparison with the rest of the population.

From Iceland there are 44 separate oval brooches with 38 being attributed to a possible burial context. An additional 6 are stray finds for which no precise archaeological context is known. Of the 38 oval brooches associated with burials, 18 brooches are from well described archaeological contexts while another 20 are not as well documented.

233

If one were to sex the graves using both grave goods (particularly on the basis of the inclusion of oval brooches in graves) and osteological sexing, one could argue that possible female graves with oval brooches amounts to 23, and those without, 16. Under this approach the total number of female graves with jewellery could be estimated at 39.

Icelandic Group 3 burials offer the same range of grave goods observed in Norway: a pair of oval brooches, the presence of a third brooch, beads, as well as an array of implements ranging from cooking utensils to agricultural equipment or weaving implements. Group 3 corresponds to what might be suggested as the wealthiest category of burial. Group 2 also displayed similarities with Norway, either one oval brooch or an other item of jewellery, beads, and one category of implement as enumerated above. Group 2 represents an in-between group. Without being very poor these graves possibly represented the graves of the female members of household's linked to ordinary free-farmers. Group 1, also in keeping with Solberg's finds in Norway, represents the least affluent group of burials.

PARTICULARITIES IN THE ICELANDIC FEMALE BURIALS

Specific behaviours unique to Iceland are apparent with regard to the presence or absence of animals as grave offerings. In female burials horses are found in all three categories, indicating that the horse held no particular significance to any specific stratum of society in early Iceland. In contrast in the Birka Chamber graves, horses are associated specifically with wealth and status and they are clearly found together with equestrian equipment and weapons that symbolise military activity (Ringstedt 1997, 70). The observations here, concerning female burials, are particular to Iceland and have been discussed by Ringstedt (1997), as well as Müller-Wille (1971). Both authors remarked on the widespread presence of horses in Icelandic burials, stating that over half of the cemeteries in Iceland which have grave goods also contained horses (Müller-Wille 1971, 120-121,123,162, 233, in Ringstedt 1997, 70).

Other unique features are apparent in Icelandic graves particularly those without oval brooches, and they offer an interesting comparison to those with. Three examples are presented here taken (one each) from Groups 1,2,3.

Group 3 graves without oval brooches. A grave from Kornsá, Austur-Hunavatnsýsla, is a higher status burial without the presence of oval brooches and on the basis of its overall assemblage could be classified as a Group 3 burial of considerable wealth (for the description of the contents of this grave see Eldjárn 1956, 96-97).

Two tongue shaped brooches with Jellinge-style decoration from this grave (similar to P137) appear to have been worn in a similar fashion to oval brooches but would have been visually distinct and rare in Iceland (Eldjárn 1956, 313). Eldjárn discussed the provenance of these tongue shaped brooches and mentioned that during Jan Petersen's classification only 8 were known from Norway, while several were said to have been found in Sweden (Eldjárn 1956, 313-314). These tongue shaped brooches have been described as being dec-

Figure 1. Tongue-shaped brooch, Kornsá, Austur-Hunavatnsýsla (drawing: M. Hayeur-Smith). Scale: 1:1.

234

orated with either foliate ornament, Borre style, or Jelling style ornament. Eldjárn knew of one example from Norway, and one from Birka that were similar to the Icelandic examples (Eldjárn 1956, 313-314). Whatever their place of origin, these brooches appear to have been uncommon in Scandinavia. A bell found in this burial has parallels in Iceland and the British Isles, where Batey (1988) identified similar bells from Caithness and England (Batey 1988, 215).

The Kornsá burial, therefore, offers evidence of unusual and foreign jewellery in a high status female grave from an early Icelandic social setting. This could reflect the internment of someone from a mixed cultural background, or be the result of trade and interaction in the Viking world. In the absence of the standard oval brooch, the deceased was granted an equally valuable item of jewellery that would serve to state her social standing in death, as well as that of her surviving kin group. In Iceland, being far rarer, tongue shaped brooches may even have been perceived as a superior alternative to the oval brooch, therefore symbolising a woman of the highest social stratum.

Group 2 graves without oval brooches. In a grave from Hafurbjarnarstaðir, Gullbringusýsla, classified as a group 2 type burial, the deceased was an adult female placed in a flexed position and was buried with the following items: a ringed pin with the ring missing, a trefoil brooch worn on her chest, a knife, a comb, two pebbles of unusual shape, three clam shells, and some iron fragments (Eldjárn 1956, 74-75). A stone slab had been placed on the upper part of her body and a whale bone plaque on the lower half (Eldjárn 1956, 74-75).

Neither of the items of jewellery from Hafurbjarnarstaðir are typically Scandinavian in origin. The ringed pin is an Irish type, and is of the polyhedral head variant, said to be the largest group of ringed pins from the Dublin sites (Fanning 1994, 25). The trefoil brooch has parallels from elsewhere in Iceland and from Jarlshof in Shetland, and it has been suggested that they were produced in the British Isles under Scandinavian influence (Paterson 1997, 649). Both items of jewellery are, therefore, not typically Scandinavian and one might speculate as to the cultural origins of this person. She may have been among those immigrants of mixed Norse/ Celtic descent, perhaps even Irish or from the northern or western Isles of Scotland.

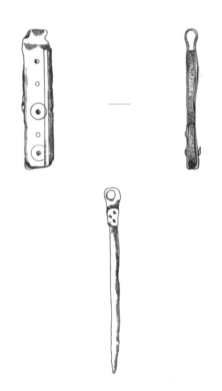

Figure 2. Strap-end from Kroppur, Eyjafjarðarsýsla (drawing: M. Hayeur-Smith). Scale: 2:1.

Group 1 graves without oval brooches. The site of Kroppur, Eyjafjarðarsýsla, revealed two burials. The female burial contained a bronze ringed pin of Scandinavian type (Petersen C), as well as what has been described as a folded bronze plate, but which has since been identified as a strap end similar to one found in a Viking burial at Kneep in the outer Hebrides (C. Paterson, pers. comm.). This type possibly originated in the British Isles. No other grave goods were found in this burial and once again, this assemblage of grave goods suggests either trade and interaction with the British isles or a person of mixed ethnic background.

Insular or foreign jewellery in Norway is not uncommon and is frequently the result of contact with the British Isles (Graham-Campbell 1984, 38). In the Birka chamber graves, Nils Ringstedt (1997), reported that high status burials for women included rare items of Insular jewellery such as crucifixes, reliquary pendants, precious stones, silver charms, and jet bracelets, and he suggested that these items reflect high status because they suggest a long distance connection and the economic ability to acquire rare products (Ringstedt 1997, 74). This does not seem to be the case in Iceland. Non-Scandinavian and Insular items do appear frequently there in combination with Scandinavian type material culture even in graves representing the lowest rank group identifiable in the burials. This combination also seems, based on the review of burial customs from other North Atlantic regions, to be something linking Iceland and Norse settlement areas in the British Isles. It is the type of Insular material mixed in which makes it unique compared to the mainland Scandinavian pattern. The inclusion of this Insular jewellery is in my opinion, the result of the incorporation of non-Scandinavian or mixed settlers from the British Isles who contributed to the colonising population of this island and who are frequently mentioned in the medieval Icelandic historical documents (Hayeur-Smith 2002a; 2002b).

Having reviewed the archaeological data from Iceland relating to status, burials, grave goods and the presence or absence of oval brooches in female graves, I would now like to turn my attention and discuss the social implications of these results. I feel it is relevant to place this archaeological data into a broader social framework in order to understand the role and place of jewellery as a status emblem. As my emphasis in this analysis has been on the presence or absence of oval brooches in graves, I will continue to focus on this type of jewellery. I believe that the oval brooch, as well as other items of Scandinavian jewellery, may have become symbols of status and cultural identity in the social reality of early Iceland.

235

Figure 3. Oval brooch from Skogar í Flókadal (no. 5030a), 10.8cm x 5.5 cm (Institute of Archaeology of Iceland; illustration: M. Hayeur-Smith).

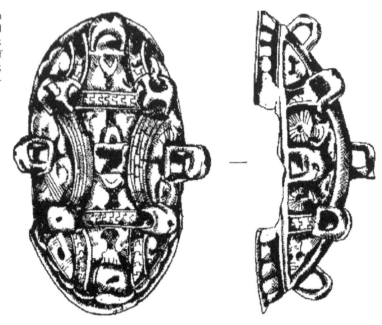

236

Jewellery as a symbol of personal, and cultural identity
The heirloom, status, and issues of cultural identity

As already discussed, jewellery, adornment, and clothing act symbolically on a person's sense of belonging. Female graves with oval brooches, as well as other items of jewellery accompanying them, or the presence of elaborately decorated sword hilts and chapes in male burials, convey this sense of belonging to a community or group. It is likely that many people continued to perform Scandinavian pagan burial practises in this new country because: (1) it was familiar and they reproduced what they knew; (2) it had enduring spiritual value to many members of the colonising population; and (3) it may also have become a special and unique way of marking their cultural heritage. This feeling of 'uniqueness' in cultural display is prevalent in the heirloom phenomenon and is intimately connected with identity. For example, there is evidence elsewhere in the North Atlantic that the dates of burials do not necessarily coincide with the dates of the jewellery incorporated in them. The Scar burial in Orkney is a case in point. In the Scar burial, an equal armed brooch (also known as a Troms type brooch) buried with the deceased woman was already of considerable antiquity when placed in the ground. It was made between the eighth and the latter half of the ninth century (Owen and Dalland 1999, 69). The dating of the grave is somewhat complex.

> [T]he most likely date for the grave is sometime between about AD 895 and 1030 and more probably after 960; while the most likely date for the grave on the basis of the artefactual assemblage is somewhat earlier, from the second half of the ninth or first few decades of the tenth century (Owen and Dalland 1999, 165).

This suggests that the brooch was an heirloom passed down to the deceased (Owen and Dalland 1999, 165).

In the Icelandic situation, although direct dates of the skeletons are not yet available (J. Arneborg, pers. comm.), it is possible that certain graves with oval brooches are later than the jewellery itself. The oval brooches from Skogar í Flókadal may be such a case (fig. 3). They are Berdal type brooches with Oseberg style ornament dated to the ninth century (Eldjárn 1956, 79). Although we know little of their context, Kristján Eldjárn considered

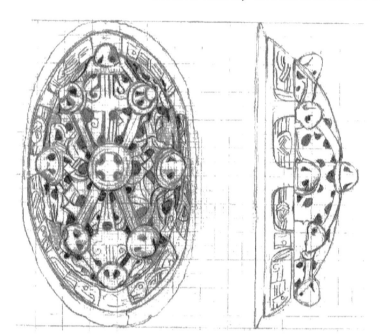

Figure 4. Oval brooch from Daðastaðir of the P51d variant, 10.9cm x 6.35cm (illustration: M. Hayeur-Smith).

237

them as belonging to a burial, and if Iceland's settlement is securely dated after AD 870, then it is likely that this burial was later than the brooches it contained.

As mentioned above, the heirloom connects with one's descent group and establishes a sense of cultural belonging for the dead and the living. In Iceland, I believe that the oval brooch, as well as other Scandinavian artefacts and the burial mode itself, became symbols of cultural identity connecting the dominant group with its origins. In this context, the oval brooch may no longer have signified simply a woman's status, as it probably did in Scandinavia, but may have come to symbolise far more: where her kin group was from and to which emerging community she belonged.

This is particularly striking with oval brooches from two graves at Daðastaðir, Norður-Þingeyjarsýsla (fig. 4), and Ketilstaðir, Norður-Múlasýsla. Both women's graves have elaborate grave goods and have been classified as higher status burials. Intuitively one would tend to equate high-quality jewellery with higher status, yet both graves produced oval brooches of relatively poor quality and poor rendering. The grave from Daðastaðir is the more elaborate of the two and contained the following grave goods: two oval brooches, a trefoil brooch, bracelet, ringed pin, bead necklace, belt clasp, agricultural implements, textile implements, a comb, one piece of flint, and a dog (Eldjárn and Friðriksson 2000, 212-213). The oval brooches from this grave are not an identical pair. While both are P51 type brooches, one is a P51d type and the other a P51b. The P51d is of poorer quality than its counterpart. This lower quality of workmanship is apparent in the rendering of the brooch itself; for example, the lack of crispness and clarity of the designs on the various panels of the oval brooch. Fuglesang (1987) enumerated a number of criteria to establish good or poor workmanship.

> Quality in this connection is taken exclusively as a criterion of craft in the rendering of ornament, eg.: Are the planes of modelling smooth and uniform or uneven and serried? Are the walls of relief smooth or jagged? Is an incised line evenly curved or angular? Are incised lines of even width and depth or are they uneven? Such criteria of technical ability reflect the amount of training a craftsman had, in other words whether he produced ornament regularly or only intermittently (Fuglesang 1987, 222).

In the case of the Daðastaðir brooches it was likely not their quality that was important but their presence in the grave.

It is likely that this sense of 'Scandinavianess' became all the more important far from the homeland, and identity in this new setting was bound to be altered and adapted to the new social environment. In effect, identity is always something in constant flux and will be affected by circumstances, such as foreign domicility due to colonisation, war, etc. (Gold and Paine 1984, 2; Amory 1997, 16). Gold and Paine (1984) have argued that particular emotions and attitudes may arise when referring to the 'homeland' or 'mother country' among people living in a new place (Gold and Paine 1984, 1). According to these authors, notions and images of the mother country may evoke a variety of responses.

> On different occasions, mother country may arouse any one or several emotions across a wide range: nostalgia or bitterness, insecurity or messianism, nationalism or international brotherhood. It is as likely to provoke feelings of elitism as of inferiority. Only exceptionally we think, is it a feeling of indifference (Gold and Paine 1984, 2).

Both the sense of cultural belonging and ideas of the mother country change with the circumstances of settlement. What people practised in Iceland as funeral behaviour may no longer have carried the same social meaning it originally had in Norway. The symbols may have been modified to suit the current reality, and certain objects placed in graves may have taken on a new symbolic meaning, to become in their own right 'status' objects worn to promote one's place in the emerging social hierarchy. After all, pagan burial, and one could say *all* burial, was by its very nature a symbolic act (Owen and Dalland 1999, 143).

SOCIAL CLIMATE OF EARLY ICELAND AND QUESTIONS OF IDENTITY

The uniqueness of early Icelandic society lay in the fact that Scandinavians arrived in a land which was essentially empty. The new society was thus forced into creating itself, not an easy task in a community consisting of a mixed group of people from both Scandinavia and the British Isles. The cultural element from the British Isles is mentioned in *Landnámabók* as well as other written sources. According to Jones the settlement of Iceland cannot be disassociated from this region, as a decade or so prior to its discovery exploratory voyages to Iceland were carried out from the British Isles (Jones 1986, 41). *Landnámabók* mentions several settlers from Ireland, the Hebrides, and Scotland whose names are Celtic. In addition, there are many examples given of Norse settlers whose spouses were non Norse or of mixed decent. Finally, we know from the written sources that most slaves brought to Iceland in the early period of the settlement were from Ireland and the British Isles (Karras 1988, 49). From *Landnámabók* there is frequent mention of Irish slaves.

> He plundered all over Ireland and took a great deal of loot, including ten slaves called Dufthak, Geirraud, Skjaldbjorn, Halldor, Dradrit—the rest of them aren't mentioned by name (Pálsson and Edwards 1972, 19).

> Hjorleif drifted west along the coast. He ran short of drinking water, and what the Irish slaves did was to knead together flour and butter saying it was good for thirst (Pálsson and Edwards 1972, 20)

> There was a man called Avang, of Irish descent, the first settler at Botn (Pálsson and Edwards 1972, 25).

Even though slavery was said to be officially abolished with the advent of Christianity in AD 1000 (Byock 1993, 123; Karras 1988, 142; Hastrup 1985, 65), Karras (1988) places the actual disappearance of slavery in Iceland roughly in the mid-twelfth century based on evidence from the Icelandic law code *Grágas* (Karras, 1988: 135). Hastrup (1985) stated that *Landnámabók* documents the abolition of slavery earlier during the *landnám* period

(Hastrup 1985, 62). What is clear from the existence of slavery and its rapid or slow decline is that from a social perspective a new social strata of freedmen emerged and were integrated into a formerly stratified social system (Byock 1993, 123; Hastrup 1985, 62. Some freedmen became tenant farmers, some became landowners (Byock 1993, 123), while others may have joined the ranks of free landless workers (Karras 1988, 144). In such a social dynamic there was bound to have been a degree of cultural demarcation at work. Cultural identity may have been affected by such a social environment when more than one social group interacted with each other, as was argued by Amory (1997):

> When two groups, whether affiliated hitherto or not, are forced into sharing limited material resources, ethnicity may assume a preponderant role in dividing and defining each of them (Amory 1997, 16).

To further complicate issues in Iceland, the society itself was undergoing rapid social change. We know that the first settlers claimed large portions of land in more advantageous agricultural regions resulting in large farms (Byock 1993, 55) and that by the first half of the tenth century humans were settled in all habitable regions of the country (Vesteinsson 1998, 4). During a later phase of settlement, newcomers were obliged to obtain land from these landowners, which gave rise to tenancy as well as small farms settling around the main farmstead units on land less favourable for agriculture. (Smith 1995, 321; Vesteinsson 1998, 2). For some authors, such as Byock and Hastrup, the large farms of the early settlement had become smaller (Byock 1993, 56-57; Hastrup 1985, 63). Furthermore, from the parcelling up of land it is said that it became increasingly difficult to distinguish the leading families among the settlers, as all landholders benefited from similar rights as freemen (Byock 1993, 56-57). Smith and Vesteinsson argued otherwise, stating that less homogenisation took place and that Iceland's élite maintained its status well into the medieval period (Smith 1995, 321; Vesteinsson 1998, 19).

239

The process of colonisation, land claiming and land negotiating did not occur suddenly and was undoubtedly gradual, resulting in some possible form of competition and the need to distinguish oneself from others. This probably took place either culturally between Norse and Celtic peoples that in turn may have been transformed and expressed by competition between social strata: élite versus entrepreneurial free farmers versus ambitious freedmen. Undoubtedly the élite tried to maintain its élite status and without a doubt jewellery and material culture in general was used to negotiate social hierarchy. The pagan burial practice, grave-goods, and oval brooches though dated prior to the introduction of Christianity, may have been one of a multitude of elements used in this socio-cultural distinction. They may have contributed to the necessity for some settlers to define themselves as 'the dominant cultural group'. Cultural identity is just one of many hypotheses worth considering when addressing 'Scandinavian' material culture and funerary display in the early settlement of Iceland.

BIBLIOGRAPHY

Amory, P. 1997. *People and Identity in Ostrogothic Italy, 489-554,* Cambridge.

Arwidsson, G. ed., 1987. *Birka II: 1, Systematische Analysen der Gräberfunde*, Stockholm.

Barley, N. 1995. *Dancing on the Grave: encounters with death*, London.

Batey, C. 1988. 'A Viking-Age Bell from Freswick Links, Caithness', *Medieval Archaeology*, 32, 213-16.

Brydon, A. and Niessen, S., eds, 1998. *Consuming Fashion, Adorning the Transnational Body*, Oxford and New York.

Byock, J. L. 1993. *Medieval Iceland*, Chippenham.

Cannon, A. 1998. 'The Cultural and Historical Contexts of Fashion', in Brydon and Niessen 1998, 23-38.

Cherry, J.F. ed., 1995. *Colonization of Islands*, London.

Clarke, H. and Ambrosiani, B. 1991. *Towns in the Viking Age*, Leicester.

Clarke, H.B., Ni Mhaonaigh, M. and O Floín, R., eds, 1998. *Ireland and Scandinavia in the Early Viking Age*, Dublin.

Crawford, B. 1987. *Scandinavian Scotland*, Leicester.

Dommasnes, L. H. 1982. 'Late Iron Age in Western Norway. Female Roles and Ranks as Deduced from and Analysis of Burial Customs', *Norwegian Archaeological Review*, 14, 1-2, 70-84.

Eldjárn, K. 1956. *Kuml og Haugfé: úr Heiðnum sið á Íslandi*, Reykjavik.

Eldjárn, K. and Friðriksson, A. 2000. *Kuml og Haugfé: ur heiðnum sið á íslandi*, 2nd edn, Reykajvík.

Fanning, T. 1994. *Viking Age Ringed Pins from Dublin*, Dublin.

Fuglesang, S. H. 1987. 'The Personal Touch, on the Identification of Workshops', *Proceedings of the 10th Viking Congress*. Oslo: Universitets Oldsakamling Skrifter, Ny Rekke 9.

Gold, G.L. ed., 1984. *Minorities and Mother County Imagery*, St John's.

Gold, G.L. and Paine, R. 1984. 'Introduction', in Gold 1984, 1-16.

Graham-Campbell, J. 1980. *Viking Artifacts*, London.

——1984. 'Western influences on Penanular brooches and ringed pins', in Arwidsson 1984, 31-38.

Gräslund, A.-S. 1980. *Burial Customs, a Study of Graves on Björkö*. Stockholm: Birka IV.

Hastrup, K. 1985. *Culture and History in Medieval Iceland*, Oxford.

Hayeur-Smith, M. 2002a. 'Viking Age Insular Jewellery from Iceland, and its Connection to the Western Isles', in the 'Proceedings from Gall-Ghaidheil: The Western Isles in the Viking World', Conference, April 3-7, 2000 Stornoway, Isle of Lewis, Hebrides Scotland (forthcoming).

——2002 b. A Social Analysis of Viking Jewellery from Iceland, unpublished PhD thesis, University of Glasgow.

Jansson, I. 1985. *Ovala Spännbucklor. En studie av vikingatida standardsmycken med utgångspunkt från Björkö-fynden*, Uppsala.

Jesch, J. 1991. *Women in the Viking Age*, Woodbridge.

Jones, G. 1986. *The North Atlantic Saga*, Oxford.

Karras, R. M. 1988. *Slavery and Society in Medieval Scandinavia*, New Haven, Conn. and London.

Kristjánsson, J. 1998. 'Ireland and the Irish in Icelandic Tradition', in Clarke *et al*. 1998, 259-276.

McGovern, T. H., Bigelow, G., Amorosi, T. and Russell, D. 1988. 'Northern Islands, Human Error and Environmental Degradation: A View of Social and Ecological Change in Medieval North Atlantic', *Human Ecology*, 16, 3, 225-269.

Müller-Wille, M. 1971. *Pferdegrab und Pferdeopfer im frühen Mittelalter. Mit einem Beitrag von H. Vierck: Pferdegräber in angelsächsischen England*. Amersfort: Berichten van de Rijksdienst voor het Oudheidkundig Bodemonderzoek 20-21.

Owen, O. and Dalland, M. 1999. *Scar: A Viking Boat Burial on Sanday, Orkney*, East Linton.

Paterson, C. 1997. 'The Viking Age Trefoil Mounts from Jarlshof: a reappraisal in the light of two new discoveries', *Proceedings of the Society of Antiquaries of Scotland*, 127, 649-657.

Pálsson, H. and Edwards, P., trans, 1972. *The Book of Settlements*, Landnámabok. Winnipeg: University of Manitoba Icelandic Studies 1.

Petersen, J. 1928. *Vikingetidens Smykker*, Stavanger.

Petré, B. 1993. 'Male and Female Finds and Symbols in Germanic Iron Age Graves', *Current Swedish Archaeology*, 1, 149-154.

Ringstedt, N. 1997. *The Birka Chamber-Graves, Economic and Social Aspects*, Stockholm.

Smith, K. P. 1995. '*Landnám*: the Settlement of Iceland in Archaeological and Historical Perspective', in Cherry 1995, 319-347.

Solberg, B. 1985. 'Social Status in the Merovingian and Viking Periods in Norway from Archaeological and Historical Sources', *Norwegian Archaeological Review*, 18, 1-2, 241-256.

Vesteinsson, O. 1998. 'Patterns of Settlement in Iceland: a study in Pre-History', *Saga Book of the Viking Society*, 25, 1-29.

240

Scandinavian Building Customs of the Viking Age:

the North Atlantic Perspective

Steffen Stummann Hansen

INTRODUCTION

The excavation of buildings became an important agendum in Scandinavian archaeology during the period between the two World Wars. The scientific potential of the morphology and layout of prehistoric and historical house structures was acknowledged. It was also realised that buildings changed over time, and that individual phases or stages of history seemed to produce their own architectural standards. Buildings, therefore, could be typologised and consequently used, not only to describe settlement and living conditions in prehistoric societies, but also as an instrument of dating. In this respect, it was simply a further development of the typological method developed in Scandinavian archaeology during the last decades of the nineteenth century.

Such a concept was, of course, of special importance to archaeological sites where the artefact assemblage contained none or only few diagnostic artefacts. This was, for instance, the situation at L'Anse aux Meadows where the morphology of the buildings played a major part in substantiating the argument of the site as being of a Scandinavian origin (Ingstad 1985).

NORSE GREENLAND

Extensive surveys were conducted in Norse Greenland in the last decades of the nineteenth century, producing a high number of site plans with house structures etc. (Holm 1884; Bruun 1895). These surveys later formed the basis for a more ambitious research campaign.

In 1921, Poul Nørlund (1888-1951), an historian and curator of the Medieval Department of the National Museum of Denmark, initiated what could be termed modern archaeological investigations into the Norse settlements in Greenland. There he soon got in contact with another young Dane, the architect Aage Roussell (1901-1972). Nørlund probably quickly realised that he, in Roussell, had met a man who could record and plan structural remains properly. Subsequently, he employed him as his assistant on archaeological expeditions to Norse farmsteads in Greenland in 1926 and 1930 (Stummann Hansen 1998a; 1999a; fig. 1).

Nørlund and Roussell excavated a number of sites in the Eastern and Western Settlements of Norse Greenland, subsequently providing us with several publications of a high standard and, importantly, in English (Nørlund 1924; Nørlund and Roussell 1930; Nørlund and Stenberger 1934; Roussell 1936; 1941).

The publications presented a detailed picture of Norse settlement in Greenland, with its farmsteads and churches. It also gave us an idea of what a Norse farmstead looked like. Thus a typical Medieval Norse farmstead in Greenland seemed to consist of a dwelling, a separate cow-byre with a barn, sheep-staples, store-houses, pens, etc. (fig. 2).

THE ARCHAEOLOGY OF BUILDINGS IN SCANDINAVIA

Contemporary with the excavations in Norse Greenland, material remains of Iron Age houses were recognized for the first time in Scandinavia. In the following years large-scale

Figure 1. Poul Nørlund (right) and Aage Roussell in the Western Settlement of Norse Greenland, 1930. Nørlund initiated modern research in Norse Greenland in 1921 and was the architect behind the Pan-Scandinavian archaeological project in Iceland in 1939. He became director of the Danish National Museum in 1938. Roussell, brought up by Nørlund, took over the research in Norse Greenland in the 1930s. He later became head of the Medieval Department of the National Museum of Denmark. By 1939 he was the leading authority on house structures in the North Atlantic having excavated extensively in Greenland and Iceland (photo: National Museum of Denmark).

excavations were executed, particularly in western Denmark, uncovering not only individual house structures but even entire village communities. These investigations were almost entirely the work of one man, the geographer Gudmund Hatt (1884-1960), of the University of Copenhagen (Hatt 1931; 1936; 1957; 1958; 1959; 1960). Hatt's work gave us a picture of the vernacular architecture of Early Iron Age society of Southern Scandinavia—apparently a peaceful rural community of farmers living in buildings characterized by having the human dwelling and cow-byre under the same roof, with the dwelling in one end of the house and the byre in the other. This type of building was referred to as the longhouse of northwestern Europe. Hatt did not confine geographically his discussion of this type of building custom to Southern Scandinavia but compared it with architecture on a wider European and almost worldwide scale (Hatt 1931).

In Sweden, Mårten Stenberger (1898-1973), in 1933, published his doctoral thesis in Swedish, *Öland under äldre järnåldern* (in English, 'Öland during the Early Iron Age'; Stenberger 1933). It was based on the impressive material of house structures, farmsteads etc, he had recorded on the island of Öland, off the coast of southeastern Sweden. This material, like Hatt's, could predominantly be dated to the Iron Age but did also contain material which was of medieval, or possibly even Viking-Age, date. Stenberger, like Hatt, demonstrated a broad European perspective in his discussion of the houses.

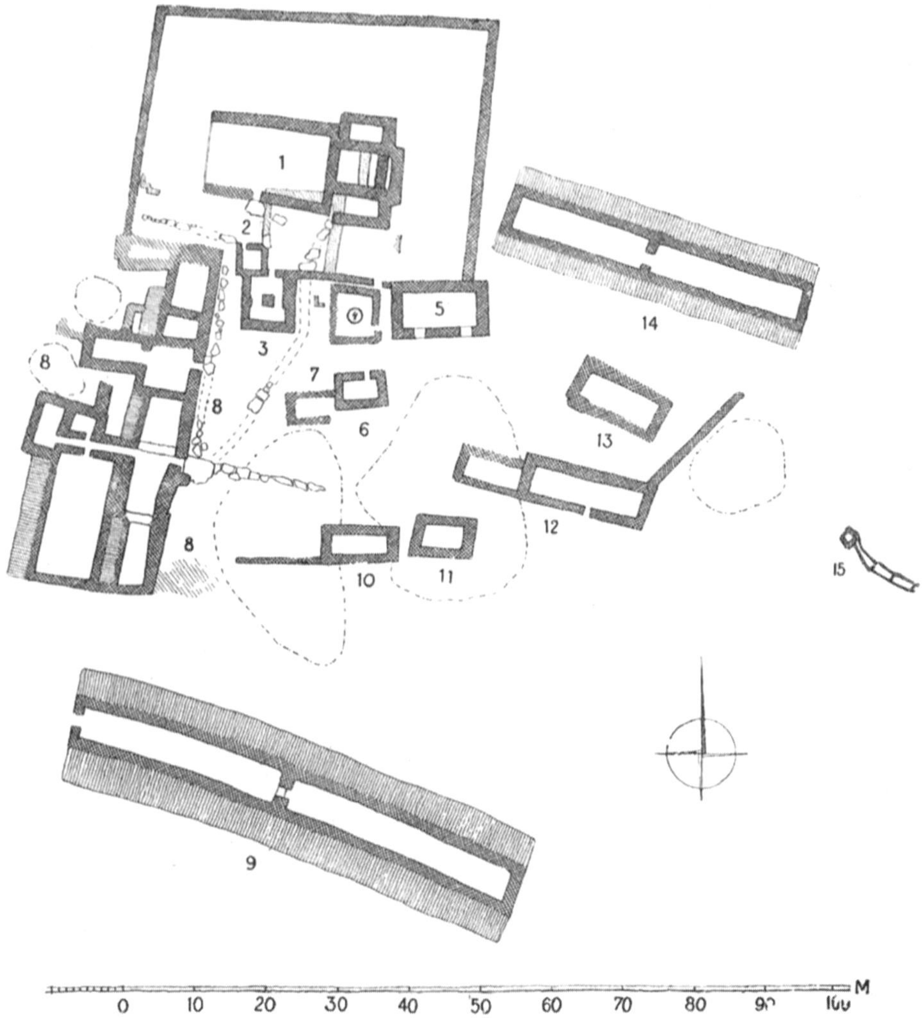

243

Figure 2. Site-plan of the bishop's seat at Garðar in the Eastern Settlement. 1: Church and Churchyard. 2: Tithe barn. 8: The bishop's house. 9 & 14: Large byres. 11: The smithy. 15: The well. Note that the byres are separate and aligned downslope while the dwelling is following the contours of the landscape (after Nørlund and Roussell 1930).

In southwestern Norway, which is assumed to be the core land of the Viking emigration into the North Atlantic, Jan Petersen (1887-1967), archaeologist and director of the Stavanger Museum, already had initiated recording of house structures still preserved in the landscape all over the region of Rogaland in the 1920s. He published his recordings, in Norwegian, in two impressive volumes (1933; 1936). These works added important materi-al to compare with that produced by Hatt in Denmark and Stenberger in Sweden. Petersen did not discuss his material in a wider European perspective but in a slightly more confined Norwegian or North Atlantic perspective which may have to be seen in the light of national trends in Norwegian archaeology throughout the 1920-30s (Brøgger 1929; 1930; 1935; 1937).

Towards a typology of houses

The intense Danish archaeological activity in Greenland produced a lot of archaeological material for which there was very little comparison with at the time. When Nørlund with the help of Roussell, published the excavation of the church and graveyard at the bishop's seat of Garðar (Nørlund and Roussell 1930), one of his conclusions, based on architectural and artefactual details, was that 'there is no doubt that, at any rate for a certain time, there has been direct communication between the Norsemen in Greenland and the Norse North Sea Islands or the British Isles' (Nørlund and Roussell 1930, 57).

The architect Roussell, Nørlund's assistant, became very interested in the morphology and structure of Norse houses, farmsteads and churches, and undoubtedly Nørlund saw the potential here immediately. Nørlund applied for money to send Roussell on a study tour to Scotland in order to record any surviving Scandinavian features in the vernacular architecture (Stummann Hansen 1998a; 1999a). Roussell published his results in a book, which was originally meant to be his doctoral thesis, entitled *Norse Building Customs in the Scottish Isles* (Roussell 1934; Stummann Hansen 2000a).

In the book, Roussell established a typology of farmsteads in the Scottish Isles, consisting of three stages, of which the oldest was represented by the so-called *black house* of the Hebrides. This house had very similar features with the Scandinavian longhouse of the Iron Age as having the dwelling and the byre under the same roof, and the building as a whole seemed to be of a very 'primitive' character (for a discussion on Roussell's view of the black house see Stummann Hansen 1998a; 1999a; 1999b; 2000b; see fig. 3). The two later stages, both characterized by not having the dwelling and the byre under the same roof, were represented by respectively the Shetland and the Orcadian farm (Roussell 1934).

Roussell's work was of pioneering importance. He was the first to categorize the form and the layout of the farmsteads and to study the geographical distribution of the different

Figure 3.   Black house in Shawbost, Lewis, 1936. Note the drain from the byre-end of the house (photo: G. Hatt).

types. The book achieved a very central role in the discussions within Scandinavia during the 1930s on the development of the longhouse from the Iron Age to the Medieval Period.

Seven years later Roussell applied this three-step evolutionary model created on the Scottish material to Norse farmsteads in Greenland, as respectively the *longhouse* (= the black house of the Hebrides), *passage-house* (Shetland), and *centralized house* (Orkney). This was outlined in his doctoral thesis, entitled *Farms and Churches in Mediaeval Norse Greenland* (Roussell 1941; Stummann Hansen 2000a).

Already in 1932, Nørlund, Stenberger and Hatt fostered the idea of a joint Scandinavian archaeological project in Iceland in order to produce material in Iceland for comparison with Norse Greenland (Keller 1989; Stummann Hansen 2001). This project, eventually, took place in the valley of Þjórsárdalur in 1939 and added a lot of fresh material, comprising important sites such as Stöng and Skallakot (Nørlund 1943; Roussell 1943a; 1943b; fig. 4).

VIKING AGE BUILDINGS IN THE NORTH ATLANTIC

When Roussell conducted his study tour to the Scottish Isles in 1931, the officials of the museum in Edinburgh were helpful and supportive in every respect, but also had very sceptical attitudes to his project. He wrote:

245

> It turned out that in archaeological circles in Scotland it was the view that the Norseman always used wood as a building material, and as every relic in Scotland is of stone and earth, it cannot be of Norse origin (Roussell 1934, 8).

Just a couple of years earlier the Royal Commission on Ancient and Historical Monuments of Scotland (RCAHMS) had published its inventory for the Western Isles where it was stated: 'the Norsemen of the Viking period were essentially builders in wood, and no edifices of dry-built stone masonry were known in Norway either of that period or of preceding ages'. A note added: 'The literary evidence puts this beyond doubt'. Furthermore, it speculated: 'The Vikings and their descendants were apparently too conservative to depart

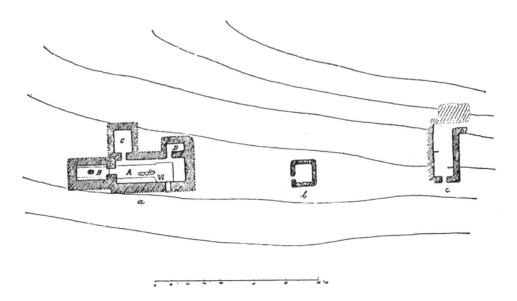

Figure 4. Medieval farmstead at Samsstaðir in Þjórsárdalur, Iceland. A: dwelling. B: outhouse. C: byre. Note that the byre is aligned downslope while the dwelling, like in Norse Greenland, is following the contours of the landscape (after Bruun 1929).

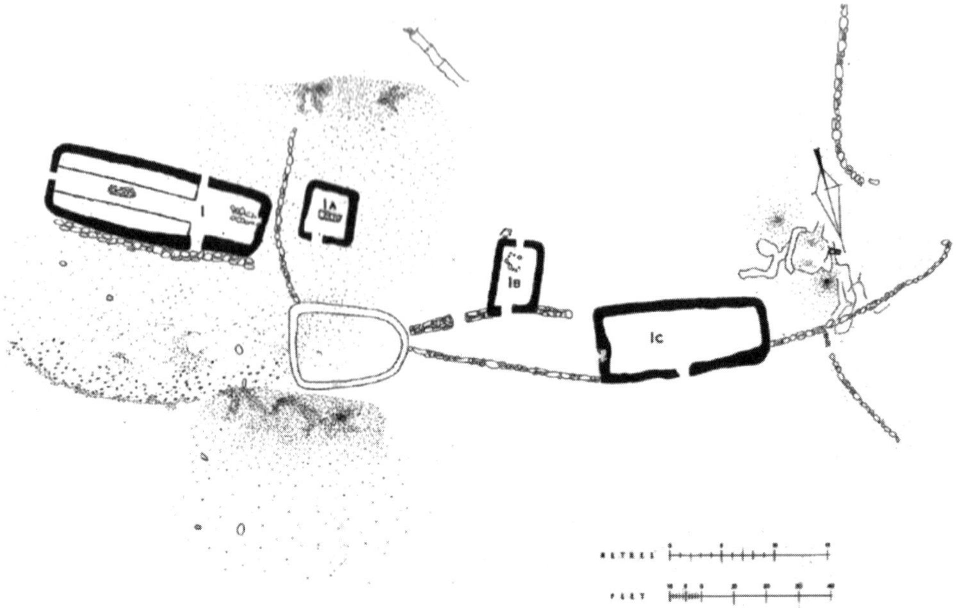

Figure 5. Site-plan of the First Phase of the Scandinavian settlement at Jarlshof, Shetland (after Hamilton 1956).

from their native practice of always employing wood. It has been suggested that they may have used low foundations of stone. Even that is doubtful.'

It should, however, only last a few years before the Scottish archaeologists had to change their minds when stone foundations of Scandinavian houses of the Viking Age for the first time were located and excavated at Jarlshof in Shetland, in 1934 (Curle 1935; 1936; Hamilton 1956), and at Brough of Birsay, in Orkney, two years later (RCHAMS 1946). How were these structures interpreted?

THE CREATING OF A MODEL OF THE VIKING HOUSE OF THE NORTH ATLANTIC

The initial phase (ninth century) at Jarlshof was interpreted as a farmstead consisting of four buildings: dwelling, byre, smithy and bath house. If one goes through Hamilton's publication it is, however, extremely difficult to find clear argumentation and documentation for his interpretation (fig. 5).

Thus there is nothing to substantiate the interpretation of one building (Building 1c) as a separate byre and if one looks at the building interpreted as a dwelling (Building 1a) it is obvious that there are problems. Hamilton refers to a door in the gable end and to evidence of benches along the walls. It is, however, much more likely that what Hamilton describes as benches are actually platforms for the cattle. The opening in the gable end is, of course, not a door but an opening where the drain from the byre goes out (Stummann Hansen 1999c).

Radford was later to argue like Hamilton when he interpreted a Scandinavian longhouse which was found and trial excavated in 1930s at Brough of Birsay (Radford 1959). Again there is no safe evidence for Radford's interpretation which must have been directed by a scholarly preconception.

In the Faroe Islands, the first proper Viking Age longhouse turned up at the site Niðri á Toft, in the settlement of Kvívík, during the Second World War (fig. 6). When it was published in 1951, it was interpreted (and later restored) exactly as first phase Jarlshof and

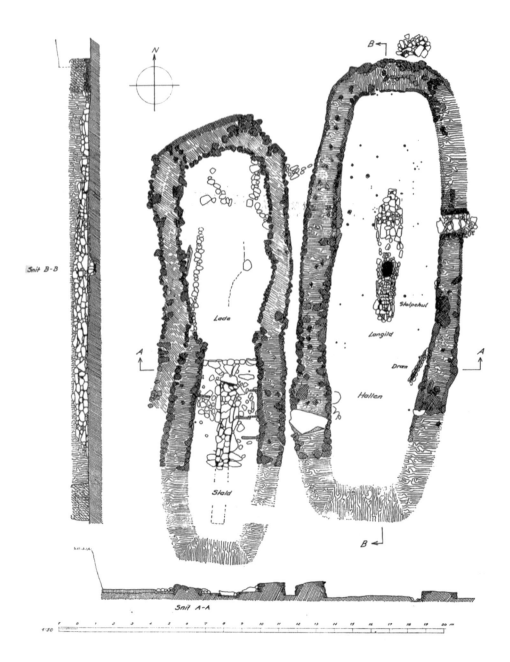

Figure 6. Viking-Age farmstead at Niðri á Toft, Kvívík, Faroe Islands. The building to the right presumably contained a byre in its lower-lying end (after Dahl 1968).

Brough of Birsay—i.e. byre and dwelling as two separate buildings (Dahl 1951; 1971a; 1971b). Recent work has indicated that there is no archaeological evidence for this interpretation and that the longhouse may have had a byre in its lower-lying end (Matras 1995).

The point, therefore, is that the interpretation of excavated Viking-Age house structures in the North Atlantic was completely based on the experience from Medieval farmsteads in Norse Greenland and Iceland. It did not take into consideration that Scandinavia had a tradition for fifteen hundred years of having dwelling and byre under the same roof.

Now, why did this happen? There is one, but probably not the only, important reason for that. The excavations in Norse Greenland were actually published, and published in English. Therefore they obtained a prominent place in the discussions crossing the borders of languages. When studying Hamilton's monograph of Jarlshof it is interesting to note that he has quite a few publications in Norwegian in his bibliography, including Petersen's important publication on the house structures of southwestern Norway. When reading through Hamilton's monograph, however, one would expect to find a discussion of Petersen's material or at least a reference to it—I have not been able to find it.

Hamilton produced a picture of the Viking Age farm in Scotland based on the experience from Medieval Norse Greenland. Since then, Jarlshof has uncritically been used as a model for a Viking farmstead in Scotland. Thus Anna Ritchie, in her book *Scandinavian Scotland* (1993), states:

248

> A typical farm of the ninth and tenth centuries consisted of a small cluster of rectangular buildings: dwelling house, byre and barn were essential elements, often with stone paving between them to reduce the problems of mud in poor weather. The dwelling had an earthen floor for warmth, although there might be paving inside the entrance where the wear from the passage of feet was most concentrated; it was designed as one large room or hall, but one end might be screened off as the kitchen. There was a large central hearth, sometimes built with a stone kerb, and low platforms or benches lined on two long walls on either side of the hearth. Traces of these platforms usually survive as lines of stones marking their inner edges, for the surface would have been wooden planking which roots away under normal conditions. Only the basal courses of the walls survive for the most part; occasionally the long walls appear to have been slightly bowed, but most buildings were straight-sided and the true boat-shaped house is not found in Scotland (Ritchie 1993, 33).

Further, Richie stated: 'In time this layout of separate dwelling and outhouses changed, first by adding the byre on to the lower end of the dwelling, thus creating the true longhouse in which humans and animals lived under the same roof' (1993, 34). This, according to Ritchie, and again based on Hamilton's dating, happened in the eleventh century (Ritchie 1993, 67).

TOWARDS A 'NEW MODEL' OF THE VIKING AGE LONGHOUSE OF THE NORTH ATLANTIC

It is, therefore, argued that there is a stratum of ninth-tenth century Viking buildings (longhouses) in the North Atlantic characterized by having dwelling and byre under the same roof, and thereby representing the terminal stage of a more than fifteen hundred years old Scandinavian tradition. These buildings are aligned downslope with the byre in the lower-lying end (figs 7-8).

By having byre and dwelling under the same roof this group of houses differs from the Early Medieval farmsteads known from Greenland (and Iceland), where the byre always occurs as a separate building. The remaining question, therefore, is whether a geographical or a chronological factor explains this.

At the site Vorbasse in Jutland, Denmark, an extensive rural Viking settlement was excavated during the 1970s (Hvass 1980). The first phase of the settlement was charcterised by farmsteads with byre and dwelling under the same roof but, when the settlement was restructured later in the Viking Age, this pattern altered and the byres became separate buildings. This phase of reorganisation can now by dendrochronology be dated to after AD 950 (Hvass 1993; Stummann Hansen 1999b). The second phase of the settlement is characterized by its famous Viking halls of the Trelleborg type (fig. 9). The earliest dates for this type of building derive from the fortresses of Trelleborg and Fyrkat, which have now been safely dated by dendrochronology to AD 980/981. Thus it seems that the change from byre-dwellings to dwelling and byre as separate buildings took place between AD 950 and 980 (Stummann Hansen 1999b).

It is up to future research to establish whether this change in architecture in Southern Scandinavia was general to the whole of the Scandinavian world of the Viking Age and the Medieval Period.

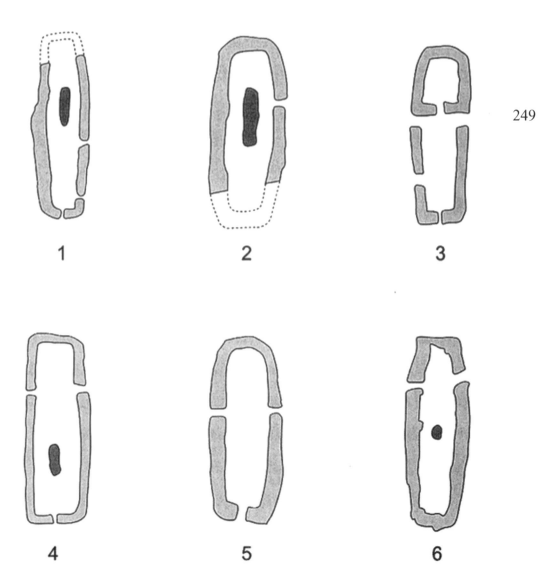

Figure 7. Viking-Age longhouses of the ninth and tenth centuries. 1: Toftanes, Faroe Islands; 2:Niðri á Toft, Faroe Islands; 3: Hamar, Shetland; 4: Jarlshof, Shetland; 5: Brough of Birsay, Orkney; 6: Oma, Norway (after Stummann Hansen 2000c).

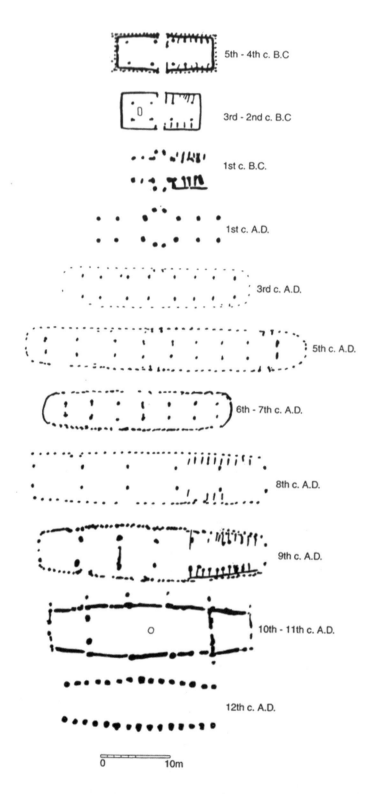

250

Figure 8. Typology of houses from southern Scandinavia from the early Iron Age to the early medieval period (after Hvass 1993).

Figure 9. Proposal for a reconstruction of a house of Trelleborg type excavated at Lejre, Seeland, Denmark. The building had a length of 48 m and 11 m width (after Draiby and Komber 1999).

251

PERSPECTIVES FOR THE FUTURE

The archaeology of buildings was established between the two World Wars, in a very intense and fruitful process which tried to tie the evidence from the Scandinavian emigrant communities of the North Atlantic together with the settlers' assumed homelands and their prehistoric traditions.

It has been demonstrated, using one example, that we still suffer from mis-interpretations on Viking Age material excavated between the two World Wars. Other examples which could have been discussed in this context, are the concept of raised benches along the walls or the possibility of the Viking Age longhouses having been two storey-buildings (Stummann Hansen 1998b; 1999c; 2003).

The early research in Norse settlements in Greenland produced a 'model' for a Scandinavian farmstead for the whole of the North Atlantic, not only for the Medieval period but even for the Viking Age. The publication of Jarlshof in Shetland (Hamilton 1956) and Niðri á Toft (Kvívík) in the Faroe Islands (Dahl 1951) are examples of that. These excavations, together with others, have since paid their contribution to reconstructions of Viking farmsteads and thereby our understanding of the architecture of that period. It is, however, obvious that a lot of these reconstructions are based on insecure or even false documentation.

What is badly needed today is a thorough, critical, re-evaluation and re-investigation of a number of the 'old' excavations of Scandinavian house structures in the North Atlantic which will help us sort out mis-interpretations and incorrectnesses in earlier excavations, interpretations, and subsequent reconstructions.

Against this background a three-year project (2000-2002) entitled, *Westnordic Building Customs in the Viking Age and Medieval Period* has been established. The project, which is mainly and substantially funded by the Nordic Research Council for the Social Sciences and the Humanities (NOS-H), is a cooperation between Orri Vésteinsson of Fornleifastofnun Íslands (Institute of Archaeology in Iceland), Jochen Komber of the Arkeologisk Museum in Stavanger (Museum of Archaeology in Stavanger) and the author, and will aim at a broad North Atlantic perspective with field-work all over the region.

The project has the subtitle 'Excavation, Interpretation and Reconstruction', which emphazises a strong link between the processes of excavation, interpretation and eventual reconstruction of house structures. While two of the participants have a rather long experience with excavations and surveys of Scandinavian sites of the Viking Age and the Medieval period, it is no coincidence that the third partner, Jochen Komber of Stavanger, besides being an archaeologist, is also a trained architect with a huge experience in reconstructions of prehistoric and historical houses in Western Norway. It is, of course, the hope that this initiative will bring us a step further in understanding the architecture of the Scandinavian emigrant communities of the North Atlantic during the Viking Age and the Medieval Period.

It is intended that the project, as a minimum, should involve surveys and excavations in Norway, Shetland, Iceland and Greenland. Surveys, to be followed by proper excavations, have been initiated this year in Þjórsárdalur in Iceland. Also in Iceland, the project is supporting the ongoing excavations at Hofstaðir. Another part of the project will be the completing and publication of surveys and excavations by the author in Unst, Shetland, since 1994 (Stummann Hansen 1998b; 2000c) and the publishing of surveys conducted in the Eastern Settlement of Norse Greenland during the years 1999-2000 (Guldager *et al.* 2002).

ACKNOWLEDGEMENTS

252

I am grateful to Kirsten E. Caning, Danish Polar Center, for improving and clarifying my text.

BIBLIOGRAPHY

Barrett, J.H. ed., 2003. *Culture Contact, Continuity and Collapse: The Norse Colonization of the North Atlantic*, Turnhout.

Bruun, D. 1895. 'Arkæologiske Undersøgelser i Julianehaabs Distrikt', *Meddelelser on Grønland*, 16, 3, (Copenhagen).

——1929. *Fra de færøske bygder*, Copenhagen.

Brøgger, A.W. 1929. *Ancient Emigrants*, Oxford.

——1930. *Den norske bosetningen på Shetland-Orknøyene. Studier og Resultater*, Oslo.

——1935. 'Den norske bosetning på Færøerne', *Norsk Geografisk Tidsskrift*.

——1937. *Hvusse Føroyar vorðu bygdar*, Tórshavn.

Curle, A.O. 1935. 'An Account of the Excavation of a Dwelling of the Viking Period at "Jarlshof", Sumburgh, Shetland, carried out on behalf of H.M. Office of Works', *Proceedings of the Society of Antiquaries of Scotland*, 69 (1934-1935), 265-321.

——1936. 'An Account of the Excavation of further Buildings of the Viking Period (Viking House No. II), at "Jarlshof", Sumburgh, Shetland, carried out on Behalf of H.M. Office of Works', *Proceedings of the Society of Antiquaries of Scotland*, 70 (1935-1936), 251-270.

Dahl, S. 1951. 'Fornar toftir í Kvívík', *Varðin*, 29, 65-96.

——1968. 'Fortidsminder', in Nielsen *et al.* 1968, 188-210.

——1971a. 'The Norse Settlement of the Faroe Islands', *Medieval Archaeology*, 14, 60-73.

——1971b. 'Recent Excavations on Viking Age Sites in the Faroes', in Foote and Strömbäck 1971, 45-56.

Draiby, B. and Komber, J. 1999. 'Rekonstruktion af Kongehallen fra Lejre', in Rasmussen 1999, 9-20.

Foote, P. and Strömbäck, D., eds, 1971. *Proceedings of the Sixth Viking Congress*, Uppsala.

Fuglestvedt, I., Gansum, T. and Opedal, A., eds, 1999. *Et hus med mange rom. Vennebok til Bjørn Myhre på 60-årsdagen.* Stavanger: AmS-Rapport 11.

Guldager, O., Stummann Hansen, S. and Gleie, S. 2002. *Medieval Farmsteads in Greenland. The Brattahlid region 1999-2000.* Copenhagen: Danish Polar Center Publications 9.

Gustafsson, A. and Karlsson, H., eds, 1999. *Glyfer och arkeologiska rum - en vänbok til Jarl Nordbladh.* Göteborg: Gotarc Series A, 3.

Hamilton, J.R.C. 1956. *Excavations at Jarlshof, Shetland*. Edinburgh: Archaeological Reports 1.

Hatt, G. 1931. 'Prehistoric Fields in Jylland', *Acta Archaeologica*, 2, 117-158.

——1936. 'Oldtidens Landsby i Danmark', *Fortid og Nutid*, 11, 97-136.

——1957. *Nørre Fjand: An early iron-age village site in West Jutland*. Copenhagen: Det Kgl. danske Videnskabernes Selskabs Arkæologisk-kunsthistoriske Skrifter, 2, 2.

——1958. 'A dwelling site of the early migration period at Oxbøl, South-west Jutland', *Acta Archaeologica*, 29, 142-154.

——1959. 'Iron Age cellars at Bækmoien, North Jutland', *Acta Archaeologica*, 30, 201-216.

——1960. 'The Roman Iron Age dwelling site at Mariesminde, Vestervig', *Acta Archaeologica*, 31, 63-83.

Holm, G. F. 1884. 'Beskrivelse af Ruiner i Julianehaabs Distrikt', *Meddelelser om Grønland* 6/3.

Hvass, S. 1980. 'The Viking-Age Settlement at Vorbasse, Central Jutland'. *Acta Archaeologica*, 50 (1979), 137-172.

——1993. 'The Settlement', in Hvass and Storgaard 1993, 187-194.

Hvass, S. and Storgaard, B., eds, 1993. *Digging in the Past. 25 years of Archaeology in Denmark*, Copenhagen.

Ingstad, A.S. 1985. *The Norse Discovery of America*, Oslo.

Keller, C, 1989. The Eastern Settlement Reconsidered, unpublished DPhil thesis, Oslo.

Matras, A.K. 1995. Vikingetidsbosættelsen "Niðri á Toft" Kvívík, Færøerne, unpublished MA thesis, Institute of Archaeology and Ethnology, University of Copenhagen.

Nielsen, N., Skautrup, P., Mathiassen, Th., and Rasmussen, J., eds, 1968. *J.P. Trap Danmark XIII (Færøerne)*, Copenhagen.

Nørlund, P. 1924. 'Buried Norsemen at Herjolfsnes', *Meddelelser om Grønland*, 67, 3.

——1943. 'Forord', in Stenberger 1943, 7-8.

Nørlund, P. and Roussell, A. 1930. 'Norse Ruins at Gardar', *Meddelelser om Grønland*, 76,1.

Nørlund, P. and Stenberger, M. 1934. 'Brattahlid', *Meddelelser om Grønland*, 88, 1.

Petersen, J. 1933. *Gamle Gårdsanlegg i Rogaland. Fra forhistorisk Tid og Middelalder*, Oslo.

——1936. *Gamle gårdsanlegg i Rogaland. Fortsettelse: Utsira, Lyngaland, Håvodl, Birkelandstølen, Hanaland*, Oslo.

Radford, C.A.R. 1959. *The Early Christian and Norse Settlements at Birsay, Orkney*, Edinburgh.

Rasmussen, M. ed., 1999. *Hal og Højsæde i Vikingetid. Et forslag til rekonstruktion af kongehallens arkitektur og indretning*. Lejre: Technical Report 5.

RCAHMS. 1928. *Inventory of Monuments in the Outer Hebrides, Skye and the small Isles*, Edinburgh.

——1946. *Twelfth Report with an Inventory of Ancient Monuments of Shetland and Orkney*, Edinburgh.

Ritchie, A. 1993. *Viking Scotland*, Edinburgh.

Roussell, Aa. 1934. *Norse Building Customs in the Scottish Isles*, Copenhagen and London.

——1936. 'Sandnes and the Neighbouring Farms', *Meddelelser om Grønland*, 88, 2.

——1941. 'Farms and Churches in the Mediaeval Norse Settlements of Greenland', *Meddelelser om Grønland*, 89.

——1943a. 'Stöng, Þjórsárdalur', in Stenberger 1943, 72-97.

——1943b. 'Skallakot, Þjórsárdalur', in Stenberger 1943, 55-71.

Stenberger, M. 1933. *Öland under äldre järnåldern. En bebyggelsehistorisk undersökning*, Stockholm.

——ed., 1943. *Forntida gårdar i Island*, Copenhagen.

Stummann Hansen, S. 1998a. 'Steep Hills, Strong Winds and Wealthy Sportsmen: Aage Roussell and his Journey to the Scottish Isles in 1931', *Review of Scottish Culture*, 11, 116-134.

——1998b. 'Scandinavian Settlement in Unst, Shetland: Archaeology (with D. Waugh, Place-Names)', in Taylor 1998, 120-146.

——1999a. 'Lange Bakker, Stærk Blæst og Velhavende Sportsmænd: Aage Roussell og hans Rejse til de Skotske Øer i 1931', *Aarbøger for nordisk oldkyndighed og historie* (1997), 185-229.

——1999b. 'En Rigdom af Oldtidsagtig Byggeskik. Gudmund Hatts Rejse til Hebriderne i 1936', in Gustafsson and Karlsson 1999, 679-698.

253

——1999c. 'I Jan Petersens Fodspor på Oma. Nyt om Vikingetidens Gårdsanlæg', in Fuglestvedt *et al.* 1999, 253-272.

——2000a. '"How to get at a man in Greenland I don't know". Aage Roussell og hans Orkney forbindelser', *Grønland*, 2000/1, 5-20.

——2000b. 'A Wealth of Ancient Building Customs. Gudmund Hatt's Journey to the Western Isles in 1936', *Review of Scottish Culture*, 13, 87-105.

——2000c. 'Scandinavian Settlement in Shetland. Chronological and Regional Contexts', in Stummann Hansen and Randsborg 2000, 87-103.

——2001. 'Settlement Archaeology in Iceland. The Race for the Pan-Scandinavian Project in 1939', *Acta Archaeologica*, 72, 2, 115-127.

——2003. 'The Early Settlement of the Faroe Islands—The Creation of Cultural Identity', in Barrett 2003, 33-71.

Stummann Hansen, S. and Randsborg, K., eds, 2000. *Vikings in the West.* Acta Archaeologica Supplementa II/Acta Archaeologica 71.

Taylor, S. ed., 1998. *The Uses of Place-names*, Edinburgh.

Games and Entertainments in Vínland

David Gardner

From single phrases in *Grænlendinga saga* ('The Saga of the Greenlanders': GLS) and *Eiríks saga rauða* ('The Saga of Eiríkr the Red': ESR), we learn that there were games and entertainments practised both in Greenland and in Vínland. What these diverse, medieval pastimes might have been is the subject of this paper which is by necessity conjectural. But, like the delightfully theatrical reenactments of daily life (*c.* AD 1000-1015) at the Norstead and L'Anse aux Meadows (LAM) sites (see Markewitz, this volume), we can only hope to compile some of the possible entertainment practices of the Viking age and let our imaginations fill in the missing details of sight and sound. For want of a better word, I have called these activities 'paratheatrical', from the Greek word *para* meaning 'beside' or 'parallel'.

In the western world, 'Theatre' (as well as 'Opera', and 'Ballet') was slow to crystallize into an art form. The accepted date is *c.* 1600, centuries after the seafaring Vikings had disappeared. So there could never be a 'Viking Theatre' *per se*. Indeed, the first recorded Scandinavian drama is *The Fall of Adam*, a liturgical folk-play written by a cathedral schoolmaster in 1562 (Lane 1988, 718). And, no permanent playhouses were built in Norway until the 1800s (Lane 1988, 718). But parallel to plays we find epic poetry and prose sagas, sung or spoken aloud, before an audience and preserved in memory by continual performance. The Viking poets or skalds were the newscasters and historians of their day, and often told their stories for payment, or the conditions of livelihood provided by the families that they eulogized. In England, by AD 1000 the adventures of the Anglo-Saxon hero Beowulf were being copied out in manuscript form, but in Iceland, the sagas of the family of Eiríkr *rauði* would have to wait another 180 to 250 years.

And, if there were no theatres at LAM, there was the single, multi-roomed longhouse. This building, in roughly cruciform shape, contains a central Great Hall or *skáli*, three living rooms boasting stone slab hearths around a sunken 'longfire', complete with cooking and ember pits. As Helge Ingstad wrote: 'Here...the Vinland voyagers must have gathered to work, eat, sing and tell tales'(H. Ingstad 1964, 708).

Parallel to the indoor pastimes were the more physical activities out-of-doors; competitive games that began, perhaps, in Grecian times as a form of military training, and would evolve, like the theatre, into public shows, and popular team and solo events. Parallel to these sporting contests were the likely, but inevitably unconfirmed, spontaneous, outdoor, busking skills of itinerant mimes and wandering vagabonds who kept the flame of entertainment alive from Roman times through the so-called Dark Ages, with their acrobatics and juggling, their wire-walking and clowning, and their dexterity with animals either trained or baited. By the nineteenth century these 'paratheatrical' busking activities would be woven into a new and recognisable entertainment form we call the circus. While there is evidence elsewhere in Europe, regrettably there is no record of buskers in Scandinavia until the high middle ages, *c.* 1200 (Lane 1988, 718).

We hear first of 'paratheatrical' entertainments in Greenland. The occasion we read of concerns the sister-in-law of Leifr *inn heppni* (the Lucky), Guðríðr, and her second marriage to Þorfinnr. We learn that the Christian feastings extended on into her wedding feast and that 'there was much chess-playing [or *tafl*, a board game] and story-telling and many other entertainments that enrich a household'(Magnusson and Palsson 1965, 92-3).

Board and dice games were popular, and I like to think of them as mini-dramas reenacted on a playing surface. Two men playing 'at board' are clearly carved into an eleventh-century Swedish rune stone, and we learn the game they are playing may be 'Nine-men's-

255

Morris'(Graham-Campbell *et al.* 1994, 65). Other games that may have been played are 'Three- in-a-row' and 'Fox and Geese'. 'Fox and Geese' has a gaming- board with 49 holes arranged in rows, 7 x 7, and is played with little bone pegs like cribbage. 'The fox starts in the middle and a team of 10 or 12 geese tries to drive him into a corner' (Simpson 1980, 149). Archaeologists at a ship-burial once unearthed two games on a single board, back to back, one on each side (Birkebaek and Barren 1975, 76).

I was intrigued to see the tiny, white, stone, triangular, gaming-piece at the LAM Reception Centre. Eleventh-century gaming-pieces were carved either in stone (often polished), wood (some even turned on a lathe), bone, or amber (H. Ingstad 1966, 213, pl. 26).

Chequers or draughts are not likely to have reached Scandinavia till the end of the medieval period (Simpson 1980, 149), but there was a war-game called *kneftafl* mentioned frequently in the Iceland sagas. Like 'Fox and Geese', a king is attacked by an army and driven into a corner (Graham-Campbell *et al.* 1994, 64). Gambling with dice was common but there was also the more serious practice of 'casting lots' to foretell the future. Special pieces of wood called 'sacrificial chips' or 'lot-twigs' were marked, sometimes with sacrificial blood, and then shaken and thrown like dice. Their positive or negative significance would then be decided (Foote and Wilson 1970, 401).

The game of chess is said to have originated in India and, because of the Viking contacts with the Arab world, may have been introduced into Scandinavia before it reached the rest of northern Europe (Simpson 1980, 149). Some exquisitely carved, realistic chesspieces have been found from the twelfth century, particularly a set of 58 from the Isle of Lewis in the Outer Hebrides of Scotland carved in walrus-tusk ivory (Arneborg 2000, 304-05). But, according to Helge Ingstad, the chessmen found in Greenland were 'simple, not shaped as human figures'(H. Ingstad 1966, 213, pl. 26).

Children had toy boats and weapons, as well as spinning tops (Graham-Campbell *et al.* 1994, 64), while woodcarving and ornamental metalworking were some of the men's domestic pastimes. Women worked, of course, sewing, spinning and weaving tapestries, but let us hope they enjoyed the craftsmanship involved in creating these household necessities. We are reminded of the significance of the spindle-whorl, and also a bone needle which was used for a form of knitting (*nålbinding*), that were discovered at LAM.

The shamanic foretelling of the future by seance was a serious practice, and may have been a Greenland rite that was also seen in Vínland. Again in ESR, we learn that Guðríðr had her fortune told by a practising pagan *völva*, in this case a woman, although the sibyl could be either male or female. While the ceremony may have had elements of performance and even diversion in it, we must remember that the spectacle underlined and embodied the faith of the participants.

Seated on a high platform with a cushion of hen's feathers, the female seer was dressed in a blue cloak with a black hood lined with white catskin. She carried a decorated staff and a pouch containing her shamanistic charms. Her gloves, too, were made of catskin, white inside and hairy. After consuming special foods made up of goatsmilk and the hearts of animals, the sibyl gathered a ring of women around her. Guðríðr, now a Christian, was persuaded, reluctantly, to sing pagan songs she had been taught as a child. Accompanied by these chants and incantations, the sibyl went into a trance to welcome in the spirits. She prophesied good fortune and then answered questions (Magnusson and Palsson 1965, 82-3; Bronsted 1980, 315). Perhaps Guðríðr learned that during the fourth expedition to Vínland she would have a child by her new husband, Þorfinnr. Indeed, in *c.* AD 1009, her son, Snorri, becomes the first recorded European child to be born in the Western Hemisphere.

The 'entertainments' at Guðríðr's wedding feast also included storytelling. At L'Anse aux Meadows, party-guests would have sat around on the outer, wooden, sleeping-platforms, which would be covered with 'patterned cloths', animal skins, or their leather sleeping-bags (Simpson 1980, 154; Morison 1971, 46; A-S Ingstad 1977, 68). The interior would have been illuminated by the longfire or by shallow lamps—wicks floating in soap-stone bowls filled with seal or whale oil. The fire was rarely out and there was a certain hier-archy about who sat closest to it. Children would most likely have been left in Greenland and women were below their husbands in rank. Those who were unduly housebound were derided as 'charcoal-chewers' (Simpson 1980, 132).

While storytelling seems self-explanatory in this age of the saga, the predilection for evenings spent with the spoken word may not be. Few people had yet learned to read or write. Foote and Wilson in *The Viking Achievement* tell us that 'people made and recited poetry, swapped verses, sometimes competed in scurrility; they asked riddles, made com-parisons...or played a similar game in which the virtues of a chosen object or person were enumerated'(1970, 187-88). (We are reminded of boasting and insulting games enjoyed by the Native Peoples in Canada.) Feasts were fuelled by food and heavy drinking; 'bawdy con-versation'(Madsen, 1970, 45), and 'lewd singing'(Foote and Wilson 1970, 401-02) could be expected. 'Sacred mead' (Simpson 1980, 164) was the drink of choice, a supersweet alco-holic beverage brewed from honeycombs and water (Lacey and Danziger 1999, 62). *Bjórr* was a stronger tipple made from fermented fruit juice (Graham-Campbell *et al.* 1994, 66) and there were berries at LAM. A supply of beer would have been limited and any wine pro-duced, from grapes collected further south, would have been laid in storage for shipment back to Greenland or Iceland (B. Wallace, pers. comm.). The liquid refreshment was kept in a communal vessel (Simpson 1980, 159), and quaffed from the hollowed horn of an animal. One illustration of a curved drinking-horn had little feet attached to keep the horn upright (Sawyer 1997, 237). In the *Saga of Arrow-Odd* there is a drinking contest in which the con-testants sang one verse of a poem and then drained a horn, the object being to see who, final-ly, could stay standing the longest (Edwards and Palsson 1970, 85-93). But the feastings were also highly ceremonial and intended to display leadership and, in the giving of gifts, to demonstrate largesse (again, very reminiscent of the early native peoples on Canada's Pacific coast). At LAM we can presume there was less incentive for one leader to outdo the other, although with the inherent frictions of the final voyage to Vínland, who could say?

257

Less is known about Viking music; perhaps because the instruments were made of more perishable materials. Still, there were harps, some form of the fiddle, pan-pipes and drums, and end-blown flutes made out of the long bones of birds or animals (Foote and Wilson 1970, 188; Klindt-Jensen 1970, 177). In the Bayeux tapestry, horns are seen, being sounded on ships (Poertner 1975, 18-9).

Often the reading of poetry and the sagas was accompanied by a harp. Singing was common, and sometimes there was dancing to the singing of love poetry between a man and a woman, with the dancers forming a ring around the singers (Birkebaek and Barren 1975, 76). With the coming of Christianity, the Icelandic Church sought to counteract such unsavoury pagan practices. They also fostered the writing down of sagas and poetry to com-bat illiteracy.

So far we have been looking at the more domestic, indoor games and entertainments that might have taken place year-round at LAM. But, of course, there were also special hol-iday occasions dotted throughout the Viking year. The three main pagan festivals were Spring, Harvest-time, and the Winter Solstice; and I think we can safely assume they were slow to die, despite the advent of Christianity.

Uppermost in the mythological pantheon of pagan gods were Þor, Óðinn, and the man and woman, or brother and sister, team of Freyr and Freyja. Gwyn Jones reminds us that 'no leading god of the Viking Age could be entirely peaceful'(Jones 1989, 323). Þor, the stormy weather-god who carries a thunderbolt in the form of a hammer, and rumbles accross the heavens in a chariot pulled by a pair of goats, is followed by Óðinn (or Wodan) the god of war and wisdom. Óðinn rides his eight-legged horse, Sleipnir, and is attended by the twelve Valkyrie handmaidens who choose which heroes are to be slain and therefore privileged to feast forever in the hall of the slain, Valhalla. Finally, we have Freyr and Freyja, the 'male and female deities concerned with peace and plenty', and the fertility of crops, animals and human kind (Simpson 1980, 161- 9). These Viking gods continue to live with us today—at least during the latter half of the week—as Wodansday, Thorsday and Freyday. Þor's hammers ceremonially blessed a bride, a newborn child, or a funeral pyre, and smaller versions of his hammer were worn as amulets (Simpson 1980, 161; Gräslund 2000, 58, 60). Óðinn was favoured by the poets and sorcerers. He also spawned a cult of 'berserkers'— naked fighters swathed in wolfskins who induced an hypnotic fighting frenzy by rhythmically howling and leaping about (Simpson 1980, 138-9). Freyr and Freyja were the orgiastic, Dionysian gods, the phallic love figures, often depicted embracing or dancing.

Naturally, these two fertility gods loved the sun and seed-time. In the spring, a farmer's wife would take meat, drink and a cake out to the fields, the cake often baked in the shape of a rayed sun. The food and drink would be shared not only with the field-hands, but the animals used in ploughing, and even the plough itself. Remnants of the cake would then be crumbled with the seed into the tilled soil to ensure a bountiful harvest (Birkebaek and Barren 1975, 72). The Scandanavian 'Maypole' was sometimes garlanded in the shape of a woman or, in coastal communities, rigged like the mast of a ship (Oxenstierna 1965, 218). Foote and Wilson inform us that penis-poles were also present (1970, 405). This type of phallic pillar (*stöng, stafr*) was painted and presumably used in fertility rituals (S. Lewis-Simpson, pers. comm.).

Sacrifice was a part of many ceremonies placating Freyr and Freyja, especially male sacrifice. Stallions were killed and parts like the liver were cooked or made into a broth for their strength-giving properties. Every nine years at Uppsala in Sweden, male representatives of nine different species were killed and hung in the trees of a sacred grove. One chilling account listed the carcasses of 72 horses, dogs, and men, found hanging (Simpson 1980, 169). Christianity, of course, would ban these sacrificial practices.

Jacqueline Simpson reveals, too, that the cult of Freyr at Uppsala involved 'some sort of dramatic performance with clapping, 'the unmanly clatter of bells' and 'effeminate gestures'(Simpson 1980, 169). She also cites a reference to the Scandinavian Varangian guard in the Byzantine court of Emperor Constantine VII providing a 'Christmas' entertainment, where men 'danced in a ring striking their shields with sticks and shouting "Yule, Yule, Yule"' (Simpson 1980, 145). Some were dressed like the 'berserkers' in furs and animal masks.

The Winter Solstice was also held in honour of Freyr and Freja (again perhaps because the question of sunlight was all-important), and its festival became absorbed into Christmas to become the Nordic 'Jul' or Yuletide. It took place during a twelve-day rest period when all 'turning action' (grinding flour, spinning, and perhaps cutting timber) ceased in the same way that the sun seemed to rest before reversing its pattern. The longest night was thought to be the 'Mother Night', since the Vikings believed that the world had been created during that night, and that all the other nights of the year came from it. A northern consciousness is apparent in the fact that for the Vikings, time was counted not in days, but nights (Madsen 1976, 16).

'Jul' was a family festival, but for the dead as well as the living. A parade of spirits and ancestors, as well as lesser gnomes and trolls, returned to visit during 'Jul'. Special tables were laid out with food and sleeping-places were prepared for the ghostly guests. Even a steam-bath was kept ready. If the visiting ancestors had been lost at sea, they usually just came to dry their clothes by the fire without saying a word (Oxenstierna 1965, 217), but the other spirits stayed throughout the feastings and enjoyed the shenanigans. The Yule games were a time of 'masquerade and the shameless behaviour that goes with it'(Foote and Wilson 1970, 399). If there was a male billy-goat in Vínland, and we recall that animals 'of all kinds' were taken on the fourth expedition, it would be especially honoured as a Þor-goat.

Even today, we are told, you see goats at Yuletide made of straw, or shaped in the form of a cookie (Oxenstierna 1965, 216-17). If no goat were present, then a couple of lads would climb under a goatskin and pretend. The Irish also had a hobgoblin spirit derived from a he-goat. In Gaelic he was a *poc* or 'pooka'. Shakespeare's 'Puck' may have been a descendant (Yeats, n.d., 88). Did the Norse bring their Þor-goat to Ireland, we have to ask? The medieval 'hobby-horse' also made the odd Viking appearance (Foote and Wilson 1970, 188), consisting of an individual under a hoop of cloth that touched the ground, with a little head and swishing tail attached, and sometimes a suggested rider on top. Sometimes, too, in the more easternly Norse settlements, a wooden statue of Freyr was wheeled around in a cart, for the Yuletide festivities often included processions and dramatic reenactments of mythological episodes (Oxenstierna 1965, 219; Foote and Wilson 1970, 39).

And there were games. On St Stephen's Day (now Boxing Day, 26 December), Vikings would saddle up their horses for a wild ride through the woods, throwing silver coins into a stream. It was a custom later attributed to St Stephen who was said to have functioned as a stable-boy (Oxenstierna 1965, 216-17). Presumably, the hope was that the coins would multiply.

At the end of August, probably after harvest, two of the favourite Norse pastimes were bareback horse-riding and the ancient spectator-sport of horse-fighting. Dating back to the sixth century, these ferocious animal battles may again have had cult origins with Freyr. Young selected stallions were specially bred to fight and there were wagers on the outcome. Kept in isolation till the battle-day, the stallions would be roused to fight 'by the sight and smell of tethered mares' (Graham-Campbell *et al.* 1994, 64). Some stallions even had horns attached to their heads (Graham-Campbell *et al.* 1994, 65). Each of the owners was allowed to be alongside with a stout stick to goad the animals to paw and bite, and ensure that they wouldn't escape. One could not strike the opponent's horse, but often the owners themselves came to blows (Simpson 1980, 146-7).

The Viking Olympics were rough and ready. Blood flowed and there were bruises, but as in all competitive games, 'nimbleness and cunning' were praised (Simpson 1980, 145). In addition to the usual running and jumping contests, they had catch-as-catch-can leg wrestling, boulder-lifting, and a kind of football, supposedly 'using the decapitated heads of enemies' (Birkebaek and Barren 1975, 76). Another ball-game played on the ice with a bat would seem to presage hockey (Foote and Wilson 1970, 189). Skis were made of pinewood two metres long and skates were fashioned from the long bones of cattle, horses or elk, with the surfaces smoothed and flattened, and then tied to the foot by a thong. The skaters and skiers propelled themselves along using iron-tipped poles (Graham-Campbell *et al.* 1994, 74). Sledges, too, have been found in some of the elaborate boat-burial sites. They would have been pulled by draught horses or oxen, their hooves studded with nails to better grip the ice (Graham-Campbell *et al.* 1994, 73). Again, it must be remembered, that many of these mainland or regional Norse practices would not necessarily be seen at LAM, even though several expeditions to Vínland did remain through several seasons of the year. It would be hoped that winter practices, for example, would be universal enough to have travelled well.

Trials of physical strength and endurance were common and one could imagine the visitors climbing the rock-faces of Gros Morne Park, or in the summer, swimming, especially long distances under the shallow waters off the coastline of LAM. Jacqueline Simpson says that 'speed was less prized than dragging one's opponent down and holding him underwater till he collapsed, without coming up for air oneself'(Simpson 1980, 145).

And there were the more traditional training competitions with weapons: throwing spears; shooting arrows; and hand to hand fighting with broadswords and the circular wooden shields covered in hide. Axe-throwing was another skill to be mastered, with the battle-axe being the favoured weapon (Foote and Wilson 1970, 189). One of the oldest sports was

259

varpa, played with flat stones weighing approximately 5 kilos (11 lbs). They were tossed underhand towards an upright pole, the object being to get as close as possible without knocking it over, a combination of cricket and horseshoe pitching. Another sport, called *stangstorting*, resembles the Scottish game of 'tossing the caber' (and we remember that the Vikings did settle in Scotland and are bound to have exerted influence). A thick tree-pole about 12 feet long and weighing nearly 50 lbs, is lifted vertically in both hands and tossed end-over-end towards an imaginary 'clock'. The pole has to land between 10 o'clock and 2 o'clock, with extra points if you can make it read exactly noon.

But my favourite sport is 'oar-walking'. While a ship was being rowed, the walker stepped barefoot from moving oar to moving oar over the swirling water. 'Sometimes the hazard was compounded by putting knives or swords on some of the oars, so that the walker had to jump over particular oars or else risk cutting his feet' (Birkebaek and Barren 1975, 77; see also Foote and Wilson 1970, 189). Even though not recorded, can you imagine a race between two oar-walkers, forward and aft on each side of the travelling ship, until one man was overboard?

Falconry was another medieval, sporting activity, with the famous white falcons of Greenland being used for hawking. One reads of the 'falcon's tree' being decorated, which would have meant a tamed falcon resting on a falconer's forearm (Simpson 1980, 156). Hunting *per se* was not a sport but a way of life for the Norse Greenlander, and a matter of trade between Iceland, Ireland, Norway and the rest of Europe. As well as timber, polar bear, reindeer and seal skins, fox pelts and walrus-tusk ivory, narwhal horns were traded for their healing and aphrodisiac powers (see Roesdahl, this volume).

Finally, in our 'paratheatrical' catalogue of games and entertainments, we must again comment on the itinerant buskers—the clowns, jugglers and acrobats of the medieval age that were found later (c. 1200) in the courts of the Scandinavian kings. Unfortunately, they are not recorded during the Vínland Viking period. And with an initial population now estimated at between only 400-500 people in Greenland (see Lynnerup, this volume), it is even less conceivable that any professional entertainers were present there, along with the sibyls, to be potentially taken to Vínland (see Lynnerup, this volume). Then, too, the wandering minstrels were not on the same social level as the sibyls or the poets. We are reminded of this in the quite amazing, 'tug-of-war' clause, or so-called 'players' statute, to be found in the older Västergötland Lawbooks. Here's what it says about the civil rights of an injured vagabond player ; I quote the *c.* 1200 law as cited in Foote and Wilson (1970, 188).

> If a player is struck, that is always invalid [that is, there is never any redress]. If a player is wounded, one who goes with a fiddle, and with viol or drum, then a wild heifer is to be brought to the raised middle of the assembly place. Then all the hair is to be shaved off its tail and the tail is to be greased. Then the player is to be given newly-greased shoes. Then he is to hold the heifer by the tail and the heifer is to be lashed with a sharp whip. If he can hold it, then he shall have this fine animal and enjoy it as a dog enjoys grass. If he cannot hold it, let him have and put up with what he got, shame and hurt.

So, despite the fact that livestock were brought to Vínland on the fourth expedition, it is doubtful that 'Holding-the-tail-of-the-heifer' would have been a spectator sport.

There was a fifth and final recorded voyage to Vínland which Eiríkr the Red's daughter Freydís and her husband, Þorvaldr, helped to organize. Her name, of course, echoes the fertility goddess Freyja, and his, the favourite pagan god, Þor. There were two ships, each with thirty men and five women (though Freydís is said to have concealed an extra five men in her vessel). The second ship carried the brothers Helgi and Finnbogi and their followers. Freydís and her party lived in Leifsbúðir, and obliged the brother's group to build places of their own 'farther inland'(Magnusson and Palsson 1965, 68). From GLS we gather that the autumn was spent amicably felling timber. Then, in a casual sentence, we learn of 'paratheatre' not just in Greenland but on North American soil, for 'when winter set in, the brothers suggested that they start holding games and other entertainments. This was done for a while'(Magnusson and Palsson 1965, 68).

This is not to say, of course, that all or even many of the Viking 'games and other entertainments' were practised at the LAM campsite. We can only presume from the borrowed compilation that I have tried to present, that some were performed and then 'only for a while', at least during the Freydís expedition. For 'trouble broke out and ill-feeling arose between the two parties. The games were abandoned', GLS tells us, 'and this state of affairs continued for most of the winter'(Magnusson and Palsson 1965, 68).

The exploratory or colonising experiment at Vínland was about to come to its infamous and bloody end. And, gradually, the Greenland colony disappeared as well. A Norwegian ship in the fifteenth century reported that 'no people were there, only cattle running wild' (Morison 1971, 60). Mysteriously, the Viking Age in the Western Hemisphere was over.

But, 'the rest is [not] silence'.

Approximately 1000 years later, in 1994, the award-winning, St. John's-based author Joan Clark would write an evocative and compassionate novel about Freydís (Clark 1994; Ward 2000, 370-71). In it she seamlessly enriched the recorded events of the Vínland sagas by fleshing out the characters and the day-to-day events into a most convincing fictional account. At the beginning of this study I said there was no Viking theatre. Now, I am happy to say, there is at least a Viking play, for three years later, Ms Clark expressionistically adapted her novel for the stage. *Eiriksdottir*, the play, was produced by Theatre Newfoundland Labrador for the Gros Morne Theatre Festival in Corner Brook and Cow Head during the summer of 1997. And for three historic matinees (30-31 July and 1 August, 1997), the production was taken north and staged out-of-doors, at the LAM site. 'Paratheatre' finally became real theatre, but it took a thousand years for it to happen.

261

BIBLIOGRAPHY

Arneborg, J. 2000. 'Greenland and Europe', in Fitzhugh and Ward 2000, 304-17.

Birkebaek, F. and Barren, C. 1975. *Sea Wolves: The Viking Era*, Gothenburg.

Bronsted. J. 1980. *TheVikings*, trans. K. Skov, Harmondsworth.

Clark, J. 1994. *Eiriksdottir*, Toronto.

Edwards, P. and Pálsson, H., trans, 1970. *Arrow-Odd: A Medieval Novel*, New York.

Fitzhugh, W.W. and Ward, E.I., eds, 2000. *Vikings: The North Altantic Saga*, Washington and London.

Foote, P. and Wilson, D.M. 1970. *The Viking Achievement*, London

Graham-Campbell, J. *et al.*, eds, 1994. *Cultural Atlas of the Viking World*, Oxford.

Gräslund, A-S. 2000. 'Religion, art and runes', in Fitzhugh and Ward 2000, 55-69.

Hutter, C. trans. and ed., 1965. *The Norseman,* Greenwich, Conn.

Ingstad, A-S. 1977. *The Discovery of a Norse Settlement in America,* Oslo, Bergen, Tronso.

Ingstad, H. 1964. 'Vinland Ruins Prove Vikings Found the New World', *National Geographic*, 126, 5, 708.

——1966. *Land Under the Pole Star, A Voyage to the Norse Settlements of Greenland and the Saga of the People that Vanished*, London.

Jones, G. 1989. *A History of the Vikings*, 2nd edn, Oxford.

Klindt-Jensen, O. 1970. *The World of the Vikings*, London.

Lacey, R. and Danziger, D. 1999. *The Year 1000*, Boston, New York, London.

Lane, H. 1988. *The Cambridge Guide to World Theatre*, Cambridge.

Madsen, O.O. 1976. *The World of the Vikings*, Geneva.

Magnusson, M. and Pálsson, H. 1965. *The Vinland Sagas, The Norse Discovery of America*, Harmondsworth.

Morison, S.E. 1971. *The European Discovery of America, The Northern Voyages, A.D. 500-1600*, New York.

Oxenstierna, E. 1965. 'The Festivals of the Vikings', in Hutter 1965, 216-19.

David Gardner

Poertner, R. 1975. *The Vikings*, New York.

Sawyer, P. ed., 1997. *The Oxford Illustrated History of the Vikings*, Oxford, New York.

Simpson, J. 1980. *The Viking World*, New York.

Ward, E. 2000. 'Reflections on an icon: Vikings in American culture', in Fitzhugh and Ward 2000, 365-73.

Yeats, W.B. n.d. *Irish Folk Stories and Fairy Tales*, New York.

From pagan to Christian—
on the Conversion of Scandinavia

Anne-Sofie Gräslund

The Christianisation of Scandinavia has many dimensions and is a very comprehensive topic. In this short article I am going to focus on how the Scandinavians perceived the conversion, as far as this can be grasped through archaeological and documentary evidence. The conversion has sometimes been described by historians as done by force. The king coerced the people to accept the new faith, since he realised that Christianity would serve his purposes—he would be on equal terms with the Continental and the Anglo-Saxon kings. Historians of religions, with the Old Norse literature as their source material, have stressed the rupture at the conversion, a 'dramatic confrontation between different ideologies' (Steinsland 1991, 345 f.). However, the archaeological material and the evidence of the rune stones tell a story that does not seem to support the idea of a cultural break. On the contrary I am convinced that the transition was gradual and that it started very early, already in the middle of the first millennium AD with the contacts between Scandinavians and the Germanic tribes on the Continent. However, this does not exclude that there was a certain moment when the people of an area could be regarded or regarded themselves as converted to Christianity. In my opinion that moment appeared when the decision was taken to use a Christian oath at the thing, instead of swearing to the pagan gods.

Runic inscriptions provide an extremely interesting and contemporary evidence of the late Viking Age society. In Sweden about 2500 Viking-Age runic inscriptions are found, with a strong concentration to the Mälar region. Most of them are datable to the eleventh century, although some of them are carved in the last third of the tenth and some in the first third of the twelfth century. Denmark (including the Old-Danish provinces which are part of modern Sweden) has *c.* 250 and Norway *c.* 65.

From different parts of Scandinavia there are three very special rune stones, one from each of the Scandinavian countries, telling us that the conversion was accomplished, that the people of a certain area had become Christian. The oldest and most well-known is the Danish Jellinge stone from Jutland (fig. 2), sometimes called the baptismal certificate of Denmark, where, on the memorial stone of his parents, king Harald Bluetooth claims that he has unified Denmark and Norway and converted the Danes. It dates from the 960s and has been regarded as the origin of the fashion of raising memorial stones with runic inscriptions. The second stone in this group stands at the small island of Frösön (Frey's island) in the province of Jämtland, Northern Sweden (fig. 3). The text states, 'Östman, Gudfast's son, had this stone raised and this bridge made and he had converted Jämtland'. Östman has been compared to king Harald Bluetooth, although in a much minor and rural perspective. On stylistic grounds the Frösö stone can be dated to the middle of the eleventh century. In Western Norway the Kuli stone (fig. 4) declares, after a memorial formulation, that 'Twelve winters had Christianity been in Norway', or according to a new technical and runological investigation (Hagland 1998), 'Twelve winters had Christianity improved things in Norway' or perhaps even 'Twelve winters had Christianity secured law and order in Norway'. Interestingly, an archaeological excavation at the site has revealed that the stone was placed at one end of the foundations of a wooden bridge over a wetland. The wood has been dendrochronologically dated to 1034, which means that the year 1022 should be the time of official conversion, a date that coincides well with historical evidence of the acceptance of Christianity at the thing in Moster (Hagland 1991, 161). The new reading strengthens the

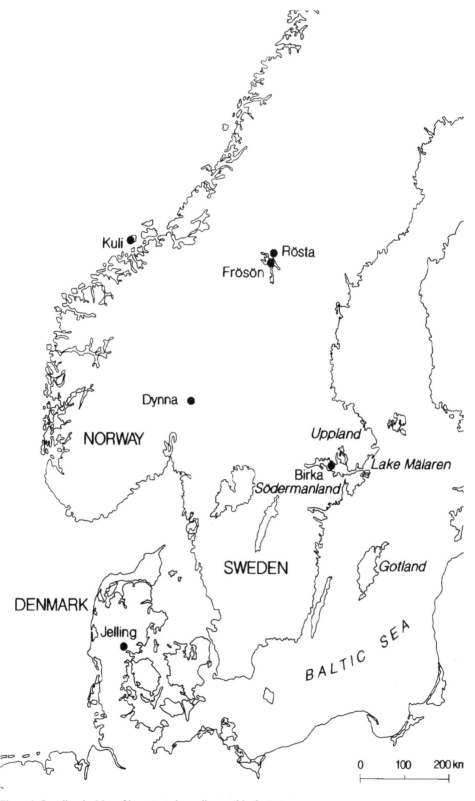

264

Figure 1. Scandinavia. Map of important places discussed in the text.

impression of the thing as the important turning-point for the question of 'momentary' conversion. It must be stressed that these three stones are unique in their mentioning of the conversion as an event; they are exceptions from the normal memorial inscriptions.

In this connection the conversion of Iceland should be mentioned, as it is said to have taken place as a special event at the Alþing in the year 1000, or possibly 999. Most probably the process of Christianisation in Iceland had started much earlier and at the time of the Alþing decision this process was almost completed—time was, so to say, ripe enough for the Icelanders to accept a compromise in order to maintain one law for the country instead of dividing it. The compromise meant that all Icelanders should be baptised but also that ancient laws about infanticide and about eating horse meat should remain valid. People were allowed to continue to sacrifice to the old pagan gods, as long as they did it secretly. This valuable information demonstrates clearly that even the stated events may be regarded as parts in a process (see Strömbäck 1975; Vésteinsson 2000).

THE EVIDENCE OF THE GRAVES

It is possible to discern a gradual transition from paganism to Christianity through the evidence of four main phases of burial customs. The earliest Viking-Age graves in older cemeteries consist of pagan cremation graves furnished with rich grave goods, artefacts of different kinds and some domestic animals. Contemporary with these cremations, or a little later, in the older cemeteries are inhumation graves, where the corpse has been fully interred, still containing grave goods. Over time, individuals are still interred in the old cemeteries, but these inhumations are oriented, indicating Christian belief, and contain no grave goods and never animals. Finally, corpses are interred in oriented graves in churchyards.

265

When we discuss grave goods, it is necessary to qualify this rather vague term. All artefacts in a grave should not to be considered as grave-goods. Objects which the deceased wore or suspended from his/her clothing, including jewellery, often of impressive quality and variety, knives, combs, etc., must be distinguished from true grave gifts such as boxes, buckets, glass vessels, pottery and metal dishes, outfits of weapons and tools. The first group implies that that the deceased was simply buried in his/her clothes, a custom that continued for a long time in both high and low social circles. The early bishops, for example archbishop Andreas Suneson (d. 1228) in Lund, were buried in full canonicals. This demonstrates that objects signifying the identity and rank of the deceased could follow him/her into the grave even in Christian contexts. On the other hand, true grave gifts, i.e. objects intended to be used in another life, must be regarded as conflicting with Christian ideas, as they express a belief in a bodily life after death where there would be a need for functional objects from our world. On the island of Gotland in the Baltic, this is clearly demonstrated by the differences between the churchyard graves from the eleventh century and the contemporary graves in pagan cemeteries: both categories contain the same type of jewellery but the pagan graves also contain metal vessels with food.

Birka in the Mälar lake can be described as a proto-town, flourishing in the ninth and tenth centuries, which the so-called Apostle of Scandinavia, Ansgar, visited twice as a missionary, in 829 and 850 (Graham-Campbell *et al.* 1994, 84). With its, at least temporarily, multi-ethnic population it must have been an important innovation center for all kinds of ideas, including religious, and therefore a crucial site for the missionary work. Through literary evidence, the biography of Ansgar, written by Rimbert, his successor as archbishop in Hamburg-Bremen, we know that there were both Christians and pagans there in the ninth century, and certainly this was the case also in the tenth century (Gräslund 1980, 83). In the end of the nineteenth century, *c.* 1100 out of a total number of *c.* 3000 graves were excavated, about 50% of them inhumations and 50% cremations. A comparison between two inhumation graves from the site, both probably datable to the middle of the tenth century shows

266

Figure 2, above.
The Jellinge stone, Denmark, set up by king Harald Bluetooth (after Brink 1990).

Figure 3, left.
The Frösö stone, Sweden (after Brink 1990).

Figure 4, facing page.
The Kuli stone, Norway (after Brink 1990).

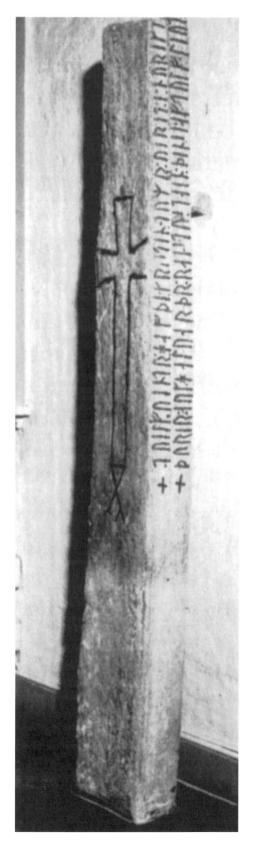

that one of them seems to be considerably more 'Christian' than the other (figs 5-6). They are one man's grave and one woman's grave, both chamber graves, roughly east-west oriented, none of them covered by a mound. All these elements in the burial custom may be regarded as influenced by Christian burials. But there is a significant difference. Whereas the woman was buried with a very rich equipment of jewellery, brooches and a necklace with various beads and pendants (one of which is a pendant cross) and small tools, all attached to her clothing, the man's grave included a full set of weapons: sword, axe, large weapon knife, two spears, a bundle of arrows and two shields as well as a big bronze bowl, probably containing food, and a set of gaming pieces of glass. Just outside the man's chamber but still in the grave pit two horses were placed on a special platform. This difference between the two graves is not only due to gender, as there are many women's graves in Birka with real grave goods such as pots, drinking vessels, buckets and boxes with content. In my view the woman got a much more Christian burial than the man, not only because she wore a pendant cross, but because all items in the grave were connected with her costume. The rich equipment of the man is incompatible with the Christian idea of afterlife, but during the transition phase status objects may occur in truly Christian graves. The crucial point, however, are the horses. Having studied the transformation of the burial customs during the conversion for many years, I have become more and more convinced that the real borderline was whether animals were allowed in the grave or not. From a comparison with Frankish material from the Continent, which has the advantage of documentary evidence of the conversion as well as archaeological evidence, it is quite clear that objects signifying rank could be deposited in early Christian graves, but never animals. The fact that the horses in the Birka chamber graves always are placed outside the proper chamber (there are 20 examples, 16 connected to men's graves, three to double graves with a man and a woman and one to a woman's grave,

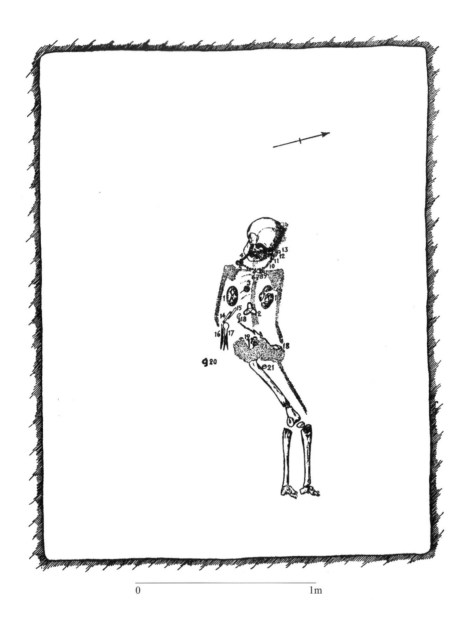

268

0   1m

Figure 5. The woman's grave Bj 968 (after Arbman 1943).

Figure 6. The man's grave Bj 581 (after Arbman 1943).

Gräslund 1980) may be a first step from the horse sacrificed into the grave towards a total separation between men and horses in graves, clearly seen in the Continental Germanic cemeteries. A good example is Childeric's grave (d. 481/482), encircled (at a certain distance) by horse graves, or rather pits, each with several sacrificed horses. Childeric himself was not a Christian, but his son Chlodwig became baptized and he got his grave in the St Genevieve church in Paris.

Another example of some of the phases of increasing Christian influence in the burial customs can be taken from northern Sweden, at the Viking-Age cemetery Rösta in Ås parish, Jämtland, with cremation graves and inhumation graves (Kjellmark 1906, 351 ff.). Of special interest in this connection are two male inhumation graves both richly furnished with weapons, horse equipment and small scales for weighing silver, an artefact that only appears in high status graves. However, the deceased men belong to different generations: the older grave is probably from the second half of the tenth century, whereas the younger grave can be dated to the middle of the eleventh century. What is the difference between these two graves, and does this support the idea of a gradually increasing Christian influence in the burial customs? Both were covered by a mound, which is presumably a pagan trait. Both men have been buried lying on a sledge. One important difference between them is that in the older grave a horse and a dog have accompanied the deceased into the grave. The younger grave contained no animals. However, close to the younger grave, at a distance of only a few metres, a grave containing a single horse was excavated. This is very unusual in the Swedish Viking Age, but well known from the Frankish and Lombard cemeteries on the Continent as well as from Anglo-Saxon England (Müller-Wille 1971).

In Rösta, the scenario could have been that at the funeral of the man in the second half of the tenth century it was still accepted that the man's horse and dog could accompany him into the grave, although there was a certain Christian influence in choosing inhumation and not cremation. A generation or two later, at the middle of the eleventh century, it was no longer acceptable to put the horse into the grave. As a compromise, the horse was buried in its own grave. It is worth noting that Rösta is situated only eight kilometers away from the above mentioned rune stone on Frösön. So we have every reason to believe that the inhabitants of Rösta were 'officially' Christians at the time of the younger burial. Presumably, the next generation of the people of Rösta were buried at the churchyard.

When discussing Christian elements in the burial customs in the context of a progressive conversion, we should not forget the remaining pagan traits. Sandra Harding has coined the phrases 'systematic knowledge' and 'systematic ignorance', meaning that the process of creating knowledge in a field is parallel to the ignorance due to the lack of attention to other sides of the field (1998, 3). The idea of the gradual process of Christianisation involves the notion that the old religion still had many adherents. As Jens Peter Schjødt writes,

> Depending upon which aspect we choose to focus on—for example the view of the missionaries or the view of the convert, the official attitude (the king) or the individual (the people), our evaluation of the extent to which something or someone was Christian or heathen will vary (Schjødt 1989, 200).

THE EVIDENCE OF THE RUNE STONES

The rune stones of Central Sweden, primarily memorial stones, show many signs of being Christian monuments, set up by landowners and their family members, not least women. If there had been a severe religious conflict in the region, this would certainly have been demonstrated in the runic texts. However, it is remarkable that there is no such evidence. Conversely, the majority of the Upplandic rune stones express Christianity. More than 50% of them are decorated with a cross and many of the inscriptions include a prayer, of which the most common one is 'May God help his or her soul' (213 examples). The prayer 'May God and God's mother help his/her soul', not as frequent as the former but still occurring in 34 inscriptions, demonstrates that Virgin Mary was worshipped in the province already before the middle of the eleventh century. In my opinion this may be regarded as a compensation for the lack of a goddess in the new religion.

About 150 of the Upplandic rune stones are erected as monuments close to bridges over wetlands or open water (Gräslund 1989, 227). From continental documentary evidence we know about building bridges as a part of the indulgence system of the early Roman Catholic church (Kinander 1935, 8). To build a bridge was an act comparable to donating land or money to churches and monasteries, giving alms to the poor, taking part in crusades, etc. The service in return by the Church was to offer prayers for the deceased's soul and/or a promise of absolution. As the texts on the bridge stones often contain a sentence, 'XX had the bridge made for YY's soul', it is clear that the ecclesiastical opinion of the importance of the bridges was known already in early eleventh-century Uppland.

Most rune stones have a zoomorphic ornamentation, a fact very helpful for their dating on stylistic grounds (Gräslund 1994), but there are also some examples of illustrations on the rune stones and they often link in with the Old Scandinavian mythology. These pagan illustrations can, in other words, be combined with an obviously Christian text. This is another argument for a gradual transition from Old Scandinavian religion to Christianity. Outspoken Christian pictures apart from crosses are very rare, but there are some examples of persons carrying a cross for processions as well as a single example of a church building and one of a bell tower (Williams 1996, 50). The famous Dynna stone is a Norwegian example. Stylistically, the stone is carved in typical Ringerike style and therefore datable to the first half of the eleventh century. It is quite clear that they knew about the Christmas gospel then—the star, Christ and the three wise men are depicted.

271

Many rune stones seem to have been set up at roads and transportation routes and, as already mentioned, at bridges. However, a large number of the rune stones were erected at pagan cemeteries, sometimes directly on a mound or in a stone-setting, judging from records left by runologists from the seventeenth, eighteenth and nineteenth centuries (Gräslund 1987). In many cases the graves have completely disappeared due to extensive cultivation. The proportion of rune stones decorated with crosses which are affiliated with cemeteries is high, *c.* 75%. This casts an interesting light on the relationship between pagan cemeteries and Christianity. The raising of a cross-marked rune stone may have served to consecrate the cemetery or a part of it. Christians could then be buried there until access was acquired to a churchyard. Many Late Viking-Age graves, often east-west oriented rectangular stone-settings, previously interpreted as pagan graves under the influence of Christian burial customs may actually be early Christian graves placed in pagan cemeteries. A drawing from the beginning of the eighteenth century is shown in fig. 7.

BREAK OR CONTINUITY?

Is it a general human tendency to avoid hard ruptures, and instead to gradually accept new ideas? I think this is often the case. Naturally, at the conversion some persons may have been very rigorous converts, totally repudiating the old religion, but it is reasonable to assume a certain remaining belief in the old ideas by most people. Many examples of such a both/and-belief could be found in the Old Norse literature. One is the Icelander Helgi the Meagre, about whom it is said that he believed in Christ, but at sea, in bad weather and at difficult tasks he invoked Þor! (*Landnámabók* 218). I think this is how it normally works, you do not leave your old ideas behind immediately. Opinions and attitudes will not be changed overnight, and one may even alter one's perception of Þor to make him look more like Christ.

Even in artefacts the mixed pagan-Christian belief can be discerned, the most striking example is a Þor's hammer amulet decorated with a cross. The pagan conception of the world can be described as complimentary rather than counting with opposite, incompatible categories. This is a reason why the pagans had no difficulties in accepting Christ as new god alongside the old ones. Confrontations presuppose clear either-or, and that was what happened later in the phase of ecclesiastical organisation in Scandinavia.

This mixture seems to be a general tendency at conversion; there are innumerable examples from the Christianisation of the Roman empire and the Germanic kingdoms. As one scholar describes it,

> Many Christians continued to take part in traditional Roman festivities; they sometimes shocked their bishops by dancing in church, getting drunk at celebrations in the cemeteries, consulting magicians, or resorting to charms to cure their troubles (Markus 1993, 74).

The question of continuity versus change has often been discussed in archaeology, and in many cases it is obvious that there is continuity even within the change, so that remaining elements from the past, even if they lose their meaning, still remain. The question of cult place continuity reflects the concept of continuity within change. Earlier research stated a bit uncritically that place continuity for the cult was normal at the transition from pagan to Christian cult in Scandinavia. In the 1960s, the Danish historian and archaeologist Olaf Olsen carefully investigated all available evidence with strong source criticism and concluded that there was no support for the idea of cult place continuity, except possibly in Old Uppsala (Olsen 1966). However, later new archaeological material has appeared that supports the old hypothesis of cult place continuity. Viking-Age offering sites have been discovered under the church of Frösön in Jämtland and in the churchyard of Estuna in Uppland. Remains of Viking Age houses/halls, where offerings took place, with finds of small fertility amulets (*guldgubbar*) have been excavated under the church of Maere in Tröndelag, Norway, and under a church in Eskilstuna in Södermanland. Viking-Age manors have been found close to several early churches in Denmark and in southern Sweden, suggesting that Viking-Age chieftains had churches built on their estates, sometimes even in their courtyards (Gräslund 1992, and bibliography). This indicates that the holiness of a place most often was not questioned by Christianity. Another argument for continuity in the transition from paganism to Christianity are the place names—very often medieval churches were built on land with theophoric place names like Torsåker, Fröstuna etc. Even the theophoric personal names are a good argument: the god Tor's (Þor's) name, is very common in both men's and women's names in Viking-Age Scandinavia as well as in the Middle Ages (and still is today): Tore, Torsten, Torbjörn, Torleif (male) and Tora, Torborg, Tordis, Torgun (female), etc.

The idea of continuity links in with the idea of a gradual transition, a long process, argued for by the Norwegian historian of religions, Fridtjov Birkeli. He suggested three successive chronological phases for the Christianisation of Norway: 1) the phase of infiltration, lasting for hundreds of years; 2) the phase of mission; and 3) the phase of ecclesiastical organisation (Birkeli 1973, 14).

This classification seems to be valid also for Sweden, Denmark and, to a certain extent, Finland. As already mentioned, the conversion of Iceland may well be comparable to that of the other Nordic countries. In the same way as in Iceland, there was certainly a moment when the people of the other Nordic countries decided to change the oath at the thing to a Christian one. The idea of the 'holy' did not change significantly, and the medieval Christian kingdom was not introduced in Iceland until the end of the so-called Icelandic commonwealth (cf. Meulengracht Sørensen 1991, 235).

Figure 7. The rune stone U 661 Håby, Håtuna parish, Uppland from the first half of the eleventh century, set up close to a Viking-Age stone-setting. The stone is decorated with a central cross and the inscription mentions that the stone was raised by two daughters in memory of their father Anund, 'who died eastwards with Ingvar. May God help Anund's soul' (after U p plands Runinskrifter).

273

Applying Birkeli's system for central Sweden (*Svealand*), the phase of infiltration could last from *c.* AD 400 (or perhaps even earlier to judge from the archaeological evidence of contacts between Scandinavia and the Roman empire and the continental Germanic societies) to *c.* 800, the phase of mission from the beginning of the ninth century (the mission of Ansgar) to *c.* 1100 and the phase of ecclesiastical organisation from the end of the eleventh century to *c.* AD 1200. Jan Arvid Hellström has objected against using such a chronological structure for larger regions, as different areas were christianised at different times (Hellström 1996, 163), which is certainly true. Instead, he suggests a model with three levels, the individual level, the collective level and the level of ecclesiastical law. However, he has obvious difficulties in placing for example the Ansgar mission in Birka in the ninth century in one of these levels. Birkeli's model may be better after all, especially if a minor region gets its own chronology. In centres of innovation as the early Scandinavian towns, visited by missionaries, where more people converted compared to rural settlements it is reasonable to believe that the rules of a Christian behaviour became generally more and faster accepted, or that other rules than those acceptable to rune stone farmers were invented in towns.

SYNCRETISM

For the historians of religions, the concept of syncretism is crucial. In a wide definition, syncretism denotes any mixture or fusion of two or more religions upon contact (Ringgren 1969, 7). It can also be used when elements from one religion are accepted into another without basically changing the character of the latter. Under what conditions is a mingling of religions possible? A very important statement is that real syncretism in the sense of fusion is only possible when the two religions are relatively similar (Ringgren 1969, 9). If they are totally different, there could not be any amalgamation; instead the two religions either continue to exist side by side or one of them turns out to be the strongest and 'wins' while the weaker one disappears.

Were there any similarities between the Old Scandinavian religion and Christianity? It is important to point out that the old religion was not static. Conversely, it was dynamic and changing over time. Most probably, during the second half of the first millennium AD it was changing under influence from the continental Christian religion—that is what Birkeli meant with his 'phase of infiltration', although infiltration is perhaps not the best word. Instead we could speak of a long phase of influence, or even interaction, heading towards mutual assimilation. In the form that the old religion has been delivered to us by Old Norse poetry and literature there are several similarities to Christianity that could be the result of such influence: the end of the world and Ragnarök, the good Christ and the good god Balder, the crucifixion of Christ and Balder's death, etc. (However, it is important to remember that these texts were recorded in vellum by Christians centuries after the Viking Age. Therefore, it cannot be said for certain whether these religious similarities were present in practice prior to the texts being committed to written form, or whether these were inserts by the Christian editors of the texts, in an attempt to interpret past pagan beliefs as being influenced by Christianity.)

There was, however, an influence the other way round as well, i.e. Christianity was influenced by Old Norse religion. The adaptation of Old Scandinavian religious elements to Christianity has been studied by the historian of religions Anders Hultgård (1992). He uses syncretism to characterise the more profound changes of a religion or of phenomena within that religion which result from the encounter with another religion; and religious accultura- tion to denote influences or modifications that do not touch the central elements of a reli- gion. As an example he takes a prescription from the Norwegian *Gulaþings* law that three farms should join in brewing a special beer and drink it together with their families with a special ritual to secure a good harvest. He concludes: 'we are certainly confronted with an old religious custom in Christian disguise' (Hultgård 1992, 101). The field processions with crucifixes or images of saints which took place in the countryside in spring from the Middle Ages up to the nineteenth century are seen by Hultgård as popular rural traditions, but a pre- Christian origin should not be excluded, given the information delivered by Tacitus about the cult of Nerthus (*Germania*, chapter 40).

REMAINING ATTITUDES

Were there similarities in attitudes by those remaining in the old faith and the converts? It has been argued that Christ must have appeared a loser to the Vikings, who were used to fighting against the Christians (Olsen 1981, 254). However, the earliest representations of the Rood in Scandinavia do not depict the suffering Christ. Instead, in accordance with West European Christian art, he is always the triumphant Christ, with the body in a completely upright position, the feet on a foot-rest and the head held high, wearing a royal crown (Larsen 1972, 134, 137). This representation of Christ as a victor is found not only in the pictorial art of the period but also in literature. Edith Marold has examined the image of God in the Old Norse poetry, which she divides into three chronological groups. During the first phase (up to *c.* 1050) God/Christ is described exclusively as a strong and mighty ruler and king. In phase two (*c.* 1050-1150) qualities like purity, wisdom and glory are added and in the last phase (up to 1200) he is presented as the Saviour, the God of atonement and for- giveness (Marold 1985, 748).

Many runic inscriptions contain pious prayers, but there is also a good example of a slowly changing mentality in the text on a fragmentary Upplandic stone probably from the beginning of the eleventh century: '......Åsbjörn and ...... land...May God betray those who betrayed him' (*Upplands runinskrifter* U 1028). Really, that sounds like the old pagan mentality, where vengeance was an important element. On a rune stone from Gotland there is a similar prayer that God shall revenge the dead person. Doubtless it is easier to introduce a new ideology than a new mentality in a society, the mentality has to settle down in people's mind, not to say their heart, and that takes time.

ABBREVIATIONS

Germania   Tacitus. *C. Germania*, trans. M. Hutton, London and Cambridge, Mass.

Landnámabók   Pálsson, H. and Edwards, P., trans, 1972. *The Book of Settlements, Landnámabók.* Winnipeg: University of Manitoba, Icelandic Studies 1.

Upplands runinskrifter   *Granskade och tolkade av E. Wessén och S.B.F. Jansson. Sveriges runinskrifter 6-9.* Stockholm, 1942-1958.

BIBLIOGRAPHY

Ahrens, C. 1981. *Frühe Holzkirchen im nördlichen Europa*, Hamburg.

Alhaug, G. *et al.*, eds, 1991. *Heidersskrift til Nils Hallan på 65-årsdagen 13. desember 1991*, Oslo.

Ambrosiani, B. and Clarke, H., eds, 1994. *Development around the Baltic and the North Sea in the Viking Age.* Stockholm: Birka Studies 3.

Andrén, A. ed., 1989. *Medeltidens födelse.* Lund: Symposier på Krapperups borg 1.

Arbman, H. 1940-43. *Birka I. Die Gräber*, Stockholm.

Birkeli, F. 1973. *Norske steinkors i tidlig middelalder. Et bidrag til belysning av overgangen fra norrøn religion till kristendom.* Oslo: Skrifter utg. av Det Norske Videnskaps-Akademi i Oslo, Hist.Filos. Klasse N.S.10.

Brink, S. 1990. *Sockenbildning och sockennamn. Studier i äldre territoriell indelning i Norden.* Uppsala: Acta Academiae Regiae Gustavi Adolphi 57.

Dybdahl, A. and Hagland, J.R., eds, 1998. *Innskrifter og datering. Dating inscriptions.* Trondheim: Senter for middelalderstudier, skrifter nr. 8.

Graham-Cambell, J. *et al.*, eds, 1994. *Cultural Atlas of the Viking World*, Oxford.

Gräslund, A-S. 1980. *Birka IV. The burial customs. A study of the graves on Björkö*, Stockholm.

——1987. 'Runstenar, bygd och gravar', *Tor*, 21, 241-62.

——1989. '"Gud hjälpe nu väl hennes själ". Om runstenskvinnorna, deras roll vid kristnandet och deras plats i familj och samhälle', *Tor*, 22, 223-44.

——1992. 'Kultkontinuitet—myt eller verklighet? Om arkeologins möjligheter att belysa problemet', in Nilsson 1992, 129-50.

——1994. 'Rune stones—on ornamentation and chronology', in Ambrosiani and Clarke 1994, 117-31.

Hagland, J.R. 1991. 'Kulisteinen—endå ein gong', in Alhaug *et al.* 1991, 157-165.

——1998. 'Innskrifta på Kulisteinen: Ei nylesing ved hjelp av Jan O. H. Swantessons mikrokarteringsteknologi', in Dybdahl and Hagland 1998, 129-139.

Harding, S. 1998. *Is science multicultural? Postcolonialisms, feminisms and epistologies*, Bloomington, Indiana.

Hartman, S. ed., 1969. *Syncretism, based on papers read at the Symposium on Cultural Contact, Meeting of religions, Syncretism held at Åbo on the 8th-10th of September 1966*, Uppsala.

Hellström, J.A. 1996. *Vägar till Sveriges kristnande*, Stockholm.

Hultgård, A. 1992. 'Religiös förändring, kontinuitet och ackulturation/synkretism i vikingatidens och medeltidens skandinaviska religion', in Nilsson 1992, 49-103.

Kinander, R. 1935. *Smålands runinskrifter, vol. 1 Kronobergs läns runinskrifter.* Stockholm: Sveriges runinskrifter 4.

Kjellmark, K. 1906. 'Ett graffält från den yngre järnåldern i Ås i Jämtland', *Ymer*, 25 (1905), 351-71.

Larsen, E. 1972. *Dansk kunsthistorie,* Copenhagen.

Markus, R. 1993. 'From Rome to the Barbarian Kingdoms (330-700)', in McManners, 1993, 70-100.

275

Marold, E. 1985. 'Das Gottesbild der Christlichen Skaldik', in *Workshop Papers I-II. The Sixth International Saga Conference 27.8-2.8 1985, arranged by Det Arnamagnaenske Institut*, Copenhagen, 717-50.

McManners, J. 1993. *The Oxford History of Christianity*, Oxford.

Meulengracht Sørensen, P. 1991. 'Håkon den gode og guderne. Nogle bemærkninger om religion og centralmagt i det tiende århundrede—og om religionshistorie og kildekritik', in Mortensen and Rasmussen 1991, 235-44.

Mortensen, P. and Rasmussen, B.M., eds, 1991. *Fra stamme til stat i Danmark 2. Høvdingesamfund og Kongemagt*. Århus: Jysk Arkaeologisk selskabs skrifter 22:2.

Müller-Wille, M. 1971. *Pferdegrab und Pferdeopfer im frühen Mittelalter. Mit einem Beitrag von H. Vierck: Pferdegräber in angelsächsischen England*. Amersfort: Berichten van de Rijksdienst voor het Oudheidkundig Bodemonderzoek 20-21.

Nilsson, B. ed., 1992. *Kontinuitet i kult och tro från vikingatid till medeltid*. Uppsala: Projektet Sveriges kristnande 1.

——1996. *Kristnandet i Sverige. Gamla källor och nya perspektiv*. Uppsala: Projektet Sveriges kristnande 5.

Olsen, O. 1966. *Hørg, hov og kirke. Historiske og arkaeologiske vikingetidsstudier*, Copenhagen.

——1981. 'Der lange Weg des Nordens zum Christentum', in Ahrens 1981, 247-61.

Ringgren, H. 1969. 'The Problem of Syncretism', in Hartman 1969, 7-14.

Schjødt, J.P. 1989. 'Nogle overvejelser over begrebet "Religionsskifte" med henblik på en problematisering av termens brug i forbindelse med overgangen til kristendommen i Norden', in Andrén 1989, 187-201.

Steinsland, G. 1991. 'Religionsskiftet i Norden og Voluspa 65', in Steinsland *et al.* 1991, 335-48.

Steinsland, G., Drobin, U., Pentikäinen, J. and Meulengracht Sørensen, P. eds, 1991. *Nordisk hedendom. Et symposium*, Odense.

Strömbäck, D. 1975. *The Conversion of Iceland: A Survey*, London.

Vésteinsson, O. 2000. *The Christianisation of Iceland: Priests, Power and Social Change, 1000-1300*, Oxford.

Williams, H. 1996. 'Vad säger runstenarna om Sveriges kristnande?', in Nilsson 1996, 45-83.

The Archaeology of *Seiðr*: Circumpolar Traditions in Viking Pre-Christian Religion

Neil Price

Introduction

For more than 120 years historians of religion, together with philologists and occasionally anthropologists, have been studying the possibility that some aspects of pre-Christian Scandinavian religion may have contained elements of shamanism. Much of this work has focused on the cult of Óðinn (Odin)—the highest god, most often associated with war, poetry and the mind—but within this field research has especially concentrated on a specific complex of rituals collectively termed *seiðr* in the Old Norse textual sources. Altogether more than 300 published works have appeared on this subject, representing the work of some 150 scholars from the disciplines mentioned above (this corpus of scholarship is fully discussed in Price 2002 but key contributions may be found in the work of Strömbäck 1935; 1970; 1975; Ohlmarks 1939a; 1939b; Buchholz 1968; 1971; Grambo 1984; 1989; 1991; Dillmann 1986; 1993; 1994).

The long time-frame of these studies is important for two reasons. Firstly, such a focus serves to dispel the idea that the study of a possible Viking shamanism results from, or is in any way connected with, the increasing popular interest in alternative religions. Medieval descriptions of Viking-Age rituals have provided inspiration for modern, neo-shamanic groups who also use the word *seiðr* to describe what they do (cf. Blain 2002), but I want to emphasise that my own research, and this paper, is exclusively concerned with the beliefs and practices of the Viking Age, with *seiðr* in its original sense. Secondly, I refer to the long history of research in this field because it is also important to stress that I am here very much following in the footsteps of others.

Interestingly, archaeologists have come relatively late to the discussion. Karl Hauck's shamanic interpretations of the Migration Period gold bracteates—a type of circular pendant perhaps worn as a mark of rank or status—first appeared in the early 1970s (e.g. 1972, 1976, 1983, 1985-89 amongst many others). However, for the Viking Age proper it is not until Bente Magnus' ground-breaking publications (1988, 1992) that we begin to see the idea of shamanism in Old Norse religion take root in archaeological circles. The present paper will primarily be concerned with these archaeological responses, but we may begin by quickly reviewing our sources for *seiðr*, and the way they have been interpreted.

Seiðr and Óðinnic magic

The most explicit descriptions all come from medieval Icelandic texts, especially the family sagas and the poetry that they sometimes contain. The most comprehensive is Snorri's *Ynglingasaga*, with especially detailed depictions from *Eiríks saga rauða* and *Hrólfs saga kraka*; these two works are those most often cited, but among the sagas of Icelanders there are in fact a great number of additional, brief mentions of *seiðr*. From the older Scandinavian sources such as the so-called Poetic Edda, a medieval collection of poems with mythological and heroic themes, there are several oblique references, especially in the poems *Lokasenna*, *Hyndlulóð* and *Völuspá*. In addition, there are other descriptions of events or practices which, although not explicitly connected with *seiðr*, also formed part of a wider complex that we might call 'Óðinnic magic' and have often been interpreted in a similar context. These especially occur in parts of *Hávamál* and *Grímnismál*, alongside many other poems and sagas (the collected sources are summarised in Dag Strömbäck's classic work on *seiðr* from 1935, newly republished in an expanded edition in 2000).

Taken together, these sources contain many descriptions of practices with parallels in shamanic cultures all across the circumpolar region. In the Old Norse texts most of these relate to the abilities and adventures of Óðinn, and include apparent initiation rites in which the god acquires sacred knowledge and the secret wisdom known only to the dead by fasting, exposure and hanging; there are descriptions of spirit journeys, states of trance and ecstasy, and shape-shifting—as for example when Óðinn sends out his soul in animal form, his body lying 'as if asleep' while he travels to other worlds for his own purposes or on behalf of others. Animal helping spirits, such as ravens and wolves, also seem to be present. On his travels between the worlds, Óðinn sometimes rides his supernatural steed, the eight-legged horse called Sleipnir (meaning approximately 'the sliding one') whose teeth are etched with runes; the god has control over the weather and the elements; he can divine the future, heal the sick and seek out the hidden.

In addition to Óðinn himself, there are also a great many human figures who are mentioned in the sources as performing *seiðr*, of whom the best known are the *völur* (sing. *völva*), women skilled in clairvoyance and the prediction of future events. The *völur* embody one of the most important elements of *seiðr*, namely the complex network of social and sexual taboos with which it was encoded. These are described at length in the written sources, but in brief they limited its 'proper' performance to women, and to a small group of men seen as different from the morally acceptable norm, either sexually or in some way we do not yet understand. This involved highly complex concepts of dishonour and a special state of being called *ergi*, and there is a suggestion of other genders, constructed in connection with this across and between the boundaries of the sexes through an induction into the mysteries of *seiðr* (see Meulengracht Sørensen 1980; 1983; and Almqvist 1965 for discussions of *ergi* and its related concept of *níð*; cf. Solli 1998). It would seem to be the apparent contradiction of Óðinn's role as both a male god and the master of *seiðr*—these rituals that were primarily the province of women—that gives him such extensive power over the minds and movements of others, and particularly over the events of the battlefield. I will return to some of these features shortly, but first I want to examine the ways in which archaeologists have approached the *seiðr* complex, its meaning and cultural context.

THE ARCHAEOLOGY OF *SEIÐR*

Since the late 1980s a number of archaeologists have worked with aspects of *seiðr* (e.g. Hjørungdal 1989; 1990; 1991; 1992; Ingstad 1992; 1995; Herschend 1997; Adolfsson and Lundström 1997; Solli 1998; Price 1998; 2000a; 2000b; these and other examples are treated fully in Price 2002), joining the comprehensive group of researchers from other disciplines mentioned above. However, only one archaeological scholar has proposed a fully-developed model for shamanic thought in Scandinavia, and this is primarily limited to a discussion of the pre-Viking period (Hedeager 1997a; 1997b).

The publications mentioned above are of high quality, but it has to be said that some of those working in this field, especially in the Viking Age itself, have not been so thorough. It would be invidious to mention names, but one can almost suggest that as what we might call the 'shamanic lobby' in Viking archaeology goes from strength to strength, the quality of the work produced seems to decline in equal measure. There would seem to be three major problems which partly develop from each other.

Firstly, there are very few, if any, of the scholars now working in this field who have tried to familiarise themselves in detail with the truly vast corpus of research on shamanism from around the world, especially concerning the cultures of the circumpolar arctic and sub-arctic region; these include in particular the Sámi people with whom the Vikings shared the Scandinavian peninsula.

Secondly, the interpretations of *seiðr* that have been put forward almost always stop at the same point, namely the relatively unsophisticated (and further undefined) suggestion that this and other forms of Óðinnic magic may have been 'shamanistic' in nature.

Thirdly, this work needs to be combined with a comprehensive understanding of the Old Norse written sources, which in philological terms involve extremely complex elements; expert guidance is needed here, as such skills are not always easy for an archaeologist to acquire.

The study of shamanism itself is a vast field, in which definition and context are of paramount importance. I will attempt no summary of this subject here (general introductions can be found in Vitebsky 1995; Lewis 1989; Larsson 2000; Price 2001) but in an archaeological context it must be emphasised that it is not sufficient to read a classic—and controversial—text such as Eliade's *Shamanism* (latest edition 1989) and to then interpret every possible sort of artefact as 'shamanic'. Regrettably, this is now occurring with some frequency.

In particular, no Viking specialist has yet ventured far into the intricacies of the Sámi belief system and its links to this wider sphere of circumpolar ritual practices. Uncritical ethnographic analogy is a constant danger in shamanic research, but I strongly believe that any meaningful study of *seiðr* must look seriously to the work being done not just in the Sámi homelands but also in Siberia, Alaska, Canada, the northern continental United States, and Greenland.

279

This introduces the core of my argument in the present paper, namely the necessity to go beyond the simplicities of a shamanic conclusion for *seiðr* if we are to understand what it may once have meant in the Viking Age. As a generalisation, I would suggest that archaeologists have largely failed to develop the idea that some form of shamanism was operating in late Iron Age Scandinavia, in that they have not gone on to ask the really vital questions about its function, social context and implications for the Viking world-view as a whole. The latter is crucial here, because in essence shamanism is a view of the world, a particular conception of the nature of reality—far more fundamentally so than many other more formalised religions—and as such has a huge influence on the actions and perceptions of those who subscribe to this kind of belief system. What that means is that if we are to take seriously the idea of Viking-Age 'shamanism' then we have to accept the interpretive challenge that comes with that suggestion.

SEIÐR AND NOAI'DEVUOTTÂ

So, how may we approach such an undertaking? As archaeologists we can start with the material culture, and before looking at finds from Nordic contexts it can be instructive to first examine the evidence from the Sámi territories.

Among the most fundamental items of equipment in the shamanic repertoire—particularly in the popular imagination—are drums. They are found in most parts of the circumpolar region, especially in Siberia, though they are by no means universal even there. In the Sámi shamanic belief system, the operative part of which was known as *noai'devuottâ*, there is no doubt that the drum was vital (for an overview of Sámi religion, see Bäckman and Hultkrantz 1978, 1985; Ahlbäck 1987). Used by the *noai'de*, the Sámi term that most closely corresponds to our understanding of a shaman, there were once many hundreds, if not thousands, of these drums. Today less than eighty examples from the post-medieval period survive, scattered throughout Scandinavia and the anthropological collections of the world. Catalogued and described by Ernst Manker (1938; 1950; see also Ahlbäck and Bergman

1991; Westman and Utsi 1999), the drums occur in several different forms with discrete distributions, the compositional variation in the images on their surfaces hinting at changing traditions and functions within Sámi ritual practice. Alongside the drums we also have several finds of the decorated antler and bone hammers used to beat them, and of the small pointers which were placed on the drum-skin during the shamanic performance (the pointer's sequential movement across the pictures on the vibrating drum-skin formed the basis for the *noai'de*'s interpretation of his visions). However, behind this corpus of material lies a far more complex picture.

A large proportion of my current research focuses on the religion of the Sámi (see Price 2002), and some brief conclusions can be presented here. In outline, we can make three main observations from a survey of Sámi shamanism which can be of relevance to its possible counterpart among the Germanic population of Scandinavia.

Firstly, *noadi'devuottâ* was not a static, orthodox entity, but in fact exhibited considerable regional variation in the form of its expression, which even in the same areas also changed over time

Secondly, the notion of the 'Sámi shaman' in fact conceals a large number of specialised types of ritual practitioner, each with their own functions and skills, including workers of specifically 'good' and 'evil' kind; there is evidence for these noai'de being 'ranked' in order of skill, and for them occasionally working magic in groups. Some of the functions these people performed can be summarised as follows:

- finding game and performing hunting-related rituals
- foretelling the future (divination)
- uncovering secrets
- healing
- bestowing good or bad fortune
- working illusions
- manipulating the weather
- causing injury to people, animals or property
- instilling fear or confusion in an enemy
- killing people
- providing protection from a hostile *noai'de*
- fighting / killing a hostile *noai'de*
- communicating / mediating with the dead
- communicating / mediating with the spirits of nature
- communicating / mediating with the unseen world(s)
- communicating / mediating with the gods

Thirdly, both sexes seem to have played an important role in *noadi'devuottâ*, again with specific and precise differences in the social functions and abilities of men and women. There may also have been a blurring of gender boundaries.

This is obviously a simplification of something very complex, and all this information is also tentative: it is very hard to gain a reliable impression of *noadi'devuottâ* when most of our data comes from the writings of the people who were trying to destroy it, namely the Christian missionaries. However, there are also linguistic sources which can support these suggestions, centring around a series of words recorded in different regions and dialects of Sápmi from the 'post-shamanistic period' of the early eighteenth to early twentieth centuries. These terms have been collated and interpreted by the comparative theologist Håkan Rydving (1987), who I should stress is not responsible for my interpretation of them and the conclusions drawn here.

Terms for male Sámi 'sorcerers' (selective list, not including alternatives and variants):

— *noai'de*	1. 'one who knows'
	2. 'shaman, diviner, magician'
— *borånoai'de*	'eater-*noai'de*'
— *piedje-nåi'te*	'sender-*noai'de*'
— *savve-nåi'te*	'wisher-*noai'de*'
— *kir'di noai'di*	'flyer-*noai'de*'
— *frimurar-nåi'te*	one who is committed to devils?
— *guwlar*	one who harms and cures by sorcery?
— *goanståsæg'gje*	one who harms by sorcery?
— *tivvo-nåi'te*	'*noai'de* who puts right'
— *juovsåhæg'gje*	one who diverts the evil of a *noai'de*?
— *oinoålma*	'one who dreams'
— *tsulidiije*	'one who whispers'
— *tsjal'bme keäi'du*	'one who creates illusions'
— *noai'dohæg'gje*	'one who causes enchantment'
— *skäddar*	'one who bewitches people's sight'
— *gæi'do*	'one who bewitches people's sight'
— *diet'te*	'one versed in magic'
— *siei'de*	'sorcerer'
— *månidæd'd'i*	'sorcerer who drives away disease'
— *sahple-lijjen-jotti*	'sorcerer that sends out his spirit in the form of a mouse'
— *judaka*s or *juraak*	'sorcerer who never chanted'
— *kiemdesniei'te*	'drum-sorcerer'
— *kairve*	'sorcerer' connected to a god?

281

Terms for female Sámi 'sorcerers' (selective list, not including alternatives and variants):

— *guaps*	'woman who could chant and divine'
— *kwepkas*	'woman versed in witchcraft'
— *gapishjaedne*	'witch, sorceress'
— *noåjdiesaakkaa*	'witch, sorceress'
— *shjarak*	female assistant to a male *noai'de*?
— *rudok*	'spokeswoman' for the female supernatural being *Årja*?

All these words describe Sámi 'sorcerers' or 'magic-workers', for want of better words. Most of the terms are gender-specific and they all seem to describe people who performed a specific function, a certain kind of magic and ritual. We do not know how many of these people were actually *noai'de*—'shamans'—nor do we know exactly what they all did, or exactly how all these different types of sorcerer worked together in the wider context of society. Most importantly, we do not know exactly how old these concepts are, though on linguistic grounds some of them are clearly of very great antiquity. Again, we are dealing with regional variation and change over time. I discuss these terms more fully elsewhere (Price 2002), but for the purposes of the present paper the detail of the practices that they represent is less important than the simple fact of their existence in such variety, emphasising the diversity and complexity of what must have actually lain behind what we conceive of today as 'the Sámi shaman'.

Neil Price

The material culture of *seiðr*

I would here ask the reader to keep this in mind as we now turn back to the Nordic cultural sphere, and back to *seiðr*. In connection with the performance of *seiðr* there are written references to several activities or pieces of equipment with circumpolar parallels, including an elaborate costume for the performer, the assistance of singers who chant songs to attract the spirits with whom the *seiðr*-performer will communicate, a ritual platform or high-seat on which the performer sits, and a special '*seiðr*-staff' of unknown function but referred to in several texts as a major component of the ritual (see the sources summarised in Strömbäck 1935, and especially the famous passage from *Eiríks saga rauða* describing a *völva* on Greenland).

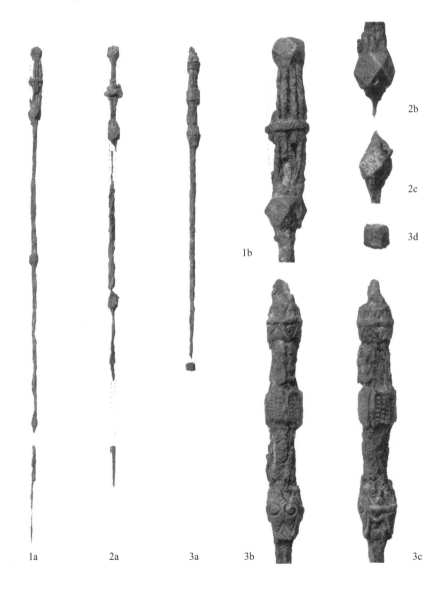

Figure 1. Three iron staffs from the Viking-Age cemeteries at Birka, Björkö, Sweden: graves Bj. 834 (1), 845 (2), 660 (3), with close-up details of their construction. The photographs were taken in the 1930s and the objects are now much deteriorated (after Arbman 1940, pl. 125).

From the archaeological sources, we can begin with these staffs, the most striking—and relatively little known—Viking artefact type which I would argue can be reasonably linked to the practice of *seiðr*. Surprisingly, quite a large number of objects of this kind have been found in Viking-Age graves. In Sweden, three examples are known from the cemeteries of Birka (fig. 1; graves Bj.760, 834, 845, in Arbman 1940-41, 277-78, 304-8, 319-20, pl. 125), together with a particularly large staff found at Klinta on the island of Öland (Sjöberg 1987, 55-62, 102-13; Petersson 1958), and another example, though simpler in form, from a mound at Aska i Hagebyhöga in Östergötland (Arne 1932). There are more than 20 of these staffs known from Norway (Petersen 1951), and at least one from Denmark, at the Fyrkat circular enclosure (grave 4, in Roesdahl 1977, 83-104). All the examples that have been dated, throughout the Scandinavian countries, belong to the tenth century.

Many of the excavated staffs resemble the Birka pieces, being about 70 cm long and made of sections of twisted iron rod, spaced at intervals with polyhedral bronze knobs decorated with dot and ring patterns, and with a handle-like feature of unidentified function at one end (we do not know which is the 'top' or 'bottom' of the object) made of several finer rods joined above and below by one of the polyhedral studs and threaded through a perforated bronze disk. Some staffs have a simpler shaft of solid iron, while others have a more complex terminal ending in an iron ring—in some cases of considerable size—on which may be threaded further iron objects, resembling amulets or pendant rattles of various kinds. The staff from Klinta on Öland is unique in that the 'handle' (of the Birka type) is surmounted by a small model house cast in bronze and resting on a flat platform, while the open iron strands of the 'handle' are clasped at both ends by animal heads, perhaps of bears or wolves; all these details are, of course, of unknown purpose. In addition to the staffs described above, there are also several earlier objects from Norwegian graves which may be wooden versions of the same thing, including one in the Oseberg ship burial (Ingstad 1992, 1995) and another from Os, near Bergen (Hjørungdal 1990). Another wooden staff of uncertain function, though almost certainly with sorcerous associations, has been found in a Danish bog at Hemdrup (Back Danielson 2001).

283

Of the metal staffs, all the Swedish and Danish examples, and 13 of the Norwegian ones, are either from female graves or from the 'female section' of a double burial containing both sexes; one is from a male grave and the others are either unsexed or from non-burial contexts. Many of the graves are very richly furnished and often include exotic imports or other unusual items, which archaeologists would normally interpret as signals of high status. The burials from Klinta and Aska i Hagebyhöga in Sweden, and at Fyrkat in Denmark, were particularly spectacular in that they contained a great many objects that were at the least out of the ordinary and in some cases unique (some of these are discussed further below). In the case of the Fyrkat grave, the woman interred there was accorded the richest burial in the entire cemetery; we should remember here that the Fyrkat enclosure was almost certainly established at the personal command of King Haraldr Gormsson, and thus it is not unreasonable to suggest that the status of this woman may have been very considerable indeed. This suggestion of wealth and status runs as a constant in the staff graves, culminating in the Oseberg ship which has been claimed as the burial of a queen (see, amongst others, Ingstad 1992; 1995).

The staffs themselves have sometimes been interpreted as meat spits, used for roasting joints over a fire. This argument has been summarised in the only catalogue of these objects, entitled *Vendel- och vikingatida stekspett* (*Vendel- and Viking-Period Roasting Spits*) which in fact contains an undifferentiated mixture of genuine roasting implements and the more problematic objects that may be *seiðr*-staffs (Bøgh-Andersen 1999). Unfortunately, and despite a nominal reference to symbolism in a general sense—the catalogue's subtitle translates as 'Not just for the kitchen: a tool with roots in Homer's time'—the author has virtually no discussion of the *seiðr*-staff interpretation, or the alternative explanations of the objects as measuring rods and processional poles. At one level, there is no doubt that the staffs described above cannot be for roasting meat. Firstly, their form is such as to make such a function impossible—joints of beef, pork, chicken, etc., could not be forced past the poly-hedral knobs without virtually destroying the meat. Secondly, several staffs have been found together with spits that undoubtedly *are* for roasting; the Fyrkat grave is the most unequiv-ocal example of the latter, although only the spit is listed in Bøgh-Andersen's catalogue. However, both the genuine meat spits and the possible *seiðr*-staffs share a great many char-acteristics, or rather combinations of them, as no two staff/spits are exactly alike. Especially close similarities are found in the 'handle' feature, which occurs both on staffs with knobbed and plain shafts, the latter being perfectly serviceable as spits. Furthermore, these 'handles' are almost identical to the grips of some types of keys found in Viking contexts, while the polyhedral knobs are similarly comparable with bronze weights.

The relationships between these different kinds of objects are difficult to understand, though the symbolic dimensions of apparently everyday activities such as cooking should not be under-estimated (see Price 2002 for a more detailed discussion of this problem). Although many of these pieces fall into the grey area between staffs and spits, those described above can be fitted with confidence into a category of their own, and a good case can certainly be made for interpreting them as *seiðr*-staffs. We have already seen the inter-estingly high status of their finds contexts, something not reflective of meat spits in gener-al, and their almost complete limitation to female graves, both of which match the textual descriptions of the *völur*. The most persuasive argument, however, must be the clear simi-larity between the excavated objects and the written descriptions of the *seiðstafr*, which specifically mention a staff ornamented with a metal knob.

There is also one further aspect of the staff graves which deserves attention, even though evidence of this kind should be treated with extreme caution (especially in a popu-lar context). In at least two instances, burials containing staffs also include remains of herbs with mind-altering properties, with obvious implications for their possible use in a ritual context. In the Oseberg ship burial, a small number of cannabis seeds had been placed with deliberate care among a pile of feathers and down (Holmboe 1927, 32-5); this is a particu-larly interesting context given the detailed description of the special feather stuffing of the *völva*'s cushion in *Eiríks saga rauða*. Similarly, the spectacular female grave at Fyrkat men-tioned above contained several hundred seeds of henbane, another herb with narcotic prop-erties (Helbaek 1977, 36; Roesdahl 1977, 104). The seeds were found grouped together near the woman's waist in a manner which suggests that they had originally been gathered in some kind of belt-pouch made of organic material that had since decayed. A similar pouch is described in *Eiríks saga rauða*. In a box at the foot of the grave were found bones of birds and small animals, which could also be interpreted as charms of some kind. Both cannabis and henbane are otherwise almost completely unknown in finds from the Viking Age, and even if we cannot be sure about their use in ritual it does seem certain that these plants were seen as special in some way that merited their inclusion in the grave assemblage.

Staffs of this kind may be what is depicted in the hands of the famous 'weapon dancers', images found in a variety of media in the Migration and Vendel periods, but in the Viking Age most often in the form of small silver pendants. Like the staffs, these pendants are largely confined to female graves, and have often been interpreted as images of Óðinn. Clearly there is a risk for circular argument here, but an identification of this object as a *seiðr*-staff would not be inappropriate in this context. The pendant found in grave Bj.571 at Birka (fig. 2; Arbman 1940-41, 185-6, pl. 92) has a particularly clearly defined staff, with notches that perhaps equate with the knobs found along the length of the excavated examples found in the female burials.

In addition to the staffs there are also several other excavated artefacts that may also be interpreted in the context of *seiðr*. The most dramatic perhaps are small silver models of

Figure 2. The silver 'weapon dancer' pendant from Birka grave Bj. 571 (after Graham-Campbell 1980, 307).

Figure 3. A miniature silver chair, found in Birka grave Bj. 968 (after Drescher and Hauck 1982, 252).

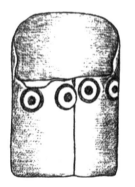

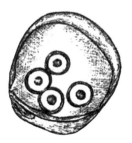

chairs, cast in silver and most often with an attached loop for suspension as a pendant. Again found exclusively in women's graves, these miniature chairs have been interpreted as representing the 'high seat' in Valhöll from which Óðinn surveys the worlds, or from which the *völur* performed *seiðr*, the *seiðhjallr* platform mentioned in saga sources. A miniature chair of this kind was found in grave 4 at Fyrkat, with the staff and pouch of bones and seeds (Roesdahl 1977, 83-104), and three are known from Birka (fig. 3; graves Bj. 632, 844, 968 in Arbman 1940-41, 210-13, 317-19, 394-6, pl. 92).

285

In one of these Birka graves with the miniature chairs (Bj.968) was found yet another artefact that may link to *seiðr*, a silver pendant figure of a woman (Arbman 1940-41, 394-6, pl. 92). This is one of a number of such images found in female graves throughout Scandinavia, and as isolated finds elsewhere in the Viking world as far afield as Russia. They are often interpreted as representing valkyries—another connection with Óðinn—but they may equally depict *völur* or any of a number of female supernatural beings.

These same female figures reoccur in another medium, in direct association with the only unequivocally shamanic image found in Viking material culture: depictions of the eight-legged horse. Such animals appear in several media, but without doubt the most prominent is its occurence as the main motif on a few examples of the so-called picture stones, set up continually since the early Iron Age as carved memorials to the dead on the Baltic island of Gotland (all the picture-stones have been catalogued by

Figure 4. Two Viking-Age picture stones from Gotland, with images of the eight-legged horse; from Alskog Tjängvide I (left) and Ardre VIII (after Lindqvist 1942, 17, 25).

286

Lindqvist 1941-42, updated in Nylén and Lamm 1987). The Viking-Age stones usually stand between two and three metres high, and most often bear an image of a rigged sailing ship on the lower half of the surface. The upper half is either divided into several lateral panels or contains a complex jumble of images, and it is among the latter that in four, perhaps five, instances we find the eight-legged horse (fig. 4; the stones in question come from Alskog Tjängvide I, Ardre I and VIII, and Lärbro Tängelgårda I and II; Lindqvist 1941, 95-6, 99-101, figs. 86, 89, 137-40, 166; Lindqvist 1942, 15-25, 92-6).

These images on the picture stones are usually interpreted as representing Sleipnir, Óðinn's eight-legged horse mentioned above. However, this apparently obvious identification is brought into serious question by other examples of similar creatures depicted on two of the five Viking-Age wall-hangings from Överhogdal in the Swedish province of Härjedalen (fig. 5; Horneij 1991; Frantzén and Nockert 1992). Like the tapestry from the Oseberg ship burial, the images on the Överhogdal weaves do not appear to be arranged in narrative sequences (as, for example, on the Bayeux Tapestry) but instead in a mass of pictures presumably combining to create a single, perhaps multi-faceted, image. In this context it is therefore striking to see that on weaves 1a and b (two portions of the same original hanging) there are no less than four eight-legged horses, depicted alongside three more with six legs and one with seven. In addition the weave shows one six-legged elk and six six-legged reindeer; a further six-legged creature may be either a horse or an elk, the tell-tale

Figure 5. Weave 1a from Överhogdal, Härjedalen, Sweden, radio-carbondated to the Viking Age (after Horneij 1991).

Figure 6. One of the two cloth masks found rolled up and used as caulking in a Viking-Age ship, wrecked in the harbour at Hedeby, Schleswig-Holstein. The upper image shows the mask as found, the lower shows it moulded into what is believed to be its original form (after Hägg 1984, 71).

head being lost where the weave has frayed. In most cases the horses are unmounted, though in a single instance a rider is shown; one of the eight-legged horses and one of the reindeer are also shown with what appears to be a prominent phallus. In addition to these, weave II contains a single image of the eight-legged horse, this time bearing two riders. It would seem difficult to interpret *all* the Överhogdal horses as representations of Sleipnir, and in fact the notion of more than one such creature accords well with ethnographic records of more recent shamanic communities. These animals are recorded as the mounts of shamans all across Siberia, for example among the Buryat, and even as far afield as Japan and India, leading some historians of religion to call this the shamanic horse *par excellence* (Elwin 1947, 150; Eliade 1989, 380; Price 2000a; 2000b). The other creatures on the Överhogdal weaves also have Siberian parallels, for example among the Khanty (Pentikäinen 1998, 68-70), and it may be that all these multi-legged animals represent different components in the shamanic complexes of the Viking Age Scandinavians and Sámi. The variety of animals depicted fits well with the more nuanced view of these belief systems advocated above.

In the written sources there are also philologically difficult references to what may be the use of masks and drums, especially in the Eddic poems *Grímnismál* and *Lokasenna* respectively. There are no recorded finds of drums from Nordic archaeological contexts, but images of masked faces are relatively common in Viking metalwork and on other media such as runestones. Even more striking are two animal-head masks made of felt, found in a Viking shipwreck in Hedeby harbour in Denmark (fig. 6; Hägg 1984, 69-72). These are intriguing objects—quite unlike the more familiar carnival masks of medieval times, and perhaps in some way associated with the idea of shape-changing, which as mentioned earlier occurs frequently in the descriptions of Óðinnic magic and shamanism. This aspect of Viking spirituality focuses particularly on the relationship between humans and animals. Due to spatial constraints it is unfortunately impossible to go very deeply into this in the present paper, but here we may almost move towards a totemistic interpretation, thinking of such figures as the *berserkir* and *úlfheðnar*, the bear- and wolf-skin warriors who served Óðinn in animal form (see Price 1998; this argument is developed at length in Price 2002). In addition to the Hedeby masks we find other images of men with the heads of wolves, such as one of the runestones from Källbyås in Västergötland (Jungner 1940, pl. 45; Svärdström 1958, 79-82) and the metal figurine found—significantly perhaps—in a woman's grave at Ekhammar (Ringquist 1969), both in Sweden. The latter grave also contained one of the weapon dancer figures, in an association with wolf-warriors which again goes back to pre-Viking times. This is seen, for example, on the helmet plaques and casting dies found at sites such as Vendel, Valsgärde and Torslunda (see Sandwall 1980); we should note that at least some of the dancers on these plaques can now be definitely identified as one-eyed (Arrhenius and Freij 1992), and thus almost certainly represent Óðinn himself.

It must be emphasised that the material presented here—the staffs, miniature chairs, eight-legged horses, female figurines, weapon dancers, masks and shape-changers—is only a small fraction of the total corpus. Many examples of these objects have been omitted for reasons of space, and several further categories of material have not been treated at all here. A full discussion will be found elsewhere (Price 2002), but even the present small sample can be combined to form a material cultural complex that may be quite convincingly be linked to *seiðr* and similar rituals. As we have done for the Sámi material, we can here too move from the archaeology to broader issues.

SEIÐR IN CONTEXT

The network of gender restrictions with which the performance of *seiðr* was encoded has been mentioned above. The emphasis on women practitioners would seem to be reflected in the archaeological record, with the overwhelming predominance of objects from female graves. However, remembering the numerous written descriptions of men performing *seiðr*, the situation may not have been so simple. This problem can be essentially reduced to a similar series of factors as we earlier saw in Sámi belief—questions of function, specific skill, variation and change. If we turn back to the Old Norse sources we find several terms for sorcerers or magic-workers, all of whom seem to use *seiðr* and the other kinds of Óðinnic magic, but in different ways. Like the Sámi terms, these are also gender-specific words, and include a range of different terms for men and women (a complete list of terms and sources is presented in Price 2002).

Terms for different types of male sorcerers recorded in the Elder Edda and other sources from the thirteenth century and later (note that the word *maðr* is of indeterminate gender, but the specific examples in this context always refer to men):

— *seiðmaðr*	'*seiðr*-man'
— *seiðskratti*	'evil *seiðr*-man'
— *seiðberendr*	'*seiðr*-carrier'?
— *vitki*	wizard?, sorcerer?
— *spámaðr*	'man who prophecies'
— *vísendamaðr*	'man who knows'
— *galdramaðr*	'spell-man'
— *galdrasmiðr*	'spell-smith'
— *galdraraumr*	'great sorcerer'
— *kunáttumaðr*	'man who knows magic'

Terms for different types of female sorcerers recorded in the Elder Edda and other sources from the thirteenth century and later:

— *völva*	seeress, sibyl?
— *seiðkona*	'*seiðr*-woman'
— *spákona*	'prophecy-woman'
— *galdrakona*	witch, sorceress
— *heiðr*	witch?
— *vitka**	sorceress?
— *kveldriða*	'evening-rider'
— *trollriða*	'rider of witchcraft'
— *myrkriða*	'darkness-rider' or 'night-rider'
— *túnriða*	'fence-rider' or 'roof-rider'
— *galdrakind*	evil witch?
— *fordæða*	evil witch?
— *flagð(kona)*	evil witch?
— *fála*	witch? (with negative connotations)
— *hála*	witch? (with negative connotations)
— *skass*	witch? (with negative connotations)

The male terms do not tell us much, other than that these people used *seiðr*, for divination amongst other purposes. The female terms are more detailed, with a group of words also refering to diviners, and an interesting quartet of terms mentioning 'Riders' of various kinds. This 'riding' would seem to refer to the soul journey in some way, and there is a verse from the Eddic poem *Hávamál* (the 'Sayings of the High One', i.e. Óðinn) which mentions the god 'seeing' such people up in the sky—presumably their spirit forms astride a shamanic steed.

There is an obvious parallel that I would draw with Sámi shamanism: the Viking-Age Scandinavians did not just have specialist ritual performers, they seem to have had *different types of them*. As with the Sámi terms that I showed earlier, we do not know exactly what all these people did, but we do know that they were associated with *seiðr* and related rituals.

Looking further at the written sources, we can draw out a similar range of attributes for these kinds of Nordic magic as for Sami religious practice (see Price 2002). Firstly, we see the same pattern of regional variation and change over time. Secondly, we can perceive the existence of different types of sorcerer with specific functions and skills, including specifically 'good' and 'evil' sorcerers. Some of the functions these individuals performed can be traced in the sources:

'Domestic' magic:
— foretelling the future (divination)
— bestowing good fortune
— bestowing bad fortune (cursing)
— manipulating the weather
— attracting game animals or fish
— causing mild harm to people, animals or property
— communicating / mediating with the dead
— communicating / mediating with the unseen world(s)
— communicating / mediating with the gods?

Battle magic:
— instilling fear and confusion in an enemy
— magically hindering an enemy's movements
— breaking or strengthening weapons and armour
— providing invulnerability in battle
— killing people
— providing protection from enemy sorcerers
— fighting / killing enemy sorcerers

Thirdly, both sexes were involved in sorcery, with evidence for different and precise social roles for men and women, together with the existence of complex sexual, social and gender constructions.

The circumpolar parallels are clearly striking in many respects, and in the Nordic culture we see a range of specialists who could perform a similar variety of different rituals according to their individual skill and disposition. This in fact is no more than we should expect, as an equal diversity of both practice and practitioners is found in shamanic belief systems throughout the northern hemisphere. However, the difference in comparison to circumpolar, and especially Sámi, shamanism comes in the context of the functions that Nordic magic of this kind seems to have performed. This is particularly important, because there is a general perception that *seiðr* was overwhelmingly used for divination and clairvoyance, and yet this is not actually borne out by an examination of the sources. *Seiðr* and Óðinnic magic was undoubtedly used for what are above called 'domestic' purposes—including divination, but also for affecting the weather to improve the crops, settling grievances and so on, all of which are mentioned in the sources. But in addition to this, we also find a different kind of magic, described in several catalogues of spells preserved in the early poetry, in the names and attributes of Óðinn, and even in the names of his servants like the valkyries, the female demons who decide the fate of warriors in battle (see Price 2002). This is a specifically violent magic, an offensive and defensive measure for active intervention in battle, for killing and shamanic combat.

In my opinion, this link between magic and aggression is the key aspect that has been neglected in many studies of *seiðr*, and goes far beyond the 'black' and 'white' forms that

Strömbäck and others have described (e.g. Strömbäck 1935; Ohlmarks 1939a; 1939b). Again, I would argue that this is in line with the other circumpolar traditions: in Sámi shamanism, for example, on the basis of a comprehensive survey of the sources I have estimated that up to 60% of rituals had an aggressive objective (Price 2002). The vital difference between circumpolar shamanism and the pre-Christian religion of the Norse is that few of the nomadic hunting cultures had a concept of organised warfare—a vital context for this aspect of *seiðr*.

But still, we must be cautious in our drawing of such parallels. Above all, we should avoid monolithic interpretations and simple definitions. We must always remember that we do not know exactly what *seiðr* meant to the early medieval Norse. At one level, this kind of belief system essentially revolves around a particular concept of the nature of the soul (human, animal and even what we would call mineral): in Viking studies it may be that we now urgently need a deeper study of Old Norse understandings of both this and the personification of luck, an update of existing work on the peculiar aspects of the self called *fylgjur* and *hamingjur* (e.g. Ellis 1943; Ström 1960; Strömbäck 1975). It should also be clear that the whole question of *seiðr* is ultimately linked to the very fabric of Old Norse society itself—how it was constructed and how the articulation of power and identity functioned within it. This should not surprise us, because—again—the shamanic belief systems of the circumpolar area are also socially embedded in precisely this way.

291

In one sense, of course, the acknowledgement of *seiðr*'s importance in the Old Norse belief system, and the whole shamanic and totemistic debate that comes with it, certainly does not fundamentally change our understanding of the Viking Age. In another sense however, the implications are profound. A close look at *seiðr* and its related rituals changes our perception of the way in which the Vikings may have thought about human beings and other living creatures, about what we would regard as inanimate objects, and even about the nature of reality itself; it changes our view of the role that ritual played in society. Faced then with a much broader field of study that opens up the idea of *seiðr* set in a universal social context for the Viking-Age North, archaeology can be seen to be of especial value, with its own particular research agenda focused on an ever-increasing database of all forms of material culture (not just that of religion), backed up by an array of theoretical tools that may be larger than those working in other disciplines realise. It may be that the archaeology of *seiðr* and its related rituals can provide one of our best hopes for the future investigation of the intricacies and sophistication of the Viking mind.

ACKNOWLEDGEMENTS

I would like to thank Jennifer Deon and the organisers of the Viking Millenium International Symposium for inviting me to speak and to contribute to this volume. My attendance at the conference was made possible by a substantial grant from the Swedish Institute, for which I am very grateful. A few paragraphs relating to the Sámi also appear in my forthcoming paper 'The archaeology of shamanism: beyond rock art', in C. Chippindale, G. Blundell and B. Smith, eds, *Seeing and knowing: ethnography and beyond in understanding rock-art* (Cambridge, 2002). Special thanks go to Shannon Lewis-Simpson for her firm but friendly editing, and her own contributions to Viking scholarship.

Finally, I would also like to record my gratitude to Magnus Magnusson, whose television programmes, books and saga translations first stimulated my interest in the Vikings many years ago, and were largely responsible for the orientation of what has now become my archaeological career. It was a great pleasure to meet Magnus at the symposium, and to at last be able to thank him for the inspiration.

BIBLIOGRAPHY

Adolfsson, G. and Lundström, I. 1997. *Den starka kvinnan: från völva till häxa*, Stockholm.

Ahlbäck, T. ed.,1987. *Saami religion*, Åbo.

Ahlbäck, T. and Bergman, J., eds, 1991. *The Saami shaman drum*, Åbo.

Almqvist, B. 1965. *Norrön niddiktning: traditionshistoriska studier i versmagi*, 2 vols, Stockholm.

Appelt, M., Berglund, J. and Gulløv, H.C., eds, 2000. *Identities and cultural contacts in the arctic*, Copenhagen.

Arbman, H. 1940-41. *Birka. I. Die Gräber*, 2 vols. Stockholm.

Arne, T.J. 1932. 'Ein bemerkenswerter Fund in Östergötland', *Acta Archaeologica,* 3, 67-112.

Arrhenius, B. and Freij, H. 1992. '"Pressbleck" fragments from the East Mound in Old Uppsala analyzed with a laser scanner', *Laborativ Arkeologi*, 6, 75-110.

Back Danielson, I-M. 2001. 'Hemdrup-staven—ett nytt tolkningsförslag', *Fornvännen,* 96, 73-7.

Bandle, O. ed., 1972. *Festschrift für S. Gutenbrunner*, Heidelberg.

Blain, J. 2002. *Nine worlds of seid-magic*, London.

Brøgger, A.W. and Shetelig, H., eds, 1927. *Osebergfundet*, vol. 5, Oslo.

Buchholz, P. 1968. *Schamanistische Züge in der altisländischen Überlieferung*, Münster.

——1971. 'Shamanism: the testimony of Old Icelandic literary tradition', *Medieval Scandinavia,* 4, 7-20.

Bäckman, L. and Hultkrantz, Å. 1978. *Studies in Lapp shamanism*, Stockholm.

——eds, 1985. *Saami pre-Christian religion*, Stockholm.

Bøgh-Andersen, S. 1999. *Vendel- och vikingatida stekspett*, Lund.

Christensen, A.S, Ingstad, A-S and Myhre, B., eds, 1992. *Osebergdronningens grav*, Oslo.

Crumlin-Pedersen, O. and Thye, B.M., eds, 1995. *The ship as symbol in prehistoric and medieval Scandinavia*, Copenhagen.

Dillmann, F-X. 1986. Les magiciens dans l'Islande ancienne, unpublished doctorat d'État dissertation, University of Caen, Caen.

——1993. 'Seiður og shamanismi í Íslendingasögum', *Skáldskaparmál*, 2, 20-33.

——1994. 'Sejd og shamanisme i de islandske sagaer', in Schjødt 1994, 23-34.

Drescher, H. and Hauck, K. 1982. 'Götterthrone des heidnischen Nordens', *Frühmittelalterliche Studien,* 16, 237-301.

Eliade, M. 1989 [1954]. *Shamanism: archaic techniques of ecstasy*, London.

Ellis, H.R. 1943. *The road to Hel: a study of the conception of the dead in Od Norse literature*, Cambridge.

Elwin, V. 1947. *The Muria and their Ghotul*, Bombay.

Fitzhugh, W.W. and Ward, E.I., eds, 2000. *Vikings: the North Atlantic Saga*, Washington and London.

Frantzén, A.M. and Nockert, M. 1992. *Bonaderna från Skog och Överhogdal*, Stockholm.

Graham-Campbell, J.A. 1980. *Viking artefacts: a select catalogue,* London.

Grambo, R. 1984. 'En seidkvinne på Grønland. Noen tanker om et avsnitt i *Eiriks saga rauda*', *Middelalderforum,* 3, 4, heft 9, 56-69.

——1989. 'Unmanliness and *seiðr*: problems concerning the change of sex', in Hoppál and von Sadovsky 1989, 103-13.

——1991. 'Problemer knyttet til studiet av seid', in Steinsland *et al.* 1991, 133-39.

Gräslund, A-S, ed., 1998. *Cult and belief in the Viking Age: a period of change*. Uppsala: EC Socrates Papers 1.

Hauck, K. 1972. 'Zur Ikonologie der Goldbrakteaten IV: Metamorphosen Odins nach dem Wissen von Snorri und von Amulettmeistern der Völkerwanderungszeit', in Bandle 1972, 47-70.

——1976. 'Bilddenkenmäler zur Religion', in Hoops 1976, 577-98.

——1983. 'Text und Bild in einer oralen Kultur. Antworten auf die zeugniskritische Frage nach der Erreichbarkeit mündlicher Überlieferung im frühen Mittelalter', *Frühmittelalterliche Studien*, 17, 510-99.

——1985-89. *Die Goldbrakteaten der Völkerwanderungszeit*, München.

292

Hedeager, L. 1997a. *Skygger af en anden virkelighed: oldnordiske myter*, Copenhagen.

——1997b. 'Odins offer. Skygger af en shamanistisk tradition i nordisk folkevandringstid', *Tor*, 29, 265-78.

Helbaek, H. 1977. 'The Fyrkat grain', in Olsen and Schmidt 1977, 1-41.

Herschend, F. 1997. *Livet i hallen: tre fallstudier i den yngre järnålderns aristokrati*, Uppsala.

Hjørungdal, T. 1989. 'Noen aspekter på tolkning av gravgods i eldre jernalder: kan gravgods belyse kult?', in Larsson and Werbart 1989, 99-106.

——1990. 'Volva frå Os-forvaltar av ein lang tradisjon', *Arkeo*, 1 (1990), 19-21.

——1991. *Det skjulte kjønn: patriarkal tradisjon og feministisk visjon i arkeologien belyst med fokus på en jernalderskontekst*, Lund.

——1992. 'Mot et nytt bilde av eldre jernalder', *Nytt om kvinneforskning*, 1, 92, 63-9.

Holmboe, J. 1927. 'Nytteplanter og ugræs i Osebergfundet', in Brøgger and Shetelig 1927, 3-80.

Hoops, J. ed., 1976. *Reallexikon der Germanischen Altertumskunde*, vol. 2: 4/5, New York.

Hoppál, M. and von Sadovsky, O., eds, 1989. *Shamanism, past and present*, Budapest.

Horneij, R. 1991. *Bonaderna från Överhogdal*, Östersund.

Hägg, I. 1984. *Die Textilfunde aus dem Hafen von Haithabu*, Neumünster.

Ingstad, A. S. 1992. 'Oseberg-dronningen-hvem var hun?', in Christensen, Ingstad and Myhre 1992, 224-56.

——1995. 'The interpretation of the Oseberg-find', in Crumlin-Pedersen and Thye 1995, 138-47.

Jungner, H. 1940. 'Västergötlands runinskrifter 1:2'. *Sveriges runinskrifter V*, Stockholm.

Larsson, L. and Werbart, B., eds, 1989. *Arkeologi och religion*, Lund.

Larsson, T.P. ed., 2000. *Schamaner: essäer om religiösa mästare*, Falun.

Lewis, I. 1989. *Ecstatic religion: a study of shamanism and spirit possession*, London.

Lindqvist, S. 1941-42. *Gotlands Bildsteine*. 2 vols., Stockholm.

Magnus, B. 1988. 'Eggjasteinen—et dokument om sjamanisme i jernalderen?', in (no editor) *Festskrift til Anders Hagen*, Bergen, 342-56.

——1992. 'A matter of literacy or magic?', in Straume and Skar 1992, 133-43.

Manker, E. 1938 and 1950. *Die lappische Zaubertrommel*, 2 vols, Stockholm.

Meulengracht Sørensen, P. 1980. *Nørront nid*, Odense.

——1983. *The unmanly man: concepts of sexual defamation in early Northern society*, Odense.

Nylén, E. and Lamm, J.P. 1987. *Bildstenar*, Stockholm.

Ohlmarks, Å. 1939a. *Studien zum Problem des Schamanismus*, Lund.

——1939b. 'Arktischer Schamanismus und altnordischer *seiðr*', *Arkiv für Religions-wissenschaft*, 36, 1, 171-80.

Olsen, O. and Schmidt, H., eds, 1977. *Fyrkat: en jysk vikingeborg. I. Borgen og bebyggelsen*, Copenhagen.

Pentikäinen, J. 1998. *Shamanism and culture*, Helsinki.

Petersen, J. 1951. *Vikingetidens redskaber*, Oslo.

Petersson, K.G. 1958. 'Ett gravfynd från Klinta, Köpings socken, Öland', *Tor*, 4, 134-50.

Price, N.S. 1998. 'Different Vikings? Towards a cognitive archaeology of religion and war in late Iron Age Scandinavia', in Gräslund 1998, 53-66.

——2000a. 'Drum-Time and Viking Age: Sámi-Norse identities in early medieval Scandinavia', in Appelt, Berglund and Gulløv 2000, 12-27.

——2000b. 'Shamanism and the Vikings?', in Fitzhugh and Ward 2000, 70-71.

——ed., 2001. *The archaeology of shamanism*, London.

——2002. *The Viking way: religion and war in late Iron Age Scandinavia*, Uppsala.

Ringquist, P-O. 1969. 'Två vikingatida uppländska människofigurer i brons', *Fornvännen* (1969), 4, 287-96.

Roesdahl, E. 1977. *Fyrkat: en jysk vikingeborg. II. Oldsagerne og gravpladsen*, Copenhagen.

Rydving, H. 1987. 'Shamanistic and post-shamanistic terminologies in Saami (Lappish)', in Ahlbäck 1987, 185-207.

293

Sandwall, A. ed., 1980. *Vendeltid*, Stockholm.

Schjødt, J.P. ed., 1994. *Myt og ritual i det førkristne Norden: et symposium*, Odense.

Sjöberg, M.B. ed., 1987. *Ölands järnåldersgravfält*, vol. 1, Stockholm.

Solli, B. 1998. 'Odin—the Queer? Om det skeive i norrøn mytologi', *Universitetets Oldsaksamling Årbok* (1997-98), 7-42.

Steinsland, G. *et al.*, eds, 1991. *Nordisk hedendom: et symposium*, Odense.

Straume, E. and Skar, E., eds, 1992. *Peregrinato Gothica III*, Oslo.

Ström, F. 1960. 'Fylgja', *Kulturhistoriskt lexikon för nordisk medeltid*, 5, 38-9.

Strömbäck, D. 1935. *Sejd: textstudier i nordisk religionshistoria*, Stockholm.

——1970. 'Sejd', *Kulturhistoriskt lexikon för nordisk medeltid,* 15, 76-9.

——1975. 'The concept of the soul in Nordic tradition', *Arv*, 31, 5-22.

Strömbäck, D. *et al.* 2000. *Sejd och andra studier i nordisk själsuppfattning*, Hedemora.

Svärdström, E. 1958. *Västergötlands runinskrifter 3:4. Sveriges runinskrifter V*, Stockholm.

Vitebsky, P. 1995. *The shaman*, London.

Westman, A. and Utsi, J.E. 1999. *Trumtiden: om samernas trummor och religion*, Stockholm.

294

Women in Viking-Age Scandinavia, or,

who were the 'shieldmaidens'?

Birgit Sawyer

I t has been generally supposed that in Viking-Age Scandinavia women had a higher status, greater freedom and fewer restraints on their activity than they had after the conversion to Christianity. This view was already current in the nineteenth century and was
closely related to the belief that the freedom and equality supposed to characterize Germanic
society survived longer in Scandinavia than elsewhere (see Jochens 1986, 36, n.4). Few
scholars still accept that interpretation of Germanic and Scandinavian society, yet belief in
free Nordic women has lasted better and continues to influence discussions of the period. It
is therefore necessary for modern students of women's history to consider how this idea
originated and on what basis.

Earlier discussions of the topic have made much use of twelfth- and thirteenth-century
literature, Icelandic sagas and the work of the Danish historian Saxo Grammaticus. Icelandic
authors who describe their pagan past let us meet many active, strong-willed, and often war-
like women, but such dominant women are conspicuously absent from the sagas written
about contemporary Iceland. In them the women are pale shadows of their predecessors;
passive, submissive, and completely subordinate to their husbands and kinsmen. The same
contrast between pagan and Christian women is found in the early major histories that cover
both periods, Saxo Grammaticus' *Gesta Danorum* and Snorre Sturlason's *Heimskringla*. The
conclusion has been that this contrast reflects real changes in women's conditions, mainly
as a consequence of Christianization. According to this view an early—pagan—ideal of
active and martial 'shield-maidens' was replaced by the passive and submissive 'madonna'
ideal favoured by the church.

Few, if any, modern scholars believe that women warriors led war bands in Viking-Age
Scandinavia; they have either been relegated to the world of amazon myths or explained in
other ways. Even so, the shieldmaidens still figure prominently both in popular beliefs and
scholarly discussions, and in this article I will address two questions: a) how are we to inter-
pet the descriptions of these war-like women in the past; and b) does the contrast between
active pagan and passive Christian women reflect real changes?

WHO WERE THE SHIELDMAIDENS?

Hitherto three kinds of answers have been presented: first that the shieldmaiden-motif
reflects pre-historic reality, secondly that it is influenced by Greek and Roman myths, and
thirdly that it expresses a pre-Christian woman-ideal.

In Icelandic literature stories about shieldmaidens are mainly found in the historically
unreliable *fornaldarsögur* (sagas about the heroic past), for example, about Hervor (in
Hervor's and Heidrek's Saga), the only child of the hero Angantyr, who fell in battle before
she was born. She took care of her father's sword (*Tyrfing*) and used it to take revenge on
his enemies. Other famous examples of war-like women are Brynhilde (in *Sigurd's Saga*)
and Freydís (in the *Saga of the Greenlanders*). Saxo Grammaticus also has many examples
of shieldmaidens and gives us a detailed description of them.

> There were once women in Denmark who dressed themselves to look like men and spent almost every
> minute cultivating soldiers' skills; they did not want the sinews of their valour to lose tautness and be
> infected by self-indulgence. Loathing a dainty style of living, they would harden body and mind with

toil and endurance, rejecting the fickle pliancy of girls and compelling their womanish spirits to act with a virile ruthlessness. They courted military celebrity so earnestly that *you would have guessed they had unsexed themselves*. Those especially who had forceful personalities or were tall and elegant embarked on this way of life. *As if they were forgetful of their true selves* they put toughness before allure, aimed at conflicts instead of kisses, tasted blood, not lips, sought the clash of arms rather than the arm's embrace, fitted to weapons *hands which should have been weaving*, desired not the couch but the kill, and those they could have appeased with looks they attacked with lances (Fisher 1979, 212; for Latin text see Saxo, 192; my italics).

It was not only the Icelanders and Saxo who wrote about such women; they are also found in earlier, foreign, sources; according to Adam of Bremen (who wrote his work about the archdiocese of Hamburg-Bremen in the 1070s) there was a region north of the Swedish lake Mälaren, the so-called 'Kvänland', populated by war-like women, and as late as the nineteenth century some historians, including Alexander Bugge and Johannes Steenstrup, maintained that such women had in fact existed in prehistoric Scandinavia.

Most modern scholars, however, do not believe this, and many explain the women warriors as a literary motif. According to some, the motif is a loan from antique traditions about the amazons (from Greek *a mazos* = without breast), women who are described as a distinct tribe in Anatolia. It was said that they cut off one of their breasts in order to be better archers, and for their survival as a tribe they were believed to couple with men from neighbouring tribes. Of the resulting children they kept only those boys that could be used for household tasks, while all girls were kept and educated in the art of warfare (Sobol 1972). The problem with this explanation, however, is that there are more differences than similarities In Scandinavian literature the female warriors are never described as a separate *tribe*; Saxo describes temporary war-bands, and in Icelandic literature we only meet single female warriors acting on their own. Another important difference is that Scandinavian shieldmaidens are characterized by their *chastity*.

According to more recent research, the descriptions of these women do reflect reality but not in such a direct way as was earlier believed. One suggested explanation is that they are based on misunderstandings by visiting foreigners who had seen temporarily man-less settlements, especially in Scandinavian coastal districts. Another suggestion, made by Carol Clover, is that the descriptions of the shieldmaidens are the literary expressions of a social reality, in which brother-less women were forced to take over the role of a son. She interprets the shieldmaidens as women who, for practical reasons, occasionally had to act like men, in taking revenge and paying or receiving wergeld (*manbót*). According to the Icelandic lawcode *Grágás* the 'ring-women', that is women who had no fathers, brothers or sons had to function like men—as long as they were unmarried. They could be seen as 'surrogate sons', and Clover explains the popularity of the motif as due to the fascination with transvestite traditions and the transgressions of sexual boundaries. Thus, according to Clover, this 'collective fantasy' tells us much about the underlying tensions of the society that produced it (Clover 1986a, 35-49).

Clover's interpretation is interesting and can explain a lot, but it does not explain why the motif remained so popular even long after the social reality had changed; most literary descriptions were written in the twelfth and thirteenth centuries when revenge and blood-feud had been forbidden and there were royal and ecclesiastical courts to regulate family conflicts. Nor does her interpretation explain the 'communities' of shieldmaidens in Saxo's work.

SHIELDMAIDEN AND MADONNA—TWO CONTRASTING IDEALS?

Whatever lies behind the descriptions of the female warriors in old Norse literature—reality and/or literary influences—we need to consider the widespread view that they express a pagan ideal of active and martial women, that was replaced by a Christian ideal of the passive and submissive 'madonna'. This view, which has greatly influenced modern women studies, is, however, highly questionable since it lacks support in other sources. Furthermore, the very concepts 'shieldmaiden' and 'madonna' create problems since they are not unequivocal, but are used by different scholars to denote different things. Sometimes the word 'shieldmaiden' is used only about female warriors, and sometimes in a figurative sense about *all* strong-willed and independent women. Further, the Church favoured not only one but *two contrasting ideals*, partly the *Virgin*, a Christian parallel to the strong, steadfast, and manlike woman ('virago'), and partly the *Wife/Mother*, the submissive and self-effacing woman, who subordinated herself to her husband and devoted her life to her children and family. Of these two, the Virgin ideal was most highly valued; in ecclesiastical literature it is the chaste woman—the widow as well as the virgin—who is honoured, but in profane literature the valuation is quite different (Strand 1980, 29-57).

We simply do not know what pre-Christian woman-ideal the Church replaced, but it is not very likely that the shieldmaiden was ever an ideal in pagan Scandinavia. Drawing their strength from chastity these female warriors were independent of men and thus uncontrollable, thereby constituting a threat to social order. I will return to the shieldmaiden-motif shortly, and now I shall concentrate on their equally strong and independent, but less warlike sisters in Viking-Age Scandinavia.

297

THE MEDIEVAL SOURCES

It is obvious that conversion to Christianity changed conditions for women as well as men, but it must be seriously doubted whether the effect of Christianity was so sudden and complete as the twelfth- and thirteenth-century authors make it appear. Instead of taking the contrasting depictions of dominant pagan and submissive Christian women at face value, we ought to ask ourselves what special purposes the authors intended with their descriptions of women. In the Middle Ages history writing was didactic, drawing useful lessons from the past. Therefore, when Saxo places almost all independent and active women in the pagan past, this serves his purpose of demonstrating that such female behaviour belongs to bygone, pagan, and thus imperfect times. It is clear that from this kind of history writing we cannot draw any conclusions about either contemporary or earlier reality. In the Icelandic sagas the descriptions of women are also subordinated to the special purposes and literary motifs of their authors. Here we often meet women as inciters, dangerous opponents and skilled in magic, and far from representing ideal women, they illustrate the ecclesiastical image of woman as a threat and danger to men. Both Saxo and his Icelandic colleagues were strongly influenced by Roman historians, and may well have used examples from Antiquity as well as from their own past as models for their descriptions of all the strong, courageous and manlike women.

Another consideration is the fact that a similar kind of contrast can be seen in English descriptions of women before and after the Norman Conquest of 1066. When describing women who had leading roles in public affairs, pre-conquest authors did not express any astonishment, while twelfth-century historians thought it was extraordinary. This change of attitude has been interpreted as a result of the actual shrinking of opportunities for women to play a political role as war and government left the home area to become genuinely public activities (Bandel 1955, 114). The fact that the contrasting attitudes in English literature before and after 1066 has nothing to do with the role of Christian influence should serve as a warning when dealing with attitudes in contemporary Scandinavian literature. Could the contrasting depictions that the Scandinavian authors give of past and contemporary women share a common origin with depictions from England? As far as *attitudes* are concerned, it is highly likely that Scandinavian authors were influenced by literary modes and conventions in other parts of contemporary Europe, but it is less likely that the contrast they presented between past and present actually reflects any shrinking of opportunities for women to take active part in public life. In twelfth-century Scandinavia the social and political developments were not yet that advanced; here war and government had not yet left 'the home area'.

CONTEMPORARY EVIDENCE

Since the literary sources from the twelfth and thirteenth centuries are so coloured by their authors' views and purposes, we will now turn to the contemporary evidence of archaeological remains, poetry, and the only written material we have from the Viking Age itself, i.e. the runic inscriptions (see further B. Sawyer, this volume).

The evidence of graves, from the third or fourth centuries to the tenth or eleventh, when pagan burial customs ended in most parts of Scandinavia, show that some women, especially older ones, were treated with great respect. In Denmark the quantity and quality of the furnishing in men's graves decreased with the age of the dead man, but some of the richest burials were of women who were 50 years old or more. This contrast shows that the elaborateness of a burial was not determined by the status of the dead person's family. What it does suggest is that respect for women increased with age and was perhaps earned by the experience gained during a long life. In other parts of Scandinavia also many of the richest burials were of women. The most lavishly furnished burial known in Sweden, at Tuna in Badelunda near Västerås, is of a woman who was buried in the fourth century with an abundance of gold and imported goods. One of the richest Norwegian graves, the ninth-century ship burial at Oseberg, was also of a woman. In Norway in this period it was women above all who were buried in large and richly furnished long-barrows (Farbregd 1988).

There are indications that some women in pre-Christian Scandinavia were highly regarded for religious reasons. Eddic poetry shows that in Nordic mythology knowledge of the past and the unknown, especially the future, was associated with female beings, as were the arts of writing, poetry and magic. The name given to this collection of poetry, *Edda*, may itself originally have meant 'great-grandmother'. If so, it underlines the role of women as transmitters of tradition, as do many of the poems (e.g. Steinsland 1985; Mundal and Steinsland 1989). In *Sigrdrifumál*, for example, when Sigurd asks the valkyrie Sigerdriva to teach him wisdom she does so by instructing him about victory runes, healing runes and runes to protect the unborn. The collection begins with *Völuspá* ('Völva's prophecy'). In it Völva, a sibyl, addresses Óðinn and describes creation, the golden age of the gods, and their corruption. In response to Óðinn's request for wisdom she prophesies *Ragnarök*, the destruction of the world of the old gods, and a new age with one powerful ruler, in which the innocent gods are resurrected and righteous men live for ever. The poem is clearly influenced by Christian ideas and its date (if it has one) is uncertain, but it is a vivid reminder of the close association of women with wisdom and prophesy.

According to Snorri the gods known as *Æsir* learned wisdom from the goddess Freyja, and it is even more significant that Óðinn is said to have done so by becoming *argr*. That word had extremely offensive implications and was used for men who took a passive, i.e. female role in homosexual relations. To accuse a man of being *argr* was a grave insult not so much because of the homosexuality, but because submission to another man implied submissiveness in other ways, cowardice and loss of honour; it amounted to declaring that a man was no longer a worthy member of society (Sørensen 1980, 24-39). It has been suggested that such insults were considered exceptionally serious in Iceland because, in the absence of a superior authority, social stability depended on the integrity of men.

The emphasis on masculine qualities is also reflected in heroic poetry and tales by the common theme of women who were not only beautiful and accomplished, but also warriors. Heroes had to overcome such women in their manly role in order to win and deserve them as partners; the proper destiny of 'shield-maidens' was marriage. Another aspect of this literature is that proud and confident women were especially attractive and highly valued as wives, not only because of the prestige of winning them but also because their sons could be expected to inherit the qualities of their mothers as well as their fathers (Mundal 1988, 24).

Once married, a woman was expected to assume a completely feminine role with her own well-defined responsibilities quite distinct from those of her husband. In Icelandic law her duties were entirely confined to the farm, where she had great authority, symbolised by the keys on her belt (for family, household, kinship and inheritance, see B. Sawyer, this volume). She could not represent the farm externally and was excluded from public life, but was involved in all family business. It was in her interest to see that the honour of the family was upheld, and the common theme in sagas about early Iceland of women urging their menfolk to take revenge probably had some basis in reality. In poetry revenge appears to have been above all the concern of women. Skalds who feared that their reputation had been damaged because they had not taken revenge as they should have done, turned to women. Most examples of skalds addressing women are in the family sagas. They are less common in the king's sagas and such poems are never in *drottkvætt*, the prestigious meter of court poetry. In general it was when a skald was most concerned about himself that he turned to a woman and spoke of his dreams and fears, or his wounds and impending death. The good opinion of women was valued. As Roberta Frank has put it,

299

> What, after all, was the point of the institutionalized male violence celebrated by the skalds, those excessive vendettas and duels, that piracy and harrying, if women were not watching you, constantly comparing you to little Alf the Stout or to Snorre Gore-Fang? (Frank 1990, 78)

Most of the literature so far mentioned was written in Iceland where conditions were in some respects very different from Scandinavia. The fact that the proportion of early medieval farms named after women was ten times greater in Iceland than in Norway may indicate that women had a higher status in the newly colonized land. It may also be significant that the most active volcanoes in Iceland all have female names (Frank 1973, 483). Archaeological evidence and runic inscriptions, however, suggest that women had much the same roles in other parts of Scandinavia as in Iceland and that at least some were highly regarded.

One way of showing concern for the honour and reputation of a family in the late tenth and eleventh centuries was to erect a rune-stone, and it is significant that almost a quarter of them were sponsored by widows. Few are as explicit as the stone from Norra Härene in Västergötland: 'Åsa honoured her husband in a way that henceforth no woman will ever do' (SR, Vg 59), but they all show family pride. One woman in Uppland erected a stone in memory of a kinsman and named his killer, apparently to keep the memory of this shameful act alive and perhaps even as an incitement to revenge. There is another inscription at Bällsta in Uppland in which a widow says that she has had a lament made for her husband. These can be compared with Icelandic laments in which widows mourn and sometimes demand revenge (Clover 1986b, 146). Carol Clover has drawn attention to other cultures with the custom of blood feud in which women had a leading role in commemorating the dead and maintaining feud. The fact that lamentation by women, often in poetic form, is a widespread feature of funeral rituals suggests that in Iceland women did so in real life as well as in literature (1986b, 180-3).

In marriage the sexes had well-defined, distinct roles, but widows and women who were unmarried or had no near male kinsmen were able, or forced, to assume some of the responsibilities that were normally men's. Some women were clearly highly regarded, whether as representatives of powerful families, or for their age and wisdom. There is no hint that women's abilities were doubted in the pagan period, and their association with wisdom and magic is notable. Their links with both nature and the supernatural were a source of power. Conversion to Christianity meant that many earlier beliefs and customs were condemned, and this gradually affected the attitude to women and their role in society. Christian authors regarded much magic as an evil to be eradicated with the result that they tended to depict women of the pagan past in the mould of Eve, the root of all evil.

WOMEN'S ROLE IN THE CHRISTIANIZATION PROCESS

There are, however, many indications that women were among the first and most eager converts; most of the early Christian graves at Birka were of women, and runic inscriptions show that the cult of Mary developed early in Sveland and was favoured by women. Further, most of the runic monuments commemorating men who were converted in their last days and 'died in white clothing' were erected by women (Sawyer 2000, 140). It is not surprising that women were especially attracted by the new faith; much Christian teaching must have been welcomed by them, a point obscured by the misogyny that colours so much medieval literature. They must have found the prospect of the Christian Paradise far more attractive than the gloomy realm of Hel to which they had previously been consigned. Many of them must also have been glad to believe that in the sight of God they were men's equals and that their worth did not depend on their fertility, family or social status; the community of Christians had room for all, including women who were barren or unmarried, as well as orphans and the poor. Christian teaching that all had an obligation to help those in need was especially welcome to women without near kinsfolk, for they had far more limited opportunities to support themselves than men in a similar situation. It may also be supposed that many mothers were gladdened by the attempts of the Church to prohibit, or at least severely restrict, the custom of infanticide, despite the increased burden that this must often have imposed.

It is no accident that one of the chapters in Rimbert's *Life of St Anskar* (VA) was devoted to the piety and steadfast devotion of Frideborg, a rich widow in Birka, and the care she took to ensure that her wealth would be distributed as alms in a suitable manner for the sake of her soul. She is said to have lived to a great age and always been a generous almsgiver. As death approached she enjoined her daughter Catla to distribute all that she possessed to the poor. According to Rimbert she said

> '...because there are here but few poor, at the first opportunity after my death, sell all that has not been given away and go with the money to Dorestad. There are there many churches, priests and clergy and a multitude of poor people. On your arival seek out faithful persons who may teach you how to distribute this, and give away everything as alms for the benefit of my soul' (VA 20).

Catla did so. Since there must have been many deserving poor in Birka and its neighbourhood, Frideborg insisted that Catla should go to Dorestad because she wanted the recipients to be Christians and the distribution to be under the guidance of clergy. She seems to have included among the poor the *pauperes Christi*, the servants of Christ who were vowed to poverty, and at the time of Frideborg's death there was only one priest in Birka. Another almost certain consideration was that Frideborg feared that, after her death, Catla would be vulnerable to pressure from relatives who did not share her enthusiasm for the new religion and were, more likely, hostile to it. By going abroad Catla could fulfil her mother's wish without interference.

It can safely be assumed that in Scandinavia, as in other parts of Europe, women were not only among the earliest converts but were also generous donors to the infant church and were also active in the work of evangelism, encouraging their husbands to convert and teaching the new faith to their children. A rune-stone at Enberga in Uppland, erected by two brothers in memory of their parents, implies that only their mother was Christian. It was erected in a pagan cemetery and the inscription reads ' Gisl and Ingemund, good drengs, had this monument made after Halvdan, their father and after Ödis their mother. May God now help *her* soul well' (SR Uppland 808).

All the prayers in the inscriptions are concerned with the soul of the dead and are based on the funeral liturgy of the western Church. The most common are 'May God help his/her soul/spirit' and 'May God and God's mother help his soul'. It is significant that Mary is never invoked as a virgin but always as a *mother*; this may have been due to the high esteem in which fertility had been held in pagan Scandinavia and facilitated the acceptance of the new faith. Britt-Marie Näsström has even suggested that Mary may have replaced the fertility goddess Freyja; many of Freyja's functions were taken over by Mary, in rites connected with childbirth, weddings and fertility of the soil (Näsström 1996, 335-48). In pagan Scandinavia women had played an important role in Fröja's cult, and it is plausible that Mary's popularity was especially great among female converts. Anne-Sofie Gräslund has pointed out a clear correlation between female sponsors and the use of the prayer to 'God and God's mother'; while 31% of the shorter 'May God help' inscriptions involve women as sponsors or deceased, women are represented in 47% of the 'God's-mother' inscriptions (Gräslund 1996, 327).

301

Conversion to Christianity meant many fundamental changes (see B. Sawyer, this volume), but the revolution was not complete. Some features of the old religion survived if in modified forms. This was partly because Scandinavian beliefs had long been influenced by Christianity. The Church condemned many rituals and practices but it had to accommodate some. The survival of magic in Christian form is well illustrated by the inscription on a Norwegian rune-stick: 'Mary gave birth to Christ, Elizabeth gave birth to John the Baptist, Be delivered in their names. Come out child. The Lord is calling you into light!' (Jacobsen 1984, 104-5). The female helpers of pagan times were replaced by Christian saints, above all by the Virgin Mary.

The 145 inscriptions that refer to bridge building confirm the leading role of women in the Christianization period. Missionaries taught that it was a meritorious act to build a bridge or causeway 'over deep waters and foul ways for the love of God'. A surprisingly large proportion of these 'bridge-inscriptions' were commissioned by, or erected in memory of, women (Sawyer 2000, 134-6). There is also one eleventh-century inscription commemorating a woman who planned to make a pilgrimage to Jerusalem (Sawyer 2000, 139-40). One Swedish inscription, sponsored by two daughters in memory of their father, reports that their father, Tore, had had a *seluhus* (soul-house) built after his wife Ingetora (SR Uppland 996: Karberga).

The inscriptions are predominantly Christian monuments, manifesting the acceptance of the new religion by the sponsors or the dead, and implying a willingness to give the missionaries active support. It is therefore significant that almost a quarter of all inscriptions involve women as property owners. Most of them were widows who could expect support from churchmen who urged them not to remarry, presumably in the hope that at least part of their property would be given to them as an endowment for their churches.

The runic inscriptions offer many examples of sole heiresses, and obviously their number increased during the eleventh century, partly because of women's higher longevity (see B. Sawyer, this volume), partly because, after the conversion, the exposure of children gradually ceased. Since female babies had run the greatest risk of being exposed (abandoned or just actively neglected), conversion resulted in an increased number of women in the population. Secondly, male mortality was very high in the early Middle Ages; apart from extremely high infant mortality, dangerous expeditions, feuds and warfare took a heavy toll. The life expectancy of women who survived their fertile period was especially favourable.

THE CONTRAST—A CONSTRUCT

Could it be concluded that in pagan Scandinavia women had a higher status, greater freedom and fewer restraints on their activity than after the conversion to Christianity? In our source material we mainly meet women from the upper stratum of society, so the answer is valid only for them, not the anonymous mass of women, who occupied less exalted positions. It is true that many pagan women had both freedom and many opportunities to act, to take responsibility, administer farms, inherit and dispose of property, *but so had their medieval successors*. The main difference seems to be the fact that after conversion women's reputation of wisdom was undermined and their magical skills were condemned. On the other hand, new opportunities for women's influence opened, e.g. as supporters of missionaries, builders of bridges, donors to the church and religious houses, and as abbesses.

The conclusion is thus that 'the strong Nordic woman' did *not* disappear after the conversion, even if they disappear in the literary sources dealing with Christian times. Why did the twelfth-century authors make them disappear?

A good starting point is to see what Saxo actually thinks about strong women. As far as the shieldmaidens are concerned he stresses how *unwomanly* they were, condemning their wish to defend their chastity with weapons. In living independently, not subordinating themselves to any man, they were presumptuously defying the order of Nature, and it is with ill-disguised satisfaction Saxo has them all defeated in the end, either in battle, or forced by male heroes to marry and become obedient wives and mothers. In his history things always turn out badly for women who want to maintain their independence. Life-long chastity is not considered a virtue; a woman's natural career is to be a wife and mother. Saxo also objects to the female inheritance rights, which guaranteed *unmarried* women a share of the family property. Apparently married women's property was not thought to be endangered as long as their husbands had control over it, and this is no doubt the implication of Saxos' propaganda for the subordination of women, a view that was supported by patristic arguments, proving that women were inferior to men in every respect. It should also be stressed that in Saxo's work contemporary chaste women, i.e. nuns, are conspicuous by their absence (as are indeed monks).

The Icelandic family sagas portray remarkably few unmarried women, and this has been explained as due to the weight the authors put on marriage and procreation (Frank 1973, 473-84). We actually only know about six Icelandic nuns altogether between *c.* 1000 and *c.* 1300; the first, Guðrun (in *Laxdœla saga*) had four husbands, a few lovers and children, and she did not become a nun until fairly late in life. Two other nuns are also said to have had husbands and children, and of the remaining three, two nuns actually lived in celibacy. The author follows up this information with anecdotes illustrating the fatal effects of such life-long chastity: one had problems with her eye-sight, and the other developed mental trouble. It is obvious that in Iceland chastity as such was not highly valued. To quote Roberta Frank, who has studied marriage in twelfth- and thirteenth-century Iceland,

> In the family sagas [...] one way to find out who is the villain is to locate the nearest bachelor, if you can find one. He is usually an outlaw, a thug, a poet, or worse [...]. When there are two unmarried protagonists in a saga, on the one hand the man who openly declares that he wants nothing to do with women will be the greater scoundrel. On the other hand, the bachelor who demonstrates his heterosexual interests—however crudely—is judged redeemable. To make a bachelor like Grettir more

respectable, the saga-author places him in a variety of amorous encounters—represented in most English translations of the saga by a series of blank spaces and dots (Frank 1973, 481).

The contempt with which the Icelanders regarded celibacy is reflected in their language: the Icelandic for bachelor (*einhleypingr*) means vagabond or scoundrel, and the term used for a spinster (*úgiptr*) also means 'one who has bad luck' (Frank 1973, 482).

Saxo and his Icelandic colleagues thus agree in their opposition to life-long chastity, and as far as women are concerned their message is simple and unambiguous: *a normal woman marries and is praiseworthy when she devotes herself to her husband.* Most ecclesiastical writings present a striking contrast; in them the ideal woman is the virgin—or widow—who, devoted only to God, withdraws from an active life and gives her property to the church. This contrast well illustrates the resistance that church still had to fight in thirteenth-century Scandinavia. The misogynistic propaganda of the day, so obvious in Saxo's *Gesta Danorum*, opaque but present in the Icelandic sagas, is, I suggest, an expression of the fear secular society must have felt for the consequences to which the economic politics and moral ideals of the church might lead. Such propaganda would not have been needed if women really were as weak, inferior and powerless as they are often said to be (Nordberg 1984, 118). Since misogynistic propaganda was obviously needed, we can conclude that women, by alienating family property to the church, were felt to constitute a real or potential threat to society.

303

As Christian writers, neither Saxo nor his Icelandic colleagues could criticize the ecclesiastical ideal of virginity openly. They had to express their disapproval in other ways. From holy virgins to pagan 'shield-maidens' may seem to be a large step, but in fact both groups shared the same basic intention, to abandon their traditional role and defend their independence, using chastity as their weapon. This is probably the reason Saxo and his Icelandic colleagues (perhaps inspired by classical traditions about Amazons) introduced female— chaste!—warriors into Scandinavian pagan history, and by criticizing their wilful strength and independence they were able to express opposition to their Christian counterparts. In doing so they created the myth of the Nordic 'shield-maiden' (Sawyer 1998).

CONCLUSION

The answers to the two questions presented in the introduction will thus be that whatever the real or literary background of the shieldmaiden motif is, these unwomanly female warriors served important purposes in twelfth- and thirteenth-century literature, illustrating the dangers with uncontrollable and independent women. The contrast between active pagan and passive Christian women was constructed by the medieval authors in order to teach their contemporaries that female activity belonged to bygone times and ought to be suppressed now that divine order had been established.

It is obvious that the high valuation of life-long chastity met with strong resistance in Scandinavia; the woman-ideal that was favoured—the wife and mother, subordinated to a man—was certainly not a novelty, introduced with the church, even if patristic teaching on women's inferiority could support and inspire authors like Saxo. A new economic reality had made a stricter control of women necessary; from the eleventh century onwards many more women reached adulthood, some of whom remained unmarried, and of those who married many survived their husbands and could as widows dispose of great properties. By means of legal rules and propaganda landowners tried to counter the threat posed by the inclination of single women to donate property to churches and religious houses.

If we are to use the concepts 'shieldmaiden' and 'madonna' at all, we can finally conclude that the woman-ideal that was honoured in pagan as well as in Christian Scandinavia cannot have been very different from the one still honoured, i.e. the wife and mother with features of the madonna in subordination and self-sacrifice, and with features of the shield-maiden in strength and perseverance!

ABBREVIATIONS

Saxo   Olrik, J. and Ræder, H., eds, 1932. *Saxonis Gesta Danorum*, vol. 1, Copenhagen.

SR   1911-. *Sveriges Runinskrifter*. Stockholm: Kungliga Vitterhets Historie och Antikvitetsakademien.

VA   Rimbert. 1961. *Vita Anskarii*, in W. Trillmich and R. Buchner, eds, *Jarhunderts zur Geschichte der hamburgischen Kirche und des Reiches*, Darmstadt, 1-133. [English translation by C. H. Robinson, 1921, *Anskar, the Apostle of the North*, London: Society for the Propagation of the Gospel in Foreign Parts].

BIBLIOGRAPHY

Andersen, R. *et al.*, eds, 1985. *Kvinnearbeid i Norden fra vikingtiden til reformasjonen; foredrag fra et nordisk kvinnehistorisk seminar i Bergen, augusti 1983*, Bergen.

Bandel, B. 'The English Chroniclers' Attitude toward Women', *Journal of the History of Ideas*, 16, 113-18.

Clover, C. 1986a. 'Maiden Warriors and Other Sons', *Journal of English and Germanic Philology*, 35-49.

——1986b. 'Hildigunnr's Lament', in Lindow *et al.* 1986, 141-83.

Farbregd, O. 1988. 'Kvinneliv i vikingtid; kven var kvinnene som ligg i langhaugar?', *Kvinner i arkeologi i Norge (K.A.N.)*, 3-23.

Fisher, P. ed., 1979. *Saxo Grammaticus History of the Danes*, vol. 1, Cambridge.

Frank, R. 1973. 'Marriage in Twelfth- and Thirteenth-Century Iceland', *Viator*, 4, 473-84.

——1990. 'Ornithology and the Interpretation of Skaldic Verse', *Saga-Book of the Viking Society*, 23, 81-3.

Gräslund, A-S. 1996. 'Kristnandet ur ett kvinnoperspektiv', in Nilsson 1996, 313-34.

Gunneng, H. *et al.*, eds, 1989. *Kvinnors Rosengård: föredrag från nordiska tvärvetenskapliga symposier i Århus aug. 1985 och Visby sept. 1987*, Stockholm.

Haug, K.E. and Mæhlum, B., eds, 1998. *Myter og humaniora*, Oslo.

Jacobsen, G. 1984. 'Pregnancy and Childbirth in the Medieval North: a Topology of Sources and a Preliminary Study', *Scandinavian Journal of History*, 9, 91-111.

Jochens, J. 1986. 'The Medieval Icelandic Heroine: Fact or Fiction?', *Viator*, 17, 35-50.

Lindow, J. *et al.*, eds, 1986. *Structure and Meaning in Old Norse Literature: New Approaches to Textual Analysis and Literary Criticism*, Odense.

Mundal, E. 1988. 'Forholdet mellom barn og foreldre i det norrøne kjeldematerialet', *Collegium Medievale*, 1988, 9-26.

Mundal, E. and Steinsland, G. 1989. 'Kvinner og medisinsk magi', in Gunneng *et al.* 1989, 97-121.

Näsström, B-M. 1996. 'Från Fröja till Maria: det förkristna arvet speglat i en folklig föreställningsvärld', in Nilsson 1996, 335-48.

Nilsson, B. ed., 1996. *Kristnandet i Sverige; gamla källor och nya perspektiv*, Uppsala.

Nordberg, M. 1984. *Den dynamiska medeltiden*, Stockholm.

Sawyer, B. 1998. 'Sköldmön och madonnan; om kyskhet som ett hot mot samhällsordningen', in Haug and Mæhlum 1998, 97-122.

——2000. *The Viking-Age Rune-stones: Custom and Commemoration in Early Medieval Scandinavia*, Oxford.

Sobol, D. 1972. *The Amazons of Greek Mythology*, New York.

Steinsland, G. 1985. 'Kvinner og kult i vikingetid', in Andersen *et al.* 1985, 31-42.

Strand (now Sawyer), B. 1980. *Kvinnor och män i Gesta Danorum*, Göteborg.

Sørensen, P. Meulengracht. 1980. *Norrønt nid*, Odense.

Christian Vikings In The North Atlantic Region

Christopher D. Morris

INTRODUCTION

W hat I presented to the Viking Millennium Conference in September 2000 represented a summary, précis or distillation of a number of communications, some
published, some (still) in press, about this very important aspect of the Viking and
Late Norse periods in the region of the North Atlantic Ocean. These other papers of mine
have inevitably gone into more detail than I can do here, and readers are referred to them for
the full critical scholarly apparatus of references, etc. (Morris 1990; 1996a; 1996b; 2001;
forthcoming; Morris and Brady with Johnson 1999). Nevertheless, I hope that, even if there
are few new ideas to report upon here, the synthesis will alert others to the importance in a
holistic view of the North Atlantic settlements, of the spiritual dimension of the lives of the
Norsemen here.

I start from a general base, concerned with the traditions of the Norse adoption of
Christianity in this region, and then focus down in more detail, upon the area formally under
the control of the Earl of Orkney, while being aware of the broader North Atlantic context.
I shall be looking briefly at some of the direct evidence from archaeology for the nature of
certain key sites in the 'Northern Isles' at this period, and the nature of parallels to them from
elsewhere in the wider region at this time. This leads logically on to both the issues of the
Norse farm-church, and of a group of possible Norse monastic sites, followed by some
reflection upon the move in the twelfth century to a more regularised parochial and hierarchical system.

TRADITIONS OF THE NORSE ADOPTION OF CHRISTIANITY IN THE NORTH ATLANTIC REGION
(see Morris forthcoming)

We begin with the importance of Birsay, the 'permanent residence' for the Norse Earls
of Orkney, and Brattahlíð in Greenland, the home to Eiríkr *rauði*, at the eastern and western
ends of the North Atlantic region within the history of the Norse expansion and settlement.
Both centres were associated with the leaders of their respective communities, and both are
associated with accounts in the sagas relating to the Norse adoption of Christianity

In *c.* 995 Ólafr Tryggvason appears to have had a key role in persuading Earl Sigurðr
to accept Christianity, and priests were also left in Orkney to 'instruct the people and to teach
them holy lore'(Anderson 1990, I, 509; Pálsson and Edwards 1978, 71). Within fifty years,
the subsequent Earl Þorfinnr had built Christ Church, 'a fine minster, the seat of the first
bishop of Orkney' in Birsay. We also hear from Adam of Bremen's *History* that 'it was
Þorfinnr's permanent achievement that Orkney became fully accepted in the Christian world
of European Christendom'(Tschan 1959, 179-81; fig. 1).

In Greenland, Leifr Eiríksson, apparently acted as a Christian emissary for King Ólafr
to Eiríkr, bringing with him a priest (or 'hurtful fellow' as his father unkindly described him)
shortly after that—probably in *c.* 1000 (contemporary with the traditional adoption of
Christianity by the Alþing of Iceland). And Þjóðhildr, his wife, built her own chapel in the
vicinity of Eiríkr's farmstead (fig. 2).

305

Figure 1. Aerial photograph of Birsay Bay, Orkney from SE with village in foreground and Brough of Birsay in background (photo: G. Moberg).

Whilst, in political terms, the Earldom of Orkney and the Eastern Settlement of Greenland were quite distinct and unconnected geo-polities, in religious terms it is manifestly the case that they both became part of a wider European Christian community across the North Atlantic region. In this, the emphasis would have been upon uniformity of ideology and practice, and within which spiritual and artistic influences, including that of the nature of church building, went from east to west. Greenland may have been at 'The World's End' and often an unpopular ecclesiastical 'posting' and elevation to the episcopate for a cleric, but it was most definitely a part of the mainstream medieval Christian European community. This community was under the See of Trondheim/Nidaros, which embraced the North Atlantic islands from Shetland in the east to Greenland in the west. Hvalsøy church, for instance, in which marriage-banns were read in 1408, could easily have been seen as Norwegian or Shetlandic in building-style, if divorced from its Greenland context.

Key Ecclesiastical Sites and their re-interpretation as Norse chapels
(see Morris 1990; 1996a; 1996b)

I have elsewhere (and at considerable length) attempted an initial re-assessment of the evidence for Norse Christianity in the 'Northern Isles' of Orkney and Shetland. In the process I hope I have demonstrated that previous associations of a number of well-known chapel-sites with the so-called 'Celtic Monastery' are no longer apposite, and instead I have proposed reinterpretation of them as Norse Christian chapels.

The key site here is the Brough of Deerness (fig. 3), traditionally seen as an Early Christian monastic site on a promontory site. Here, my excavations (Morris and Emery 1986) showed it had two major building-phases, both of which could be from the period of Scandinavian control.

This then raises questions about other well-known alleged pre-Norse chapel-sites such as the Brough of Birsay and St Ninian's Isle in Shetland. At Birsay, there has been a debate about the original location of the 'Christ Church' associated with Earl Þorfinnr in

Figure 2. Aerial photograph of Brattahlíð / Qagssiarssuk, Greenland from SE (photo: C.E. Batey).

Figure 3. Aerial photograph of the Brough of Deerness, Orkney, from the north (photo: J.D.H. Radford).

Orkneyinga saga (Pálsson and Edwards 1978, chapters 31-2). There are proponents for both the site of the current St Magnus Church in the village and for the chapel on the Brough of Birsay. Under the former, John Barber found the remains of an earlier building, probably twelfth-century in date (Barber 1996). At the latter, both the RCAHMS (1946, II, no. 1) and Dr Ralegh Radford have claimed the site of an earlier chapel from the pre-Viking period (Radford 1959; Cruden 1965).

At St Ninian's Isle, the stone chapel excavated by Professor Alan O'Dell has usually been related to that from the Brough of Birsay (Cant 1975). But there were also the remains of an earlier chapel, interpreted by both Professor Charles Thomas and Alan Small as pre-Viking (Small 1973; Thomas 1973; 1983). However, on the basis of analogy with Deerness and the evidence from the site of Norse activity (such as the presence of a hogback stone), I suggest it might well be seen as Viking or Late Norse in date.

The dating in all three cases has previously been presented by Dr Ralegh Radford in terms of a pre-Norse 'Celtic church' (i.e. Pictish) in the 'Northern Isles' (Radford 1962a; 1962b; 1983). However, there are good arguments now for a Christian Viking context before AD 1000. The Anglo-Saxon coin at the Brough of Deerness between the two major phases; the parallel here for the early chapel; the so-called 'Celtic enclosure' at the Brough of Birsay now proving to be enigmatic (if not fugitive!); the parallel at St Ninian's and the presence of a hogback stone, all point in this direction. This is not as impossible as it may seem; there is other material (not discussed here) also pointing in the same direction, e.g. Stevenson's analysis of a small group of the sculpture in Shetland (Stevenson 1981); and the general lack of pagan burials.

309

I have also now compared these sites with examples in the North Atlantic from Faroe, Iceland and Greenland and the period of Norse control there (e.g. Sandur church on Sandøy in the Faeroe Islands: Krogh 1975). There is of course a tradition of stone or turf churches in the North Atlantic region, and recent excavations in both Iceland and Greenland have demonstrated the existence of such in the Norse period e.g. Stöng (Vilhjalmsson 1996) and Brattahlíð (Krogh 1967; 1982). Also the remains of decorated wooden panels from Flatatunga and Bjarnastadalíð have been known for some time, and are quite evidently remains from chapels (Eldjarn 1953).

It would be straightforward enough to suggest that these relate to a post-995/1000 chronology, to fit in with our written accounts from the sagas etc. of the adoption of Christianity across the region. However, I consider it to be likely that we have been too obsessed with the AD 1000 date for the Scandinavian organisation of religious control. This would parallel, in my opinion, the way in which we have been too obsessed with the recorded dates of formal recognition of the Scandinavian organisation of *political* control in the North Atlantic islands. I have argued elsewhere for an 'informal' period of settlement in the Northern Isles preceding the formal recognition in the written sources (Morris 1985), and I would propose that it is the same with the religious organisation.

THE NORSE 'FARM-CHURCH' IN THE 'NORTHERN ISLES'
(see Morris forthcoming)

We can, in my opinion, expect Christian chapels well before AD 1000, especially in the context of the Norse equivalents of *eigenkirchen* or private chapels of chieftains, adjacent to their halls and farmsteads. Examples of major high status sites would be at the Brough of Birsay in Orkney; at Sandøy in Faeroe; at Stöng in Iceland; and at Brattahlíð in Greenland. In all cases, there is a clear relationship of chapel to farmstead i.e. effectively a chapel or *eigenkirch* of the landowner of the area.

The formal adoption in *c.* AD 995/1000 need, then, be no more than the official *de jure* recognition of a *de facto* situation with existing groups of Christians. It need not be the act of a missionary church in a hostile religious environment—and may then be marked by further chapel building (or re-building). Certainly, even apart from the Cathedral buildings, there could be quite impressive stone structures as we move on into the Late Norse/ later Medieval periods. The following are a few examples: Brattahlíð and a group of other Greenland Medieval churches (Krogh 1967; 1982); and Egilsay and Orphir in Orkney. Again, recent work has emphasised the wider contacts. In the case of Egilsay in Orkney, Eric Fernie has drawn attention to influences from Southern Denmark and Schleswig (Fernie 1988). In the case of the Orphir round church, also in Orkney, Ian Fisher has suggested parallels with other round churches in southern Scandinavia (Fisher 1993).

It is worth adding that, quite independently, very similar ideas are being brought forward now in Scandinavia by Professor Stefan Brink (forthcoming), emphasising the presence of early, small churches on farms in the tenth century, perhaps particularly associated with estates in the southern part of Scandinavia. Clearly both Brink and I, in our separate areas, are bringing forward perhaps heretical ideas in seeing the gradual adoption during the 'pagan' Viking Age of Christianity at the local private landowner level. This would be reflected in small chapels at a date significantly earlier than that indicated by the written sources for the adoption of Christianity at the higher political level.

310

THE SHETLAND CHAPEL-SITES PROJECT
(see Morris and Brady with Johnson 1999; Morris 2001)

This outline is at least a hypothesis now to explore, and the Viking and Early Settlement Archaeological Research Project (VESARP) intend in the next phase of research to explore the concept of Norse Christianity in the eastern North Atlantic region. This will be through a programme initially of fieldwork and then followed by selective excavation. In some areas, of Northern Britain, practically nothing has been undertaken on chapel-sites and buildings since the pioneering work of Sir Henry Dryden in the 1860s and 1870s and that of other contributors to the overall survey of ecclesiastical sites in the 1890s by MacGibbon and Ross. The programme has begun, initially, in the northern isles of Shetland but we intend, in the future, to extend our survey-project from here to the northern mainland of Scotland (in Caithness and Sutherland), as well as to the *Suðreyjar* or Hebrides (hopefully perhaps in Lewis/Harris).

There are many of these small chapels and chapel-sites—literally hundreds in Orkney and Shetland (although often modest in character)—most of which do not appear in documentary sources (fig. 4). Although in Shetland many sites are obvious in terms of upstanding ruins, many others are not. So, there is a good basis for further work in the Island of Unst, where we have carried out follow-up survey work on twenty-five known sites (Morris and Brady 1998; Brady and Johnson 1998; Brady and Johnson 2000). However, in the adjacent islands of Fetlar and Yell we have had to undertake very basic documentary research to identify potential sites before even venturing out onto the ground (Brady 1998; Brady 2000a). In Fetlar, up to nineteen sites were identified from various sources to be investigated; and in Yell it was perhaps thirty-one sites (figs 5 and 6). We completed 'audit surveys' of these sites in 1999 and 2000 (Brady and Morris 2000; Brady 2000b).

As well as identifying these on the ground, we shall be following up some of the previous work undertaken by historians on issues such as the relationship of these sites to land-units known as 'scattalds' in these islands (Smith 1984). It also has to be added that in areas such as these islands, there are very strong folk-traditions, which are of considerable assistance. On Unst, for instance, Dr Christopher Lowe in the 1980s was able to follow up the

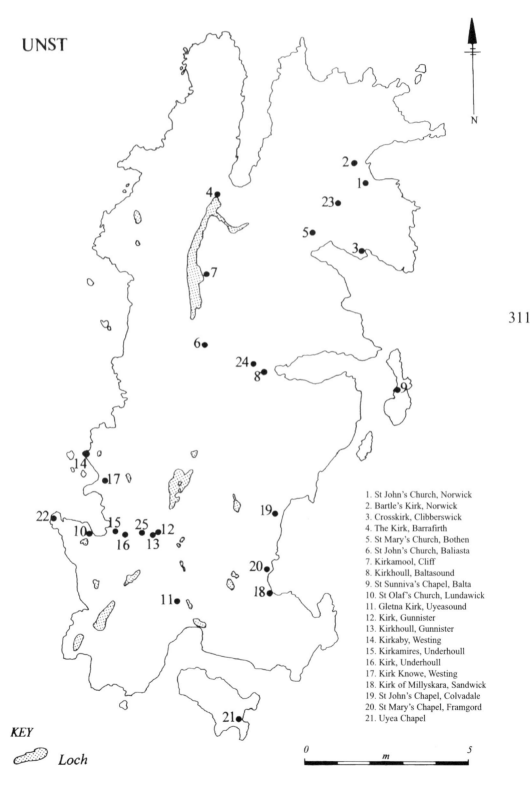

UNST

N

311

1. St John's Church, Norwick
2. Bartle's Kirk, Norwick
3. Crosskirk, Clibberswick
4. The Kirk, Barrafirth
5. St Mary's Church, Bothen
6. St John's Church, Baliasta
7. Kirkamool, Cliff
8. Kirkhoull, Baltasound
9. St Sunniva's Chapel, Balta
10. St Olaf's Church, Lundawick
11. Gletna Kirk, Uyeasound
12. Kirk, Gunnister
13. Kirkhoull, Gunnister
14. Kirkaby, Westing
15. Kirkamires, Underhoull
16. Kirk, Underhoull
17. Kirk Knowe, Westing
18. Kirk of Millyskara, Sandwick
19. St John's Chapel, Colvadale
20. St Mary's Chapel, Framgord
21. Uyea Chapel

KEY

Loch

0   *m*   5

Figure 4. Overall map of chapel sites, Unst, Shetland. 22. Blue Mull and 23. Papil: other sites identified as having potentially ecclesiastical associations. 24. Kirkton and 25. Crosbister: potentially promising place-names on the Ordinance Survey map.

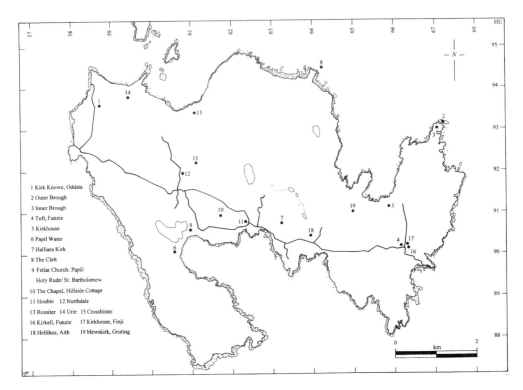

1 Kirk Knowe, Oddsta
2 Outer Brough
3 Inner Brough
4 Toft, Funzie
5 Kirkhouse
6 Papil Water
7 Halliara Kirk
8 The Clett
9 Fetlar Church: Papil/
   Holy Rude/ St. Bartholomew
10 The Chapel, Hillside Cottage
11 Houbie 12 Northdale
13 Rossiter 14 Urie 15 Crossbister
16 Kirkell, Funzie   17 Kirkhouse, Finji
18 Hellihus, Aith   19 Mewskirk, Gruting

Figure 5. Overall map of chapel sites, Fetlar, Shetland.

work of Mrs Jessie Saxby from earlier this century identifying traditional sites of old chapels (Lowe 1988; Saxby 1905). There is also an interesting relationship between the scattalds in Fetlar and social obligations in relation to burials—as elucidated by Dr Margaret Mackay (1987). Further, Dr Doreen Waugh is currently investigating the place-name heritage of these areas (Waugh 2001): already in addition to the obvious Kirkja names, she has identified in the documents a 'Binnas' on Unst, presumably a 'prayer-house' or *Boen-hus* which is known elsewhere in the North Atlantic (e.g. in Leirvik, Eysturøy, Faeroe). Such evidence can give pointers to the earlier existence of an archaeological site.

Further, there is the issue of the relationship of these chapels to earlier foci such as brochs, explored to some degree by Drs Lamb, Lowe and Thomson (e.g. Lowe's demonstration of sites at Marykirk and Grimeston, Harray; Lyking and Stackbrue: Lowe typescript). Excavations at St Boniface, Papa Westray by Lowe has examined this further (Lowe 1998). Our surveys have turned up a number of such possible sites (e.g. Vollister, Yell; Kirkaby, Unst).

Another question relates to the relationship of the chapel-sites to the Papa- type names. The known presence of a 'Papil' name (i.e. *Papa-byli* = 'buildings of the priests') on each of the three northerly Shetland Islands is itself of considerable interest. It is a linguistic relic of the church structure that the Scandinavians encountered on their arrival here, i.e. as names given by the Norsemen of the peoples they came into contact with (Lamb 1995). Of relevance here is the changing interpretation of such names from an eremitic model to an economic one, i.e. in the 'Northern Isles' at least, names representative of a previous system of organisation of landed estates under/for the Church. They have been described as 'A power to be reckoned with' on the arrival of the Vikings (Lamb 1993; 1995). It is not without significance that at the most southerly Papil church/site in Shetland, on Burra, there was distinctive high quality sculpture, which seems to have been copied, perhaps in the Viking period, at a site on Bressay. In Orkney, there is, then, the St Findan story to support the concept

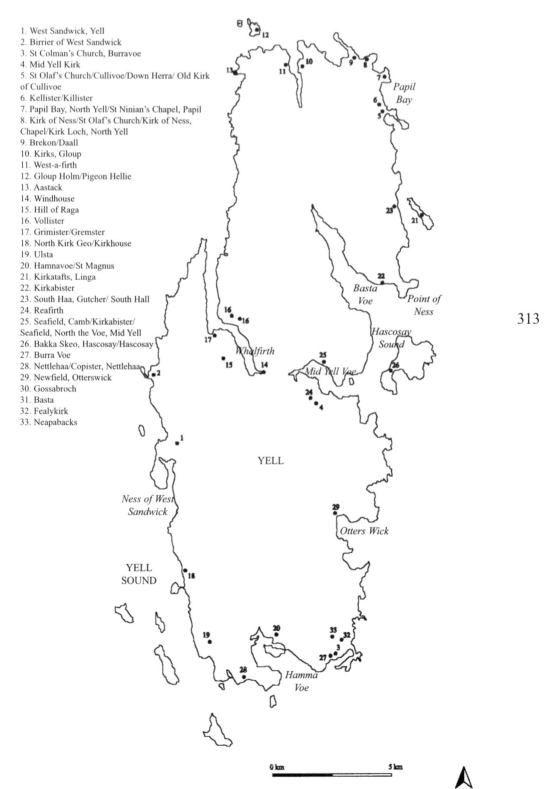

1. West Sandwick, Yell
2. Birrier of West Sandwick
3. St Colman's Church, Burravoe
4. Mid Yell Kirk
5. St Olaf's Church/Cullivoe/Down Herra/ Old Kirk of Cullivoe
6. Kellister/Killister
7. Papil Bay, North Yell/St Ninian's Chapel, Papil
8. Kirk of Ness/St Olaf's Church/Kirk of Ness, Chapel/Kirk Loch, North Yell
9. Brekon/Daall
10. Kirks, Gloup
11. West-a-firth
12. Gloup Holm/Pigeon Hellie
13. Aastack
14. Windhouse
15. Hill of Raga
16. Vollister
17. Grimister/Gremster
18. North Kirk Geo/Kirkhouse
19. Ulsta
20. Hamnavoe/St Magnus
21. Kirkatafts, Linga
22. Kirkabister
23. South Haa, Gutcher/ South Hall
24. Reafirth
25. Seafield, Camb/Kirkabister/ Seafield, North the Voe, Mid Yell
26. Bakka Skeo, Hascosay/Hascosay
27. Burra Voe
28. Nettlehaa/Copister, Nettlehaa
29. Newfield, Otterswick
30. Gossabroch
31. Basta
32. Fealykirk
33. Neapabacks

313

Figure 6. Overall map of chapel sites, Yell, Shetland (T. Simpson). Although there has been some literary/historical tradition for Sites 30 Gossabroch and 31 Basta, extensive local survey has revealed no archaeological evidence. The two positions given for Site 16 are due to some confusion over the grid reference for this site.

of continuity of ecclesiastical institutions into the Viking period (including even a bishop), which further implies perhaps a degree of co-existence of pagan and Christian (Thomson 1986).

Finally, in this regard, we can also chart the development of certain forms of distinctive stone sculpture or graveyard furniture. There is the St Ninian's hogback, for instance; the presumably related (although similar and smaller) monuments known as 'Keelstanes' from Framgord and Baliasta; and the cross-heads of distinctive form from e.g. Uyea Island; Framgord, Norwick and Lundawick, Unst; and West Sandwick and Kirkhouse, Yell.

Of course, this work needs to be put in a broader context, and it also needs to be seen in the broader North Atlantic context. So it will be vital to link this with similar evidence in other areas of the North Atlantic (i.e. Faroe, Iceland and Greenland) and to exchange information with, if not collaborate with, colleagues in these other islands. This would be a project hopefully both in the spirit of, and under the aegis of, the North Atlantic Biocultural Organisation (NABO).

'NORSE MONASTIC SITES'

A sideline in this study concerns a particular group of sites, first identified by Dr R. G. Lamb in the early 1970s as Norse monastic sites (Lamb 1973), as against popular identification of them as pre-Norse chapels. In recent years it has been part of the VESARP project to record these sites alongside chapel-sites in the northern three islands in the Shetland archipelago. Sites such as Blue Mull, Unst; Strandibrough, Fetlar; and the Birrier of West Sandwick, Yell are sites which fall into this category—not to mention even more inaccessible sites such as Aastack, Yell and the Clett, Fetlar (see reports cited above).

Also, in 2000, a small-scale survey and excavation project was mounted by VESARP under the direction of Kevin Brady on the top of another site, this time off the coast of Papa Stour (Brady 2000c). Again, nearby, there is another site, of even more difficult access: Maiden Stack. In brief, the work demonstrated that there was a sub-surface reality to the features identified on the surface during surveying, but also that there was evidence of structures, both roughly rectangular in form and also of earlier ones, more cellular in form. Although the excavation was simply based upon trial-trenches, a greater complexity of structural form was encountered than had been expected. Dating evidence has yet to be properly examined and the results assimilated, but there appears to have been both Viking/Late Norse and earlier Iron-Age pottery, in addition to other material.

THE MOVE TO A PAROCHIAL AND HIERARCHICAL SYSTEM IN THE TWELFTH CENTURY

The map produced by Dr Ronald Cant of major ecclesiastical sites in Medieval Shetland (fig. 7) shows a significant diminution of the numbers of chapel-sites with the changeover to an all-embracing parochial system, i.e. there were now just three parishes in each of Yell and Unst, and only one on Fetlar. Undoubtedly, some of these parish churches were simply some of the farm-churches upgraded. But, also, some were built *de novo* on other sites. Either way, the net result is the abandonment of *most* Norse chapel-sites. The twelfth century onwards sees the period of assertion or re-assertion by the clerical authorities, at the expense of the landowners. Further, in addition, we get the erection of grand *cathedrals*— and here we are back to comparisons between Birsay and Brattahlíð. In Orkney, the bishopric was moved to Kirkwall and a major Romanesque cathedral dedicated to St Magnus and built in the twelfth century (Crawford 1988). Similarly in Greenland, the focus shifted

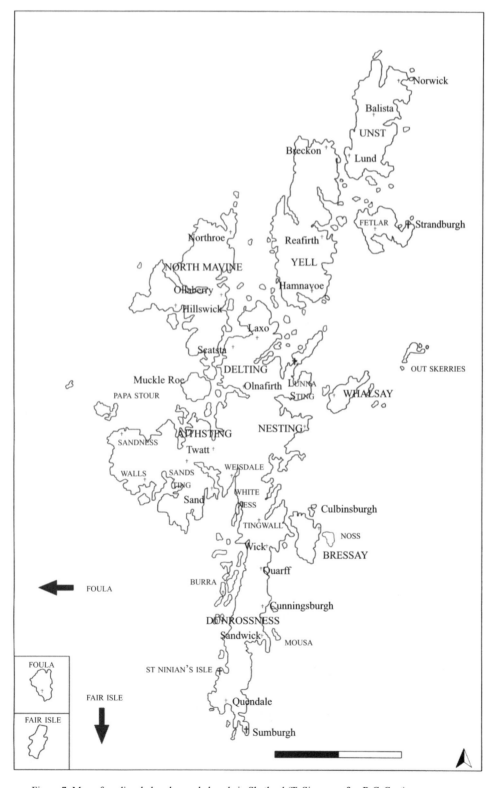

Figure 7. Map of medieval churches and chapels in Shetland (T. Simpson after R.G. Cant).

✝ other major foundations   † head (parish) churches.

from Brattahlíð to Garðar, where a complex of episcopal buildings was erected, in addition to a cathedral (Nørlund 1936).

CONCLUSION: THE WIDER PERSPECTIVE

Ultimately, the lives of all those who lived in the North Atlantic region between the eleventh and the fifteenth centuries were radically affected by the power, spiritual, social and economic, of the Church. At first, the Church acquired converts and then status through the good offices of the ruler(s) concerned, and would often be looking to them to provide the material manifestation of Christianity through the building or re-building of private chapels on their lands or of those of their major followers. Later, though, as the Church's power and influence grew, as the formal ecclesiastical structure began to emerge, then these private benefactors and their successors were essentially pushed to one side, as firstly a new parochial system, and then the full hierarchy above it was put into place.

It seems to me no coincidence, then, that both at Birsay and at Brattahlíð homes of arguably some of the earliest and most important of the Christian Vikings, the influence of the hierarchy was gravely affected by a shift in focus to a physically separate site. The secular power was now to be metaphorically in the shadow of a greater, if not higher, power! The bishop at Garðar had enormous storage barns and byres—far larger than any such buildings found at Brattahlíð. As for Birsay, it became so unimportant following the move of the bishopric to Kirkwall, that in time people referred to 'The back o' Birsay', i.e. one step on from 'the back of beyond' (see Morris 1989, 15)!

316

ABBREVIATION

RCAHMS   Royal Commission on the Ancient and Historical Monuments of Scotland, 1946. *Twelfth report with an Inventory of the Ancient Monuments of Orkney and Shetland*, 3 vols, Edinburgh.

BIBLIOGRAPHY

Adams, J. and Holman, K., eds, forthcoming. *Scandinavians and Europe 800-1530*, Turnhout.

Anderson, A. O. ed. and trans., 1990 [1922]. *Early Sources of Scottish History AD 500-1286*, 2 vols, Edinburgh 1922 [Stamford 1990].

Barber, J. W. *et al.* 1996. 'Excavations at St Magnus' Kirk, Birsay', in Morris 1996c, 11-31.

Batey, C.E., Jesch, J. and Morris, C.D., eds, 1993. *The Viking Age in Caithness, Orkney and the North Atlantic*, Edinburgh.

Berry, R.J. and Firth, H.N., eds, 1986. *The People of Orkney*, Kirkwall.

Brady, K.J. 1998. *Fetlar Chapel Survey. Desk-top Assessment 1998* (GUARD 636), Glasgow.

——2000a. *Yell Chapel-Sites Survey. Desk-Top Assessment 1999* (GUARD 733), Glasgow.

——2000b. *Yell Chapel-sites Survey 1999-2000*, Glasgow.

——2000c. *Brei Holm Survey and Excavations, Papa Stour, Shetland*, Glasgow.

Brady, K.J. and Johnson, P.G.1998. *Unst Chapel Survey 1998* (GUARD 515.3), Glasgow.

——2000. *Unst Chapel-Sites Survey 1999* (GUARD 515.4), Glasgow.

Brady, K.J. and Morris, C.D. 2000. *Fetlar Chapel-Sites Survey* (GUARD 636.2), Glasgow.

Brink, S. forthcoming. 'Some new perspectives on the Christianisation of Scandinavia and the organisation of the early Church', in Adams and Holman, forthcoming.

Cant, R.G. 1975. *The Medieval Churches & Chapels of Shetland*, Lerwick.

Crawford, B.E. ed., 1984. *Essays in Shetland History. Heiðursrit to T M Y Manson*, Lerwick.

——ed., 1988. *St Magnus Cathedral and Orkney's Twelfth Century Renaissance*, Aberdeen.

——ed., 1995. *Northern Isles Connections. Essays from Orkney and Shetland presented to Per Sveaas Andersen*, Kirkwall.

——ed., 1996. *Scotland in Dark Age Britain.* Aberdeen: St John's Papers 6 St Andrews.

Cruden, S.H. 1965. 'Excavations at Birsay, Orkney', in Small 1965, 22-31.

Eldjarn, K. 1953. 'Carved Panels from Flatatunga, Iceland', *Acta Archaeologia*, 24, 81-101.

Fellows-Jensen, G. ed., 2001. *Denmark and Scotland: the cultural and environmental resources of small nations.* Copenhagen: Historisk-filosofiske Meddelelser 82.

Fernie, E. 1988. 'The Church of St Magnus, Egilsay', in Crawford 1988, 140-61.

Fisher, I. 1993. 'Orphir Church in its South Scandinavian Context', in Batey *et al.* 1993, 260-71.

Krøger, J.F. and Naley, H-R., eds, 1996. *Nordsjøen. Handel, religion og politikk. Karmøyseminaret 1994 og 1995*, Stavanger.

Krogh, K.J. 1967. *Viking Greenland*, Copenhagen.

——1975. 'Seks Kirkjur Heima a Sandi', *Mondul*, 12, 21-54.

——1982. *Erik den Rødes Grønland / Qallunaatsiaaqarfik Grønland*, Copenhagen.

Lamb. R.G. 1973. 'Coastal Settlements of the North', *Scottish Archaeological Forum*, 5, 88-93.

——1993. 'Carolingian Orkney and its Transformation', in Batey *et al.* 1993, 260-71.

——1995. 'Papil, Picts and Papar', in Crawford 1995, 9-27.

Lowe, C.E. 1988. Early Ecclesiastical Sites in the Northern Isles and Isle of Man: An Archaeological Field Survey, 2 vols. Unpublished PhD thesis, University of Durham.

——1998. *St Boniface Church, Orkney. Coastal erosion and archaeology*, Stroud and Edinburgh.

——typescript. 'The Early Historic Church Sites of the Northern Isles and Isle of Man: Problems of Identification, chronology and interpretation'(paper presented to Shetland conference in 1989).

Macafee, C. and Macleod, I., eds, 1987. *The Nuttis Schell: essays in the Scots Language*, Aberdeen.

MacKay, M. 1987. '*The Sib and the Fremd*, Country Life in the Dictionaries', in Macafee and Macleod 1987, 211-18.

Morris, C.D. 1985. 'Viking Orkney: A Survey', in Renfrew 1985, 210-42.

——1989. *The Birsay Bay Project. Volume 1. Brough Road Excavations 1976-1982*, Durham.

——1990. *Church and Monastery in the Far North. An Archaeological Evaluation. Jarrow:* Jarrow Lecture 1989.

——1996a. 'From Birsay to Tintagel: A Personal View', in Crawford 1996, 37-78.

——1996b. 'Church and Monastery in Orkney and Shetland: An Archaeological Perspective', in Krøger and Naley 1996,185-206.

——1996c. *The Birsay Bay Project Volume 2. Sites in Birsay Village and on the Brough of Birsay*, Durham.

——2001. 'Norse Settlement in Shetland: the Shetland chapel-sites project', in Fellows-Jensen 2001, 58-78.

——forthcoming. 'From Birsay to Brattahlíð. Recent perspectives on Norse Christianity in Orkney, Shetland and the North Atlantic region', in Adams and Holman forthcoming.

Morris, C.D. and Brady, K.J. 1998. *Unst Chapel Survey 1998* (GUARD 515.3), Glasgow.

Morris, C.D. and Brady, K.J. with Johnson, P.G. 1999. 'The Shetland Chapel-sites Project 1997-98', *Church Archaeology*, 2, 25-33.

Morris, C.D. with Emery, N. 1986. 'Excavation of a chapel and churchyard on the Brough of Deerness, Orkney 1975-77', *Proceedings of the Society of Antiquaries of Scotland*, 116, 301-74, microfiche sheets 2-4.

Nørlund, P. 1936. *Norse Ruins at Garðar, the Episcopal seat of Medieval Greenland, Meddelelser om Grønland*, 76 part 1.

O'Connor, A. and Clarke, D.V., eds, 1983. *From the Stone Age to the 'Forty-Five': Studies presented to R.B.K. Stevenson*, Edinburgh.

Pálsson, H and Edwards, P., trans, 1978. *Orkneyinga Saga: The History of the Earls of Orkney*, London.

Radford, C.A.R. 1959. *The Early Christian and Norse Settlements at Birsay*, Edinburgh.

——1962a. 'The Celtic monastery in Britain', *Archaeologia Cambrensis*, 111, 1-24.

——1962b. 'Art and architecture: Celtic and Norse', in Wainwright 1962, 163-87.

317

——1983. 'Birsay and the spread of Christianity to the North', *Orkney Heritage*, 2, 13-35.

Renfrew, A.C. ed., 1985. *The Prehistory of Orkney BC 4000-1000 AD*, Edinburgh.

Saxby, J.M.E. 1905. 'Sacred Sites in a Shetland Isle', *The Antiquary*, XLI (1905), 133-8 (also published in *Saga Book of the Viking Society for Northern Research*, IV (1904-5), 24-35).

Small, A. ed., 1965. *The Fourth Viking Congress, York, August 1961*. Edinburgh and London: Aberdeen University Studies 149.

——1973. 'The site: its history and excavation', in Small, Thomas and Wilson *et al.* 1973, 1-7.

Small, A., Thomas, A.C. and Wilson, D.M. *et al.*, eds, 1973. *St Ninian's Isle and its Treasure*, 2 vols. Oxford: Aberdeen University Studies 152.

Smith, B. 1984. 'What is a Scattald? Rural Communities in Shetland, 1400-1900', in Crawford 1984, 99-124.

Stevenson, R.B.K. 1981. 'Christian sculpture in Norse Shetland', *Fróðskaparrit*, 28, 283-92.

Thomas, A.C. 1973. 'Sculptured Stones and Crosses from St Ninian's Isle and Papil', in Small *et al.* 1973, 8-44.

——1983. 'The Double Shrine "A" from St Ninian's Isle, Shetland', in O'Connor and Clarke 1983, 285-92.

Thomson, W.P.L. 1986. 'Introductory Note to Appendix B. St Findan and the Pictish-Norse Transition', in Berry and Firth 1986, 279-87.

Tschan, F. J. trans., 1959. *Adam of Bremen, History of the Archbishops of Hamburg-Bremen*. New York: Records of Civilisation Sources and Studies 53.

Vilhjálmsson, V.Ö. 1996. 'Gård og kirke på Stöng i Þjórsádalur. Reflectioner på den tidligste kirkeordning og kirkeret på Island', in Krøger and Naley 1996, 119-39.

Waugh, D.J. 2001. '*Fae da nort tae da suddart*: Norse settlement in Shetland with special reference to Unst and Old Scatness', in Fellows-Jensen 2001, 47-57.

Wainwright, F.T. ed., 1962. *The Northern Isles*, Edinburgh and London.

Vínland or Vinland?

Magnús Stefánsson

THE PROBLEM

A thousand years ago, Icelandic and Greenlandic seafarers came to the New World. The saga tradition, as recorded in *Eiríks saga rauða* (ESR), says that the country was called Vínland: 'There were fields of wild wheat growing there, and vines, and among the trees there were maples'(ESR 211, 415; Magnusson and Pálsson 1965, 86).

The search for traces of Norse settlement led the late Norwegian explorer Helge Ingstad to L'Anse aux Meadows (LAM) on the far northern tip of Newfoundland. In the years 1961-68 he prepared and directed seven archaeological seasons there. His wife, the late Anne Stine Ingstad, led the excavations undertaken by an international team of experts. The excavations showed that the sites were authentically Norse. Radiocarbon analyses gave a mean date of around AD 1000 or even older (Ingstad 1996, 256; see Wallace, this volume).

LAM, however, lies in a subarctic area where neither wild wheat nor vines grow. Ingstad cited a neglected Swedish theory, maintaining that the mention of vines and grapes was due to an etymological misunderstanding, first propounded by Adam of Bremen. The place-name should be spelt *Vinland*, in which *vin* with a short i referred to 'natural meadow, pasture'. The name had nothing to do with wine or vines—Old Norse *vín*, with a long í (Söderberg 1910).

The name Vínland became controversial.

Did tradition confuse the two name forms *Vínland* and *Vinland*? What characteristics of the new land were the ancients familiar with, and what was most valuable to them? I shall examine the names philologically, historically and according to Norse naming practice.

TRADITIONS OF THE PROMISED LAND

In his history of the Archbishopric of Hamburg-Bremen, written in the 1070s, Adam of Bremen mentions

> Insulam...in...oceano, quae dicitur Winland, eo quod ibi vites sponte nascantur, vinum optimum ferrentes
> [An island...in that ocean...called Vínland [Winland] because vines producing excellent wine grow wild there] (Schmeidler 1917, 275; Tschan 1959, 219).

Adam makes it clear that this is not based on 'fabulous reports' but comes from a trustworthy Danish King. What he goes on to say, however, makes the account problematic:

> Post quam insulam, ait, terra non invenitur habitabilis in illo oceano, sed omnia, quae ultra sunt, glacie intolerabili ac calgine immensa plena sunt
> [Beyond that island, the King said, no habitable land is found in that ocean, but every place beyond it is full of impenetrable ice and intense darkness] (Schmeidler 1917, 275; Tschan 1959, 219).

According to Adam, Vínland is therefore a mythical paradise on the margin of the habitable world, beyond which lie ice and darkness (fig. 1).

But Adam is in no way trustworthy and is in fact an unusable source with regard to geographical knowledge. Recent studies show that he envisaged Vínland to be placed at the outlet of the river Dvina into the White Sea (Jackson 1992). He is nonetheless relevant because the authors of *Grœnlendinga saga* (GLS) and ESR, collectively termed the 'the Vínland

Sagas', knew Adam's work when referring to vines growing wild (Jóhannesson 1956, 127; 1974, 103). Ari the Learned also knew Adam's work when he wrote his *Íslendingabók* (The Book of the Icelanders), in the 1120s (Ellehøj 1965, 66, 78). All we can say is that rumours of the discovery of Vínland had reached Adam's ears (Jóhannesson 1956, 127; 1974, 103).

Adam here falls into an etymological misunderstanding. He could hardly have known the Norse word vin, 'natural meadow, pasture'. Instead, he must have understood the first syllable of the name as derived from the Latin *vinum*, 'wine', which gives the Norse form vín in Vínland. I claim that the confusion of the two Norse words vin and vín was understandable, since the difference between Old Norse i and í concerned the length, not the quality, of the vowel. The short i in vin was pronounced [vin] as in English 'think', whereas the long vowel í in vín [vi:n] was pronounced as in English 'feel'. Both were close, tense monophthongs. Later, the short Norse i developed into a lax monophthong [I], lowered to become a sound between [i] and [e], rather like the i in English 'sit'. Norse í, on the other hand, remained a close, tense monophthong (Benediktsson 1959; 1962). In Modern Icelandic the í in Vínland is only halflong [] (Blöndal 1920-24, 947). If this was the case in Old Norse as well, it might perhaps have facilitated the confusion of the two sounds in more or less careless pronunciation.

320

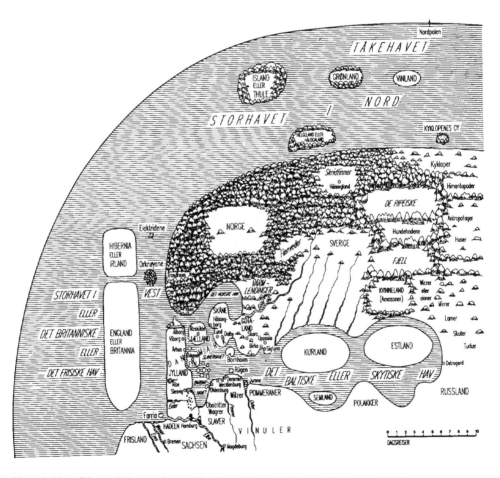

Figure 1. Map of the world in accordance with Adam of Bremen's *History* (after Ingstad 1960).

Ari the Learned mentions Vinland without explaining the reason for the name (ÍF 1, 13; Hermannsson 1930, 64). He also mentions *skrælingar*, and knew Vinland to have been inhabited by the same kind of people who were supposed to have lived in Greenland, that is the paleo-Dorset. The settlers in Vinland discovered artefacts of the same kind as found in Greenland (ÍF 1, 13-14; Hermannsson 1930, 64). Ari's statement is important because there is no reason to doubt its validity. He was in a very good position to obtain reliable information on the early explorations. Ari's uncle had himself been to Greenland where he gathered information on the settlements in the west (Jóhannesson 1956, 127-28; 1974, 103).

In 1996, the late Erik Lönnroth published an article, entitled 'The Vinland Problem' (Lönnroth 1996). He pointed out that in Adam's days there was a tenth-century account of a paradisal island, *Navigatio Brendani*, translated into vernacular languages such as Low German and Norse (*Navigatio Brendani* 53ff). It does not mention grapes—just grape-like fruits in such quantities that the trees were borne down by the burden. Lönnroth wondered whether Adam's island could simply be a 'vulgarization' of this myth.

Such descriptions probably go back to ancient notions of a promised land, or an island kingdom in the west or northwest, like Atlantis. They were known in learned circles throughout Europe including Iceland. Among these is Isidore's description of the 'Fortunate isles', where the ridges are covered with wild vines and cereals and vegetables growing like grass (*Etymologiarum* 6, 8 in Dahlerup 1889).

321

GLS was contemporary with but composed independently of ESR, and both narratives differ. Leifr Eiríksson and his men go ashore on an island where there was 'dew on the grass, and the first thing they did was to get some of it on their hands and put it to their lips, and to them it was the sweetest thing they had ever tasted' (GLS 250). Matthías Þórðarson, the editor of GLS in Íslenzk fornrit in 1935, made an almost prophetic comment in light of later archaeological knowledge. He suggested that the dew-rich island could have been Belle Isle north of Newfoundland: 'This hints that they had now come to Vínland' (GLS 250, n. 4). When Leifr and his men sailed into a sound between the island and a headland jutting northwards, Þórðarson comments that they could have sailed through the Strait of Belle Isle, 'north of the northernmost promontory of Newfoundland' (GLS 250, ns 5-6). And LAM lies on this northernmost tip of Newfoundland! Leifr named all the places *eptir landkostum*, 'after the natural resources of the land'. Is it reasonable that they named the land after wine, which was not wine, but dew?

The accounts of vines and grapes come later in the narrative of GLS. They are legendary, revealing a fundamental ignorance of vines and grapes, as for instance the tale of filling their tow-boat with vines and grapes before returning to Greenland and the tale of Leifr's foster-father, Tyrkir, returning in high spirits (*mjök skapgott*) after having been missing for a while. He had found vines and eaten grapes, first speaking for a long time in German, rolling his eyes in all directions and pulling faces, and no one could understand what he was saying. After a while he spoke in Norse (GLS 252-253). This episode may remind us of the narrative in *Navigatio Brendani*, the last of the Greek vine-god Dyonysos, who found vines and ate grapes when strolling around. They were filled with the sweetest wine and put him into high spirits.

The northern limit for wild North American grapes lies between the 44th and 45th parallel (fig. 2), and the following species grow wild in North America (Arnfinn Skogen, pers. comm.). The *Riparia*-grapes are both small (6-12 mm) and quite sour, with the northern limit of its growth running from Quebec to Ontario to northeastern New Brunswick. The *Æstivalis*-grapes are also small (5-10 mm) and quite sour. Their northern limit is Ontario. The two species of grapes big enough and sweet enough to be 'nutritionally interesting' are the *Rotundifolia*-grapes (10-25 mm), known as 'muscadine grapes', and the *Labrusca*-grapes, one of the two 'fox grapes'. Both have southern Maine as their northern limit (Gleason 1952; Svensson 1961; Heiser 1973; Adams 1985).

It has been asserted that the name *Vinland* cannot be correct as it should have been *Vinjarland* or *Vinjaland*, depending on whether the reference is to a singular or a plural genitive of vin. Let me remind the reader of the name Markland, the Norse seafarers' name for Labrador, and the only existing stem-compound with *mörk*. In Iceland there are at least twelve names derived from the noun mörk, the best known being *Markarfljót* (Rangárvallasýsla) and *Breiðamerkursandur* (Austur-Skaftafellssýsla), and they invariably have a flexional ending between the elements. The others are:

Merkurbœir (Rangárvallasýsla)
Merkurengjar (Rangárvallasýsla)
Merkurengjar (Rangárvallasýsla)
Merkurheiði (Vestur-Skaftafellssýsla)
Merkurhraun (Árnessýsla)
Merkurjökull (Rangárvallasýsla)
Merkurnes (Rangárvallasýsla)
Merkurrani (Rangárvallasýsla)
Merkursel (Rangárvallasýsla, Þórsmörk)
Merkurvöllur (Kjósarsýsla) (Landið þitt. Ísland, Lykilbók 1985, 162).

322

But the name in question is Markland, not Markarland or Merkurland. If we refuse Vinland, we have to explain Markland.

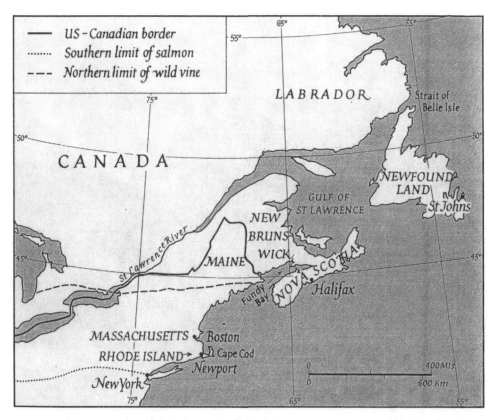

Figure 2. Map of Eastern North America, demonstrating the southern limit of salmon and northern limit of wild grape vines (after Wahlgren 1986).

However, most recently the Norwegian place-name scholar Frode Korslund has point-ed out seven and perhaps as many as 19 Norwegian stem-compounds with *vin* (Korslund 2001, 33-39) including:

Vinangr (Sør-Trøndelag)
Vináss (Vestfold, Telemark, Nord-Trøndelag twice; probably also Oppland; Buskerud twice; Telemark twice; Møre and Romsdal, three times)
Vinhólar (Oppland)
Vinvangir (Nord-Trøndelag)

Other *vin* names probably include *Vinhóll* (Hedmark) and *Viney* (Sogn and Fjordane). Furthermore a poetic name for Sjælland, Zealand in Denmark, is *Viney*, Vin-island, a paral-lel to Vinland (Egilsson and Jónsson 1931, 618; *Norrøn ordbok* 502). Compounds could be made in different ways, and is a warning against one-sided linguistic postulates. Korslund has also maintained that, as far as he knows, names were *not* given after man-made products like food/victuals or beverage/drinks, which could also be used in trade/commerce. This is for instance true for *öl*, beer, *mjöðr*, mead, *brauð*, bread. The quite exceptional place-name *Vínland*, named after *vín*, would break with this apparent rule. On the other hand, place-names were named after constructions like *hús*, house, *hof*, pagan temple, *skáli*, dwelling house or a house containing a large hall for festive use, *borg*, fortification, *brú*, bridge, and others. The same is true for laudatory names like *smjör*, butter, and names used for compar-ison such as *spjót*, spear, *hjalt*, hilt of a sword, *hjálmr*, helmet, *skjöldr*, shield, and so on.

323

FUNCTIONAL NAMEGIVING

The Vínland Sagas again and again emphasize that the Norsemen gave names to places *eptir landkostum*, 'according to the natural resources of the land'. A name like *Vínland* would be strictly opposite to functional namegiving, as wine was a foreign element in the drink culture of Icelanders and Greenlanders.

The sagas agree in saying that Icelandic and Greenlandic seafarers discovered three lands on the east coast of North America. First, according to GLS, they came to a land with-out grass: 'The hinterland was covered with great glaciers, and between the glaciers and the shore the land was like one great slab of rock. It seemed to them a worthless country, [*gæðalaust*]. They therefore called the country *Helluland*, literally "Slab-land".' (GLS 249). Scholars agree that this must have been Baffin Island.

South of *Helluland*, the seafarers after two days reached a land which was 'flat and wooded, with white sandy beaches wherever they went; and the land sloped gently down to the sea.' They therefore called the country *Markland*, literally 'Forest-land', after its natural recources, *af kostum* (GLS 250). Scholars are likewise in agreement that this must have been Labrador.

From *Markland* to *Vinland* it was *two days' sail* with a northeast wind. The seafarers named the land *eptir landkostum* (GLS 253).

THE ICELANDIC 'SKÁLHOLT MAPS'

Let us now consider two early maps mentioning Vinland and pointing to Newfoundland. The so-called 'Skálholt Map' was produced around 1590 at Skálholt in Iceland. The original has disappeared, but two copies exist, the older from 1669 (fig. 3).

Figure 3 shows 'Helleland', 'Markland', and 'Promontorium Winlandiæ', the Vinland promontory. The adjacent mainland is called 'Skrælinge Land', after the name given by the Norsemen to the natives of North America. The map says:

Hic proxime est Vinlandia quam propter terræ fæcúnditatem et utilum rerúm ube rem proventúm Bonam dixere.
[*Closest lies Vinland*, which on account of the fertility of the soil and other useful things is called Vinland the Good (my emphasis); Hogg 1989, 22ff.]

It was precisely good soil, *landkostir*, which was most important to the Norsemen.

Figure 4 is the younger 'Skálholt Map'. This map may have been drawn by Þórður Þorláksson, a master at Copenhagen University and Bishop of Skálholt 1674-1697, during his stay in 1669 on the island of Karmøy, Norway, with the Icelander Thormod Torfæus (Þormóður Torfason), a former Royal antiquary. It was first published in Torfæus' work, *Historia rerum Norvegicarum* (1695-1715). Here 'Promontorium Vinlandiæ' has been given a slightly different shape. On this map, the Norwegian historian and philologist Gustav Storm suggests: 'one must identify Vinland with Newfoundland, Markland with Labrador, and Helluland with the southernmost parts of Baffin Island' (1888, 32). Yet Storm claimed that 'this is impossible'. He thought that Vinland should be located a little south of Cape Breton in Nova Scotia.

324

Figure 3. The 1669 version of the 'Skálholt Map' (after Hogg 1989).

A medieval *Itinerary*, a booklet on geography, tells: 'South of Greenland is Helluland, then comes Markland, then it is *not far* to Vinland the Good' (*eigi langt til Vinlandz ens goda*: AM 194 8vo; Halldórsson 1978, 79; *Alfræði Íslenzk* 12; my emphasis). This description is attributed to Abbot Nikulás Bergþórsson of Munkaþverá, who died in 1159 (*Alfræði Íslenzk* 23).

Is it reasonable to interpret the name of the promontory of Vinland, not as adjacent to the 'Skrælingeland' of the hinterland, but as the referring to southern Maine, 1000 kilometres or 600 miles away? Or as a gateway to the whole region of the Gulf of St Lawrence? The grapes in northeastern New Brunswick are, however, the small and quite sour *Riparia*-grapes. Is it reasonable to believe that these grapes were interesting enough to become the source of the namegiving? In that case, the name *Vínland* would not have been given before the Norsemen had reached the southern outskirts of this supposed *Vinland* region, 800 kilometres or 500 miles away. Furthermore, it would also mean that place-names were derived from a man-made product, wine. Indeed nothing indicates that the Norse people at that time

325

Figure 4. The younger, 1706 engraving of the 'Skálholt Map' (after Hogg 1989).

knew the art of wine-making. Indeed, permission was asked of the pope to use beer in the communion instead of mass-wine. If they had known the art of wine-making, they would certainly have used that technique to make mass-wine of crowberries or blueberries. It is not likely that people in Iceland and Greenland knew how to make wine before the Greenland bishop Jón taught people in Iceland how to make wine from crowberries around 1200; he had learned the art from King Sverrir (*Páls saga biskups*, Ch. 9; ÍF 16, 311). This art of wine-making was obviously considered so important that it was mentioned in several Icelandic annals (*Islandske Annaler* 23, 62, 122, 181, 254, 324). The use of wine was rare also in Norway. On festive occasions it would scarcely have been consumed anywhere except at royal and episcopal courts, perhaps not before the thirteenth century, and in aristocratic circles not until the late Middle Ages. The exception to this rule appears to have been Bergen, where wine was no more expensive than home-brewed beer (KLNM 20, cols. 73ff).

The words which I have italicized above also point to Vinland as lying *not far* from Helluland and Markland. Furthermore we have no information of Leifr and his men leaving the Vinland area. Indeed GLS says:

> When they had finished building their houses, Leifr said to his companions, 'Now I want to divide our company into two parties and have the country explored; half of the company are to remain here at the houses while the other half go exploring— but they must not go so far that they cannot return the same evening, and they are not to become separated' (GLS 251-52).

Is it reasonable to assume that Leifr did not give a name to the land where they had come ashore and built their houses and wintered? The other two names, Helluland and Markland, would have been given where they came ashore. Of course the whole area where the Norsemen travelled *might* have *gradually* come to be known as *Vinland*, meaning pasture-land. Indeed the houses built by Leifr and his men were called *Leifsbúðir*, and *búðir* was primarily used for temporary dwellings. Most likely the houses were a base or a camp for further travels as several scholars have assumed (e.g. Haugen 1981; see Wallace, this volume). Helge Ingstad claims that the Norse site at LAM can hardly be anything but Leifsbúðir in Vinland (Ingstad 1996, 186). I am convinced that he must be right.

GLS narrates the measuring by Leifr and his men of the length of the day at winter solstice: 'The days and nights were much more equal in length than in either Greenland or Iceland. In the depth of winter the sun was aloft by midmorning and still visible at midafternoon' (GLS 251). Most recently the scholar Páll Bergþórsson has been able to show that this refers to the approximate latitude of LAM at 50 degrees 30 minutes (1997).

All these indications most naturally point to Newfoundland as being Vinland.

Rather ironically professor Erik Lönnroth in a recent study, *The Vinland Problem: on the discovery of America* (1998), asks why the Norsemen for some incomprehensible reason sailed all the way to Maine, penetrated the forests, and discovered vines which made them so enthusiastic that it overshadowed all other impressions! Yet the *verifiably* visited Newfoundland was left without a name! A land all ships in the area had to pass (fig. 5)! Can this fit northeastern New Brunswick as well?

On the other hand the name *Vinland* as a name for Newfoundland, derived from the Norse word *vin*, 'natural grassland', would agree with Norse settlement culture and name-giving. A passage in GLS indeed confirms this interpretation:

> The quality of the land (*landkostr*) seemed to them so good that no winter fodder would be needed for livestock; there was never any frost during the winter and the grass hardly withered at all (GLS 251).

The Swedish professor Valter Jansson states that *vin* occurs as the *first* element of compound names in both Norway and Sweden. He moreover speculates that *vin*-names *may* have existed as nature-names in Iceland and the Faroes, but later disappeared, presumably when the appellative *vin* died out in Norway. On the age of the *vin*-names, Jansson concludes: 'On these grounds I believe that the oldest vin-names are probably no earlier than from around the birth of Christ ... The youngest place-names ending in *-vin* are probably about a thousand years younger' (Jansson 1951, 29ff, 43ff, 391, 415, 423). The Norwegian philologist Magnus Olsen draws attention to a number of *vin*-names from historical times in West Norway (Olsen 1926, 170).

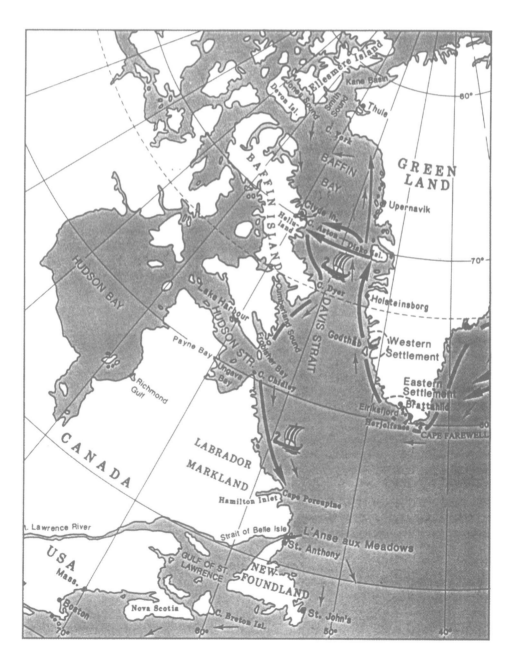

327

Figure 5. The Eastern Arctic region (after Dahls 1993).

Conclusion

For the time being, we should stick to what actually has been discovered archaeologically, and interpret it in terms of what we know about the culture and way of life of the Norsemen.

It is risky to draw conclusions from the saga accounts of vines and grapes. The descriptions are too similar to the narratives of fabulous countries in the western ocean given by classical and medieval authors. The sagas never mention winemaking. Drinking wine was extremely rare. People drank beer. Wine is never mentioned in the main texts of the Vínland Sagas, and only once in the Icelandic family sagas as a whole, in connection with Norway in *Egils saga* (ÍF 2, 42). It is mentioned twice in *Prestsaga Guðmundar góða* and *Þórðar saga kakala* in connection with Iceland and in both cases as an import (*Sturlunga saga* I, 136; II, 84).

The confusion of *vin* and *vín* led to the interweaving of the two traditions, orally and in the *Vínland sagas*. On the one hand, the tradition of rich grasslands important for settlers accustomed to animal husbandry, and opportunities for hunting and fishing: Newfoundland was a land which fitted Norse cultural patterns perfectly, and this gives the name *Vinland*. On the other hand, the anachronistic traditions about a mythical paradise with grapes and wine, with entertainment value for people who told stories or read them aloud to brighten their drab existence. The fables caught on and were later perceived as the true explanation for the name in question. This gives the name *Vínland*, a poetic and mythical saga-name.

In the Vinland discussion, narratives of vines, grapes and wild corn have played a major role, even after Anne Stine and Helge Ingstad discovered the Norse house foundations at LAM. I believe that the confusion of *vín* and *vin* can be explained linguistically, and in terms of functional namegiving. Using *vín*, wine, to name a place would neither have been functional, according to the natural resources of the country (*eptir landkostum*), nor would it have been in accordance with Old-Norse namegiving. In addition comes the influence from Adam of Bremen's work and the fact that around 1200, when the two *Vínland sagas* were written, the word *vin* had fallen out of use a long time previously.

Viewing the situation as a whole, the most important fact must be that Norse houses have actually been discovered in North America. The site at LAM is internationally recognized as Norse, the one and only authenticated Norse ruins dating from the time of the Vinland voyages.

Abbreviations

Alfræði Íslenzk	Anon. 1908. *Alfræði Íslenzk* I, Copenhagen.
ÍF 1	Benediktsson, J. 1968. *Íslendingabók-Landnámabók*. Reykjavík: Íslenzk fornrit 1.
ÍF 2	Nordal, S. 1933. *Egils saga Skalla-Grímssonar*. Reykjavík: Íslenzk fornrit 2.
ÍF 16	Egilsdóttir, Á. 2002. *Biskupa sögur* II, *Páls saga biskups*. Reykjavík: Íslenzk fornrit 16.
Islandske Annaler	Storm, G. ed., 1888. *Islandske Annaler*. Christiania: Det norske historiske Kildeskriftfond.
KLNM VII	Benediktsson, H. 1962. 'Islandsk språk', *Kulturhistorisk Leksikon for nordisk middelalder* (KLNM) VII, cols 486-493.
KLNM XX	Molland, E. 1976. 'Vin I', *Kulturhistorisk Leksikon for nordisk middelalder* (KLNM) 20, cols 73-75.
Navigatio Brendani	Selmer, C. ed., 1959. *Navigatio Sancti Brendani abbatis*, Notre Dame, Indiana.
Sturlunga saga	Anon. 1946. *Sturlunga saga* I-II. Reykjavík: Sturlunguútgáfan.

BIBLIOGRAPHY

Adams, L.D. 1985. *The Wines of America*, New York.

Benediktsson, H. 1959. 'The Vowel System of Icelandic: A Survey of its History', *Word*, 15, 282-312.

Bergþórsson, P. 1997. *Vínlandsgátan*, Reykjavík.

Blöndal, S. 1920-24. *Íslensk-Dönsk Orðabók/Islandsk-Dansk Ordbog*, Reykjavík.

Dahlerup, V. 1889. *Physiologus i to islendske bearbejdelser*. Copenhagen: Aarbøger for nordisk Oldkyndighed og Historie.

Dahls, T. 1993. *Adam av Bremen*, Oslo.

Egilsson, S. and Jónsson, F. 1931. Lexicon Poeticum, 2nd edition, Copenhagen.

Ellehøj, S. 1965. *Den Ældste Norrøne Historieskrivning*, Copenhagen.

Gleason, H.A. 1952. *The New Britten and Brown Illustrated Flora of the Northeastern United States and Adjacent Canada*, vol. 2, New York.

Halldórsson, Ó. 1978. *Grænland í miðaldaritum*, Reykjavík.

Haugen, E. 1981. 'Was Vinland in Newfoundland?', *Proceedings of the Eighth Viking Congress*, 3-8.

Heggstad, L., Hødnebø, F. and Simensen, E. 1975. *Norrøn Ordbok: Gamalnorsk Ordbok*, Oslo.

Heiser, C.B. 1973. *Seeds to Civilization: The Story of Man's Food*, San Francisco.

Hermannsson, H. ed. and trans., 1930. *The Book of the Icelanders*, Ithaca, London, Oxford.

Hogg, P.C. 1989. 'The prototype of the Stefánsson and Resen charts', *Historisk Tidsskrift*, 68, 1, 3-27.

Ingstad, H. 1960. *Landet under leidar-stjernen: en ferd til Grænlands norrøne bygder*, Oslo.

—1996. *Oppdagelsen av det nye land*, Oslo.

Jackson, T.N. 1992. 'Location of Bjarmaland, Suomen Varhaishistoria', *Tomittaja Kyösti Julku*, 122-130.

Jansson, V. 1951. *Nordiska vin-namn*, Uppsala and Copenhagen.

Jóhannesson, J. 1956. *Íslendinga saga,* I, Reykjavík.

——1974. *A History of the Old Icelandic Commonwealth:* Íslendinga saga, trans. H. Bessason. Winnipeg: University of Manitoba Icelandic Studies, 2.

Korslund, F. 2001. 'Vinland, "Beitelandet"', *Maal og Minne*, 33-39.

Jósephsson, Þ. and Steindórsson, S., eds, 1985. *Landið þitt. Ísland, Lykilbók*, Reykjavík.

Lönnroth, E. 1996. 'The Vinland problem', *Scandinavian Journal of History*, 21, 39-47.

——1998. 'Problemet Vinland. Om upptäkten av Amerika', *Tidens flykt*, 109-23 (Stockholm).

Magnusson, M. and Pálsson, H., trans, 1965. *The Vinland sagas: The Norse Discovery of America,* Harmondsworth.

Olsen, M. 1926. *Ættegård og helligdom*, Oslo.

Schmeidler, B. ed., 1917. *Magistri Adami Bremensis Gesta Hamburgensis Ecclesiae Pontificum*, Hannover and Leipzig.

Söderberg, S. 1910.'Professor Sven Söderberg om Vinland', *Sydsvenska Dagbladet Snällposten*, 295, 30.

Storm, G. 1888. *Studier over Vinlandsreiserne, Vinlands Geografi og Ethnografi*, Copenhagen.

Svensson, H. 1961. *Vin og brennevin*, Oslo.

Thormod Torfæus. 1695-1715. *Historia rerum Norvegicarum*, Hafniæ.

Tschan, F.J. ed., 1959. *Adam of Bremen, History of the Archbishops of Hamburg-Bremen*, New York.

Wahlgren, E. 1986. *The Vikings and America*, London.

329

Arguments Against the *Vinland* Hypothesis

Alan Crozier

The *Vinland* hypothesis is the claim that the name *Vinland* originally had nothing to do with Old Norse *vín* 'wine' but instead derives from a rare word with a short vowel, *vin*, meaning 'pasture' or 'meadow', recorded in writing only once, in the conservative language of the old Norwegian law of *Gulathing* (Cleasby and Vigfusson 1957). The asterisk in *Vinland* indicates that the form is not actually attested in any text; it is conjectured or reconstructed. The hypothesis was first propounded in 1898 in a lecture by Sven Söderberg, Professor of Scandinavian Languages at Lund University, who never published it in any scholarly forum; the lecture was printed in the local newspaper in 1910, nine years after his death. Since then, to my knowledge, no scholar working in the field of Old Norse philology has endorsed the hypothesis, mainly because there is no evidence that the word *vin* 'pasture' was still in use at the time Norsemen settled Iceland or Greenland. The hypothesis has nevertheless been revived from time to time, but never by linguists. It has been argued by a geographer (Tanner 1941), by an archaeologist (Meldgaard 1961), and most forcefully by Helge Ingstad (1985, 307-313), who discovered the Norse site at L'Anse aux Meadows (LAM) in Newfoundland. Of the linguistic authorities cited by Ingstad in support of his claim, Magnus Olsen (1926, 164-173) argues that the word *vin* may have survived in Iceland, although it was not used to name any places. Olsen's point is that some Norwegian names with this element may be later than is generally assumed; he says nothing at all about *Vinland*. Valter Jansson (1951, 105-106), author of the definitive study of Nordic place-names with *vin*, merely includes a dutiful reference to Söderberg's hypothesis as a possibility. Numerous scholars—not just linguists—have rejected the whole hypothesis (e.g., Magnusson and Pálsson 1965, 58, n. 1; Jones 1986, 123-4; Wahlgren 1986, 141; Holm 1997; Durand 2000, 30).

It is easy to understand the renewed attraction of the *Vinland* hypothesis, since a name meaning *'Pastureland'* would no doubt have been more appropriate for the climate and topography of northern Newfoundland. For Ingstad, the obvious absence of vines around LAM, and the lack at that time of any material evidence to show that the Norsemen had sailed south to more temperate climes, must have made the hypothesis seem like a neat way to eliminate the missing link between Newfoundland and the parts of North America where grapes do in fact grow wild. However, it is founded on a mere assumption: that the site at LAM is the place that gave rise to the name *Vinland*.

Because of Ingstad's great influence, the *Vinland* hypothesis is now often presented in popular works as if it were an undisputed fact (e.g., *The Viking* 1975, 116), and it has recently been put forward again independently by two distinguished historians, Erik Lönnroth (1996) and Magnús Stefánsson (1998). It was the publication of their articles in the respected *Scandinavian Journal of History* that provoked me to enter the debate and publish a detailed reply to the historians' arguments (Crozier 1998).

My ambition to put an end to the *Vinland* hypothesis once and for all is probably fruitless, because it is unlikely that the issue will ever be proved one way or the other, on account of our lack of conclusive evidence. Söderberg knew that the word *vin* 'pasture' does not occur in the historical literature from Iceland, but he believed that the word could have survived without being recorded in any of our sources (1910). In contrast, many scholars believe that the Norsemen did discover some place in North America where grapes grew wild, and that it received the name *Vinland* 'Wineland' for that reason, and I think that there is good enough justification for that belief despite the lack of concrete physical evidence. In other words, both sides of the debate rely in some measure on the old axiom, 'Absence of evidence is not evidence of absence.' It is my purpose here to examine the arguments on both sides in the light of this axiom. I shall begin with the **Vinland* hypothesis.

Here, however, I must immediately qualify the axiom. Absence of evidence may not be *proof* of absence, but it can be *evidence*. If we consider that we have a large corpus of Old Icelandic literature and a representative body of early Icelandic place-names, then the absence of a single example of **vin* 'pasture' is a fairly strong argument that the word was extinct. However, it must be admitted that there is always a possibility that it did survive unrecorded. Yet even if it did, this is not enough on its own to corroborate the **Vinland* hypothesis, since more links are required in the chain. We have to assume that the word was also used to name a place discovered in North America. Let us be generous and admit that this too is possible. Perhaps, as Söderberg and Tanner suggested, the word referred to a kind of grassland that did not exist in Iceland or Greenland, but when the Norsemen came across this grassland in America, they remembered the old word that had been used for it back in Scandinavia. Sigurdur Thorarinsson (1942, 44) calls this 'armchair reasoning' (*skrivbords-resonemang*).

Then we have another problem for which the hypothesis has to provide an answer: how did the unrecorded **Vinland* change into the form *Vínland* that we find in the Icelandic sagas, where it is associated with grapes, not grassland? Söderberg's answer to this was to ascribe the change of the name to Adam of Bremen, who wrote his history of the archbishops of Hamburg-Bremen around 1075. The German historian certainly did have a penchant for fanciful etymologies, and it is possible that if he heard the opaque name **Vinland* he could have interpreted it as *Vínland*—even though his own German had a similar distinction between long and short *i*—and was thus prompted to invent the vines and the wine. If this is the case, then Adam did not just imagine the reason why a place called *Vínland* was given its name, he also lied about his source. Adam says that his main informant was the Danish king, Svein Estrithson (known in Icelandic sources as Sveinn Úlfsson). The king

> spoke of yet another island of the many found in that ocean. It is called *Vinland* because vines producing excellent wine grow wild there. That unsown crops also abound in that island we have ascertained not from fabulous reports but from the trustworthy relation of the Danes (Tschan 1959, 219).

Adam's history is full of fantasies, but by no means everything in it is false. Nevertheless, let us for the sake of argument grant that it may be possible that Adam corrupted **Vinland* to *Vínland*.

But that is not the end of the story. The new name had to get back to Iceland somehow, and it had to displace the old name. How could this happen? If the word **vin* 'pasture' was still alive in Iceland, surely it would have been less likely that the Icelanders could have allowed the name **Vinland* to be corrupted. Would Icelanders and Greenlanders familiar with tales of the voyages of discovery, familiar with the name **Vinland* and perhaps knowing why it had been called **'Pastureland'*, have willingly accepted not only a new story, but also a new name with a change in pronunciation? For there is no doubt that **Vinland* and *Vínland* would have been pronounced differently in Old Icelandic, just as they are pronounced differently in Modern Icelandic. Magnús Stefánsson (1988, 140) may be right to say that the difference in Old Icelandic was only one of quantity—a short vowel versus a long one, a distinction not systematically indicated in the medieval manuscripts (Crozier 1998, 39)—but that difference is important enough not to be dismissed with an 'only'. As for Erik Lönnroth's argument that the change was due to the 'lack of linguistic schooling that characterized the Viking Age Norsemen' (Lönnroth 1998,122, my translation), he is really saying that the Norsemen did not know their own language—one of several preposterous statements he makes.

The **Vinland* hypothesis thus relies on a chain of assumptions. Each one in itself may be possible; this must be admitted because we cannot prove otherwise. Yet the chain inevitably grows weaker for each unlikely assumption that is added to it. Absence of evidence may not be evidence of absence, but this hypothesis invokes so many absent pieces of evidence that one wonders why it appeals to historians trained in the Scandinavian school of source criticism. As Mats G. Larsson puts it (1999, 33), the skeptics sometimes go to such extremes in their disbelief that their theories become totally unbelievable.

Let us now look at the other position. No one has as yet found any incontrovertible traces of Norse presence in any part of North America where wild grapes grew—a brief stop may not have left anything for archaeologists to find. And if they brought back grapes from the south to the site at LAM, then no trace has been found of them—grape seeds are very small and could have totally decomposed after a thousand years. Yet this understandable lack of evidence does not mean that they did not discover a land with vines. Let us look at the indications that they did.

First we have the two early thirteenth-century sagas telling of the voyages, *Grænlendinga saga* (GLS) and *Eiríks saga rauða* (ESR). Many historians, of course, like Erik Lönnroth, would simply dismiss these as fiction, allegedly inspired by Adam of Bremen or by legends of a paradise across the ocean, the bountiful islands of Brendan and Isidore. Most scholars, however, feel that there is some core of truth concealed amidst the confusions, distortions, and fantasies in the sagas. One way to attempt to get at this core of truth is to compare the two sagas (Table 1).

One striking difference is that ESR has fewer voyages than GLS, and the number of people who are said to have sailed with Þorfinnr Karlsefni (160) happens to equal the number of people on separate voyages said in GLS to have been undertaken by Leifr Eiríksson, Þorvaldr, Þorfinnr, and Freydís (35 + 30 + 60 + 35). Since there is other evidence that ESR was written to glorify Þorfinnr Karlsefni's descendants, we may suspect that the saga has compressed all these voyages into one and given the credit to Þorfinnr. It also looks as if ESR has shifted the sequence of events: Þorfinnr is said to have named Helluland and Markland (and Kjalarnes), but it is likely that an earlier version of the story, better reflected in GLS, attributed this to Leifr Eiríksson (and to Þorvaldr Eiríksson in the case of Kjalarnes). To compensate for this—for it would scarcely have been possible to go against the tradition and deny Leifr any credit—ESR does say that Leifr was the first to discover vines, but that this happened when he came off course and discovered the new lands by accident. Leifr is thus put back earlier in the story, totally displacing Bjarni Herjólfsson. At the same time, the writer of ESR incorporates several different accounts of the discovery of wild wheat and vines, as if not wanting to omit any of the stories he knew. Leifr finds these resources when blown off course on his way to Greenland, which would mean that he strayed very far to the south. The fabulous Scottish runners Haki and Hekja find grapes and wheat not far beyond Markland (which is probably Labrador), but this also seems like a dubious location, just as the whole episode is obviously legendary (Almqvist 1997, 235-247). Finally, Þorfinnr himself discovers these abundant resources, at a place called Hóp, located well south of his initial settlement at Straumfjörðr.

The partially parallel account in GLS seems in many ways to be more plausible. Yet here the discovery of the grapes comes in an unlikely location: on a grassy headland just south of an island which seems to fit the position of Belle Isle, at the mouth of the strait between Labrador and Newfoundland. A comparison of the two sagas suggests that in this case it is ESR that best preserves an earlier version. I think that the episode of Þórhallr going missing and being found mumbling discontentedly has been incorporated in GLS in a more entertaining and fanciful version. The distinctive figure of Þórhallr, who had been in the service of Eiríkr *rauði* for a long time and who was brought along because of his experience of wild regions, has been turned into the equally distinctive figure of Tyrkir, Leifr Eiríksson's German foster-father, indicating that Tyrkir likewise had a close relationship to Eiríkr. Instead of complaining that he finds no wine, when Tyrkir goes missing he discovers

333

Grænlendinga saga	*Eiríks saga rauða*
Bjarni comes off course, sights land.	Leifr comes off course, finds land with wild wheat, vines, and mazer. He collects samples.
Leifr Eiríksson sets off with 35 men (including Tyrkir). Eiríkr stays in Greenland.	Þorsteinn Eiríksson sets off while Eiríkr stays in Greenland, but fails to find Vínland because of a storm.
Leifr explores and names Helluland and Markland.	Þorfinnr Karlsefni sets off with Þorvaldr and Freydís for Vínland, with 160 men (including Þórhallr). He explores and names Helluland and Markland, Kjalarnes and Furðustrandir. Haki and Hekja find grapes and wheat.
Leifr lands on an island with rich dewy grass, north of a headland.	Þorfinnr lands on Straumey, an island in a fjord, rich in birds' eggs.
Leifr builds booths for the winter on land just south of the island. They find plenty of grass and salmon. They explore.	Þorfinnr settles at a nearby grassy site they call Straumfjörðr. They explore and find a stranded whale. A severe winter is followed by fish and game in plenty.
Tyrkir goes missing but returns, talking incoherently, with grapes. They sail home from Vínland with grapes and timber.	Þórhallr goes missing, but is found mumbling, and complains that he has not had any wine; he sails off north with a few men.
	Þorfinnr Karlsefni sails far south to Hóp, finds wild wheat, vines, fish, game. They have their first encounter with *skrælingar*. They sail past Kjalarnes to the land of the Unipeds and home to Greenland.
Þorvaldr Eiríksson sails to Leifsbúðir in Vínland with 30 men. They explore the coast to the west and east. Their ship is damaged at Kjalarnes, which Þorvaldr names. He dies of a *skræling* arrow. The crew sails home from Krossanes with grapes and vines.	
Þorsteinn fails to find Vínland because of a storm.	
Þorfinnr Karlsefni sails to Leifsbúðir with 60 men. They find grass, timber, grapes, game, skins, and a stranded whale.	
Freydís with 35 men and Helgi and Finnbogi with 30 men sail to Leifsbúðir.	
Later in Norway: Þorfinnr sells his *húsasnotra* of unknown mazer wood from Vínland to a Bremen merchant.	*Alfræði Íslenzk*: Þorfinnr felled trees for a *húsasnotra*, then went in search of Vínland but could not explore it or find any of its resources.

Table 1. A comparison of key events in the accounts of the voyages.

grapes, and he can invoke his experience of southern vine-bearing regions, as if to certify the genuineness of the find. The account in GLS is not only more exotic; the events have also been compressed, so that the discovery of the grapes comes immediately after the building of the first settlement, instead of, as in ESR, after a southward passage from the first settlement. I think that the version in ESR is closer to the original story—which is of course not to say that it is necessarily closer to an original factual event, but the account of the southward journey could be a factual detail.

The description of *Leifsbúðir* in GLS seems to square well with LAM, but the story of the discovery of grapes nearby is impossible—a circumstance that is eagerly invoked by advocates of the **Vinland* hypothesis. However, in the parallel account in ERS, where the first settlement at Straumfjörðr also fits LAM quite well, the grapes are found only after a further journey southwards. This means that the combined evidence of the sagas, interpreted in this inevitably selective way, allows us to believe that the Norsemen's explorations brought them some distance south beyond the northern tip of Newfoundland. And I believe that in the original story it was Leifr Eiríksson, not Þorfinnr, who made this discovery.

Proponents of the **Vinland* hypothesis have made much of the fact that stories of wild grain and grapes growing in abundance are frequent elements in medieval legends of blessed islands across the ocean. Yet if the reports in the sagas are inventions, then it is a remarkable coincidence, as Sigurdur Thorarinsson says (1942, 44), that grapes actually do grow wild in this region of North America, as do plants which early European visitors could have mistaken for self-sown wheat; perhaps the most likely candidate is wild rye (*Elymus virginicus*) (Larsson 1992, 314). Jacques Cartier, the Frenchman who explored the St Lawrence in 1534, made special mention of the fields of 'wild wheat that has an ear like barley and the grain like oats' (Hermannsson 1936, 70; Magnusson and Pálsson 1965, 86), as well as abundant grapes on both sides of the river (Durand 2000, 32-33). It is interesting that Cartier reported finding wild wheat and grapes on the same decidedly non-legendary voyage up the St Lawrence. This shows that we need not be suspicious every time grapes and grain occur together in the same account. Any similarity to the legends does not necessarily imply that everything is borrowed from them. Those who heard a factual report of the Norsemen's discovery of grain and grapes could have taken it as confirmation of the legends, if they knew them; it would thus have been natural for them to use wording similar to that of the legends, and it would have been easy for the author of ESR to incorporate legendary episodes, such as the tale of Haki and Hekja.

It should not be forgotten that a third natural resource occurs alongside the wild vines and wheat in the sagas, but not in the accounts of Brendan, Isidore, and Adam of Bremen. I am referring to the kind of wood known as *mösurr*, for which I will use the archaic English cognate *mazer*. According to ESR, Leifr Eiríksson discovered mazer in the same place as the wheat and vines, while GLS tells us of Þorfinnr's piece of carved mazer wood from *Vínland*, a *húsasnotra*, some sort of decoration for a house, perhaps a weathervane (Ingstad 1985, 142-5) or a gable-end (Magnusson and Pálsson 1965, 71, n. 1). Þorfinnr sold this to a merchant from Bremen. This artefact is mentioned in a third Icelandic source which I have added to the table above, the encyclopaedic work *Alfræði Íslenzk*, compiled by Abbot Nikolaus of Þverá, who died in 1159:

> It is said that Þorfinnr Karlsefni felled trees for a weather-vane (*húsasnotrutré*) and then set out to search for Vinland the Good, and that he came to where he thought this land lay, but was unable to investigate it or procure any of the produce of the land (Ingstad 1985, 344).

Here is one source which, besides casting doubt on Karlsefni's achievements as described in ESR, confirms that some remarkable timber was felled and worked in North America.

335

I think that this detail tallies very well with some concrete evidence excavated at LAM. I am referring to the butternuts and the burl of a butternut tree bearing the marks of a sharp tool—as if someone had tried carving it but given up. The butternut tree or white walnut (*Juglans cinerea*) does not grow anywhere in Newfoundland. Its northern limit in Canada coincides roughly with the northern limit of wild grapes (*Vitis riparia*). These resources must have been brought here from the south (Wallace 1990, 193).

Old Norse *mösurr* is often translated as 'maple', but it does not necessarily refer to any particular species. The original meaning of the Germanic word seems to be 'excrescence'. The modern Swedish cognate *masur*, now borrowed into English, refers to an abnormal growth in the annual rings of certain deciduous trees (e.g. birch, maple, elm), giving mottled, wavy figures. The archaic English *mazer* denotes a bowl carved of such wood, as well as the wood and the tree itself; according to the Oxford English Dictionary, the wood is properly maple, but one quotation from *c.* 1500 describes how mazer trees can be grown from soaked walnuts.

> Take many rype walenottes and water hem a while, and put hem in a moiste pytt, and hile hem, and there shalbe grawe thereof a grett stoke that we calle masere (*Oxford English Dictionary* s.v. *mazer*).

This beautifully grained walnut wood that lends itself to carved and turned objects must be the *mösurr* that is mentioned in the sagas. We have here a rare example of perfect agreement between a written source and an archaeological find, and that find clearly indicates that the Norsemen who built their booths at LAM sailed further south in search of useful resources. The physical evidence, while not providing us with grapes, shows that the Norsemen reached a latitude where they could have found grapes. This means that there is no need to doubt that they could have called that land *Vínland*, just as Cartier called an island *Isle Bacchus* (now Île d'Orléans up the St Lawrence estuary near Québec), and French settlers gave the name *Baie de vin* ('Wine Bay') to the area near the mouth of the Miramichi River in north-eastern New Brunswick, on the southern shores of the Gulf of St Lawrence (Durand 2000, 30; B. Wallace, pers. comm.). The finding of grapes is evidently enough to bring thoughts of wine to people's minds. It is unlikely that the French explorers tried to make wine before they bestowed these names, and we are certainly not forced to believe that the Norsemen ever made wine from the grapes they discovered in the New World; reports of the excellence of the wine were no doubt embroidered by Adam of Bremen or his informants. There is enough evidence that Norsemen reached a part of North America where grapes grew wild. We do not need to believe that they sailed as far south as New England, let alone New York, since wild grapes could have been found in present-day Canada. The sailing distances are so short that even the skeptics should find it hard to deny the possibility that some Norseman—perhaps Leifr Eiríksson himself—could have landed in a place with vines. It is quite likely that this happened only once and that later Norse explorers—perhaps like Karlsefni—failed to repeat the find. The name *Vínland* could have been bestowed on the basis of a single discovery, and it would have lived on as the name of a land—*Vínland hit góða* 'Wineland the Good'—that enticed people to sail in quest of it, just as sixteenth-century explorers searched for El Dorado.

To conclude, let us perform a mental experiment and imagine that absent evidence turned up. Suppose that a hitherto unknown Old Icelandic manuscript was discovered, containing the word **vin* 'pasture'. This would confirm that the word had survived, but it would not confirm the **Vinland* hypothesis—it would merely strengthen the first link in that very weak chain of assumptions. On the other hand, if grape seeds were excavated in a Norse context at LAM it would surely dispel all the skeptics' doubts. But we do not need grape seeds to believe in *Vínland* as a 'Wineland'. The butternuts and the burl from the white walnut tree—the probable *mösurr* of the sagas—are a very adequate substitute.

ABBREVIATIONS

ESR   Þórðarson, M. ed., 1935. *Eiríks saga rauða*, in *Eyrbyggja saga: Grænlendinga sögur*. Reykjavík: Íslenzk fornrit 4.

GLS   Þórðarson, M. ed., 1935. *Grænlendinga saga*, in *Eyrbyggja saga: Grænlendinga sögur*. Reykjavík: Íslenzk fornrit 4.

BIBLIOGRAPHY

Almqvist, B. 1997. 'Before Columbus: Some Irish Folklore Motifs in the Old Icelandic Traditions about Wineland', in Josephson 1997, 225-252.

Cleasby, R. and Vigfusson, G. 1957. *An Icelandic-English Dictionary*, 2nd edn, Oxford.

Crozier, A. 1998. 'The *Vinland* Hypothesis: A Reply to the Historians', *Gardar*, 29, 37-66.

Durand, F. 2000. 'L'Anse aux Meadows, porte océane de l'Amerique norroise', *Proxima Thulé*, 4, 9-33.

Hermannsson, H. 1936. *The Problem of Wineland*. Ithaca, NY: Islandica 25.

Holm, G. 1997. '*Vínland*: "Vinrankornas land"', *Gardar*, 28, 47-53.

Ingstad, H. 1985. *The Norse Discovery of America*, vol. 2. *The Historical Background and the Evidence of the Norse Settlement Discovered in Newfoundland*, Oslo.

Jansson, V. 1951. *Nordiska vin-namn: En ortnamnstyp och dess historia*, Uppsala.

Jones, G. 1986. *The Norse Atlantic Saga: Being the Norse Voyages of Discovery and Settlement to Iceland, Greenland, and North America*, Oxford.

Josephson, F. ed., 1997. *Celts and Vikings: Proceedings of the Fourth Symposium of Societas Celtologica Nordica*, Meijerbergs arkiv för svensk ordforskning.

Larsson, M.G. 1992. 'The *Vinland* Sagas and Nova Scotia: A Reappraisal of an Old Theory', *Scandinavian Studies*, 64, 3, 305-35.

——1999. *Vinland det goda: Nordbornas färder till Amerika under vikingatiden*, Stockholm.

Lönnroth, E. 1996. 'The Vinland Problem', *Scandinavian Journal of History*, 21, 1, 39-47.

Magnusson, M. and Pálsson, H., trans, 1965. *The Vinland Sagas: The Norse Discovery of America. Grænlendinga Saga and Eirik's Saga*, Harmondsworth.

Meldgaard, J. 1961. 'Fra Brattalid til Vinland', *Naturens verden*, 353-385.

Olsen, M. 1926. *Ættegård og helligdom: Norske stedsnavn sosialt og religionshistorisk belyst*, Oslo.

Murray, J.A.H. *et al.*, eds, 1933. *Oxford English Dictionary*, Oxford.

Söderberg, S. 1910. 'Professor Sven Söderberg om Vinland', *Sydsvenska Dagbladet Snällposten*, 295 (30 October), 3-4.

Stefánsson, M. 1998. 'Vínland or Vinland?', *Scandinavian Journal of History*, 23, 3-4, 139-52.

Tanner, V. 1941. 'De gamla nordbornas Helluland, Markland och Vinland', *Budkavlen*, 20, 1-70.

Thorarinsson, S. 1942. 'Vinlandsproblemet: Några reflexioner med anledning av V. Tanners skrift', *Ymer*, 62, 39-46.

Tschan, F.J. trans., 1959. *History of the Archbishops of Hamburg-Bremen, by Adam of Bremen*, New York.

The Viking. 1975. Chief contributor B. Almgren, New York.

Wahlgren, E. 1986. *The Vikings and America*, London.

Wallace, B.L. 1990. 'L'Anse aux Meadows: Gateway to Vinland', The Norse of the North Atlantic, *Acta Archaeologica*, 61, 166-197.

337

Section Three:
Exploration, Navigation and
Cultural Interaction

Did the Vikings Reach North America without Discovering It?

The Greenland Norse and Zuan Caboto in the Strait of Belle Isle

Peter Pope ✓

The word 'discovery' carries a lot of freight. So much freight that some doubt whether we should talk as if Europeans discovered other continents. Nine or ten thousand years ago, as the glaciers of the last Ice Age melted away, the Maritime Archaic Indians of Atlantic Canada colonised Labrador and eventually Newfoundland (Tuck 1976). We know that medieval sagas about Greenlandic voyages to these same lands can be taken seriously, thanks to the archaeological investigation of the Norse site at L'Anse aux Meadows, Newfoundland, located in the 1960s by the remarkable Norwegian couple Helge and Anna Stine Ingstad, following the earlier (and too often forgotten) research of the Danish archaeologist Jorgen Meldgaard (Ingstad and Ingstad 1985; Wallace 1986; 1991; Meldgaard 2000). A few years ago we celebrated exploration of the same region by the Venetian master mariner Zuan Caboto in 1497. How could Cabot discover something that had already been discovered 500 years earlier by the Greenlanders and thousands of years before that by Canada's first peoples? With due respect to native peoples (and the Norse), in whose wake he sailed, Cabot's expedition was also a voyage of discovery. To deny that Europeans discovered North America at the end of the fifteenth century is an effective way to criticize modernist euro-centred history and geography—but it is also a way to lose sight of the fact that it was, for better or for worse, early modern western Europeans who discovered that the world has many continents and that it is possible to reach and exploit them by sea (Parry 1981). The relationship of Old World and New was asymmetrical: European mariners visited North America, returned with news of it and began to exploit it; not the other way around. I ask whether we can seriously consider the Greenlandic Norse 'Vikings' in the same light.

Like the first voyage of Columbus, Cabot's expedition of 1497 gave rise to a significant historical tradition precisely because it could be taken to symbolize the moment when Europe appropriated North America. These discoveries have often been used, by Europeans or North Americans of European descent, as precedents or justifications for possession. Because of this, the concept of 'discovery' bears with it a contextual burden: the European appropriation of new territory, sometimes loosely summarized as 'conquest'(Seed 1992). With respect to northern North America, this burden is something imposed by later events. For several centuries, Europeans and native peoples were interdependent and one could hardly be said to have conquered the other (Bailey 1969; Hoffman 1961; Trigger 1985). The situation changed after significant numbers of Europeans colonized North America in the eighteenth century. Cabot's discovery was used as a precedent for possession and, in the nineteenth century, the location of his landfall therefore came to seem symbolically significant to the historians and geographers of the new colonial states of Canada, Newfoundland and the United States (Pope 1997). A hundred years later it would seem that there are those who would like to put the medieval Norse Vínland voyages to the same use. One way of putting this kind of myth-making in perspective is to look at the invention of tradition associated with Cabot's voyage. This will also serve to introduce a review of the evidence linking his geographical notions of the North Atlantic with the Norse traditions of Vínland.

An obsession with Cabot's landfall characterized the historiographic aftermath of the 1897 quadcentenary of his voyage and generated a great deal of self-assured speculation (fig. 1). These landfall theories seem to have as much to do with national myth as they do with the history of navigation. At any rate, the national origin of scholars is an accurate pre-

Figure 1. Some of the places that have been claimed as Cabot's landfall.

342

dictor of their landfall geographies. For Americans, Columbus is a founder hero (Bushman 1992). For them, it does not make mythic sense for another discoverer to approach American waters as early or as closely as he did. Obeying the logic of myth, American scholars have therefore generally preferred to remember Cabot as a northern mariner, placing his landfall in Labrador or nearby (Harrisse 1892 [1961]; Morison 1971). It is the British who like to imagine an American landfall in Maine or even farther south, bringing King Henry's navigator as close to the heart of 'Columbia' as possible, so to speak (Quinn 1968; 1977; Wilson 1991;1996: I have heard Prof Quinn has repented of these views). Canadian scholars have shown little interest in that theory, although it was rehearsed for them in the *Dictionary of Canadian Biography* by the late keeper of maps in the British Library, R.A. Skelton (1966 [1979]). Until Confederation with Newfoundland in 1949, Canadians generally preferred a landfall near Cape Breton, in Nova Scotia. On this interpretation, the beginnings of the British Empire could be found on Canadian territory, which delighted British North American nationalists, with the added bonus that it enraged French-Canadian intellectuals, for mythic infringement on the Gulf of St Lawrence, territory explored in the mid-sixteenth century by their own founder-hero Jacques Cartier (Pope 1997). In reaction to the Anglo-Canadian mythology of a Nova Scotian Cape Breton landfall, Newfoundlanders fixed on their own Cape Bonavista, which is more plausible geographically, though the cartographic evidence is similarly ambiguous. Since Newfoundland joined Confederation, mainland Canadian scholars have become more broad-minded about landfalls in Newfoundland. To the extent that there is a Canadian scholarly consensus about John Cabot's landfall, it is that he landed near the Strait of Belle Isle, between continental Labrador and insular Newfoundland— in effect, a nice Canadian compromise (Ruggles 1988; McGhee 1991). Participants in these debates gave the virtually contemporary explorations of the Corte Reals and other Azorean

Portuguese captains little attention, again probably on the principle of mythic exclusion. Perhaps one discoverer is as much as the average nationalist is willing to remember at one time (although we Newfoundlanders seem to be pretty adept at moving smartly along from one to another).

The Cabot celebrations in 1997 provoked another shorter round of mutually-exclusive claims about where he sailed and where he made land. On this occasion we found ourselves celebrating his ship, the *Matthew*, rather than his landfall, perhaps for reasons having to do with our newly-developed sensitivity about the political correctness of 'discovery' (Cuthbertson 1997; Williams 1996; Wilson 1996; Firstbrook 1997: at the 'Cabot and His World' symposium sponsored by the Newfoundland Historical Society in 1997, the folklorist Gerald Pocius drew attention to the contemporary tendency to focus on the ship). The present paper takes up a somewhat different issue, somewhere between the vessel and the landfall, and that is the question of Cabot's itinerary. Despite the many landfalls proposed by scholars, there are really only two theories about how the *Matthew* made its way from Europe to North America. The argument here is simple: the northern and southern alternatives for the *Matthew*'s itinerary express profoundly different ways of remembering Cabot's voyage. The northern itinerary would give some long-term historical significance to Norse geographical traditions. This in turn raises the question I have posed by my argumentative title: does it make good historical or anthropological sense to think of the Norse Greenlanders as the discoverers of North America?

343

Anyone interested in Cabot's itinerary in 1497 have a significant advantage over the scholars who puzzled over the handful of Cabotian documents available a century ago (Winship 1900 [1967]). The single most informative contemporary report of his trans-Atlantic voyage was not discovered until the middle of the twentieth century. The crucial document was identified in the Archives at Simancas, Spain, by Louis André Vigneras and first published in 1956 (Vigneras 1956; Williamson 1962). It consists of an intelligence report, written soon after the 1497 voyage, by the London merchant John Day, addressed to the 'Grand Admiral' of Spain, probably Columbus himself. Day was a well-educated man from an influential family who had lived and worked in Bristol and was well qualified to gather and to understand intelligence about Cabot's North American adventure (Ruddock 966; see Williamson 1962, 29).

More recently Edoardo Guiffrida and others have brought to light a number of other documents which shed significant light on Cabot's early commercial career, indicating that he traded in furs or skins, among other things (Giuffrida 1999; Tiepolo 1973). These more recently-published documents do not deal directly with the voyage of 1497, however. While other documents, published in the nineteenth century, have information about the voyage, the Day letter provides several very useful clues about the expedition missing from previously-known contemporary accounts of the Cabots. In my view, these implications were not clearly recognized by the scholars who originally did such a good job of bringing the Day document to wider attention. Vigneras himself continued to take a Cape Breton landfall for granted, despite the challenge to that interpretation posed by explicit geographic detail given in the Day letter (Day in Williamson 1962, 25; Vigneras 1957). Despite protestations that they took the document seriously, R.A. Skelton and James Williamson, in the latter's invaluable collection of Cabotian documents, are forced to ignore the same specific details (in the Day Letter), the better to defend a voyage to Maine and Nova Scotia, an interpretation they had already adopted, based on their reading of the la Cosa map (Williamson 1962, 54-83; Skelton 1962). It is, perhaps, easier for later generations of scholars to make sense of the Day Letter. For us it has always been part of the data, making it easier to give it the central place that it deserves in interpreting the voyage.

What does Day's letter tell us about Cabot's itinerary in 1497, that is, within the context of the other key contemporary sources on the voyage, the letters of the Milanese ambassador Raimondo de Soncino and the Venetian merchant Lorenzo Pasqualigo (de Soncino in Williamson 1962, 24; Pasqualigo in Williamson 1962, 22)? Cabot set out from Bristol in a vessel of about 50 tons, with provisions for seven or eight months, in May 1497 (cf. Williamson 1962, 61; Toby in Williamson 1962, 19; Quinn 1967). He took the *Matthew* to the west of Ireland, then headed north before striking west again (de Soncino in Williamson 1962, 24). This was latitude sailing, an important technique for trans-oceanic navigation which became more practical in the late fifteenth century with the development of reliable instruments for better determining latitude at sea: the quadrant, the astrolabe and the cross-staff (cf. Morison 1971, 170). Latitude sailing involved observation of the altitude of a celestial body, in northern waters generally Polaris (the North Star). In the northern hemisphere the altitude of Polaris, with some correction for the time of night, equals terrestrial latitude. The altitude of the sun at noon is related to the observer's latitude in a more complex way, requiring adjustment for the time of year. The ability to make reasonably accurate observations of *altura* meant pilots could make good estimates of their north/south position (Waters 1967, 200-7, 219). This technique of running down the latitude called for charts with a scale of latitude and the first such charts date *c.* 1500 (Waters 1967, 219; Campbell 1976). Pilots did not yet work with a numerical concept of latitude but instead identified their position by saying, for example, that Polaris had the same altitude as it did at such-and-such a point on the coast of Europe. Deducing the exact altitude of the North Star actually required further skill in celestial navigation, since Polaris is just off the celestial North Pole and rotates in a tight circle around it, every twenty-four hours. Its position relative to true north can be deduced from the position of the nearby stars in Ursa Minor, called by navigators 'the Guards', and early modern pilots devised another simple instrument, the nocturnal, to do this. These refinements in navigation were as useful in their way as the magnetic compass, which had already become a standard instrument in the late middle ages (Lane 1965).

Although Cabot could estimate his position north or south, he would not have been able to estimate accurately his east/west position. The determination of longitude requires precise ship-board timekeeping, which had to await the invention of the marine chronometer in the eighteenth century (Taylor 1971, 245-63). Since longitude was uncertain, it made sense to sail first, in known waters, north or south to the latitude of the intended landfall and then to head east or west, staying as close as possible to the chosen latitude so that the ship's position was known, at least in one dimension, somewhere on a particular east-west line. It is, therefore, essential to discriminate among late fifteenth-century sources on the basis of the kind of navigational data they report. Indications of latitude can be taken seriously, within a degree or so. East/west distances given in contemporary reports of Cabot's voyage, on the other hand, would have been based solely on his estimates of wind, current, and speed over the sea-bottom and would therefore be subject to much larger error. The Day letter gives us several estimates of latitude, expressed as equivalence to a European location, in the style of the period. Some other contemporary reports of the 1497 voyage estimate distances covered in the trans-Atlantic passage and in coasting the North American littoral. The latitude data in the Day letter are more trustworthy than these distance estimates—not because of the special virtues of that document but simply because this was a kind of data obtainable with some precision in the period, while exact distance figures were not. The fact that Day does not bother to mention distances, except as days sailed, is a mark of his own navigational sophistication and of the navigational experience he assumed for his correspondent (Columbus?) (Ruddock 1966).

If Cabot had no preference for any particular line of latitude, as an east/west course, he would likely have departed Europe from one of the headlands on the west of Ireland. If he sailed further north, out of sight of land, his position became less certain. On these assumptions he would have begun his trans-Atlantic crossing somewhere on the Irish coast between about 51° and 55° N. One maritime historian argues that he would have departed from

Dursey Head, at the southwestern extremity of Ireland at about 51½° N; others that he must have departed from Achill Head in western Connacht, at 54° N (Morison 1971; Jackson 1963; Markham 1897, 608). These are reasonable speculations but there is no reason Cabot might not have chosen any other prominent Irish headland as his point of departure (cf. Harrisse 1892 [1961], 7). Western Ireland is a potentially treacherous coast in the prevailing onshore winds: good reason for any sailor to stand off from it as soon as convenient. Nevertheless, Cabot sailed north 'some days' before putting 'the north on his right hand' and heading westward, timing which would favour a change of course at one of the northern headlands, or even farther north, beyond St. Kilda and the Hebrides (de Soncio in Williamson 1962, 24).

There is a small but significant clue in the Day letter, not often remarked, which sheds light on his itinerary. According to John Day, the *Matthew* ran before an east-north-easterly wind on its outward passage. This was a very convenient but very curious wind. A steady east-north-easterly off the west of Ireland in late May, or in fact at any other time of the year, is an unusual wind. Despite this, R.A. Skelton thought that early Bristol traders used 'the northeasterly winds of early summer...westward from southern England or Ireland' (Skelton 1995, 234). In many months of the year, sailors have to run to about 65° N, the latitude of Iceland, to find prevailing easterlies, although this is not necessary in May, when easterlies blow regularly at about 60° N (Isemer and Hasse 1986, 189, chart 152). Medieval traders venturing from Norway to Greenland certainly knew about this wind, which is recorded in the fourteenth-century *Hauksbók*:

345

> From Hernar in Norway sail due west for Hvarf in Greenland; and then will you sail north of Shetland so that you can just sight it in clear weather; but south of the Faroe Islands, so that the sea appears half-way up the mountain slopes; but steer south of Iceland so that you may have birds and whales therefrom (HB, 4).

This itinerary for a voyage from southwest Norway to Cape Farewell at the southern tip of Greenland, is latitude sailing at 61° N, in the middle of the easterlies that can be expected there in late spring (Marcus 1981; fig. 2). Cabot made land after thirty-five days at sea, which was not bad for a westward trans-Atlantic passage and an indication that he had followed some such efficient course rather than bucking headwinds in lower latitudes (Morison 1971, 168-9). The old Norse itinerary would have been known in fifteenth-century Bristol, which traded with Iceland and Greenland and which was home to dozens of Icelanders (McGhee 1991, 90). The indications in the Day letter that Cabot followed some such northern itinerary are consistent with the context of the voyage.

Cabot's itinerary west of Greenland is more obscure. By June, the winds there are confused westerlies (Isemer and Hasse 1986, 190, chart 153). A heading roughly southwest is probably the best the *Matthew* could have done on any one tack and would be a likely course, given that the expedition was looking for temperate Japan and not arctic Tartary. On 24 June, 1497, Zuan Caboto and his companions made their North American landfall ([Sebastian Cabot?], Paris Map [1544], Legend 8, in Williamson 21). The Day letter is silent on the landfall but tells us that Cabot found a 'mainland' and some islands, one of which he identified as the Island of the Seven Cities, a common feature of late medieval legendary Atlantic geography, often known as Antillia (Williamson 9-10; Johnson 1994, 131-50). Cabot reported the southern limit of his Island of the Seven Cities as being in the same latitude as the River of Bordeaux which would make his island discovery either Cape Breton Island or Newfoundland's Avalon Peninsula. (The Avalon was consistently mistaken for an island until the later sixteenth century (Harrisse 1900 [1968], 203-13). According to the Day letter, Cabot and his crew 'landed at only one spot of the mainland, near the place where land was first sighted'. The landfall, then, was not one of the islands discovered but some part of the 'mainland', which means that Day's letter tells us what geography has always

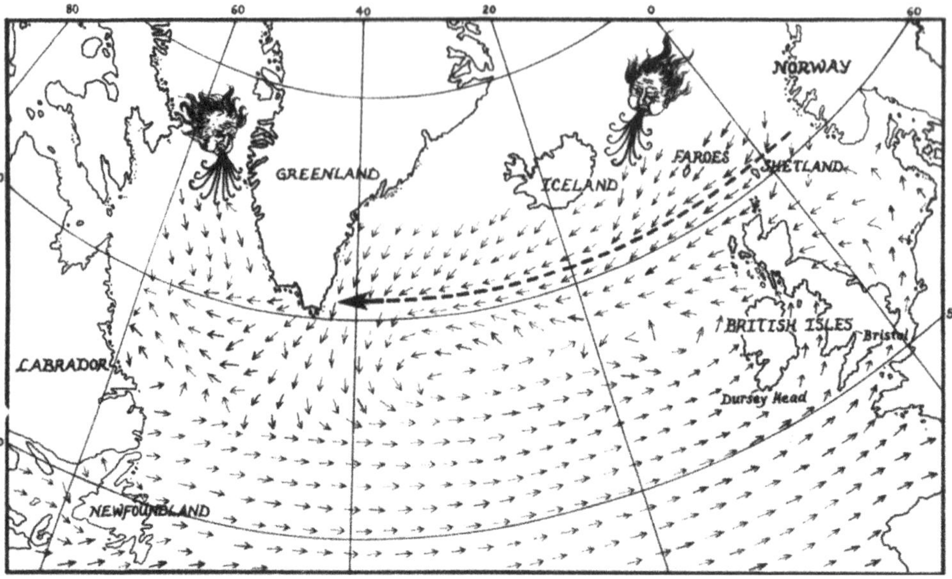

Figure 2. The traditional Norse sailing itinerary with the winds prevailing in May.

346

suggested: Cape Breton is an unlikely landfall for a westward expedition departing from Ireland. If the Island of the Seven Cities was Newfoundland's Avalon Peninsula rather than Cape Breton Island, then we must look even farther afield for a 'mainland'.

Where was Cabot's 'mainland'? The only other latitude information that has come down to us from the voyage of 1497 is also contained in the Day letter, which reported that 'the cape nearest to Ireland is 1800 miles [*millas*] west of Dursey Head'. We have to take such distance information with a grain of salt, although the identification of a cape at the latitude of Dursey Head is easy enough: at 51½° N, this would be prominent Cape Dégrat, near the more low-lying Cape Bauld in the Strait of Belle Isle, at the northern end of Newfoundland's Great Northern Peninsula (Morison 1971, 172-3). (There are no other prominent capes in the region.) Cape Dégrat is about 3000 km from Dursey Head, close to Cabot's estimated 1800 miles. This assumes Cabot used the generally accepted Ptolemaic mile of 5000 feet. The nautical mile of 6080 feet was a seventeenth-century invention (Waters 1958, 423-425 and 487-488). Cape Spear, just south of St. John's, is actually slightly closer to Ireland, although in quite the wrong latitude. Pasqualigo thought Cabot's 'mainland' was '700 leagues away'—not a bad estimate, if Pasqualigo expressed himself in land leagues of three miles; if he used sea leagues of four miles, it was an overestimate (Taylor 1963). Neither the 'Island of the Seven Cities' nor 'the cape nearest Ireland' are necessarily candidates for the much-debated landfall though. The fact that they are mentioned but not specified as such rather argues against them. They do provide us with some sense of the coast explored by Cabot in 1497. He was, after all, an expert navigator and he thought he had been in the latitudes of the Strait of Belle Isle and of the south Avalon or Cape Breton Island. 'All along this coast', Day reported, 'they found many fish like those which in Iceland are dried in the open and sold in England and other countries, and...called in English "stockfish"'. Cabot himself told Soncino that the sea was swarming with so many fish that they could be taken 'not only with the net, but in baskets let down with a stone'(de Soncino in Williamson 1962, 24). On the evidence of the Day letter, his 'mainland' was, paradoxically, the Island of Newfoundland (cf. Quinn 1967, 112-19).

John Cabot's 'mainland' probably also included southern Labrador, for it is unlikely that he distinguished between the island of Newfoundland and coastal Labrador. He and his son Sebastian, who later explored the same area, seem to have treated the Strait of Belle Isle between Labrador and Newfoundland as a bay in a continuous 'mainland' coastline rather than as a body of water opening into the Gulf of St. Lawrence, separating continental Labrador from insular Newfoundland. This is how Joannes Ruysch showed the area in his world map of 1508 and other early sixteenth-century cartographers, like Robert Thorne, followed suit (Ruysch in Nordenskiöld 1889 [1973], pl. xxxii; Harrisse 1897, 5; 1900[1968]). Indeed, the Basque whalers who exploited these waters in the mid-sixteenth century continued to refer to the Strait of Belle Isle as 'La Gran Baya'. Interestingly, this is also how early modern Norse maps depict the region. Whatever the origins of this conception of the Strait of Belle Isle as a bay in a continental coastline, we know that Cabot visited the region. This is food for thought.

The tip of Newfoundland's Great Northern Peninsula in the Strait of Belle Isle is the one part of North America with which we are absolutely certain that the Norse were familiar. This was not barren Helluland, which can be interpreted as Baffin Island or northern Labrador; nor wooded Markland, which sounds like Labrador south of the tree line; nor was it, likely, the original Vínland, which must have been somewhere south of the St Lawrence, if grapes were really part of the reconnaissance described in the sagas. The only archaeological evidence of Norse occupation of a New World site was located on the Newfoundland side of the Strait at L'Anse aux Meadows (LAM: Sutherland 2000). Birgitta Wallace's research for Parks Canada suggests that this site was occupied for several seasons, at most. It was not a colony but a base camp for exploration and ship repair. The recovery of an American butternut from a good Norse context at the site indicates that the Greenlanders had managed to reach south across the Gulf of St Lawrence in a kind of foraging survey. In the Bay de Chaleurs in northern New Brunswick, they would have found not only butternuts but grapes, as well as an indigenous maritime people, the ancestors of the native Mi'kmaq people of Canada's maritime provinces (Wallace 2000a). The LAM site is likely the remains of what the sagas call Leifsbúðir, roughly 'Leif's Camp', rather than of Vínland, at least as Leif or his contemporaries would have understood the term (Wallace 2000b).

347

This is quite a coincidence. Zuan Caboto's American 'cape nearest Ireland' of 1497 looks to have been about 10 km from Leifsbúðir, which Greenlanders had used half a millennium earlier. Can we jump from the fact that the Greenlanders knew the area in the tenth and eleventh centuries to the conclusion that there must have been a wider late medieval northern geographic tradition of western lands with which Cabot was somehow familiar? (cf. Quinn 1961; Skelton 1995; Marcus 1981, 164-73; McGhee 1991, 81-92; Seaver 1996a, 305-06). The relevant documentary evidence is limited and problematic.

The Icelandic sagas of Eiríkr the Red (ESR) and of the Greenlanders (GLS) describe the Norse voyages to the west and are, in this sense, part of a geographical tradition about the location of Vínland. GLS recounts four separate voyages towards Vínland; ESR presents these as one, emphasizing the historical role of Karlsefni (Wallace 2000b). The descriptions of Leifsbúðir and nearby Straumfjörðr fit a site on the Great Northern Peninsula well, at the mouth of a strait with a strong current opposite a large island. GLS makes some observations about day length at the winter solstice which can be variously interpreted, but northern Newfoundland is a reasonable interpretation of this evidence (Sigurdsson 2000). The sagas, in other words, express the idea that there were inhabited temperate lands to the west; they are consistent with the archaeological evidence from LAM; but they are too vague geographically to be of much to pilots. In any event, the itinerary they seem to suggest for the Vínland voyage, from Disko Island off the coast of Greenland, across the northern Davis Strait to Baffin Island and south along the coast of Labrador, would have been impossible for Cabot in a June voyage, even if he had somehow heard of it. In the end, it seems doubtful that the Vínland sagas alone could have lead Cabot to the Strait of Belle Isle, except in the general sense that the idea of Vínland might have acted as confirmation of his belief in lands to the west. Neither saga is clear about the location of Vínland, apart from a sense that it is beyond Straumfjörðr and Leifsbúðir. Together, the two sagas give the impression that the toponym 'Vínland' had already become ambiguous by the time the sagas were written down sometime in the thirteenth century. Whether we treat the late medieval sense of 'Vínland' as important or irrelevant depends on our attitude to the two or three maps that use the name.

Yale University's 'Vínland Map' is the most notorious of these (Skelton, Marston and Painter 1995; see Seaver, this volume). The document has been subject to some formidable criticism, much of it so intemperate as to raise the question of why the idea of a genuine mid-fifteenth-century map depicting part of North America generates such offense, given that we now know the Norse actually visited the area depicted. The vague provenance of the document, Yale's initial secrecy about it, and the manner in which it was then promoted have doubtless exacerbated the vehemence of the debate; but one hopes that the document will stand or fall for scientific and historical reasons and not because one faction of scholars finds a more colourful way of labelling the other as charlatans. The fact that the map resembles *mappe mundi* securely dated to the fifteenth and early sixteenth centuries is an objection only if forgery is presumed (McNaughton 2000). Some critics of the map have used the depiction of Greenland as an island as evidence against authenticity; but this argument is not very convincing, for several reasons (Taylor 1974). The map-maker was clearly willing to jump to insular conclusions, since Vínland is shown as an island; besides, Greenland is sometimes shown as an island on early modern maps (Painter 1995a). Furthermore, by the fourteenth-century the Inuit knew the true form of Greenland and they could have communicated that perception to the Norse (McGhee 1991; Brown 1999). Some have argued that the medieval Norse did not generally make maps and that the Vínland Map must therefore be suspect on these grounds (Seaver 1996a, 164). About 1605, the Danish Bishop Resen made a map depicting the North Atlantic, which he claimed was based on a late-medieval Icelandic original, which would be one counter-example, at least, to the supposed rule that the medieval Norse did not make maps (Painter 1995b, 252). In any event, its proponents do not actually claim that the Vínland Map is Norse, but defend it as Germanic, suggesting some connection with the Upper Rhineland and the Church Council of Basle, of 1431-1449, which is a context in which disparate scraps of geographical knowledge might plausibly have come together (Painter 1995a; Marston 1995).

The Vínland Map depicts *Vinilandia Insula* as a large island in the latitudes of Newfoundland and Labrador, with a large fjord on the northern part of the coast leading to an inland lake, just as Hamilton Inlet actually leads into Lake Melville. It also shows a prominent peninsula, separated by a large embayment, pointing northwards from the southern part of the land mass, the northern tip of which is shown at the same latitude as southern Ireland—that is to say, as a reasonably accurate depiction of the Great Northern Peninsula with the Strait of Belle Isle as a bay (cf. Skelton 1995; Seaver 1996b). This would be a suspiciously accurate depiction of the region, if the map had been recovered after the identification of the LAM site. Since the Yale map actually surfaced first, this relative accuracy tends to authenticate it. The most telling initial objections to the Vínland Map have been to the ink, although re-analysis has satisfied some that the materials may be authentic. It would be fair to say that opinions are once more divided on this score (Cahill and Kusko 1995; McNaughton 2000). This means that the Yale map is not effective evidence for an explicit northern geographic tradition of Vínland, because the strongest evidence for its authenticity remains its depiction of the region we know the Norse to have frequented: a circular argument which will be difficult to escape unless a positive consensus emerges about the chemistry of the inks (cf. Skelton 1995).

Scholars intent on detecting a geographical tradition have also looked for evidence of Vínland in a pair of early modern post-Cabotian maps: the Resen map of *c.* 1605 and a map drafted by Sigurdhir Stefánsson around 1590, although unpublished until 1668 (Ingstad and

Ingstad 1985, 323). A recent paper argues that legends on the Resen map were added after it was originally drafted, which would weaken conclusions based on the occurrence of the toponym 'Vinland'(McNaughton 2000). The authenticity of Stefánsson's map is more widely accepted, although its significance has been questioned. This map shows a *Promontorium Winlandiae* running north to the latitude of the Strait of Belle Isle. Many scholars have seen the Resen and Stefánsson maps as derivative essentially of the geographical content of the sagas (Ingstad and Ingstad 1985, 323-37). These early modern northern maps can certainly be understood as an attempt to repudiate Spanish and Portuguese claims in the New World by symbolizing Protestant Scandanavian precedents recorded in the sagas and it seems fair enough to say that cartographic accuracy was subsidiary to the aim of staking a cultural claim to territory (McNaughton 2000). In this sense, these maps remained medieval in character (Edson 1998). Yet both maps do incorporate, with remarkable clarity, a geographic feature not clearly described in the sagas and rarely summarized clearly in southern European sixteenth-century maps of a more modern character. This feature is what Stefánsson calls the *Promontorium Winlandiae*, that is to say, Newfoundland's Great Northern Peninsula (Ingstad and Ingstad 1985, 323-37; Harrisse 1900[1968], 273-80). Where does this feature come from, if not from a northern geographical tradition of Vínland?

There are several lines of evidence here. The sagas tell us that there was a place, Leif's Camp, in what sounds like the Strait of Belle Isle, at the northern gateway to Vínland, a geography substantiated by the archaeological record at LAM. If we are not inclined to dismiss the Yale map as a forgery, it records a late medieval conception of Vínland, in which the Great Northern Peninsula and the strait of Belle Isle are among the most prominent geographical features. (And, if we dismiss the Yale map, it is irrelevant.) The post-medieval Stefánsson map depicts this *Promentorium Winlandiae* and a similar feature is shown on the Resen map of the same period, whether or not it was actually labelled *Vínland* in the original draft. The Day letter strongly suggests that John Cabot's itinerary in his voyage to the New World involved latitude sailing on the old Norse route to Greenland. One of the very few locations identified in the accounts of his discovery is a cape (likely Cape Dégrat) in the latitude of the Strait of Belle Isle. Together these are significant pieces of information.

349

The suggestion of a northern itinerary for Cabot's voyage of 1497 is not new. The Newfoundland nationalist, Bishop Michael Howley, argued for it a century ago (Howley 1903). Scholars have been making the suggestion of a conceptual connection between the Norse and Cabot for at least fifty years: notably R.A. Skelton, David Quinn, G.J. Marcus, Robert McGhee and, in her distinctive way, Kirsten Seaver. To these suggestions, I would add that the navigational details in the Day letter, about the easterly winds which brought the *Matthew* across the ocean and about a visit to the Strait of Belle Isle, are important, because they suggest familiarity with Norse navigational traditions. This fits nicely with the new evidence that Zuan Caboto was as a trader in skins and woolfells, with their implication that he may have traded in England before 1496, perhaps in Bristol (Giuffrida , 66). A mass of circumstantial evidence suggests that a northern rather than the southern itinerary is most likely for Cabot's voyage to the West in 1497, as a return trip from Cape Dégrat, latitude sailing at 51° N would be a sensible use of the prevailing westerlies.

The northern and southern itineraries are profoundly different ways of remembering the voyage. The southern route proposes a new Renaissance vision, often attributed to 'Giovanni' Caboto, with emphasis on his supposed origins in Genoa, the home of Columbus, celebrated by nineteenth-century hagiographers as the scientific dispeller of medieval obscurity. The northern route represents a kind of additive European effort, in which a Venetian merchant with Valencian experience found English backers (and a Burgundian barber) to build on the geographical knowledge of medieval Norse mariners, using Mediterranean and Portuguese navigational skills (derived we must remember from Islamic and even Chinese precedents). In such an historical mythology the discoverer-hero might be better remembered by his own name, Zuan Caboto, rather than assimilating him to one particular nineteenth-century nationality or another. We might think of Zuan Caboto's achievement as the successful application of rapidly-evolving, southern European, navigational techniques to a vernacular, northern, geographical tradition.

As the medieval historian Henri Pirenne observed, Europe found America in the tenth century, only to lose it again. In this and other ways the idea of Norse 'discovery' is problematic. Leaving aside the issues raised by the fact that native people already had millennia of experience navigating our coasts, it is worth noticing how the Vínland voyages differed from early modern voyages of discovery, even when they covered the same ground. While the itinerary of Zuan Caboto's voyage is much debated, there are strong reasons to accept an arctic crossing above the 60th parallel, running ahead of prevailing easterlies—that is, on the old Norse route to Greenland. The only geographical reference in the surviving documentation of Cabot's voyage is to Cape Dégrat / Cape Bauld, in the Strait of Belle Isle, while the sole known Norse archaeological site in the New World is also located in the Strait of Belle Isle. Why doubt that the Norse expeditions of *c.* 1000 were voyages of discovery, if we are willing to so describe a voyage to the same place that happened 500 years later—particularly if a vernacular memory of their geographical traditions survived to help inform Cabot's conception of the West? Norse techniques of navigation and sailing differed, of course, from those developed in the late middle ages. The Norse achievement in gradually extending their range to Iceland, Greenland and, for a while at least, to Markland and Vínland, is in some ways therefore even more impressive. What makes medieval Norse voyages different from the early modern western European voyages is that the former consisted of kin groups, moving for a year or two at a time, as part of normal resource foraging, which sometimes resulted in migration. To the extent that these were colonising ventures, they were part of what archaeologists would call a wave of advance. The north Atlantic crossings of the early Renaissance were completed within a few months and were not intended to found colonies but to establish trade links, initially with Asia. Navigators like Cabot raised capital for their ventures, which were manned and provisioned using the new commercial tool of the charter party. These were voyages of discovery because they were conceptualized as a means of reaching around the globe, for a very modern mixture of national, commercial and scientific reasons. The earlier Norse voyages were none of these things, but are better understood as a late stage in the gradual spread of our species into new environments. They succeeded in closing human occupation of the northern hemisphere, as the Newfoundland Museum's recent exhibition rightly emphasized (cf. McGhee 1991, 50). They were the end of an era rather than a beginning.

ABBREVIATION

HB   *Hauksbók*. 1892. ed. F. Jónsson, Copenhagen.

BIBLIOGRAPHY

Bailey, A.G. 1937 [1969]. *The Conflict of European and Eastern Algonkian Cultures 1504-1700*, Toronto.

Brown, G.W. and Trudel, M., eds, 1966 [1979]. *Dictionary of Canadian Biography*, vol. 1, Toronto.

Brown, S.C. 1999. 'Review: The Vinland Map and the Tartar Relation, R.A. Skelton, T.E. Marston and G.D. Painter', *Newfoundland Studies*, 15, 1, 115-24.

Bushman, C. 1992. *America Discovers Columbus: How an Italian Explorer Became an American Hero*, Hanover, New Hampshire.

[Sebastian Cabot?]. 1962. 'Paris Map [1544], Legend 8', in Williamson 1962, 21.

Cahill, T.A. and Kusko, B.H. 1995. 'Compositional and Structural Studies of the Vinland map and Tartar Relation', in Skelton, Marston and Painter 1995, xxix-xxxix.

Campbell, E.M.J. 1976. 'Discovery and the Technical Setting 1420-1520', *Terrae Incognitae*, 8, 11-17.

Cuthbertson, B. 1997. *John Cabot and the Voyage of the* Matthew, Halifax, Nova Scotia.

de Soncino, R. 1962. 'Letter to the Duke of Milan, 18 December 1497', in Williamson 1962, 24.

Edson, E. 1998. *Mapping Time and Space: How Medieval Mapmakers Viewed their World*, London.

Firstbrook, P. 1997. *The Voyage of the* Matthew: *John Cabot and the Discovery of Newfoundland*, Toronto.

Fitzhugh, W.W. and Ward, E.I., eds, 2000. *Vikings, the North Atlantic Saga,* Washington and London.

Giuffrida, E. 1999. 'Richerche Cabotiane, Nouve Prospettive Storiografiche'/ 'New Documents on Giovanni Caboto' (trans. P.C. Clarke), in Zorzi 1999, 47-60/61-72.

Harris, R.C. and Matthews, G.J., eds, 1988. *Historical Atlas of Canada, vol. 1, From the Beginning to 1800*, Toronto.

Harrisse, H. 1892 [1961]. *The Discovery of North America, a Critical, Documentary, and Historic Investigation*, Amsterdam.

——1897. *L'atterage de Jean Cabot au continent américain en 1497*, Göttingen.

——1900 [1968]. *Découverte et évolution cartographique de Terre-Neuve et des pays circonvoisins 1497-1501-1769*, Ridgewood, NJ.

Hoffman, B.G. 1961. *Cabot to Cartier: Sources for an Historical Ethnography of Northeastern North America 1497-1550*, Toronto.

Howley, M.F. 1903. 'Latest Lights on the Cabot Controversy', *Proceedings and Transactions of the Royal Society of Canada*, 9, 205-215.

Ingstad, A-S and Ingstad, H. 1985. *The Norse Discovery of America*, 2 vols, Oslo.

Isemer, H-J and Hasse, L. 1986. *The Bunker Climate Atlas of the North Atlantic Ocean, vol. 1, Observations*, Berlin.

Jackson, M. 1963. 'The Labrador Landfall of John Cabot, 1497', *Canadian Historical Review*, 54, 122-141.

Johnson, D.S. 1994. *Phantom Islands of the Atlantic*, Fredericton, New Brunswick.

Jones, G. ed., 1986. *The Norse Atlantic Saga*, London

Lane, F.C. 1965. 'The Economic Meaning of the Invention of the Compass', *American Historical Review*, 68, 605-617.

Marcus, G.J. 1981. *The Conquest of the North Atlantic*, New York.

Markham, C.R. 1897. 'Fourth Centenary of the Voyage of John Cabot, 1497', *Geographical Journal*, 9, 6, 604-620.

Marston, T.E. 1995. 'The Manuscript: History and Description', in Skelton, Marston and Painter 1995, 1-16.

McGhee, R. 1991. *Canada Rediscovered*, Ottawa.

McNaughton, D. 2000. 'A World in Transition: Early Cartography of the North Atlantic', in Fitzhugh and Ward 2000, 257-269.

Meldgaard, J. 2000. Searching for Vinland—Myths and Realities, unpublished lecture, Canadian Archaeological Association, Ottawa.

Morison, S.E. 1971. *The European Discovery of America: The Northern Voyages*, New York.

Nordenskiöld, A.E. 1889 [1973]. *Facsimile-Atlas to the Early History of Cartography*, New York.

Painter, G.C. 1995a. 'Introduction to the New Edition', in Skelton, Marston and Painter 1995, ix-xx.

——1995b. 'The Tartar Relation and the Vinland Map', in Skelton, Marston and Painter 1995, 241-262.

Parry, J.H. 1981. *The Discovery of the Sea*, London.

Pasqualigo, L. 1962. 'Letter to his brothers in Venice, 23 August 1497', in Williamson 1962, 22.

Pope, P.E. 1997. *The Many Landfalls of John Cabot*, Toronto.

Quinn, D.B. 1961. 'The Argument for the English Discovery of America Between 1480 and 1494', *Geographical Journal*, 127, 227-285.

——1967. 'John Cabot's Matthew', *Times Literary Supplement,* 8 June 1967, 517.

——1968. *Sebastian Cabot and Bristol Exploration*, Bristol.

——1977. *North America from Earliest Discovery to First Settlements: the Norse Voyages to 1612*, New York.

Ruddock, A.A. 1966. 'John Day of Bristol and the English Voyages across the Atlantic before 1497', *Geographical Journal*, 132, 224-233.

351

Ruggles, R.I. 1988. 'Exploring the Atlantic Coast', in Harris and Matthews 1988, pl. 19.

Ruysch, J. 1889 [1973]. *Universalior Cogniti Orbis Tabula ex Recentibus Confecta Observationibus* [1508], in Nordenskiöld 1889[1973], pl. xxxii.

Samson, R. ed., 1991. *Social Approaches to Viking Studies*, Glasgow.

Seaver, K.A. 1996a. *The Frozen Echo, Greenland and the Exploration of North America,* ca *A.D. 1000-1500*, Stanford, CA.

——1996b. 'The Mystery of the "Vinland Map" Manuscript Volume', *The Map Collector*, 74, 24-29.

Seed, P. 1992. 'Taking Possession and Reading Texts: Establishing the Authority of Overseas Empires', *William and Mary Quarterly*, 49, 2, 183-209.

Sigurdsson, G. 2000. 'The Quest for Vinland in Saga Scholarship', in Fitzhugh and Ward 2000, 232-37.

Singleton, C.S. ed., 1967. *Art, Science and History in the Renaissance*, Baltimore.

Skelton, R.A. 1962. 'The Cartography of the Voyages', in Williamson 1962, 295-325.

——1995. 'The Vinland Map', in Skelton, Marston and Painter 1995, 107-240.

Skelton, R.A. 1966 [1979]. 'Cabot (Caboto), John (Giovanni)', in Brown and Trudel 1966 [1979], 146-52.

Skelton, R.A., Marston, T.E. and Painter, G.D., eds, 1995. *The Vinland Map and the Tartar Relation*, 2nd edn, New Haven.

Sutherland, P.D. 2000. 'The Norse and Native North Americans', in Fitzhugh and Ward 2000, 238-47.

Taylor, E.G.R. 1963. 'Where Did the Cabots Go? A Study in Historical Deduction', *Geographical Journal*, 129, 339-341.

——1971. *The Haven-finding Art, a History of Navigation from Odysseus to Captain Cook*. London: Institute of Navigation.

——1974. 'The Vinland Map', *Journal of Navigation*, 27, 2, 195-205.

Tiepolo, M.F. 1973. 'Documenti Veneziani Su Giovanni Caboto', *Studi Veneziani,* 15, 585-597.

Trigger, B.G. 1985. *Natives and Newcomers: Canada's 'Heroic Age' Reconsidered*, Montreal and Kingston.

Tuck, J.A. 1976. *Newfoundland and Labrador Prehistory*. Toronto: National Museum of Man.

Vigneras, L.A. 1956. 'New Light on the 1497 Cabot Voyage to America', *Hispanic-American Historical Review*, 36, 4, 503-506.

——1957. 'The Cape Breton Landfall: 1494 or 1497: Note on a Letter from John Day', *Canadian Historical Review*, 38, 3, 219-228.

Wallace, B. 1986. 'The L'Anse Aux Meadows Site', in Jones 1986, 285-304.

——1991. 'The Vikings in North America: Myth and Reality', in Samson 1991, 207-19.

——2000a. 'The Viking Settlement at L'Anse aux Meadows', in Fitzhugh and Ward 2000, 208-216.

——2000b. 'An Archaeologist's Interpretation of the Vinland Sagas', in Fitzhugh and Ward 2000, 225-31.

Waters, D.W. 1958. *The Art of Navigation in England in Elizabethan and Early Stuart Times*, London.

——1967. 'Science and the Techniques of Navigation in the Renaissance', in Singleton 1967, 189-237.

Williams, A.F. 1996. *John Cabot and Newfoundland*, St. John's, Newfoundland.

Williamson, J.A. ed., 1962. *The Cabot Voyages and Bristol Discovery Under Henry VII*, London.

Wilson, I. 1991. *The Columbus Myth: Did Men of Bristol Reach America before Columbus?*, London.

——1996. *John Cabot and the Matthew*, Tiverton.

Winship, G.P. 1900 [1967]. *Cabot Bibliography with an Introductory Essay on the Careers of the Cabots*, New York.

Zorzi, R.M. ed., 1999. *Attraversare Gli Oceani: Da Giovanni Caboto al Canada Multiculturale*, Venice.

Skrælingar Abroad—Skrælingar at Home?

Kevin McAleese

Introduction

W hen the Viking-Age Norse disembarked from their ships at L'Anse aux Meadows (LAM) approximately 1000 years ago, they did not step onto a land empty of people. Indigenous people inhabited the Island of Newfoundland, like those Þorvaldr Eiríksson supposedly first noted in Markland during his initial southward voyage:

> [U]pon coming closer they saw there were three hide-covered boats [on the beach] with three men under each of them. They divided their forces and managed to capture all of them except one, who escaped with his boat (*Grænlendinga saga* (GLS) in Sigurðsson 2000, 220).

During Þorfinnr Karlsefni's expedition to Vinland, the *skrælingar* were described as being 'short in height with threatening features and tangled hair on their heads. Their eyes were large and their cheeks broad'(*Eiríks saga rauða* (ESR) in Sigurðsson 2000, 223). According to the sagas the new countries of Markland and Vínland were home to more indigenous groups, as was Helluland (the Baffin Island region) to the north.

353

In the sagas all these peoples are called *skrælingar*, a term with no single accepted definition and with unclear origins. The sagas indicate that these *skrælingar* threatened the Norse in their quest for new lands to settle and resources to acquire for trade. However there is little archaeological data to inform us about the early direct Norse-*skræling* contact *c*. AD 1000. There is more archaeological data for the later centuries when later Europeans were in contact with a variety of Aboriginal groups. Therefore the archaeological record, documentary accounts and circumstantial evidence are all relied on here to present a brief overview of the way of life of the groups who inhabited the territory we know as Newfoundland and Labrador, and its surrounding territories.

Most saga accounts about Norse-*skræling* contact generally describe mistrust and conflict. There are a few instances of relatively peaceful trade between them, with most trade episodes apparently ending in violence. This contrasts with trading relationships the Norse had with their 'homeland' neighbour groups, specifically the ancestors of the Sámi. Both the archaeological and historic evidence indicate that the Norse traded with, competed with and taxed the ancestors of the Sámi (Seurujarvi-Kari *et al.* 1997, 10, 11). Yet despite these unequal relations they generally cooperated with each other. This contrast is noteworthy in terms of inter-cultural conflict. Therefore Norse-*skræling* conflict will be compared with the relative peaceful Norse-Sámi coexistence, as the one situation may inform the other.

The Business of Naming

General similarities between all circumpolar, northwest Atlantic peoples may have formed a conceptual basis for the Norse to label them all *skræling*. But it is unclear how broadly this West Old Norse term was used. Research on Nordic Peninsula cultures of a thousand years ago indicates that ethnic identities and lifestyle that we generally label Viking and *skræling* were probably not as well defined at the time (Price 2000a; Olsen 2000). In fact ethnic identities in the Nordic Peninsula *c*. AD 1000 appear to have been blurred and changeable, at least along the edge of Norse homelands (Price 2000a; Olsen 2000). In contrast, the sagas have reified the Viking-Age *skræling* for all indigenous people of the circumpolar, northwest Atlantic.

Figure 1. The North West Atlantic and northeast North America: the arena for *skrælingar* and Norsemen, *c.* eleventh to fourteenth centuries AD (courtesy of Provincial Museum of Newfoundland and Labrador).

This reification process is also evident with the term 'Viking' itself. It was not used by the people who referred to themselves as Danes, Goths and Rogalanders (Wallace 2000a, 51). Their victims and trade partners referred to them as 'Northmen' or 'Norsemen' or 'Viking'. Viking is also a fairly recent 'popular culture' and 'academic' label that appears to have been less used *c.* 1000 AD. (Price 2000b, 25). In reality it referred to the pirates or raiders from the north, and was not complementary. But then neither was *skræling*—a harbinger of other non-complementary names given Aboriginal people centuries later by the Basques, Dutch, French and English.

In fact, ethnic 'slandering' is a relatively common phenomenon in history, where 'others' in a frontier situation get blamed, mistreated and negatively labeled for their strange/difficult behaviour and actions. For example, even during the late Roman Empire many Roman accounts about indigenous people were quite ethnocentric. The 'tent dwellers' or indigenous people from the Near East to Gaul where described in unflattering terms, especially when they posed a threat to the safety and security of Romans (Wiseman 2000, 13).

Security and safety issues appear to have been a significant factor for the Norse in Vínland. In fact, incidents of conflict appear to have been one of the most important factors that persuaded them to withdraw from Vínland:

> Karlsefni and his men had realized by now that although the land was excellent they could never live there in safety or freedom from fear, because of the native inhabitants. So they made ready to leave the place and return home (ESR in Magnusson and Palsson 1965, 100).

In contrast, security and safety issues do not appear to have been significant in the Nordic Peninsula for Norse chieftains and their Sámi ancestor trading partners. They are one of the indigenous groups of northern Scandinavia, who by *c.* AD 1000 were recognized by their neighbours as a distinct people (Price 2000a, 38-39). They may have been one of the semi-nomadic peoples of the Nordic Peninsula whom the Norse called 'Karelians' (Fitzhugh 2000, 1).

Like many subarctic Eurasian people in band-level societies, the ancestors of the Sámi practised a mixed hunting/fishing way of life. Their material culture included a variety of metal objects made of iron and silver, as well as a mix of tradtional implements of wood, bone and antler. Many historic Sámi implements generally resemble those of North American *skræling* groups, especially ones that deal with hunting, fishing and travel. They lived liked *skrælingar* even if they were not actually called *skrælingar*. It is unlikely that similarities with the latter would not have gone unnoticed by observant Norsemen, especially given Norse-Sámi economic relations.

The Norse and Sámi were both neighbours and competitors with a well developed exchange 'code' (Olsen 2000, 33). Their successful trade included wilderness resources such as furs, bird down and walrus tusks offered to the Norse, who saw them as 'luxury goods.' In exchange the Sámi ancestors received Norse/European manufactured goods such as iron and silver (Seurujarvi-Kari *et al.* 1997, 10, 11). Both groups had well developed reciprocal relations, even to the point where the Norse and the Sámi ancestors may have occasionally intermarried (Olsen 2000, 32-35).

The business of trade, regardless where it occurs, requires a shared, mutually understood language, code, or means of communication. Without it misunderstandings arise which can result in conflict and escalation to violence. According to the sagas this appears to have been a common result during trading episodes with the Vínland *skrælingar*. Since the Norse occupation of Vinland was only about two decades, and then only intermittently, a common Norse-*skræling* trade code never appears to have developed between them. Trading activity would be indicated if many Norse and/or *skræling* artefacts were recovered from each others' living sites, but that is not the case. In fact virtually none have been recovered (McGhee 1993, 49; Cox 2000, 206-207; Wallace 2000b, 213).

355

But apparently not all culture contact was negative, as in ESR Norse-*skræling* trade in red cloth and milk products for furs is described (McGhee 1993, 48; Sigurðsson 2000, 221). Productive trading is suggested to a greater degree in the eastern Arctic, given the many Norse objects found there in Thule Inuit sites, and a few in Dorset ones. This proliferation of objects indicates that there was at least occasional trade, possibly through direct contact. This is not surprising given the long term Norse occupation of south-west Greenland and their activities in 'Norðsetur', a hunting area north of the Disko Bay region of west Greenland. Though they hunted in this area for about five centuries, this initial settlement of Greenland by Europeans is brief in comparison to the millennia of settlement by *skrælingar* and their ancestors.

ANCIENT PEOPLES AS *SKRÆLING* ANCESTORS

Aboriginal people of a culture known today as 'Maritime Archaic Indian', crossed over from Labrador to the Island of Newfoundland about four millennia earlier than the Norse. These people were probably descended from people of a culture archaeologists call 'Palaeoindian', whose ancestors originally discovered North America more than 12,000 years ago after crossing the Bering Sea 'land bridge' which then joined Siberia and Alaska (Renouf 1999, 20). Groups of Maritime Archaic Indians first occupied Labrador's Strait of Belle Isle coast about 9000 years ago (Tuck 1976, 107), and crossed the Strait to occupy various areas of the Northern Peninsula about 5000 years ago (Renouf 1999, 20).

These Indian people were followed at LAM by an entirely different lineage of people known as the Palaeoeskimos. They were an arctic-adapted people who originally migrated out of northeast Asia, and who spread across the arctic over 4000 years ago. One group whom archaeologists refer to as 'Groswater' Palaeoeskimos arrived in Labrador about 4,000 years ago, followed by the 'Dorset' Palaeoeskimos at about 3000 years ago (Renouf 1999, 10; Odess *et al.* 2000, 193-197). Both groups occupied LAM, the Groswater at 3000-2600 years ago and the Dorset at 1500-1300 years ago (Wallace 2000b, 214).

A later arctic culture, the Thule Inuit, occupied northern Labrador about 700 years ago, then spread southward to the Strait of Belle Isle (Tuck 1985, 236, 237) by *c.* AD 1500. These ancestral Inuit did not live at LAM nor on the Island of Newfoundland, but they were trading Norse goods near Baffin Island and in Greenland by the thirteenth century AD (Schledermann 1993, 56-63).

When the Viking-Age Norse arrived at LAM, only people of what archaeologists call the 'Recent Indian' cultures were living on Newfoundland's Northern Peninsula. 'Recent', in terms of cultural chronology, contrasts with the region's earlier 'Intermediate' and even older 'Archaic' cultures. The descendants of Recent Indians on the Island of Newfoundland were the Beothuk, and in Labrador they are the Innu (Pastore 1992, 9-12; Loring 1992, 451, 459, 462).

Recent Indians had occupied LAM about a century prior to the Norse (Wallace 2000b, 214), and *c.* AD 1000 they seasonally occupied Bird Cove and Port au Choix, between 150 and 175 km southwest of LAM. Given their proximity to LAM these '*skrælingar*' were 'neighbours' to the Norse, though no saga account clearly documents their meeting in the region. Further to the west in the Maritime Provinces of Canada, or 'western' Vínland (Sigurðsson 2000, 236, 237), the archaeological record suggests *skrælingar* were the ancestral Mi'kmaq people.

In summary, most of these circumpolar and North West Atlantic indigenous people were '*skræling*-like' during the Viking Age. That is, many sub-arctic and arctic people were hunters/ fishers/fur trappers who participated in short and long distance trade networks. They were not farmers and their ethnicity appears to have been distinctly non-European. They also shared, at a general level, beliefs in a spirit world that was largely animistic, with animal spirits and land/sea spirits providing conditional support in a risk-filled geographic region.

SKRÆLINGAR AS MI'KMAQ ANCESTORS (VÍNLAND)

The ancestors of the Mi'kmaq Indians probably moved into the Maritimes about 3500 years ago, and were well established by 2700 years ago. By 1000 years ago, the Miramichi River and its estuary was one area occupied by these people. They appear to have had a rich and comfortable way of life. During spring and summer they lived in or near a few relatively large villages along the rivers flowing into Miramichi Bay. These settlements, some near the coast, could support many extended family groups as they were excellent fishing stations, particularly for sturgeon. Fish was dried or smoked, then stored for winter in birchbark boxes set in the ground in cache pits.

There were also smaller camps near coastal marshes and lagoon/estuary areas that were used for spring/summer egg gathering, fall bird hunting and collecting wild fruits and vegetables. Hunters might travel fifty to sixty kilometres from their large, riverside camps to these select hunting locations. Over the winter people moved into more sheltered locations near stored food surpluses, from which they could hunt moose, deer and caribou (Whitehead 1980, 8, 9).

Like other Aboriginal people who practiced hunting and fishing, the ancient Mi'kmaq made ground and chipped stone knives, scrapers and projectile points. Unlike other ancient people of the Atlantic region, the Mi'kmaq ancestors were distinguished by their participation in a ceramic industry. While many other Aboriginal people used only birchbark or soapstone for containers, the Mi'kmaq ancestors made pots for both cooking and storing food (Petersen and Sanger 1991, 118-152).

The Mi'kmaq appear to have been a vibrant people with an economy that included trade with each other and with their neighbours. Some of this trade is indicated by pieces of

Ramah Chert, a valuable flint-knapping stone recovered from ancient Mi'kmaq sites but only originating in northern Labrador. Other imported trade objects include grave offerings such as tubular pipes, copper beads and exotic shells, some probably from present-day Ohio (Whitehead 1991, 227-229).

Although no archaeological evidence exists, trade between the Mi'kmaq ancestors and the Norse is suggested from saga accounts and environmental factors (Sigurðsson 2000, 236, 237; Whitehead 1991, 227). The floral remains and 'ecofacts' recovered from LAM indicate a Norse familiarity with the landscape of the Mi'kmaq ancestors. Butternuts, cut butternut wood and cedar tree pieces were recovered from the Norse occupation at LAM (Wallace 2000b, 214-216). Yet the Island of Newfoundland has no wild grapes nor butternut trees, nor would it have a thousand years ago (see Bell *et al.*, this volume).

Although the Mi'kmaq ancestors and the 'Recent Indians' of the Island of Newfoundland participated in a trade network, it is unlikely they traded nuts and wood or travelled between those regions. The apparent vector for the transfer of nuts and wood from the mainland to the Island then is the Norse (Wallace 2000b, 213). While traversing Vínland in their quest for resources, the Norse must have noted that the Island of Newfoundland landscape was significantly different from that on the mainland. This difference, especially the absence of wild grape habitat on the Island, makes it problematic to include it in Vínland ('Wineland'). Yet the Island's west coast landscape bears some resemblance to the Atlantic mainland, and the settlement/subsistence pattern of its 'Recent Indian' inhabitants, resembles that of *skrælingar* on the mainland.

Skrælingar as 'Recent Indians' (Vínland/Markland)

At or near LAM the sagas suggest the Norse interacted with Aboriginal people, though interestingly there is no archaeological evidence for this. However, archaeology does indicate that during the 'Recent Indian Period' the inhabitants of Labrador and the Island of Newfoundland's west coast lived a similar way of life. Their stone tool technology supports the view that these peoples were related (Pastore 1992, 9-11), but there are other similar cultural elements.

In terms of tools and weapons, chipped stone arrow and spear points had corner notches for hafting. Both Labrador and Newfoundland Recent Indians manufactured relatively large knives and relatively small scrapers for butchering and skinning land animals, sea mammals and fish. Many Labrador Recent Indian tools, in particular notched flake points, are strongly similar to Recent Indian projectile points from the Island. They have been excavated from sites at Bird Cove and at Port au Choix, on Newfoundland's Northern Peninsula. At both locations they are primarily made from the distinct Labrador stone called 'Ramah Chert,' which indicates a trade and transport network for this material

Settlement pattern research suggests they never numbered more than a thousand in Labrador, and less on the Island. Recent Indian bands were probably extended families who lived both on the coast or in the interior, moving between camps on a seasonal basis. They occupied sites near river mouths in the bottoms of bays/inlets or, seasonally, out on coastal headlands. Their occupation and use of these sites depended on the kinds of animals they were trying to capture, such as seals or caribou (Loring 1992, 334-342). Both seals and caribou would have provided meat and marrow for food, skins for shelter and clothing, sinew and tendons for sewing/binding and for many other things.

In order to move between these sites, both riverine and/or coastal ones, these *skrælingar* would have required boats. Like canoes of the Labrador Innu, descendants of the Recent Indian people, their boats were likely made of sewn birchbark or skin. These Innu canoes are recorded in the ethnographic literature from at least the early eighteenth century. They

357

measure about 14 feet long, and made adequate temporary shelters during travel periods (McGhee 1993, 48).

As for Labrador Recent Indian dwellings, comparisons again with the Labrador Innu suggests the dwellings probably took the form of small, conical-shaped tents made of poles and animal skins, or larger, more dome-shaped structures (Loring 1992, 267-277). On the Island of Newfoundland there is little evidence to suggest Recent Indian dwelling types, though shelters/tents made of poles covered in birchbark and animal skins would conform with the ethnographic record.

In terms of 'ceremonial' architecture, a Recent Indian linear hearth feature was uncovered at 'Winter Cove 4' near the mouth of Hamilton Inlet. Dating to about 450 years ago, it appears to be the remains of a ceremonial structure called a *shaputuan* (Loring 1992, 341-351, 358-361). Crushed and burned caribou bone was been found in abundance in this hearth (Pastore 2000, 44). Similar features have been recorded for the Recent Indians on the Island of Newfoundland (Gilbert 2001, 2). Feasting ceremonies were held in honour of the caribou in these structures, an important cultural activity well documented for the Labrador Innu. Arguably, the large number of shared cultural elements amonst these groups over centuries suggests they are all part of one cultural tradition.

A Norse account which appears to summarize elements of this tradition can be found in GLS. Norse sailing directions and landscape descriptions, combined with southern Labrador geography, suggest the Norse sailed into Hamilton Inlet. There the Norse describe meeting *skrælingar* who lived in 'mounds'. These 'mounds' may have been the elongated, dome-shaped superstructure of light branches and animal skins which probably covered a shaputuan (McGhee 1990, 48). However this meeting, like many others, was not peaceful. It ended with the Norse killing a number of Aboriginal people who were apparently sleeping beneath boats (Sigurðsson 2000, 220-224), probably canoes of the type documented ethnographically.

Skrælingar as Dorset Palaeoeskimos (Helluland)

As Palaeoeskimo people, the Dorset and their ancestors occupied most of the high Arctic from about 3800 years ago until about 800 years ago. They were one of the many groups of Siberian people who migrated across the Bering Strait into Alaska and the western Arctic about 4500 years ago. The Palaeoeskimos who appear to have been the most successful are called the 'Dorset' by archaeologists. This name stems from the Cape Dorset location, which contains many of their definitive archaeological sites.

The Dorset were able to exploit a variety of sea mammals, birds and land mammals such as caribou and musk-ox. They reached the Island of Newfoundland about 2800 years ago. Here, over time, they focused more on marine mammal hunting, a technological and economic distinction characteristic of the Dorset culture.

Their technology was extremely innovative and efficient. Using the bones and hides of their prey animals they were able to clothe and house themselves, as well as make boats and sleds for travel. In this regard whales, walrus, seals, musk-ox and caribou were all utilized. Seal bone, whale teeth and walrus ivory were also used to fashion harpoons, tool handles, snow knives and goggles, as well as needles and their cases.

Stone was manufactured into projectile points and carving tools. The latter were also used to produce intricate and detailed bone and antler animal carvings of the important prey species hunted and respected by the Dorset. They also carved soapstone into pots and lamps for cooking their food and lighting their dwellings, respectively.

Depending on the season a Dorset dwelling might be a tent, a snow house or one made of sod, wood, bone and animal skin. In these Dorset dwellings located on headlands or on islands, a few extended families would live. These were seasonal occupations closely coordinated to the availability of resources.

For example at Port au Choix, Newfoundland, Dorset family groups lived in dozens of semi-subterranean houses found at the Philip's Garden site. These were somewhat circular dwellings with interior raised benches/platforms around the periphery. In these the Dorset spent the late winter season, over a period from about 2100 to 1300 years ago. They exploited the rich harp seal populations which whelp on the sea ice in March. Seals provided meat, hides for clothing and house roofs, and blubber for lighting their lamps (Renouf 1999).

Despite their pan-Arctic settlement, including as far south as the Island of St. Pierre (LeBlanc 2000, 97-103), by 1200 years ago the Dorset abandoned the region and were living only in northern Labrador and parts of the high Arctic. Climatic change, particularly warm periods in the Northwest Atlantic, may have been a factor (Frydendahl 1993, 91-93). These warm periods may have negatively influenced the distribution of Arctic prey species on which the Dorset depended. For example, if sea ice formation and patterning was effected, then good seal hunting sites may have diminished. A retreat northward to Labrador to hunt those species, as well as connect with other Dorset people, may then have been the result.

It is likely the Dorset and Norse met in Helluland. There is no Norse saga account describing contact, but the Norse would certainly have passed Dorset camps as they sailed along the Helluland (Baffin Island and area) and Markland coasts during their trips between Greenland and Vínland. The same warm periods which may have had a negative effect on the Dorset had a positive effect for Norse expansion westward across the Atlantic. A more stable climate with less ice appears to have been an effect of these warm periods, thus making trans-Atlantic voyaging more feasible (Frydendahl 1993, 91-93).

359

Dorset-Norse contact may also have occurred in northern Labrador. At the Avayalik site spun cordage of musk-ox wool has been identified (Sutherland 1999, 166). This is not generally recognized as a Dorset artefact type, so a working hypothesis is that it represents Dorset-European trade, probably with Norse Greenlanders. But the cordage initial dating at between the late seventh-early eighth centuries AD (Sutherland 1999, 164-167) does not fit with the known occupation of Norse Greenland, *c.* AD 985-1450.

This example of possible early Norse-Dorset contact may have occurred as a result of Norse wood harvesting. In 1347 a written account describes some Norse Greenlanders getting blown off course on their return from a wood collecting trip to Markland, and landing back in Iceland (Seaver 1996, 108). It is possible the Norse met the Dorset on these trips as a few Norse artefacts have been found in close association with Dorset ones in Helluland (Sutherland 2000, 160-167; Odess *et al.* 2000, 195-197) and elsewhere, but some of those associations are weak.

For example, the Dorset soapstone bowl excavated at LAM (Odess *et al.* 2000, 197) was not recovered from the Norse occupation layer, so later inhabitants must have scavenged it from a Dorset camp and deposited it there. In addition, the site's only recovered soapstone spindle whorl, once thought to represent contact with the Dorset, is apparently made from a piece of a Norse soapstone vessel (B. Wallace pers. comm.). If and when it did occur, Dorset-Norse contact was likely brief as virtually all the Dorset appear to have been replaced throughout the eastern Arctic by the Thule Inuit by *c.* AD 1500 (McGhee 1996, 231).

Skrælingar as Thule/Inuit (Helluland and Greenland)

The 'Thule' people migrated out of the far western Arctic 1000 years ago, and moved into northern Labrador via Baffin Island about 700 years ago. The name 'Thule' stems from an archaeological site in west Greenland where early twentieth-century scientists discovered important settlements with artefacts typical of this culture. The Thule are the direct ances-tors of the modern-day Labrador Inuit and all the Canadian and Greenland Inuit.

Thule Inuit settlement and subsistence patterns are characterised by regular, seasonal travel in search of animals for food, tools, clothing, warmth and light. Like the Dorset Palaeoeskimos who they replaced, the Thule were skilled sea mammal hunters who used skin boats to hunt bowhead whales. In fact they relied heavily on animals from the sea for subsistence such as seals, walrus, whales, cod, char and salmon.

Summer travel on water was by kayak and umiak, skin-covered boats which carried one to twenty people, respectively. From these vessels hunters chased their sea mammal quarry, harpooning and spearing them with weapons made of stone, bone and animal thong/line. The line was attached to an inflated seal bladder and used as a 'drag' to slow down a wounded animal.

Kayaks were also used by hunters to lance caribou as they crossed ponds or inlets close to Thule camps, where the animals were butchered with stone knives. This food was then cached for later use, or brought back to their dwellings. Of the land animals, caribou was the primary species, usually hunted late in the summer. Other food sources included lake trout, birds and berries.

'Early' Thule settlements in the central arctic were relatively large and characterised by substantial houses made of whale bone and sod. Winter travel between these settlements and/or hunting sites was by komatik, a large sled pulled by a dog team. Dogs were not only crucial for travel, but they were 'partners' in the hunt for polar bears and seals and, occasionally, eaten as emergency food.

Using skin covered boats and dog traction, the Thule Inuit expanded across the high Arctic and into north Greenland by the early thirteenth century (Schledermann 1996). As the Thule slowly moved south into what the Norse Greenlanders called 'Nordsetur' they would likley have met the Norse (Schledermann 1993, 60-65).

Indirect trade between the Thule and the Norse is suggested by Norse artefacts found in Inuit sites scattered throughout the eastern arctic (Schledermann 1993, 56-59). These include: a bronze balance arm (Sutherland 1987); a portion of a cast bronze bowl (McGhee 1976); a bronze pendant and pieces of smelted copper (McGhee 1984); a copper pendant (Harp 1975); various pieces of iron, some smelted

360

Figure 2. This delicate driftwood carving, with distinctly non-Inuit features, was likely a portrait of a Norse visitor, c. mid-thirteenth century AD (after Schledermann 1997).

(McCartney and Mack 1973; McGhee 1976); and a wooden figurine (Sabo and Sabo 1978), possibly a representation of a hooded Norse Christian. The Norse origin of these objects is indicated by their shape and composition, especially the smelted metals, a non-Thule Inuit technology.

These objects were not deposited by the Norse however, given the objects' great geographic range around the eastern arctic and the many centuries of occupation of the find sites. The greater number of Norse finds from Inuit sites on the east coast of Ellesmere Island, particularly from Skraeling Island south of Ellesmere's Bache Peninsula does, however, suggest direct trade (Schlederman 2000, 251). 'Skraeling Island,' named for the many Inuit sod houses noted by Otto Sverdrup (1904) during his substantive geographical surveys along Ellesmere's east coast, has a few Thule sites. Many Norse metal and wood items have been recovered from these, including ship rivets.

Some of the most significant Norse items in that collection include a clump of chain mail, a piece of an iron blade from a carpenter's plane, knife and spear blades, an awl, ship rivets and pieces of woolen cloth, perhaps from a sail (Schlederman 2000, 250). They came from Thule Inuit sod house floors, hearths and interior cache pits, along with a few unmodified ship rivets and a wooden face carving of a Norseman. These last items are more suggestive of direct contact (Schledermann 1997, 36).

Iron is generally modified as it passes through trade networks, as some ship rivets were. But unmodified rivets had to be removed from intact Norse ship planks. They suggest a Norse ship ventured far north into this region and never returned (Schledermann 1993, 64-65). In turn, the wooden carving has a person's recognizable features which must have been known, in some fashion, to the Skraeling Island Inuit.

361

Most of these artefacts date to the mid-thirteenth century AD, as does a similar collection from Thule Inuit sod houses on Ruin Island, directly east of Skraeling Island off the Greenland coast. The Ruin Island pieces include a lump of chain mail with rings virtually identical to the Skraeling Island find, as well as pieces of woven cloth, a comb and a gaming piece, all closely dated to the Skraeling Island finds. These objects further support the contention that a Norse vessel ventured north to Skraeling Island, a risky voyage in ice-filled waters.

In Markland/Labrador, more than 2500 km to the south, Thule Inuit-Norse contact did not occur. The earliest Labrador Thule Inuit settlement dates to the mid to late thirteenth century (Fitzhugh 1994, 258), long after the initial and fairly brief Norse travel to the region. By the fourteenth and fifteenth centuries, the Inuit replaced the Norse in Greenland. Climatic cooling, along with a variety of European trade factors, may have persuaded the Norse to abandon their farms (Seaver 1996, 12-13, 115; see also Lynnerup, Arneborg this volume). This cooling was an environmental development for which the Thule Inuit were well adapted.

Figure 3. Dorset amulet made from a piece of smelted sheet copper possibly from Norse Greenland found in Richmond Gulf, Hudson's Bay (Ministère de la Culture et des Communications Laboratoire et Réserve d'archéologie du Québec).

CONCLUSION

The Norse sagas' relating of *skrælingar* may be seen to represent a collective memory based on actual incidents. These incidents are believed to have occurred around AD 1000 in Vínland, the name the Norse gave to the region many scholars believe was insular Newfoundland's west coast, Labrador's Strait of Belle Isle coast and much of mainland Atlantic Canada (Wallace 2000b). Yet currently there is no archaeological evidence for these cultural interactions.

The people who lived along the Island's west coast were of 'archaeological' cultures of the Recent Indian Period. These people were likely the ancestors of at least two different Indian cultures: Beothuk and Innu. Based on Atlantic Canada history and archaeology, the ancestors of the Mi'kmaq of present day Nova Scotia and New Brunswick were likely perceived as *skrælingar* by the Norse as well. People of two arctic cultures, the Dorset Palaeoeskimos and the Thule Inuit, also appear to have been *skrælingar*.

362

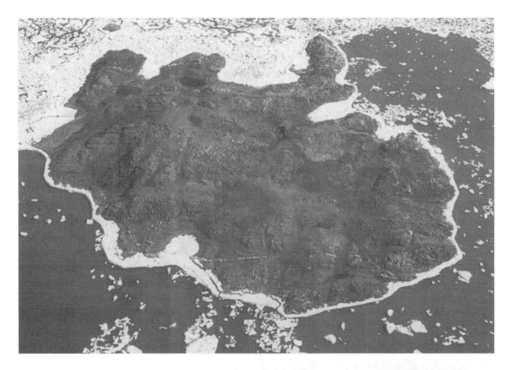

Figure 4, above. Skraeling Island, in Alexandra Fjord, Ellesmere Island was named by Otto Sverdrup in 1898-1899 while exploring the Arctic in his boat *Fram*. The island was home to thirteenth-century Thule Inuit, and a place visited then by the Norse (after McAleese 2000, 57).

Figure 5, left. Iron ship rivet, *c.* AD mid-thirteenth century, found in a Thule Inuit winter house ruin on Skraeling Island (after McAleese 2000, 57).

The Norse who contacted these *skrælingar* between the eleventh and fourteenth centuries AD were from the Eastern Settlement in Greenland, and from Iceland. Based on the trans-Atlantic Norse economy and society, they probably knew of *skræling*-like indigenous peoples of the Nordic Peninsula, some of whom may have been called Karelians.

One nineteenth-century saga translation documents the labelling of Nordic Peninsula people as *skrælingar*:

> There was a man called Þorbjorn, with the last name Karlsefni. He said he would explore Greenland and go places where no one had ever gone before. He sailed from the South West of Greenland until the landscape started changing and he discovered places where no one has been since. He met *skrælingar* and these people are in some books called Lapps (Rafn 1867, AM 770c).

Yet labelling Nordic Peninsula people as *skrælingar* was apparently a rare occurrence. This was probably because of the fairly positive and structured economic and social relations Nordic Peninsula people had with the Norse. In contrast, the Norse collective memory reifies *skrælingar* as the people who prevented the Norse from obtaining new resources to trade and lands to settle, though we have only saga accounts to indicate that outcome. Slandering these indigenous people may have been a Norse way of rationalizing a period in their history when people for whom they had little respect, curtailed their *landnám* (land taking) and stymied their business interests.

363

Trade and exploitation were fundamental characteristics of Norse cultural relations with indigenous people, apparently facilitated by a common language and/or a code of exchange. North American *skrælingar* and the Norse appear to have had neither.

BIBLIOGRAPHY

Appelt, M., Berglund, J. and Gulløv, H.C., eds, 2000. *Identities and Cultural Contacts in the Arctic*, Copenhagen.

Clausen, B.L. ed., 1993. *Viking Voyages to North America*, Roskilde.

Cox, S. L. 2000. 'A Norse Penny from Maine', in Fitzhugh and Ward, 206-07.

Deal. M. and Blair, S., eds, 1991. *Prehistoric Archaeology in the Maritime Provinces. Past and Present Research,* Fredericton, New Brunswick.

Fitzhugh, W. W. 1994. 'Staffe Island 1 and the Northern Labrador Dorset-Thule Succession', in Morrison and Pilon 1994, 239-68.

Fitzhugh, W.W. and Ward, E.I., eds, 2000. *Vikings: The North Atlantic Saga*, Washington and London.

Frydendahl, K. 1993. 'The Summer Climate in the North Atlantic about the year 1000', in Clausen 1993, 90-4.

Gilbert, B. 2001. 'Dildo Island, Cupids and Surveys in Conception and Trinity Bays' in Archaeological Work Carried Out in Newfoundland and Labrador, 2001. Ms. on file, Provincial Archaeology Office, Government of Newfoundland and Labrador, St. John's.

Harp, E. 1975. 'A Late Dorset Copper Amulet from Southeastern Hudson Bay", *Folk*, 16/17, 33-44.

Loring, S. 1972. Princes and Princesses of Ragged Fame: Innu Archaeology and Ethnohistory in Labrador, Unpublished Phd Dissertation, University of Massachusetts.

Magnusson, M. and Pálsson, H. 1965. *The Vinland Sagas: The Norse Discovery of America*, London.

Maxwell, M.S. ed., 1976. *Eastern Arctic Prehistory: Palaeoeskimo Problems*. Washington: Memoirs of the Society of American Archaeology 31.

McAleese, K. ed., 2000. *Full Circle—First Contact: Vikings and Skraelings in Newfoundland and Labrador*. St. John's: Exhibit Catalogue, Newfoundland Museum.

McCartney, A. P. and Mack, D.J. 1973. 'Iron Utilization by Thule Eskimos of central Canada', *American Antiquity,* 38/3, 328-339.

McGhee, R. 1976. 'Palaeoeskimo Occupations of Central and High Arctic Canada', in Maxwell 1976, 15-39.

——1984. 'Contact Between Native North Americans and the Medieval Norse: A Review of the Evidence', *American Antiquity*, 49/1, 4-26.

——1993. 'The Skraelings of Vinland', in Clausen 1993, 43-53.

Kevin McAleese

——1996. *Ancient People of the Arctic*, Vancouver.

Morrison, D. and Pilon, J-L., eds, 1994. *Threads of Arctic Prehistory: Papers in Honour of William E. Taylor Jr.* Hull: Canadian Museum of Civilization, Mercury Series, Archaeological Survey of Canada Paper 149.

Odess, D., Loring, S. and Fitzhugh, W.W. 2000. 'Skraeling: First Peoples of Helluland, Markland and Vinland', in Fitzhugh and Ward, 193-205.

Olsen, B. 2000. 'Belligerent Chieftains and Oppressed Hunters?—Changing Conceptions of Inter-Ethnic Relationships in Northern Norway during the Iron Age and early Medieval Period', in Appelt, Berglund and Gulløv 2000, 28-42.

Pastore, R.T. 1992. *Shanawdithit's People—The Archaeology of the Beothuks*, St. John's, Newfoundland.

——2000. 'Recent Indian Peoples and the Norse', in McAleese 2000, 43-7.

Petersen, J.B. and Sanger, D. 1991. 'An Aboriginal Ceramic Sequence for Maine and the Maritime Provinces', in Deal and Blair 1991, PP??.

Price, N.S. 2000a. 'The Scandinavian landscape: People and Environment', in Fitzhugh and Ward 2000, 31-41.

——2000b. 'Drum-Time and Viking Age: Sámi-Norse Identities in early Medieval Scandinavia', in Appelt, Berglund and Gulløv 2000, 12-27.

Rafn, C.C. 1837. *Antiquitates Americaenae*, Copenhagen

Sabo, D. and Sabo, G. 1978. 'A Possible Thule Carving of a Viking from Baffin Island, NWT', *Canadian Journal of Archaeology*, 2, 33-42.

Schledermann, P. 1996. *Voices in Stone—A Personal Journey in the Arctic Past*, Calgary.

——1997. *The Viking Saga*, London.

Seurujarvi-Kari, Pedersen, S. and Hirvonen, V. 1997. The Sámi—The Indigenous People of Northernmost Europe, Brussels.

Sigurðsson, G. 2000. 'An Introduction to the Vinland Sagas', in Fitzhugh and Ward, 218-24.

Seaver, K.A. 1996. *The Frozen Echo—Greenland and the Exploration of North America* ca *AD 1000-1500*, Stanford, California.

Sutherland, P. 1987. 'Umingmaknuna: Its People and Prehistory', *Inuktitut*, 66, 46-54.

——2000. 'Strands of Culture Contact. Dorset-Norse Interactions in the Canadian Eastern Arctic', in Appelt, Berglund and Gulløv, 159-69.

Thomson, J.S. and Thomson, C., eds, 1985. *Archaeology in Newfoundland and Labrador 1984, Annual Report 5*, St. John's.

Tuck, J. 1985. '1984 Excavations at Red Bay, Labrador', in Thomson and Thomson 1985, 224-247.

Wallace, B. L. 2000a. 'Vinland's Place in the Viking World', in McAleese 2000, 51-55.

——2000b. 'The Viking Settlement at L'Anse aux Meadows', in Fitzhugh and Ward 2000, 208-16.

Whitehead, R.H. 1980. *Elitekey. Micmac Material Culture from 1600 A.D. to the Present*, Halifax.

——1991. 'The Protohistoric Period in the Maritime Provinces', in Deal and Blair 1991, 227-58.

Wiseman, J. 2000. 'Barbarians at the Gate', *Archaeology*, 53/6, 12-14.

Humour, Irony, and Insight:

The first European Accounts of Native North Americans

Kenneth Baitsholts

T he Norse inhabitants of Greenland were the first Europeans to encounter native peo-
ple in North America. They, or rather their cousins in Iceland, were also the first
Europeans to record accounts of that contact, in the form of what are known as the
Vínland sagas.

Like later Europeans, the Norse made no distinctions between the various peoples with
whom they interacted. They referred to them, collectively, as *skrælingar*, a term with a dis-
puted etymology. Ásgeir Blöndal Magnússon (1989, 869) and Alexander Johannesson
(1956, 828) relate the word to *skrá* 'dry, wrinkled skin.' Sayers derives the word from Old
Irish (1993, 9).

While Norse interactions with the First Peoples of Atlantic Canada, and perhaps New
England, were of brief duration, it is with these, almost exclusively, that the Vínland sagas
deal. Were it not for these sagas, inaccurate though they may be, we would know next to
nothing about these interactions. It is also unlikely that the Norse site at L' Anse aux
Meadows would have been located without the information provided in the Vínland sagas
(Ingstad 1985, 9-10).

Norse contact with the Thule Inuit, in Arctic Canada and Greenland, may have continued for several centuries. There is little evidence of this contact in the sagas, but literary, linguistic, and most importantly, archaeological evidence can be utilized to better understand
the nature of this interaction.

I will first discuss the saga evidence for native-Norse contact. Next, I shall briefly discuss the historical sources relating to that contact. I will then deal with linguistic and cultural borrowings, which may give some indications as to the nature of native-Norse interaction. Finally, I will mention, briefly, the archaeological evidence of contact.

LITERARY EVIDENCE

Both *Eiríks saga rauða* (ESR) and *Grænlendinga saga* (GLS) describe episodes of
peaceful trading between the Norse and the natives. The saga writers found the behavior of
the natives to be peculiar, and to increase the entertainment value of their stories, they
employed humour to mock that behavior.

In ESR, Þorfinnr Karlsefni Þórðarson and his men traded with *skrælingar* who appeared
in the spring. For their pelts, the *skrælingar* accepted red cloth, though they initially wanted swords and spears. As the Norse began to run short of this cloth, they cut it into small
strips, for which, the saga writer mockingly reports, the *skrælingar* traded as many pelts as
before, or even more (ESR 228). To the Norse who heard this story, and to Icelanders who
later read the saga, the *skrælingar* were made to appear silly and foolish.

Bruce Trigger reports that eighteenth-century officials of the Hudson's Bay Company
were also puzzled when the natives of subarctic Canada, with whom they were trading,
offered fewer pelts for sale, when they were given a higher price for them. He says:

> it made sense for native traders to collect fewer furs when those were sufficient to satisfy their needs.
> Under these circumstances, minimizing effort made more sense than maximizing profits (Trigger 1997,
> 195).

It is reasonable to conclude that the converse was true with the *skræling* traders in ESR. If it was necessary to provide more pelts to obtain the quantity of cloth they desired, the *skrælingar* were willing to do so. It would have been difficult for the Norse, as it certainly was for later Europeans, to accurately judge the value their goods held in native society. This varied from nation to nation, and changed with time. Verazzano discovered this in 1524. To the natives of southern New England, probably Narragansett and Wampanoag, he traded 'little bells, blue crystals and other trinkets' (*Cellere Codex* 1910, 191; Quinn 1981, 15). He claimed that they were uninterested in steel, iron, or arms.

In Cape Breton, however, the Mi'kmaq would accept only knives, fish hooks, and sharp metals, and when Verazzano had run out of these, the Mi'kmaq scorned him and his men by showing them their buttocks and laughing (Calloway 1991, 32, 264, n.11; Marshall 1996, 17; Hoffman 1961, 112).

The color red had special meaning to the First Peoples of Atlantic Canada (Marshall 1996, 287). When Panoniac, a respected leader of the Mi'kmaq was killed around 1615, his body was wrapped in red cloth obtained from the French (Ricker 1997, 42).

GLS also contains a description of trading. Again the *skrælingar* are mocked for their seemingly foolish behavior. After being frightened by a Norse bull, they traded their valuable pelts for nothing more than dairy products. As before, they initially wanted weapons, but Karlsefni would not allow the Norse to sell them.

A Norse audience would not have missed the humour in the saga writer's remark that, while the Norse got valuable furs, the *skrælingar* carried away the goods which they received in their bellies (GLS 261-2). We should take into account, however, that fat, in the form of butter, or from other sources, was highly prized by arctic and subarctic peoples. Hermann Pálsson cites several examples, taken from the sagas, of the value placed upon imported fat by the Sámi of northern Norway (Pálsson 1997, 25).

The lack of familiarity with iron among the *skrælingar* is also mocked in both sagas (ESR 230; GLS 263). They are depicted as being so simple as to not know the use of an iron axe. They must have learned quickly, however, because both sagas tell us that they sought to buy weapons.

From Columbus in the south, who reported that the natives there, being unfamiliar with iron, cut their hands upon his dagger (Houben 1935, 126), to Frobisher in the north and the infamous iron blooms (Olin 1993, 49), iron has been a recurrent theme in European-native relations. When GLS tells of a *skræling* trying to steal Norse weapons (GLS 263), it is merely the first in a long series of such European accounts. Inuit in the Godthåb area of Greenland even managed, in 1586, to steal an anchor from the ship of John Davis (Oswalt 1999, 39). Different concepts of ownership and of community property were most likely at the root of the misunderstandings which arose over such acts (Birket-Smith 1936, 149).

As would often be the case with later European expeditions to America, peaceful relations involving trade developed into hostile confrontations. While ESR claims that the bull incident, which it also reports, was the cause of this (ESR 228), GLS gives a more plausible explanation that the killing of a *skræling* man was the cause (GLS 263). ESR does report that Karlsefni kidnapped two *skræling* boys, but this is said to have taken place after the hostilities had already begun (ESR 233). Corte Real, Cartier, and Frobisher all kidnapped native people on their expeditions in Atlantic and Arctic Canada (Biggar 1911, 64; Hoffman 1961, 136; Hulton 1964, 13). Such kidnappings would naturally have caused the populations of the people affected to become hostile toward Europeans (Marshall 1996, 17).

The confrontation which has gained the most attention is the one involving Freydís Eiríksdóttir. In this episode, a pregnant Freydís frightens off her *skræling* attackers by slapping a bare sword on her exposed breast (ESR 229). This episode has entertained generations of Icelanders, and puzzled generations of scholars. It is unfortunate that most of those who have commented upon Freydís' action have been far more familiar with the world of

Greek antiquity, than they have been with the First Peoples of North America (Wolf 1996, 469; see B. Sawyer, 'Women in Viking-Age Scandinavia', this volume).

James Howley, in his monumental work *The Beothuck or Red Indians*, gives examples where Beothuk women, when confronted by hostile European men, exposed their breasts to indicate their sex (Howley 1915, 34, 93; see also Winter 1975, 7; Horwood 1959a, 41; 1959b, 82; Marshall 1996, 292). Among the Beothuk, there appears to have been a strong taboo against harming women, and the women in these cases obviously believed, or at least hoped that this taboo was also observed by the Europeans. Although the pre-Christian Norse did have a similar taboo (cf. *Eyrbyggja saga* 36, 54; *Gísla saga* 101), later European settlers did not. Howley gives an example where a pregnant Beothuk women, much like Freydís, is left behind by her kinsmen fleeing their attackers. Rather than exposing her breasts, she pointed to her stomach. The European fishermen, in this case, however, took no pity (Howley 1915, 34).

While it is true that Freydís is described as having Amazon-like attributes, I think that the episode is better explained if we assume that the Norse settlers in Newfoundland actually observed the behavior in proto-Beothuk women. They, then, incorporated accounts of it into their stories. The saga writer, two hundred years later, either misunderstood, or purposely embellished upon these stories, coming up with the Freydís incident. (I have been unable to document this behavior among women of other First Nations, but it is certainly possible that the practice was not confined to the Beothuk.)

367

We find examples of shamanism, Norse and *skræling*, in both Vínland sagas. The affinities between Norse and Sámi shamanism are well known (Pálsson 1997, 85; Price 2000; see Price, this volume), and it appears that some type of shamanism was practiced by most circumpolar peoples (de Laguna 1994, 7). In ESR, Þorbjörg *lítil-völva* (Little Sibyl) and Þórhallr both function as shaman (ESR 206 and 224), while *skræling* shaman in Vínland apparently employ 'optical illusions' to trick the Norse into believing that their attackers are more numerous than they were (ESR 230). The heavy sleep which falls upon Þorvaldr and his men, together with the mysterious voice which warns them to flee, may be seen as a shamanic effort to drive away the Norse (GLS 256). In the early 1600's, Abenaki told the French that their shaman had used magic to bring about the failure of the English colony on the Kennebec river (Calloway 1991, 41-8).

While some of the narrative in the sagas concerning the *skrælingar* may at first seem to be fabricated or totally inaccurate, upon closer examination it sometimes emerges that the accounts correspond, as well as can be expected, to what we know about the First Peoples of Atlantic Canada and New England at the time. In the Vínland sagas, we find a description of *skræling* food, said to have been: 'animal marrow blended with blood' (ESR 230), a *skræling* man with a beard (ESR 233), and a nation ruled by 'two kings' (ESR 233). All of these descriptions could be based upon actual experience. Howley gives examples where Beothuk food is described in much the same way (1915, 12 , 77; Gathorne-Hardy 1921 [1970], 178), while an account of the Scots colony in Nova Scotia from 1629 mentions an encounter with a shaman, who has a beard (Griffiths and Reid 1992, 508). Verazzano also uses the phrase 'two kings' in describing the leaders of the natives he encountered in southern New England. It seems that dual chieftainship was a feature of leadership among these people (Quinn 1981, 16). We can conclude by saying that the Vínland sagas, though somewhat bias and inaccurate, are the results of actual personal experience with the First Peoples of North America. The saga descriptions, however, do not enable us to determine the tribal affiliations of the peoples with whom the Norse interacted.

Before moving on to the historical evidence, I would like to discuss, briefly, the Greenlandic Inuit oral traditions, relating to the Norse. Norse interactions with the Thule Inuit may have lasted for several centuries. Inuit oral tradition in Greenland has preserved several stories about the Norse. While it is proper to be somewhat skeptical regarding the accuracy of these traditions, one should not forget the story of Charles Francis Hall. Working among the Inuit in Baffin Island in 1862, he was able, from their stories, to reconstruct the details of a previous European expedition to the area. The people knew how many ships had come, what the Whites had brought with them, and where they conducted their activities. This may not seem very impressive, until we realize that what these Inuit were 'remembering' were details of the Frobisher expeditions, which had taken place almost three hundred years before (Rowley 1993; Jones 1997, 33).

The interpretation of Greenlandic Inuit oral tradition is complicated by several factors. A large degree of mobility among the Thule (Nørlund 1936, 137), and later colonisation by Europeans (McGovern 1979, 173), introduce added uncertainties about the locations and time frame of the events described in the stories (see Arneborg, this volume). Some of these traditions, however, do seem to be based upon actual meetings between the Thule and the Norse. One story tells of a bow shooting contest, said to have occurred in what was the Western Settlement, when the two cultures first came into contact (Rink 1875, 317-19). The place, located near several Norse ruins (Krogh 1982, 194-5, map 2), is called Pisigsarfik, 'the shooting place.' The first meetings between the Norse and the southerly-migrating Thule could have taken place in such a location. It must be admitted that the mountain, upon which the story is said to have occurred, and which bears the name Pisigsarfik, has the shape of a bow (Bruun 1918, 81, fig. 11). It is possible that the place-name arose instead for this reason. Nevertheless, had there not been peaceful interactions between the two cultures, it is unlikely that the story would have arisen.

Rink (1875, 308) and Rosing (1963, 39) both recount stories of Thule-Norse encounters which were not so peaceful. The interpretation of the traditions recorded in these stories, however, is also difficult. What we can say is that Inuit oral traditions may give a general idea about the nature of Thule-Norse contact.

Moving now from story to history, what evidence is there for Norse-native interaction? Unlike the sagas, the historical evidence relates almost exclusively to the Thule people of Greenland. Adam of Bremen mentions Vínland, but seems unaware that it was inhabited (Tschan 1959, 219). Ari *inn fróði* Þorgilsson ('the Wise') says nothing about them though he does tell us that there were people there (*Íslendingabók* 48). The earliest source to provide information about the inhabitants of Greenland is the late twelfth-century *Historia Norvegiae*. There we find:

> Beyond the [Norse] Greenlanders to the north, hunters have found small people whom they call Skraelings. They are thus made that when they receive a wound that is not life-threatening, their wounds turn white without bleeding; but when they are mortally wounded, their bleeding scarcely stops. They completely lack iron; they use walrus tusks for throwing-weapons and sharp stones as knives (cited in Seaver 1996, 48).

'Beyond the Greenlanders to the north' seems to indicate the Norðsetur hunting grounds—Disko Bay and farther north. It was here, most likely, that the Norse obtained, from the Thule, valuable trade goods, such as walrus ivory (Arneborg 2000, 306; see Roesdahl, this volume).

Gulløv believes that most of the contact activities between the Thule and Norse took place in this region (2000, 326). These 'activities', as the account illustrates, were not always peaceful. The historical evidence, supported by the archaeology, indicates that the Western Settlement ceased to exist sometime in the mid-fourteenth century (Seaver 1996, 104; see also Lynnerup, Arneborg, this volume). The historical sources for the period, however, are often confused, contradictory, or outright falsifications.

The account attributed to Ívarr Bárðarson is the most well-known of these. He is thought to have visited the Western Settlement sometime before 1349 (Seaver 1996, 104). It is claimed that he went north to drive the *skraelingar* out of the settlement, but that he found neither heathen, nor Christian. He did, however, find livestock (Halldórsson 1978, 136-7). How much of the Western Settlement did Ivàrr actually visit? The livestock could not have survived without people to attend to it; where were they?

Gísli Oddsson of Skálholt, who wrote in the 1630s, stated that in the year 1342:

> The inhabitants of Greenland of their own free will abandoned the true faith and the Christian religion, having already forsaken all good ways and true virtues, and joined themselves with the folk of America (cited in Seaver 1996, 86).

This statement cannot be verified. In 1630 the extensive archives at Skálholt burned. It is possible that Gísli had access to information now lost (GHM, III, 459).

There are many entries in the Icelandic annals which deal with remote Greenland, but few of these provide any information about Norse contacts with native people. The Skálholt annals for the year 1347 record that a small, anchorless, Greenlandic ship, which had been in Markland, drifted to Iceland with 17 men on board (Storm 1888 [1977], 213). The Gottskalks annals for 1379 tell of a *skraeling* attack which resulted in the killing of 18 Norsemen, and the kidnapping of two boys (Storm 1888 [1977], 364). It is uncertain how this information fits into the larger picture. This historical evidence is very tantalizing. It leads us to ask: what became of the two kidnapped boys? What was the Greenlandic ship doing in Markland? What did Gísli know that we do not? While we cannot answer any of these questions, there are other types of evidence available to us, which may help us to better understand what took place when the Norse came into contact with the *skrælingar*.

369

Linguistic Evidence

Interactions between different cultures often lead to linguistic and cultural borrowings. These can sometimes tell us a great deal about the nature of the interactions. Despite Leland's opinion that Norse mythology influences Wabanaki religion (Leland 1992, 6), no evidence has yet emerged demonstrating that the Norse had any lasting impact upon the First Peoples of Atlantic Canada or New England. It is extremely unfortunate that ethnocentrism and gullibility, rather than scholarship, have guided much of the discussion on these matters (Redmond 1979).

In Labrador and Baffin, Norse contact with the inhabitants may have been somewhat more intense, but as Fitzhugh suggests, such contact was probably 'brief and had little effect on the native peoples' (1985, 29). In Greenland, however, where the interactions were of a much longer duration, we do find evidence of linguistic, and perhaps even of cultural borrowings.

The Greenlandic word *kuanniq* 'angelica' is one of the few Inuit words thought to have been borrowed from Old Norse (Fortescue *et al.* 1994, 179). Although the Norse did not introduce the plant, as was once believed (Iversen 1953, 98), the migrating Thule first encountered it at the same time they first encountered the Norse. It grows at approximately the same latitudes as the Norse cultural areas (Grøntved 1942). Angelica has medicinal value (Bjarnarson 1994, 228), and was considered, in the Middle Ages, to be the best defense against plague (Meldgaard 1977, 165). There may have been good reason for the Thule and Norse to discuss this plant.

Another Old Norse loanword in Greenlandic is *niisa* 'porpoise' (Bergsland 1986, 55). This is found only in Greenlandic, which lacks both of the terms used in other Inuit languages (Fortescue *et al.* 1994, 46, 191). That a marine mammal hunting culture like the Thule would borrow such a word may seem odd, but as Bergsland explains, the species is found, not in northern areas, whence the Thule came, but rather to the south, where they also met—and obviously spoke with—the Norse (Bergsland 1986, 59).

It has been alleged that the Greenlandic words for sheep, child, and wife/woman were borrowed from the Norse (McGovern 1979, 176; Petersen 2000, 348). These, however, were borrowed later, or derive from a common Inuit root (Kleivan 1984, 549). Without a doubt, the most unexpected Norse loanword found in Greenlandic appears to be the term which Greenlanders apply to themselves: *kalaaliq*, in the singular. It derives from the Old Norse term *skraelingar*. In 1750 Poul Egede wrote:

> This, they themselves claim, is what they were called by the Christians who once inhabited the land (cited in Bergsland 1986, 61; Fortescue *et al.* 1994, 153).

Though the term *skraelingar* might have been derogatory to the Norse, it, apparently, was not to the Thule. Bergsland believes that the borrowing demonstrates that the Thule of southwest Greenland had 'more or less firm connections with Eastern Settlement farms' (1986, 63).

The Greenlandic word *mussak* 'silverweed' (*Potentilla anserina*) also appears to have been borrowed from Norse (Bergsland 1986, 57). It is another plant with medicinal value (Bjarnason 1994, 126), and Greenlandic stories and place-names connect it with the Norse (Bergsland 1986, 57).

No one ever collected a Greenlandic Norse vocabulary, and the last speaker of that language probably died in the fifteenth century. Consequently, although it is quite likely that the Norse did borrow Thule words, the evidence for these borrowings has disappeared. The closest thing that we do have are fjord-lists from late sources. In his *Greenland Annals*, Björn Jónsson records a place called Utibliksfjordur (Halldórsson 1978, 39). At first glance, the name may appear to make perfect sense in Norse. There is an Icelandic farm called Útiblikstaður (Benediktsson 1957, 351). The name, however, bears a striking similarity to the Inuit term *itiblik* 'portage' (GHM, III, 233), found in several Greenlandic place-names. There is, indeed, a portage to be found in this fjord (Krogh 1982, maps 4 and 5).

In *Gronlandia*, completed about 1602 (Halldórsson 1978, 229), Arngrímmr Jónsson calls this same fjord Makleiksfjordur (Halldórsson 1978, 235). This name makes no sense in Norse, but may be related to the proto-Eskimo root *magaq*—'carry on head (*kayak*),' (Fortescue *et al.* 1994, 193), as well as a modern Greenlandic word, *makigiak*, meaning 'portage' (Schultz-Lorentzen 1926 [1967], 156). Place-names ending in *-lik* are common in many Inuit areas.

Rather than resulting from a simple misreading of Utibliksfjordur, as has been suggested (Halldórsson 1978, 237; Benediktsson 1957, 351), it appears possible that Makleiksfjordur, as well as Utibliksfjordur, were originally Inuit place-names which found their way into Icelandic sources, sometime before the seventeenth century. We know neither how, nor when, this might have occurred.

The Norse were great lovers of games, as are the Inuit today. It is possible that, in addition to the alleged bow shooting contest, one of the games which they played together was a type of hopscotch. Stone rows have been found at several places in the Western Settlement (Bruun 1918, 60, 75, 80). According to Bruun, the Greenlanders told him that the stones

> were made by the Norse who, while they dwelt at the fishing-places, entertained themselves by competing to see who could best hop on one leg, from stone to stone, along the whole row. The Greenlanders maintain that their forefathers learned the game, or sport, which they call 'Nangissat', from the Norse (Bruun 1918, 60).

In Denmark and Norway, a similar game is called *hoppe paradis*, 'to hop paradise' (Nielsen 1999, 105; Enerstvedt 1971, 25) In Iceland there is a game called *að ganga heljarbrú*, 'to go over hell's bridge' (Gotlind 1933, 31). De Vries even describes a version played with a piece of wood, incised with a cross (1957, 19). The game seems to have symbolized the striving of the soul to attain heaven (Gomme 1894, 226-7; Enerstvedt 1971, 31).

Because these stone rows appear to be found only in the Western Settlement, near to where the Moravian mission was later established, and because of the nature of the game, it is proper to suspect that it was later missionaries, rather than the Norse, who introduced the game. Missionaries would not, however, have introduce the ring dance, which is known from old drawings, as well as modern tradition, among the Inuit in Greenland. It is quite similar to the ring dance, which is still performed in the Faroe Islands. Nielsen thought this to be a survival from Norse times (Gruner 1933, 155), and Birket-Smith calls the dance 'quite un-Eskimo' (1936, 155).

The linguistic borrowings which have been documented, (and there is good reason to suspect that they represent only a fraction of those which actually occurred), and the cultural borrowings, which are less certain, indicate that Norse interaction with the Thule people was more intimate than the historical evidence would lead us to believe.

ARCHAEOLOGICAL EVIDENCE

Lastly, I would like to briefly say something about the archaeological evidence of Norse-native contact. Few native objects have been found in Norse sites. Roussell found an arrowhead at the Western Settlement farm of Sandnes, which he believed originated with the ancestral Innu people of Labrador (1936, 107). It was found in the churchyard, leading Seaver to postulate that it may have come to Greenland in the body of a Norsemen (2000, 275). The spindle whorl from L'Anse aux Meadows appears to be a Norse reworking of a Dorset pot (Wallace 2000, 215). A beautiful Late Dorset lamp was found, oddly enough, in the roof turf of a Norse house at the same site (Wallace 2000, 216). The excellent condition of the lamp, and the unusual find location, are perplexing. I suggest that it may have been deposited there by Dorset for a ritualistic purpose. Oil lamps in Inuit tradition are thought to symbolize the soul (Feinup-Riordan 1994, 272), they play an important role in the bladder festival (Feinup-Riordan 1994, 140), and appear, for example, in Yup'ik oral tradition, as an aid to a person returning from the dead. The soot from such a lamp enabled a girl to enter an, otherwise inaccessible, *qasgiq*, or men's house (Feinup-Riordan 1994, 4).

At the Eastern Settlement farm of Herjólfsnes, Nørlund found a bear's tooth, and an oval, whalebone box, containing animal tissue and dried blood. These were found in two separate graves within the church (Nørlund 1924, 68). The bear's tooth may be viewed as a charm, as Nørlund suggested. In *Flóamanna saga* we are told that Eiríkr *rauði* worshipped bears (*Flóamanna saga* 303-4), not an uncommon thing among circumpolar and subarctic peoples (Fleischhut 1989, 1). The whalebone box shows a relationship to Inuit culture (Nørlund 1924, 68), and both objects are unusual finds from the graves of Christian Norsemen. We should remember that Herjólfsnes was the farm where Þorbjörg conducted her shamanism.

Many more Norse objects found their way into native sites. Almost all of these are Dorset and Thule sites. One notable exception is the Norse coin, minted sometime between 1065 and 1080 in Norway. It was found in a Late Ceramic Period site in coastal Maine (Cox 2000, 206-7). Several factors make it clear, however, that it arrived at the site through trade, most probably with other native groups, rather than from contact with the Norse. An amulet of smelted copper was found by Harp in a Late Dorset site on the east coast of Hudson Bay (Harp 1974/1975, 33). Again it is likely that it arrived there through trade.

Norse metal has been found throughout the Eastern Arctic and in Greenland. Meldgaard expressed the opinion that iron was the only Norse commodity which had any economic value in Inuit society (1977, 161-2). Arneborg records 70 sites in Canada and Greenland

371

where Norse objects have been found (cited in Seaver 1999, 536), while the Greenlandic sites alone have produced approximately 170 Norse objects (Gulløv 2000, 325). It is not possible to determine how these objects were obtained by the Dorset and Thule. Trade played a role, as did the scavenging of Norse sites and shipwrecks (Gulløv 1997, 18-19). Ship rivets, and a woolen cloth, which may have been a sail, have been found in High Arctic Canada (McCullough 1989, 235). Appelt *et al.*, excavating a Late Dorset winter house in northwest Greenland found, in addition to the Dorset objects which were to be expected, Early Thule Culture objects, as well as a thirteenth-century European bronze pot (Appelt *et al.* 1998, 17).

Finally, there are the Inuit carvings that are believed to depict Norsemen, of which Gulløv gives a good overview (1982). The one that has drawn the most comment was found on Baffin Island (Sabo and Sabo 1978, 33). There is a faintly incised cross on its chest, leading some to call the figure the 'bishop of Baffin' (Sutherland 2000, 239). This 'cross', however, may in fact be a soul mark, well known in Inuit carvings and having nothing to do with Europeans (Gulløv 1982, 232).

SUMMARY

372

The Vínland sagas provide a good starting point for an understanding of Norse interaction with the native peoples of North America, despite a clear bias, and many inaccuracies. Historical, linguistic, and archaeological evidence enables us to develop a picture of Norse interactions with the Dorset and the Thule people.

In many ways, these first European encounters with native peoples, and the accounts which stem from them, are similar to what was to be experienced 500 years later. In several ways, however, they are unique. Medieval Norse Greenlanders had a culture which was quite different from that of the sixteenth-century Europeans, later to explore and colonise the Americas. Although the Vínland sagas were written long before the accounts of these later explorers, they form an important part of the same history: the history of European interaction with native North Americans.

ABBREVIATIONS

Cellere Codex Verrazzano, Giovanni da. *Giovanni da Verrazzano and his discoveries in North America, 1524, according to the unpublished contemporaneous Cellere Codex Rome, Italy*, ed. A. Bacchiani, trans. E.H. Hall. Albany, NY: American Scenic and Historic Preservation Society, 1910.

ESR Þórðarson, M. ed., 1935. *Eiríks saga rauða* in E. Ól. Sveinsson and M. Þórðarson, eds, *Eyrbyggja Saga, Brands Þáttr Orva, Eiríks saga rauða, Grænlendinga saga ok Grænlendinga Þáttr*. Reykjavík: Íslenzk fornrit, 4, 193-237.

Eyrbyggja saga Sveinsson, E. Ól. and Þórðarson, M., eds, 1935. *Eyrbyggja Saga, Brands Þáttr Orva, Eiríks saga rauða, Grænlendinga saga ok Grænlendinga Þáttr*. Reykjavík: Íslenzk fornrit, 4, 1-184.

Flóamanna saga Vilmundarson, Þ. and Vilhjálmsson, B., eds, 1991. *Harðar saga, Bárðar saga, Þorskfirðinga saga, Flóamanna saga*. Reykjavík: Íslenzk fornrit, 13.

GHM *Grønlands Historiske Mindesmærker*, 1845-1976. Copenhagen: Det Konglige Nordiske Oldskrift-Selskab.

Gísla saga Þórólfsson, B.K. and Jónsson, G., eds, 1958. *Vestfirðinga sögur, Gísla saga Súrssonar, Fóstbroeðra saga, Þáttr Þormóðar, Hávarðar saga Ísfirðings, Auðunar Þáttr vestfirzka, Þorvarðar Þáttr Krákunefs*. Reykjavík: Íslenzk fornrit, 6.

GLS Þórðarson, M. ed., 1935. *Grænlendinga saga* in E. Ól. Sveinsson and M. Þórðarson, eds, *Eyrbyggja Saga, Brands Þáttr Orva, Eiríks saga rauða, Grænlendinga saga ok Grænlendinga Þáttr*. Reykjavík: Íslenzk fornrit, 4, 238-369.

Íslendingabók Benediktsson, J. ed., 1968. *Íslendingabók, Landnámabók*. Reykjavík: Íslenzk fornrit, 1.

BIBLIOGRAPHY

Appelt, M., Gulløv, H.C. and Kapel, H. 1998. 'De sidste palaeoeskimoer i Grønland. Nyt lys over den gadefulde Dorsetkultur', *Nationalmuseets Arbejdsmark* 1998, 11-26.

Arneborg, J. 2000. 'Greenland and Europe', in Fitzhugh and Ward 2000, 304-17.

Benediktsson, J. ed., 1957. *Arngrimi Jonae. Opera Latine Conscripta*, vol. 4, in *Bibliotheca Arnamagnaeana*, vol. 12.

Bergsland, K. 1986. 'De Norrøne Lånord i Grønlandsk', *Maal og Minne*, 1, 2, 55-9.

Biggar, H. P. 1911. *The Precursors of Jacques Cartier 1497-1534*. Ottawa: Publications of the Canadian Archives, 5.

Birket-Smith, K. 1936. *The Eskimos*, trans. W. E. Calvert, London.

Bjarnason, A.H. 1994. *Íslensk Flora með litmyndum*, Reykjavík.

Bruun, D. 1918. *Oversgt Over Nordboruiner i Godthaab—og Frederikshaab—Distrikter*, Meddelelser om Grønland 56, 3.

Calloway, C.G. 1991. *Dawnland Encounters. Indians and Europeans in Northern New England*, Hanover and London.

Cox, S.L. 2000. 'A Norse Penny from Maine', in Fitzhugh and Ward 2000, 206-7

de Laguna, F. 1994. 'Some Early Circumpolar Studies', in Irimoto and Yamada 1994, 7-44.

de Vries, J. 1957. *Untersuchung über Das Hüpfspiel Kinderspiel—Kulttanz*, Helsinki.

Dumas, D. ed. 1984. *Handbook of North American Indians*, vol. 5: *Arctic*, Washington.

Enerstvedt, A. 1971. 'Hoppe Paradis, en barnelek', *Tradisjon*, 1 (1971), 25-36.

Feinup-Riordan, A. 1994. *Boundries and Passages. Rule and Ritual in Yup'ik Eskimo Oral Tradition*, London.

Fitzhugh, W.W. 1985a. 'Early Contacts North of Newfoundland before AD. 1600: A Review', in Fitzhugh 1985b, 23-43.

Fitzhugh, W.W. ed., 1985b. *Cultures in Contact*, Washington and London.

Fitzhugh, W.W. and Olin, J.S., eds, 1993. *Archaeology of the Frobisher Voyages*, Washington.

Fitzhugh, W.W. and Ward, E.I., eds, 2000. *Vikings: The North Atlantic Saga*, Washington and London.

Fleischhut, S. 1989. *Der Barenjagdkomplex bei den Iyiyuc (East Main Cree) and Ilnuc (Montagnais)*. Bonn: Mundus Reihe Ethnologie, 27.

Fortescue, M., Jacobson, S., and Kaplin, L. 1994. *Comparative Eskimo Dictionary*, Fairbanks, Alaska.

Foster, R. ed., 1997. *European and Non- European Societies, 1450-1800*. Hampshire: An Expanding World, 27.

Gathorne-Hardy, G. M. 1921 [1970]. *The Norse Discoverers of America*, London.

Gomme, A.B. 1894. *Dictionary of British Folklore*, London.

Gotlind, J. 1933. 'Idrott och Lek', *Nordisk Kultur*, 24, 10-53.

Griffiths, N.E.S. and Reid, J.G. 1992. 'New Evidence on New Scotland, 1629', *William and Mary Quarterly*, 49 (1992), 492-508.

Grøntved, J. 1942. *The Pteridophyta and Spermatophyta of Iceland. The Botany of Iceland*, vol. 4, pt. 1, Copenhagen.

Gruner, N.H. 1933. 'Dans paa Faeroerne', *Nordisk Kultur*, 24 (1933), 150-55.

Gulløv, H.C. 1982. 'Eskimoens syn på europaeren—de såkaldte nordbodukker og andre tvivlsomme udskaeringer', *Grønland*, 30, 5-6-7, 226-34.

——1997. *From Middle Ages to Colonial Times. Archaeological and ethnohistorical studies of the Thule culture in South West Greenland 1300-1800 AD*. Copenhagen: Meddelelser om Gronland, Man and Society 23.

——2000. 'Native and Norse in Greenland', in Fitzhugh and Ward 2000, 318-26.

Halldórsson, O. 1978. *Grænland í Miðaldaritum*, Reykjavík.

Harp, E. 1974/1975. 'A Late Dorset copper amulet from southeastern Hudson Bay', *Folk*, 16/17, 33-44.

Hoffman, B.G. 1961. *Cabot to Cartier. Sources for a Historical Ethnography of Northeastern North America 1497-1550*, Toronto.

Horwood, H. 1959a. 'The people who were murdered for fun', *Maclean's*, 10 October.

——1959b. 'The people who were murdered for fun', *Maclean's*, 21 November.

Houben, H.H. 1935. *Christopher Columbus. The Tragedy of a Discoverer*, trans. J. Linton, London.

Howley, J.P. 1915. *The Beothucks or Red Indians*, Cambridge.

Hulton, P. and Quinn, D.B., eds, 1964. *The American Drawings of John White 1577-1590*, London.

Ingstad, H. 1985. *The Discovery of a Norse Settlement in North America*, vol. 2, Oslo.

Irimoto, T and Yamada, T., eds, 1994. *Circumpolar Religion and Ecology. An Anthropology of the North*, Tokyo.

Iversen, J. 1953. 'Origin of the Flora of Western Greenland in the Light of Pollen Analysis', *Oikos*, 4, 2 (1952-53),

Johannesson, A. 1956. *Islandisches Etymologisches Wörterbuch*, Bern.

Jóhannesson, J. 1945. 'Reisubók Bjarnar Jorsalafara', *Skírnir*, 119 (1945), 68-96.

Jones, H.G. 1997. 'An Early Meeting of Cultures: Inuit and English, 1576-1578', in Moss 1997, 33-41.

Kleivan, I. 1984. 'History of Norse Greenland', in Dumas 1984, 549-55.

Krogh, K.J. 1982. *Qallunaatsiaaqarfik Gronland/ Erik den Rødes Grønland*, Copenhagen.

Leland, C.G. 1992. *Algonquin Legends*, New York and London.

Magnusson, A.B. 1989. *Íslensk Orðsifjabók*, Reykjavík.

Marshall, I. 1996. *A History and Ethnography of the Beothuk*, Toronto.

McCartney, A.P. ed., 1979. *Thule Eskimo Culture: An Anthropolgical Retrospective*. Ottawa: National Museum of Man, Mercury Series, Archaeology, 88.

McCullough, K.M. 1989. *The Ruin Islanders. Thule Culture Pioneers in the Eastern High Arctic*. Hull, Quebec: Archaeological Survey of Canada, Mercury series 141.

McGovern, T.H. 1979. 'Thule-Norse Interaction in Southwest Greenland: A Speculative Model', in McCartney 1979, 171-88.

Meldgaard, J. 1977. 'Inuit-Nordbo projektet. Arkaeologiske undersøgelser i Vester bygden i Grønland', *Nationalmuseets Arbejdsmark* 1977, 159-69.

Moss, J. ed., 1997. *Echoing Silence. Essays on Arctic Narrative*, Ottawa.

Nielsen, E.K. 1999. 'Hopscotch Games in Denmark. A Report on Tradition and Innovation with a Brief Look At Other Scandinavian Countries', *Arv*, 55, 105-26.

Nørlund, P. 1924. *Buried Norsemen at Herjolfsnes,* Meddelelser om Grønland, 67,1.

——1936. *Viking Settlers in Greenland*, London.

Olin, J. S. 1993. 'History of Research on the Smithsonian Bloom', in Fitzhugh and Olin 1993, 49-55.

Oswalt, W.H. 1999. *Eskimos and Explorers*, Lincoln, Nebraska

Pálsson, H. 1997. *Úr landnorðri. Samar og ystu rætur íslenskrar menningar.* Reykjavík: Íslenzk fræði 54.

Petersen, H.C. 2000. 'The Norse Legacy in Greenland', in Fitzhugh and Ward 2000, 340-9.

Price, N. 2000. 'Shamanism and the Vikings?', in Fitzhugh and Ward 2000, 70-1.

Quinn, D.B. 1981. *Sources for the Ethnography of Northeastern North America to 1611*. Ottawa: National Museum of Man, Mercury Series, Canadian Ethnology Service, 76.

Redmond, J. R. 1979. *'Viking' Hoaxes in North America*, New York.

Ricker, D. 1997. *L'sitkuk. The Story of the Bear River Mi'kmaw Community*, Lockport, NS.

Rink, H. 1875. *Tales and Traditions of the Eskimo*, Edinburgh.

Rosing, J. 1963. *Sagn and Saga from Angmagssalik*, Copenhagen.

Roussell, Aa. 1936. *Sandnes and the Neighbouring Farms, Meddelelser om Grønland*, 88, 2.

Rowley, S. 1993. 'Frobisher Miksanaut: Inuit Accounts of the Frobisher Voyages', in Fitzhugh and Olin 1993, 29-32.

Sabo, G. and Sabo, D. 1978. 'A Possible Thule Carving of a Viking from Baffin Island, N. W. T.', *Canadian Journal of Archaeology*, 2 (1978), 33-42.

Sayers, W. 1993. 'Vinland, the Irish, 'Obvious Fictions and Apocrypha'', *Skandinavistik*, 23, 1, 1-15.

Schultz-Lorentzen, C.W. 1926 [1967]. *Den Grønlandske Ordbok. Grønlandsk-Dansk*, Copenhagen.

Seaver, K.A. 1996. *The Frozen Echo. Greenland and the Exploration of North America, ca. 1000-1500*, Stanford, CA.

Seaver, K.A. 1999. 'How Strange is a Stranger? A Survey of Opportunities for Inuit-European Contact in the Davis Strait before 1576', in Symons 1999, 523-52.

Seaver, K.A. 2000. 'Unanswered Questions', in Fitzhugh and Ward 2000, 270-9.

Storm, G. 1888 [1977]. *Islandske Annaler indtil 1578*, Oslo.

Sutherland, P.D. 2000. 'The Norse and Native North Americans', in Fitzhugh and Ward 2000, 238-47.

Symons, T.H.B. ed., 1999. *Meta Incognita: A Discourse of Discovery. Martin Frobisher's Arctic Expeditions, 1576-1578*, vol. 2. Hull, Quebec: Canadian Museum of Civilization, Mercury series 10.

Trigger, B. 1997. 'Early Native American Responses to European Contact: Romantic Versus Rationalistic Interpretations', in Foster 1997, 191-211.

Tschan, F.J. ed., 1959. *History of the Archbishops of Hamburg-Bremen*, New York.

Wallace, B.L. 2000. 'The Viking Settlement at L'Anse aux Meadows', in Fitzhugh and Ward 2000, 208-16.

Winter, K. 1975. *Shananditti. The Last of the Beothucks*, Vancouver, BC.

Wolf, K. 1996. 'Amazons in Vinland', *Journal of English and Germanic Philology*, October 1996, 469-85.

375

Vínland and the death of Þorvaldr

Birgitta Wallace

> Þorvaldr now inquired among his men whether anyone was wounded. Not a wound among them, they assured him. 'I have got a wound under my arm,' he told them. 'An arrow flew in between gunwale and shield, under my arm. Here is the arrow, and it will be the death of me. I command you, make the fastest preparations you can for your return. As for me, you shall carry me to that headland where I thought I should so like to make my home. Maybe it was truth that came into my mouth, that I should dwell there awhile. For there you shall bury me, and set crosses at my head and feet, and call it Krossanes for ever more' (*Grænlendinga saga* in Jones 1986, 196).

As told in *Grænlendinga saga* (GLS), so ends the first episode of the Norse meeting with the people already living in the land the Norse had only now discovered. The aggression was instigated by the Norse, who, unprovoked, had killed eight out of ten men sleeping under three canoes the previous day. In *Eiríks saga rauða* (ESR), Þorvaldr also dies from an arrow fired at him by an indigenous person, but here the episode has a mythical touch as the one shooting the arrow is an *einfœtingr* (uniped):

> Þorvaldr Eiríksson was sitting by the rudder, and the uniped shot an arrow into his guts. He drew out the arrow. 'There is fat round my belly!' he said. 'We have won a fine and fruitful country, but will hardly be allowed to enjoy it.' Þorvaldr died of this wound a little later (Jones 1986, 229).

377

Where did this encounter take place? In order to arrive at an answer, we will first look at the sagas, then the archaeological evidence at the L'Anse aux Meadows (hereafter LAM) site.

THE SAGAS

The historicity of the Vínland sagas has been debated for well over a century. Some scholars have read them as objective historical documents (Rafn 1837; 1838; Reeves 1890; 1906; Storm 1887; Bergþórsson 2000). Others have rejected them as medieval fantasies about a far-away paradise (Nansen 1911). The current view lies somewhere between total faith and total rejection. It maintains that the sagas reflect actual events, skewed by the fact that they were written to serve thirteenth- and fourteenth- century religious and socio-political purposes. However, it is difficult to distinguish fact from fiction in this net of tales (Halldórsson 1978; 1992; Þorláksson 1999). My view is that the archaeological evidence at LAM combined with recent archaeological, anthropological, and demographic research on eleventh-century and medieval Iceland and Greenland can help to define the actual events behind the sagas.

GLS and ESR describe the same events, but with discrepancies. GLS describes the finding and naming of Vínland. ESR describes a *search* for Vínland. GLS has one single settlement, Leifsbúðir, Leifr's Camp. ESR has *two* major locations, Hóp, Tidal Lagoon, and Straumfjörðr, Fjord of Currents (*Skálholtsbók* has Straumsfjörðr, the meaning is the same). Generally, these locations have been regarded as three separate settlements. I suggest that they are not three separate spots but two, Hóp and Straumfjörðr, and that *Leifsbúðir* is a conflation of the two. ESR describes Straumfjörðr as a base in the north from which expeditions leave in the summer to explore in all directions, returning there to spend the winter. Hóp is a summer camp in the south where grapes are collected and lumber harvested. Leifsbúðir has elements of both. Like Straumfjörðr it is a base for explorations in several directions, but many of its physical characteristics are close to those of Hóp, and both grapes and lumber are harvested there. This conclusion is a logical extension of what the Icelandic saga scholar, Ólafur Halldórsson, concluded (Halldórsson 1992) that the purpose of ESR was to magnify Guðríðr's role to establish the proper credentials in support of the proposed canonization of Bishop Björn Gilsson, a direct descendant of Þorfinnr Karlsefni Þórðarson and Guðríðr Þorbjarnardóttir. As pointed out by Ólafur, the need for glorifying the ancestor of this bishop has affected the content of ESR. As for the two versions of ESR, *Skálholtsbók* (hereafter SB) and *Hauksbók* (hereafter HB), Sven B. F. Jansson (1945, 168-171) has shown that HB was both a more edited and informed rendition of the original material. Although this can be explained by the greater erudition of Hauk than that of the compiler of SB, his direct descendance from Þorfinnr Karlsefni and Guðríðr may be a contributing factor.

In GLS Leifr bestows all the names on the regions visited, beginning with Helluland: 'I shall now give the land a name' (Jones 1986, 192), or in the original wording, *Nú mun ek gefa nafn landinu, ok kalla Helluland* (GLS 249). Formal name-giving can be equated with the laying of a conventional claim to the areas named. ESR simply says 'They' gave a name to the land (*Þeir gáfu þar nafn*: ESR 222). The same is true for Markland. '"This land", said Leifr, "shall be called... Markland"'(Jones 1986, 192; GLS 250). Again ESR just says 'They' or *þeir*. In GLS, Kjalarnes, or Keelness, receives its name during Þorvaldr's expedition, when a keel is broken and set up as a marker on a cape north of Leifsbúðir. In ESR, this keel is encountered by Karlsefni's expedition on a cape north of Straumfjörðr, and Karlsefni and his crew therefore call the place Kjalarnes. This makes sense only if others have been there before Karlsefni.

Many writers have assumed that Karlsefni's expedition did not find Leifr's Vínland (Hovgaard 1914, 237; Sigurðsson 2000, 236). I disagree. The HB version of ESR says very clearly that Straumfjörðr is part of Vínland. As the expedition leaves Straumfjörðr and steers north to Markland, the text says, 'When they sailed from Vínland' (Jones 1986, 230), *Þa er sigldu af Vínlandi toku þeir sudrön vedr* (HB; Jansson 1945, 77).

There are other reasons for thinking that we are dealing with the same locations in both sagas. The parallels of events are striking, and the descriptions do more to complement than to contradict each other as has been pointed out by Crozier (see this volume). Þorvaldr's death is a case in point. In both GLS and ESR, Þorvaldr is killed by an arrow fired by an indigenous person. In GLS, his death takes place east and north of Leifsbúðir. In ESR his death takes place far north of Straumfjörðr and north of Kjalarnes. Þorvaldr cannot have died in two different places. This suggests a correspondence between Leifsbúðir and Straumfjörðr. Another parallel is in the encounters with the *skrælingar*. In both GLS and ESR, the most prolonged encounters take place during Karlsefni's expedition. They begin with trade, and only the commodities offered in trade by the Icelanders differ: milk in GLS, cloth in ESR. In both versions, the *skrælingar* want weapons; in both versions Karlsefni says no to this, and in both versions the bull plays a role. In both sagas the *skrælingar* are amazed at the Icelandic iron axe. In GLS these events occur at Leifsbúðir. In ESR they are at Hóp. These things are too specific to reflect two separate locations, and the correspondence between Leifsbúðir and Hóp is clear.

The physical descriptions for Straumfjörðr and Hóp are more detailed than those for Leifsbúðir. Straumfjörðr gets its name from a fjord with an island at its mouth. Strong currents surrounded the island. On this island were so many seabird (HB says 'eider') nests that a man could hardly set foot between the eggs. Landing on the shore of the fjord, they found abundant grass (SB adds 'mountains'). Later on we learn that there were cliffs, plenty of game, sea fish, and several islands. Winters were so mild that the cattle could graze out of doors on an island. Straumfjörðr was not a forbidding place. The reason peopled starve the first winter is not because of harsh weather but because they had been too busy to lay up provisions for the winter. For the other years HB informs us that there was abundance of everything they had need of (*ok voro þar fyri allz gnottir þess er þeir þurftu at hafa*: HB in Jansson 1945, 74).

Straumfjörðr	*Leifsbúðir*
Winter base for voyages north and south	Base for summer-long travels west, east, and north
No *skrælingar*	No *skrælingar* except during Karlsefni's stay; no skrælings in westward direction
Fjord	Point of land projecting north
Island off the mouth of the fjord	Island north of point
Other islands nearby	Settlement on bay west of the point
Strong currents	Lake a bit inland
Sea birds (HB: eiders) and their nests completely covering the island	Sun rises earlier and sets later than in Greenland or Iceland on the shortest day of the year
Mountains (only in SB)	
Abundant grass	
Livestock grazed on the island all winter	Livestock grazed out of doors all winter
Fishing	Fishing
Hunting	Hunting
Stranded whale	Stranded whale
Snorri born at Straumfjörðr	Snorri born at Leifsbúðir

Table 1. A comparison between Straumfjörðr and Leifsbúðir.

379

Hóp	*Leifsbúðir*
Summer base for part of the expedition	Base for summer explorations
River estuary with lagoons sheltered by sandbars; lagoon can be entered only at high tide. Some have considered the differences between high and low tide to have been significant (Berg 1955). However, the text does not speak of drastic tidal drops but tidal shallows. The GLS text states *þar var grunnsævi mikit at fjoru-sjóvar* (GLS, Reeves 1890, 146), and the ES *ok matti eigi komaz i ana vtan at haflöðvm* (HB, Jansson 1945, 68).	Stream, shallows so low that the ship went aground a long distance from the shore at low water and could be brought in only at high tide. Point of land project-ing north
A river flowed from the land into a lake and from it to the sea	A river flowed out of a lake
—Self-sown wheat	—Grapes
—Grapes	—Lumber, *vínvíð*
—Lumber, *vínvíð*	—Salmon
—Brooks full of fish	
—Halibut caught in tidal pools	
Karlsefni's expedition meets many *skrælingar* in canoes. They trade red cloth for fur.	Karlsefni's expedition meets many *skrælingar* in canoes. They trade milk for fur.
Fight between the Norse and *skrælingar*. Þorbrandr Snorrason killed. *Skrælingar* amazed by iron axe	Fight with the *skrælingar*. *Skrælingar* amazed by iron axe.

Table 2. A comparison between Hóp and Leifsbúðir.

Given the above, I think it futile to try to locate Leifsbúðir since in my opinion there was no one such site. A more worthwhile exercise is to look for Straumfjörðr and Hóp, which probably do represent actual locations.

One curiosity generally taken at face value is the story told in ESR of the breast-slapping Freydís, who had a hard time keeping the same pace as the men because she was pregnant. One would assume that her pregnancy was far advanced for this to be the case. Yet the only baby said to have been born in Vínland was Snorri Þorfinnsson (Karlsefnisson) to Guðríðr. There is no indication that Freydís also gave birth to a baby in Vínland, or that she was pregnant there. Is this a case of personal names being confused? For example, in another context where SB has Freydís, HB has Guðríðr: 'It is some men's report that Bjarni and Freydís had remained behind there, and a hundred men with them' (SB, Jones 1986, 229). HB has the same statement, but here the names are Bjarni and Guðríðr (HB, Jansson 1945, 74).

In my early days at LAM, I believed that LAM was an anonymous site, perhaps not mentioned in the sagas. Over the past couple of decades important archaeological research on the Greenland colony and Iceland has taken place, which furnishes a new perspective on LAM and makes it possible to place the site in its proper context. I am thinking of the work by Niels Lynnerup, Jette Arneborg, Joel Berglund, Christian Keller, Tom McGovern, Astrid Ogilvie, Orri Vesteinsson and many others. The archaeological knowledge of the Aboriginal populations along the eastern seaboard has also been expanded. This, too, has a bearing on LAM. By now, thanks to the findings at LAM, I think that we can arrive at conclusions regarding the location of Straumfjörðr and Hóp. This in turn, gives clues to the area where Þorvaldr was killed.

LAM is a highly organized outpost. It is far too substantial and complex a site not to be mentioned in the sagas. Let us consider the physical construction. Calculations based on post moulds in combination with material requirements to build the replicas in the A-B-C complex give an estimate that at least 86 tall trees had to be felled for the posts of the three large halls plus large amounts of wood for the huge roofs and all the smaller buildings. Calculations based on wall widths and lengths, their estimated heights (average of 1.5 m) and estimated sizes of roofs give an estimate that about 1100 cubic meters of sod were used in the construction. Based on the amount of labor expended on the three house replicas at LAM, we can estimate that it would have taken a labor crew of sixty at least two months to build the whole settlement, or a crew of ninety at least a month and a half, not including the time spent on the actual cutting and transportation of the sod. This is the better part of summer. Another indication that LAM represents a major effort on the part of the Greenland colony comes from Niels Lynnerup's research on the Greenland population. Lynnerup has convincingly demonstrated (1998, 115; see this volume) that in its first decades the Greenland colony had only 400 to 500 inhabitants. LAM, which dates from the same time, was built to shelter seventy to ninety people, equivalent to fourteen to twenty-two percent of the entire Greenland colony. Even if two-thirds of the crew were Icelanders, the remaining third constituted at least five percent of all Greenlanders. In terms of labour, the percentage is higher, as the Vínland voyagers were primarily men in their best working age. For demographic and economic reasons, the Greenlanders would simply not have had sufficient labor to form additional settlements of this magnitude (fig. 1).

LAM forms a remarkable parallel to Straumfjörðr in terms of function, type of occupants, social organization, climate, and even physical description—although most of the physical descriptions in the Vínland sagas are so general that they can fit any number of locations along the eastern seaboard. As for climate, livestock could indeed have grazed outside all winter as shown by the winter of 1998, when a temperature difference of only a couple of degrees above normal for our era resulted in an almost total lack of snow at LAM.

Figure 1. Reconstructed sod houses at L'Anse aux Meadows National Historic Site of Canada (photo: A. Croneiller, courtesy of Canadian Parks Service).

Figure 2. Lagoons in Kouchibouguac National Park, New Brunswick (photo: A. Dufresne).

According to Ogilvie *et al.* (2000, 43), the climate in the North Atlantic was particularly favourable in the period AD 800 to 1100.

Like the occupants of Straumfjörðr, the Norse at LAM also ventured south to areas where grapes grew wild and good lumber could be had, as will be shown later.

The area closest to LAM which displays all of the characteristics of Hóp is northeastern New Brunswick. Here extensive sandbars shelter shallow tidal lagoons along the entire coast (fig. 2). Butternuts, wild grapes, and hardwood forests grow in the Miramichi area, especially along its southwestern branch, more dominant in the eleventh century than now. The Miramichi area was also home to large Aboriginal populations, the ancestors of the Mi'kmaq.

Although Prince Edward Island and the Gulf shore of Nova Scotia are likely to have been visited on the way, neither of these areas contained butternut trees nor wild grapes (Hosie 1979, 134; Zinck 1998, I, 576). The species was introduced there in later, colonial times.

Another feature of Hóp was self-sown wheat. In a paper published in 1859, F. C. Schübeler (Schübeler 1858-1859) suggested that the self-sown wheat was Indian wild rice, *Zizania aquatica*. This suggestion has been repeated by later researchers (Holand 1940, 37; Bergþórsson 1997, 181-185). In order to know what cereal the Norse may have had in mind, we have to look at what they called wheat. It was not our modern type of wheat but earlier forms such as emmer. American dune grass, *Elymus mollis*, looks very much like Norse wheat (fig. 3). It is common in both coastal and inland locations in eastern North America. It is related to Icelandic lyme grass, *Elymus arenarius* (which the Norse called *melr*: Hovgaard 1914, 161), which has always been a flour substitute in Iceland, but sufficiently distinct from it (Roland and Smith 1969: 94) that the Norse would have noted the difference, so this plant is a strong contender for self-sown wheat. In 1534 Cartier (Cook 1993, 18) described American dune grass in neighbouring Chaleur Bay, also in New Brunswick, as 'wild oats like rye, which one would say had been sown there and tilled'. Also the Linnæus' disciple Peter Kalm saw this plant as the self-sown wheat of the sagas when he encountered it near the mouth of the St. Lawrence River in 1749 (Kalm 1972, 460). Wild rye, *Elymus virginicus*, is another possibility. Wild rice, on the other hand, bears no similarity to wheat, and, at the time, the Norse were unfamiliar with rice. Wild rice grows in lakes, usually in inland locations in New Brunswick and along the St. Lawrence River and regions to the west of there. Unlike the *Elymus* species, it does not form 'fields' of wheat.

The presence of the butternut pieces in the Norse deposits at LAM is testimony not only to voyages south, but to the Norse encounter with grapes. Wild grapes grow, or rather grew, in the same areas as the butternut tree: the St. Lawrence River Valley west of St. Paul Bay, on the Miramichi and the Saint John River. They possibly grew in the Pictou area in Nova Scotia (this is on the Gulf of St. Lawrence side of Nova Scotia) and in southern Maine, coastal New Hampshire and New England, but not between these areas and the Saint John River. According to some Nova Scotia botanists (Roland and Smith 1969, 507; Zinck 1998, I, 576), the wild grapes growing in Nova Scotia now, were introduced, by the French in 1605 and later. Although both Champlain (Langdon and Ganong 1922, I, 368) and Nicolas Denys (1672, I, 55-6) talk about wild grapes and butternut trees growing at what now is Fort Anne in Annapolis Royal in Nova Scotia, they were clearly mistaken, as noted by William Ganong (1922, 368, n. 1). Ganong refers to Lescarbot as the more accurate observer. Writing in 1606, Lescarbot (1928, 107) states emphatically that since grapes grow wild on the New Brunswick side of the Bay of Fundy, they could be *planted* at Port Royal. He gives an amusing vignette of Poutrincourt planting grapes there and getting tipsy like Father Noah. As for Nicolas Denys, it is clear that he speaks of New Brunswick and his description of the Port Royal area is an almost verbatim repeat of a statement about New Brunswick in the same volume a few pages back (1672, I, 46-47).

Where grapes grow wild, the vines look nothing like those in a vineyard. Instead they wrap themselves around any tree or bush that happens to be nearby, often all the way to the top of the trees. These are the *vínvið*, the grapewood-trees of the sagas, the lumber harvested and brought back to Greenland by every Vínland expedition (fig. 4).

Vis-à-vis the *vin/vín* controversy, that is whether *vin* in Vínland means 'grasslands' or 'wine,' it is significant that the *vínvið*, the grape-trees, are every bit as important as the grapes. This makes no sense if we interpret *vin* as pasture.

In looking at the sagas we have also to take into account recent North American research on Aboriginal sites. An important feature in the stories of Hóp is that the *skrælingar* there travelled in skin-covered boats, or canoes. Over the past twenty years, American archaeologists such as Bert Salwen (1978, 68) and Dean Snow (1978, 164), have documented that canoes were rarely used by native people south of central Maine, and not at all south of Boston, where the watercraft used were hollowed-out logs. However, canoes were a prime means of transportation among the Mi'kmaq. Although made of birch bark in later times, a Mi'kmaq named Arguimaut told Abbé Maillard, around 1740, that in his ancestors' time the canoes had been of 'moose skins from which they had plucked the hair, and which they had scraped and rubbed so thoroughly that they were like your finest skins' (cited in Whitehead 1991, 20).

ESR does not speak of salmon, and it is not clear if the salmon at Leifsbúðir in GLS is found at the base camp or in the areas of the grapes. It is worth noting, however, that the Miramichi has been the richest salmon river in eastern North America at least since the seventeenth century, in spite of industrial development and changes to the river bed. In 1672 Nicolas Denys (1672, I, 185-186) complained that he could not sleep because of the noise created by the multitude of salmon jumping in the Miramichi, and an eighteenth-century fisherman took 700 salmon in a 24-hour period. In the 1960s about 30,000 salmon were caught yearly in the Miramichi (Russell 1970, 96). The Mi'kmaq on Chaleur Bay encountered by Chrestien LaClerq in 1677 had salmon as their totem (in Whitehead 1991, 64, 66). This speaks for a long tradition of salmon-fishing.

By contrast, recent research by the Canadian zoo-archaeologist Catherine Carlson (1996) indicates that salmon were not present as far south as New England before the seventeenth century. She bases this on both archaeological investigations and written documentation. She found no salmon bones among the 30,000 fish bones from twenty-one precontact sites she examined in Maine and New England (salmon which are now found in New England rivers such as the Connecticut River are recent introductions for sport fishing).

The combined evidence points to Hóp being in the general area of eastern New Brunswick, in particular the Miramichi. Everything is there: a large population of indigenous inhabitants, canoes, grapes, good lumber, shallow tidal lagoons, sandbars, and salmon. The area is rich in resources compared to northern Newfoundland and to the home settlements in Greenland and Iceland. Why would anyone seek further afield?

The similarity between ESR's description of Hóp and Jacques Cartier's depiction of the Miramichi is striking. Ólafur Halldórsson (1992) has even pointed out that if ESR did not predate Cartier, one would think that its passage about Hóp had been copied from Cartier's journal for his 1534 voyage.

> We went out in our longboats to the cape on the north and found the water so shallow that at the distance of more than a league from shore there was a depth of only one fathom...a bay...ran back a long way; and so far as we could see the longest arm stretched northeast. This [Miramichi] bay was everywhere skirted with sandbanks and the water was shallow....The land on the south side of it is...full of beautiful fields and meadows...and it is as level as the surface of a pond...on the north side is a high mountainous shore, completely covered with many kinds of lofty trees...near the water's edge...were meadows and very pretty ponds (Cook 1993, 18-19).

Figure 3. North American dune grass, *Elymus mollis* (photo: R. Ferguson).

384

Figure 4. Grapevines growing on trees, the Saint John valley, New Brunswick (photo: K. Leonard).

Also Cartier's first contact with Aboriginal people on Chaleur Bay, just north of Miramichi is striking in its similarity with Karlsefni's experience:

> ...we caught sight of two fleets of savage canoes that were crossing from one side to the other, which numbered in all some forty or fifty canoes...landed a large number of people, who set up a great clamour...holding up to us some skins on sticks...They bartered all they had to such an extent that all went back naked without anything on them (Cook 1993, 21).

These people were Mi'kmaq who had come to Chaleur Bay to fish. I suggest that the similarities arise because they describe the same area.

The map of Vínland is beginning to take form. Helluland, I think we can all agree, is the area north of latitude 58, that is from the Cape Chidley peninsula in northern Labrador, and everything north of there. (During the symposium Mats Larsson pointed out that sea ice along the coast of Baffin Island and northern Labrador would have prevented the Norse from following the coast here. However, a drastically different view of the coastline as richly forested was presented at the same symposium by Alexander Robertson. Modern sea-ice maps show the coasts as ice-free in late July, and this was certainly the way the crew of the replica Viking ship Snorri experienced it in 1998. Furthermore Ogilvie *et al.* (2000) indicates that the Arctic Greenland waters may have been relatively free of sea ice at the end of the tenth and early eleventh century.) It follows that Markland is the extensive forested area of Labrador which is the next extremely distinct geographical feature facing the traveller from the north, or rather northeast, for here the Labrador coast bends sharply to the east. Clumps of forest are visible on the coast south of Nain, but do not become consistent until the Kiglapeit Mountains stood directly in the way for the southbound travellers (Grenfell 1934, 62-63). The distance covered is 650 km or 338 nautical miles, with another 250 km to the Strait of Belle Isle, if one sails in a straight line. This would be about two days of sail under average conditions. However, obviously on voyages of exploration, or for that matters on ships depending entirely on wind propulsion, one does not sail in a straight line. What is the point of exploring if one sails too far from the coast to observe land forms and resources?

385

South of Markland was a cape and *Furðustrandir*, or Wonder Beaches. These beaches are described as being on the starboard side and being 'long and with sand banks' (*voru þar strandir langar ok sandar*: HB, Jansson 1945, 62, l. 286), with SB adding *þar var avrœfi*, ('there were no harbours'). The name was given because it took such a long time to sail by them. Going ashore, presumably on the cape, as the name that reflects such a feature, the expedition finds the broken keel and names the place Kjalarnes, or Keelnes.

Many writers have commented on the long harbourless Porcupine Beach with its sandy bottom and sand beaches up to 100 m wide, and Cape Porcupine, a prominent point of land (Hovgaard 1914, 223-224; Munn 1914, 19; Tanner 1941, 23; Meldgaard 1961; Morison 1971, 42-43). This is south of Hamilton Inlet in Labrador. It is a spectacular series of open sandy beaches along an 80-km stretch, so unusual that special note has been given to it by people approaching both from land and sea. If the winds were favourable, it would have taken a Viking *knörr* about five hours to sail by them, a considerable length of time, and there are no real harbours along this stretch. Páll Bergþórsson comments that *strand* in Old Norse does not necessarily mean sandy beach and that we therefore do not need to think of Furðustrandir as sandy beaches. This leads him to the conclusion (Bergþórsson 2000, 62-63) that Furðustrandir is the Atlantic coast of Nova Scotia, all 670 km of it, as the crow flies, or nearly 3000 km if one follows the coastline. In the English language, however, a beach can also be rocky or cobbly, so we are not dealing with a mistranslation as inferred by Bergþórsson. More importantly, it is obvious that Furðustrandir were thought of as one particular feature, not a diversified, broken coastline such as the Atlantic coast of Nova Scotia. It is just more of the same kind of coast as along the shores of Newfoundland. Its beaches are relatively small, scattered and less spectacular and only short stretches lack good harbours. A more credible identification has been made by Mats Larsson (1999, 70-72) who suggests that a forty-kilometer stretch south of Cape Garbarus on the southeastern shore of Cape Breton is Furðustrandir. However, in order to get there, the Norse explorers would already have sailed along the unique Porcupine Beach and would thus have been less likely to note similar but less impressive beaches.

Continuing south from Furðustrandir, we arrive at *Straumfjörðr*. Straumfjörðr lies at the mouth of a fjord (after a stretch of coast indented with bays). An island surrounded by strong currents is at the entrance to the fjord. I believe the description fits the Strait of Belle Isle and the island of Belle Isle. The Labrador coast between Porcupine Beach and the Strait is indeed heavily indented. As one enters the Strait, it does have the appearance of a fjord, indeed a fjord can be open on both ends (B. Ralph, pers. comm.). About twenty kilometers wide at Belle Isle, it narrows to only fourteen kilometers further south. The Labrador Current discharges into the Gulf on the Labrador side at the same time as water from the Gulf pours out on the Newfoundland side, creating complex multidirectional currents accelerating to a speed of 3.6 km an hour (Farmer 1981). Others (Larsson 1999, 70-72; Bergþórsson 2000, 69-71; Sigurðsson 2000, 237) have suggested that the fjord must be the Bay of Fundy because its twelve to fifteen meter tides, the highest in the world, create strong currents. This bay is nearly fifty to eighty kilometers wide, and if Straumfjörðr had been located here, it would have been the tide, not the current that had been noted. Given that we have the physical evidence of LAM on the Strait of Belle Isle and that it corresponds to the description of Straumfjörðr, I think that this northern ascription is more feasible.

There is another point in the sagas that supports the hypothesis that the main base at Straumfjörðr/Leifsbúðir was LAM. In the GLS, Þorvaldr spends his first summer of exploration going west but encountering no humans. The only sign that the area was inhabited is a wooden structure, a *kornhjálm*, that he, coming from an agricultural background, interprets as a hayrick. About the only place along the eastern seaboard where a ship crew could explore for an entire summer without seeing people would have been the eastern Quebec shore, Quebec's 'North Shore', west of the Strait of Belle Isle. This is a desolate area, which is sparsely populated even now and which seems always to have been sparsely populated in pre-contact times. The Labrador coast, Nova Scotia, New Brunswick, the rest of Quebec, Maine and New England all had large Aboriginal populations spending the summers on the coast where encounters between groups would have been likely to occur.

To get to Vínland, we should look at a map with Greenlanders' eyes, not the modern way with north at the top. Vínland encompasses the shores of the Gulf of St. Lawrence, from the Strait of Belle Isle in the north, to Nova Scotia and New Brunswick in the south. The journey begins in Greenland and goes across Davis Strait (fig. 5). There we begin the southward journey, except that in order to proceed, one has to veer to the east. From there one enters the Strait of Belle Isle and the Gulf of St. Lawrence, where, as I have suggested, we find Hóp in eastern New Brunswick. The alternative route south would have been along the eastern coast of Newfoundland, an island the size of Iceland, but this is much longer, more exposed and less inviting, with extensive coastal stretches of rocky coast and scrub forests. If explored, this route would probably quickly have been abandoned. The distance south to Nova Scotia from there would also be much greater than from the southwest corner of Newfoundland and less clear that land lay ahead.

We must also bear in mind that all exploring was confined to the summer months as much of the Eastern seaboard as far as New Jersey is covered in snow during the winter. The range of the ships was limited by the winds. The ships could tack to 60° against the wind, but this could slow them down to a crawl of 1.2 to 2 knots (Andersen and Andersen 1989, 318). As the crew of the replica *knörr Snorri* learnt, sometimes there is no wind at all.

386

Figure 5. The route to Vínland (map: J. Ertzmann and B. Wallace). The shaded areas indicate Helluland, Markland, and Vínland.

Figure 6. Grand Lake, Hamilton Inlet, Labrador (photo: W. Fitzhugh).

If one accepts the Gulf route but wants to place the Norse further south, one has to contend with the geography of Nova Scotia. Nova Scotia is a peninsula running almost east-west, adding considerable distance to the voyage. In addition, the Atlantic coast of Nova Scotia is mostly rocky, with scrubby softwood forest and swampy areas, exactly the same landscape as northern and eastern Newfoundland. Why continue this way when southwestern Newfoundland and the Gulf side of Nova Scotia have already demonstrated richer hardwood forests, warmer waters and more varied resources? And here also are other land masses to explore: the Magdalen and Bird Islands, Prince Edward Island, and all the inviting lagoons along New Brunswick.

Now finally to the location of the death of Þorvaldr. The route he took to his death in ESR varies in detail from that in the GLS, but in both cases it takes place north of Kjalarnes. In GLS they leave Kjalarnes and 'they sailed away and east along the land, and then into an entrance of two adjoining fjords, and to a headland jutting out there which was entirely covered in forest' (Jones 1986, 196).

In ESR they left Straumfjörðr and

> ...went north past Kjalarnes, and then bore west, with the land on their port side. There was nothing but a wilderness of forest-land [HB: 'to be seen ahead, with hardly a clearing anywhere']. And when they had been on their travels for a long time, there was a river flowing down off the land from east to west. They put into the river-mouth and lay at anchor at the southern bank. [HB adds: They concluded that those mountains...were one and the same and that they therefore stood opposite each other and lay the same distance on both sides of Straumfjörðr] (Jones 1986, 229).

SB simply states 'they moved away and back north....They proposed to explore all the mountains, those which were at Hóp and those they now discovered' (Jones 1986, 229).

I suggest that Þorvaldr's death took place in Hamilton Inlet, or in this general region. This is both north and west of Cape Porcupine. The land is heavily forested, and there are indeed rivers running from east to west, although we must always take the saga's compass directions with a pinch of salt, as pointed out by Sven B. F. Jansson (1945, 270-271). Along the southern shore of Hamilton Inlet is the Mealy Mountain range. With a maximum height of about 1132 m, it is comparable to the Chic-Choc mountains near the mouth of the St. Lawrence River (1248 m), in coastal sailing terms, at a comparable distance from LAM/Straumfjörðr. It is somewhere in the Hamilton Inlet area that Þorvaldr met his death, perhaps near English River, which runs east to west (fig. 6). The people who shot the arrow into Þorvaldr would have been the ancestors of the Algonkian-speaking Innu, formerly known as Montagnais and Naskapi and related to the Newfoundland Beothuk.

So will we find Þorvaldr's grave? I think not. In GLS Þorvaldr asks that he be buried with a cross at his head and one at his feet. However, the sole purpose given for his brother Thorsten's expedition the following year was to collect Þorvaldr's body. ESR does not mention either burial or retrieval, but if we assume that Þorvaldr was Christian, it would have been a necessity to bring his body back to consecrated soil in Greenland, or for a priest to return to perform the proper rites. Þorvaldr's wish to 'stay for a while' was cut short.

BIBLIOGRAPHY

Andersen, B. and Andersen, E. 1989. *Råsejlet—Dragens Vinge*, Roskilde.

Berg, H. 1955. 'Vínland og tidevannet', *Det Kongelige norske videnskapsselskap*. Museet, Årbok 1955.

Bergtórsson, P. 2000. *The Wineland Millennium. Saga and Evidence*, Reykjavik.

Carlson C.C.1996. 'The (In)Significance of Atlantic Salmon', *Federal Archaeology*, Fall-Winter, 23-29.

Cook, R. ed., 1993. *The Voyages of Jacque Cartier*, Toronto, Buffalo and London.

Denys, N. 1672. *Description geographique et historique des costes de l'Amerique septentrionale. Avec l'Historie nautrelle du Pais,* in d'Entremont, C-J. 1982, 63-269.

d'Entremont, C-J. ed., 1982. *Nicolas Denys, sa vie et son oevre*, Yarmouth, NS.

Farmer, G. H.1981. 'The Cold Ocean Environment of Newfoundland', in Macpherson and Macpherson 1981, 56-82.

Fitzhugh, W.W. and Ward, E.I., eds, 2000. *Vikings: The North Atlantic Saga*, Washington and London.

Halldórsson, Ó. 1978. *Grænland í miðaldaritum*, Reyjavík.

——1992. 'The Vínland Sagas', unpublished lecture typescript.

Holand, H. 1940. *Norse Discoveries and Explorations in America. Leif Erikson to the Kensington Stone*, New York.

Hosie, R. C. 1979. *Native Trees of Canada*, Ottawa.

Hovgaard, W. 1914. *The Voyages of the Norsemen to America*, New York.

Jansson, S. B.F. 1945. *Sagorna om Vínland. Handskrifterna till Erik den rödes saga*, Stockholm: Kungliga Vitterhets Historie och Antikvitets Akademiens handlingar 60, 1.

Jones, G. 1986. *The Norse Atlantic Saga. Being the Norse Voyages of Discovery and Settlement to Iceland, Greenland, and North America*, Oxford and New York.

Langdon, H.H. and Ganong, W.F., eds, 1922. *The Works of Samuel de Champlain*, Toronto.

Larsson, M.G. 1999. *Vínland det goda. Nordbornas färder till Amerika under vikingatiden*, Stockholm.

Lescarbot, M. 1606. *Nova Francia. A Description of Acadia*, trans. [1609] P. Erondale, London.

Lynnerup, N. 1998. *The Greenland Norse. A Biological-anthropological Study*. Copenhagen: Meddelelser om Grønland. Man and Society 24.

Macpherson, A.G. and Macpherson, J.B., eds, 1981. *The Natural Environment of Newfoundland Past and Present*, St. John's.

Meldgaard, J. 1961. 'Fra Brattahlid til Vínland', *Naturens Verden*, 45, 353-385.

Morison, S. E. 1971. *The European Discovery of America. The Northern Voyages A.D. 500-1600*, New York.

Munn, W. 1914. *The Wineland Voyages. The location of Helluland, Markland and Vínland from the Icelandic sagas*, St. John's.

Nansen, F. 1911. *In Northern Mists*, vols 1-2, London.

389

Ogilvie, A. E. J., Barlow, L.K. and Jennings, A.E. 2000. 'North Atlantic Climate *c.* AD 1000: Millennial reflections on the Viking discoveries of Iceland, Greenland and North America', *Weather*, 55, 2, 34-45

Rafn, C.C. 1837. *Antiquitates Americanæ sive scriptores septentrionalies rerum ante-columbianarum America. Samling af de I Nordens Oldskrifter indeholdte Efterretninger om de gamle Nordboers Opdagelsereiser til Amerika fra de 10e til det 14de Aarhundrede.* Copenhagen: Det Kongelige Nordiske Oldskriftselskab.

——1838. *Discovery of North America*, New York.

Reeves, A. M. 1890. *Finding of Vínland the Good. The History of the Icelandic Discovery of America, edited and translated from the earliest records. To which is added biography and correspondence of the author by W.D. Foulke. With phototype plates of the vellum mss. of the sagas*, London.

——1906. *The Norse Discovery of America. Translations and Deductions, London.*

Roland, A. E and Smith, E.C. 1969. *The Flora of Nova Scotia*, Halifax, NS.

Sigurðsson, G. 2000. 'The Quest for Vínland in Saga Scholarship', in Fitzhugh and Ward 2000, 232-37.

Storm, G. 1889. *Studies on the Vínland Voyages/ Mémoires de la Société Royale des antiquairies du Nord, 1884-1889: 307-370.* Copenhagen: Kongl. nordiske Oldskriftselskabet.

Salwen, B. 1978. 'Indians of Southern New England and Long Island', in Trigger 1978, 160-76.

Schübeler F.1858-1859. 'Om den 'Hvede', som Nordmændene i Aaret 1000 fandt vildtvoxende i Vínland', *Christiania Videnskabs-Selskabs Forhandlinger*, 1859, 21-31.

Snow, D.R. 1978. 'Late Prehistory of the East Coast', in Trigger 1978, 58-69.

Trigger, B. 1978. *Handbook of North American Indians,* vol. 15: *Northeast*, Washington, DC.

Wawn, A. and Sigurðardóttir, Þ., eds, 2001. *Approaches to Vínland*. Reykjavík: Sigurður Nordal Institute Studies 4.

Whitehead, R. 1991. *The Old Man Told Us: Excerpts from Micmac History, 1500-1950*, Halifax, NS.

Þorláksson, H. 2001. 'The Vínland Sagas in contemporary light', in Wawn and Sigurðardottir 2001, 63-77.

Zinck, M. 1998. *Roland's Flora of Nova Scotia. Based on materials written by A.E. Roland*, vols 1-2, Halifax, NS.

390

The Vínland sagas and the actual characteristics of Eastern Canada—some comparisons with special attention to the accounts of the later explorers

Mats G. Larsson

T he two main Icelandic sagas concerning Vínland, *Eiríks saga rauða* (ESR) and *Grænlendinga saga* (GLS), include many obvious similarities. That is true especially of how they account of the first real exploration of the newly-found areas in the west Atlantic. The landings on the different coasts are described in a similar way, and the leader of the expedition is told to have given the lands the same name in both versions: *Helluland* ('land of rocks'), *Markland* ('land of forests') and *Vínland* ('land of grape vines'). Moreover, the final landing place, *Leifsbúðir* or *Hóp*, has more or less exactly the same characteristics in both sagas—a lake with a river running through it, which is navigable from the sea into the lake only at high tide and which has large sand banks outside its estuary at low tide; geographical conditions which are also in accordance with the place-name *Hóp*.

These descriptions probably derive from the same tradition, retold by one or several of the participants when returning home. The similar descriptions also seem to indicate that they refer to one and same expedition, although in ESR assigned to Þorfinnr Karlsefni and in GLS to Leifr Eiríksson.

To which of the explorers does this tradition thus belong? No certain answer can of course be given to that question, but the fact that both sagas survived in Iceland must definitely be considered. Is it probable that an expedition lead by Leifr Eiríksson, a Greenlander with a Greenlandic crew, would survive in detail in Icelandic tradition? Instead it seems more in accordance with the circumstances that the members of Karlsefni's expedition gave a detailed description of their own experiences of the journey when they returned to Iceland, and that it was these experiences which survived in the oral tradition on the island. A further support for that conclusion is that GLS, although assigning the explorations to Leifr Eiríksson, remarks that the tradition about the voyages was brought to Iceland by Þorfinnr Karlsefni.

It may be objected that the description still may be true even for Leifr Eiríksson's expedition if both voyages went the same road. It is, however, highly improbable that two sailings would sight and make landings on the same coasts in these difficult waters, and it is also clearly indicated in the descriptions that they deal with the first exploration of the three lands. We must also bear in mind that Þorfinnr Karlsefni, although related to Leifr Eiríksson by marriage, was an Icelandic magnate with his own ambitions who would probably not be satisfied with settling down in an area already taken into possession by an other man.

Thus, when we try to identify the different lands as they are described in the Vínland sagas, it is probably the trails of Þorfinnr Karlsefni we are following—the details of the landing places of Leifr Eiríksson are likely to have been forgotten in Greenland. The remaining memory of them might in fact be only the short remark in ESR that Leifr discovered lands with vines, self-sown wheat acres and *mösurr* trees.

But perhaps one of Leifr's settlements has been found after all, due to Helge Ingstad's explorations and investigations. For L'Anse aux Meadows, although not in correspondence with the saga tradition of *Hóp* or *Leifsbúðir*, may well be the place in North America where Leifr first landed and settled. The datings are definitely in favour of such an hypothesis, and the finds of butternuts indicate that expeditions really took place from this settlement to the coasts where both the grapes and the butternuts grow, probably the St. Lawrence area.

When trying to reconstruct Þorfinnr Karlsefni's expedition, we should consider a fact that is often disregarded by scholars, although it is stated in both sagas as well as in the Old Icelandic geographic work *Landafræði*: that all the discovered lands—including Helluland—were situated *south* of Greenland and were reached with *southern* courses. This general picture of the expedition, indicated in *all* the sources, should in my opinion be considered more trustworthy than the sole contradiction to it, namely the information in GLS that there were glaciers in Helluland, which has lead so many scholars to identify it with Baffin Island.

In fact, a voyage to Vínland along the arctic coasts of Canada has more or less been taken for granted by today's scholars. When assuming this, however, it seems to have been forgotten that the ice conditions do not favour such a sailing course from southern Greenland.

The Strait of Belle Isle usually becomes free of sea ice in May, and the most southern part of Labrador in the beginning of June (fig. 1). However, the northern part of Labrador is not accessible from the sea until the last week of July, and not until early August the ice has left the most southern part of Baffin Island (fig. 2).

Thus, already in the beginning of the summer it would be possible to land in southern Labrador, while it would be necessary to wait for almost two months longer—the main part of the short summer—to reach Baffin Island. And even if the ice may have left earlier in the eleventh century, the difference in time between the southern and the northern coasts would probably still be substantial. Considering that the arctic route also would more than double the sailing distance compared to a direct course to the southern areas, it does not seem probable that experienced sailors would choose it for a voyage with a lot of people—and cattle—on the ship.

Southern Labrador is also the area which is best in correspondence with the information in GLS that it was situated southwest of southern Greenland on a four day's sailing distance with a good wind. It would furthermore be the first area sighted on an approximately southerly sailing from the Godthaab area, as stated in ESR, even though it must be admitted that the sailing distance given there, two days, is too short to be true (fig. 3).

The general description of Helluland and its large rocks, accounted of in both sagas, is well in accordance with a landing in southern Labrador. The Norse explorers could only see the coastal area from their ships and did not visit the interior. Their impression of the land would thus be the rocky coast of this region with its tundra vegetation, and not the forests in the interior.

If we want to imagine how the Norsemen themselves reacted in the face of the new lands, one method is to compare the traditions of their voyages with the reports given by later explorers of the same general area. For southern Labrador we have the well-known statement by Jacques Cartier—almost identical with the Norse description of Helluland—in which he does not even want to call it a land, only stone and dreary rocks, and says that it must be the land God gave Cain.

Regarding the second land, Markland, the sailing distances from Helluland is between two and three days according to the sagas, but the courses differ between southwest and southeast (fig. 3). The only general conclusion that could be drawn from this is that Markland was situated on a not too long distance south of Helluland. That would evidently give Newfoundland as the most probable alternative. With a sailing along the Atlantic coast of that island—which seems to have been the general view of both sagas—the Norse would be bound to encounter the part jutting out to the northeast from Fogo Island to Cape Freels, with its long sandy shores and its vast lowland, characteristics of Markland according to GLS.

Newfoundland also gives good reason for the name Markland, as it is rather heavily forested and probably was much more so in former times. And, again, the early historic

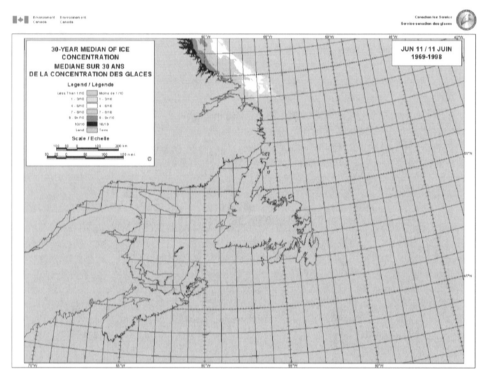

Figure 1. 30-year median of ice concentration along Eastern Canada in the beginning of June (Environment Canada, Canadian Ice Service).

Figure 2. 28-year median of ice concentration along Baffin Island and Northern Labrador in the beginning of August (Environment Canada, Canadian Ice Service).

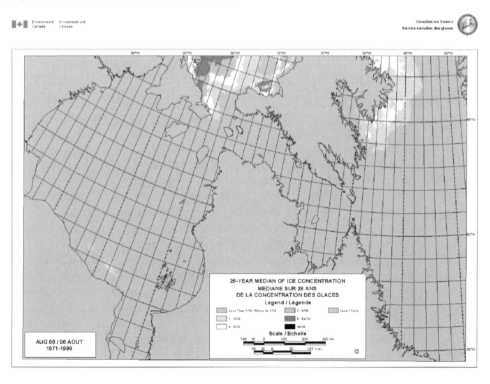

Figure 3. Sailing courses and distances in 'days' from Greenland to Helluland, Markland and Vínland, according to *Grænlendinga saga* and *Eiríks saga rauða*.

GREENLAND

HELLULAND — 2 days

HELLULAND — 4 days — 2 days

MARKLAND — 2 days

394

MARKLAND — 3 days — 2 days

KJALARNES — 2 days

VÍNLAND

LEIFSBÚÐIR

?

KJALARNES

FURÐUSTRANDIR

STRAUMSFJÖRÐR — STRAUMSEY

VÍNLAND

HÓP

GRÆNLENDINGA SAGA　　　　*EIRÍKS SAGA RAUÐA*

explorers give exactly the same reports on their first impression of this region as the sagas do of Markland—dense woods, large trees and good bear hunting.

The last of the discovered lands, Vínland, was according to the sagas situated on a two days sailing distance from Markland with a southerly or southwesterly course. With a departure from Newfoundland this leads us to Nova Scotia, and especially Cape Breton, one of the earliest discovered parts in this area made by the later explorers.

Only in ESR we have a description of the northern part of Vínland, with the promontory *Kjalarnes* ('Keelness') in the north, followed by *Furðustrandir*. The promontory Cape Breton itself or Cape Gabarus a short way south of it would correspond well with *Kjalarnes*, but what about *Furðustrandir*, mostly translated as 'wonder beaches' with reference to their great extension? The name has always been regarded as disputable, as the word *furða* ('something that goes before, portent, wonder'), although frequently used as a strengthening before adjectives is never used in that way before nouns.

A more probable interpretation may be the one recently hinted by the Swedish philologist Jan Paul Strid. He compares the name with the many place-names for breaking rocks in the Swedish archipelagos, *både*, also meaning 'portent' and referring to the possibilities to notice the shoal before hitting it.

This interpretation would in the opinion of Strid correspond very well with the extended barrier beaches of gravel and sand dominating the coast of eastern Cape Breton Island from Cape Gabarus down to Point Michaux: far-stretching sandbars running outside land and causing the sea to break offshore (fig. 4). The northernmost of them has a length of 20 kilometers, and the next one of 15 kilometers, i.e. approximately the same extension as the beaches around Cape Porcupine, so often pointed out as *Furðustrandir* although they do not have any particular characteristics.

One of the most striking characteristics of Vínland according to the saga tradition is the different hints of very high tides and strong currents. The estuary of the river at *Hóp* or *Leifsbúðir* was navigable only at high water and there were large sandbanks outside the estuary at low water: although the ship had safe depth under its keel when the tide was in, the sea was on a long distance when the tide was out. And there was a bay, *Straumsfjörðr* ('Stream Bay'), where the currents were very strong both in the bay and around an island off it, *Straumsey* ('Stream Island').

These characteristics point at a location south of Bay of St. Lawrence, with its rather low tidal ranges. The same applies to the mild winter climate described in the sagas, contrary to the cold and snowy winters in the St. Lawrence area.

395

There are two bays or bay-like places in Nova Scotia noticed for their strong currents by the early French explorers. One is the Strait of Canso, parting Cape Breton Island from the mainland. Before it was closed by a causeway the tidal currents through it was up to four knots, and it was accordingly called *Le passage courant* ('The streaming strait') by Samuel de Champlain. However, it is not a bay, and in Chedabucto Bay outside its mouth the currents are much less. The strait also lacks an island off it with such strong currents and such a tremendous amount of sea-fowl as described in ESR.

Figure 4. The barrier beaches south of Cape Gabarus, Cape Breton Island.

The other place mentioned by Champlain is more interesting. He calls it *Baye courante* ('Stream Bay'), i.e. the same name as the Norse one. It is today called Lobster Bay and is located a bit west of the southern tip of Nova Scotia. The currents in this bay have a rate of three knots, but the most interesting detail is maybe that there is an island off it called Seal Island, where the currents have a rate of four knots. And on this and the adjacent islands both Champlain and Denys in the first part of the seventeenth century report such large amounts of sea-fowl that 'no one who had not seen it would believe it possible'.

There have been ongoing discussions about the former existence of wild grape vines in Nova Scotia. However, Scoggan in his *The Flora of Canada* (1978-79) sets the northern limit of the species *Vitis riparia* through the southern part of the province, referring to a specimen collected in 1924 close to Bridgewater by the La Have River (where it is still flourishing).

With this one and only specimen we must of course consider the possibilty that it was once planted on the spot, but fortunately we have several older reports on wild grapes in the province. Champlain and Denys reported them in several habitats, both in the southwestern and in the northern part of the peninsula. These reports have sometimes been regarded as mistakes, but there exists in fact an interesting confirmation of them from the end of the nineteenth century.

396

When the botanist Lawson arranged an inquiry about wild vines by help of the Nova Scotian newspapers he received reports from several individuals. These reports were evidently independent of the ones from the old explorers, but still pointed out exactly the same

Figure 5. Reports of wild grape vines in Nova Scotia.

o = 17th century report.
+ = 19th century report.
x = still existing specimen.

Figure 6, above. The tidal flats at the estuary of Chegoggin River.

Figure 7, right. Reconstruction of the former tidal lake at Chegoggin River. The darker area shows the extension of the lake after dyking.

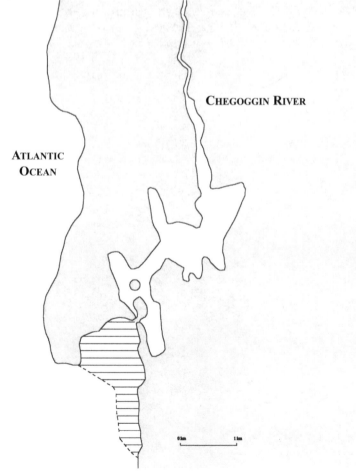

CHEGOGGIN RIVER

ATLANTIC
OCEAN

areas for the habitats (fig. 5). This gives a mutual strengthening of the information and increases the probability that wild grapes were growing in Nova Scotia during the Viking Age, especially considering the warmer climate during that period. Together with the other characteristics this makes Nova Scotia a strong candidate for the Vínland of Þorfinnr Karlsefni.

The most carefully described place in the Vínland sagas is the river estuary with the lake mentioned above. The fact that this place is so special and that it is similarly characterized in both sagas gives the tradition of it a high probability to reflect a real place. If we really want to find the spot where Þorfinnr Karlsefni and his crew built their camp, it is in my opinion such a place we should look for.

So far no one has, to my knowledge, pointed out any spot with more than a minor similarity to these descriptions. I have myself during several years looked for such places in Nova Scotia, especially in the southern part, where the tides starts to be high enough. During these investigations I have only been able to locate one place with all the characteristics given in the sagas. That place is the estuary of Chegoggin River, a few kilometers northwest of Yarmouth and thus in the very vicinity of Lobster Bay and Seal Island. It has still extensive tidal flats outside it (fig. 6), but the tidal lake in the lower part of the river has since a long time been dyked and is now almost completely vanished. However, it can still be reconstructed by help of air photographs and maps, showing that it once stretched about four kilometers up the river (fig. 7).

Unfortunately, almost all the land around this former lake is cultivated and ploughed since centuries, and all possible traces of prehistoric buildings would have been levelled with the ground. Thus, more sophisticated investigations than ocular inspections must be used to find out if they are there; such as phosphate mapping, special air photographing and electromagnetic investigations, all rather expensive. Such investigations have started, but so far only a minor area close to the sea has been investigated with phosphate mapping. However, I hope to be able to go further in the near future.

BIBLIOGRAPHY

The content of this paper is mainly based on the research published in my article, 'The Vínland Sagas and Nova Scotia. A Reappraisal of an Old Theory', *Scandinavian Studies,* 1992, 3, and in my 1999 book, *Vínland det goda. Nordbornas färder till Nordamerika under vikingatiden*, Stockholm, where further references may be found.

A Core Condensation of My Ideas Concerning the Locations of Sites Mentioned in the Voyages of Leífr Eiríksson, Þorvaldr Eiríksson and Þorfinnr Karlsefni

George M. Shendock

What is factually known at this time about Viking sites in North America, is that a sizable group, at least the size of Karlsefni's, established a settlement on the northern tip of Newfoundland in the early eleventh century. None of the other sites mentioned in both sagas have ever been verified. Through eleven individually planned, funded, and executed field expeditions, and my extensive research, which included a trip to Iceland, I have developed an original, unique theory to identify several of the other sites mentioned in the sagas.

In dealing with Leifr's and Þorvaldr's voyages I will be primarily citing *Grænlendinga saga* ('Greenlanders' Saga: GLS). This is the older of the two, is considered by most scholars to be the more historically accurate, and has been called Leifr's saga. In dealing with Karlsefni's voyages I will be primarily citing *Eiríks saga rauða* ('Eiríkr the Red's Saga: ESR), which has been referred to as Karlsefni's saga (Ingstad 1969, 32-33).

As best as I can determine in about AD 1003 Leifr set sail in early summer and followed Bjarni Herjólfsson's route in reverse back to North America. In the area he named Markland (Labrador), GLS states: 'This country was flat and wooded, with white sandy beaches wherever they went; and the land sloped gently down to the sea' (GLS 55). I think the section '[...] with white sandy beaches wherever they went' implies not a single landfall in Labrador but rather a few. The thirty mile or so beach near Cape Porcupine almost certainly was viewed, but there are quite a few other smaller, white sandy beaches in southern Labrador on the Strait of Belle Isle. These can be found at Pinware, Forteau, and Blanc Sablon. Indeed Blanc Sablon means 'white sand' in French. I, unlike most investigators, believe that Leifr turned into the Strait of Belle Isle and did not cross the strait to Newfoundland. I believe there may be two reasons for this. One may have been expediency. The current is very strong and can travel both into and out of the strait, depending upon the tide. It may have been an incoming strong current at the time Leifr arrived at the strait that caused him to turn into the strait rather than cross it at that time, despite the fact he could easily see the shore of Newfoundland across from him.

A second reason for entering into the strait instead of crossing it at this time, may be due to the Norse perception that the strait was the entrance to a huge fjord or bay as evidenced in the Skálholt Map. There is very little evidence that they ever realized that what we now call Newfoundland was indeed an island.

I believe Leifr made at least one landfall on the Labrador side of the strait at either Forteau or Blanc Sablon. Both have white sand beaches at their head and both offer good anchorage. Both, especially Forteau Bay, are very impressive looking from the sea, and Forteau would have been the nearer of the two for Leifr. After this landfall GLS simply states, 'They hurried back to their ship as quickly as possible'(GLS 55). Could it have been they discovered the area was already inhabited by natives and this was the cause of them hastening back to the ship? This coastal area was indeed inhabited by natives at the time of the voyages.

GLS then states:

> [they] sailed away to sea in a north-east wind for two days until they sighted land again. They sailed towards it and came to an island which lay to the north of it (GLS 55).

I maintain as part of my original theory that Leifr sailed 'before a north-east wind' and in a southwesterly direction from Forteau or its vicinity; and following the prevailing current which runs southwest, sailed non-stop to Ille Sainte au Marie, a distance of *c.* 140 land miles, in two days. Although some Norse *knarrar* could sail more than 100 miles per day, I believe there were several factors influencing their speed. Firstly I don't believe they were under sail a full 48 hours (*tvær doegri*). He and his crew had already gone ashore in daylight hours in Labrador, thus part of the first day was already lost. Secondly, it is doubtful whether they sailed in a perfectly straight line from Forteau to Ille Sainte Marie. Thirdly, as I have personally experienced several times, June and July are the worst months for fog along this coast and these are the months he would be sailing. It is also quite possible the ship was under sail only during daylight hours-due to the unknown nature of these waters, the possible fog, or both.

Ile Sainte Marie is in reality east not north of Pointe-à-Maurier. However, I think there is an explanation for the Norse tendency to shift their daytime perception of north to the north-east in their more southerly latitudes at least during the summer months. If they based their direction upon the rising of the sun on or about the summer solstice (21 June), their estimation of north would shift gradually to the northeast as the sun would be rising further down on the horizon the farther south they traveled. This in effect would make the St. Marie appear to be north north-east of Pointe-à-Maurier. This tendency to shift north toward the northeast can be seen in the so-called Western and Eastern Settlements in Greenland and in the Skálholt Map. The Western Settlement is actually north-west of the Eastern Settlement and the huge bay between Markland and Vínland runs nearly due north/south on the Skalholt Map, when in reality the separating body of water between the two runs northeast/southwest (fig.1).

An argument can be made that Pointe-à-Maurier is merely a point of land jutting out into the Gulf of St. Lawrence and not a true cape. However, I myself have seen it from Ile St. Marie and I believe it can be taken for a cape, because it is a few miles in width and south of it the land mass abruptly turns west.

GLS then states,

> They steered a westerly course round the headland. There were extensive shallows there and at low tide their ship was left high and dry, with the sea almost out of sight. But they were so impatient to land that they could not bear to wait for the rising tide to float the ship; they ran ashore to a place where a river flowed out of a lake (GLS 56).

This description fits well with the mouth of the Etamamiou River on the North Shore of Québec. There is a shallow bay at its mouth which lowers to just a few feet at low tide (Canadian Hydrographic Service, Chart 4440). The river empties into and then out from Lac Volant to the sea after a short distance. Lac Volant is a tidal lake 1-1/4 miles wide and 1 mile long. I observed the northern shores of the lake in 1996, but under my compressed schedule could not observe the southern end. The northern end is very shallow, but a channel runs along part of the south side, where I was able to observe some good grass growing in an open area. I think this area warrants further investigation by the proper agencies.

GLS then goes on to state, 'There was no lack of salmon in the river or the lake, bigger salmon then they had ever seen'(GLS 56). The Etamamiou is indeed one of the major salmon rivers along the North Shore.

There is no mention of Leifr encountering any natives at the site just described above. It is highly unlikely that he and his crew never saw any natives along the length of their entire voyage. However it is just as unlikely he would have wintered over at a location where there were natives in the vicinity. The Etamamiou may not have been occupied during this period, despite its rich fisheries, and hundreds of sea birds (important as a source of eggs and down) and seals along its adjacent coasts (Jones 1984, map 14).

Another fascinating bit of information contained in the saga is that, 'On the shortest day of the year the sun was visible in the middle of the afternoon'(Ingstad 1969, 42). Gustav Storm and H. Geelmuyden believed the Old Norse term used in this passage referred to a

Figure 1. The 1669 version of the 'Skálholt Map' (after Hogg, 1989).

point on the horizon and not a time of day. Basing their calculation upon this belief, they mentioned the settlement was at 49°55'N (Storm 1886, 121-131). Lac Volant is located at 50°17'N. Another ineresting observation is that the rest of North Shore is at roughly this same latitude for nearly 150 miles to the west of Lac Volant.

What I am alluding to in this last statement is that although Lac Volant fits well into the saga, it is by no means the only possible candidate for Leifr's wintering site along the North Shore. I have made some quick on site observations here and at Lac Coacoachou, somewhat further west. But I think Lac Volant would make a good starting point for any further investigations westward along the North Shore up to perhaps Kegaska. Any investigation of these areas would have to be executed by sea, as there are no roads, and the airline servicing some of these outlying areas does not stop at every area with a possible site (fig. 2).

402

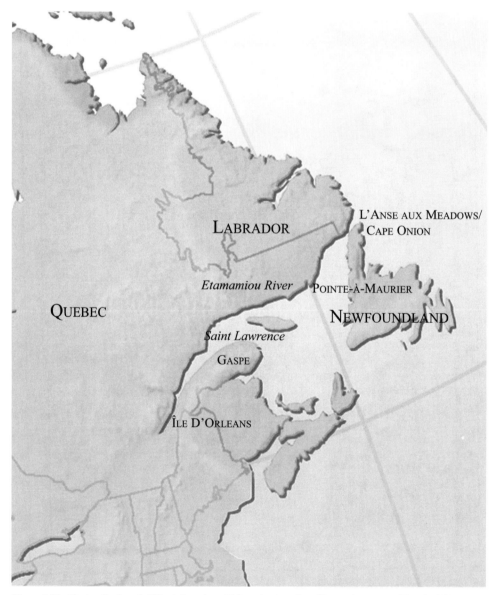

Figure 2. The Eastern Seaboard of North America with key sites mentioned in text (courtesy of Provincial Museum of Newfoundland and Labrador).

With this in mind let us analyze further the saga content. In GLS we are told that first the permanent houses are built and then explorations of the land begin. In one of these explorations the famous grapes are found. It is my contention that the exploration that produced the grapes was not undertaken on foot, but was instead the result of a sea reconnaissance of significant duration. It appears both the main ship and boat were used. I come to this conclusion from the statement in GLS, 'It is said that their tow-boat was filled with grapes'(GLS 57). If their tow-boat was filled with grapes, and they were as I suspect traveling by sea, then the main ship was also used and the after-boat used as a cargo holder for the fragile grapes. I have difficulty accepting the idea as some have accepted that the grapes, which ripen at the very end of summer or early fall, were stored in the boat until spring, at which time Leifr hauled them back to Greenland.

In the previous passage in GLS it reads,

> They slept for the rest of the night [where the grapes were found], and next morning Leifr said to his men, "Now we have two tasks on our hands. On alternate days we must gather grapes and cut vines, and then fell trees, to make a cargo for my ship." This was done (GLS 57).

It appears we have another implied contradiction with the first line, 'They for the rest of the night'—referring to where or near where the grapes were found—and another previous line referring to the missing character, Tyrkir. When Leifr and twelve other men went looking for the detained Tyrkir, it reads, 'They had gone only a short distance from the houses when Tyrkir came walking towards them'(GLS 57). Why they felt it necessary to sleep there that night would seem to me to be more logical if they were indeed nowhere near their permanent winter quarters but rather a short distance from an improvised camp near their ship. Another possible clue to the possibility they were not in the same climatic zone as their permanent camp lies in the fact Leifr is also having timber felled at the same location. It is stated earlier in the saga the original area where the permanent houses were built was 'well wooded, some of it suitable for housebuilding'. If he were near his permanent settlement one would think this task could be accomplished in autumn or winter—but Leifr instead divides his crew evenly for the two tasks of grape gathering and timber cutting. Could it be that he had ventured to an area further south that contained northern hardwoods, such as red oak, maple, and other very valuable species which would be superior in ship building and repair compared to the more northerly soft wood conifers, which were probably present at his permanent site?

Now arises the perennial question, where was the original Vínland? If at least for the time being one accepts the possibility the original base was on the North Shore, it would be a prudent move to explore the coast further to the southwest, within constant site of land. This of course would take them into the St. Lawrence Estuary. I would like once again to refer to the Skálholt Map. It clearly shows *Markland/Skrælinge Land* separated from Promontorium Winlandiæ by a huge bay or estuary narrowing to the south and eventually merging with Promontorium Winlandiæ. It is likely this geographical conception was arrived at through experience rather than mere speculation. Not only does it closely resemble geographic fact (St. Lawrence Estuary) in configuration, but if one looks at proportionate distance, for example, from the tip of Promontorium Winlandiæ to the Ile D'Orleans and compare this with the distance from Promontorium Winlandiæ to the area between Markland and Helluland, we find a very close match in distance which is the case in reality.

I've mentioned the Ile D'Orleans specifically because it is my belief this is the location of the original Vínland from Leifr's first voyage. My reasons for concluding this are as follows: The Ile was called Ile de Bacchus by the earliest French explorers. Jacques Cartier writing in the early sixteenth century has this to say about the immediate area,

403

> We found on both sides the most beautiful and best land we could hope to see-filled with the most won-
> derful trees in the world, and so many grape-vines weighed down with grapes that they appeared to have
> been planted by man and not growing wild, but because they have not been cultivated or grafted, the
> grapes are not as large or as sweet as ours (cited in Ingstad 1969, 125).

Indeed today there are at least two commercial vineyards on the island. Also mentioned by Cartier is an area 'filled with the most wonderful trees in the world', which can still apply today. The area around Québec City and especially Ile D'Orleans is the northern limit of many hardwood species such as butternut, examples of which have been found at L'Anse aux Meadows, Newfoundland. These have been radio-carbon dated to the early eleventh century. There are no butternuts to be found from L'Anse aux Meadows until one reaches the area around Québec City. Also, as was mentioned earlier, there are a variety of other northern hardwoods present on Ile D'Orleans which are near their northern limit, such as sugar and red maple, and red oak which would be prized in ship building for its water resistance and strength. Although some species, such as red oak, can be found as far to the northeast as Gaspe, the point I am trying to make is that these hardwoods, and the butternuts and grapes all could be found in this location. There is also another tree, with whitish bark, which the Québecois call *boulaau*. Here I am going to make one departure in exclusively using GLS in researching Leifr's voyage.

In ESR there is one curious reference to Leifr finding *masur* trees in Vínland. Although it is generally accepted that M. L. Fernald has shown *masur* trees as being birch, I can't help but wonder about the similarity of the relatively uncommon characteristic of *boulaau* having white bark. In any case it's a minor point, but worth mentioning (Fernald 1910; see Crozier, this volume).

I'm sure there will be criticism against my choosing Ile D'Orleans as the original Vínland site on the basis of the large native population found along both shores of the estuary at this point in time. There were as many as fifty villages strung out along both shores (Ministre de la Culture et des Communications, Quebec, pers. comm.). But, to date, archaeological evidence on any possible native sites on the island during the early eleventh century is fragmentary and uncertain, although some evidence of perhaps earlier and later native visits or occupation is present (Ministre de la Culture et des Communications, Quebec, pers. comm.). That the Norse did in fact reach the mouth of the St. Lawrence in the immediate vicinity of Ile D'Orleans in the early eleventh century can be supported by the radio-carbon dating of the butternuts found at L'Anse aux Meadows.

The Norse voyagers and the indigenous native population were undoubtedly aware of each others' presence. However, what safer place other than an island could the Norse have chosen for their reconnaissance of the area. Their superior vessel and the width of the river would be to their advantage in the event of an escape. I believe their stay, however, was of a prudently short duration; and gathered what resources as they could (grapes and timber) as quickly as possible, and left for their permanent camp on the Cote Nord in early fall. One can imagine the awe these intensely self-sufficient explorers from the ice clad coast of Greenland felt after having witnessed the bounty of this land.

I am left with the impression that after Leifr's initial visit to Ile D'Orleans there were no others for at least ten years. I base this upon the sagas where, when grapes are further mentioned, it is in a contradictory and unconvincing manner in context to the rest of the information in the sagas (Þorvaldr Eiriksson in GLS and Þorfinnr Karlsefni in ESR).

But by AD 1070 Adam of Bremen's accounts given him by the Danes of the wonderful quality of the Vínland wine are probably not based on the chance finding of grapes on a single voyage, but rather multiple voyages which helped establish somewhat of a reputation.

Also the discovery of a silver Norse coin (dating from the 1070s) at the eastern mouth of Penobscot Bay at a large native American trading site is significant. Because it is the only European object found at the site it is considered to have arrived by trade over a considerable distance (Logan 1992, 105). The presence of Labrador ramah chert at the site has some investigators speculating the coin may have also been transported from this area. I believe I have come up with a unique, possible alternative. The site, located on the largest bay in Maine, certainly was a center for sea-born trading along an extensive part of the northeast coast of North America. I perceive that the prevailing opinion is that it arrived by sea. My apparently unique speculation is that it could just as easily, if not more easily, have arrived overland along a well established trade route following the Penobscot River, Chesuncook Lake, and the Chaudiere River located less than ten miles of Ile D'Orleans on the Saint Lawrence. A map outlined with this route and others in the State of Maine was kindly provided to me upon request by Mr. Steven L. Cox of the Maine State Museum (Maine State Museum 1998, pl. 7). If the Norse did penetrate as far as the mouth of the St. Lawrence, which would seem likely as evidenced by the solitary, but highly significant butternuts, it would also seem likely they would return to this abundantly rich area as long as their nautical capabilities and resources permitted.

On the Ile D'Orleans itself, I would choose a small, somewhat crescent shaped cove near Ste. Petronille on the south-west coast as a possible starting point for any archaeological evidence of Norse contact. There is a large estate located there which originally was built by a businessman who controlled a fair amount of traffic on the river. The property then passed on to the Catholic church, and from what I understand, is today administered by a business affiliated with the church. The land rises in three tiers or small plateaus from the shore and gives an excellent view of any river traffic. A small spring brook runs adjacent to the property.

405

As I mentioned earlier, there appears to have been a period of some years before this possible site was revisited by the Norse. Although Leifr's brother, Þorvaldr, led a two-year expedition (AD 1005-1007) to North America, I am unconvinced that he ever explored the area around the mouth of the St. Lawrence. I believe he did arrive and stay at his brother's permanent camp on the Cote Nord, but it appears he found no grapes. GLS states,

> They spent the winter there [at Leifsbúðir] and gathered grapes and vines as cargo for their ship. In the spring they set off on the voyage to Greenland (GLS 61).

It is highly unlikely they used grapes from the previous fall as a cargo for their departure in the spring. It is quite possible Leifr kept the location of grapes a secret, and swearing to secrecy the twelve or so members of his crew who were with him at the time. When Þorvaldr left on his voyage he may have only taken members of the original crew who had been left behind at Leifr's permanent camp. In such a case all these men would know about the location of the grapes is that Leifr sailed from the permanent camp in a westerly direction and returned from the same direction. The very first exploration Þorvaldr undertakes from the permanent camp is in a westerly direction. He and some of his men take the pinnace or afterboat and sail 'west along the coast'(GLS 59). The Cote Nord runs due west for over 300 miles. GLS further describes the land as having 'white sandy beaches. There were numerous islands there, and extensive shallows'(GLS 59-60). This description also fits well with the Cote Nord. It further states, 'They found no traces of human habitation or animals except on one westerly island, where they found a wooden stackcover'(GLS 60). Parts of this territory would have been populated by the ancestors of today's Montaignais Indians, a branch of the Algonquin Group of tribes.

What is called a stack-cover or grain holder made of wood was probably a cone-shaped temporary hunting wigwam; which does to a large degree resemble an ancient Norse grain storage bin. That would explain its solitary and apparently abandoned state.

Another reason for Þorvaldr turning back at this point might be found in geography. If he had followed the coast as far west as say, Harve Sainte-Pierre, he might be of the impression he was coming to the end of this huge bay or fjord. To the south he could detect the north coast of huge Anticosti Island making itself more and more apparent as he continued. Thus he may have miscalculated the head of this huge 'fjord' by at least 350 miles. And today, as in the eleventh century, no grapes could be found along this coast.

GLS then tells us: 'Next summer Þorvaldr sailed east with his ship and then north along the coast'(GLS 60). This sailing information fits in perfectly if Þorvaldr is leaving from the Cote Nord. First of all it is significant that Þorvaldr, 'sailed east with his ship', because if he were sailing eastward from the Cote Nord, he would be crossing approximately 100 miles of open sea in the Gulf of St. Lawrence before making landfall halfway up the west coast of Newfoundland. Keep in mind the previous year's expedition to the west 'along the land' in the much smaller ship's boat.

And it states, 'then [they sailed] north along the coast'. This could only be the Great Northern Peninsula of Newfoundland. Next, GLS states: 'They ran into a fierce gale off a headland and were driven ashore; the keel was shattered and they had to stay there a long time while they repaired the ship'(GLS 60). Then Þorvaldr named the cape Kjalarnes (Keelness). Two very good candidates for the location of Kjalarnes are the Port-au-Choix Penninsula and the area near Reefs Harbour located fairly close to each other. Summer storms in this area usually blow from the west, this part of Newfoundland experiencing 3-4 thunderstorms each summer. Traveling north along the Northern Peninsula and encountering a storm blowing from the west could easily run them aground with land on their starboard side.

When the ship had been repaired, 'they sailed away eastward along the coast. Soon they found themselves at the mouth of two fjords, and sailed up to the promontory that jutted out between them'(GLS 60). Now from sailing northward along the land the sailing direction shifts to the east. There is only one place on the entire east coast of North America from which one could sail first westward along the land, then eastward to northward along the land and then eastward once again along the land; and this starting place must be located at the Cote Nord. As far as I know I am the first to make this proposal and I think because of the relative historical accuracy of GLS, plus the importance of the individuals involved, my proposal warrants consideration (fig. 2).

If the fjord Þorvaldr turned into at this point was Sacred Bay, then the headland he stepped ashore on was Cape Onion. I investigated Cape Onion and the western side of Sacred Bay in the summer of 1999. I specifically made the 1500 mile journey in search of information that would support my proposal for locations of saga sites. I was not disappointed. Onion Cove next to the cape is one of the most beautiful places I have seen in Newfoundland (fig. 3). There is a beautiful meadow containing hay and wild flowers about a half mile in length, and on the higher ground there is a huge carpet of what the local people call blackberry; there are also strawberries and partridgeberries. A large spring provides fresh water at its lowest point. A fair-sized vessel up to the size of a Viking *knörr* could come in quite close to shore in this cove and would be protected by a northwest reef and several islets (Canadian Hydrographic Service, Chart 4509). One of the largest islets is called the Mewstone, or molting stone. Local people say years ago the islet would be covered in molting season by hundreds of eider ducks. Eider down was prized by the Norse and they avidly collected it in large quantities (Wahlgren 1986, 135). The saga reports the headland had plenty of forest and even today there are thick stands of spruce on both hills of the headland. It was here Þorvaldr wished to settle. However there was an encounter on the way back to the ship with natives whereupon eight of the natives were killed. The natives retaliated by sending a fleet of skin boats against their ship, mortally wounding Þorvaldr. Following this they may have taken refuge on Great Sacred Island. As Þorvaldr lay dying he requested to be taken back to the headland and to be buried there.

I thought if my choice of Cape Onion as Þorvaldr's famous cape were correct, some vestige of his interment may still exist. I climbed the cape and found myself looking at a large oval-shaped pile of stones approximately 25 feet long, 14 feet wide and 6 feet high. It runs in roughly a northeast/south westerly direction and there is a commanding view to Great Sacred Island, Belle Isle, the Strait of Belle Isle to the Labrador coast, and even across Sacred Bay to Epaves Bay—indeed L'Anse aux Meadows itself is visible six miles away. Part of this structure appears to be natural, but a large portion of it seems to have been man-made. For one thing all the rocks on the northwest side are within a particular range in size. All of them are small enough to have been transported by human beings. To the best of my knowledge this structure has not been investigated—it may have been, but I have seen nothing in references used by me. Even if it is the original place of internment of Þorvaldr, it may well be empty today. Þorvaldr's brother Þorsteinn and his wife Guðríðr launched an ill-fated expedition in or near AD 1008 to retrieve Þorvaldr's body and bring it back to Greenland; perhaps so it could be buried in consecrated ground, since the Norse were now Christian. They were tossed around at sea all that summer and returned to Greenland, never having made landfall. The body may have finally returned to Greenland with Karlsefni in about AD 1012 after he and his group departed from L'Anse aux Meadows, a mere six miles from Cape Onion.

407

Other information concerning Old Norse burial practices would make this a prime location for such an internment. As Rudolf Poertner writes, 'the mortal remains were buried in a mound, because of the widespread belief in a mound as a center of energy. Mounds varied in position and form, depending on the locality. Rocky promontories overlooking the sea ... were preferred sites'(Poertner 1975, 245). I am of the opinion Cape Onion is the Crossness of GLS.

The next attempted Vínland voyage, Þorsteinn's, has already been mentioned. When Þorsteinn dies that winter (*c.* AD 1008) Þorfinnr Karsefni, a newly arrived Icelander, marries Þorsteinn's widow. Karlsefni of course has heard of the great resources of the newly discovered land, and being a successful businessman, attempts to exploit them by establishing a permanent colony. There appear to have been at least three ships, with the number of people involved varying from 60 to 160. In any case most scholars are of the opinion that a group of Norse settlers numbering at least 60, if not more, inhabited L'Anse aux Meadows in the early eleventh century.

As I mentioned at the beginning of this paper, I will be using primarily ESR when referencing passages concerning Karlsefni's voyages. It is by far the more confusing and self contradicting of the two sagas, due in part that it exists in two variant forms, *Hauksbók* and *Skalholtsbók*. To use this saga as an informative source one must take many risks in trying to decide which passages are a viable source of information and which are either placed out of context, fragmented, or just plain fabricated out of hand. Herein of course lies the danger-attempting to use speculation, albeit based upon logic, in making to a large extent a subjective evaluation on the validity of the material. This method, plus the sparse archaeological evidence is all we have to work with, more particularly in ESR, than in the more historically accurate GLS.

In about AD 1009, Þorfinnr Karlsefni, his wife Guðríðr and at least 60 other people, along with livestock, sailed down the Coast of Labrador. When passing Cape Porcupine, Karlsefni probably noticed the shape of the Cape reminded him of an upturned boat and this is the probable reason he named it Kjalarnes (Keelness). It is doubtful to me, as I explained earlier, that this cape is the same Keelness as Þorvaldr's, for reasons which I explained earlier. Below the cape, the long stretch of sandy beach is named Furðustrandir (Wonder Beaches) by Karlsefni. Soon afterwards they reach their destination, which was almost certainly L'Anse aux Meadows. When I say they reached their destination, I believe they left Greenland with the intention of sailing to this very spot; not because Leifr had built his house here, but because of accounts from members of Þorvaldr's expedition of the advantages of the area around Great Sacred Bay especially the relative abundance of grass. Karsefni's voyage was the first expedition which had as its goal permanent settlement, which of course included livestock. Leifr and Þorvaldr's expeditions were one of exploration, and the existence of good strands of grass where their dwellings were located, would have been of less importance. Two other considerations for not choosing Leifr's houses may have the apparent lack of grapes in the vicinity of Leifr's houses and the greater sailing distance involved getting there. One other possibility is that northern Newfoundland is ideally situated to be reached by direct sail from Iceland, by-passing Greenland altogether. Karsefni was an Icelander, not a Greenlander and indeed, after his attempt at colonising, did return back to Iceland where he lived. That such a voyage could be made was a fait accompli by the Norse (Herjolfsson's voyage).

After the first year of settlement, Karsefni decided to explore southward along the coast (Ingstad 1969, 54). For reasons I will explain shortly, I believe they first explored southward along the west coast of the Great Northern Peninsula. If my calculations of Þorvaldr's last voyage are correct, then the northern third of this coast had already been viewed by Þorvaldr's crew. They may have given Karsefni a favorable account and he was prepared to attempt a second settlement. The word settlement is significant here; it was not simply a voyage of exploration, judging from the fact they brought livestock with them. Once again, as in the case of L'Anse aux Meadows, the possibility exists they had a specific destination or at least a pre-chosen area in mind.

Karlsefni called his second settlement Hóp, or 'Sheltered Bay'. There are several examples of this on the northwest coast of Newfoundland. Despite its apparent advantages, Hóp had one large disadvantage-native populations lived nearby. Armed clashes developed between the two groups, and although the Norse temporarily hold their own, they know the natives have superiority of numbers. The one advantage the Norse do have are their iron weapons. However, as Magnus Magnusson states, 'although the iron weapons of the Norsemen were superior to those of the Stone Age Indians, they were not superior enough to be decisive in the long run'(1973, 133).

After leaving Hóp and now sailing north along the coast toward their base (Straumsfjörðr), they come across a headland of note with large numbers of animals. Could this be Point Riche on the Port-au-Choix Peninsula? Large numbers of caribou were known to migrate here in the past.

In attempting to glean some information dealing with events, directions, and places in the remainder of ESR, I have found it necessary, as stated earlier, to disregard certain passages which are contradictory or fictitious.

Karlsefni then undertakes a second voyage ostensibly to find Þórhallr the Hunter; but in reality I believe it was to explore the other side of the Great Northern Peninsula. I shall give three reasons for coming to this conclusion: First the passage about Þórhallr sailing north past Furðustrandir and Kjalarnes to search for Vínland there and then having Karlsefni follow this route some time later doesn't make sense. They had all viewed this coast on their way to Straumsfjörðr, and should have had a fair idea of what it offered and didn't offer. Þórhallr and his men may have indeed sailed this route, but in an attempt to return to Greenland.

Secondly, the saga states, 'When they had sailed for a long time, they came to a river which was flowing from east to west down from the high land'(Ingstad 1969, 58). If one travels southward down the east coast of the Great Northern Peninsula you will arrive at

White Bay. On the northeast corner of the bay is a small river running from east to west and emptying into the bay. It is several miles south of a tiny village called Seal Cove.

Thirdly, the saga reads, 'They thought the mountains at Hop and those they now discovered belonged to the same mountain range, and that these places therefore were directly opposite each other, and that the distance from Straumsfjörðr was the same in both directions'(Ingstad 1969, 59). This is from the *Hauksbók* version. The Long Range Mountains run down the length of the peninsula and are visible from both the east and the west coasts. Of interest here also is the statement that Hóp and the second location are directly opposite each other and the distance from their base at Straumsfjörðr was the same in both directions. The saga has this to say when they leave the second location to return to Straumsfjörðr, 'Then they sailed away and back to the north'(Ingstad 1969, 58). This would fit in well with a location at White Bay (fig. 2).

After approximately a three-year stay, Karlsefni and his group decide to return to Greenland. His decision was probably the result of several factors, none of which I will attempt to explore in this paper.

Before leaving, it would seem logical to me that Karlsefni and Guðríðr would retrieve the body of Þorvaldr if it were anywhere nearby for reinterment in Greenland. This would seem likely in light of the previous, harrowing voyage Guðríðr made with Þorsteinn five years earlier. It would also help explain why ESR claims Þorvaldr was killed on Karlsefni's expedition. Karlsefni was indeed returning to Greenland with Þorvaldr's body—but he had died six years earlier on his own expedition.

Epilogue

The conclusions and speculations I arrive at in this paper are the result of nearly thirty years of independent research, eleven self-planned and self-funded expeditions from Chateau Bay, Labrador, along the Cote Nord to Québec, and the Northern Peninsula and west coast of Newfoundland. Most of the expeditions were conducted by sea in dories or small open vessels, and I know what it is to be caught in the arctic ice on the Coast of Labrador and to be nearly capsized in thunderstorms along the Cote Nord. I have willingly risked my life more than once in pursuit of at least a partial solution to the Vínland enigma. I, and anyone else who has made a serious investigation of the problem, knows the difficulties involved in attempting to piece together events of a thousand years ago; the arduous task of combining probable facts from the two frequently contradictory saga accounts and what we know from the sparse archaeological evidence. We must take into account information from a myriad of other sources such as locations of native populations at the time, to climatic conditions at the time, to prevailing winds, currents, weather, present and past fauna and flora, and personal on site observations. All this information we must use as an overlay in determining what we may consider probable or improbable. It is to a very large extent a personally subjective evaluation. But barring any other hard evidence of major importance since L'Anse aux Meadows, what other approach can be taken at this time? So I ask the reader to forgive my many inferences and assumptions (which are less hazardous to an amateur archaeologist, like myself, then to a professional) and allow me more latitude to express my views on the subject if for nothing more than creating food for serious consideration. I am acutely aware that anything new I have stated here in my paper would have to be corroborated by hard archaeological evidence by designated authorities to achieve credence. However, I have mentioned some specific sites for investigation in this paper that may stir some interest to attempt just that.

409

ABBREVIATIONS

ESR   *Eiríks saga rauða*, in Ingstad, H. 1969. *Westward to Vinland*, New York.

GLS   *Grœndlendinga saga*, in Magnusson, M. and Pálsson, H., trans, 1965. *The Vinland Sagas: The Norse Discovery of America*, 75-105.

BIBLIOGRAPHY

Canadian Hydrographic Service, Chart 4440.

Canadian Hydrographic Service, Chart 4509.

Fernald, M.L. 1910. *Notes on the Plants of Wineland the Goo*d, Boston.

Hogg, P.C. 1989. 'The prototype of the Stefánsson and Resen charts', *Historisk Tidsskrift*, 68, 1, 3-27.

Ingstad, H. 1969. *Westward to Vinland*, New York.

Jones, G. 1984. *A History of the Vikings*, Oxford.

Logan, D.F. 1992. *The Vikings in History*, London.

Magnusson, M. 1973. *Viking Expansion Westwards*, New York.

Maine State Museum, Plate Seven, 1998.

Poertner, R. 1975. *The Vikings*, New York.

Storm, G. 1886. 'Om Betydningen of Eyktarstadr i Flatobogens Beretning om Vínlandsreiserne', *Arkiv for Nordisk Filologi* (1886), 121-131.

Wahlgren, E. 1986. *The Vikings and America*, New York.

The Forests of Iceland at the Time of Settlement:

Their utilisation and eventual fate

Þröstur Eysteinsson and Sigurður Blöndal

DESCRIPTION OF THE FORESTS AND WOODLANDS OF ICELAND

Í þann tíð var landit viði vaxit milli fjalls ok fjöru.
'At that time the land was wooded from beach to mountain'.
—Ari *inn fróði* Þorgilsson, 1120

Ari was describing conditions in Iceland at the time of Norse settlement almost 250 years earlier. The words 'at that time' and 'was' indicate that by 1120 a large part of the original forests and woodlands had disappeared, perhaps most of them. Independent evidence in the form of palinological studies paints the same picture with grasses and sedges replacing birch as the dominant pollen type over a period of less than 200 years directly after settlement (Einarsson 1963; Vasari 1972). Evidence in the form of place names is also convincing with names or suffixes such as *skógar*, *mörk* and *holt*, all of which mean 'forest', being common throughout Iceland. Today, we have deserts named the Blue Forest and the Land's Forest. However, the most convincing direct evidence for a wooded Iceland are the ubiquitous charcoal pits, found all over Iceland at elevations from sea level to over 400 m (Guðbergsson 1992).

411

Several people have estimated the extent of woodlands at the time of settlement based on various evidence and all have come to similar conclusions, that one quarter to one third of Iceland's land area was wooded. The most recent estimate is 27% of the total land area or roughly 27,000 km^2 (Blöndal and Gunnarsson 1999).

Descriptions of what these forests looked like are few in the sagas and early ecclesiastical inventories. There is, however, one mention of a boat being built of Icelandic birch and forests were to some extent classified according to their stature. The classification *raftskógur* or 'rafter forest' indicates that boles were thick enough, straight enough and long enough to be used for supporting the turf roofs of buildings. A 2 m long rafter requires a tree that is at least 4-5 m tall. However, the best description can probably be deduced based on modern Icelandic birch woods and a knowledge of history, genetics, tree physiology, and forest ecology.

Today, most Icelandic woodlands are composed of low-growing, scrubby and crooked downy birch (*Betula pubescens* Ehrh.). The trees are mostly rather young, having regenerated from stump sprouts after winter sheep grazing generally ceased around the middle of the twentieth century. Most woodlands are still utilised for summer grazing accounting for some of the scrubbiness, with sheep having pruned the trees often before they exceeded sheep-height. Another reason for small stature and crooked habit is genetic introgression with dwarf arctic birch (*Betula nana* L.), a species that seldom reaches 50 cm in height, is more resistant to grazing and is now more common than downy birch (Tómasson 1994). Some introgression probably took place before human settlement, for instance at the upper elevational limit of downy birch or on exposed peninsulas. However, in the absence of sheep, hybrids would have been at a disadvantage at lower elevations and been shaded out by taller trees. It is therefore likely that much of the introgression has taken place since settlement.

Besides downy birch, only three other tree species were native to Iceland; rowan (*Sorbus aucuparia* L.) which is widespread but uncommon, aspen (*Populus tremula* L.)

which is rare and tea-leaved willow (*Salix phylicifolia* L.) which is common and attains tree size when growing amongst birch on rich sites.

The first settlers of Iceland found a land dominated by birch forests. Scrubby birch woodlands were found on exposed peninsulas and at elevations of 400-600 m, above which they were replaced by willow scrub and tundra. Relatively tall birch forests inhabited the lowlands with a larger component of rowan than exists today since rowan is favoured by both people and sheep. Birch and tall willows occupied wetter sites that today are mires with only the wettest fens being treeless (Bjarnason 1974).

The forests were mostly uneven-aged with regeneration occurring after windthrow or snow breakage of individual trees. Lightning is very rare in Iceland so even-aged regeneration after large scale fires would not have taken place although in some places avalanches could have resulted in regeneration of even-aged stands. Unlike some old-growth forests, the forests of Iceland did not have a park-like appearance due to the absence of grazing animals. Thus the forest floor was occupied by shade tolerant but grazing intolerant forbes such as *Geranium sylvaticum* and *Rubus saxatilis,* and shrubs such as *Juniperus communis* and *Vaccinium myrtillus*.

The tallest birch and rowan trees in Iceland today are close to 15 m tall. Thus, it is likely that trees reached 15 m or more on good sites in sheltered valleys. It is also likely that on such sites the birch was reasonably straight due to competition for light.

412

Today, forests and woodlands cover only 1.2% of the land area of Iceland with only 0.2% being forest over 5 m in height. Thus only 5% of the original woodland cover remains and most of that is in a state of genetic, physiological and ecological degradation. As a result of this deforestation and continued overgrazing, massive erosion has taken place leading to the desertified Iceland we know today (Bjarnason 1942).

FOREST AND WOODLAND UTILISATION

People do not change the way they do things just because they move to a new place. The settlers of Iceland were agriculturists practising animal husbandry with cattle, swine, horses, sheep and goats and growing grain, flax and various herbs (Jóhannesson 1974). They knew how to create better land for agriculture and grazing by burning woodland. Thus, large areas of forest were cleared immediately after the arrival of humans to create conditions suitable for agriculture. Among these were probably the tallest and best forests since those sites were also best suitable for agriculture.

The settlers were fishermen utilising fish, seabird eggs and other resources along the coast. This required boats, but it is likely that most boats were imported from Norway or the British Isles since pine and especially oak are much more suitable than birch for boat building.

The settlers were traders and occasionally Vikings needing ships (*knarrar* and longships). There is not much evidence of ship building in Iceland and if ships were built, the wood would have been imported.

The settlers were craftsmen (carpenters, blacksmiths, shipwrights, weavers, etc.). The most used raw materials were turf for building houses, wool for clothing and wood and iron for practically everything else.

Forests and forest products were essential to their way of life. Forests and woodlands were:

— burned and roots removed to make way for grain and hay fields;

— burned to improve grazing land and to keep from losing livestock;

— used for animal fodder (birch and willow shoots were both consumed directly by livestock and cut for winter fodder); and

—cut for wood.

The main uses for wood were for fuel for cooking, building material, tools and utensils and charcoal for iron smelting and working.

Medium to small dimension birch was preferred for fuel. As woodlands became scarce, other sources of fuel were available, such as dung and peat. Therefore, wood was not absolutely essential for cooking. When birch and willow shoots were no longer available for fodder and dung used for fuel in stead of manure for hayfields, cattle farming became more difficult and Icelanders turned increasingly to the more economical but less productive sheep. This transition took place mostly during the thirteenth century (Ingimundarson 1995).

Even though Icelandic buildings were made mostly of turf, wood was required for rafters and support posts as well as doors and furnishings. Driftwood (mostly larch, pine and spruce) was utilised for doors and furnishings but was too expensive to be used as building material, with the exception of churches (Eggertsson 1993; Ingimundarson 1995). Birch was used for rafters and support posts until the nineteenth century when wood started to be imported as building material. In fact, birch rafters were used in outbuildings for as long as they were built of turf or well into the twentieth century.

By far the most important use for wood was for making charcoal, which was needed for iron smelting and ironworking. Evidence of bog iron smelting in the form of slag piles is common in Iceland and it seems that this was practised at most main farmsteads during the first 100-200 years after settlement. During the twelfth and thirteenth centuries, iron smelting seems to have become more specialised and restricted to fewer places (Þórarinsson 1980).

413

Iron was needed for weapons, various tools, and various hardware such as door hinges and locks. By far the most important of these were scythes. Scythes, not swords, were absolutely necessary for survival. Even though sheep are better at fending for themselves than cattle, there are periods during most Icelandic winters when even sheep cannot find anything to eat, and if the sheep starved, human starvation was not far behind. Therefore, it was essential for people in most parts of Iceland to make hay for their sheep as well as for their cow (if they had one). This required scythes (Þórarinsson 1974).

Iron scythes were soft and quickly lost their edge so that during hay making, a new edge had to formed every morning. This entailed firing the scythe in a bed of charcoal and working the edge with a hammer. Þórarinsson (1974) calculated that the amount of charcoal required for iron smelting and working from the time of settlement to 1870 (when steel scythes began to be imported) would have required clearfelling of about 1000 ha of birchwoods annually during the first 600 years and about 640 ha annually thereafter due to a smaller population. This makes a total of at least 8,200 km^2 of birchwoods required for charcoal alone or about one third of the original wooded area.

THE FATE OF ICELAND'S FORESTS

Most of Iceland's forests and woodlands were wiped out during the first 200-300 years after settlement.

It is likely that regeneration of birch from stump sprouts after cutting was often successful during the early period. However, as Icelanders became more dependent on sheep and the climate worsened, regeneration failure became more common due to the need for birch shoots as fodder. Also, as times got tougher, it was considered a waste to not utilise all the wood in a forest so it became the general practice to rip up the roots as well. In fact, this practice is mandatory according to the legal code *Jónsbók* from 1261 but is not mentioned in *Grágás*, which is roughly a century older (Guðbergsson 1999).

The thirteenth century in many respects marks a turning point in Icelandic history. Historians tend to emphasise the social upheavals and loss of independence as well as the subsequent rise of the Church to power (Jóhannesson 1974). Anthropologists see a drastic change in the social fabric, a decline in the standard of living possibly due to decreasing foreign trade and a change from diverse agriculture to subsistence farming based primarily on sheep (Ingimundarson 1995). Sheep went from being a cash crop (wool for export) to being survival food. A worsening climate is often cited as at least a partial explanation for these events but an equally important environmental factor is that forests had become a rare resource (Bjarnason 1974). It is our contention that forests did not become rare because of climate change but because of overexploitation and that the lack of forests exacerbated the effects of a cooling climate.

To get necessary fuel as well as fodder for sheep, farmers practised *hrísrif* (*hrís* = low-growing or regenerating birch, *rif* = ripping). Charcoal was bought at a high price, often in the form of labour, from the few remaining forest owners, mostly the Church. Those who could not afford charcoal starved during bad years when they could not procure fodder for their sheep and the sheep could not fend for themselves. For example, because of heavy snow during winter and the late arrival (lack of arrival) of spring. The term *Úrkula vonar* is a term meaning 'hopeless' in modern Icelandic. Translated literally, it means to be 'out of coal'. If you couldn't make or obtain charcoal, you were without hope (Þórarinsson 1974). Forests, had they still existed, could have prevented much starvation.

414

Population decline in the fifteenth century due to the bubonic plague and continued low population until the early nineteenth century due to famines and volcanic eruptions decreased the pressure on the remaining birchwoods and many were able to regenerate. Increased population in the nineteenth century reversed this trend again. In the early 1700's 73% of the districts in Iceland had at least some birchwoods, but by 1888 only 34% of the districts had wooded areas. This trend seems to have continued to about 1940 with woodland owners cutting and selling fuelwood to heat the new and colder wooden and concrete houses being built in the towns (Guðbergsson 1998).

Conclusion

The Norse came from a forested environment in Scandinavia and the forest resource was extremely important to them. They knew how to utilise the forest, what tree species were good for what purposes and how to make forest into farmland and grazing land. Icelandic forests, being solely composed of tree species of good use to humans and palatable to livestock, were not able to withstand the pressure and regeneration failed. Society was able to adjust to the demise of woodlands and worsening climate in most respects, with the exception that the scarceness of charcoal seems to have been exceptionally difficult to cope with.

Abbreviation

Íslendingabók   Jónsson, G. ed., 1946. *Íslendingabók*, Reykjavík.

Bibliography

Bjarnason, H. 1942. 'Ábúð og örtröð', *Ársrit Skógræktarfélags Íslands*, 1942, 8-40.

——1974. 'Athugasemdir við sögu Íslendinga í sambandi við eyðingu skóglendis', *Ársrit Skógræktarfélags Íslands*, 1974, 30-43.

Blöndal, S. and Gunnarsson, S.B. 1999. *Íslandsskógar—Hundrað Ára Saga*, Reykjavík.

Einarsson, Þorleifur. 1963. 'Pollen-analytical studies on the vegetation and climate history of Iceland in late Pleistocene and post glacial times', in Love and Love 1963, 355-65.

Eggertsson, O. 1993. 'Origin of the driftwood on the coasts of Iceland; a dendrochronological study', *Jökull*, 43, 15-32.

Guðbergsson, G. 1992. 'Skógar í Skagafirði', *Skógræktarritið*, 1992, 74-85.

——1998. 'Hrís og annað eldsneyti', *Skógræktarritið*, 1998, 23-31.

——1999. 'Til varnar Íslands skógum', *Skógræktarritið*, 1999, 103-107.

Ingimundarson, J.H. 1995. Of Sagas and Sheep: Toward a Historical Anthropology of Social Change and Production for Market, Subsistence and Tribute in Early Iceland (tenth to the thirteenth century),unpublished PhD dissertation, University of Arizona.

Jóhannesson, J. 1974 [1954]. *A History of the Old Icelandic Commonwealth (*Íslendingasaga*)*, trans. H. Bessason, Winnipeg.

Love, A. and Love, D., eds., 1963. *North Atlantic Biota and their History*, New York.

Tómasson, Þ. 1994. 'Af ástum fjalldrapa og birkis', *Skógræktarritið*, 1994, 35-47.

Vasari, Y. 1972. 'The History of the Vegetation of Iceland During the Holocene', *Acta Universitatis Ouluensis*, Series A, *Scientum Rerum Naturae*, 3, *Geologica* 3, 239-252.

Þórarinsson, Þ. 1974. 'Þjóðin lifði en skógurinn dó', *Ársrit Skógræktarfélags Íslands*, 1974, 16-29.

——1980. 'Ísarns Meiður á Eiðum', *Múlaþing*, 10, 31-55.

A Mathematical Search for

Viking Navigational Practices

Curt Roslund, Søren Thirslund and Emília Pásztor

T he Norse people were great seafarers, but in describing their exploits and adventures, the Icelandic sagas only incidentally mention details of navigational interest. Certain statements in the sagas do convey the circumstantial impression that the Norsemen mastered some elementary knowledge of celestial navigation and possibly knew how to use a simple navigational device. For instance, *Hauksbók*, compiled in the twelfth century, says that the Norsemen had to steer a course due west after leaving Hernar Island (60°41' N) in the archipelago west of Bergen in Norway in order to reach Cape Farewell (59°50' N) on Greenland nearly 1500 nautical miles away (Thirslund 1997a, 59), and *Grænlendinga saga*, written in the late twelfth century, recounts how Bjarni Herjólfsson and his crew being lost in dense fog for several days south of Greenland finally got their bearings when seeing the sun again (Magnusson and Pálsson 1965, 52-53).

Only one explicit reference to an instrument used in navigation has been found in Icelandic medieval sources through the meticulous research of Uwe Schnall (1975, 74-115). The reference is to the *leiðarsteinn*, 'guiding stone', which most likely was the magnetic compass. Another reference in connection with sea and seafaring is to the *sólborð*, 'sun-board', the purpose of which is not made clear. A *sólarsteinn*, 'sun-stone', is probably a ball of crystal with interesting optical properties for sunlight but hardly of any use in navigation. Not mentioned by Schnall is the *húsasnotra* that Þorfinnr Karlsefni brought to Norway as mentioned in *Grænlendinga saga*. *Húsasnotra* is usually translated as an ornate house or ship panel, possibly a weather vane (Fritzner 1891, 103), while Mowat (1965, 354-355) has presented linguistic evidence for a navigational instrument.

417

STEERING BY THE NOON SUN AND THE POLE STAR

There seems to be a general consensus of opinion among historians of navigation that before the advent of the magnetic compass, the Norsemen practiced latitude sailing whenever practicable and steered by the wind, the waves and the ocean swell, occasionally correcting their steering by taking observations of the noon sun in daytime and the pole star at night. In the view of navigational experts like Geoffrey Marcus (1953, 122-123) and Eva Taylor (1971, 79-81), such observations could not only give the helmsman his bearings but also some notion of his northing or southing to assist him in keeping the course set out.

It is a straightforward affair to take readings of the noon sun from the bridge on a modern ocean liner. The navigation officer has only to follow the slow rise of the sun before noon with his sextant until the sun starts to descend. The observations give him not only the exact moment of the sun's meridian passage but also the sun's noon altitude within one or two minutes of arc to enable him to compute the direction of due south and his latitude with great precision. The case is not so simple from the deck of a small boat in heavy seas. The observer seldom gets the chance of riding the crest of a wave long enough to make a reliable reading with reference to the horizon even with the finest instruments available. This would have been true for the Norsemen too. In addition, their lack of precision altitude-measuring instruments would have prevented them even in calm weather from observing the slow change in the sun's altitude around noon, necessary for determining the south direction with any claim to accuracy.

In order to keep track of the movement of their ships in latitude by observations of the midday sun, the Norsemen would have needed not only instruments capable of obtaining measurements within fractions of a degree but also knowledge of the seasonal changes in the sun's declination, i.e. in the sun's angular distance from the celestial equator. Although learned men in Iceland in the beginning of the twelfth century had recorded the weekly changes in the sun's declination (Zinner 1933, 302; Roslund 1989, 498), which can amount to as much as nearly three degrees a week in spring and autumn, it is doubtful that the Norse navigators knew about them and how to apply them correctly for finding their latitude.

The situation is not much different when it comes to the pole star. Contrary to common belief, this star does not mark the stationary point in the sky around which the stars move. That imaginary point is called the north celestial pole. A millennium ago, the pole star circled the celestial pole at an angular distance of 6°15' which meant that the altitude of the pole star changed by a full twelve and a half degrees during twenty-four hours! In order to follow the ship's movement in latitude, the altitude of the pole star should always be measured at the same instant of sidereal time when it is in the same position in its daily path around the celestial pole. To these difficulties, the usual problems of obtaining accurate altitudes from a small boat should be added. On the other hand, on a calm night it would have been quite possible for an observer with keen eyesight and thoroughly familiar with the starry sky, with no mist or clouds obscuring the horizon, to discern shifts in latitude as small as one or two degrees just by noting which stars seemed to touch the horizon in the north and the south.

418

Despite the frequent mention of the pole star in the Icelandic written sources as the 'guiding star' (Marcus 1953, 123), its importance for pointing out the north direction is much overstated. Its high elevation in the sky, about 60°, makes it unsuitable as a reference star for bearings along the horizon. True north can only be obtained when the pole star is either at its highest or lowest point on its daily circle around the celestial pole. The polar nights above latitude 60°N are also too bright in high summer for the pole star to be seen at all.

Fortunately for the Norsemen, the pole star was seen at its most westerly point at sunset in spring and at its most easterly point at sunrise. Steering errors arising before midnight would therefore largely be cancelled by those occuring after midnight, provided the sky remained clear all night. In autumn the pole star attained its most easterly point at sunset and its most westerly at sunrise with the same cancelling effect. More important was probably the reassuring constant sight at night of the pole star on the starboard side of the ship as a source of relief to people on their long westward trek across the North Atlantic.

DIRECTIONAL SUN DIALS

The magnetic compass quickly proved so efficient and trustworthy, functioning in every kind of weather, that other methods for obtaining bearings may well have been completely forgotten soon after its introduction. Even historians of navigation seem largely unaware of the fact that there exist simple and ingenious methods for obtaining directions of the sun at any time of the day. These methods are mainly based on sundials where the shadow of a stylus or gnomon marks the direction of the sun. Such sundials date from classical antiquity (Gibbs 1976, 39-56) and were widely used by Muslims in the Arab world during the time of the Norse penetration into the North Atlantic (King 1975, 51-53).

In the most basic form, sundials consist of a shadow pin erected vertically on a horizontal plane surface. During the day, the sun's shadow of the pointed end of the gnomon traces a hyperbola on the surface, which is called a day curve or a gnomon curve and whose line of symmetry is orientated north-south. The shape and location of a day curve for a specific latitude and gnomon length depends only on the season of the year. In the summer half

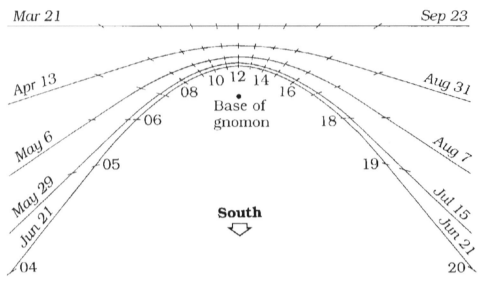

Figure 1. Gnomon curves for selected dates for a horizontal sundial at latitude 61°N. Numerals below the summer solstitial curve mark local true solar times.

year, the day curves open up towards the south and in the winter half year towards the north. At the equinoxes the day curve degenerates into a straight line orientated east-west. The network of day curves for some selected dates are shown in figure 1 for latitude 61°N.

As the line of symmetry for the gnomon curves is orientated north-south, a portable sundial of this kind, small enough to be held in the palm of one's hand, would have served as an accurate sun compass for latitude sailings. The navigator had only to hold the dial plate horizontally and to turn it around a vertical axis until the shadow of the gnomon point touched the morning or afternoon branch of the gnomon curve relevant for that day and the latitude sailed. The day curve could easily have been obtained by tracing the shadow of the sun on a level surface at the place of departure prior to sailing or drawn according to an existing prototype. As the gnomon curve only changes slightly with date, especially near midsummer, the same curve could be used for voyages of up to two or three weeks of duration, depending on the season of the year. Due to the symmetry of the day curves, a steering error in the morning caused by a slightly out of date day curve or by the ship veering from its proper latitude, would in the afternoon largely be cancelled by a steering error of the opposite sign.

The performance and proficiency of such a simple device have been tested with computer derived gnomon curves on several occasions (Thirslund 1993; 1997b, 23-32). The navigator of the *Gaia*, a replica of the famous Gokstad ship, reported that the sun compass had been accurate within two to five degrees on a voyage in 1991 on the old Norse route between Norway and Greenland. In 1995, the master mariner Sir Robin Knox-Johnston managed to sail 50 nautical miles, missing his target by no more than half a mile, i.e. with a navigational error of about half a degree, steering only by the wind and by means of a sun compass with a gnomon curve obtained on the day before sailing.

A NORSE BEARING DIAL?

It would be tempting to suggest that it might have been the ancient horizontal sundial used as a compass which made possible regular sailings to Greenland. Two artifacts unearthed in the Eastern Settlement on Greenland do indeed display a gnomon-like curve on a horizontal plane, which by design or by pure chance, resembles a day curve for midsummer at latitude 61°N. One object is part of a circular wooden disc from the Norse site Ø149 at Narsarsuaq on the Uunartoq Fjord (Vebæk 1992a, 14-19), and the other a triangular plate of steatite from the site Ø71 at Russip Kuua on Lake Saqqata Tasia (Vebæk 1992a, 14-19; 1992b, 77-78), both measuring about 7-10 cm.

Before the significance of the gnomon-like curve was realised (Ramskou 1982, 30-37), the wooden disc had already been identified as a probable bearing dial by the navigational expert Carl Sølver (1953) on account of triangular notches cut along the rounded outer edge of the disc and arranged like compass points in later compasses (fig. 2). Although it has been conclusively shown that the gnomon-like curve on its front surface was cut twice, probably intentionally with a sharp-edged tool (Thirslund 1991, 71), the incision is rather vague and shallow for marking the length of the sun's shadow. Alternatively, it might have been a boy's play thing modelled after a genuine bearing dial or a discarded dial that had failed to meet quality requirements.

In the first century BC, the Roman architect Vitruvius in his famous book *De architectura* is in effect describing a sun compass for finding the proper direction for setting out streets in town planning (Morgan 1914, 26-27). Islam adopted the Greek and Roman horizontal sundials by incorporating on their dial face hour lines for prayers and the local direction, *qibla*, of the holy city of Mecca, in which direction all worshippers should turn while praying. The Duke of Saxony owned a magnetic compass with gnomon curves depicted on the compass card (Schück 1915, 23), which shows that sundials remained a complement to magnetic compasses in Europe as late as the sixteenth century.

It is altogether possible that Arabic travellers and visiting merchants could have brought with them to the North their knowledge of how to find one's bearings from a sundial. A medieval manuscript tells the tale of an official at the court of the caliph of Córdoba, a certain Ibrahim Ibn Ahmed at-Turtuši, who is said to have visited the Norse trading centre Haithabu on the Jutland peninsula in the middle of the tenth century (Jacob 1927, 29). Devout Muslims would surely have tried to establish the *qibla* for their prayers when visiting new and unfamiliar territories, possibly by the use of a sundial. If this procedure happened to be witnessed by curious and intelligent native seamen, they might have grasped the importance of a sundial for latitude sailings. Three Moorish sundials have been preserved to the present. One of these is dated to the early eleventh century and one other has an arrow pointing out the direction of Mecca (Cabanelas 1958; King 1978).

If a horizontal sundial really was used by the Norsemen in navigation, it is remarkable that its time-measuring ability was not employed on shore. All extant early medieval sundials in Scandinavia and on the British Isles with few exceptions are

420

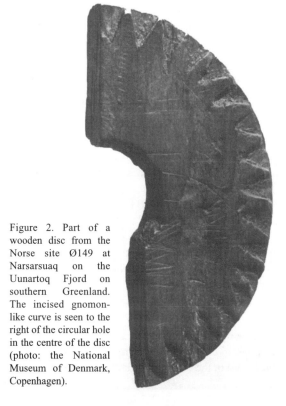

Figure 2. Part of a wooden disc from the Norse site Ø149 at Narsarsuaq on the Uunartoq Fjord on southern Greenland. The incised gnomon-like curve is seen to the right of the circular hole in the centre of the disc (photo: the National Museum of Denmark, Copenhagen).

of a much simpler design than the ancient ones (Daniel 1986, 5-10; Vellev 1988). As long as no archaeological object with a full family of gnomon curves for different dates has been retrieved in a firmly established nautical context, navigation with sun compass by the Norsemen must remain a tentative proposition.

COMPUTER TESTS

The sun's daily path across the heavenly vault can be expressed by a few simple trigonometrical equations which are easily adapted for work with a computer. The computer can promptly calculate and print out day curves and hour lines for any orientation of the shadow-receiving dial face for any latitude north or south of the equator. The computer is also well suited for studying the effect on bearing-readings of small changes in the tilt and orientation of the sundial, simulating the difficulties of properly handling the object on deck of a heaving and rolling ship without the risk of the investigator falling seasick or getting saltwater spray into his eyes.

It should be borne in mind that the sun compasses discussed here have been invented by us and not necessarily by the Norsemen, no matter how useful they might have been to them. The primary object of this paper is to demonstrate the existence of simple and direct methods for steering by the sun at sea in order to assist archaeologists in correctly identifying a navigational instrument as such if one should ever be excavated.

421

The computer simulations showed that the horizontal planar sundial would give reliable bearings on North Atlantic voyages from sunrise to sunset except around midday. Contrary to the view of most experts, the course of a ship at high latitudes cannot be accurately determined at noon with crude instruments due to the small change in altitude of the sun close to the south meridian. An important aspect of the horizontal sundial is the ease with which the eye can judge a plane to be level with the horizon even on board a ship in unruly seas.

Two other types of planar sundials were popular in antiquity. One type had its shadow-receiving surface parallel to the meridian plane, showing the morning or the afternoon hours, depending on whether the dial surface faced east or west. The meridian sundial complements the horizontal one in that it can provide accurate bearings closer to midday, but it is of little use early in the morning or late in the afternoon (fig. 3).

The other type of sundial had its shadow-receiving surface parallel to the prime vertical, that is a vertical plane orientated east-west. Computer simulations showed it to be far inferior to the other types discussed for finding one's bearings. A computer search for deviating sundials with improved features for compasses proved negative.

There are countless solutions to the mathemathical equations describing the sun's motion in the sky that would answer the requirements of a sun compass. Although ancient portable sundials show many innovative and unconventional designs (Price 1969), it was here decided to investigate only those devices known to have existed or to have had their origin in one form or other during the Viking Age, for ways of transforming them into bearing-measuring instruments.

CANTERBURY TYPE OF SUN COMPASS

In 1938 a unique piece of silverware of undoubtedly Anglo-Saxon origin from the early eleventh century was fortuitously unearthed during work in the cloister court yard of the Canterbury Cathedral. It forms a solid block only 5 cm in length. Its top end is connected with a chain from which it can hang freely. Each of its two main sides are divided into three long vertical panels, each of which is furnished with an upper hole for inserting a 25 mm long metal pin and with two lower holes probably once set with chips of coulored glass. On

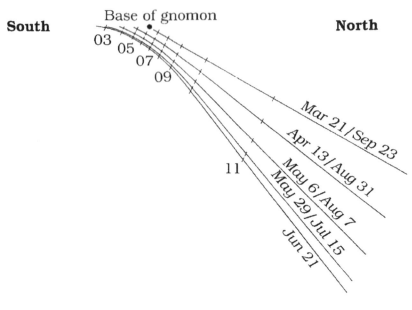

South

Base of gnomon

North

03 05 07 09

11

Mar 21/Sep 23

Apr 13/Aug 31

May 6/Aug 7

May 29/Jul 15

Jun 21

422

Figure 3. Gnomon curves for selected dates for an east facing meridian sundial at latitude 61°N. Numerals to the left of the summer solstitial curve mark local true solar times.

Figure 4. The Canterbury sundial showing three dial faces for the summer months from left to right: April and September, June and July, and May and August. The lowest point on each dial shows the length of the shadow of the shadow pin at time of noon and the middle point mid-morning or mid-afternoon (photo: the Dean and Chapter of Canterbury).

each panel are engraved the names of one spring month and a corresponding autumn month with respect to the solstices (fig. 4).

The object is unquestionably a portable sun dial of a novel design. It was made for the latitude 53°N, to indicate the time of midday and the times halfway between sunrise and noon and halfway between noon and sunset (Binns 1971). To read the time of day, the pin had to be inserted into its hole in the panel for the appropiate month, and the dial swung to face the sun. When the shadow of the pin reached the lower jewelled point it was midday and when it touched the upper point mid-morning or mid-afternoon.

Contrary to Alan Binns's ascertion (1971, 24), it is not necessary to know the local time in order to derive the sun's azimuth. The astronomical term azimuth of a celestial object refers to the angular distance along the horizon counted clockwise from the direction of north to the projection of the object onto the horizon. For a specific latitude and date of the year, there is a simple relationship between the sun's altitude and its azimuth. As the Canterbury sun dial essentially is an altitude-measuring device for the sun, the length of the shadow of the pin on the dial face can be converted into a scale of compass points for any date of the year for its latitude. It would have been a convenient instrument for use at sea, as it suspended from the chain could be read off quickly when the wind happened to bring it for a short instant to face the sun. There would have been no need for any theoretical calculations to obtain the scale of compass points, as these could be established on shore from known directions of familiar landmarks.

When comparing computer-made scales of compass points for different dates of the year, it was apparent that the marks for the compass points appeared in the same relation to each other for all the summer months for the latitude 61°N for the Norse Greenland route. By making the scales of compass points of the same length from the east-west mark to the south mark for all dates in the summer half year, the length of the shadow pin and its position on the dial face had to change with the season of the year as seen in Table 1. In this way there would no more be any need for monthly dial faces, but instead one would have had to know what pin to use and where to place it. Such an instrument would certainly seem both complicated and sophisticated, but it could easily have been constructed by an observant mariner who had noticed the similarity of azimuth scales for different months.

423

QUADRANT TYPE OF SUN COMPASS

The portable quadrant for measuring altitudes of celestial objects was in all likelihood adopted from the astrolabe in the tenth century (Zinner 1956, 154). It is not known with certainty when it was introduced at sea, but it was in general usage by Portuguese navigators in the early part of the Great Age of Discovery in the fifteenth century. As the quadrant seems to have been known on Iceland in the Middle Ages (Schnall 1975, 54), it cannot be wholly excluded that it was used there in navigation.

The quadrant got its name from its geometrical shape of a quarter of a circle. It has a graduated scale on the curved edge and two pinhole sights on one of the radial straight edges. A plumb line hangs from the centre of the circle.

The quadrant is an altitude-measuring instrument. The observer aligns its sights on a celestial object and reads its altitude from the point where the plumb line intersects the scale. As the sun's altitude varies with azimuth in a well-known manner on a specific date and latitude, the altitude scale can be converted into a series of azimuth scales for different dates and latitudes.

When analysing computer printouts of the variation of the sun's altitude with azimuth, a remarkable result appeared for the latitude of the Greenland route at 61°N. The change in the altitude of the sun, when the sun moves from one particular azimuth to another, is then

Points of the Compass	June 21	July 15	Aug 7	Aug 31	Sept 23
	May 29	May 6	Apr 13	Mar 21	
Length of gnomon	50	53	59	66	72
Top of dial face	0	0	0	0	0
Base of gnomon	0	1	5	14	25
NE NW	3	3	-	-	-
ENE WNW	13	13	12	-	-
E W	26	26	26	26	26
ESE WSW	40	40	40	40	41
SE SW	53	53	53	53	54
SSE SSW	62	62	62	62	62
S	65	65	65	65	65

Table 1. Position of marks of the sun's bearing on selected dates at latitude 61°N as shown by the sun's shadow of the point of a horizontal gnomon on a Canterbury type of sun compass. The position of the marks are expressed in millimetres as measured from the top end of the dial face.

424

almost independent of the date in the summer months as can be seen from Table 2. This very unique behaviour of the sun makes it possible to transform the altitude scale of the quadrant at this important latitude into an azimuth scale valid for the whole summer but for a shift of zero point with the date of the year. The simplest way to take care of this drift in zero point is to leave the azimuth scale fixed and instead to move the rear sight of the quadrant every day into such a position that the plumb line falls on the south mark when taking the noon altitude of the sun (fig. 5). The azimuth scale is then valid year after year and can be obtained on shore at the right latitude on any day of summer.

The quadrant is, however, an unsuitable instrument for taking observations of the sun at sea. Because of its blinding light, the sun cannot be sighted through pin hole sights without damaging the eye. Instead, the quadrant has to be aimed at the sun by adjusting it by hand until the sunrays pass through both sights, making a bright spot of light on a screen behind it, an operation that is seriously impaired by the movement of the ship.

STAFF TYPE OF SUN COMPASS

A computer search was made for transforming altitudes of the sun obtained with a staff into compass points. For a staff held vertically by the hand at its lower end, no way was found for overcoming the problem that the scale of compass points changed with the season of the year and had to be replaced every now and then for the same latitude. In order to observe the summer solstitial sun at noon, the staff had to be of unwieldy length, about 80 cm, making it hard to balance in the wind.

The matter is quite different for a staff held vertically by its own gravity at its upper end at arm's length at the same elevation of the arm as at noon for all observations of the sun until noon the next day. The azimuth scale at latitude 61°N is then almost independent of the date during the summer half year as can be seen from Table 3. This method for obtaining bearings was first suggested by Svend Aage Saugmann (1981, 61-62) but unfortunately not described by him in full detail.

In order to ensure that the staff is held in the same way all day when making observations, a marker can be used to line up with the horizon by adjusting it up or down the staff when the sun at noon passes behind the south mark on the staff. If the compass point marks

Points of the Compass	June 21	July 15	Aug 7	Aug 31	Sept 23
		May 29	May 6	Apr 13	Mar 21
NE NW	49	49	-	-	-
ENE WNW	38	38	39	-	-
E W	25	26	27	28	29
ESE WSW	14	14	15	16	17
SE SW	6	6	6	7	8
SSE SSW	1	1	2	2	2
S	0	0	0	0	0

Table 2. The sun's altitude below its noon altitude expressed in degrees at various points of the compass on selected dates at latitude 61°N.

Points of the Compass	June 21	July 15	Aug 7	Aug 31	Sept 23
		May 29	May 6	Apr 13	Mar 21
NE NW	349	350	-	-	-
ENE WNW	295	295	298	-	-
E W	224	223	223	228	238
ESE WSW	144	143	142	143	149
SE SW	70	70	69	69	71
SSE SSW	19	19	18	18	18
S	0	0	0	0	0

Table 3. Position of marks of the sun's bearing on selected dates at latitude 61°N on a staff held vertically by its upper end when sighting the sun behind the staff. When making measurements, the staff should be held at arm's length at the same angle of the arm as at the sun's meridian passage of that day. The position of the marks are expressed in millimetres as measured from the top of the staff.

are placed around the staff in their angular positions in relation to the south direction, and the horizon marker is set as an arrow at a prearranged angle to the south, the marker will always point in the same direction, no matter behind which compass point mark the sun is observed (fig. 6). By connecting the compass marks with a continuous curve, the navigator does not have to wait for the exact moment when the sun passes behind the few compass points marked on the staff. Bearings can then be obtained at any time on any day at latitude 61°N during the whole summer without the navigator ever having to know the precise compass points of the sun.

The staff suffers from an inconvenience, however, in that the scale of compass points is related to the length of the navigator's arm and can only be used by the person for whom it was made. The navigator also runs the risk of being blinded by the sun when trying to get it behind the staff for taking measurements.

Apart from these few drawbacks, the sun staff is an excellent example of a geometrically sophisticated and aesthetically pleasing design for a simple but dependable instrument whose function could easily be grasped by most seamen. But was it ever contrived and used for its purpose by the Norsemen?

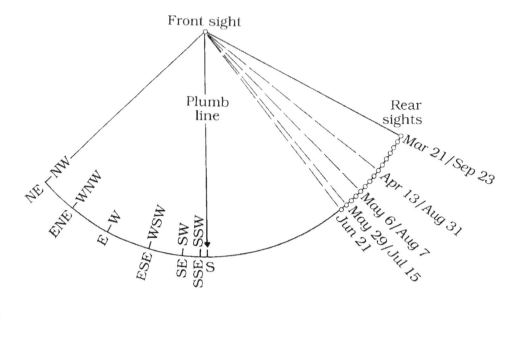

Figure 5. A seaman's quadrant transformed into an instrument for finding the sun's bearing at latitude 61°N.

Figure 6. A staff made for obtaining the sun's bearing at sea at latitude 61°N.

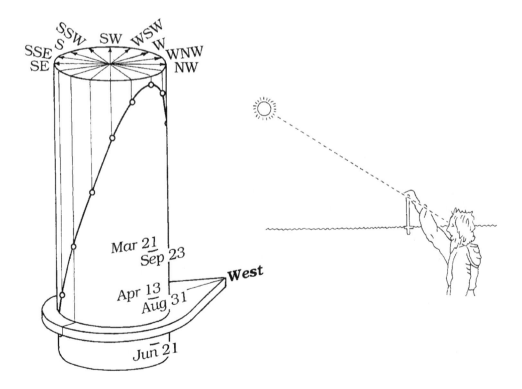

CLOSING WORDS

In our modern age we are completely accustomed when travelling to rely on precision navigational instruments to take us from the point of departure to our destination. It has not always been so. It is perfectly conceivable that a noninstrumental navigator, painstakingly trained to be keenly observant of every possible clue in nature and whose life depends on the right interpretation of these clues, can develop a sense of orientation by a brief glance at the sun at any time of the day and season (Mowat 1965, 358). However, his ability to find his bearings would unwittingly be based on the same principles that govern the design of the instruments discussed here.

ACKNOWLEDGEMENTS

The authors would like to express their sincere gratitude for financial support from the *Swedish Institute* (C.R.), the *J P Hempel Foundation* (S.T.), and from the *Hungarian Arts Foundation* (E.P.) that enabled them to take part in the Symposium.

BIBLIOGRAPHY

Aveni, A.F. ed., 1989. *World Archaeoastronomy*, Cambridge.

Binns, A. L. 1971. 'Sun Navigation in the Viking Age, and the Canterbury Portable Sun Dial', *Acta Archaeologica*, 42, 23-34.

Cabanelas, D. 1958. 'Relojes de Sol Hispano-Musulmanes', *Al-Andalus*, 23, 391-406.

Daniel, C.St.J.H. 1986. *Sundials*, Aylesbury.

Fritzner, J. 1891. *Ordbog over Det gamle norske Sprog* 2, Kristiania.

Gibbs, S.L. 1976. *Greek and Roman Sundials*, New Haven.

Jacob, G. 1927. 'Arabische Berichte von Gesandten an germanische Fürstenhöfe aus den 9. und 10. Jahrhundert', *Quellen zur deutschen Volkskunde*, 1, 1-50.

King, D.A. 1975. 'On the Astronomical Tables of the Islamic Middle Ages', *Studia Copernicana*, 13, 37-56.

——1978. 'Three Sundials from Islamic Andalusia', *Journal for the History of Arabic Science*, 2, 358-392.

Magnusson, M., and Pálsson, H. 1965. *The Vinland Sagas. The Norse Discovery of America*, Harmondsworth.

Marcus, G.J. 1953. 'The Navigation of the Norsemen', *Mariner's Mirror*, 39, 112-131.

Morgan, M.H. trans., 1914. *Vitruvius. The Ten Books on Architecture*, Boston.

Mowat, F. 1965. *Westviking*, Toronto.

Price, D.J.de S. 1969. 'Portable Sundials in Antiquity', *Centaurus*, 14, 242-266.

Ramskou, T. 1982. *Solkompasset*, Copenhagen.

Roslund, C. 1989. 'Sun tables of Star-Oddi in the Icelandic sagas', in Aveni 1989, 498.

Saugmann, S.A. 1981. *Vikingernes tidsregning og kursmetode*. Maritim Kontakt 2.

Schnall, U. 1975. *Navigation der Wikinger: Nautische Probleme der Wikingerzeit im Speigel der schriftlichen Quellen*. Oldenberg: Schriften des Deutschen Schiffahrtsmuseums 6.

Schück, A. 1915. *Der Kompass* 2a, Hamburg.

Sølver, C.V. 1953. 'The Discovery of an Early Bearing-Dial', *Journal of the Institute of Navigation*, 6, 294-296.

Taylor, E.G.R. 1971. *The Haven-Finding Art.*, 2nd edn, London.

Thirslund, S. 1991. 'A presumed sun compass from Narsarsuaq', in Vebæk 1991, 65-71.

——1993. 'The Discovery of an Early Bearing-Dial: Further Investigations', *Journal of the Institute of Navigation*, 46, 33-48.

——1997a. 'Sailing Directions of the North Atlantic Viking Age', *Journal of the Institute of Navigation*, 50, 55-64.

——1997b. *Viking Navigation*, Humlebæk.

Vebæk, C.L. 1991. *The Church Topography of the Eastern Settlement and the Excavation of the Benedictine Convent at Narsarsuaq in the Uunartoq Fjord*. Man & Society 14.

——1992a. 'The two bearing-dials from Uunartoq and Vatnahverfi in the Norse Settlements in South Greenland', in Vebæk and Thirslund 1992, 14-19.

——1992b. *Vatnahverfi. An inland district of the Eastern Settlement in Greenland*, Man & Society 17.

Vebæk, C.L. and Thirslund, S., eds, 1992. *The Viking Compass*, Humlebæk.

Vellev, J. 1988. 'Middelalderens solure', *Hikuin*, 14, 173-198.

Zinner, E. 1933. 'Die astronomischen Kenntnisse des Stern-Odde', *Mannus*, 25, 301-306.

——1956. *Deutsche und niederländische astronomische Instrumente des 11.-18. Jahrhunderts*, München.

428

The Uunartoq 'Bearing-Dial'—

not an Instrument for Ocean Navigation?

Christian Keller and Arne Emil Christensen

INTRODUCTION

When Danish archaeologist Christen Leif Vebæk excavated a Norse site in the Uunartoq fjord in south west Greenland in 1945-48 he uncovered a find which did not attract much attention at the time. Excavating what was believed to be the ruins of a Benedictine convent, a small wooden object was uncovered in the lower cultural layers which were assumed to predate the convent. It was a semi-circular disk, 7 cm across. Around the curved edge, triangular notches had been carved, creating an image not unlike a half-finished cog-wheel (fig. 1).

Vebæk published it as an object for unknown use in *The Illustrated London News* (Vebæk 1952). The article caught the attention of a Danish compass manufacturer and maritime historian Captain Carl V. Sølver, who suggested the disk to be the remains of a sun-compass (Sølver 1953; 1954). There is a general consensus that the magnetic compass (Old Norse *leiðarsteinn* = magnet) was not known in Northern Europe until after the Viking Age (KLNM 12, 260), and so the findings of a suggested sun-compass in far-away Greenland appeared to offer a solution to the lost secret of Viking navigation: how to cross the North-Atlantic without modern navigational instruments.

429

Sølver's solution gained in popularity, and was presented as a fact in several prestigious works (KLNM 12, 261; Graham-Campbell *et al.* 1994, 80-81). For a while it was also presented on posters in the exhibition of the Viking Ships Museum in Oslo. Recently, the disk has been presented as a controversial object (Seaver 2000, 274).

The ambiguity of the original object was perhaps lost on the way, and people seemed to have forgotten the basics of experimental archaeology: the distinction between exploring what might have happened, and seeking evidence for what probably did happen.

The purpose of this paper is not to discourage future research in ancient navigation, nor to bar speculation in this fascinating field. Ancient navigation is indeed a subject for interdisciplinary studies.

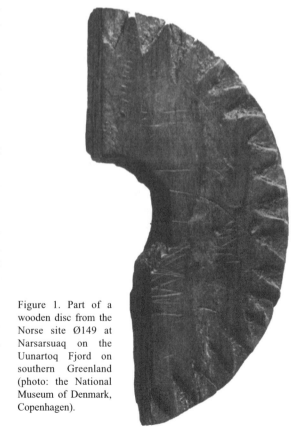

Figure 1. Part of a wooden disc from the Norse site Ø149 at Narsarsuaq on the Uunartoq Fjord on southern Greenland (photo: the National Museum of Denmark, Copenhagen).

Still, it is important to try to separate the plausible from the possible. This is an attempt to find a different interpretation of the Uunartoq disk through a more conventional archaeological approach: by looking for similar or related objects within the same cultural sphere.

It is suggested the Uunartoq-disk is a so-called 'confession-disk', a mnemonic device used to record certain clerical services, preparing people for a totally different journey than the one across the North Atlantic. The suggestion is tentative, since little is known about the use and dating of confession-disks, and the examples stem from the seventeenth and eighteenth centuries, which makes them post-Reformation Lutheran. A troubling fact, since Medieval Greenland was undisputedly Catholic.

The first part of this paper will therefore deal with the find, and the discussions about solar navigation. The second part will focus on confession-disks, and the status of the confession in the Nordic churches before and after the Reformation.

THE DISCOVERY AND DATING

As already mentioned, the disk was found at site Ø-149 Narsarsuaq in the Uunartoq Fjord in south west Greenland (Vebæk 1991; fig. 2). This fjord is located roughly in the middle of the so-called Eastern Settlement, which was colonised by Norse immigrants around AD 1000 and deserted some 400 years later.

430

The site was well-preserved, and featured an infield and a fence, a church and a churchyard, several house ruins, and a large ruin-complex which was called called Ruin 2. Vebæk

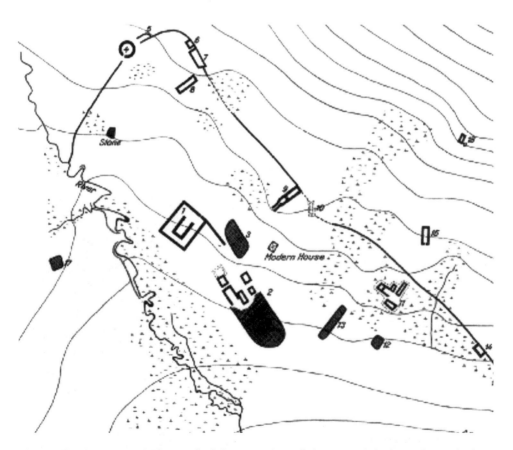

Figure 2. Site 149 Narsarsuaq in Uunartoq fjord, the presumed Benedictine convent is the dense ruin complex down right from the church, indicated by the large rectangle (drawing by Vebæk 1948; after Vebæk 1991).

argued that this was the location of the Benedictine Convent which was mentioned in two fourteenth century sources, although he did admit there were some problems with the interpretation, one of them being the lack of a fireplace.

Below this complex, visible in what was called Room III and Room IV, an older settlement phase was discovered in a cultural layer stretching under the walls of the two rooms. Radiocarbon dates indicate that the settlement started as early as the eleventh century, while the relationship between this early settlement and that of the later suggested convent seems unclear.

The Uunartoq disk was discovered under Room III during the excavation of the lower cultural layer, and has therefore been regarded as belonging to the early settlement phase, perhaps even to the *landnám* period. The Norse colonisation (*landnám* or 'landtaking') in Greenland is traditionally set to AD 985 (fig. 3).

This identification of layer is important, because it led to the conviction that the disk belonged to the first settlers, and thus originated in the Late Viking Period. A closer reading of Vebæk's 1991 publication raises some questions concerning this conclusion. Vebæk says:

> It should be noted that the objects and animal bones found in 2-III were nearly all lying above the gravel—at least (as far as I know) all the objects of steatite; but regrettably I was not at first aware of the special stratigraphical problems, so finds were not kept separate, and when the conditions became evident, everything above floor level had been dug away. So nothing certain can be said about the finds in 2-III. In the eastern part of the room, where there was no gravel, the upper and lower cultural strata merged without any separation (Vebæk 1991, 73).

431

Figure 3. Ruin complex 2 at Ø-149 Narsarsuaq in Uunartoq, during C.L. Vebæk's excavations. Room III, where the disk was found, can be seen as a dark depression top right in the ruin. It must have been difficult to have full control of the stratigraphy in a rocky site such as this (after Vebæk 1991, fig. 69).

This is in contrast to most of the literature on the disk, where its Viking-Age dating remains unquestioned. In all fairness, it must be pointed out that this was written by Vebæk in 1991, in a chapter which appears to be an addition written much later than the rest of the text. The doubts about the stratigraphy seem to have been expressed only late in Vebæk's life, which may be why they have not been noted earlier. Today, it must be concluded that the stratigraphy simply did not support rock-solid dating in the Viking period.

HIGHLIGHTS OF THE DEBATE

The disk was first published by Vebæk in the *Illustrated London News*, 3 May 1952, in an article called 'A New World Nunnery before the Days of Columbus', as an object for unknown use. The title is interesting for two reasons. Firstly, he regarded Greenland as part of the New World, and secondly, his main subject was the convent and its finds. The article caught the attention of Danish Captain Carl V. Sølver, who suggested the Uunartoq disk was a sun-compass first in 1944 (Sølver 1953). His book on Viking navigational techniques, *Vestervejen* (1954) caused international reaction. His ideas were referenced as facts by Jørgen H.P. Barfod in *The Cultural Encyclopedia for the Nordic Middle Ages* (KLNM 12, 260-63).

Later Dr Curt Roslund, of the Technical Highschool of Chalmers in Gothenburg suggested that a line on the top-side of the dial was a gnomon-curve (explained below; Roslund 1985; see also Roslund *et al.*, this volume). The Danish archaeologist Thorkild Ramskou presented these ideas in his book *Solkompasset* (Ramskou 1982).

Opposition against Sølver's ideas was made as early as 1954 (Taylor *et al.* 1954; see also Christensen 1993). Over the last decades Søren Thirslund and to some extent Curt Roslund have been the foremost advocates for the solar-navigation theories (Roslund 1985; Thirslund 1987; 1993; Thirslund and Vebæk 1990).

LATITUDE NAVIGATION

Coastal navigation was the oldest way of getting a ship from one point to another, simply by using known landmarks on shore to determine the ship's position. Crossing the open sea is different. A traditional method was latitude navigation, where courses over open water were laid out east or west by sticking to the same latitude, using the elevation of the sun for guidance. Medieval sailing descriptions typically described where on the Norwegian west coast to start when sailing (due west) to Iceland, and where on the Icelandic west coast to start when heading for Greenland (see KLNM 15, 68 for an overview). The height of the mid-day sun indicates the latitude; if the sun is too low one is further north, higher means further south. Not surprisingly, a number of ancient navigational instruments are designed precisely for determining sun height but none of these date from the Viking Age.

One problem is that such observations must be taken at noon, leaving 24 hour gaps between each time the course (and latitude) may be checked and adjusted. The use of gnomon curves eliminates part of this problem, at least in daylight.

At night, sightings of the North Star (Polaris) will serve a similar purpose, since it is located in a stable position over the geographic North Pole. It therefore indicates north. The further one travels south towards the Equator, the lower the position of the star over the horizon, so it is a good latitude indicator. Unlike the sun, the North Star does not appear to move, so its position can be checked throughout the whole night, as long as it is dark, that is. (In actual fact, it moves in a very small circle.) In bright northern summer nights it is invisible and nor does it cast a shadow, so the gnomon is of little use.

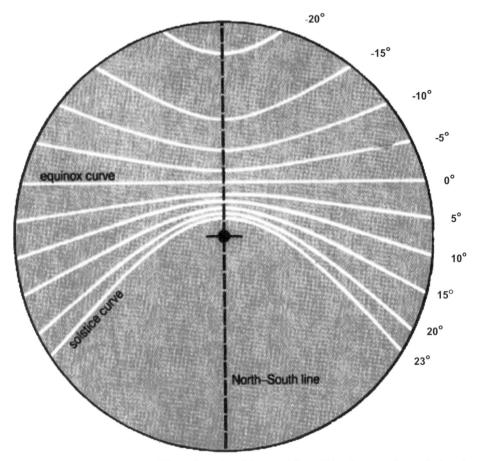

Figure 4. Gnomon curves. The plate will be horizontal, and the central line will be aligned north - south. A vertical pin (called a gnomon) in the center casts a shadow. During the day, the tip of the shadow will travel across the plate, making an arc called the gnomon curve. The curve will change with the latitude and time of year (after Graham-Campbell *et al*. 1994, 181).

GNOMON CURVES

A gnomon curve may best be understood if one imagines a sun-dial in its simplest form; a vertical pin or stick called a gnomon, casting its shadow on a horizontal surface. In the early morning sun, the stick which will cast a long shadow. Towards mid-day, the shadow will have moved, but also shortened. By sunset, the shadow will have moved further and be quite long again.

Imagine that a mark is made at the tip of the shadow at regular intervals between sunrise and sunset. Connecting the dots, one will observe that the tip of the shadow has described an arc during the day. This arc is called a gnomon curve. The shape of the curve will be specific for the latitude and the time of year. Hence it may be used in reverse order, to determine the latitude by help of the sun (fig. 4).

A sun-compass is simply a disk with an incised gnomon curve and a pin (gnomon) in the middle to cast the shadow. This requires an idea of where north is, and some marks along the edge of the disk to indicate north and roughly the time of day. Using this device, one may check one's latitude several times during the day. With a rough feeling for the time of day, it may also be used to indicate the sailing direction.

The shape of the gnomon curve will vary throughout the year, but it will be the same shape for one geographical location over a given period of time. Around mid-summer the variations are negligible, so one single curve may be used for navigation in June-July, say between Norway and Iceland.

The accurate use of gnomon curves in reality is dependent on many factors. For example, the user must hold the disk horizontally, which is difficult in heavy seas. One must see the sun, difficult when overcast, to both see the gnomon curve and to determine the position of north, which is opposite of the sun at noon. Further, one must determine what time of day it is (or at least determine noon), and then determine what time of the year it is. This is of less importance in the summer.

There is only one drawback to this method: nobody has been able to deliver absolute proof that Norse navigators knew about gnomon curves, although medieval sailing descriptions suggest latitude navigation (KLNM 15, 68). In recordings by the Icelander Oddi Helgasson from the middle of the twelfth century are calculations of sun directions and meridian heights in a table for the full year (KLNM 12, 260-61). However, extrapolating this table back to the Viking Age is not as straightforward as it may seem. European navigational techniques were to a great extent learned of from the Moslems during the crusades, and Star-Oddi lived roughly half a century after the First Crusade of AD 1096-99).

434

THE POTENTIAL OF THE UUNARTOQ DISK AS A PRECISION INSTRUMENT

In 1991 Søren Thirslund described the disk as follows:

> At the rounded outer edge on one side there are sixteen or seventeen triangular notches arranged like the compass points in later compasses, and ten of these are in fact placed at angular intervals of about 11.5 degrees, which is the way the 32-point compass card is divided up. The remaining notches are confusing, as their division is irregular, and one may have been erased—hence the alternatives sixteen or seventeen (Thirslund 1991, 65)

On inspection of an enlarged photograph of the original, there are 17 notches making out slightly less than half a circle, which makes a full circle of 32 notches almost impossible. 35 is probably closer to reality (fig. 5).

The notches bear no signs of having been carved according to a pre-drawn plan, but seem to gradually twist 'off-center', as if the carver lost track of the disk's center, making the incisions more and more askew while working his way around the edge. The error then had to be corrected before going on.

Measuring the gaps between the notches, a substantial variation in gap span is revealed, ranging from 4-9 mm (fig. 6). This is not what would be expected from a precision instrument. Rather, the triangular notches appear to be carved at random, as if the final number of notches was not known to the carver before the piece was finished.

The overall impression is that this is the product of an amateur carver, perhaps imitating something he or she had seen, such as a real instrument. Or, this may have been an object made for a totally different purpose than that of solar navigation, one that did not demand a high degree of accuracy.

It should also be noted that the whole piece creates only half a circle. It is by no means certain it ever consisted of a full circle, even though this is a likely assumption.

The traditional archaeological approach to identify such an object would be to look for similar finds in other Norse contexts, in either Greenland, Iceland, Scandinavia or the British Isles. Unfortunately, no obvious parallels have presented themselves, as least not to the present author, except in much later ethnological collections in Iceland. It is to these discs where we shall now turn our attention.

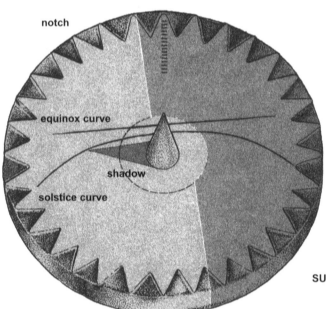

Figure 5. Reconstruction of the Uunatoq disk as a sun-compass or bearing-dial. The preserved part is the dark half to the right, and the reconstructed part the one to the left. The triangular notches of the original have been 'improved' to create a more regular pattern (after Graham-Campbell *et al.* 1994, 180).

SURVIVING FRAGMENT

435

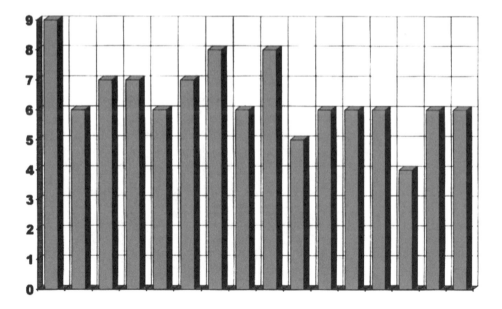

BEARING DIAL
Millimeter gap span

Figure 6. Bar graph indicating the gap span between the notches on the Uunartoq disk. The smallest gap is 4 millimeters, eight gaps are 6 millimeters, three are 7, two are 8 and one is 9 millimeters. The disk has probably been shrinking during its time in the ground and subsequent conservation, but the relative distance between notches are hardly that much affected.

Figure 7. Confession disk
(Icelandic Skriftaskífa)
from the Church of
Draflastaðir in Iceland.
Numbered 1 - 55. No.
3925 National Museum
of Iceland (photograph:
Ívar Brynjolfsson).

436

Figure 8. Confession disk
from the Church of Nés
in Iceland. Numbered 1-
30. No. 11278, National
Museum of Iceland
(photo: Ívar
Brynjolfsson).

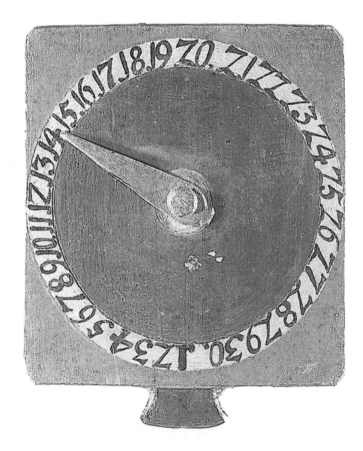

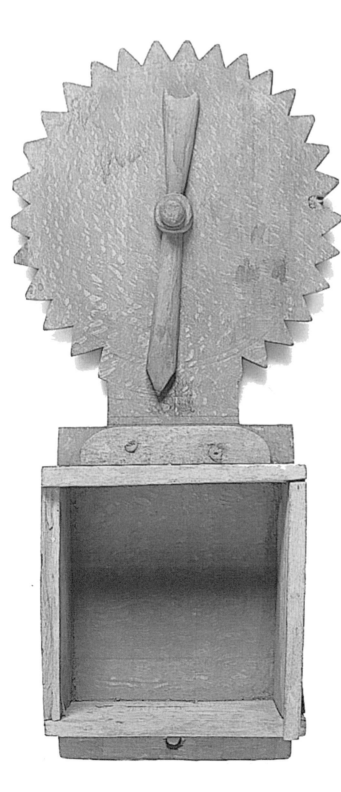

Figure 9. Confession disk from the Church of Glæsibær in Iceland. Diameter 16-16.5 cm, 26 notches. No 6456 National Museum of Iceland (photo: Ívar Brynjolfsson).

Figure 10. Confession disk from the Church of Skútustaðir in Iceland, 26 cm in diameter, numbered 1-38. No. 6351 National Museum of Iceland (photo: Ívar Brynjolfsson).

ICELANDIC CONFESSION DISKS

In the National Museum of Iceland are some objects which vary considerably in shape and design, but which all have been collected from parish churches around the country. Their name in Icelandic is *skriftaskífar*, which translated to English means 'confession disks' (figs 7-10).

A few similar objects are preserved in Denmark and Norway, although mostly with a different design than the Icelandic ones, mostly a rectangular slab with numbers and a hole for a peg outside each number. There are not many of them, and they all seem to date from the seventeenth and eighteenth centuries. The Icelandic ones, however, have one interesting feature: they consist of a wooden disk with some kind of notches or numbers around the edges.

The similarity to the Uunartoq disk is striking, but the photographs are misleading, as they tend to hide the fact that the Uunartoq disk is so much smaller than the others being only 7 cm in diameter, as opposed to 16-26 cm for the Icelandic ones.

Compared to the Uunartoq disk, the craftsmanship on the confession disks is much more precise, but then nobody have ever claimed them to be navigational instruments! Similarities in shape and design are traditional archaeological criteria for establishing similarities in dating and function. The confession-disks do, however, represent a great variety in types and design, making such conclusions difficult. It is therefore relevant to have a closer look at their function.

There is some knowledge about their use, but very little about their initial date. They must, however, be classified as mnemonic tools, for that is what they are. As such, they compare to other mnemonic instruments like those designed for navigation.

Quickly described, the confession disks were instruments used by the parish ministers or priests to count how many parishioners were taking confession. This was done in one of two ways: either by twisting a dial on what resembles a clock face, or by putting a little peg in a hole next to a number.

The clever thing with some of these objects is that they may be used even in a room too dark to actually see the numbers, simply by running a finger over the notches or holes. They could even be used by persons who were numerically illiterate.

According to the National Museum in Iceland, at least four confession disks are known from there. There are also six or eight from Denmark, and at least two are known from Norway, both from the Church of Vestre Moland in Aust-Agder. At least two of the Icelandic disks are made from beech wood, which is not native to Iceland, nor a common driftwood there. As this wood is common in Denmark, these disks were either produced there or made in Iceland from imported Danish material.

439

The function of the disks is strikingly obvious. Two Danish examples feature self-explanatory texts. One reads *Numerus confidentium*, i.e. number of confessants, and *Helt Borgs Schriffte Taffle* ('Heltborg's Confession Disk'). The Icelandic name is as mentioned *skriftaskifa*, in Danish / Norwegian *skriftetavle*. The Icelandic and Scandinavian words for confession—*skrifta* or *skrifte*—derive from the Old Norse noun *skript*, or verb *skripta*, which in turn is derived from the Old English word *scrift*.

The dates of these confession disks are also reasonably clear. Besides the stylistic evidence, the shape of the Arabic numerals (in particular the digit '4') indicate they date from the fifteenth century or later (see KLNM 18, 119). Some of the objects have a year painted or carved directly on them. Thus one of the Norwegian examples carry the text: *1781 Westre Molans Soun* ('1781 Vestre Moland's parish'), while two Danish examples bear the dates 1695 and 1696.

The key issue, of course, is to establish whether confession disks were used in the Nordic countries under the Roman Catholic Church, or were these a post-Reformation phenomenon.

A new understanding of the Uunartoq disk will demand more than a superficial likeness with some seventeenth century Icelandic objects for clerical use. Although it is tempting to argue that it was found in what was believed to be a convent, it is unclear whether it belonged to the convent itself or to an earlier phase of settlement.

Museum Director M. Mackeprang, who wrote about confession disks in a small article from 1916, assumed they all dated from the period after 1685, when the rules for a new Church Ritual for Denmark and Norway were introduced (which, by the way, also included Iceland). These rules stated,

> The clerk should keep track of how many persons from the Parish are taking confession, to write this down in a book, so one may know the absentees, and to calculate how much host and wine may be needed for the communion. For this purpose every priest shall have a board with him in the confessional, onto which he shall draw the number of confessors (Anon. 1685, 149-150; translated to English by C. Keller).

One may ask if this book from 1685 described a new ritual, as Mackeprang apparently believed, or whether it confirmed an already established practice. There is evidence for the latter. In an Icelandic description of the confession from 1593, when people could still remember Catholic times, the clerk is said to follow the priest and count the number of confessors on a string of pearls (obviously a rosary), so one would know exactly how much host to prepare for the Eucharist (Bull 1912, 171).

Archaeologically it may be suggested that the confession disks represent a very new type of object, which, by the time of the seventeenth century, had not yet found a stable form. The great variation in pattern and design, even down to the technical devices for recording the numbers, may indicate this was a new apparatus, where the practical design was left to individual creativity. On the other hand, it may be argued that the need for such instruments would disappear when most men of the cloth had learned to read and write. Also, the variation in design may indicate that the disks simply falls into a larger category of mnemonic aids, known for a variety of purposes. Both arguments could indicate that this type of instrument originated in the Middle Ages.

Today, most people would argue that the personal confession is one of the Sacraments in the Roman Catholic Church, but not in the post-Reformation, Lutheran Church. Tempting as it is to use this to propose a medieval origin of the Confession Disk, it is too much of a simplification. A closer look at the practice of confession is needed.

CONFESSION IN THE MEDIEVAL CHURCH

440

In the very early Christian Church, confession was done in public, in front of the congregation. In the Middle Ages, this practice was replaced with the private confession, usually to the Parish Priest.

In 1215, the Fourth Lateran Synod was held in Rome, under the direction of Pope Innocent III. The synod issued the decree *Omnis utriusque sexus* where a formal link was made between the confession and the Eucharist—Holy Communion. It imposed upon everybody to confess to a parish priest at least once a year, and to make confession during Lent, prior to taking the Eucharist at Easter. Not doing so implied exclusion from the church and the denial of a Christian burial. Without confession, one did not have access to the Eucharist (Swanson 1995, 33, see also Bull 1912, 93-94).

This practice was introduced very fast in the Norwegian Church, which at that time included Iceland. In Norway proper it was embedded in the New Christian Laws of Magnus the Lawmender's National Law from 1267-68. In Iceland, it was confirmed in Bishop Magnus of Skálholt's 'Rules' dating from 1224, and confirmed by Bishop Arne in 1269 (Bull 1912, 129, citing *Diplomatarium Islandicum* vol. 1, 17, vol 2, 7). Ash Wednesday in Iceland was typically called *Skriptinsdagr* after the Old English / Old Norse terms for confession.

Today Holy Communion implies two elements, host and wine, which through transubstantiation becomes the Body and Blood of Christ. In the Middle Ages, the wine was consumed by the clergy on behalf of the congregation, while the ordinary parishioners had to make do with the host. It is interesting, therefore, to observe that two of the Icelandic confession disks (from Skútustaðir and Glæsibær) are attached to a small wooden box, supposedly containers for the host.

In the wake of the new decree from 1215, the need to keep a closer tab of the parishioners taking confession and communion arose. Confessions should be made to *your own priest*. Confessing to someone else than the parish priest was considered spiritual adultery (Swanson 1995, 236). This rule was practiced even in Iceland (Bull 1912, 103). However, with the development of religious orders during the High and Late Middle Ages, it was permitted to confess to monks or nuns, thus undermining the authority of the parish priest. This came to be a recurring topic for debate throughout the rest of the Middle Ages.

It may therefore be argued that after the decree of 1215 (or its implementation within the next 60 years or so), parish priests had to keep count of how many parishioners that confessed, both to prepare the right amount of host, and to exert a certain control. This probably created the need for an account system like rosaries or confession disks. Absence from confession and communion over more than three years led to exclusion from the Church. Whether the confession disks were used this early and as far away as in thirteenth-century Greenland is impossible to say without further information.

With the Reformation, the obligatory confession was abolished, along with the right of the priest to prescribe penance. The practice of taking confession before communion was, however, continued, in some places as late as the nineteenth century. Thus the need for confession disks may theoretically have lasted that long.

FINAL COMMENTS

The suggestion of the Uunartoq disk as a Viking-Age navigational instrument originated from its likeness to a modern ship compass. Its explanation as a sun compass is based on the assumption that latitude-navigation was used during the Viking Age. Such navigation is collaborated by written sources from the middle of the twelfth century onwards, but it is difficult to find older evidence, simply because older written sources are extremely rare. The technique of latitude navigation does not demand a sun-compass, however, other means of determining the sun-height or height of the North Star were available. The question of navigation based on gnomon curves is even less substantiated.

441

The stratigraphic problems admitted by Vebæk also cast severe doubts upon the Viking-Age dating of the Uunartoq disk, it may very well have come form the second settlement phase of the suggested Benedictine convent. It is not known for certain whether such confession disks were used during the Middle Ages, although the confession practices of the Roman Catholic Church certainly opens the possibility. The fact that the disks could be operated in the dark, and by the illiterate, would have made them highly useful in marginal areas with a (supposedly) less educated clergy.

It is unlikely that confession-disks were developed before the Fourth Lateran Synod in 1215. This means that any possible confession disks at the site of Ø-149 Narsarsuaq in Uunartoq must be associated with the second settlement phase, i.e. with what Vebæk believed to be the Benedictine convent. If the disk in question was designed for something else, such as a navigational instrument, this reasoning does not apply.

The identification of a new artifact type such as the Uunartoq disk will first of all demand a sober use of archaeological methods, where comparisons with identified, known objects of a similar or related form will have to be a core issue. The time-span between the Uunartoq disk and the Icelandic confession dials is 300 years at a minimum, perhaps twice as much. This is obviously a problem, even though it may be argued that the cultural contexts are related.

The conclusion must be that the final interpretation of the Uunartoq disk has not yet been reached. The present article has offered some new alternatives, and so maybe the puzzle will be solved by a new find in a clearer context somewhere. Maybe it was designed for some mnemonic purpose, maybe for navigation, or perhaps it was a toy?

How the Vikings navigated across the North Atlantic is still a bit of a mystery. Maybe they used the North Star, maybe solar navigation with or without gnomon curves, maybe a variety of techniques. The lack of conclusive evidence should not stop us from speculating. We may need the answers, but we also need the mysteries.

ACKNOWLEDGEMENTS

This paper was written in cooperation with Professor Arne Emil Christensen of the University's Cultural History Museum in Oslo and Museum Director Guðrún María Kristinsdóttir of the Akureyri Museum, Iceland. Great help has also been received from Curator Þóra Kristjánsdóttir and Photographer Ívar Brynjolfsson, both of the National Museum of Iceland. Thanks also to Director Bård Kolltveit of the Norwegian Maritime Museum, to Professor Jan Schumacher, at the time of writing of the Center for Viking and Medieval Studies, University of Oslo, presently of the Norwegian Lutheran School of Theology in Oslo, to Librarian Mette Røkke, also of the Norwegian Lutheran School of Theology, and to Ann-Turi Ford of Ford Formgiving Fortissimo Forlag at Nesodden.

ABBREVIATION

KLNM   *Kulturhistorisk Leksikon for Nordisk Middelalder* 1956-1978, 2nd ed. 1982, vols 1-21, Copenhagen.

BIBLIOGRAPHY

Anon. 1685. *Danmarks og Norgis Kirke-Ritual*, Copenhagen.

Bull, E. 1912. *Folk og kirke i middelalderen*. Kristiana and Copenhagen: Studier til Norges Historie.

Christensen, A.E. 1993. 'Vikingenes verdensbilde, skipsbygging og navigasjon', *Norsk Sjøfartsmuseum Årbok 1992*, 151-160.

Clausen, B.L. ed., 1993. *Viking Voyages to North America*, Roskilde.

Fitzhugh, W.W. and Ward, E.I., eds, 2000. *Vikings. The North Atlantic Saga*, Washington and London.

Graham-Campbell, J. *et al.*, eds, 1994. *Cultural Atlas of the Viking World*, Oxford and New York.

Mackeprang, M. 1917 'Skriftetavler og skriftestoler', *Foreningen til Norske Fortidsmindesmærkers Bevaring, Aarsberetning* (1916), 115-117.

Ramskou, T. 1982. *Solkompasset*, Copenhagen.

Roslund, C. 1985. 'Hur hittade Vikingerna till Vinland?', *Forskning och Framsteg*, 5, 4-11.

Seaver, K. 2000. 'Unanswered Questions', in Fitzhugh and Ward 2000, 270-279.

Swanson, R.N. 1995. *Religion and Devotions in Europe* c. *1215-* c.*1515*, Cambridge.

Sølver, C.V. 1944. *Vestervejen. Om Nordboernes Navigering over Atlanteren. Det Grønlandske Sclshabs Aarsskrift*, Copenhagen.

——1953. 'The discovery of an ancient bearing dial', *Journal of the Institute of Navigation*, 6, 294-6.

——1954. *Vestervejen. Om Vikingernes Sejlads*, Copenhagen.

Taylor, E.G.R., May, W.E., Lethbridge, T.C., and Motzo, R.B. 1954. 'A Norse Bearing Dial?', *Journal of the Institute of Navigation*, 7, 78-84.

Thirslund, S. 1987. *Viking navigation. Sun-compass guided Norsemen first to America*, Humlebæk, Denmark.

——1991. 'A presumed sun compass from Narsarsuaq', in Vebæk 1991, 65-71.

——1993. 'Navigation by the Vikings on the Open Sea', in Clausen 1993, 109-117.

Thirslund, S. and Vebæk, C.L. 1990 *Vikingernes kompas: 1000-årig pejlskive fundet i Grønland*, Kronborg, Denmark.

Vebæk, C.L. 1952. 'A New World Nunnery before the Days of Columbus', *Illustrated London News*, 3 May 1952.

——1991. *The Church Topography of the Eastern Settlement and the excavation of the Benedictine convent in Uunartoq Fjord*. Copenhagen: Meddelelser om Grønland, Man & Society 14.

Vebæk, C.L. and Thirslund, S. 1992. *The Viking compass guided Norsemen first to America*, Humlebæk, Denmark.

The 'Vínland Map':

Faith, Facts, and Fables

Kirsten A. Seaver

At a symposium with the discovery of the L'Anse aux Meadows site at its heart, it seemed fitting to discuss the so-called 'Vínland Map' which Yale University acquired about forty years ago. If this Norse site had not been found between the time the map arrived in New Haven and the time it was ready for public consumption, would the map have been more convincing as evidence of Norse discovery in America? Or would the absence of competition have led to a softer sell on Yale's part, with less acrimonious battle lines as a result?

We'll of course never know. There are some certainties, however. One is that the publicity in favor of the map's authenticity has been as determined as it has been under-scrutinized. A second is that since Yale's 1965 announcement, faith in the map's authenticity as a mid fifteenth-century artifact has been pitted against growing skepticism and evidence of its fake nature. A third is that this debate has included little knowledge about the medieval Norse in Iceland and Greenland, although the map's claim to importance is based on its supposed association with the Norse discovery of America from these two countries.

443

As we know, faith is not a product of cold reason. A rational discussion confronting fables with facts may lead people to change their thinking, but faith is essentially based on the will to believe and on trust. When trust fails, faith is likely to suffer.

In 1965, members of the public placed their trust in assurances by the Yale University Library and Yale University Press that they had acquired a manuscript world map, from around 1440, showing the Norse discovery of Vínland. If genuine, it would be a rarity indeed, because the earliest known cartographic appearance of the 'Vínland' name was on the speculative map Sigurður Stefánsson drew in Iceland around 1590. Indeed, the medieval Norse had no cartographical tradition. If the pragmatic sailing knowledge of the medieval Norse had been communicated to European geographers at any time between the eleventh and fifteenth centuries, the resulting maps would have shown the various northern regions very differently.

Yale's claim could nevertheless expect to find believers among people who had always been convinced by the saga accounts. Their number might well include many not taken in by the Kensington Runestone, the Newport Tower, and similar non-evidence of Norse presence on the American continent, because the story of Norse activities in America had recently gained the respectability of demonstrable fact. In November of 1964, *National Geographic* had described the genuine Norse site which Helge and Anne Stine Ingstad had found at L'Anse aux Meadows four years earlier and were still in the process of excavating (Ingstad 1964).

However, this very discovery also threatened to make the map superfluous as supposed evidence of Norse exploration in North America and as a rallying point for those who had maintained their belief in this Norse achievement. In a moment, we'll look at how those with a vested interest in securing the Vínland Map as an icon in this debate dealt with the situation. But first, we'll go back to the pre-L'Anse aux Meadows days of 1957, when the map surfaced in the European antiquarian market and was rejected as suspect by the British Museum after a brief look by manuscript experts there (Wallis *et al.* 1974, 186).

At that time, the sellers' chief obstacle was the lack of proper provenance for the map. It is a major sticking point to this day and has not diminished with the inconsistent stories told by Laurence C. Witten II, the New Haven antiquarian book dealer and Yale alumnus who eventually brokered the deal that resulted in Yale's ownership.

We know the identities of several dealers involved at one point or another in 1957, but not necessarily all the names. Fingerpointing is therefore unwise. We can say with certainty, however, that the map and its companion manuscripts appeared on the antiquarian market after 1955, when the Allied authorities had handed over to the Germans and the Austrians the task of reuniting Nazi loot with former owners. Oversight with such loot became even more diffuse in post-war Europe, with the result that antiquarian items from any source could change hands and cross borders with greater ease.

A case in point are several stolen codices from the Cathedral Library of Zaragoza, which had been cataloged as recently as 1954. They, too, appeared on the European market in the second half of the 1950s, with the marks of former ownership removed or defaced. Several of these volumes passed through the hands of three or four of the people most directly involved in the Vínland Map transactions, including Witten's (Grosz 1996; Nichols 1996; Saenger 1998, 202; Shailor 1987). However, Witten vehemently denied that the Vínland Map volume had come from the Biblioteca Capitular de la Seo, and I believe him because of the indications I have found of the volume's two previous homes—a subject to which I shall also return later. Witten's and his colleagues' involvement with the Zaragoza codices and similar deals nevertheless suggests that they were not always particular about the source of their merchandise.

444

Witten's own explanation for why he had not insisted on 'pedigrees' for the Vínland Map and many other items he purchased in Europe during the same period was that in the chaotic conditions of post-war Europe, these niceties were on the whole not observed. People turned a profit where they could (Skelton *et al.* 1995, xlii-xliii).

Witten was six years into his career as an antiquarian book dealer in 1957, when he first met and traded with Enzo Ferrajoli de Ry, a colorful Italian dealer who often left his home in Barcelona to search for books throughout Western Europe, and who eventually served a prison sentence for his part in the sale of the Zaragoza codices. Witten met him in Geneva, Switzerland, in the shop belonging to Nicolas Rauch, another key figure in the Vínland Map transactions. According to Witten, 'Rauch's shop had a special importance in the antiquarian book world, because in Switzerland Rauch was in the ideal position to make banking arrangements for dealers and private clients in other European countries'(Skelton *et al.* 1995, xli-xlii). Indeed! Switzerland had managed to stay neutral during the war, its bank accounts remaining the very model of discretion. After the war, the country retained the advantages of its banking system, of its neutral stance, and of course of its strategic location.

Witten bought the volume containing the Vínland Map from Ferrajoli the same year they met and by his own account paid $3,500 for it (Washburn 1971, 26). When the volume eventually was resold to another loyal Yale alumnus, Paul Mellon, widely known for his quiet and generous philanthropy, the price was $1,000,000, according to Wilcomb Washburn, late of the Smithsonian Institution. He said this in an early 1996 PBS interview connected with his renewed efforts to declare the map authentic. When I asked the map's current curator at Yale's Beinecke Library to confirm these figures, he replied that he was unable to do so (R. Babcock, pers. comm.).

Barbara Shailor, a cataloger of medieval codices at the Beinecke, recently stated that the volume with the Vínland map

> was acquired from a private collection in Europe by L.C. Witten, who subsequently determined that the Vínland Map and the *Ystoria Tartarorum* were once bound together with another manuscript then in the possession of Thomas E. Marston.... Presented to the Beinecke Library by an anonymous donor in 1965 (Shailor 1987, II, 183-86).

We do not know Paul Mellon's reaction in 1974 when it became clear that not just one, but two European book dealers who had sold the volume to Witten retained a financial interest in it until the inflated resale price had been effected. In any event, this circumstance triggers questions about the miraculous reunion of the two volumes owned respectively by Thomas E. Marston, the Curator of Medieval and Renaissance Literature in the Yale University Library, and by Witten—or, more accurately, by his wife (Saenger 1998, 201)—because this fortuitous linking appeared to provide the reassurance about the map's authenticity which the lack of provenance had so far denied it. The two textual portions involved already appeared to be related and to be genuine mid fifteenth-century works. That judgement, at least, has held up to scrutiny during the ensuing decades. Now that the worm holes reportedly matched in key places that also involved the map, these texts seemingly legitimized the map.

Marston had a number of business dealings with Witten just at that time. They have told similar stories about their wonderful luck in matching up the worm holes in the volume containing the map and its companion manuscript and in an incomplete manuscript version, in a fifteenth-century binding, of the *Speculum historiale* by Vincent of Beauvais, which Mr. Marston purchased for $75 from the London dealer Irving Davis and soon afterwards donated to Mrs. Witten. This completed her collection prior to Mr. Mellon's purchase of all three manuscript items. Davis was the same dealer who had tried to persuade the British Museum to buy the volume containing the Vínland Map; he had obtained the *Speculum* fragments he now sold to Marston directly from Ferrajoli (Washburn 1971, 26).

445

The cartographic star spotted through the worm holes was not deemed ready for the public telescope until October of 1965, when the map was announced in the United States with great fanfare just before Columbus Day. The carefully planned launch suggests that the people in charge knew that the intervening discovery of L'Anse aux Meadows might dampen public excitement about an artifact to which so many troublesome questions still attached. There were the press announcements and on-the-spot publicity commensurate with any well-run public relations campaign, but there was also an earlier stage so discreet as to be virtually unknown to this day.

On the Friday immediately before the map's existence was announced in the US, the Norwegian Academy of Sciences in Oslo hosted a gala event where Helge and Anne Stine Ingstad were among the guests especially invited to a presentation by Chester Kerr, the Director of Yale University Press. He announced Yale's ownership of the Vínland Map and gave a lengthy description of it. Yale billed this as a 'courtesy visit' to the homeland of Eiríkr *rauði*. If you wonder why a similar courtesy visit was not made to Iceland, Leifr Eiríksson's birthplace and home of the Vínland sagas, just remember that in all the world at that time, Helge and Anne Stine Ingstad were the two people most likely to be heard if they raised questions about Yale's new acquisition after merely reading about it in their morning paper.

A long article in *Aftenposten* for 11 October 1965 shows that Kerr came well prepared with handouts for the press, including a tasteful account of how Yale had acquired the map. When the *Aftenposten* reporter asked Ingstad about his reaction to the news, he replied that since he did not yet know any of the background material, he did not want to judge this strange map prematurely and could only note that it was certainly interesting. He then added

> The value in this presentation of the map comes from the fact that an institution like Yale stands behind it, together with such authorities as one of the world's most highly regarded cartographic scholars, R.A. Skelton at the British Museum. I am given to understand that their final report is the product of many years of research and many investigations.

Neither Ingstad nor anyone else at that time could possibly know that the sole objective of the 'research and investigations' had been to promote the map as genuine, and that neither then nor later did those two institutions lend their approval to the Vínland Map.

Throughout, public efforts on behalf of the map have involved just a few individuals who made sure that their respectable institutional ties were always mentioned.

Mr. Kerr then hurried back to New Haven, because his Press was publishing a handsome book simultaneously with the announcement about the map. The authors of *The Vinland Map and the Tartar Relation* were three scholars of blameless reputation, but with little applicable expertise. R.A. Skelton, the Superintendent of Maps at the British Museum, was an authority on printed, not manuscript, maps. Thomas Marston, Witten's friend, had a doctorate in nineteenth-century British history (Saenger 1998, 199). He also collected printed books from the fifteenth and sixteenth centuries with a special interest in ancient Roman poets, as well as fifteenth-century textual manuscripts from Italy (Shailor 1992, III, xviii). The third author, George D. Painter, was Assistant Keeper in charge of *incunabula* in the British Museum, of which the present British Library was still a part at the time.

Not one of these three men was versed in medieval Norse history and culture nor did they possess the languages needed to supplement their knowledge. Nor did they have palæographical expertise—a necessary skill when judging a manuscript of any sort. They could not consult other scholars, because they had been sworn to secrecy during their work. It is unfortunate that this secrecy also prevented an independent peer review prior to publication. An unbiased, knowledgeable reader would have found much to worry about in that manuscript. It was surely an extraordinary decision by a prestigious academic press and not very good soil for trust to grow in.

In a second edition of this work, published in 1995, Kerr and his successor at Yale University Press, John Ryden, expressed the hope that this new edition would rehabilitate 'one of history's most important cartographical finds.' There seems to have been some ambivalence on Mr. Ryden's part, however, because on 23 March 1996, the *Star Tribune* of Minneapolis, Minnesota quoted him as saying that 'the cumulative weight of the evidence is that the map is authentic. But I don't mind that some mystery remains. It's sexier that way'.

Kerr and Ryden considered a news story on the front page of the *New York Times* and the book's distribution through both the Book-of-the-Month Club and the History Book Club as evidence of the original edition's immediate success, rather than as testimonies to a well-run public relations campaign by an institution unlikely to be ignored in the first place. Their preface also mentioned the 'leading attention paid to the book in *American Heritage Magazine*'. Interestingly, one of the magazine's associate editors was Chester Kerr's wife. Furthermore, the October issue was published almost simultaneously with Yale's announcement and featured not only an editorial introduction, but substantial articles by both Skelton and Painter.

Actual book reviews were not invariably supportive, especially outside the United States. Wilcomb Washburn wrote one of the less critical ones, published early in 1966 in the *American Historical Review* (1966). That same year he arranged a major conference at the Smithsonian Institution, where an international assortment of scholars expressed a broad spectrum of opinions about the Vínland Map and its companion manuscripts. The *Proceedings,* which Washburn later edited, constitute a valuable record of early reactions (Washburn 1971). It was also Washburn who masterminded the quietly prepared second edition of the book which, like the first edition, was launched with much media attention. At that time, George Painter was the only one of the original authors still alive.

The book was in fact unchanged except for five essays added as frontal matter, not one of which reflected thirty years of progress in Norse and cartographic research. In his own new essay, Painter restated his reasons for believing that the map is a 'major and authentic message from the middle ages on a hitherto unknown moment in the history of the world and American discovery'(1995). Unfortunately, his new essay presented no evidence for the map's authenticity.

That 'moment in the history of the world and American discovery' was discussed quite a bit during the Symposium. Before we analyze the map and what it reveals about its creator, let us just note that since Norse voyages to North America continued for several centuries, they constituted rather more than a moment in history, except perhaps to students of trilobites.

Fortunately, in the original 1965 volume Painter wrote about a subject he understood well, namely the 'Tartar Relation.' A formerly unknown version of this account of a papal mission to Mongolia during 1245-47 was bound with the Vínland Map, in a relatively recent binding, when Yale acquired it. Despite the volume's hazy provenance, there is little reason to question Shailor's judgment that this version of the 'Tartar Relation' is a genuine, mid fifteenth-century companion piece to the Vincent of Beauvais *Speculum historiale* fragments, with similar handwriting and identical watermarks in the paper portions of the mixed paper and vellum quires. However, although the map was drawn on an old piece of vellum that could have come out of the same volume, and despite a share of those handy worm holes, there is no evidence that the map formed an original part of the volume.

Those who are interested in these and other physical details will find plenty to read on the subject. Summing it up here, the evidence suggests a Germanic origin for the manuscripts and an association with the general Upper Rhine region, with which the maker of the Vínland Map was thoroughly familiar.

Marston confidently stated that the 'Upper Rhineland bastard (or cursive) book hand' was 'apparently' the same in all three works. All the palæographic experts who have seen the map disagree with him. In fact, one does not need to be an expert to see that there are two different handwritings in the map. One hand uses larger, inconsistently shaped letters varying in slant from 90 to about 105 degrees. The other is small and formal with ruled lines exactly two millimeters apart—rather an unusual measurement for the fifteenth century. There is no reason to suppose that the same hand could not have created both kinds of writing. My son's professional lettering as a graphic designer is exquisite, but I would not use that adjective about his regular handwriting!

447

We'll focus on the northwestern corner of the map because it suffices to reveal the work's fake nature. Once you know that the map is fake, its many anomalies and teasers are secondary, more important is the context of the person who made the map and of the time it was created. When we discuss the faker himself, we'll look at issues such as the ink, at the map's cartographical and cosmographical antecedents, and of course at the reason for making the map.

Here we have three northern islands: *Vinilanda/Vimlanda Insula*, *Gronelãda* and the curiously named Iceland: *Isolanda Ibernica*—the Irish Island. There will be an explanation for this last feature as well, but let us start with Vínland, shown as an island with two deep bays in its eastern coast. Some have suggested that this almost tripartite delineation indicates Markland and Helluland as well, but the two legends here don't support that theory. The short legend says: 'Island of Vínland, discovered by Leif and Bjarni together.' In case we missed the point, the longer legend says, according to the translation in *The Vínland Map and the Tartar Relation*:

> By God's will, after a long voyage from the island of Greenland to the south end of the most distant remaining parts of the western ocean sea, sailing southward amidst the ice, the companions Bjarni (*byarnus*) and Leif Eiriksson (*leiphus erissonius*) discovered a new land, extremely fertile and even having vines, the which island they named Vínland. Eric (*Henricus*), legate of the Apostolic See and bishop of Greenland and the neighboring regions, arrived in this truly vast and very rich land, in the name of the almighty God, in the last year of our most blessed father Pascal, remained a long time in both summer and winter, and later returned northeastward toward Greenland and then proceeded in most humble obedience to the will of his superiors (Skelton *et al.* 1995, 140).

The last part of this translation was skewed to fit with Skelton's mistaken views here, as we shall see later. Let us take the main issue first, namely the perplexing notion that Leifr Eiríksson and Bjarni—presumably Bjarni Herjólfsson—discovered Vínland together. This runs counter to the saga information, which distinguishes sharply between the two men's voyages and accomplishments. Skelton reassured his readers: 'If this be fact, it is unrecorded in any surviving textual source for the voyage and must derive from an oral or written tradition otherwise lost'(Skelton 1995, 223).

The Vínland sagas remain our earliest descriptions of the circumstances around the Norse discovery of America and of the principal persons involved. Actually, the source of the information in this map legend is both extant and identifiable. The first time Leifr and Bjarni sailed together was in 1765, when the German Moravian Brother David Crantz published his *Historie von Grænland*. It was intended as a report on the new German missions in Greenland, about which he presumably knew something, but the Danish missionary H.C. Glahn found Crantz generally ill prepared for his task (Lidegaard 1991), and that was without addressing the book's perfunctory summary of Greenland's Norse period, where Crantz wrote that after Bjarni Herjólfsson had reported drifting off to unknown lands in the west on his way to Greenland to join his father, Leifr Eiríksson 'fitted out a ship with 35 men, and went to sea with Biærn' (Crantz 1767, I, 254-55).

On the continent, the book quickly gained a wide audience as the only work about the recently recolonised Greenland available to non-Scandinavian readers. Soon translated into French and English, it was still considered current in 1864 when Charles Francis Hall published his *Life with the Esquimaux* and tossed in an account of the medieval Norse, citing Crantz as the source for his story about 'Bjorn's' discovery of 'a new country covered with wood' in 'the year 1001'. Hall added: 'On his [i.e. Bjarni's] return, Leifr fitted out a vessel, and with Bjorn as pilot, went in search of this new land'(Hall 1864, 39-41).

Crantz conscientiously attributed his information about Bjarni and Leifr to Paul Henry Mallet's *Introduction à l'histoire de Danemarc* (1755-56), and to Bishop Erik Pontoppidan's *Natural History of Norway*, published in Norwegian in 1752 and translated into English in 1755. These two men, Crantz assured us, had transcribed their information from Arngrim Jonas [sic] and Torfæus and confirmed it with Adam of Bremen.

Mallet indeed noted that he relied on Arngrímur Jónsson's *Gronlandia*, first written in Latin around 1600, for information about Greenland, and on Torfæus' later works for Vínland. After giving Arngrímur's version of *Grænlendinga saga*, in which Bjarni Herjólfsson drifted within sight of those unknown western coasts while on his way to Greenland to join his father, Mallet continued: 'The following summer, viz. in the year 1002' Bjarni went to Norway to see 'count' [Earl] Eric and told about his sighting of the unknown land in the west, upon which he was chided for not being more curious. On Bjarni's return to Greenland, 'he [here clearly referring to Leifr] began to think seriously of exploring those lands with more attention. Leif, the son of that same Eric rufus who had discovered Greenland..., being desirous of rendering himself illustrious like his father, formed the design of going thither himself; and prevailing on his father Eric to accompany him they fitted out a vessel with five and thirty hands.' Still following *Grænlendinga saga*, Mallet then related that Eiríkr fell off his horse on the way to the ship, and that the superstitious Leifr decided to set sail without his father (Mallet 1770, 279-83). There was no pilot named Bjarni aboard.

Mallet had understood his source Arngrímur correctly. Nowhere does Arngrímur hint of subsequent exploration fever in Bjarni, but Leifr Eiríksson, we are told, went at his father's urging with a ship and 35 men to the new lands Bjarni had seen, where Leifr found Helluland, Markland and Vínland (Jónsson 1732, 43-5). Nothing that Arngrímur wrote can be construed as that Bjarni and Leifr sailed off together. Nor did Thormodus Torfæus say so (BL 152.a.8.(1)). An Icelander born and bred, and well educated in Copenhagen, Torfæus had no trouble reading his sources in both Latin and Old Norse. He conveyed the saga information as we know it today.

Considering that Crantz's French was so bad that he misread Mallet, it is not surprising that he got Pontoppidan wrong as well—presumably in English. The good Norwegian bishop also relied on Arngrímur Jónsson in telling how Leifr Eiríksson sailed off on his quest with 35 men, not one of whom was Bjarni (Pontoppidan 1755, 228-29).

In short, the Nordic sources so confidently cited by Crantz fail to corroborate any joint cruise by Bjarni and Leifr. As for Adam of Bremen, his history of the Bremen Archbishopric, completed around 1075, does not even mention who discovered Vínland. Crantz's explicit statement about Bjarni's and Leifr's joint discovery therefore does not go back beyond 1765, which means that those two Vínland map legends don't antedate 1765, either. If a map of North America purporting to be from the mid-sixteenth century showed Washington D.C. on the mid-Atlantic east coast, such an anachronism would condemn that map as a fake, and the same standard should be applied to the Vínland Map.

Adam of Bremen's eleventh-century geographical notions were vague, but he did his best with information that came his way, including about 'yet another island of the many found in that ocean. It is called Vínland because vines producing excellent wine grow wild there. That unsown crops also abound on that island we have ascertained not from fabulous reports but from the trustworthy relations of the Danes' (Tschan 1959, 219). Note the similarity here to the Vínland description in the longer legend. It is not surprising that there is much of Adam in this map, because it was made by a German Catholic priest some 800 years Adam's junior, who considered his fellow ecclesiastic not only the first, but also the most reliable historian of Norse American discovery.

449

The same trustworthy Danes probably inspired Adam's explanation for Viking raids. Describing the Norwegians as living in a cold and unproductive country, he noted that

> poverty has forced them [...] to go all over the world and from piratical raids they bring home in great abundance the riches of the lands. In this way they bear up under the unfruitfulness of their own country.... Since accepting Christianity, however [...] they have already learned to love the truth and peace and to be content with their poverty-indeed, to disperse what they have gathered, not as before to gather what has been dispersed. [...Except, that is, for those] who are removed beyond the arctic tract along the ocean. [...] I have heard that women grow beards in the extremely rough alps of that region and that the men live in the woods, rarely exposing themselves to sight. They use the pelts of wild beasts for clothing and in speaking to one another are said to gnash their teeth (Tschan 1959, 211).

Caution is also needed before attributing factual knowledge to Adam in other areas. He designated as islands not only Vínland, Greenland, and Iceland, but also the Baltic country of Estonia and many other well-anchored areas (Tschan 1959, 194-8). Adam's supposed knowledge therefore does not explain why Greenland was shown as an island on the Vínland Map, especially given the uncannily informed outline of the place. Greenland's true shape was slow to emerge on maps, and the country was not circumnavigated and proved to be an island until early in the twentieth century. The fact that Helluland and Markland are missing from both Adam's work and the Vínland Map nevertheless suggests a tie between Greenland's island status and Adam, but those vaguely modern delineations have another source.

The Danish cartographic historian Axel Anton Bjørnbo, with whom the maker of the Vínland Map corresponded for some years, believed that the Dane Claudius Clavus, who first introduced Greenland to European cartography around 1424 during a sojourn in Rome, had personally visited Greenland, where the Norse Greenlanders had conveyed to him information about their country's shape which their forebears had obtained by circumnavigating their island during a particularly warm early period. Bjørnbo changed his mind shortly before he died in 1912, but he never had a chance to inform his German correspondent, who remained convinced that Claudius Clavus had in turn shared his knowledge with continental churchmen during the first quarter of the fifteenth century.

During their exchange of letters, Bjørnbo's German colleague wrote on 3 January 1911:

> I am very glad that [Nansen] is bringing out the information about the ancient Irish. It has always been my view that the Irish who removed to Iceland, also sought out the Westland [i.e. Greenland]. But I lacked convincing historical evidence (Fischer 1911).

This was, of course, a reference to the Irish hermit monks the Norse found when they first settled Iceland, supposedly in such numbers that they spilled over into Greenland, and it explains the name *isolanda Ibernica* for Iceland. Innumerable statements which Bjørnbo's German correspondent published about the Norse demonstrate shaky knowledge. In 1902 he wrote: 'The majority of scholars now lean to the theory that both of the Norse settlements lay on the west coast of Greenland.' Clearly unable to distinguish between the Eastern Settlement and the East Coast: five pages later he praised Finnur Jónsson for having identified 'the 12 churches of the east coast'(Fischer 1903, 23, 28).

The correspondence between Bjørnbo and the well-known German cartographic historian Father Josef Fischer, S.J. is still at the Royal Library in Copenhagen (Bjørnbo and Fisher; Seaver 1997, 42-7). Fischer posed many questions concerning his forthcoming book *Claudius Clavus, the First Cartographer of America*, and interspersed them with pedantic notes about the early Ptolemaic maps on which he considered himself more expert than Bjørnbo. He also made frequent references to his own work on Norse discovery.

As I already noted, inconsistent lettering is a feature of the informal Vínland Map legends. A handwriting sample from a letter by Fischer, datelined Feldkirch, 25 May 1904, also reveals much inconsistency in the lettering, especially in upper case letters. There is quite a contrast between an elaborate 'F' in Feldkirch and one in 'Funde.' It is a firm handwriting with determined downstrokes and a horizontally looped and somewhat impatient 'd' very much like the one used on the Vínland Map. The evenly spaced lines in this letter are due to the line guide with a ten millimeter spacing which Father Fischer normally used to control a tendency to the up-down wavering—a feature of the larger writing on the map. A postcard from the Wolfegg Castle archives shows both the result when Father Fischer did not use his line guide and his ability to write perfectly shaped, tiny letters.

However, it was not Fischer's handwriting which led me to think that he made the Vínland Map. I reached that judgment only after scrutinizing Continental scholars interested in the Norse discovery of America—a search I began as soon as I had found the literary evidence that the map is fake and then determined that the cartographical and historical ideas evident in the map are typical of Continental Norse scholarship in the late nineteenth and early twentieth centuries. I looked for someone with the shortcomings evident in the map legends, but who nevertheless had considerable cartographical and historical expertise. Those criteria further narrowed my search, because my suspects—who otherwise ranged widely on the competence spectrum—so far showed little or no cartographical expertise. However, when I followed up their footnotes, Father Fischer's name turned up so often that I realized I must look at other aspects of his work than the cartographical analyses I normally associated with his name. I then discovered innumerable links between the cartographical and textual messages in the map and the information—and misinformation—found in Father Fischer's less known published writings.

The son of a decorative painter and gilder, Fischer was born in 1858 and died in 1944, after a long career as a teacher of the history of geography and cartography at the Austrian Jesuit college of Stella Matutina in Feldkirch. Throughout his adult life he was sustained by his love for the Roman Church and by his passion for early maps, especially fifteenth-century ptolemaic world maps. Both interests are reflected in the Vínland Map, which contains more pedantic cartographical teases than I can tell about here, and which demonstrates the early missionary reach of the Roman Church, not only through its many indirect references to Adam of Bremen, but in quite overt ways.

While the Bishop Henricus referred to in the longer Vínland legend on the map was just a blip of recorded religious enterprise in a great void, he was useful as a reminder of papal influence in the farthest known northwest corner of the world. In the name *isolanda Ibernica* we are reminded that Irish monks beat the Norse to Iceland, and the 'Great St. Brendan's Isles, also called Brasil' serve as a similar reminder of far-flung Christian travels. On the Asian continent, in the extreme southeast, there is a reference to Prester John, and in the far northeast, right below the name *Thule ultima*, there is a direct reference to the Carpini journey described in the 'Tartar Relation'.

Those familiar with early cartography know that *Thule* usually is shown as an island in the North Atlantic, although as something of a movable feast. On the Vínland Map, Thule is in the middle of the Eurasian land mass, at a latitude somewhat above the north coast of Iceland, i.e. at about the Arctic Circle, the latitude assigned by Ptolemy. There is no island on this map named *Thule* or *Tile*, however. Yet Fischer's trusted source, Adam of Bremen, wrote about two islands named Thule. Referring to ancient sources, he noted that one Thule 'is now called Iceland', but the other, remote from all other regions, is 'situated far off in the midst of the ocean'and reached by a voyage of nine days from Britain, after which there is one more day's voyage to the permanently frozen sea. He also noted specifically that it lies beyond Vínland, where no habitable land is found, and where 'every place beyond is full of impenetrable ice and darkness'(Tschan 1959, 216 and Schol. 152, 154; 219 and Schol. 159). Where does this get us on the Vínland Map?

451

Northeast of the Great Tartar Sea lie two large islands found on no other map. In fact, they baffled Skelton so much that he passed hastily over them both (Skelton *et al.* 1995, 137). *Insule sub aquilone zamogedorum* means 'The island under the dark cold north and associated with the Samoyeds' and *Postreme insula* means 'Outermost Island.' Placing the short ends of the maps together top form a cylinder provides ample explanation for these islands and for the awkward, off-center design of the map. The *Insule sub aquilone* now lies west-northwest of Vínland in the outermost cold regions and represents Adam of Bremen's Thule, while the *Postreme insula* is the outermost land or island in a world seen as having a strip of ocean east of Asia, beyond which lies more land. What we call the American continent, Father Fischer represented by means of the Island of Vínland, which to his way of thinking demonstrated continuously transmitted knowledge about Norse discovery, here supposedly interpreted about 450 years later by a continental European cartographer.

Aside from this Vínland intrusion, such a vision of the habitable world is in keeping with Cardinal Pierre d'Ailly's fifteenth-century reiteration of the Aristotelian concept that 'the end of the habitable earth on the east and the end of the habitable earth on the west are "moderately close" (*sunt satis prope*); and in between is a small sea (*parvum mare*) as to its breadth, although over the land there is a larger area that extends over half of the earth's circumference (*per terram sit majus spacium quam sit madietas circuitus terrae*). Therefore...it follows... that there are vaster habitations still beyond'(*Imago Mundi*, ch. 11). D'Ailly died in 1425, but his cosmographical ideas were still important to Columbus' thinking in 1492, and they were certainly current in 1436, when Andrea Bianco drew a world map with many acknowledged similarities to the Vínland Map.

In terms of what the maker of the Vínland Map clearly set out to accomplish, there is far more to this depiction of east-meeting-west than adherence to mid fifteenth-century cosmographical notions: it symbolizes the globe-spanning influence of the Roman Church, and it illustrates the longer 'Vínland' legend's 'explanation' for what happened to Bishop Eirik of Greenland. Instead of Skelton's skewed translation, which says that Eirik 'later returned northeastward toward Greenland and then proceeded in humble obedience to the will of his superiors', that part should read: 'later returned toward Greenland and then proceeded to the wintry east in obedience to his superiors'. In other words, he went east (in the Cabotian and Columbian sense of east, i.e. to Asia) to the *Insule sub aquilone zamogedorum*, in order to be a missionary to the Samoyeds, as the Carpini Mission were to the Tartars over a century later.

Another baffling place name is the *Magnum Mare Tartarorum*—the Great Tartar Sea. As far as anyone knows, the first time a Tartar Sea in that region appears on a map is in Tommaso Porcacchi's 1572 world map, where the feature is called *Mare di Tartaria* (Porcacchi 1572, 109). This oddity makes sense, however, when we know that Father Fischer all his life was a great believer in lost maps and preoccupied with finding the first map to name or delineate a particular location. In 1903, Father Fischer gained international notice with his discovery, at Wolfegg Castle, of two early maps by the German cartographer Martin Waldseemüller. This discovery resulted in a book entitled *The Oldest Map with the Name America of the Year 1507 and the Carta Marina of the Year 1516 by M. Waldseemüller* (1903). While corresponding with Bjørnbo, he was working on *Claudius Clavus, the First Cartographer of America*, and he subsequently wrote numerous articles about cartographical 'firsts'.

In other words, Father Fischer designed the Vínland Map to show a number of cartographic 'firsts,' and he did so in the firm belief that there had been cartographic precedents, now lost, but reconstructable from written sources. He did not see such reconstructions as falsifying the cartographic record. From the sagas, he knew exactly where the Norse had sailed—'Vínland' was Cape Breton and Nova Scotia combined (Fischer 1903, 97; 1907, 419). He was also sure that the Norse had explored the American mainland, which accounts for the baffling phrase 'this truly vast and very rich land' in the longer Vínland legend. As we know, islands tend to be somewhat limited in scope.

Fischer's convictions came from combining the saga information with modern cartographical knowledge, and from his certainty that there had once been cartographical representations which took into account information reaching Rome directly, beginning with Guðríðr Þorbjarnardóttir's pilgrimage in the eleventh century and with Adam of Bremen and his Danes. 'The mediæval cartographers must have had opportunities of hearing full details of the discoveries of the Vikings in the west,' Fischer wrote. 'Nordenskiöld cannot be far wrong in supposing that Columbus may have seen a representation of the Norse discoveries in America'(Fischer 1903, 101-02, 106).

The actual reason for Fischer's research at Wolfegg, which led to his discovery of the Waldseemüller maps, was his hope of finding cartographical evidence of the Norse discovery of America. Indeed, his 1902 book on Norse discovery referred to a number of fifteenth-century maps he thought carried vestigial knowledge of Norse discovery in Greenland and/or Vínland, in large part inspired by the Claudius Clavus maps on which the German cartographers Nicolaus Germanus and Henricus Martellus later elaborated. He noted that because Claudius Clavus had visited Greenland only, Helluland, Markland, and Vínland were not on his map, but other pre-Columbian European maps had also transmitted Norse knowledge of the American coast (Fischer 1903, vii, 35, 41, 46 n.2, 56-7; 1906; 1907, 420-22). In fact, Fischer was sure that a specifically German cosmography had existed, based on numerous older and newer authors and with evidence of exploration in a number of areas (1910). His many publications show his efforts to trace the cartographical links of a lost, mid fifteenth-century work by Cardinal Nicolaus Cusanus with pre-Columbian maps by Donnus Nicolaus Germanus, Henricus Martellus Germanus, Hieronymus Münzer—and last, but not least, with the Norse world as revealed by Claudius Clavus.

For twenty years after Bjørnbo's death, Fischer was nevertheless forced to abandon active work on Norse exploration, because he knew none of the Scandinavian languages. Nor did he understand Icelandic and medieval Norse naming customs—a good example being the longer Vínland legend calling Leifr Eiríksson *Leiphus erissonius*, instead of

Leiphus Erici filii. A more important link between this legend and Father Fischer, however, is the use of Crantz's story about a joint voyage by Leifr and Bjarni. Father Fischer listed Crantz's work in the expanded bibliography accompanying the English translation of his book, *The Norse Discovery of America*, first published in Germany in 1902 (Fischer 1903). In other words, he considered Crantz's book a scholarly work, and in giving joint credit for Vínland's discovery to Bjarni and Leifr, he could expect the two map legends to be read by other Germans familiar with Crantz's well-known work. But why not follow the saga version?

The main reason is that Fischer himself was ambivalent about the credit for the discovery of Vínland. In 1902 he wrote, 'The authorities differ entirely as to the name and person of the first discoverer, as to the time and circumstance of the discovery and subsequent exploration'(Fischer 1903). Fellow pedants might easily argue about this technicality and consider that both Bjarni and Leifr might be credited with first discovery, i.e. first sight, as opposed to the first planned expedition to explore America, with which both sagas credit only Leifr. It needs noting, however, that not a single known work from the time of the sagas to Fischer's own time considered the point worth making, and we should also be aware that semantic arguments over the word 'discovery' is a relatively modern pastime.

Everything about the Vínland Map shows that it was intended to tease, and the quantity of published opinions about the map during the last 35 years suggests success beyond the fondest dreams of an old priest. Father Fischer must have anticipated that if this map came to light after his death, it would be analysed by the so-called culture bearers of Hitler's Third Reich. He therefore put in the biggest tease of all: those anti-Catholic Nazis with their much-touted 'Nordic' ancestry would have to deal with a map showing the wide and early influence of the Roman Church, while specifically noting the prowess of those Norse heroes. It could not be dismissed out of hand.

453

Making the map would also have satisfied Fischer's penchant for lost cartographical links, and given what he thought he knew, not even the drawing of 'Vínland' would have struck him as dishonest. Far from being random, the map's cartographical messages reflect a composite cosmography which, to his way of thinking, might credibly be assigned to around 1440. The choice of this particular time frame might strike one as odd unless one knows that the original paste-downs on the inside covers of the binding that still held four books of the *Speculum historiale* when Yale acquired its treasured trio, was a document associated with the Council of Basle and dated 1437 (Painter 1995, xvi-vii). The binding had been interfered with and the paste-downs replaced when Yale acquired the volume, so that only a mirror image of the originals remained upon inspection. There is good reason to believe that these were still in place when Father Fischer acquired the dilapidated *Speculum* manuscript and the 'Tartar Relation' and that he knew exactly which period to aim for. In addition, the Council of Basle association would have dovetailed with his conviction that in one way or another, information about the Norse in Greenland and Vínland had chiefly been funneled through the Church and through Nicholas of Cusa.

Father Fischer probably made the map in 1934 or shortly thereafter, during a period of converging motives and opportunity. A 1932 article on a manuscript copy of an early edition of Ptolemy's *Geografia*, which was subsequently offered for sale in Lucerne, Switzerland, by the exclusive auction firm Gilhofer & Ranschburg, shows that the auction house had allowed him to keep the manuscript at Stella Matutina for the better part of a year (Fischer 1932a). Fischer appreciated this singular mark of trust, especially since he was certain that an unnamed northern peninsula sticking out from the edge of a map in this work represented Greenland. His early interest in the Norse was now revived after a dormancy of twenty years.

Also in 1932, he finished his *magnum opus* on early Greek ptolemaic maps in the Vatican Library (Fischer 1932b). He was shocked and saddened to the point of insomnia when a noted cartographic scholar publicly slaughtered it early in 1933 (Bagrow 1933). This was just when Hitler came to power and almost immediately began to arrest Catholic priests in southern Germany. Stella Matutina, still Fischer's home, soon felt the heavy hand of Nazi rule. Pressure of a more local kind had made the Catholic heirs to the splendid library at Mikulov Castle in Brno decide to disband the collection as early as in 1931 and to let the firm of Gilhofer & Ranschburg sell the more important items during the same auction that featured the manuscript edition of the *Geografia* lent to Father Fischer (Seaver 1996).

Item 292 in the catalogue for the June 1934 auction was a single book from the Vincent of Beauvais *Speculum historiale* which had clearly fallen out of its original volume and been rebound. Sequentially, it came right after the four books which Yale had obtained with the Vínland Map trio. Neatly written in two columns in black ink touched with red, the fragment was judged to be from the fifteenth century, and its description matched Yale's fragments so well that it is frustrating not to have the dimensions listed. This particular book concerns the threat to Christian Europe from the heathens to the east. Together with the four preceding books, it would have formed a logical introduction to a version of 'The Tartar Relation' commissioned by an East European prince.

Father Fischer had made repeated use of the Mikulov library during his research on early German cartography. He combined this interest with an equally strong passion for medieval travels in Eastern Europe and Asia and would have accepted with alacrity if either Gilhofer & Ranschburg or the heirs to the castle had offered this respectable old scholar an incomplete, dilapidated volume containing a copy of the already well-known 'Tartar Relation' along with a very incomplete *Speculum historiale*. The circumstantial evidence is very strong that this is what happened, and that Fischer, by this time in his late seventies but still intellectually active, subsequently relieved anxious hours by making the Vínland Map, either using ink of his own making or mixing easily available commercial ones.

The scientific studies of the ink's composition are by no means complete. I hope they will continue until there is some unanimity on the subject, and until we know a great deal more about how to spot fakes by means of ink analysis.

In 1967, two scientists at the British Museum found the Vínland Map's ink to be unlike any other known medieval ink, but they did not have an opportunity to analyse the ink further. In 1972, the Chicago scientists Walter and Lucy McCrone found that the ink contained anatase in a molecular form developed for the paint industry around 1916—in my Norwegian home town, as it happens. The structure of these molecules was subsequently confirmed by another scientist and has not been disproved by later studies.

When the Nazis closed down Stella Matutina completely in 1939, the ageing Father Fischer was forced to leave for Munich and to leave virtually all his notes and books behind. We know that the sorting and restoration of the former Stella Matutina library did not begin until the early 1950s; we also know that at least one map his school had acquired for his research, and subsequently pilfered, was offered for sale by Christie's of London in 1984. In 1941, with the war raging all around him, Fischer was given shelter at his beloved Wolfegg Castle, where he died in 1944 and was buried in a grave already holding two of his brother Jesuits.

While visiting Wolfegg Castle five years ago, I learned that neither the Prince nor his archivist objected to my conclusions about Father Fischer. Nor have the many German Jesuits who have helped me accused me of heaping shame on one of their own. Indeed, anyone with direct experience of the Nazi regime would see the Vínland Map for what it is: a pious old scholar's quiet protest in the great sea of resistance to the inhumanity of those years. The legacy of shame here surely belongs to those who have stood behind the marketing of the Vínland Map volume with its distorted view of Norse exploration in America.

Acknowledgments

I am grateful to Peter Barber of The British Library Map Library for lending me the 1996 Christie's catalogue. The author thanks Professor Philippe Buc at Stanford University, California, for verifying a point through an independent translation of the long Latin caption on the Vínland Map.

Abbreviations

Bjørnbo and Fischer   'Correspondence between Axel Anton Bjørbo and Fr Joseph Fischer, SJ', The Royal Library, Copenhagen, Ny kgl. Samling 2508. 2o, folder III.

Imago Mundi   Petrus Ailliacus [Pierre d'Ailly, Cardinal]. *Imago Mundi*, trans. E.F. Keever, 1948. Wilmington, North Carolina. Typescript. (Copy used: British Library 10002.i.18.)

Bibliography

Bagrow, L. 1933. 'Review (no. 89)', *Petermanns geographische Mitteilungen*, Gotha, Justus Perthes [Dr. A Petermanns Mitteilungen aus Justus Perthes geographischer Anstalt], 73, 1, 51-52.

Crantz, D. trans., 1767. *History of Greenland*, 2 vols. London: Printed for the Brethren Society for the Furtherance of the Gospel among the Heathen.

Fischer, J. 1902. *Die Entdeckungen der Normannen in Amerika*. Freiburg in the Breisgau: Supplementary vol. 81, Stimmen aus Maria-Laach.

Fischer, J. 1903. *The Norse Discovery of America*, trans. B. Soulsby, London.

——1906. 'Die kartographische Darstellung der Entdeckungen der Normannen in Amerika', *Proceedings, 14th International Congress of Americanists*, 1904, vol. 1, Stuttgart.

——1907. 'America, Pre-Columbian Discovery of', *American Catholic Encyclopedia*, vol. 1, New York.

——1910. *Der deutsche Ptolemëus aus dem Ende des XV. Jahrhunderts (um 1490) in Faksimiliedrück*, Strassburg.

——1932a. 'Die Ptolemëushandschrift des Georgius Schbab (nach 1513)', *Zeitschrift für Buchdrück-, Bibliophilie- und Pressegeschichte* (Schwiezerisches Gutenbergmuseum), 18, 212-221.

——1932b. *Claudii Ptolemaei Geographiae Codex Urbinas Graecus 82*, 4 vols, London and Leipzig.

Fischer, J. and Wieser, R.v. 1903. *The Oldest Map with the Name America of the year 1507 and the Carta Marina of the year 1516 by M. Waldseemüller (Ilacomilus)*. Innsbruck: Wagnersche Universitáts-buchhandlung [Copy used: British Library, Map Ref. C.9. (2)].

Grosz, P. 1996. 'Introduction', *Catalogue of the Mauerbach Benefit Sale 29-30 October 1996*, Christie's, Vienna.

Hall, C.F. 1864. *Life with the Esquimaux: The narrative of Captain Charles Francis Hall of the Whaling Barque 'George Henry' from the 29th May, 1860, to the 13th September, 1862*, London.

Ingstad, H. 1964. 'Vinland ruins prove Vikings found the New World', *National Geographic Magazine*, 126, 5, 708-35.

Jónsson, A. 1732. *Grónlandia: Eller Historie om Grönland af Islandske Haandskrevne Historie-Böger....og först i det Latinske Sprog forfatted af Arngrim Jonsson*, trans. Einar Eyjolfsson, Copenhagen.

Lidegaard, M. ed., 1991. *Glahns anmærkninger. 1700-tallets Grænlændere. Et nærbillede*. Copenhagen: Det Grönlandske Selskabs Skrifter 30.

Mallet, P.H. 1770. *Northern Antiquities. A Translation of Introduction à l'Histoire de Dannemarc*, 2 vols, London.

Nichols, L.H. 1996. 'Preface', *Catalogue of the Mauerbach Benefit Sale 29-30 October 1996*, Christie's, Vienna.

Painter, G. D. 1995. 'Prefatory article to *The Vinland Map and the Tartar Relation*', in Skelton, Marston and Painter 1995, xvi-vii.

Pontoppidan, E. 1755. *The Natural History of Norway*, London [1752. *Norges Naturlige Historie*, Copenhagen].

Saenger, P. 1998. 'Vinland Re-read (review article)', *Imago Mundi*, 50, 199-202.

Seaver, K.A. 1996. 'The Mystery of the "Vinland Map" Manuscript Volume', *The Map Collector*, 74, 24-29.

——1997. 'The Vinland Map: A $3,500 duckling that became a $25,000,000 swan', *Mercator's World*, 2, 2, 42-47.

455

Shailor, B. 1987-92. *Catalogue of Medieval and Renaissance Manuscripts in the Beinecke Rare Book and Manuscript Library, Yale University*, vols 2-3. Binghamton, New York: Medieval and Renaissance Texts and Studies.

Skelton, R.A., Marston, T.E. and Painter, G.D. 1995. *The Vinland Map and the Tartar Relation*, 2nd edn, New Haven, Connecticut.

Thomaso Porcacchi da Castiglione. 1572. *L'Isole piv famoso del mondo, arretino e intagliate dà Girolamo Porro*, Venice [Copy used: British Library Maps C.7.b.19].

Torfæus, T. 1706. *Gronlandia antiqua*, Copenhagen [Copy used: British Library 152.a.8. (1). Translated as *Det gamle Grönland* by the author and published in Copenhagen in 1706. Reissued 1947, Oslo: Etnografisk Museum].

Tschan, F.J. trans., 1959. *History of the Archbishops of Hamburg-Bremen*. New York: Records of Civilization Sources and Studies, Dept. of History. Columbia University, 53.

Wallis, H. *et al.* 1974. 'The strange case of the Vinland Map', *Geographical Journal*, 140, 7 (June), 186.

Washburn, W.E. 'Review, *The Vinland Map and the TartarRelation*', *American Historical Review*, 71 (April, 1966), 927-28.

——ed., 1971. *Proceedings of the Vinland Map Conference*, Chicago.

456

Afterword:

Where's Vínland?

Trond Woxen

I've lived a life of seeking
All knowledge I could find,
But there's just one nagging question
That's always taxed my mind:
    Where's Vínland?

I've searched the written pages
I've been around the globe
I'm totally frustrated
I'm suffering like Job!
    Where's Vínland?

And so it finally happened
A conference on the way
To be about old Vínland
Up in Canada, eh?
    Where's Vínland?

Now perhaps I'd get my answer
I'd learn secret Viking lore
Way up there in Newfoundland
And foggy Labrador.
    Where's Vínland?

But my question wasn't answered,
It was driving me insane!
And so I brought the problem
To Karl, a somewhat great a Dane:
    Where's Vínland?

He told me not to ask him
Not even on his life
For the reason that he came here
Was to escape his wife!
    Where's Vínland?

I then approached M. Magnusson
The Icelandic-Scottish bard
But Sandy blew his bagpipes
So hearing M. was hard.
    Where's Vínland?

457

To a nice bow-tied Icelander
A famous meteorologist
I posed the question to him
But he gave me this long list:

'Vínland', says he,
'Learn this first,
then you'll find Vínland:

History, Navigation, Mathematics,
Meteorology, Oceanography, Astronomy,
Archaeology, Anthropology, Architechtural History,
Chemistry, Botany, Marine Biology,
Hydrology, Morphology, Pathology,
Linguistics, Physics, Psychology,
Et cetera, Et cetera, Et cetera....'

Numb, I asked dear Kirsten:
'Could you lead me out of this maze?'
But she pulled out her Vínland Map
and talked for three full days!
    Where's Vínland?

So I finally did surrender
The problem would not bend
My very simple question
Remains unanswered to the end:
    Where's Vínland?

They put me in the asylum
A madman's part of hell
They all declared me crazy
In my padded cell.

Why? Because I said...ha...ha...ha...ha...

That I had found Vínland!

Index

461

AGMV Marquis

MEMBRE DE SCABRINI MEDIA

Québec, Canada
2003